4th Edition

GUN
DIGEST
TREASURY

The Best from 25 Years of GUN DIGEST

Edited by John T. Amber

Follett Publishing Company / Chicago
T- 0359

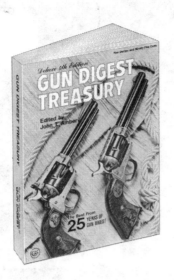

OUR COVER

Twenty-two caliber versions of two famous Colt single action revolvers adorn the cover of the fourth edition Gun Digest Treasury. The New Frontier 22 (left) features a ramp front and adjustable rear. The Peacemaker 22 (right) is an all steel version of the famed 45 caliber Peacemaker. Both guns have color case hardened frames and are available with magnum cylinders.

GUN DIGEST TREASURY STAFF

EDITOR
John T. Amber
ASSOCIATE EDITOR
Harold A. Murtz
INDEX EDITOR
Lilo Anderson
PUBLISHER
Sheldon L. Factor

ISBN 0-695-80359-X   Library of Congress Catalog Card #61-9610

CONTENTS

GENERAL

COLLECTORS

HANDLOADING

RIFLES

SHOTGUNS

HANDGUNS

EXPLODED VIEWS

It Ain't So, Mac!

by WARREN PAGE

WILL ONE SHOTGUN shoot the same shell harder than another one? Is the autoloader less "powerful" than the bolt action? Do you hold over or under when the target is up on a hill? Down in a canyon? Do duck loads shoot harder straight up, or on the flat? Does this rifle of mine shoot just as fast as the ballistics tables say it does? Does the 12 gauge kill birds farther or more easily because it spreads the shot more widely? Will bullets glance away from a tree trunk they almost but not quite hit? How far does a high-velocity bullet travel from the gun muzzle before it begins to fall?

Questions like these are cause for puzzlement and mighty strenuous argufying even among pretty smart shooters. These and forty-'leven others, the old wives' tales of gunnery, have had shooters fooled for years—and have kept more hot-stove sessions going through more midnights than any other questions of gun facts. I know, because in my job I answer stacks of letters on 'em, and settle some red-faced disagreements on the facts. Facts? Certainly. Who wants to referee a set-to that's a matter solely of personal opinion? The common fallacies and misunderstandings referred to in that opening paragraph, and a score more like them, are matters of proven fact, or at least they can be.

If a chap wants to know whether the grouse is a better game bird than the quail, or the 270 a better all-round caliber than the 30-06, it's easy to offer an opinion, and probably not too hard to make it stand up, whichever side of the fence we're on—but we can't *prove* absolutely that we're right. The answer in either case depends on what we expect of a bird or a rifle, or the circumstances under which we shoot either one.

More Power from Semi-Auto or Bolt Action?

But if the point at issue is whether a blowback 22, for example, develops as much or less "power" than a bolt action 22 of similar barrel dimensions using the same cartridges—and there are thousands of shooters who are tripped up on that one—on such a question we can dig up some hard facts.

You won't dig 'em up in your back yard; at least I was never able to arrive at anything significant from shooting into chunks of timber and measuring penetration. Few of us have the laboratory chronograph equipment which is the only way of getting exact checks on velocity, hence on "power." So, being fortunate in knowing the ballisticians who toil in the ranges under Winchester's New Haven plant, and also Dr. C. (for Chuck) Cummings, who has charge of all those fancy gadgets in the Remington lab, I spent some time and some loading-company money finding out. The answer is: Stop worrying; there isn't any difference in any practical sense.

Let's look at some facts. Up at Remington, they took one of their Model 550 22 semi-autos (the rifle that has a little "kicker" or sliding inner chamber so that its blowback action will function with either shorts, longs, or long rifles) and two boxes of long rifle fodder from the same carton. The first box of 50 was fired with the gun operating normally; the second with the action blocked up, so that the gun was performing just like a locked-breech bolt action. Several thousand dollars' worth of Potter electronic counter chronograph revealed a difference of 12 f.p.s. instrumental speed in favor of the action *when it blew back normally!* Then Doc Cummings tried it with a Colt Woodsman, a 4½-inch-barreled model. Another 50 with the action opening normally, followed by as many more shots with it blocked up, tallied an average 12 f.p.s. higher from the locked breech. Ah-HAH! says the proponent of the bolt or locked-breech action. But that differential is of absolutely no significance in any practical shooting sense, since if the loading companies could turn out 22 long rifle fodder that would deliver the same speed every shot, plus or minus *twice* 12 f.p.s., they'd be very happy indeed. The difference is probably not even significant to a hair-splitting laboratory technician, guns and ammunition being what they inevitably are.

Just to put the clincher on, I got the dope on experiments the Winchester people had run with one of their Model 74 semi-auto 22 rifles. They fired 20-round strings, standard production ammunition from the same box. When the action was permitted to blow back as designed, the average 15-foot instrumental velocity for that fodder was 1,226 f.p.s. With the action jimmied so that it could not blow open, the speed averaged 1,219 f.p.s., 7 f.p.s. *slower*. Again the difference, imperceptible even had it been the other way around, is no more than a variation normal to all ammunition.

In all common sense, there is no particular reason to expect a blowback 22 to be less powerful than a similar bolt, lever, or trombone type. True, the breechblock is free to move backward, save for its own inertia and the light thrust of the counter-recoil spring, when the powder goes off and the bullet starts on its way. But, since the bullet weighs 40 grains, and the breechblock many times as much—the Colt Woodsman slide weighs about 6½ ounces or 2,844 grains, 70 times more than the bullet—it starts back mighty slowly in comparison. Furthermore, the cartridge case itself is held tightly to the chamber walls for an instant by pressure. The bullet, therefore, is beyond the muzzle, or at least way beyond the point of pressure and velocity build-up, before the back door opens, so to speak, to cause any velocity loss.

Figuring that an autoloading shotgun is puny as compared to a pump, with the same loads and barrel length, is equally wrong—and for even stronger reasons, since in the typical Browning-designed action the barrel and the breechblock are firmly tied together until they have moved nearly all the way back into the receiver, where they are separated by a tripping action so that the barrel can go back into battery, the spent shell be kicked out, and the breechblock come forward later to pick up a fresh round. Clearly the inertia of barrel plus chunk of breechblock is so vastly greater than that of the accelerating shot that the pellets will be gone before there's any speed loss because of the breech opening. Taking shot velocities with absolute accuracy is a tough job—but it's a cinch that if we fired a Browning type autoloader both locked and unlocked, any difference would come within the speed variation limits natural to shot shells.

Now there may be certain peculiar actions, and individual loads, where the flat statement that there is no sensible "power" differential doesn't hold water. Winchester found that the Garand gained some 28 f.p.s. when the action was locked shut, for example; so the situation in gas-operated guns, where pressure is tapped off behind the slug, well ahead of the chamber, may be different. But for the 22's and shotguns, which are the pieces whose "power" people worry about, there's no meaningful difference.

Except with a dud round, you'll never find these exaggerated differences in velocities with any rifle, autoloading, bolt, or whatever.

Rifle shooters are pretty hard to get along with on occasion, but if you rib a smoothbore artist about the hard-shooting qualities of his pet shot-squirter, there's apt to be blood on the floor. Most riflemen will grudgingly admit that their game rifle doesn't shoot any harder than the next guy's in the same caliber—just straighter—but the shot-gunner is plumb hardheaded about his long-range killer.

Ballistics tables are reliable—to a point—but you'll know more about YOUR rifle by shooting it.

Do Rifle Velocities Agree with Ballistics Tables?

The rifleman, however, is likely to be a slave to the ballistics tables, to accept their figures for his own rifle without question, assuming that it has a barrel of standard length. That's not, as a matter of absolute truth, quite correct, although for purposes of doping trajectory, sighting in rifles, or comparing loads, it's good enough in a practical sense.

A couple of years ago I carted up to the Remington ballistics labs three rifles in 270 caliber, plus a batch of factory ammunition of a lot which had given me excellent accuracy, hence must have been uniform in delivered velocity. I was primarily interested in the relationship between barrel length and speed; consequently the three guns were picked for their 24, 22, and 19-inch lengths. All were apparently standard save that the 22-incher was cut with a 1-in-12 twist.

When the smoke had cleared away and the figures were averaged up, it appeared that identical factory ammunition fired from the standard length 24-incher gave a 60-foot instrumental speed of 2,980 f.p.s.; the 22-inch sporter, 3,031 f.p.s.; and the stubby 19-inch barrel, 2,793 f.p.s. Note these points. First, the barrel of 24 inches, the standard length used in all the ballistics tables for 270 caliber, could not by any stretch of the slide rule deliver the 3,140 f.p.s. calculated muzzle speed published for the load. Second, the barrel 2 inches shorter gave higher speeds with the same load!

Now you can draw any conclusions you want to about the barrel-length vs. velocity business, but this little incident points up what Phil Sharpe's extended experiments have developed more fully—that the inevitable variations in the inside dimensions of rifle barrels, of chamber, throat, and bore, are productive of very considerable pressure and speed differences with the same loads, sometimes even greater differences than those caused by a couple of inches of barrel length, which latter variations or losses are usually less important than we think anyway. In practice, of course, if rifle A starts its slug 50 feet faster than rifle B, the buck doesn't much care which slug misses him, and he won't know the difference if both hit him, not out at a couple of hundred yards. Those ballistic table figures are evolved from tests with precisely made laboratory barrels—not with smokesticks bored and reamed to ordinary production tolerances—so treat the figures with the merest pinch of salt.

While the matter of barrel length and velocity in center fire rifles is an engrossing subject, and one on which many shooters are either confused or full of opinionated beans, it would take a whole article to skim around its edges. Let's save it, and say that the old rule of thumb for so-called "high-power" cartridges, which calls for a velocity loss of 25 f.p.s. per inch of barrel removed, in terms of ordinary sporter lengths, is only the roughest kind of approximation. With the extremely hot loads using high pressures clear out to a standard length muzzle, this figure is usually too low; with the 35,000 to 45,000-pound loads, it's usually too high. Exact chronograph checks often reveal that other factors in a barrel's innards or in the load—inside dimensions all the way out, bullet type and diameter, ignition, the burning qualities of the specific powder—are more important than a couple of inches of muzzle end. In common-sense terms, we are not going to skimp too much on the velocity delivered *at the animal* if we make our barrel for the 270 to 30-06 type of cartridge 22 inches long; for the Magnums, 24 inches; for the 30-30, 32 Special, 35 Rem, even the 300 Savage with the heavier bullets, a handy 20 inches. A lot more noise when we cut 'em back from standard, but not a catastrophic speed loss.

Does One Shotgun Shoot Harder than Another?

Now that character with the hard-shooting shotgun is itching to get in his two-bits' worth. The heck of it is, in a laboratory sense, if not in a practical sense, he has some right on his side. For example, I have data showing average shot velocities delivered over 40 yards, same loads of course, by a couple of shotguns with identical barrel lengths and almost exactly the same amount of choke constriction. One gun shot 38 f.p.s. faster than the other. Why? Perhaps because the cylindrical section of its barrel was 9/1,000 of an inch smaller. Or mebbe it was a difference back at the forcing cone. No telling. BUT, when the loading companies can put out shot shells which will constantly stay within a 25 f.p.s. velocity tolerance, there'll be dancing on the green. It isn't practical.

The duck couldn't care less which pellet hits him, but the slower ones may make the difference between kills and misses.

As a matter of fact, since the difference in speed between the fastest and the slowest pellets in any one shot shell is fully 25 f.p.s., and since the loads themselves vary more than that out of the same box, and since 1/1,000 of an inch of choke constriction (in a tight-bored gun there may be nearly 40/1,000) means one added foot per second of average speed over 40 yards, and since temperature and humidity affect speed almost as much as some of the individual gun measurements, it is quite possible that from one combination of guns and conditions we could get from 50 to 100 f.p.s. of difference in speed. That would show nicely on labo-

ratory equipment, but it would be pretty tough to measure it by shooting at either telephone books or high-flying ducks. This velocity business, then, is apt to be rather academic, even if it is rather nice to know that from two barrels absolutely identical save that one is 26 inches, the other 30, the average shot speeds over 40 yards will be between 25 and 30 f.p.s. less for the shorter barrel. But it is not yet established what even this means to a duck of average intelligence and sensitiveness to chilled shot.

There is actually a very great difference in how hard individual shotguns will shoot, even though seemingly much alike. Velocity is not the only element in shotgun power if we assume the same shot size and charge; delivered pattern density is a much more important one. Counting patterns is an easy way to go nuts, but I have many times observed that certain of my guns patterned certain shot shells much closer than others marked as having the same choke. Up in New Haven not long ago they counted 200 patterns from eight different "full-choke" guns of assorted makes, all pump guns as I remember it, and found that with the same duck load of No. 6 shot the 40-yard, 30-inch patterning circles were perforated by anything from 66 percent to 75 percent averages from the different guns. Now the 66-percenter would put 185 shot into the circle; the 75-percenter, 211. Those extra 25 or so pellets *might* be just the ones to kill the duck! Shotguns *do* have individually hard-shooting qualities sometimes, even in standard factory borings, depending on just how the fickle fowling pieces will throw their patterns.

Does the 12 Throw a Bigger Spread than the 20?

And that brings us to a question on which there is a very wide range of misunderstanding—the width of the spreads thrown by 12, 16, and 20-gauge guns which are of the same degree of choke, when fired with comparable loads. This is a real whing-ding. Ask any confirmed 12-bore shooter and he will swear that his full-choke gun will spread its shot over more of the barn door—or more of the covey of quail, chukars, or what have you—than a full-choked 20 gauge. He may even want to fight about it. In a practical sense, he's completely wrong. The man who holds coats during fist-fights just stepped out, so wait a minute, friends, let's see what the figures say. Cold-turkey data from the ballistics labs will prove more than any casual one- or two-shot guesstimates.

Winchester was inquisitive on this point, among others, and fired both Super-X and Ranger loads, No. 6 shot, from full-choked 12's, 16's, and 20's, Model 12 pump guns. With the heavy loads, all three gauges put from 72% to 74% into 30 inches at 40 yards; with the lighter loads, 69% to

You could get plenty of spread with a blunderbuss, but the killing range and pattern density would be lousy.

70%. If we count 90% of all the shot holes on the pattern board—no sense in looking at *all* the shot holes, since in any charge there are some deformed shot that go flying off south-southeast—maximum diameters would range between 46 and 50 inches with the easy load, 48 to 50 inches with the duck load, *regardless of the gauge fired.*

When I put the proposition up to Cummings at Remington, he burned up a lot of green shells to arrive at virtually identical results. He drew 40-inch circles on the papers bearing the patterns, (25 from each gauge) shot with a fully choked 20 gauge handling an ounce of 6's, a 12-gauge choke-bore firing duck loads, 1¼ ounces of the same shot, and the same 12 gauge firing a one-ounce dose of 6's at a speed identical to the 20-gauge setup. Inside those 40-inch circles *all* three guns put from 81% to 86% of their shot, and the averages were even closer on 10, 20, and 30-inch inner circles. Obviously, except for odd stray pellets, the guns were throwing the same overall spread.

The bigger hole in the 12 bore therefore does not, assuming the same choke, throw any wider slather of shot than the smaller bores—but it does throw more shot into the same area, for a denser pattern that will hold together further out. Consequently, choke for choke, it will have greater killing power. To put it another way, at a given range we can use roughly one degree less choke with the bigger bore and get similar pattern density with larger overall spread. Catch on?

There is no practical difference in velocity when shooting straight up or on the level.

Do Shotguns Shoot Harder Straight Up, or On the Level?

Now one more common question about shotgun performance. This is one you can figure out yourself. Why is it that a load of 4's or 6's seems to hit a duck less hard when he's crossing straight overhead than when he's at the same range out over the decoys? The answer is, it doesn't.

The argument that shotgun shells somehow have less "oomph," their shot less striking velocity, when fired straight up than they do when fired on the level or up at a shallow angle, is an old-timer—wrong as can be, but popping up perennially. The reason why it crops up, particularly after some half-frozen duck-shooter has had a very tough day in the blind, is one of the reasons for his tough day—faulty range estimation. When a bird is up over us, where there are no ground points or known objects against which to judge his apparent size, it's a lot easier to figure the 70-yard cloud-splitter at a shootable 50 yards than when he is nearer the water. There we have our decoys, the next point, possibly trees, to go by and can guess his distance that much more accurately. A shot charge doesn't slow noticeably faster than normal just because we shoot it straight up.

There can't be any difference save that exerted by the force of gravity, which on a straight-up shot does help slow the pellets. A maximum load of 6's is in flight .167 seconds, or thereabouts, in traveling 50 yards. The downward acceleration of gravity, at the accepted rate of 32 feet per second per second, would therefore slow the straight-up pellets so that they'd smack the duck approximately 5 f.p.s. slower than they would if he were on the level in front of the blind. That speed difference is *not* going to be the difference between two teal and a full limit of black ducks, however, not when human eyes are judging the range!

Where Should We Aim on Uphill or Downhill Shots?

Gravity does play some rather odd tricks in respect to rifle trajectory. Not only does it continue to pull every bullet downward, at a rate of acceleration remarkably constant regardless of bullet weight, from the very instant it leaves the muzzle; but it also, in this constant pull, can lead us to some long-range misses even with carefully sighted and held rifles. Probably such misses, although they are uncommon with high-velocity, flat-trajectory cartridges, give rise to the common questions regarding the proper point of aim on uphill or downhill shots at long range. The mathematics of these questions is tough, the logic a bit easier.

Those who remember trigonometry well enough can not only prove that for large angles of elevation or depression (greater than 10°) the slant hitting range of a rifle sighted in on the horizontal is greater than the hitting range of that same rifle on a horizontal, flat-country shot, but he can also rough out the error. The ordinary guy, who relies on trigger-nometry rather than trigonometry, can also grasp the idea this way.

Assume our rifle to be zeroed in at 200 yards. In that distance the bullet has risen above our line of sight, by virtue of the original sight correction for the effect of gravity, and has just come back down to it again. Hence on a 300-yard target, straight out on the flat, we'd have to hold over to allow for the continuing effect of gravity—in the case of the scope-sighted 30-06 with 180-grain bullet, about 11 inches. Now if our 300-yard target, a sheep for example, is perched up on a shale slide above us by some 45°, the pull of gravity, still straight down, is working in reference not to a roughly horizontal line through the center of our rifle bore, but to a line tipped up slightly more than 45°. Hence its effect on the bullet in relation to that line is not as great, and we won't have quite as much drop to worry about on that 300-yard sheep. That is, the slant hitting range is increased. Matter of fact, instead of needing to hold over by 11 inches, under the simple conditions outlined we'd need to figure as if we were shooting on the flat at 213 yards, and hence would need only a couple of inches of hold-over, which in a practical shooting sense is nothing at all. The conclusion

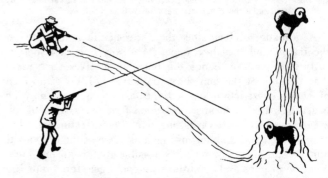

When in doubt on uphill or downhill shots, aim a leetle low.

we have arrived at here is that on shots sharply uphill or downhill we should hold *under* the point of aim we would think correct for that range on the flat.

To estimate the effective range over which we are shooting, as distinct from the actual distance from our own case of buck fever out to the trophy sheep, try to imagine how far it would be from you on the horizontal to a point straight into the hill under the sheep up there, and figure your hold accordingly. Too tough? Well, with modern cartridges like the 270, 30-06, 257, 300 Magnum, and so forth, when the rifles are properly sighted in for the big and rough country where such problems are likely, just forget the whole deal and hold a leetle low.

But if you're the type of character who carries a pad and pencil up the mountain, or can do rapid calculation, you can arrive at your effective range (the one according to which you should sight or hold) in terms of a formula in an informative book by ballistician C. S. Cummings, entitled *Everyday Ballistics*, published by Stackpole & Heck:

Effect of Slope Angle on Effective Range

Angle of Slope (up or down)	Divide Estimated Range by
15°	1.04
20°	1.06
25°	1.10
30°	1.15
35°	1.22
40°	1.31
45°	1.41

In actual hunting, any such mathematics may go with the wind, either literally or figuratively. Your dope may also be upset by the different sling tension put on your rifle by the peculiar way the rocks make you belly down; or you may make a bum guess—and this is a very important point—as to just where on that odd-looking critter way up or down there the bullet should hit to drive into his boiler room. Try looking at a mule deer from 45° above him sometime, and you'll discover that the bull's-eye isn't painted on him in the same place it usually is! The ideal hitting point for a heart shot—how would it shift under those conditions?

Can Bullets Bounce from Trees They Don't Hit?

While that last line is being stewed over, let's move to another subject for hot-stove-league arguments. Is a bullet deflected off course away from a tree or a rock or a fence post between you and the target, when it comes whisker-close to that tree but doesn't actually tick it?

It is often argued, with plenty of convincing table-thumping, that in passing very close to an object, the bullet in flight compresses a thin pad of air between it and the object and so is bounced a bit off line. Or mebbe the shock wave tearing along with the bullet has something to do with it. At any rate, the chap who is banging the table is convinced that some such mysterious effect caused him to miss the trophy shot of a lifetime. Not so.

If the slug even just barely touched the branch, it was probably deflected some, perhaps a lot. Long and heavy bullets with round noses plow through the shrubbery better than light, short, or pointed ones; ultra-fast projectiles may be completely broken up even by light impact. But if it didn't actually touch—bullet weight, speed, or shape has nothing to do with the case—the bullet will keep on as straight as it ever did.

To check on this, I did what has already been done before. I set up a target at 100 yards, locating it so that the bark of an 8-inch rock maple 60 yards out was a-a-almost exactly in line with it and my rifle on the sandbags. The rifle (a supremely accurate 220 Wilson Arrow, whose Pfeifer target-weight barrel and FN action had been put together and chambered up by L. E. Wilson himself, the stock beautifully inletted and designed for sandbag work in bullet testing by Bill Humphrey of Virginia) had earlier been targeted against another marker on the same board and had made three 5-shot groups from 6/16″ to 11/16″ extreme spread. These groups centered 1¾″ above the aiming point, a strong ¼″ right of center.

Unless the bullet actually hits the tree, the deflection shown by the dotted line would NOT occur.

Then I fired ten shots at the marker, which was located so that all ten must just squeeze by the tree. But two didn't. They *hit* the bark, one flying off into the butts somewhere, the other keyholing into the target about 5 inches out of the group. The other eight, which did not hit the rock maple, but must have come within an inch or less of it, printed up a nice group only ⅝″ across, centering 1¾″ high, perhaps ⅜″ right. The tree was on the right side. Was any bullet in the least deflected which did not actually contact the tree? Was either the accuracy of the rifle or its point of impact altered when the bullets skimmed the mid-range obstacle? The answer is *No* in both cases, and there's every reason to feel that it would be *No* in other similar ones, regardless of bullet weight, shape, speed, or even proximity to the obstacle, so long as there is no actual contact.

However, it must be admitted that the great ballistics experimenter, F. W. Mann, working with cast bullets at velocities under 2,000 f.p.s. (slow by today's standards), turned up some evidence of bullet deflection in his plank-shooting tests. His bullets shifted impact away from or toward the plank according to whether their distance from it was greater or less than half an inch. But his bullets were fired to pass alongside flat planks *4 to 16 feet long*; they were not zipping past tree branches. Even Mann noted no deflection when his "plank" was a 4″ block. Hence his experiments do not controvert but rather support those made with modern high-speed loads.

Every batch of mail that shooters send to gun editors, and every session of chin-music among shooters either amateur or expert, will turn up more of these odd questions. When they are matters of opinion, let it be every man to his own, and long may we shooters rave—but when the debate hinges on matters of fact, let's turn either to the professional ballistician's gadgets or to the back-yard laboratory to find the right answer.

A Shotgun is a

You may not agree with the author's premises

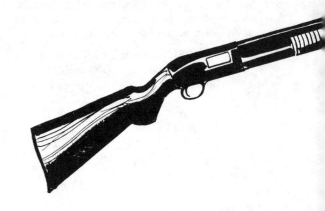

REMEMBER Mark Twain's famous account of Tom Sawyer, the board fence, and the whitewash? If you're half as smart as Tom was, not in bamboozling other people to do a painting job for you, but in handling a whitewash brush with ease and accuracy, you can be a wingshot. Swinging a scattergun and wielding a juicy-wet paintbrush have a lot in common, a slapdash sort of artistry.

The average shotgunner is all too often like the duffer at golf, so hamstrung by the effort to recall, all at once, instructions to keep his head down, his eye on the ball or target, to grip his weapon not that way but exactly this way, to waggle his fanny not both ways but the other way, that he can neither shoot nor drive for little green apples. The golfer has an advantage in applying a book-learned technique because he has all afternoon to set himself to whack that little pill. It doesn't fly away while he's getting ready. The would-be wingshot has to apply his studies instanter, in one smooth flow of instinctive reaction, or his bird is long gone. He has no time for thinking out the shot. Which is one reason why I think wingshooting has been made, for all too many people, entirely too complicated. Their scattergun lives would be simpler, more fruitful, if they remembered only to think of the gun as a paintbrush and slapped away at their target accordingly.

Before the shotgun sophisticates overwhelm me with a barrage of tired clichés about stance, hand position, coordination of eye and hand, lead calculations and ballistic data, let me clarify that paintbrush business. All the other elements in wingshooting have their place, an important place but not nearly as vital as this paintbrush concept. And what is it? If you imagine that your scattergun is the handle of a brush and *wipe* it through the bird as it goes, cutting loose at that instant the "paint" would be smearing him thickest if you were using paint instead of pellets, you'll kill more birds, break more targets. Ballistics and scattergun choreography can go and be hanged.

Actually, what we're getting at here is the effectiveness of what those people who must have exact terms for every human move call swing-through shooting. It is the style of scattergunnery used by nearly every fine shot, whether his target be a disc of tarred clay or a full-feathered cock. The top-notch shooter, with a minimum of flumdummery, does these things: he gets his gun-muzzle moving along the bird's line of apparent motion as soon as possible, and keeps it pursuing that bird while his right hand is bringing the gun butt up into position with cheek and shoulder. He is speeding his swing as the gun settles to rest and the eye into alignment with the barrel. As the muzzle wipes across the bird and passes it he cuts the charge loose, and as the gun sets

Pointing Out

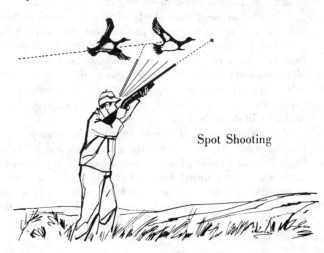

Spot Shooting

Paintbrush

by JOHN MAYNARD

or conclusions, but he's shot scads of shells.

back in recoil he continues the swing or swipe through a full stroke—exactly as you would in whitewashing the fence.

Brings Hits

And that brings hits because the lead necessary to hit any flying target has been automatically calibrated to hit that particular target by the amount of gun-swing speed necessary to catch up to and pass it, to *swipe through it*. No need to defend that reasoning, though it can be done, with Einsteinian mathematics regarding shot speed, target speed and range, reaction and lock times. It works. Just watch half a dozen fine shots in action. They are swipers.

The average beginning wingshooter starts out shooting at a spot. The need for throwing his charge of pellets ahead of the target has been dinned into him; so he responds by pointing his smoothbore at an area in space somewhere in front of the bird and cutting loose. His shot string will cut the line of target flight or intersect it at the right moment only by purest chance, even though that pellet swarm is roughly a dozen feet long and four feet fat at the forty yard marker. The novice misses and has no idea why he flubbed, no concept of where he was in relation to the target.

Only the most expert scattergunner can get away with spot-shooting, only the confirmed grouse-hunter, for example, in whom long and bitter experience has drilled reflexes to guess gun angle and bird flight exactly on the nose. Many of our top-flight skeet competitors break crossing targets with uncanny speed, while the clay is still, to most of us, a blurred line fleeing the trap arm. They may seem to be spot-shooters; they're not. Gifted with the Ted Williams brand of visual speed and eye-to-hand reaction time, they actually do track the target, zip the gun through it, pull, and follow through in the one slick motion. They're swipers of the most skilled sort—they have to be. A spot-shooter operating that fast would be hopelessly whipped in skeet competition by the few targets in a hundred-round event that are set wrong on the trap, blown off line by wind.

Clay Targets Help

Many accomplished wingshots, bird-slayers par excellence, insist that either skeet or trap, or any of the less formalized clay target games set up to synthesize field gunnery, are little or no help to the starting shooter. That I can't ride with. It may be negative reasoning to argue that the phony-bird games are the only possible substitute, in these days of scrimpy bag limits of four ducks or a couple of cock pheasants, for the extensive game-killing practice our granddaddies enjoyed. But it is positive reasoning to point out that seasons and bird populations and limits have nothing to do with the *preliminary* training needed for a wingshot, the drill that makes gun-mounting and swinging automatic, the experience to turn up faults not only in technique but in gun-fit as well. Trap targets from the 16-yard line offer least help to the beginner because the shooter starts with his gun cheeked and ready as it never is a-field; skeet does the next best job with its gun-handling training and wide variety of target angles; a hand trap slung by a patient and strong-armed friend is the best clay-target deal of all for the novice.

Learning to hit the stylized trap and skeet birds passing

Swing Through or
Paintbrush

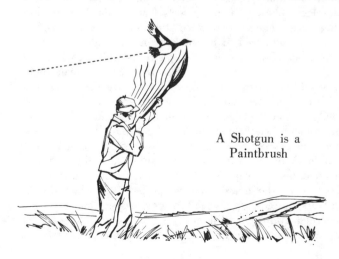

A Shotgun is a
Paintbrush

well is no great stunt, shouldn't take a man of normal vision and health too many shells. In the process of teaching aerial free gunners for Uncle Sam's Navy planes, we could take young radiomen or mechs and in some twenty hours of class shooting have them smashing 80% or better of the targets thrown. Some of these men had never so much as busted a shell at a rabbit before. To get above 90% and stay there was quite another problem, but a good start was both easy and quick. Yet in any of the stylized gun games there is one danger, a danger especially notable in starting a wingshot on the skeet field.

Since each target's flight line and speed are fixed, it is possible to calculate leads on the skeet field and so to tell a man at Station 2 outgoer, for example, to keep his muzzle a couple of feet ahead and a few inches under the clay; or at Station 4 to double that lead. Such instruction, while it's vastly better than encouraging the novice to shoot at some blindly guessed spot, has two bad effects. First, it makes him a *thinking* shooter, one who pokes and calculates and ends up, after he has maintained the "proper" lead for an interminable time, with a stopped swing, missed bird. Second, such drilling has him completely snafued when he encounters quail that buzz up and off in all directions. They pay no heed to the set lead situations he has learned.

The maintained-lead or pointing-out scheme of scatter-gunnery works fine on waterfowl, where the gunner has, relatively speaking, all afternoon to watch his target as the pintails swing over the decoys, to get the gun up and out ahead by two or six or fifteen duck lengths. On slow-flying pheasants in open cover, where the flush is close to you and the dog, there's similarly time for elaborately thought-out maintained-lead shooting. Practice in the pointing-out method is part of an accomplished wingshot's arsenal—but he leaves it at home when he steps out for grouse, quail, any of the now-or-never winged targets, and he found long ago that this method was no good on targets such as can be hand-thrown by a cooperative, evil-minded partner.

A Swiper Doesn't Know

The really fine wingshot is a *swiper* who can, for neither love nor money, tell you how much he leads any one target. He doesn't know. Even excluding the variation in shot flight time over various ranges—and the difference between twenty and fifty yards of ranges, in terms of pellet speed alone, means for a canvasback drake crossing at 60 per a difference in theoretical lead of some nine long feet—no two men have either the same triggering speed or the same idea of what a duck looks like two, four, or forty feet behind their moving gun muzzles. The ace shot doesn't think of lead as distance but rather as gun speed, if he thinks about it at all.

Last fall in an Illinois goose pit yours truly was fit to be tied the first morning. The geese were coming over high, paying little attention to calls or decoys because this was a firing-line situation on the fringe of a reserve. The general bombardment kept 'em up. With the birds in sight for an interminable length of time, I was calculating leads in distance, and thereby wasting heavy loads of 2's. Disgusted, I went back to the swipe method, waiting until the very last moment before rearing out of the pit, then swinging and shooting as the muzzle was swept past the white throat-markers, building up the lead by a swipe-speed automatically governed by the birds' flying speed. Fifteen minutes later I was through for the day, with all the goose dinners I was

entitled to. The field-shooting method paid off in the pit, as it always does on upland birds.

You may be able to paint a ceiling upside down or cover cupboard shelves while tied in a knot, but you can't swing a shotgun, you can't swipe-shoot effectively, with your feet fouled up or your upper body locked. The broadbill gunner who sits up in his scooter to take a bunch can swing to his left and kill birds; but those two scaup that broke sharp right are safe because his right swing is hopelessly cramped. He can swipe only from the waist up. As every upland gunner knows, after he has flubbed two pheasants in a row because his size 12's were tangled in the raspberries, flexibility clear down to the feet is of the essence.

A right-handed boxer moves around with his left foot leading slightly, so that he can hit with either hand, swing either way. So must a scattergunner. On clay targets, skeet for example, he can set his soles comfortably apart some 12-18 inches, the left foot leading so that it is only five or ten degrees left of the imaginary line out to where he expects to break the target. That gives him ample elasticity all the way from his toes to his left or gun-pointing hand, rubbery freedom to pick up the target well right, swipe through it and continue swinging into the follow-through. Nor will his hips lock in a full swing the other way. The trap-shooter can easily plant his dogs to give him swing ease anywhere in the 90-degree cone of flight of legal targets. The field gunner must set his feet right to swing properly, yet he cannot, like the clay targeteer, anticipate the line his chink or chukar is going to follow.

Does that change matters regarding foot position? Not at all. The upland shooter, save in the rarest instances where tree-dodging ruffed grouse or quail diving into thick brush demand ultra-fast shots, has at his disposal plenty of time to

Ewing Galloway

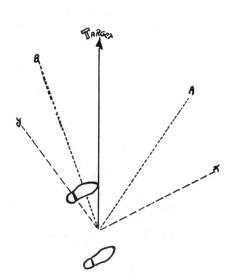

1—Normal "fighter" stance, easily assumed in field shooting, puts leading or left foot slightly off left of expected target line. It permits fairly free swing from X to Y, perfect swing ease from A to B, which is in target area.

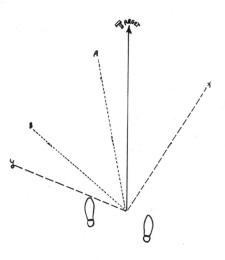

2—Excessively closed stance, with left foot on or right of line to expected target, puts easy-swing arc between X and Y, best swing area between A and B. Hence anticipated target is in poor area, one where free gun swing begins to cramp.

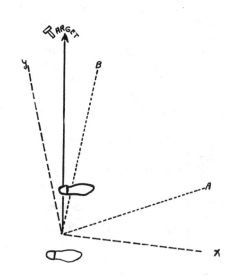

3—Unduly open or square stance, more directly facing the likely target, may permit swing between X-Y, Y-X, but the least cramped, smoothest swing area is between A and B. That arc does not include the likely target area, hence the position, an improvement over 2, is not as good as 1.

take the extra step or make the shuffle that will line his boots in the same relationship to the feathered bird as he would assume to a trapped clay. The thunderous outburst of a covey of quail, while faster and certainly more furious than the cackling get-off of a ringnecked rooster, actually does permit that time. With modern loads or close-bored guns, indeed, we'd better count off a few more second-fractions before blasting away, or we'll pick up only pheasant hash.

In a number of years of acting as a gun at field trials for spaniels and retrievers, a kind of high-pressure bird-shooting which is as much hard work as it is fun because the guns must not only connect, but must drop the bird as the judges wish, I've watched some top wingshots in action. An ace like Ernest Burton, no matter how foot-tangling the cover, will never cut loose until his feet are spotted for a comfortable swing. That final adjusting step is one part of the tracking-swinging-shooting move that is a blended unit of scattergun accuracy and deadliness.

Free to Swing

When the feet are positioned right, the weight forward on the leading leg is a 60-40 distribution which comes naturally, the wingshot's hips are free to swing, as are indeed his shoulders. No problems? Only one. Too many embryonic scattergunners recall their rifle training, G.I. style, and they cock out that right elbow like a shelf. Result—their shoulders become as inhibited, in respect to swing, as a Boston spinster. Since the scattergun is a weapon of movement, the trigger-arm position must be comfortable, with the elbow only half-raised, the shoulders not lifted but relaxed, fluid.

Most treatises on shotgun techniques, no matter which gun-pointing methods they may uphold, spend a good many inches of type on the important left hand. It is, to be sure, the hand that points the gun; though at least two amazingly deadly wingshots, left sleeves emptied by military wounds,

have gunned beside the author, taking bird for bird. They were forced to shoot with only the right hand. Yet for ninety-nine per cent of us, it is the left hand that kills the cock. Novices in the scattergun game, often because the double they inherited from Uncle Harry came fitted with an antiquated and abominable splinter fore-end, tend to crook the elbow, to grab the gun so far back toward the center of balance that they achieve gun-swinging speed without any control. Conversely the shotgunner long trained on clay targets tends to straighten the left arm, muscle onto the gun as far out as he can reach, for precise control but a very limited free-swing radius. There's no positive prescription. The point you palm on the fore-grip is dependent on your arm length, your personal compromise between the exaggeratedly short or long holds. Just one tip—the left hand goes *under and along* the gun, not squarely across or around it, so that the barrel is pointing off the second knuckle of your index finger, not being pried at like a crowbar.

Too little attention is paid to the right or triggering hand, it seems from this corner. With the slow passing from the scattergun scene of the side-by-side double, conventionally built with two triggers and a straight wrist or grip, we have become a nation of pistol-grip-grabbers. Our over-under guns, our pumps and semi-automatics all come with one bend or another of pistol handle, and of course they are single-triggered. With the left or pointing hand spotted a couple of inches below the sight line, as it must inevitably be for either the repeating single-barrel or the vertically framed double, that right hand becomes more important in proper gun line-up than is generally realized. Sometime experiment with your Old Betsy pump or that engraved over-under that you just got back from Pachmayr's. Shift your trigger-hand position high on the grip and notice how you push the butt down, the muzzle up, when you mount the gun fast; drop it low on the curve and see how you automatically force the gun to shoot low. There's one exactly right position of the triggering hand, only one, and getting it right every time the covey busts out is the result only of long gun-handling experience and drill.

Even before sales of double guns began to slump, of course, a revolution had taken place in wingshooting methods. Forty years ago, and for two hundred years before that, a proper fowling piece was so stocked that a proper gentleman gunner shot standing up, straight-necked. Drops of over two inches to the comb edge and over three inches to the heel of the stock were normal. With this dog-legged weapon Nimrod, upright in every sense, pointed out his game. Today scattergunners find Granddad's crook-stock handy on rabbits, impossible on flushing game because he undershoots with it by a matter of yards, not feet or inches. We no longer stand straight-necked, nor do we put our cheek down on the comb as we mount the gun. Not, that is, unless we are an over-serious trapshooter who winds himself up, in, and on his weapon with enough tension to ensure a droned "Lost!" from the referee. Today, with chin slightly forward, neck slightly bent, we bring the gun up to the cheek.

Potentially Faster

To the starting wingshot, this has two meanings. First, it means that with straighter stocks, conventionally made with some $1\frac{1}{2}''$ to $1\frac{5}{8}''$ drop from sight line to comb and $2\frac{1}{2}''$ to the heel, he is potentially a faster game shot than his sainted Granddad because he has faster-handling equipment. Second, it means that until he has established basically sound gun-pointing techniques, gained a proper idea of swing, he doesn't have to sweat over the niceties of gun-fit. Certainly

not unless he departs widely from the average male physique, is a five-by-five or a pole-long refugee from the basketball court. Why not? Because by adjustment of the position of his head as the gun is brought up to his cheek, by eventually learning in the muscles, as it were, of an habitual head position which is adapted to the gun, he can accommodate himself to a so-called standard stock.

In the dusty quiet of the Purdey or Holland & Holland showrooms, certainly at their shooting schools, this idea of fitting the man to the stock is outrageous heresy. The English technique for centuries has been to mate to the shooter, be he grouse-killing expert or fumble-fingered novice, a stock derived from experiment with a try-gun. How this precise fit can be accomplished on a subject who knows a shotgun only as a subject for jokes about forced weddings, who has no idea of the why's and wherefore's of the weapon he's handling, this uncouth Yankee has never quite understood. Time enough for the try-gun when a wingshot has developed nonchalance if not great skill. We have no more than half a dozen try-guns in this whole country anyway, all in expensive gun stores where the average scattergunner seldom treads. He will do as well by adapting himself to a standard stock until, come that day when long practice and many dead birds, perhaps many whittlings so the stock is no longer even remotely standard, he has a clear idea of the shape of his gun-handle ideal. Then and only then can he know the pleasure of a stock that fits to perfection, that is a completely unnoticed cog in the gun-pointing sequence, a symphony composed in walnut.

But, as a skilled wingshot, he'll still be using it just like the handle of a paintbrush!

The 18th century gent, shooting a stock with deep drop, stood straight and unbending, not to say stiff, when birding.

The modern gunner, using a straighter stock, leans slightly forward, head down, to meet the rising gun.

Picking the right bullet for *your* hunting needs is more
important than choosing a caliber. Here's the lowdown on—

Bullet Bustup

by WARREN PAGE

A FIVE-HUNDRED-DOLLAR rifle, when you get right down to the killing it was built for, isn't worth a penny more than a five- or ten-cent bullet. Engraving will make a rifle pretty and a fine barrel will make it accurate, but all this handsomeness is history when the projectile hits. From there on out it's the bullet, not the rifle, that determines whether you walk over to pose beside a trophy neatly dispatched or have to hunt over half a mountain range to finish off an animal messily shot up. The best bullet in the world, to be sure, won't kill clean if you and your rifle don't drive it into the right spot; but the best rifle and rifleman are going to fail on cleanly sure kills if they aren't shooting the right bullet.

The sad tales you read condemning ultra-velocity weap-

ons because their bullets "explode on impact, blowing out a fist-sized chunk of meat" always damn rifle or caliber. They never spot the blame where it belongs, on the *wrong* bullet as chosen by a lunk-headed rifleman. As I type this, I bleed for a chap who has already left for Africa with, as part of his arsenal, a super-hot 25 caliber. Its bottle-big cases are crammed with powder and fragile little 87-gr. pills meant for crows and woodchucks. At 3700 f.p.s. they'll burst like bombs and he'll bloody up the camp meat, make sieves of a few trophy capes, have to chase some worthwhile beast halfway across Kenya, and end up cursing out the rifle. He and his bullets really rate the profanity. Bullet selection, which is a combination of experience and common sense, can make all the difference on his or anybody

The European roebuck, show in various attitudes of collapse and shock as it is hit in the liver, the lungs, the heart, etc. From the RWS *Mitteilungen* No. 6 (July 1956, Nürnberg).

To really know bullet performance the rifleman must himself perform careful autopsies, mostly a bloody job of work, seldom the easy one that *Field & Stream's* Gun Editor Warren Page is here knifing out on a New Zealand red deer of the transplanted *hirsch* or European type. The 175-gr. 7mm Nosler bullet from the Mashburn Magnum was lodged just under the off-side hide of this 13-point stag.

else's expensive hunt.

The average bloke would be several lifetimes accumulating enough bullet performance dope, on even two or three calibers, to mean much more than what we read in the advertisements; even a man in my spot, one who more or less hunts for a living, would mine such data very slowly if it were not for the mob of gun cranks who own pencils, paper, and a yen for letting-writing. A file of their comments on what bullet X did inside a critter's boiler room at range Y is more precious than gold. At least it would be if more correspondents would give forth with *all* the story, and would go to *all* the gory trouble of carving up animals to find not only the battered projectile, but also to trace its wound channel through innards and muscle, skin and bone. The serious hunter who isn't compiling his own private file is losing half the fun anyway, especially if he's a handloader and has a host of bullets to choose from.

The 6mm in New Zealand

The shooting world by this time knows that I'm a 6mm bug, can therefore understand that, for a seven-week hunt in New Zealand recently, one of the rifles toted was a 240 P.S.P. On the hunting menu were Jap, fallow, whitetail, Axis deer and chamois on the light animal side; pigs in the middle; sambur, red deer or hirsch, and Himalayan tahr on the heavier end of the list. My loads would drive the 105-gr. Speer bullet at about 3200 f.p.s., and the 100-gr. Nosler at roughly the same speed. Reasons for taking the 240? First, I like the rifle; second, I wanted to see how

those two pills performed on a lot of kills, get more data than I could hope to collect in the states in several seasons. And I also had a sharp knife ready to do a lot of autopsies. Answers? That's easy. First, the 240 P.S.P. killed like lightning even on red deer of 350-400 pounds, though this can't be the whole story because of the two dozens beasts the caliber took all but one were hit with vital precision. Second, the two bullets performed with characteristic consistency. That is, on broadside or slightly angling lung-area hits from 50 to 250 yards, the 105 Speer would usually be found under the hide on the off side, expanded way back, weighing some 50 grains of its original 105. The wound channel would show early opening, a tearing and explosive effect as the bullet shed lead or forepart, but seldom did the pill hold enough weight to break out through the cushion of off-side skin, unless it missed all bone on the way through. The action of the Nosler semi-spitzer bullet was a bit different. None of these could I recover from pigs, deer, or whatever, because at ranges out to 200 yards, where the impact speed was still fairly high, the butt section (that below the partition which beefs up Noslers in all calibers) always tore out a fifty-cent-size exit hole. But the thin-tapered forepart was obviously expanding; in one instance, where the bullet hit shoulder bone immediately under the skin on the impact side, actually shattering, because in careful autopsies the latter half of the wound channel showed the ripping and outspread tearing of tissue we always get from a bullet that has turned into a buzz-saw.

What use in all this? Now I know, or at least have an

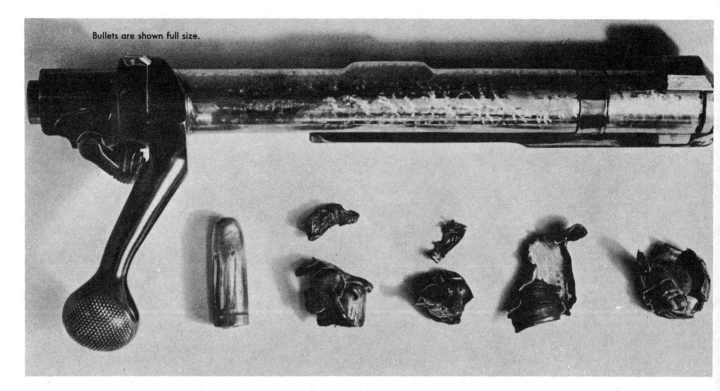

Bullets are shown full size.

Bullets recovered from African-Asian big game. Left to right, (1) 300-gr. 375 Kynoch solid hit Indian gaur at about 65 yds., smashed shoulder and spine, slug found under hide at far side. Almost no bullet deformation. (2) 300-gr. 375 W-W solid fired into large rhino at about 60 yds., entering behind shoulder. Found fully smashed in joint bone of other shoulder, gilding metal jacket not performing as true solid should. (3) 300-gr. Silvertip fired from Weatherby 375 Magnum into tiger at 25 yds. Hit and broke shoulder, rest of bullet found in diaphragm. Excess velocity smeared rather tender bullet. (4) 300-gr. S'tip fired at 375 Weatherby speed into lion's shoulder at 100 yds. smashed up squarely on big bone, though jacket material found loose in lung area. Leo ran, hit again in fore-quarter. Bullet bustup showed too much speed for type of construction. (5) 300-gr. 375 S'tip fired from Weatherby at 2775 f.p.s. into neck of great bull eland at about 250 yds. Bullet broke spine, lodged in off-side flesh, kill was instant. Moderate impact speed insured excellent expansion, performance. More shooters should make these autopsies, report their findings.

opinion, as to how these two bullets stack up against the normally fast-opening Hornady 100-gr. roundnose, the tough-jacketed Sierra spitzer of the same weight. Next time the 240 P.S.P. goes hunting with me, be it for white-tail at woods ranges, antelope far across the flats, muleys in the sagebrush or chamois on some crag in Austria, I'll be able to pick the pill which should be the proper medicine.

Nosler and Hornady 7mm's

That same hunt — remember that New Zealand has no closed season on deer, no limit, no license, and the government employs "cullers" to destroy deer at the rate of 100,000 a year — also gave me an opportunity to check on the action of two 7mm bullets as they worked on heavier game out of my 7mm Mashburn Magnum, which pushed the 175-gr. Hornady and Nosler types at 3050 clocked muzzle speed. The Nosler bullet, which has accounted for the majority of the 160-175 world-wide big game kills that belong to that trusty musket, is a known quantity. It has consistently refused to smash up even when slammed into the heavy shoulder bone of rutting bull moose or chunky stud zebra at short range and high impact speeds; it has expanded forward to create deep-penetrating destruction even on hits at bad angles, and has proved its ability to expand to at least two calibers at low impact speed by its performance on an African greater kudu at 600 yards. Action on 400-500 pound red deer stags simply reasserted the earlier evidence. First-lot Hornady 175-gr. soft points used on game of 300-800 pounds weight had shown a tendency to open fast at magnum speeds, and to shed their cores at the end of penetration, so in New Zealand I wanted to try a later type, one which Hornady had made tougher in jacketing, with a core-binding cannelure rolled on. The first try of the new type bullet involved a big red deer or hirsch, up in the Dart Valley. From some 175 yards I deliberately angled the shot through the short ribs into the off shoulder. The new bullet — and it was re-checked on other game — showed the effect of its redesigning by opening more slowly but fully, holding its core intact below the cannelure, and so giving far deeper penetration than the original type. Now we know another 175-gr. slug of .284″ diameter which will stand up to magnum velocities.

There's no agreement as to the qualities of the the-roetically perfect game bullet, but from where I sit, the projectile for critters above varmint size should be: (1) *accurate;* (2) *sure* to start expanding at velocities as low as the 400-yard impact speeds of the rifle or cartridge from which it is fired; (3) so *controlled* in its expansion that, save for certain exceptions, it will not smash or fly to pieces even if it smacks bone early in its passage through the animal; (4) capable of enough *penetration* in the game for which its caliber and weight are intended so that its extensive wound channel will either end with an exit hole on broadside hits or will extend to an off-side under-hide position on all but the shallowest angling hits.

It's axiomatic that no slug fulfills all requirements to perfection, but bullet makers and designers keep trying, even if they are stringently limited by cost factors — the

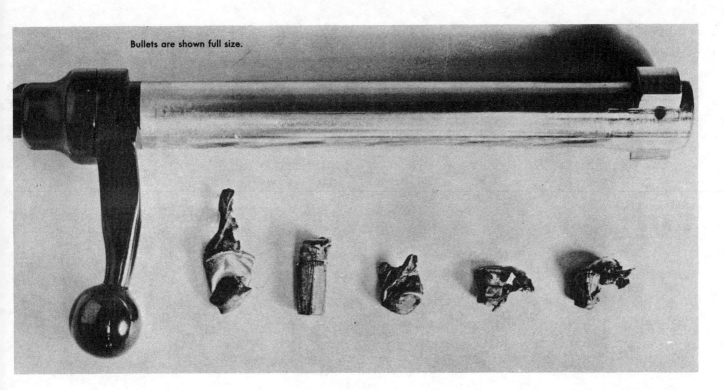

Bullets are shown full size.

From left to right, a group of busted-up slugs from Page's kills. (1) 180-gr. Remington Bronze Point taken from 1500-pound Alaskan brownie. Bullet struck at 75 ft. into shoulder bone, smashing it, then blew up in the lung area. Impact speed, perhaps 3200 f.p.s., too high for a bullet designed for 30-06 velocities, though bear was kaput instanter. (2) 180-gr. Remington P C L, fired from a 30-06 at 150 yds. into a caribou, ahead of shoulder. It hit a big bone, was deflected, lodged in rear of far shoulder. Death in seconds. (3 and 4) Two Speer 105-gr. 6mm's, fired into red stags (350 lbs.) at 200-250 yds. Both broadside hits through the lungs, both found under far-side skin. Consistent, complete expansion, with only rib bones hit. (5) 243 Winchester 100-gr. hit mule deer at 200 yds., entering just ahead of ham, lodged in left shoulder. Remarkable penetration for this type of bullet, though no bones were struck until final moment.

Nosler 30 caliber bullets, for example, cost about a dime each — and by the rather few available techniques for building into a bullet specific functional features.

Bullet Design

No matter how you cut it, there are only three basic methods of starting bullet expansion. First is the exposed lead tip, tried and true and used by Speer, Sierra, Hornady and others as well as by the big arms plants — the Silvertip bullet is in this category since the tipping of white gilding metal is merely a point protector. Second is the hollow point, sometimes appearing with a false nose of thin metal for magazine protection, which works devastatingly at high speeds but is unreliable when the steam is gone. Less often appear the peg, wire, or wedge point design such as the present Remington Bronze Point in which a wedge is driven back by impact to split the fore-section of the bullet. For all its tendency to batter in the magazine, the old lead point is still probably the surest to start opening at any impact velocity.

Nor do we seem to have evolved any radical schemes for controlling the rate of expansion in its early stages. The fracture-line scheme used by Winchester-Western in their redesigning of the Silvertip line some years back, which by drawing jackets (the fore-section only) through a hexagonal die creates little folds or break-lines, is just a modern version of the cut-nosed dum-dum bullet. So in a sense, is the similar fracture-line method used by Remington in their Pointed Core-Lokt series, or even the scalloping used on jacket edges of their basic round-nosed soft point which

is preferred for woods use. There's nothing new about tapering jacket metal so that it is thinnest near the exposed point, a method most skillfully used in Hornady bullets but practiced by most other manufacturers. The one great exception is Fred Barnes, who swages his slugs out of lead plus copper tubing with the point thicker than the shank. Yet he manages to get expansion, the Barnes pills having a neat habit of wadding up into a misshapen ball that does killing damage, as certain heads and hides adorning my gun room testify. Few shooters, of course, realize the great effect on expansion rate of the controlled hardness of jacket metal and lead cores. Home-swaged bullets made for bench rest accuracy in 224, 243, or 257 diameters, if their jacket metal is work-hardened by too many passes through dies, will often punch caliber-sized holes through either varmints or game despite soft lead cores. The problem with certain lots of Remington PCL bullets, way back when, was cores made needlessly tough by certain hardening agents used in the lead. Adjusting the metallurgy of a bullet to give both accuracy and proper expansion under all the variables of range or impact speed, plus all the infinite variables of those layers of skin, flesh, bone, and tissue which develop varying resistances in assorted game animals — this is a problem which will never be ideally solved.

Magnum Matters

The development of "magnum" cartridges in recent years, whether these be labeled Weatherby, wildcat, Winchester, or RWS, has brought with it progress in the matter of controlling expansion to retain bullet weight, thereby to increase the penetration which is *usually lessened,* not increased, by high muzzle and impact speeds. The RWS H-jacket method employed in Germany had its heyday when standard 8x57mm speeds were souped up by the 8x60 "magnum bombe" and the 8x68mm hotshot loomed up. It works just dandy but it costs too much for American manufacture. The Nosler partition-jacket method, in which a closed wall of heavy gilding metal is formed across the inside of the heavy jacket, to separate the frangible front and the durable rear sections of the bullet, achieves the H-jacket aims. It also probably produces a better and more accurate (because simpler) bullet, but is still relatively costly. When the sliding outer belt used by Peters in its 220-gr. 30 caliber slug proved too tough for anything save the biggest brownies or really rugged African antelope types, it went out, in favor of an inner belting or canneluring — now also used by Winchester-Western under another name in some calibers and weights. This works efficiently unless we really overdrive such 30-06 pills, say, by at least the five or six hundred foot-seconds feasible with a Weatherby-type loading. The solid-based slugs Ackley experimented with would hold their base weight regardless of speed, but ran up pressures and never gave much real accuracy in any rifle I tried them in; and the double-jacketed slugs, a bullet within a bullet, which experimenters Bert Shay and Al Cosentino have tried in 257 and 284 calibers, have never been used in quantity enough for any real assessment. Magnum-velocity bullets are a lot more common today than ten years ago, however, and will continue to be developed as powders improve and speeds increase.

To assess each and every bullet available to both the hardware store patron and the handloader is a job that would fill this issue of the GUN DIGEST, a stuffing of which Editor Amber might disapprove. Let's however, try it for one or two sample situations. Say you're a 270 shooter, willing to shoot either factory ammo or reloads. You have coming up a Wyoming trip which will involve antelope and muleys in open sagebrush country. One of the quickest killers on antelope or small deer, a bullet which will open and usually smash up at any likely game yardage is W-W's 130-gr. O P E, a hollow-point with fracture-nicked foresection. A bomb, and also a meat-spoiler, as its long kill history out of my Pachmayr-built 270 indicates. You prefer to eat those forequarters or want to make a shockingly sudden kill? The 130-gr. spire point by Hornady, or the Sierra and Speer bullets at this weight, will give less rapid blow-up, might be better bets on the mule deer. Now you've decided to add a pack trip for elk to that Wyoming deal? Well, any good 130-gr. 270 will drop wapiti fast if you slip it between the forward ribs without angling through any quarters, but you'll be better able to cope with a tough bull, long range, and the need for shooting him at some screwy angle if you handload the 150-gr. boat-tail by Sierra, the 150 Nosler spitzer or the 150 Speer flat-based spitzer, and use enough 4350 or 4831 to give close to 3000 foot-seconds. Any one of these three pills will hold together to let out his life after a hit on the bias, and such a load is infinitely better across a canyon than the 150-gr. factory slowpoke, in trajectory better beyond 300 yards than the 130-gr. combinations.

Part of Page's recovered bullet collection. From left to right, (1) 175-gr. 7mm Nosler, fired into greater kudu at 600 yds., went into the short ribs at an angle, then through liver, lungs, etc., to break a rib, lodged under skin at far side. (2) Ditto Nosler shot at high velocity into a bull elk at some 450 yds. Bullet drove in behind shoulder, was found under hide of other shoulder, busting ribs and top of the heart en route. Death was right now! (3) Ditto Nosler at 3050 f.p.s., dug from a 400-lb. New Zealand red stag. Impact was into rear ribs, quartering to opposite shoulder, which it broke, bullet found under skin. An instant kill. (4) 175-gr. Hornady fired into greater kudu at magnum speed at 150 yds. Hit broadside in heart and lung area, ribs on both sides were broken, bullet found under hide of fore-quarter. This newest Hornady 7mm gave excellent killing effects. (5) 275-gr. Hornady from 35 Mashburn Magnum dropped very big Alaskan moose. Bullet went into ribs, smashed two of them, diaphragm, lungs, lodged in opposite shoulder. Heavy damage, good penetration, an instant kill.

Or suppose you're a 30 caliber bug and want to go varminting. The factory 100-gr. bullets from either red or green boxes have a quaint habit of tossing two or three well out of a group of ten shots, so you'd better reload. While the assorted 110-gr. pills available up to a year ago weren't much for accuracy either, Sierra has a new hollow point that is a tackholer in all good 30 caliber rifles, regardless of their 1-in-10 standard twist. Too, the 30 caliber Speer and Hornady 130-gr. open-enders will both shoot and bust up on chuck or clod.

Say you were going to Africa? Lucky fellow. Am I to understand you want some solids for your 300 Weatherby, just in case? Then we run into some facts of life. In the first place, neither Kenya nor Tanganyika legally sanctions the use of any caliber less than a 375 on the kind of critters — rhino, elephant, possibly buff — where solids are indicated. In the second place, those round-nosed 220-gr. bullets left over from Krag days aren't true solids, any more than is any other bullet fully patched with mere gilding metal, like match and military ammo. In fact, since even the conical-nosed 308 slug developed by Winchester-Western is a full-patch rather than a *true* solid, your only bet is a box of the 30 calibers jacketed in thick mild steel, copper-plated, of which Hornady has made a few.

Note I said true solid. There are only two real solids made in any commercial quantity in this country, the factory slug for the 458, and Joyce Hornady's bullet for the 375 H&H or the 378 Weatherby. To be a true solid, a bullet capable of resisting bending, riveting, or any other form of deformation when it whonks into an elephant's noggin, the slug must be round or bluff-nosed, must be jacketed in mild steel from .05- to .10-inch thick. The Rigby and Kynoch or ICI types made in England qualify; our 375 "solid" as loaded in East Alton doesn't because its jacket is gilding metal and that will smash. I crunched one into confetti on a Kenya rhino's shoulder joint, on the off side where it had slowed down, so that's that. Winchester-Western will probably be making a proper steel-coated slug for the 375 H&H soon, probably also for the 338 Magnum when this Newton-type job hatches.

The only real test of game bullets, expanding bullets, is on the game for which they are intended. Putting a slug in a vise and setting up on it to check expansion control is interestingly irrelevant. Shooting bullets at known impact speeds into nearly incompressible water, as the arms companies do, will give us handsome pictures of how bullets open up in a homogenous medium, pretty pictures for advertising — but water ain't what a bullet smacks into when it punches into a bull elk's shoulder. It whacks into thick neck hair, then rut-toughened hide, probably either cracks or deflects off a sizeable chunk of bone, slices through muscle and finally, we hope, buzz-saws through a lot of soft lung and arterial tissue before it runs into the thin flesh, rib, and stretchy skin of the distant side. Or the procedure may be reversed, with no bone or hard muscle being encountered until the slug has done its business and crossed the vital area. Or — and this heaven forbid — it may plop into a paunch stuffed with half-digested grass that makes an excellent bullet-swallower and is unlike either shoulder beef or any tank of

water. It's only the careful autopsy, bloody-handed and messy, that proves the pudding for a game bullet — I'll never forget hacking up a very dead tiger's carcass to prove what I had suspected, that the 300-gr. 375 Silvertip is a more fragile bullet than the 270-gr. soft point.

Varmint shooters are in a better fix. With a long shooting season, a lot of targets, and hardly need for amateur surgery to discover what their bullet did or didn't do, it usually doesn't take them long to make up their minds on the right pill for the job. Just because a bullet happens to be .224-inch in diameter, for example, doesn't automatically fit it for every varminting job. It's no great secret that before the 222 Remington was announced, the factory put up some combinations involving the 48-gr. Swift bullet at 3135 f.p.s. These I tried out on some fifty chucks. The result was some Bridgeport hair-tearing and assorted telephone conversations, ultimately the revamping of that bullet to one with a Hornet-thin jacket at a bit higher speed. Obviously no projectile meant to start at 4100 is going to perform correctly if it sets forth a thousand feet slower.

This cuts both ways, in that using Hornady's new pill designed for normal 222 speed out of your 22-250 or 220 Swift can bring only disappointment. At 3800-plus it probably will blow up short of the target, however devastating it may be when started six or seven hundred feet slower. But most varminteers run into the opposite problem, that of projectiles too tough for their hitting speed. Sierra 55-gr. spitzers or the stout Sisk Express pills blow the backside off chucks out of my 220 Arrow, often let them reach their holes when loaded to only just over 3000 f.p.s. from a 222.

And when the varminter moves into one of the justly popular 6mm cartridges, he runs into much of the same thing. Both the 75-gr. Remington and 80-gr. Winchester bullets, at normal factory speeds, have seemed to smash handsomely on chucks or crows I hit, or bust themselves into non-dangerous pieces on the ground I hit when the chucks were missed, clear out of the 350-yard mark. There velocities have dropped to the 2000-foot-second mark, the usual bust-up minimum. Yet neither of the heavier 90- or 100-gr. factory bullets can be relied on to avoid ricochet. Neither will the 90-gr. Speer, which is really intended as a game bullet, or for that matter the 85-gr. Sierra which will do a surprising job of penetration on critters like antelope, for example. Gardiner's 6mm bullets come in two jacket weights, or used to, and where the thin ones are junior bombs on a varmint, the thick ones can make you mighty unpopular with farmers or ranch owners.

So even the varmint hunter has to exercise judgment on qualities other than accuracy when he buys a box of ammo or a box of bullets, however much simpler his problem is than that of the Nimrod after larger game. It's this latter gent who must really use his thinker — No, sir, there's not much choice for the 30-30; just use the 170-gr. soft point of any make and try to dodge the trees — when he decides on loads for that hunt of a lifetime.

The Nosler Partition-Jacket bullet.

Cornel Klett, Hofbüchsenmacher

The story of a rare two=caliber wheellock

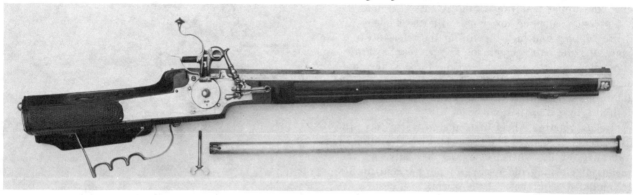

by STEPHEN V. GRANCSAY,
Curator of Arms and Armor, Metropolitan Museum of Art

ONE OF THE most unusual and interesting guns in the Metropolitan Museum of Art is a wheellock with two rifled barrels whose large-caliber fixed barrel .contains a smaller barrel, removable at will. The main barrel is dated 1653 and is signed by Cornel Klet (or Klett—as usual in that period there were variant spellings), a gunmaker who belonged to a distinguished family of firearms craftsmen and inventors. The stock is identified as the work of the unidentified master, H N, who worked for the Austrian court and nobility.

While the wheellock mechanism has been described many times, it is not usually illustrated in detail. For this reason, the lock of our Klett rifle has been dismantled, and drawings[1] have been made to show each step in reassembling the elements. These drawings should be helpful to collectors who are unfamiliar with the mechanics of the wheellock, and also to anyone who wishes to make a missing part so that an incomplete lock can be made to function.

The drawings illustrated in figs. 1-9 show the numbered elements of our Klett rifle as they were assembled. The simple wheellock consists of a grooved steel wheel, to the axis of which a powerful spring is attached by a short chain. It is spanned or wound up clockwise (usually through about

[1] The drawings were made under the supervision of Rudolph Bullock and Leonard Heinrich of the Metropolitan Museum of Art.

Fig. 1. 1. Lockplate; 2. Wheel cover; 3. Thimble
4. Slide support of pan cover; 5. Bridge support post
6. Support for release sear and mainspring
7. Mainspring guide and pivot

Fig. 2. The elements of Fig. 1 are in position.

8. Wheel with grooved edge
9-9A. Trigger sear and pivot.

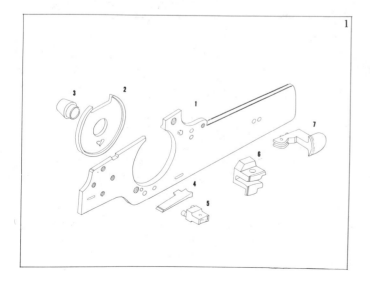

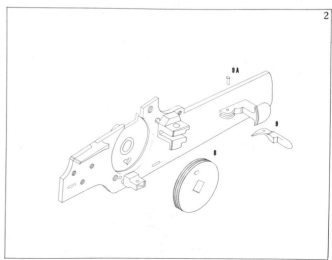

280° to 320°) by means of a spanner or key and retained in that position by a supported sear.[2] The sear catch in the wheel is a shallow, beveled depression, and the nose of the release sear is short and rounded. When the piece is spanned and the nose slides into the shallow sear catch it is prevented from sliding out by a supporting trigger sear which slips automatically in place. A single double-action spring actises the release sear and the trigger sear; when the wheel is wound, the upper leaf presses the release sear into the wheel depression, and the lower half tilts the trigger sear forward to support and lock the arm of the release sear.

On touching the hair trigger, the trigger sear is thrown back, unlocking the release sear, and the force of the compressed mainspring pulls the wheel counterclockwise, and the cam on the axle throws open the pan cover; the pyrites slides off the retreating pan cover on to the serrated edge of the already rotating wheel of tempered steel, thus producing a stream of sparks. The heart-shaped perforation in the lower part of the wheel cover was decorative as well as a means of cleaning the residue of powder and pyrites that accumulated at the base of the wheel.

Our rifle is equipped with a two-sear hair trigger which is both a release and a safety device. The wheellock could be carried safely when it was spanned, and the hair trigger had to be cocked before the piece could be fired. Safety devices designed to prevent the accidental discharge of loaded weapons have been among the most important me-

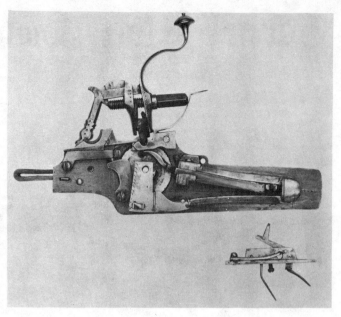

Fig. 15. Interior of Wheellock, also hair trigger.

chanical improvements in the gradual evolution of firearms. The hair trigger is in principle an additional lock which delivers its hammer blow on the sear tail, and effects a lighter and far more precise release than can be achieved by trigger pressure alone. When cocked, a light touch on the hair trigger will release the firing mechanism.

The trigger pull in the original and early wheellock mechanisms was heavy. It had an unsupported sear—that is, the nose of the sear fitted into a depression in the wheel deep enough to hold the nose of the one-piece sear, without the supporting or locking sear. Considerable pressure had to be exerted on the trigger in order to disengage the unsupported sear, which naturally tended to deflect one's aim. Our rifle has both the supported sear and the hair trigger, features that were decided aids to accurate marksmanship.

---

[2]There is a Nuremberg 17-century double-barrel side-by-side wheellock pistol in the Metropolitan Museum of Art (51.176.3) with a lock on each side; the left-hand lock is naturally wound counterclockwise since the mainspring and chain are behind the spindle. When released the wheel of the lock turns clockwise.

A wheellock rifle in the Metropolitan Museum of Art (26.268.2) has a large cogwheel on the spindle which winds approximately 260°: When released this causes a small joined cogwheel to revolve through 610°. The small cogwheel and the grooved wheel turn on the same spindle, the square section of the spindle fitting into the usual square opening in the grooved wheel.

Fig. 3. The preceding elements are in position.

10. Spindle with chain of three links attached to cam.
11-11A. Release sear and pivot screw.
12. Double-action spring for release and trigger sears.

Fig. 4. The preceding elements are in position.

13. Pan with flash protector.
13A. Screw to secure pan to lockplate.
14. Mainspring.

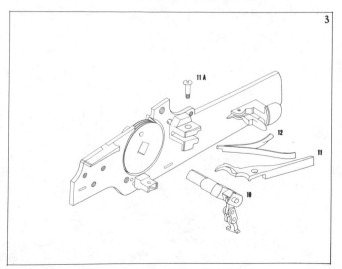

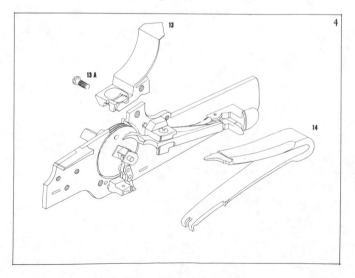

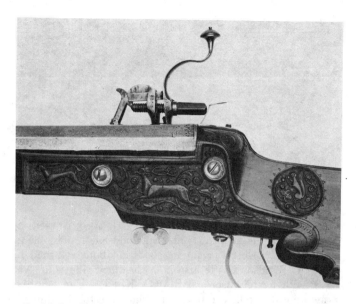

Fig. 14. Details of stock carving show the work of the Salzburg (Austria) stock master **H N**.

Springs play an important role in the wheellock mechanism. The strong hairpin mainspring revolves the wheel; the doghead spring, smaller than the mainspring, but of the same type, firmly presses the pyrites held in the jaws against the pan cover and then against the serrated wheel when the cover is thrown open by the cam on the revolving wheel spindle; the trigger and wheel hairpin spring is pivoted at the bend to move two pieces of mechanism; a flat steel spring holds opened or closed the pan cover, which in this piece is activated by hand. In many wheellocks the pan cover is closed by pressing a button which releases a spring that locks the pan cover in open position and a second spring automatically presses against a lug at the base of the pan cover arm, throwing the pan cover in closed position.

While the lock mechanism of our rifle is a common type, the disposition of the double barrel is unusual, and there are comparatively few examples of similar construction extant.

Fig. 5. The preceding elements are in position.

The T link of the chain fits into the notched end of the lower leaf of the spring. 15-15A. Pan cover with pivoted arm, and screw.

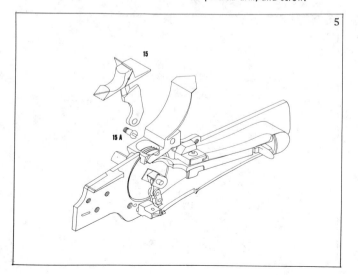

The main barrel is octagonal, 26¼ in. long, caliber 75, rifled with eight grooves, right-hand twist rifling making one-half turn in the length of the barrel, weight four lbs. It is dated and inscribed 1653 CORNEL · KLET, and is equipped with a twin leaf-sight and elongated brass fore sight. Three pierced lugs are swaged at intervals to the under facet for the transverse pegs which secure it to the stock. The tang screw passes upward from the under side of the stock and also secures the fore end of the iron trigger guard which has three indentations for the second, third, and fourth fingers to aid in steadying the piece.

A small removable rifled barrel fits within the large rifled barrel, so that the piece can be used for hunting large or small game. It is 25¾ in. long, caliber 39, rifled with seven grooves, making three-quarters turn right twist, weight 2 lbs. 2 oz. A guide lug on the breech end turns the small barrel into proper position when it is inserted in the upper groove of the large barrel. The removable barrel is locked by a long screw with wing head which fits in the under side of the stock and is screwed through the under side of the main barrel and fits into a depression on the under side of the removable tube. When assembled, the octagon end of the small barrel corresponds to the octagon shape of the large barrel.

So far as is known to me only ten examples of this type of double-barrel have been recorded, six of them by the Klett masters. In the Waffensammlung or Arms Museum in Vienna there is a pair of wheellock guns (D.292-293), dated 1652, and a wheellock gun (D.294) dated 1653, all signed by Sigmund Klett. In the collection of Prince Thun of Teschen, which was auctioned at the Dorotheum in Vienna on October 24, 1933, there was a piece inscribed SIGMUND KLETT INVENTOR 1653, and in Windsor Castle (Laking, Catalogue, No. 309) there is a wheellock rifle with barrel inscribed SIGMVNT KLET INVENTOR 1652. The only piece with a rifled barrel within a rifled barrel that is signed by Cornel Klett is the one that is the subject of this article. Dr. Arne Hoff, Curator of Small Arms of the Tojhusmuseet, Copenhagen, writes that there are other examples of this type (but not by members of

Fig. 6. The preceding elements are in position.

16-16A. Pan cover spring and screw.

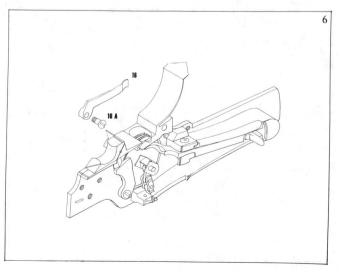

the Klett family) in the Tojhusmuseet in Copenhagen (B 1394:1), in the Oruzheinaya Palata in Moscow (No. 6626), in the Royal Armory in Stockholm (No. 1797), and one is believed to have been in the former Armee Museum in Munich. The Danish ambassador Just Juel in 1709 saw one in the royal stables in Berlin.

Gunmaking is an old trade, but fine gunmaking is a highly specialized art. The gunsmith requires an extensive knowledge of mechanics. Not only must he be a toolmaker, but he must also be able to adapt himself to almost any type of work—barrel, sight, and spring making, coloring of barrels, and engraving, chiseling, and gilding. Our rifle represents the highest technical skill of the era in which it was made, and the ingenious double-barrel mechanism is made with great care. By way of comparison, we might recall that when James Watt conceived the basic idea for his steam engine he could find no one with the skill or the means to bore a true cylinder 6 in. in diameter by 24 in. in length. A cylinder bored on Smeaton's machine was ⅜ inch out of true.

We have already noted that our rifle is the work of Cornelius Klett, a member of a distinguished family of gunsmiths. His father, Johann Paul Klett (1636-1663), left Suhl with his family in 1634 and settled at Ebenau near Salzburg, where in 1636 he became the barrelsmith of the Prince Archbishop. There he worked in the same workshop with his three sons, Cornelius, Johann Paul II, and Sigmund, and also with the gunsmith and stockmaker Hans Krach, who married Klett's daughter, Elisabeth. The combined mark (P S C K) of the three brothers appears on a wheellock gun dated 1646 in the Waffensammlung in Vienna (D.286). In the same collection in Vienna there is a self-spanning wheellock gun with gear rack (D.99) marked (P S K) for Paul and Sigmund Klett and with a stock by the master H N. Cornelius ran the workshop until his death in 1661, from which time his widow (Susanna, born Wallinger) continued the profession with her brother-in-law Johann Paul II, and after completing his apprenticeship,

Fig. 16. Inscription on main barrel.

the son of Cornelius, Johann Paul III, also worked in Ebenau until his death in 1692. Sigmund Klett and Johann (Hans) Krach left Ebenau in 1663 and both returned to Suhl. At Windsor Castle also is a wheellock rifle (Cat. No. 310) with barrel inscribed SIMON KLETT. The heraldic arms upon the butt are those of Prince Elector Ferdinand, Archbishop of Cologne (1612-50). Prince Prelates of the House of Bavaria ruled at Cologne from 1583 to 1650.

Although the Kletts were primarily barrelsmiths for the court of the prince archbishop, they also worked for the imperial court in Vienna and the electoral court in Munich. Lazarino Cominazzo, who worked in the village of Gardone near Brescia, was also a barrelsmith. And the barrels made at Sedan in Flanders and at Aquisgrana (Aix-les-Bains) are highly esteemed and valued. However, unlike any other gunsmith family of their time, the Kletts also devoted themselves to various designs and improvements in firearms. A variety of the most interesting multifiring constructions, which are found in several collections, witness the inventive genius of these masters. Count Raimondo Montecucculi, one of the greatest military commanders of his time, who was in the service of Austria, refers to a multifiring carbine that was made by Cornelius Klett. In the Royal Ontario Museum in Toronto is a flintlock repeating magazine gun by Cornel

Fig. 7. The preceding elements are in position.

17. Dog spring; 18-18A. Bridle connecting dog and dog spring, also bridle screw.
19. Bridge supporting spindle and enclosing chain and end of mainspring. 19A. Pin for securing bridge.

Fig. 8. The preceding elements are in position.

20. Dog with lower jaw; 20A. Dog pivot screw; 21. Upper jaw of dog
22. Dog screw (adjusts both jaws) 23. Iron pyrites.
24-25. Strips of leather (often lead) for chocking pyrites.

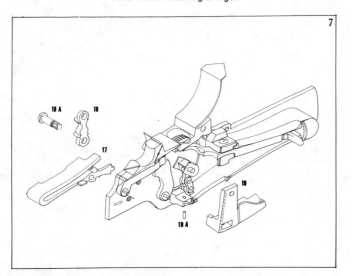

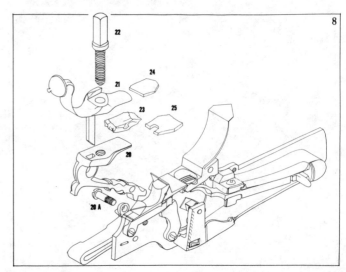

Klett dated 1653. The trigger guard of this gun acts as a lever, moving from side to side. One motion of the lever to the right and back to the normal position, loads the barrel, primes the pan, sets the frizzen, and draws the cock. The inscription on the butt plate reads: HAT MICH GE-MACHT CORNEL KLETT AUF DER HOCH FÜRST-LICHEN ZU SALTZBURG IN EBENAU ROHRSCHMITEN (Cornel Klett made me in the gunsmithy in Ebenau of the archducal court in Salsburg). Below this is a rhyming proverb: DER MIT MIR KAN UMBGEEN DEN LAS ICH NIT VEL STEEN. This may be roughly translated as: He who knows how to work me, I do not let him down. This gun apparently came from Schloss Sighartstein. Bearing the CK mark of Cornelius Klett was a wheellock revolver in the Prince Thun auction at the Dorotheum in Vienna, Lot 40. Other works by Cornelius Klett in the Waffensamm-lung in Vienna are: A wheellock gun (D.110), with stock by the unidentified master I M and dated and inscribed 1657 CORNELYUSS KLETT SALTZBURG; four flintlocks with the Bavarian arms on the butts (HGK 583); and a four-barreled flintlock carbine (D.374). Formerly in the collection of Prince Thun at Schloss Tetschen were a pair of double-barreled flintlock pistols (over-and-under) with locks inscribed CORNELYUS CLETT.

The gun industry comprised the crafts of barrelsmiths, locksmiths, and stock makers. It was in the workshop of the stock maker that the separate parts of the gun were assembled—the barrel produced by the barrelsmith, the lock made by the locksmith. By means of the stock made by himself, the stock maker had to assemble the gun and to test the separate parts. Dealers in guns derived from the guild of stock makers. These dealers, experts in their line, saw to it that the guns delivered were of first quality. Only after careful testing would the gun be accepted by the dealer.

The stock of our rifle is of walnut carved in relief with a scale pattern and animals of the chase—hound, stag, hare, also squirrels; on the under side of the stock is a shallow punched rosace. It is ascribed to the master H N, an able carver whose work was in great demand. Some 30 extant firearms have been ascribed to him, with locks and barrels by various masters, notably Hans Faschang of Vienna and the Klett gunsmiths. A characteristic of the work of the master H N is the vine motifs that terminate in animal and grotesque heads, as may be seen on our rifle (fig. 14). While it is not common to find signed firearm stocks, many instances are recorded. For example, a wheellock rifle (26.261.6) in the Metropolitan Museum of Art has the initials H N carved in the stock, and there is also in the same museum a small unsigned wheellock pistol by the same master, as well as the Klett rifle.

In this article an effort was made to call attention to the work of one member of the Klett family of gunsmiths, i.e., Cornelius. There are extant many samples of the work of the other Klett gunsmiths, and it is hoped that this article will cause some student to publish a more extensive and well illustrated article dealing with the works of the various members of the Klett family. The name is sometimes spelled Klet or Clett (often misread Cleft or Cleff). About fifteen different masters are referred to in the various publications.[3]

The time-consuming loading of the wheellock was one of several reasons why it never came into general use except as a hunting weapon—cost of making, relative fragility of parts were others. In good hands, shooting game with such a rifle was easy. In the Bargello in Florence is a repeating magazine gun by Sigmund Klett with the inscription WER GUT MICH BEDIENT, MACHT KEINEN FEHL-SCHUSS (Who uses me rightly, makes no misses). In fact, contemporary writers tell us that "just as it was considered no art to live well with wine, so too it was no art to shoot well with grooved and rifled guns."

[3] I am greatly indebted to Hans Schedelmann of Salzburg, Austria, for many notes on the activities of the Klett gunsmiths. Unfortunately I have not had an opportunity to consult the following publication which deals with the activities of the Klett gunsmiths: Oskar Seefeldner, "Die bürgerlichen Büchsenmacher im Lande Salzburg vom 17. Jahrhundert an." in Salzburger Museumsblatter, 1933, vol. 12, nos. 5-6.

Fig. 10. Isometric Perspective of Klett Barrels.

26. Breech plug; **27.** Breech end with touch hole.
28. Section of barrel with rear sight.
29-31. Three sections of barrel showing lugs (in different positions) for fastening barrel to stock.
32. Muzzle end of large barrel showing front sight, also inner barrel inserted showing guide lug, touch hole, and locking indentation.
33. Breech plug of inner barrel; **34.** Muzzle end of inner barrel.
35. Breech end of barrel with inner barrel secured by wing-headed bolt which passes through under side of stock.
36. Muzzle end with inner barrel in place.

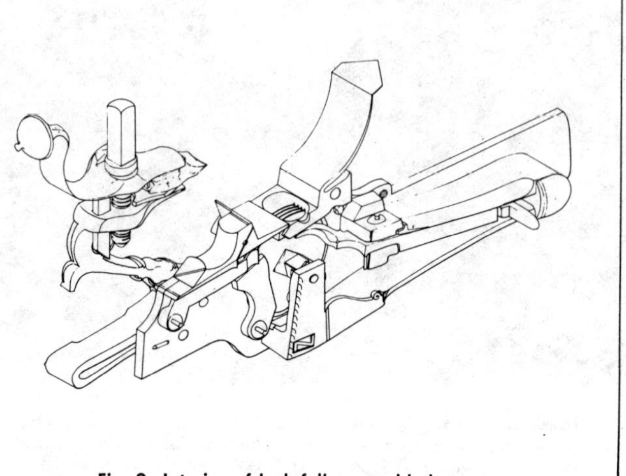

Fig. 9. Interior of lock fully assembled.

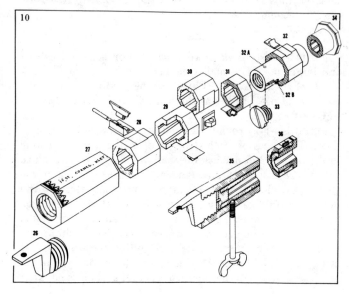

A Code for Muzzle Loaders

by KENNETH L. WATERS

WITH THE WIDESPREAD REBIRTH of interest in shooting the muzzle-loading rifle, there has come a whole new legion of beginners. Quite frequently these new-comers are experienced shooters in other fields, either target or hunting. Nevertheless, if their previous shooting has been confined to the use of fixed ammunition—cartridges—then they have an entirely new experience ahead of them, involving the learning of a completely new technique.

While there are some excellent books covering this subject at great length in all its aspects, the "nerve-center" or controlling factor of this game lies in the selection and preparation of components, and the procedure of loading them into the rifle. It was felt that a condensed list of instructions outlining these operations would prove helpful as a starting point for the novice muzzle-loading shooter.

These instructions are offered as a guide and are not intended to be all-inclusive. As the shooter progresses he will undoubtedly become enthused with his subject and want to know more, at which point a book such as *The Muzzle Loading Cap Lock Rifle* (Harrisburg, 1950), by Ned Roberts, is recommended.

Material

POWDER—Use black powder *only!* For bores 45 caliber and larger use FG; smaller calibers use FFG. For flintlock rifles, FFFG (or even FFFFG) may be used for priming the pan. Don't use FFFFG as the main charge. FG is coarsest, FFG less so, etc.

PATCHES—For round balls: Today, invariably, cloth is used. Thickness of cloth depends upon the depth of rifling in the barrel, thin patches for shallow rifling and vice versa. Linen is recommended, though a good grade of strong broadcloth is excellent if washed first to remove any starch. And don't be afraid of the sales girl laughing at you when you pull out a micrometer to measure the thickness of the cloth! Patches should be cut with some care to achieve uniformity. A shotgun wadcutter will help in cutting patches. Or the cloth may be laid over the rifle muzzle (after pouring in the powder charge), a ball placed upon the cloth, and after

pushing down with the thumb or "short starter" until flush with the muzzle, trim off the excess cloth protruding from the bore with a razor blade or sharp knife. Try different thicknesses of cloth.

For "picket" or cylindrical bullets: Almost always these are used in rifles with a false-muzzle, and the picket or "sugar-loaf" bullet used a round cloth patch, cut with a patch- or wad-cutter. If you have a false-muzzle with 2 or 3 grooves cut across the top, then a 2- or 3-strip paper patch is indicated. Shallow rifling will also be found when the rifle is intended for paper patches. Paper must be a good

Lower left, picket ball used in medium twist (24"—36") rifles. Cross patch was used with picket ball or "slug" rifles, round patch used with round balls. At lower right, Minié type bullet, hollow based and lubricated. Top, later cylindrical paper patch bullet, with extra patches used. Two caps are shown.

The false muzzle, patented in 1840 by Alvan Clark, was necessary to load picket or cylinder bullets without damage to their bases, which would have impaired accuracy. The false muzzle is rifled and coned, permitting easy entrance of bullet.

grade of tough "bond" paper, and should be cut with the grain. A fair amount of trial may be needed to determine the best paper thickness, but it will frequently measure from .002" to .004".

LUBRICANT—As a general rule, use greased patches for hunting and "spit" patches (saliva) for target shooting; wet patches tend to be more accurate, but will rust the bore if left loaded for long. Try wet "green" soap or one of the liquid dishwashing soaps for target work, but never for hunting. Do not use any mineral oil for patches; sperm or animal oil may be used.

THE BALL—Use soft, scrap lead, not hardened, for casting round balls. For long bullets a little tin added to the lead—say 1 part to 40—makes for a harder bullet less apt to upset. An easy method of proportioning is to melt a 1-ounce block of tin with about 3 pounds of unhardened lead. "Slug" and "mike" the bore, and obtain a mould of the proper size, allowing for the thickness of patch to be used. If the breech plug can be removed, drive a soft, oversize lead ball through the bore, then measure across widest part. This will be groove dimension. If breech plug can't be got out, drive a snug fitting cork down the lightly oiled barrel a few inches, first attaching a stout retrieving rod to the cork. Now heat some Cerro-Safe (or other low melting bismuth compound, obtainable from dental supply houses) and pour into muzzle. Let cool, withdraw and "mike."

CAPS—Be sure to use percussion caps of the proper size to fit firmly over the nipple. Cap should not be loose. The larger caliber military rifles generally took the split musket or "top-hat" cap, while the hunting and target muzzle loaders use the smaller caps, numbered 9 (small) to 13 (large).

Shooting the Muzzle Loader

Wipe the bore free of oil. Be *sure* false-muzzle is on while cleaning (if rifle is so equipped), and it's a good idea to tie the false-muzzle to the loading bench! These irreplaceable items have been shot away and lost.

Place the hammer at half-cock and blow through the barrel. If air doesn't come from the nipple, either nipple or bore or both are blocked. An old load may still be in the breech, and if so must be cleared out either with a "worm" from the muzzle or by removing the breech plug. If nipple is clogged up, remove it and clean vent.

Snap several caps with gun *unloaded* to clean vent of oil and moisture. If all is now clear, a slight wisp of smoke will emerge from the muzzle, or a piece of paper placed on the muzzle will be lifted off.

Raise the hammer to half-cock. Load a small charge of *powder only*, with a wad of cloth or paper, and fire into the air. If that charge fires, you are then ready to load the gun with powder and ball.

For target shooting, a long loading tube extending down the bore is helpful, possibly with a small funnel attached at top. This prevents powder grains from sticking to the sides of the bore.

To determine the charge of black powder, try the following old formulas; the "right" load will shoot the cleanest and the rifle will *crack* when fired. A round "boom" is your tip to try more powder.

(a) 1 grain of powder per caliber: (38 grs. for 38 caliber). Short range.

(b) 1½ grains of powder per caliber: (57 grs. for 38 caliber). 200 yds.

False muzzle and funnel in place, black powder is being poured into adjustable measure.

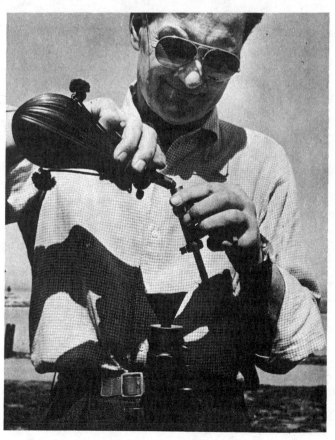

Rifling form shows range from deep, narrow grooves, a style popular 1700-1840, to the wide, shallow grooves of the later muzzle loaders; the latter are not unlike modern rifling.

Combination starter—the short plug positions round ball for trimming patch, the longer stem drives ball down 6"-8", ready for ramming "home."

(c) 3 grs. powder for each 7 grs. of round ball: (42 grs. for 38 caliber).

(d) 3 grs. powder for each 17 grs. bullet, when a long, heavy bullet is used: (45 grs. for 38 caliber with 255-gr. bullet or 71 grs. for 45 caliber with 405-gr. bullet).

Place oiled or wet patch accurately centered on the muzzle.

Place bullet on center of patch and start into muzzle with the fingers. With round balls, keep the "sprue" (or cut-off) on *top*, preferably.

Unless round-cut patches are used, cloth patches must be trimmed at the muzzle level to insure center patching. See "Patches" above. Patch must be wide enough to go well up the sides of the ball when in the barrel, that is, nearly three times the diameter of the ball.

Hold the bullet starter down tightly, squarely over the bullet with the left hand, and strike the knob of the starter plunger *one* blow with the right hand. If one blow is not enough to force the bullet the length of the starter, then the patch is too thick or the bullet too large.

Push the ball down the barrel with the ramrod, using a uniform pressure. Do *not* ram or pound the ball on the

powder charge; this will distort the ball, affect accuracy.

Be *sure* that the ball is actually seated down *on the powder.* If fired with ball only partly down, the barrel may become "ringed."

Remove the false muzzle (if one is used) and place a percussion cap firmly on the nipple.

After Firing

Wipe muzzle of rifle clean or apply the false muzzle. Most target shooters clean the bore after every shot, using a damp (not wet) patch, some pet "score improver," or a bristle brush with soap solution.

Recover and examine the fired patches, and look for signs of cutting. It may be necessary to change the material or thickness of patch.

For day's end cleaning, attach a rubber tube to the nipple, then pour hot water down the muzzle and scrub. Oil the gun well, afterward.

Now that you have passed these 21 (steps), you should have "come of age" in the muzzle-loading fraternity, and be well on your way in the pursuit of a fascinating sport.

Picket ball, centered in round cloth patch, is seated in false muzzle. Piston type bullet starter, coned to conform to bullet nose, ready to be placed over bullet.

Starter in place over bullet, the plunger should be driven to limit of its travel by one sharp blow with heel of palm. Bullet is then seated (firmly but not pounded) on powder with wooden cleaning rod or ramrod. →

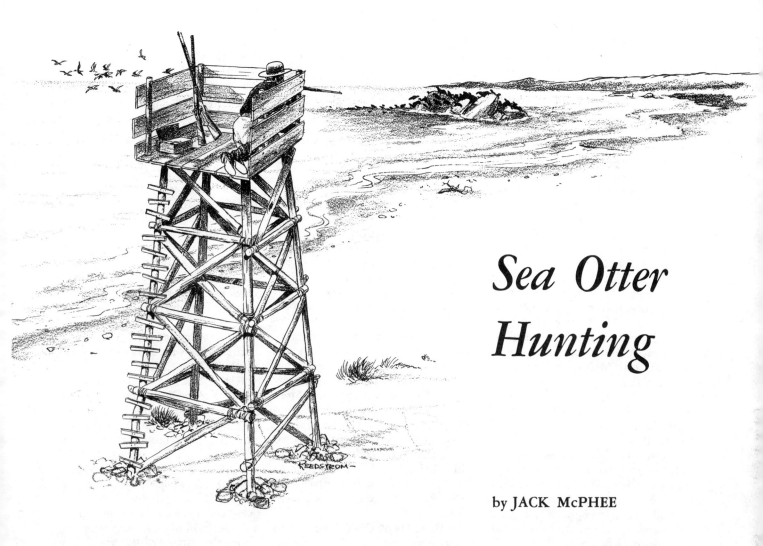

Sea Otter Hunting

by JACK McPHEE

IT HAD BEEN raining steadily and the wind blew in gusts, dashing its wetness into the gaunt face of a man who watched the waves about two hundred yards off shore. Finally his vigil was rewarded — several black forms were tossing in play on the incoming tide. His muzzle-loading caplock rifle, which he'd kept under his coat to keep dry, was raised to his shoulder. Blowing the water out of the rear-sight notch, he set the trigger, leaned against a huge drift log for steadiness, aimed most carefully and touched her off. The roar of black powder answered the trigger-pull and the wind dashed smoke into his face, but not before he had seen his bullet fall short of its mark.

The group of sea otters continued their frolic, undisturbed by the shot. Carefully measuring the powder, the hunter poured it down the barrel, placed the wet patch he had been holding in his mouth on the muzzle,

The last half of the 19th century saw the infamous slaughter of the buffalo, but what is less well-known was the near-extinction of the sea otter in the same period. Pat Roundtree started hunting the sea otter about 1860 —here's his story.

---

then put a ball in the center of the patch; he rammed the cloth-covered lead ball down the barrel until it rested firmly on the powder. Removing the hickory gun-stick from the barrel, he placed a fresh cap on the nipple, rested his body against the log and fired again. Another miss.

Again the rifle was loaded and fired, but a splash in the water to leeward of the target showed yet another miss. Loading again, the hunter held the rifle at his shoulder until a lull in the wind came. As one of the otters rose on top of a wave,

the rifle spoke and the animal relaxed on the water in death. The man relaxed as well, heaved a sigh of contentment and went about cleaning the fouled bore of his weapon; the incoming tide would bring his quarry to the beach.

The hunter was Patrick Henry Roundtree,[1] who had come across the plains in 1859 and settled in Washington Territory at Pacific Beach. Always a hunter, he had turned to pursuing the sea otter as a means of supporting himself and his family while he gained a foothold in the new country. The skin of one of these valuable furbearers was then worth from $50 to $100; a lot of money in those days, especially to a young man with a wife and growing family. Pat was successful in his hunting, for from it he paid for the clearing of his farm as well as supported himself and his family.

In Pat's early hunting days, the late 1850's and early 1860's, sea otters around Pacific Beach were very plentiful. The herd he worked seemed to range between Gray's Harbor and Point Grenville, a distance of about thirty miles. From observation he believed that they fed on such marine life as clams, crabs and sea-urchins, diving to the bottom and bringing their catch to the surface. There it was held on their chests while they seemed to pick it apart, lying on their backs with head and hind legs out of the water. It is asserted today, by trained observers who have watched them through powerful binoculars, that these animals — at least in other parts of their range — have been seen to dive to the bottom, bring up a crustacean and a rock at the same time, then use the rock to break the shell of their catch. One observer of a herd ranging near Monterey, California, told me that he had watched them feeding in this manner and had heard a continual pounding from the battering together of the rocks and the shellfish.

Those who have only seen the raw otter skins after removal from the carcass and stretched have described the animal as much larger than he actually is. A full-grown sea otter will measure, from nose to tip of tail, about 4-4½ feet. The otter's skin is very loose on the body and, after skinning and stretching, the pelt will often measure 7x3 feet or a

trifle more. The head is round, the ears small, eyes black, whiskers coarse and white, growing like those of a common house cat. The front legs are short and thick, the toes not webbed, its hind legs long and shaped like flippers. The toes of the hind feet, longest on the outside, are thinly webbed and fur-covered, except for five spots at the ends of the toes; these areas are covered with black, granular skin. The forepaws are used like hands and the animals are very clever with them; the hind legs are mostly used in swimming. Because of the great length of the hind legs and their doubling under of the hind toes while walking, the gait of a sea otter on land is awkward. The tail, which seems to be used mostly as a rudder, is flat, probably about three-quarters of an inch thick and two and one half inches wide. The fur of the sea otter is very fine, very dense, soft and silky. From white near the skin it shades into brown at the ends and, in some skins, black. White hairs generally cover the head, and the body generally has white hairs distributed all through the skin about an inch apart. On some otters the belly fur is almost white.

In those far off days there was no more alluring target than the sea otter — to a rifleman the thought of $100 every time he hit the mark was extremely attractive — and lots of

them were drawn to the game. Yet few otters were taken compared to the number of shots fired; most hunters soon gave it up. Only the most expert riflemen could shine in such shooting; there were always plenty of sea otters — in 1863 and 1864, hundreds of sea otters could be seen most any day — but they presented such a difficult target, bobbing around in the surf, that misses were common. Strong, gusty winds, blowing constantly, were a big problem that only the good riflemen solved.

A head-shot otter floated, but one hit through the body generally sank. However, the latter could almost always be recovered if the beach was patrolled carefully on the next high tide.

To Pat Roundtree it was a fascinating game, with a big reward when his bullet rang the bell.

His 46 caliber caplock muzzleloader had been a good deer killer back east and, while crossing the plains to the Pacific Coast, he had thrown many a buffalo in its tracks. It was a time-tried and well-beloved arm, but its weaknesses speedily showed up when it was used at ranges of two hundred yards and over, and on such small targets as an otter's head and body showing above the surface of the sea. A buffalo at 200 yards, probably a standing animal at that, was vastly different from a sea otter capering and tumbling among the waves and buffeted by the winds, tides and currents common on the western shores of the Pacific.

In those old days it was Pat's custom to cast about a hundred balls each night, all of which would probably be fired at otters during the next day's hunt. Though all shots were fired with great care, always from a rest when it was possible and with careful thought as to the exact range, misses were more plentiful than hits. When a count of otters brought to bag over a month's shooting was compared with the number of shots fired, the average was found to be some 200 balls to one sea otter! Clearly something ought to be done — if the range could be cut down and if the rifle could be fired from an elevation, more otters might be taken, and with less ammunition.

Finally, in 1863 or 1864 — Pat was not sure about the year — he de-

Sea otters on Amchitka Island, Alaska.

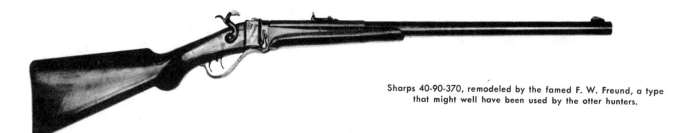

Sharps 40-90-370, remodeled by the famed F. W. Freund, a type that might well have been used by the otter hunters.

cided to try to set up a tripod of poles as far out on the beach as the receding tide would allow. On top of the tripod he would build a platform and there he intended to sit while the otters came in on the tide. A fellow hunter, John Thompson, helped him to erect the first tripod or, as they were always referred to by the hunters, "derricks." This was made of stout poles about 22 feet long, planted as firmly as they could manage. One of the three poles was placed forward of the other two, against the incoming tide, with the two rear poles bracing it against the force of the waves. However, after sizing up their finished product, neither man felt inclined to stay on the platform while the tide came in. Retreating to shore they watched with dismay as their brain-child shuddered, then collapsed under the pounding of the mighty ocean. Thankful they had not been on their derrick, they felt they'd learned a lesson in the construction of shooting platforms.

During the ensuing months they tried various ideas, finally Thompson was able to anchor a derrick firmly by tying the three legs to stakes set solidly into the ground. After it had survived a few tides, a platform was built on top and a ladder made up one of the legs. The day of the first hunt from the new derrick dawned wet and windy, and Thompson walked toward the platform with mixed hope and fear — the destruction of their first platform was fresh in his mind. As the day wore on, his anxiety fled while shooting improved remarkably — three were taken that

first day, an unusually high number, and with fewer balls!

At Pacific Beach, where the terrain is fairly flat, Pat built a derrick 200 yards from the beach and 65 feet in height. Well-anchored and well-built, its four-foot square platform was accessible through a hole in the bottom. Around all four sides cedar boards formed a wall to break the wind and hide the hunter. Inside was a seat for the rifleman and a rest for his rifle, making this, in reality, a sheltered bench rest. All in all, a pretty snug spot to shoot from, and a far cry from leaning against a drift-log on the beach, thought Pat.

Still, while shooting from this high platform did kill more otters, the number of shots needed remained high — the derrick wasn't all Pat had hoped for.

About this time, Pat bought a new rifle from a man who had just crossed the plains from St. Louis. Stamped on the top flat of the heavy, octagon barrel were the magic words: "S. Hawken, St. Louis." Of about 55 caliber and slow twist, it fired its heavy, round ball with best accuracy when loaded with 125 grains of Fg black powder. The heavy 250-grain ball with the big charge of powder bucked the wind better than had the lighter 46 caliber and, as it weighed 11 pounds — most of which was in the barrel — it shot more accurately, too.

The best hunting spot in Pat's territory, he recalled, was near Copalis Rocks; there Henry Blodgett,[2] built a shooting house of the finest. The stone was drilled deep enough for metal bolts to be sunk and to these

the sills were anchored fast. Topped by a good roof and fitted with a really solid shooting bench, it was the most successful derrick in the whole section.

Pat's new rifle, fired from the vantage point of the derrick, answered the veteran otter hunter's prayers. Shooting from his new derrick, high above the water and often only some hundred yards from the quarry, the Hawken was deadly. Instead of the old kill-ratio of 200 balls to one otter, the St. Louis rifle made it possible to knock over an otter every few shots. Often Pat was able to kill several of them in one day. As the fame of the Hawken spread along the coast, more hunters took up the business, armed with Hawkens and other heavy-ball rifles. Under the increased fire, the otters grew warier.

Now, too, the otters were being harried at sea as well as on the feeding ground — ships for the express purpose of hunting them sailed from Seattle, Portland and San Francisco and, across the Pacific, the sea ports of Japan sent forth many vessels to pursue the unlucky otters.

The Indians, too, started hunting the sea otters in family groups, from their canoes. The poor animals, driven away from their feeding grounds by the intensive hunting, had learned to stay beyond rifle range. The Indians, using several canoes bow to bow, would paddle along until an otter was sighted, the one first seeing it silently pointing it out with his paddle. Instantly the canoes would race toward the otter and, when within range, the Indians would all shoot. Firing was kept up

"S. Hawken, St. Louis" rifle, a prime favorite of mid-19th century western hunters.

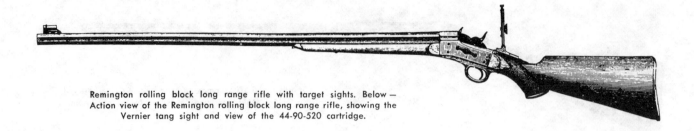

Remington rolling block long range rifle with target sights. Below —
Action view of the Remington rolling block long range rifle, showing the
Vernier tang sight and view of the 44-90-520 cartridge.

every time the animal surfaced until, after a long last dive, the exhausted otter came to the surface and the kill was made.

The ranks of the otters thinned and, though their scarcity drove the price up, hunting them hardly paid. The old days were gone. When the take got down to about two a month, both Pat and Henry Blodgett quit hunting them and turned their attention to shooting deer for the market. Long range Sharps and Remington rifles appeared on the beaches about this time, highly accurate and chambered usually for the 40-90-370, 44-77-470 and 44-90-520 cartridges; some even had telescope sights. A heavy-calibered Remington, Pat remembered, became known as "The Sea Otter Special."[3]

Liddle and Kaeding, gunmakers of San Francisco (1874-1876) offered their own "Sea Otter Special," a side-lever, tipup-actioned rifle using the 44-90-370 cartridge of buffalo

REMINGTON CREEDMOOR RIFLE.

fame.

With the advent of these more powerful and longer ranged rifles, the derricks were moved back to high-tide line and built more sturdily, now with four legs instead of three.[4] Yet, with all these aids, otter hunting was a losing, dying game. At last, all along the Pacific strand

and far out to the last island of the Aleutians, the sea otter was seen no more. Many believed it to be extinct.

On July 7, 1911, an International Treaty restricting the killing of sea otters was signed by Great Britain, Japan, Russia and the United States. To the best of my knowledge, this treaty has been rigidly enforced, and the otters have increased under its protection. During the Japanese occupation of the Aleutian Islands during World War II, some otters were undoubtedly killed by the invaders and, about at the end of that conflict, the Fish and Wild Life Service in Fairbanks, Alaska, arrested a fur buyer with two sea otter skins in her possession. These had probably been taken in the Aleutians and brought to Fairbanks by a returning soldier.

Happily, we do know that the sea otter, like the buffalo, is on the road back, though it won't, most probably, ever again reach its vast numbers of the 19th century.

---

[1]Patrick Henry Roundtree was born in Knox County, Illinois, on February 18, 1843. He died at Bois Fort, Washington, in April of 1929. He was named for his famous cousin, the great orator, Patrick Henry. Pat's father came from Kentucky and his mother from Ohio. They were early settlers of Knox County, moving there in 1835.

All of Pat's close relatives crossed the plains in 1852 and 1853, settling on the Chehalis River at Bois Fort. Family letters induced Pat to start his long wagon train trek to Washington on April 4, 1859. With Pat was his uncle, A. J. Roundtree, who had crossed the plains to Washington in 1852, and had returned east via the Isthmus of Panama. Others in the party were T. J. Spooner, his mother and two sisters; J. N. Reynolds and his family, and one Ben Benson, all of whom became pioneer settlers in the Bois Fort country.

Enroute west the wagon train met a Major Reynolds and his artillery battery, both groups then traveling together as far as the site of present day La Grande, Oregon.

Evidently experienced frontiersmen, the party defeated several Indian at-

tacks; on one occasion, after their animals had been run off, the men tracked the marauders down afoot and recovered all the stock without loss of a man.

[2]Pat Roundtree and Henry Blodgett were close friends and partners in hunting from young manhood. Pat's life was one life-long hunt — in addition to hundreds of otters killed, he remembered killing over a hundred cougars and literally countless deer and black bear. The largest of several grizzles shot — 13 bullets were found in the bear later, after a running battle that lasted over three hours — entirely filled an 11 foot wagon box, with the hind feet hanging over the tailgate some 20 inches. This great bear was shot with Pat's first muzzle-loader in 1868.

[3]While Pat used muzzle-loaders in his otter shooting and the large-calibered black powder cartridge rifles during his market-hunting days, his first 30-30 Winchester was a revelation to him. Never before had he owned a rifle with the flat trajectory and velocity of this arm. He often told his son Bert that had he owned a 30-30 in the sea otter days, he could have kept a crew of skinners and stretchers busy all the

time. The 30-30 cartridge of his day shot a 165-grain bullet at 1960 foot seconds velocity, much less powerful than the 30-30 sold today. Yet he considered it a much more powerful rifle than any of his former arms. Too, it was much lighter, something to be considered when one had to pack his game out of the woods on his back. The 30-30 came long after the grizzlies had been killed, so he never had an opportunity to try it out on such tough game.

[4]The last of the sea otter hunters around Pacific Beach was a man who is remembered today as "Shorty Axtell." His was the last derrick in that country and was still standing about 1900. While he killed few otters in his time, his skins brought much larger prices than any killed by Pat. Often good skins brought Shorty from $400-$500. Shorty used a breechloader, probably a 40-90 Sharps, by all accounts.

I am indebted for all information to Mr. Bert Roundtree, one of Pat's sons, now 75 years old, and to a small pamphlet Pat wrote and published on his life and adventures. I have read Bert Rountree's copy several times.

A Genealogy of Colt Longarms

Drawing and text by James M. Triggs

Paterson Arms

Paterson Ring Lever Rifle, First Model

Calibers—34, 36, 38, 40, 44 — Barrel, 32"
Cylinder—8 shots (Note bridge over cylinder)
First production revolving longarm, manufactured at Paterson in 1837 and 1838.

Paterson Ring Lever Rifle, Second Model

Calibers—36, 38, 40, 42, 44, 46 — Barrels, 24", 27½" and 32"
Cylinder—8 shots, rounded rear face
Manufactured from 1838 to 1840. Most produced with a permanently attached loading lever on right side of barrel lug as shown.

Paterson Carbine and Rifle, Model of 1839

Caliber—525 smoothbore — Barrels, 24", 28" and 32"
Cylinder—6 shots, rounded rear face
Later models produced with permanently attached loading lever as on second model ring-lever rifles.

Paterson Shotgun

Caliber—50 to 70 smoothbore — Barrels, 24" and 32"
Cylinder—6 shots, rounded rear face
Follows the design of the model 1839 carbine except for heavier cylinder; relatively few manufactured.

Whitneyville—Hartford Transition Model

Produced experimentally, the 44 cailber rifle was based on the Dragoon revolver design. Never put into production.

Hartford Revolving Cylinder Arms

Patent Sporting Rifle and Carbine, First Model

Caliber—36 — Barrels, 15", 18", 21", 24", 27" and 30"
Cylinder—6 shots, plain round
First sidehammer production model manufactured at Hartford, this arm had a detachable oiler and cleaning rod attached at left side of frame and barrel. Manufactured between 1856 and 1859.

Fullstock Sporting Rifle, Second Model

Caliber—36, 40, 44 — Barrels, 21", 24", 27" and 30"
Cylinder—6 shots, full fluted (plain round cylinders on some early models)
Also produced in this pattern were full-stock military rifles with barrel lengths from 24" to 37½" in 40, 44, 50, 56 and 64 calibers. Most cylinders were full fluted; five shots in 56 or 64 calibers, six shots in smaller calibers.

Revolving Cylinder Carbines

Caliber—36, 44, 56 — Barrels, 15", 18", 21" and 24"
Cylinder—6 shots (5 shots in cal. 56)

Halfstock Sporting Rifle, Third Model

Caliber—36, 44, 56 — Barrels, 24", 27" and 30"
Cylinder—6 shots (5 shots in cal. 56), full fluted

Shotgun, Model of 1859

Caliber—60, 75 smoothbore — Barrels, 27", 30", 33" and 36"
Cylinder—5 shots, full fluted

Military Arms

Rifled Musket, Models of 1861, 1863, 1864

Caliber—58 — Barrel, 40"
Based on the Springfield Model 1861 rifled musket, a great number of these arms were produced during the Civil War; a number of minor variations exist.

Colt-Berdan Military Rifle & Carbine

Caliber—42 — Barrel, 32½"
Essentially an experimental arm, a number of these rifles were produced for Russia. Few were sold domestically.

Colt-Franklin Military Rifle

Caliber—45-70 — Barrel, 32½"
An experimental magazine rifle produced in very limited number for military field trials.

Sporting Arms

Colt-Burgess Lever-Action Rifle

Caliber—44-40 — Barrels, 20" and 25½"
Based on the Andrew Burgess patents, approximately 6400 of these arms were manufactured.

Lightning Magazine Rifle

Calibers—22, 32, 38, 44, 38-56, 40-60, 45-85, 50-95
The Lightning magazine rifle was produced in light, medium and heavy weights in a number of variations.

Breechloading Shotgun, Model 1878

10 and 12 gauge — Barrels, 28", 30" and 32"
Produced from 1878 to 1891. Slightly over 22,600 of these hammer guns were made.

Breechloading Shotgun, Model 1883

10 and 12 gauge — Barrels, 28", 30" and 32"
Produced until 1900, approximately 8000 of this hammerless model were manufactured.

Double Barrel Rifle

Calibers—45-70, 45-85 Express, 45-90, 45-100 — Barrels 28"
One of the rarest Colt longarms, it is estimated that only slightly over 30 of this model were actually produced. This type is based on the Model 1878 shotgun frame.

A GENEALOGY of Colt Longarms

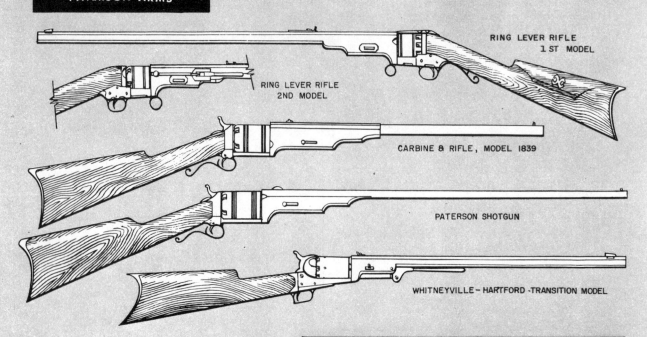

RING LEVER RIFLE
1ST MODEL

RING LEVER RIFLE
2ND MODEL

CARBINE & RIFLE, MODEL 1839

PATERSON SHOTGUN

WHITNEYVILLE – HARTFORD – TRANSITION MODEL

HARTFORD REVOLVING CYLINDER ARMS

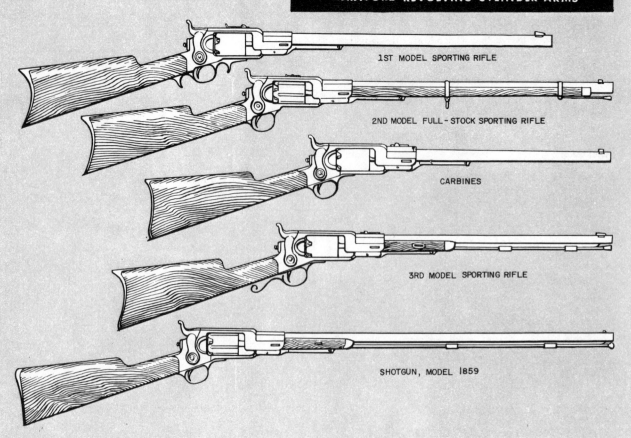

1ST MODEL SPORTING RIFLE

2ND MODEL FULL – STOCK SPORTING RIFLE

CARBINES

3RD MODEL SPORTING RIFLE

SHOTGUN, MODEL 1859

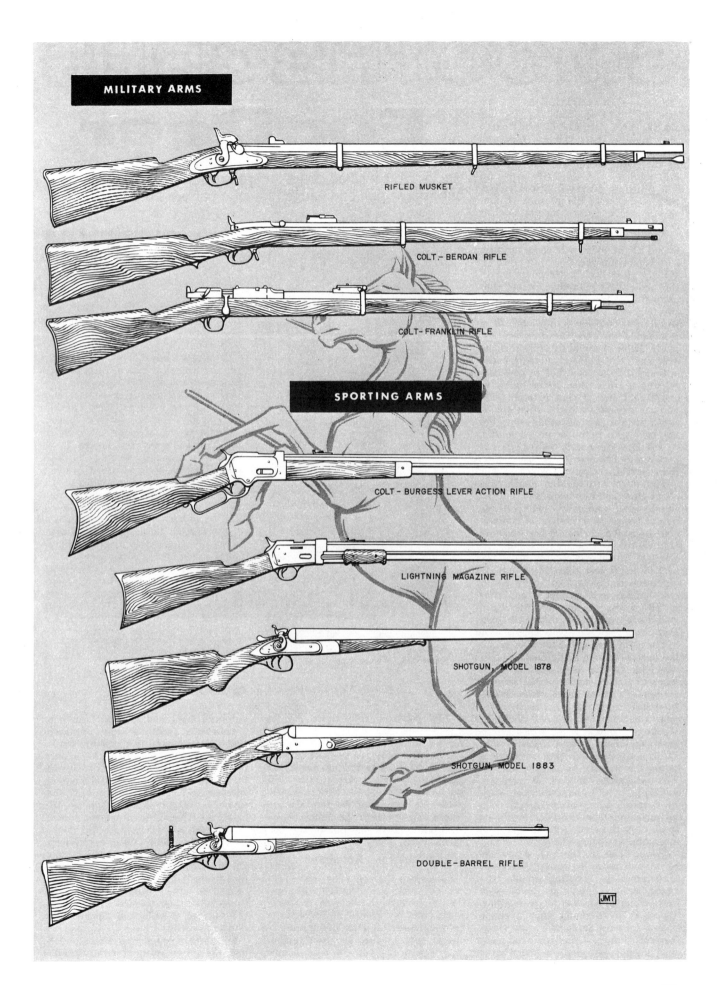

MILITARY ARMS

RIFLED MUSKET

COLT - BERDAN RIFLE

COLT - FRANKLIN RIFLE

SPORTING ARMS

COLT - BURGESS LEVER ACTION RIFLE

LIGHTNING MAGAZINE RIFLE

SHOTGUN, MODEL 1878

SHOTGUN, MODEL 1883

DOUBLE - BARREL RIFLE

JMT

TWO-FISTED HANDGUNNING

The pistol has always been a one-hand weapon — which doubtless
explains why so few people can hit anything with
one. Unless you're a top gunslinger, grab ahold with the
other mitt, too, says Askins,   and watch your scores zoom!

by Col. Charles Askins

THE COPS, who are pretty wise about such things, shoot their sixguns with two hands. Over at the University of Indiana, where the National Police Pistol Combat championships are banged out every year, the John Laws get a two-fisted grip on the 38 whenever the rules say they can. They shoot better that way.

Bill Jordan, whose book, *No Second Place Winner*, tells how to hit with the six-shooter when the chips are down, also advises the two-handed grip. Bill put in 30 years with the Texas Border Patrol, so you can be sure his advice about how to hit with the handgun is backed up by a plentitude of powder burning.

More lately, the Army has relented on a long-standing reg which insisted that all troopers when firing the high-bucking old 45 service gun had to use only one hand. Now our GI can double-grip it and to hell with stance. It may be the doughboys took a leaf from the Marines' book, for the USMC now shoots the big pistol two-handed. Their double-clutch is a recent change.

It stands to reason that the shooter —any shooter, whether the champ or the rawest dub—is going to shoot better, hit closer, score higher and step up his lethality with two hands. The pistol is a good deal like the rifle, and with the latter we shoot better because, among other things. it is held with both hands. It seems sort of stupid to me that someone hasn't pointed out long before this that all 10 fingers should be entwined around that sixgun stock.

Target match shooting, the kind the boys do in the competitive wars, is governed by an NRA rule which says the pistol has got to be supported by only the one hand. This rule is an archaic holdover from the days when the Code Duello was in flower. It specifically enjoined participants from gripping the pistol with both fists. The duellist took up the classic pose which saw his body edged to that of his adversary, thus presenting the smallest possible target. To have double-gripped the duelling weapon would have necessitated a full-face stance and given his opposition a lot more target to pink.

It might be well for the NRA fathers to give some thought to knocking this antiquated rule out of the book. It is apropos to point out that the National Rifle Association sanctions the National Police Matches, and here the gendarmes rap both fists around the stock in a number of the events.

Two-Handed Advantages

There are highly obvious advantages which accrue to the gunner who bangs 'em out two-handed. To begin with he faces his target squarely and brings the pistol onto the target directly before both eyes. If he is the kind of a shooter who aims with both eyes open he will like the two-fisted handgunning. It permits him to see gun and target just as freely and as easily with one eye as the other, and for this reason he is quicker and more sure of his aim.

A further advantage is that when the gun recoils it cannot buck so high. Since the up-flip is damped the marksman can get back on the mark faster for the follower shots. This can very well be a life-or-death matter with the law enforcement officer. With the casual shooter it is not nearly so critical, but he will instantly approve of a shooting style which allows him more time to aim and squeeze the trigger and which requires less time and effort to fight the recoiling handgun back down on the target again.

Apart from these major advantages there are some pretty obvious minor ones. Among these is the fact that the pistol can be held with a more steady aim in two hands than in one. Never is this more apparent than when shooting in the wind. Too, there is less fatigue in firing with two hands, and, as well, scores run higher and with less effort expended. Shoot all day, firing with one hand as we usually do, and you will wind up in the evening a very tired boy. Do the same stint two-handed and you will find your fatigue measurably less.

Sometimes I sit back and am a bit confounded that we did not swing over to two-fisted handgunning a long time ago. This reflection of mine will draw a lot of derisive snorts from the fraternity who hunt with the handgun. These gentry have always fired two-handed. An indication maybe that they are away ahead of the rest of us on the score of practicality.

I do not believe there is any argument but that we can all shoot better and hit closer with the handgun—any caliber, 22 to the magnums—using two hands rather than one. But just how much better?

Can the laddy-o who shoots an 8-inch group at 50 yards, one-handed, tighten that cluster to 4 inches if he double-fists the gun? Can the hotrock

Askins found he could get tight groups on the 7-yard silhouette target when firing with two hands, even though he banged out 6 shots in 3 to 4 seconds.

who knocks out a score of 95 out of 100 at rapid fire, sink 'em all and come up with a possible when he gets both hands on the gun butt? Can the police marksman who triggers off 6 rounds in 7 seconds at 7 yards on the Colt silhouette target—and puts 'em all in the "K" area—expect to two-fist the 357 and then put the group into the head portion of that target?

How Much Improvement?

If we grip the handgun with all 10 fingers, can we improve the group, or the score, or the hits by 50%? or 25%? Or is it only good for a 10% betterment? The fact is, no one seems to know just what the improvement may be. Everyone is in agreement that it is a surefire way to higher results, but no one seems to have pinned down just how much better. I determined in my own case to find out.

Each week for a lot of years I've shot the pistol two or three times. This has always been one-handed. Now when I swung around and squarely faced the mark, clamping my idle hand on the stock, I was thrilled at how steady the grip seemed. I have always been one of those gunners who pretty generously faced 'round toward the target, and to swing a little bit more was not difficult. The really satisfying part of the equation was the staunchness of the pose. I am a southpaw and so the left hand went first on the grip. I overlaid it with the right fist. The two together gave me a steadiness which I had

never before attained, and I have been shooting with a monotonous regularity for the last 30 years.

I commenced to do a lot of dryfire practice, two-handed. I liked the experience right from the beginning. To shoot proficiently with the handgun it is essential that you not only stand almost perfectly still, but you must also be capable of holding the outstretched arm and hand practically motionless. Few people can do this, at least to the degree necessary to hit close, and do it round after round. Most handgunners shoot like the shotgun marksmen—they touch off the shot as the sights come winging by. The gun never really stops in the center of the mark long enough to achieve a decent trigger squeeze. The reason is, in great part, a continuous swaying movement in the body and a resulting lack of steadiness in the shooting arm and hand.

When dry firing with the two-fisted grip, I found that I was very much steadier. Not only did it seem to me that the gun rocked less but there also was a noticeable lack of body movement. It is the most natural thing in the world to squarely face whatever we are watching, with the feet widespread, and this was precisely the new stance with the pistol in both balled fists.

I could not do any rapid dry fire practice because I am a shooter of automatics, and when you get all 10 fingers wrapped around the stock there isn't any known method for

yanking the hammer back in simulation of actual firing. Still, I was so elated with the feel of the gun, its steadiness and surety in the dry firing I'd done deliberately, I had no doubt the rapid fire would shape up all right. I was ready to move onto the range.

I proposed to fire 10 times over the Police Course, which is 10 shots at 25 yards slow fire, 10 shots timed fire and 10 shots rapid fire, on the Standard American target, first two-handed and then on the same day to go over the course with the one hand. I'd first shoot the 22, switch over to the 38 and wind up with the 45. This would amount to 900 shots with two hands and an equal number with one hand. It would cover our more common calibers and should tell me in exact percentages just how much better I could expect to be with the new two-fisted shooting.

After the strictly target shooting, I planned to do an extensive test on silhouette targets and here, too, I expected to spell out in percentages just how much advantage the one style had over the other.

Handguns Used

For this shooting I selected three good guns. The first was the High Standard Supermatic Trophy 22 with 7¼" barrel, 2¼-lb. trigger pull and standard factory stocks. For the stint with the medium bore I set aside S&W's 38 wadcutter automatic, the Model 52, with 3 lb. 2 oz. trigger and

In slow-fire, two-handed shooting, Askins found it easy to stay in the 10-ring of the 25-yard Standard American target with 45 ACP.

The double-grip helped hold the big 45 auto down during recoil, gave an average group of 5¼″ for 6 shots at 7 yards, in only 3.8 seconds.

the as-issue stocks. The 45 was an Elliason-tuned job with Herrett's customized stocks. Federal cartridges were to be fired throughout.

The first 10 shots at 25 yards on the Standard American target, two-handed, resulted in a score of 100. It was easily done and I was elated of course but not at all surprised. If I'd shot any less score I'd have been disappointed—and surprised. The timed fire, 5 shots in 20 seconds in two strings, resulted in a score of 95. This was not so hot. The group had sunk into the 5 o'clock corner of the bullseye. I made a sight correction. It was a timely change for in the rapid fire, 5 shots in 10 seconds in two strings, I accounted for a very acceptable 99. The total score, 294. This is about all I can shoot and I was happy with the results. It looked to me like this two-fisted shooting really had something!

I immediately swung over and shot the course one-handed. The slow fire scored 97, the timed fire 96, and the rapid 97. Total, 290. Clearly the second hand on the stock was going to keep right on showing this difference. An improvement of 4 points may sound like very little, but when you intend to shoot over the Police Course 60 times, as I planned to do, a difference of 4 points each 30 shots would amount to a very considerable margin at the end of the stint.

Each day thereafter I fired once over the course using two hands and once over with the one hand. The totals totted up thusly:

		Slow	Timed	Rapid	Total
One	Hand	97	96	97	290
Two	Hands	100	95	99	294
One	Hand	97	99	97	293
Two	Hands	99	97	91	287
One	Hand	94	98	98	290
Two	Hands	98	100	100	298
One	Hand	98	95	97	290
Two	Hands	99	100	93	292
One	Hand	98	97	96	291
Two	Hands	97	98	98	293
One	Hand	98	98	96	292
Two	Hands	99	99	98	296
One	Hand	99	97	97	293
Two	Hands	98	100	97	295
One	Hand	98	98	100	296
Two	Hands	99	99	99	297
One	Hand	99	96	100	295
Two	Hands	98	96	100	294
One	Hand	99	96	100	295
Two	Hands	98	96	100	294
Ave. (one hand)		97.6	97.2	97.7	292.5
(two hands)		98.6	98.3	97.1	294.1

The difference here in favor of the two-handed hold was 1.6 points. This is only .5% and was a disappointment to me. I hadn't been so sanguine as to expect I was going to better my totals by anything like 10%, but I had, confidentially, thought I could prabably add not less than a 2% betterment. In my case this would have been considerable.

I immediately commenced with the S&W 38 wadcutter automatic and some finely selected Federal match. The routine was precisely the same as with the 22. I shot a slow fire string two-handed, and then the same string

with one hand. This was repeated timed fire and then rapid. After 5 times over the course with each method, I stopped and took tally. I had an average of 291 with the one-hand and 291.2 with the two-fisted approach. I found I was shooting slightly better slow fire using both hands; the timed and rapid fire were running neck and neck. I had been quite certain in my estimate of the forthcoming shooting that as the recoil increased the two-handed clutch would show it was the better. However, in rapid fire with one hand I had an even 97 average; with two hands only 95.4.

I found, having by this time shot 450 carefully aimed shots with the two hands, that there were problems that did not show themselves in dry-fire practice. For instance, when you squarely face the mark and extend both hands before the body and those hands grasp a 40-oz. shooting iron, there is a tendency to tip over on your face. Or at least lean forward. This causes a swaying motion. In slow fire you can fight this but in rapid fire there isn't the time. Along with this back-and-forth sway there is a marked tendency of the knees to buckle ever so little in rapid fire. The gun kicks upward and the force has a more pronounced effect on the knees than on any other part of the body.

I learned, too, that it is just as easy to flinch with two hands as with one. Too, it seems that when you goose the trigger with both hands on the gun you can move it just a little bit farther out of the 10-ring!

I was disgusted with my firing of the 38. I'd had some theories about how it would perform and these had not proven out at all. I concluded that the 5 times over the course had given me usable averages both with the one hand and with the two, so I put the S&W aside and went to work with the 45. I shot it 10 times over the course with each grip. This was a full 600 shots and averages at the conclusion looked like this:

	Slow	Timed	Rapid	Total
One Hand	97.1	97.5	96.5	291.1
Two Hands	98.7	97.6	96	292.3

The only significant difference here was in the slow fire averages, where holding the pistol with both fists appeared to be a slight advantage. The timed fire and rapid fire showed no material differences. With the three guns the slow fire had usually been slightly ahead using both hands on the grip. At the same time the rapid fire was a mite the better with only one hand at the helm, a result which I had confidently expected would go quite the other way.

I now commenced to fire on the silhouette targets at 7 yards. In the police matches this is usually fired 6 rounds in 7 seconds. I shot considerably faster, using from 3 to 4 seconds for the string. I tried the 22 and then the 38 and finally finished with the 45. I shot the latter pistol 10 strings with the one-hand grip and 10 two-handed.

Here the advantages in favor of

M/Sgt. Ted Stafford, one-time British Commando, upped his score from 231 to 261, using the two-handed grip for the Police Course.

gripping the weapon with both paws became apparent. It was not evident in the 22 and barely perceptible with the 38, but with the 45 it was spelled out not only in a greater percentage of hits in the very center of the silhouette but also was fired in shorter time limits. Along with these obvious improvements were noticeably smaller shot groups. The sum total of the 120 45-cal. shots at 7 yards looked like this:

One Hand		Two Hands	
Time (Sec.)	Group (Ins.)	Time (Sec.)	Group (Ins.)
4.1	7.5	3.5	5.0
4.1	7.8	3.4	4.9
4.5	8.5	3.7	5.5
3.9	8.1	3.9	6.1
4.0	7.0	4.1	5.2
4.6	6.5	3.8	4.6
4.2	8.0	3.8	4.3
4.1	7.3	3.7	5.2
4.3	7.5	4.0	5.8
3.8	6.6	4.1	5.7
Ave. 4.16	7.48	Ave. 3.80	5.23

Here, then, I had, after a considerable amount of firing over an extended period, found what I was seeking. When the big-caliber pistol is fired really fast, as in defensive firing, it is a distinct advantage to double-grip it. Not only had it proven it was capable of tighter groups but the time limit was distinctly bettered.

It was obvious to me in an analysis of my shooting, however, that I was a poor guinea pig. Over the past 35 years or so I've probably shot away a million handgun cartridges—and almost all of them with the left hand. To have expected to noticeably improve my shooting by the double-fist grip was a bit too much. But what about some other handgunner? A fellow who was a good but not necessarily an expert marksman. How much would the two-handed approach help him?

I enlisted a couple of shooting cronies. M/Sgt. Ted Stafford, who made the landing with me in Africa in '42, one of the original 1st Rangers, a real hardcase character and a good pistol shot, was the first choice. With him he fetched along Bill Manual. Bill totes a sixgun all the time, using it on armadillos, jackrabbits and rattlesnakes. When I explained what I wanted, both of them snorted about holding a pistol in two hands.

"Sissy stuff," said Stafford, "but I'll do it just to humor you."

The Police Course was fired. Stafford went first and shot 231 with one hand. With two hands he got a 261. This really opened his eyes—and I was elated! "Maybe you've got something here," he grudgingly admitted.

Bill Manual then shot, getting 215 with one hand and 246 with two. The day following they again fired, Stafford turning in 227 with the one hand

Bill Manual, who likes to turn his handgun on jackrabbits, rattlesnakes and similar critters, cranked up his scoring by an average of 20 points when he fired two-fisted.

and 258 with the two-fisted grip. Manual came up to 237 with one hand and 259 with the two. The third and last day of the target work, Stafford had 240 and 268, Manual, 235 and 251, first with one hand and then with the two. Both were enthusiastic about the possibilities of the double grip by this time.

"I'm going to shoot a whitetail this fall with my 357 and this two-hand stuff," Manual enthused. "It ain't as good as a rifle, but it's sure a lot better than trying to make like Matt Dillon."

We then swung over to the Colt silhouette target and rapid fire. After 50 shots one-handed, Stafford had a group which showed 11 shots completely off the silhouette, 19 in the silhouette but outside the kill area. The remaining 20 were all K hits. Bill Manual had 24 K hits out of his 50 shots, one-handed.

Using two hands, Stafford, a short powerful man with strong hands and great muscular forearms, had all 50 hits in the K area. It was a spectacular show of good shooting. Time limits had run well under the 7 seconds prescribed for 6 shots. Bill Manual had 42 of his 50 shots in the K area and the remaining 8 had struck the silhouette but not within the vital zone. His, too, had been excellent shooting and indicated a marked improvement over his shooting with the one hand.

Here, then, was the place for the double grip. Though no great help to the hotshot, the average fair-to-good pistol marksman obviously can do markedly better if he will take a two-fisted grasp on the pistol or revolver. ●

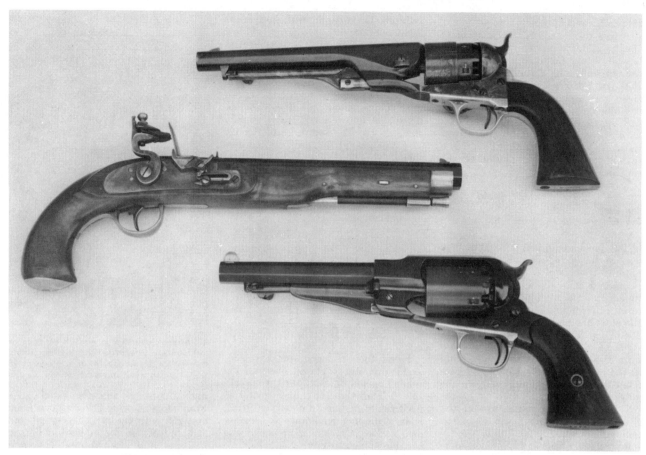

Three replica handguns that are excellent shooters: Centennial Arms 44-cal. Army Colt, Dixie Gun Works 40-cal. Kentucky flintlock and Navy Arms 36-cal. Remington Belt Model.

RELOADING SANS

Four typical replica muzzle-loading long guns: Navy Arms' 58-cal. Remington Zouave rifle-musket, Dixie Gun Works' 20-gauge double barrel percussion shotgun, Kentucky rifle made from Dixie Gun Works kit (40 cal.) and Numrich Arms' Hopkins & Allen 45-cal. underhammer rifle.

Large "top-hat" percussion caps are used on muskets and rifle-muskets, but smaller caps are used for nearly all other percussion rifles, pistols, revolvers and shotguns. The Witt capper provides convenient storage for 18 caps and makes capping safer. Another type of capper is available for "top-hat" caps.

CARTRIDGE CASES

by ROBERT E. COLBY

A full-scale, extensive and comprehensive essay on black powder shooting. Complete details on the loading, care and cleaning of flintlocks and caplocks that cover rifles, shotguns and handguns—muzzleloaders all.

"ACCURACY AIN'T so bad for an old muzzleloader." There's a comment often heard when a modern cartridge shooter first encounters a blackpowder gun. It's assumed that front feeders are inaccurate and unreliable. Not so! Properly loaded and handled, a muzzleloader, antique or replica, shoots as well—and sometimes even better—than an equivalent cartridge gun. Accuracy and reliability, however, do not come without effort and patience, for muzzleloaders can be temperamental and cantankerous.

(*Muzzleloader* includes all non-cartridge arms using blackpowder, lead balls or bullets, and usually of flint-lock or percussion ignition. Most often the components are loaded separately, but powder and ball may be contained in a non-metallic (paper) cartridge or loading tube.)

In reality, blackpowder shooting is nothing more than reloading without the customary brass cartridge case and a workbench full of expensive tools. It is reloading in the shooting environment, and this has definite advantages, especially when developing a load or varying loads for specific targets and ranges. Consider the barrel or chamber as the cartridge case, the percussion cap or priming powder the primer and the similarity between

muzzle-loading and cartridge reloading is obvious.

Loading time for a muzzleloader appears to be considerably longer than the time required to load a cartridge gun, but this is misleading. When you consider the hours spent hunched over the cartridge reloading bench manipulating measures, scales, presses, dies, and all sorts of other tools, the time equals out. There is also something to be said for spending one's time outdoors in the shooting environment.

Muzzle-loading is usually less expensive than cartridge reloading since less and cheaper equipment is re-

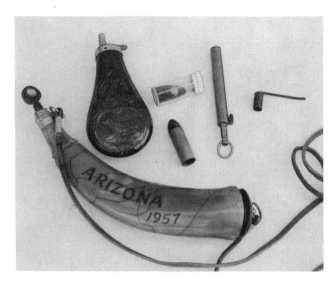
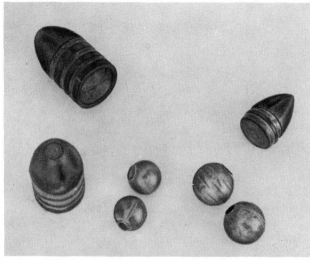

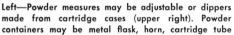

Left—Powder measures may be adjustable or dippers made from cartridge cases (upper right). Powder containers may be metal flask, horn, cartridge tube or plastic vial. ● Right—Bullets and balls used in muzzleloaders: the famous hollow-base Minie ball; 36- and 44-cal. round balls, and 44-cal. conical ball.

quired, and there is no need for that most expensive of cartridge components, the brass case. Fifty dollars will buy every blackpowder loading accessory you will normally use (target shooting with a slug rifle may cost and require more). For the ordinary shooter, the job actually can be done for less than $10. For cartridge loading on any but a very limited scale, $50 buys you only the essential equipment. $100 is a more reasonable figure for a relatively complete cartridge setup and it can go much higher as the equipment becomes more sophisticated.

Obviously, muzzle-loading has economic advantages. It's also a lot of fun, and it provides considerable satisfaction and a feeling of achievement when you have loaded and hit the mark as the frontiersman and soldier did a century or more ago.

Types of Guns

The only blackpowder guns practicable to shoot use flintlock and percussion ignition systems. Table 1 shows the general types of guns and their use. The number of checks indicates relative frequency of use, though all types have been and are being used for all kinds of shooting, regardless of suitability. The author

Table 1   Commonly Used Blackpowder Guns

Type	Ignition System		Use		
	Flintlock	Percussion	Hunting	Casual	Target
Patched-ball rifle	X X X	X X X	X X	X X X	X X
Rifle-musket		X X	X	X X X	X
Smoothbore musket	X X	X		X	
Patched-ball rifled pistol	X X	X X		X X	X
Smoothbore pistol	X X	X		X	
Revolver		X X X	X	X X X	X X
Shotgun	X	X X	X	X	X
Custom target pistol & rifle	X	X X			X X

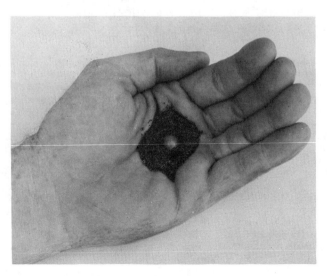
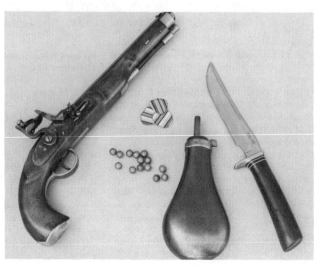

Left—An early rule of thumb for determining how much powder to use in a rifle was to lay the ball in a slightly cupped hand and cover it with powder. ● Right—Dixie Gun Works' flintlock pistol and the accessories required to load and shoot it. A small flask for priming powder is often used also. The same equipment, plus a ball starter, is required to load a patched-ball rifle. Properly loaded, this pistol will shoot groups of less than 1½ inches at 25 yards.

knew of one individual who shot an original 57-caliber, rotating, double barreled flintlock pistol! Such use of a collector's item is unusual, and something at which most blackpowder shooters would shudder. Custom-built target guns are used by a few serious match shooters.

Ignition Systems

Percussion and flintlock ignition systems are quite reliable when properly used. The percussion cap consists of a bit of fulminate lying at the bottom of a copper cup, thimble-like, which is pushed onto the nipple and struck by the hammer. Caps come in various sizes; see Table 2.

Table 2   Small Percussion Caps

Cap. No.	Nipple Size, ins.
9	.152-.158
10	.159-.164
11	.165-.169
12	.170-.174
13	.175-.179

Military muskets and rifle-muskets usually use the large "wing" or "top hat" percussion cap.

While No. 11 caps usually fit most percussion revolvers, ideally the cap should be fitted to each gun, as there are no real standards for nipple sizes or between different brands of caps. Nipple diameter can be measured about halfway up the side of the cone. Measurement of length is usually done by trying different sizes of caps. (Cap sizes for most muzzleloaders used today are shown in Table 4.)

Fitting caps to revolvers is rather critical because poorly fitted caps can cause a multitude of problems. For instance, undersize caps which do not seat completely on the nipple may drag on the recoil shield and jam the action or even detonate. On any gun, under-size caps may cushion the hammer blow and cause misfires or hangfires. Overly long caps may cause these problems also. Oversize (diameter) caps on revolvers may cause multifires as the flash jumps from one loose cap to the next. They may also fall off the nipples.

The brand of caps is a matter of personal choice. American caps are usually noncorrosive and quite reliable. European caps often produce a hotter flash, but are sometimes less reliable, more corrosive. European caps are generally shorter, which can be important with smaller percussion guns.

Flint, frizzen and pan, while the most difficult ignition system to cope with, are still quite adequate when loaded and handled properly. The first consideration is the flint itself. It must have a beveled or angled edge and be clamped securely in the jaws of the cock with beveled edge up. The jaws must be lined with leather or sheet lead to keep the flint from slipping. A sharp, properly adjusted flint

should last for 50 to 60 shots; a dull or poorly adjusted flint may produce too few sparks to ignite the priming powder. Poor ignition is also caused by weak springs, binding parts, misaligned cock and frizzen, or a soft frizzen. (Correction of such mechanical difficulties is covered in various sources listed in the bibliography.)

Most flintlock pistols use FFFg powder for both propelling charge and priming powder. However, if the pan flashes without igniting the propelling charge, the finer FFFFg may be required. It pays to check the flash hole for blockage and the priming powder for dampness before changing to a finer powder granulation.

Powder

The first and foremost thing to remember in shooting muzzle-loaders is: *use only blackpowder.* The second is: keep blackpowder away from open flames or sparks; it is much more readily ignited than smokeless powder. Aside from the obvious "No Smoking" rule, be sure to close tightly any blackpowder container when through loading and ready to shoot.

Table 3
Blackpowder Granulations and Use

Fg	Rifles over 58 caliber and large bore shotguns.
FFg	Rifles 41 to 58 caliber, pistols over 50 caliber, and most shotguns.
FFFg	Rifles through 40 caliber, pistols under 50 caliber, and all percussion revolvers.
FFFFg	Priming for flintlocks and very small-caliber pistols.

These uses can be varied somewhat. For instance, FFg usually works as well as FFFg in most percussion revolvers, and FFFg is sometimes used in rifle-muskets because it reduces fouling.

Powder charges are usually measured in grains, just as in smokeless powder reloading. However, powder flasks and loading instructions sometimes give charges in drams: 1 dram = 27.3 grains.

Powder containers and measures range from cartridge tubes with pre-measured charge and ball to powder

horns and flasks. A flask or horn has advantages as it stores, measures and funnels the powder; those with an adjustable spout can be used to vary the powder charge. Cardboard or paper cartridge tubes and plastic vials are quite useful in the field once the proper load is developed. It is debatable whether paper cartridges are worth the effort.

Balls and Bullets

The basic rule is to use pure lead balls or bullets, though some shooters add a minute amount of tin for better casting. Round balls are used in most patched-ball rifles, pistols and revolvers. Conical bullets can be used in revolvers, but their shape makes them difficult to load. Rifle-muskets use the famous hollow-base Minie ball, although they will shoot well with patched round balls.

Some shooters feel that modern wadcutters provide greater accuracy than round balls. From a ballistics

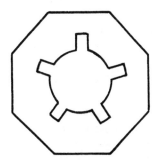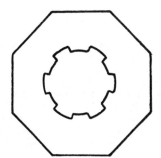

Rifling common in patched-ball rifles. The deep groove type is virtually limited to original rifles while the generally superior shallow groove rifling is found in both original and replica rifles.

standpoint this seems logical as the wadcutter, or the conical ball, for that matter, has a higher sectional density and better aerodynamic shape than the round ball. Wadcutters, however, unless beveled at the base, may present the same loading difficulties as do conical balls. Wadcutters cast from Lyman 454309 (44-cal.) and 358425 (36-cal.) moulds look like good bullets to try. Experimentation may prove loads with these bullets to be the most accurate yet.

With the exception of martial arms, round ball diameters are not fixed, even in guns of the same caliber. For pistols and rifles the most common way to determine correct size is to push a lead slug through the oiled bore from breech to muzzle, then measure the land and groove impressions on the slug. This provides a starting point from which to determine the proper size. An old rule of thumb which can be applied here is that the ball diameter should be about a half-thousandth less than the bore (not groove) diameter expressed to the 3rd decimal place. Thus for a 40 caliber

The rifle-musket is a favorite of blackpowder loaders because of its ease of loading and good accuracy. While a powder flask or horn can be used, the most convenient way to load is with the cartridge tube holding bullet and powder.

(.400″) bore, a .395″ ball is about right.

The critical dimension of revolvers is not the bore, but the chamber. The ball must fit the chamber snugly to seal-off the powder charge. To determine the diameter, measure the chamber about ¼-inch below the mouth. Bore size on shotguns and other smoothbore guns can be measured with a taper gauge or small-hole gauge and a micrometer. Table 4 also gives ball sizes for commonly used muzzleloaders.

Moulding is not covered here because the procedures are the same as those used in conventional reloading. Round ball moulding is, in fact, somewhat easier since balls have no grease grooves and sizing is not required. The old original iron, brass or bronze moulds are seldom satisfactory. They often lack sprue cutters, any provision for bleeding-off air, and become much too hot to touch unless wooden handles are added or asbestos gloves are used. The Lyman Gunsight Co. fur-

nishes moulds for nearly all sizes of round balls required and some conical bullets. If you want to do it the old way, however, such sources as Dixie Gun Works, Navy Arms, Centennial Arms or Replica Arms offer replica moulds.

Developing Loads

There is a lot of tradition and very little documented data on blackpowder loads. Nobody publishes a reloaders handbook dedicated to loads, components, ballistics, and procedures for muzzleloaders. There are, however, numerous sources of information if you know where to look. One is the Dixie Gun Works catalog, which contains much muzzle-loading data along with photos and descriptions of guns, parts and accessories. Another source is one chapter in the Lyman Reloading Handbook. The numerous books on muzzle-loading guns often contain some load data, and replica makers sometimes furnish such information. Some military service data is avail-

able for originals, and there are the growing number of articles on blackpowder shooting in gun magazines. The information in Table 4 is drawn from such sources. It is intended to serve as a guide, not as the final word on loads.

Since most of the load data is of the "hand-me-down" or "in-grandpa's-day" nature, there are many rules of thumb, some of which are quite useful. However vague, such rules provide a point from which to begin developing a load. Here are some rules for determining the optimum powder charge for rifles:

Use one grain of powder for each caliber of the ball, i.e., 40-cal./40 grains.

• Lay the ball in a slightly cupped hand and cover with powder.

• Use one third the weight of the round ball as the powder charge.

• A sharp crack is heard from an

The 44-cal. round ball (right) shows the rifling ring typically found on a properly fitted round ball fired from a revolver. The dark ring on the left side of the ball was impressed by the rammer during loading.

optimum load. Conversely, a hollow boom results from a less than optimum load. (A hollow boom can also indicate a ball that is not fully seated on the powder charge—a dangerous condition.)

Before discussing loads, though, a word of caution. Often heard is: "A muzzleloader can take all the blackpowder you can stuff in it and still not blow up." If this is not completely false, it certainly is not sensible. The only result guaranteed from a heavy overload is much recoil and poor accuracy. Again, *use only blackpowder* in muzzleloaders.

Patched-Ball Loads

Guns that use the patched ball include flintlock and percussion rifles and pistols. While inherently the most accurate of load/gun combinations, they present the greatest challenge because of the very critical patch and the lack of standardization in bore size and type of rifling in these typically civilian guns. (Military muskets and rifle-muskets of particular model are usually uniform in caliber and original loading data is often available.)

Centennial Arms' 44-cal. Colt Army revolver is one of the more popular replicas loaded and shot today. Considerable loading data is available for this gun. Besides the caps, balls and powder shown, grease is an important loading component.

Table 4   Common Loads for Muzzleloaders

	Cal.	Gun	Ball Size (in.)	Ball Type	Recommended charge (grs.)	Ignition Cap or Flint
Original Army	69	U.S. muskets	.680	round	80 FFg	musket
	58	U.S. rifle-muskets	.570-5	Minie	60 FFg	musket
	577	Enfield rifle-musket	.570-5	Minie	60 FFg	musket
	54	U.S. Mississippi rifle-musket	.535	Minie	75 FFFg	musket
	54	U.S. Harpers Ferry pistol	.535	round	35 FFg	flint
	44	Colt Dragoon revolver	.454	round	40 FFFg	No. 11
	44	Colt and Remington Army revolvers	.454	round	28 FFFg	No. 11
	36	All other percussion revolvers	.376	round	22 FFFg	No. 11
	31	All other percussion revolvers	.321	round	15 FFFg	No. 10 or 11
Replicas Arms	67	Tower flint pistol	.650	round	65 FFg	flint
	58	Remington-Zouave rifle musket	.575	Minie	60 FFg	musket
	54	Harpers Ferry and Virginia flint pistols	.550	Minie or round	35 FFg	flint
	44	Colt Walker revolver	.451	round	50 FFFg	No. 12
	44	Colt Dragoon revolver	.451	round	40 FFFg	No. 11
	44	Colt Army revolvers	.451	round	28 FFFg	No. 11
	44	Remington Army revolvers	.454	round	28 FFFg	No. 11
	36	Colt and Remington revolvers	.371-5	round	22 FFFg	No. 11
	36	Colt Paterson revolver	.378	round	22 FFFg	No. 11
	31	Colt Wells Fargo and Baby Dragoon revolvers	.316	round	13 FFFg	No. 11
	44	Kentucky flint pistol (Navy Arms)	.430	round	24-40 FFFg	flint
	40	Dixie Kentucky pistol (Dixie Gun Works)	.395	round	25 FFFg	flint or No. 11
	40	Dixie Kentucky rifle (Dixie Gun Works)	.395	round	47-70 FFFg	flint or No. 11
	45	Hopkins & Allen rifle (Numrich Arms)	.443	round	65-95 FFg	No. 11
	36	Hopkins & Allen rifle (Numrich Arms)	.347	round	40-65 FFg	No. 11
	41	Philadelphia derringer	.395	round	48 FFFg	No. 11

Kentucky-type rifles and non-martial pistols are omitted due to the almost total lack of standards

 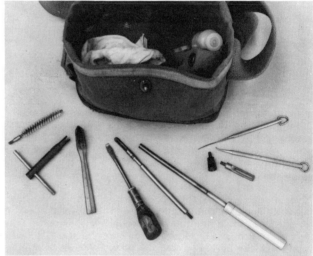

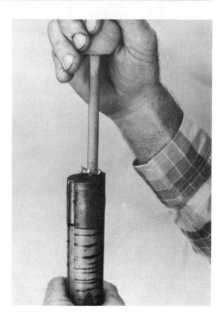

Above left—Components required to load this Dixie Gun Works' double barrel shotgun are powder, shot, caps, over-powder and over-shot wads. ● Above right—If you are going to do much shooting in the field, where mobility is required, a shooting pouch is a very useful accessory. Required tools include, from left: bore brush, nipple wrench, tooth brush, screwdriver, cleaning rod and attachments, various picks. The cone-shaped item is a tulip-head attachment to convert a 50-cal. cleaning rod into a ramrod for the rifle-musket. ● Below right—The ball starter is a useful tool. After it is used to start the patched-ball into the bore, the ramrod completes the job by seating the projectile on the powder.

In the patched-ball gun, an under-sized ball is spun by rifling it never touches! Gripping the patch tightly, the patch takes the rifling and imparts spin to the ball. As the spinning ball leaves the muzzle, the patch falls free. Why is the patch used? Because it would be very difficult to ram a ball down several feet of bore, as the lead takes the rifling, even when the bore is clean. Another major purpose of the patch is to act as a gas seal. Thus the thickness of the patch and its relationship to the depth of rifling

and size of ball, along with the powder charge, determine the accuracy possible with a patched-ball gun.

Originally patches were leather, buckskin or linen. Of these only linen is still used today, with muslin or Indian Head sometimes substituted because of the high cost of linen. Denim, bed ticking, canvas, sail cloth and cotton flannel are used when thicker patches are needed. Linen may be .005″ or less thick while canvas may be as thick as .020″. Paper is used in some special target or "slug" rifles,

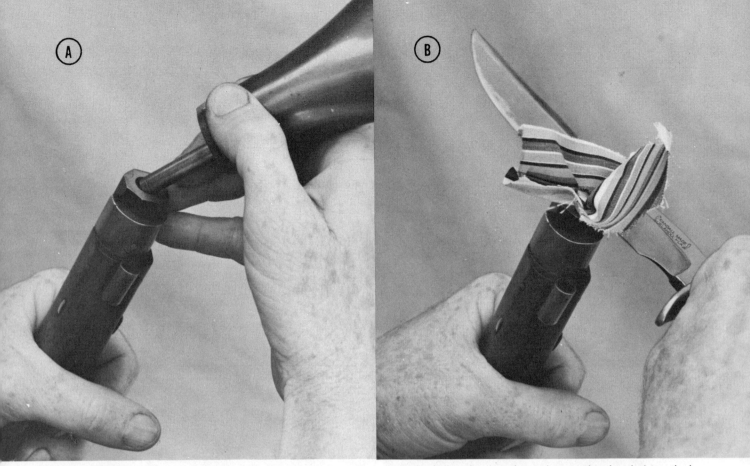

A) After placing the hammer at halfcock and the frizzen forward, pouring a measured charge down the bore is the first step in loading a flintlock. ● B) The ball is placed on the patch material and pushed into the bore. Then the excess patch material is trimmed off flush with the muzzle. ● C)

usually a thin, tough bond paper made from linen or rag base. Nearly any strong, closely-woven material will work as long as it can withstand being shot down the bore without burning or wearing through.

Patches must be lubricated to ease their passage down the bore during loading and to soften and remove fouling. Saliva, a traditional favorite, is still much used. However, saliva may rust the bore and wet the powder if the gun is not shot for a long time, as during hunting. In such cases, tallow, Vaseline, cup grease, vegetable oil, sperm oil, even graphite, can be used. Whatever the lubricant, enough should be applied to completely wet the patch though not to excess. With pre-cut patches, oil and grease may well be applied when the patches are cut, giving the lubricant the opportunity to evenly disperse through the material.

The thickness of the patch depends on the depth of rifling, diameter of bore and size of ball. For a given bore size and rifling depth, the patch thickness increases as the ball size decreases and vice versa. The patch must completely fill the grooves and be under considerable compression by the rifling in order to obtain a good gas seal. Obviously a perfect seal is desirable, but you still must be able to push the patched-ball down the bore without using extreme pressure

or deforming the ball. Thus a trade-off must be made between sealability and loadability. For practical purposes, only the pressure of the fingers on the ramrod should be required to push the patched-ball down the bore to seat on the powder.

Each gun requires its own patch and ball combination, and there may also be more than one acceptable combination. The following combinations generally apply, and can be used as a starting point:

1) Narrow lands and wide, deep grooves: bed ticking or canvas patch of a thickness about twice the groove depth; ball diameter nearly equal to bore diameter, that is, between lands.
2) Narrow lands and wide, shallow grooves: linen or muslin patch about .007″ thick; ball diameter .002″ to .005″ less than bore diameter.
3) Wide lands and shallow grooves: linen patch about .005″ thick; ball diameter about one patch thickness less than bore diameter.
4) Wide lands and deep grooves: canvas or bed ticking about .02″ to .025″ thick; ball diameter about .01″ less than bore diameter.

To see if your combination is ok, recover and "read" several fired patches. The following general rules apply:
1) Clean cuts where patch touched lands: lands are too sharp; try a stronger patch or lap the bore carefully with fine to medium steel wool.

2) Hole burned in center of patch by gas blow-by: patch is much too thin to act as gas seal; try a thicker patch.
3) Over-all blackening, but no holes burned in patch: patch is still too thin to seal the bore.
4) Torn or frayed where patch engaged lands: material not durable enough or bore is excessively rough.
5) Circular cut on patch where ball rested on muzzle: edge of muzzle is too sharp; try a stronger material or chamfer muzzle.
6) Blackened circle where ball rested, minor powder soiling, and minor powder burn streaks at groove marks: patch fits well and seals bore properly.

While reading a fired patch is best, the ball and patch combination also can be checked by driving a patched ball through the bore from the breech. If the ball shows heavy cloth marks where the lands pressed, alternating with lighter marks over the grooves, the combination is correct. However, if the ball has cloth marks (lands) alternating with unmarked areas (grooves) the patch is too thin.

While patch diameter is much less critical than thickness, the patch must completely cover the circumference of the ball where it contacts the bore. During a typical loading sequence, the patching material is placed over the muzzle, the ball seated in the bore flush with the muzzle, and the patching material cut off flush. If pre-cut

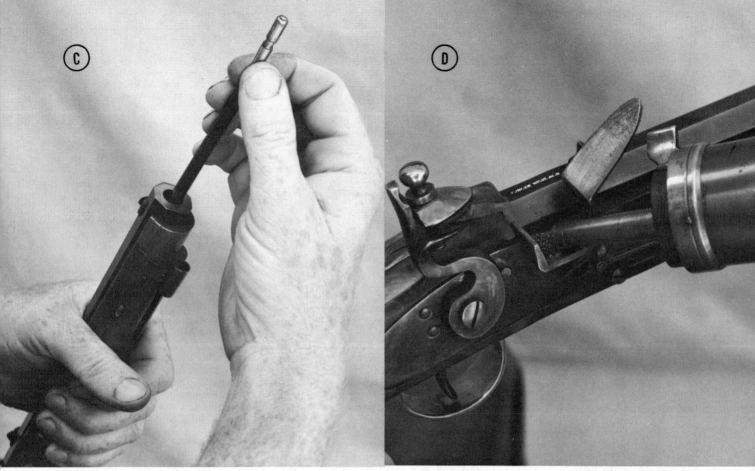

The ball and patch are pushed down the bore to seat firmly on the powder. Only moderate force should be required on the ramrod. ● D) Priming the pan and lowering the frizzen to firing position completes loading. Only enough powder to fill the pan to the touch-hole level should be used.

patches are desired, the material is not cut off; instead the outline of the bore edge is marked on the material. The material and ball are removed from the bore and the material is cut along the circular outline to form a pattern for other patches.

Smoothbore muskets and pistols were generally fired with unpatched balls. If a paper cartridge was used, the paper was often shoved down the bore as a wad between powder and ball to act as a gas seal and clean the bore. However, a greased patched ball in smoothbore guns helps keep powder fouling soft and the bore clean as well as providing lubrication and easier loading. A ball slightly smaller than the bore is usually required to compensate for the patch thickness.

Quantity and granulation of the powder affect accuracy, and the powder charge for each gun is also an individual thing because of the lack of standardization. This makes recommendation of specific charges difficult, but the loads given in Table 4 can be used as a starting point, or the rules of thumb given earlier can be used.

To develop a load you must juggle ball, patch and powder charge simultaneously. As an example, let's take a flintlock such as the Dixie Kentucky pistol. This pistol has relatively wide lands, shallow grooves, and a land-to-land diameter of .400″. Using Rule 3 of patch selection, a .395″ ball with

a .005″ thick linen patch looks like a good choice. We verify the ball size by referring to Table 4, our choice agreeing with that listed in the Table. (Wherever possible, information on replica guns in this Table is based on recommendations of the distributors.) Let's also start with the 25-gr. FFFg powder charge given in Table 4.

Load her up (using the procedures described in the next section) and fire at least 5 shots from a rest. This will give some idea of the sight picture/bullet impact point relationship, then fire another 5 shots to check grouping and accuracy. Vary the powder charge by 1- or 2-gr. increments up and down. (Lighter charges usually are more accurate.) For general shooting there is usually no need to vary the charge by fractions of a grain, but for target shooting this is not unusual.

An overly heavy powder charge is indicated by heavy recoil and continued poor accuracy. To verify this, fire the gun from the prone position with several pieces of white paper spread on the ground in front of the muzzle. If you find many unburned powder grains on the paper, the charge is much too large.

Retrieve several fired patches and "read" them as described previously. If the results are unsatisfactory, take the indicated action. A change in patching material will probably change

accuracy and grouping so you must continue the test fire sequences. Continue reading patches and varying powder charges until the most accurate load is achieved.

Powder granulation can also be changed, especially if coarser granulations are used initially. Ball size also can be varied, but try this last as several ball moulds are required. If the ball was carefully selected in the first place, changing to another size is usually unnecessary.

With all these variables, more than one "optimum" load may exist. Moreover, when developing a hunting load, some accuracy may have to be sacrificed for lethality. With the Dixie flintlock pistol one of the more accurate loads is:

.395″ round ball, .004″ linen patch, saliva lubricated; 20 grams FFFg main charge and FFFg primer.

Note that it differs somewhat from the load tried initially.

Loads for other patched-ball guns are developed in the same way, using data from Table 4 and/or the various rules of thumb. With the proper load, a patched-ball hunting rifle should make 1.5″ to 2″ groups at 50 yards, and the average target rifle 0.5″ to 1″ groups at the same distance.

Rifle-Musket

58- and 54-cal. rifle-muskets, both firing the famous Minie ball (bullet, really), are used by many shooters. The Minie requires no patching material and, as it is undersized, it is easily pushed down the bore. The bullet has a cup-shaped depression in its base. As the powder charge is ignited, the expanding gases press the rear flange of the bullet into the rifling. It was this type of bullet that made it possible to rapidly load rifles, which had led to the adoption of rifles by the military, which previously had used smoothbore muskets. Today the rifle-musket is a popular shooter because it is almost as accurate as a patched-ball rifle, easy to load, and standard loads are available. As with any muzzleloader, however, each gun has its own peculiar load.

While original rifle-muskets are quite satisfactory, the Navy Arms replica of the 58-cal. Remington Zouave is the shooter's choice. Handsome and less expensive than any original in good shooting condition, its 33" barrel is considerably handier than the longer standard rifle-musket.

Of the several Lyman Minie bullets available, the 505-gr., .575" diameter bullet cast from the No. 575213 mould is an old favorite. However, a relatively new bullet, the 530-gr., .580" bullet cast from the No. 57730 mould may give slightly better accuracy.

The standard load for a rifle-musket is usually between 50 and 60 grains of FFg powder. However, lighter loads and sometimes finer powder granulation often give better accuracy. Some typical loads are shown in Table 5.

The tested loads were fired from a bench rest at 50 yards. In the offhand position you must be able to hold at least 3" groups to qualify for the North-South Skirmish matches.

Minie ball grooves are ordinarily filled with grease to provide lubrication and keep fouling soft. A mixture of 40% beeswax and Crisco is good, and for additional lubrication the bullet's base cavity can be filled with the same material just before loading. Some shooters feel that the best accuracy is achieved by lubricating the base of the bullet *only*. The entire load can be conveniently packaged in a cartridge tube.

Round, patched balls can also be shot in the rifle-musket. A good load is a .562" round ball with a .013" thick, saliva-lubricated ticking patch and 65 grains of FFg. Another is a .575" round ball with an .007" linen patch and 87 grains of FFFg.

Percussion Revolvers

Percussion revolvers are among the most popular muzzleloaders, with the 36 and 44 calibers generally the best shooters. However, the little 31-cal. revolvers are very pleasant to shoot and would probably be more so if there were more than one type of replica available. (The author would like to see a 31-cal. Remington Pocket Model replica in addition to the Colt Pocket offered.) Considerable loading data is available for the 36- and 44-cal. revolvers from numerous sources; but, as with any muzzleloader, each revolver requires its own optimum load.

Although chamber diameters can vary as much as .01", the balls listed in Table 4 will work satisfactorily in most percussion revolvers, at least for casual shooting. A ball of the correct size will rest with about one-quarter of its diameter in the chamber mouth of a revolver. When rammed down onto the powder charge, it is not uncommon to have a small ring of lead remain around the rammer. Only moderate force on the loading lever should be required.

Round balls are used by most shooters because they are the easiest to cast and load, and generally give the best accuracy. _____ require a smaller powder charge, but are prone to tip and load eccentrically, causing fliers. Moreover, the small loading cut-out in the barrel web of some revolvers almost precludes the use of anything but a round ball, whose diameter is always less than the long dimension of a conical bullet.

If you don't want to cast your own lead balls, you can use No. 0 buckshot in 31-cal. and No. 000 buckshot in 36-cal. revolvers. Buckshot, seldom perfectly round, may be slightly harder than a ball should ideally be, but it works reasonably well.

While a percussion revolver in good condition can handle all the blackpowder you can cram into the chamber, but still leave room for a ball, the charges given in Table 4 provide good accuracy for casual shooting. These charges can be worked up or down for the best load, with lighter loads usually giving the best accuracy. For example, the author's Centennial Arms 1860 Army Colt replica shoots a 2.3" group at 50 yards with 22 grains of FFFg pushing a 138-gr. round ball. With a 28-gr. charge, the group is about 5". In the same gun, the 168-gr.

conical bullet propelled by 22 grains of FFFg gives a group of 4.3" at 50 yards. If you are looking for pure power, try the 44 Colt Walker replica. Loaded with a 219-gr. bullet and 50 grains of FFg, it almost equals a 44 Magnum in performance.

Very light loads, however, may cause erratic performance if the ball does not seat snugly on the powder charge. To insure that the powder is slightly compressed by the ball, the extra space between powder and ball can be filled with an inert substance such as Cream-of-Wheat. Enough is added to fill the chamber until the ball can be seated ⅛" to ¼" below the chamber mouth without crushing the powder grains. Another way to fill this space is to use a greased felt filler wad; this helps lubricate the gun and prevents multifires from one chamber to another.

Seating the ball just below the chamber mouth is supposed to give the greatest accuracy, all other factors being equal. However, for casual shooting, the ball can be seated to the end of the rammer stroke. No filler is needed as long as at least 20 grains of powder are used in a 36-cal. revolver and 25 grains in a 44-cal.

FFFg powder is used most often in revolvers because it burns faster and cleaner than a coarser granulation. FFg, however, is sometimes used in the large Colt Walker and FFFFg can be used in revolvers under 31-cal. When it comes to percussion caps, one brand may fit better and give more uniform results in one revolver than in another. The only way to be sure is to try several types.

While developing the load, vary charges one grain at a time. Shoot at least 12 rounds with each load and, when you feel that the optimum load is reached, shoot an additional dozen to verify results.

Shotguns

Of all muzzleloaders, shotguns are probably used the least, even though they are good hunting weapons and provide a lot of fun at minimum cost. Furthermore, shotgun load development is easier because bulk proportions of powder charge and shot charge are equal. As in any shotgun, the load consists of powder charge, over-powder wad, shot charge and over-shot wad.

Powder and shot charges can be selected from Table 6 or can be determined by using an old saw which says that the depth of the powder charge and the depth of the shot charge each should equal the bore diameter. To determine what weights of powder and shot equal these dimensions, fill a plastic vial, whose inside diameter nearly equals the bore diameter, to the appropriate depth and then weigh the charge.

Table 5   Rifle-Musket Loads

Mould No.	Wt., grs.	Diam./ins.	Charge/grs.	Group/ins.
575213	505	.575	35 FFFg	1.8
575213	505	.575	50 FFg	1.9
575213	505	.575	60 FFg	2.7
57730	530	.580	70 FFg	—

Table 6 Common Muzzle-Loading Shotgun Loads

Gauge	Bore dia., ins. (nominal)	Powder charge (drams FFg)*	Shot charge (ozs.)**	Load type
410	.410	1¼	½	Light
		1½	½	Medium
		1½	⅝	Heavy
28	.550	1¾	⅝	Light
		2	⅝	Medium
		2	¾	Heavy
20	.615	2	¾	Light
		2¼	⅝	Medium
		2½	⅞	Heavy
16	.662	2¼	1	Light
		2½	1	Medium
		2¾	1	Heavy
14	.693	2½	1	Light
		2¾	1	Medium
		3⅛	1⅛	Heavy
12	.729	3¼	1⅛	Light
		3¾	1¼	Medium
		4⅛	1⅜	Heavy
10	.775	4	1¼	Light
		4½	1½	Medium
		5	1¾	Heavy

*1 dram = 27.3 grains   **1 ounce = 436.8 grains

FFg powder is used in nearly all loads. As in any shotgun load, the size of the shot depends on the use of the load.

The over-powder wads may consist of a card wad and one or more filler wads. The card wad is often used when lubricated felt is used as the filler wadding. The card stock, about ⅛-inch thick, is positioned directly over the charge to provide a gas seal and help prevent lubricant from reaching the powder. If commercial fiber shotgun wads are used as the over-powder wad, no card wad is needed.

The filler wad(s) cushions the effect of the expanding powder gases and helps prevent disruption of the shot pattern. Its thickness depends on the bore size, as the old rule used for the powder charge also calls for a wad thickness about equaling the powder depth. Commercial wads are the easiest to use, but are restricted to guns with standard sized bores. Felt wads usually must be hand-cut, but when lubricated they help clean the bore, making swabbing between shots less necessary. Soluble machine oil or water are common lubricants. However, water should not be used unless the gun is to be fired immediately or it may wet the powder charge. Commercial wads are not ordinarily lubricated.

The over-shot wad, usually ¹⁄₁₆"-⅛" thick, contains the shot charge. If too thin it may not do this, while if too thick it may distort the shot pattern. It may be made from card stock or be a commercial wad. It must seat tightly over the shot charge, especially in a double barrel gun, where the recoil from one charge could jar loose the charge in the other barrel.

Both over-powder and over-shot wads should require no more force to seat them than can be applied with thumb and fingers. When the entire charge is loaded, it should be firm enough to make the ramrod bounce when dropped on the over-shot wad.

If commercial wads are not used, do-it-yourself wads can be cut with a wad cutter. Such cutters are normally available for conventional-sized wads only; they must be made for non-standard sizes. Sharpen the outer edge of a steel pipe of appropriate inside diameter to make such a cutter.

Based on the loads given in Table 6 and the foregoing wad considerations, the following load was developed for a Dixie Gun Works replica 20 gauge double to use on quail and dove:

2½ drams FFg; one ⅛" card wad and one ⅜" felt wad, oil-lubricated; ⅞-oz. No. 9 shot; ¹⁄₁₆" over-shot card wad.

Two ⅜" commercial wads could be substituted for the card and felt over-powder wads.

Once a load is decided upon, the gun can be patterned much like a modern shotgun. With the modern gun, the pattern is tested in a 30" circle at 40 yards. However, since most all but the finest muzzle-loading shotguns have cylinder bores (no choke), the pattern should be fired at 25 yards. A good load should place 60% to 70% of the shot in the 30" circle at this range.

There is no accepted way to determine how hard the shot is hitting except to try the load on the intended target. Turner Kirkland of Dixie Gun Works, however, suggests a unique method. Fire the shotgun at a regular tin can from 20 yards. If the shot penetrates the can, then it is hitting hard enough to kill rabbits, doves, and even ducks.

Loading Procedures

Uniformity in the loading procedure, as well as in the load itself, is the key to consistent accuracy in muzzle-loading—just as in modern handloading. Muzzle-loading uniformity is sometimes harder to achieve as the muzzleloader is subjected to vagaries of the shooting environment (wind, temperature, etc.). Moreover, the muzzleloader does not have the handloaders' carefully engineered loading press, powder measure, scale, etc. But to the muzzleloader, the challenge of overcoming these handicaps is half the fun of blackpowder shooting. The look of amazement on a cartridge shooter's face when for the first time he sees a muzzleloader equal or better his performance makes it all worth while.

Muzzle-loading operations can be divided into three similar, but different types: those for rifles and pistols; shotguns; revolvers. The differences depend on the mechanics of the gun and the type of projectile. False muzzle target rifles, such as the "slug" guns, possibly can be considered as a fourth type, but the over-all loading procedure still is basically the same as for any rifle. However, before discussing specific loading procedures, a number of items which apply to all must be covered.

Safety Check the condition of the gun, especially if an original. Perform a mechanical and functional check and then test-fire it. Specific items that

After one barrel of a double barrel muzzle-loading shotgun has been fired, be sure to remove the cap from the unfired barrel before reloading! If it's a double flintlock, empty the unfired pan.

must be checked and methods of checking are given in several of the sources listed in the bibliography. If in doubt, have a gunsmith who knows muzzleloaders check the gun or do not use it at all.

Always point the muzzle away from you and anyone else. Do not lean over the bore while loading; keep well back. Do not hold your fingers over the bore any longer than necessary. Hold the ramrod with thumb and fingers only; never put your palm over the end of the rod.

Do not leave a muzzle-loader unattended while it is loaded, but if you must, remove the percussion cap or empty the pan. Moreover, it is poor practice to leave a load in the gun any longer than necessary. The components of the load often cause rust and corrosion in the bore or chamber and even deterioration of the load itself.

Ball Starter A tool commonly used with patched-ball rifles to start the ball and patch down the bore with uniform pressure. Placed on the ball, seated flush with the muzzle, the starter is hit a sharp blow with the hand or a mallet, driving the patched ball several inches into the bore. The shaft of the starter is about 4″ long, 1/16″ smaller than the diameter of the bore, and cupped on the end to fit the ball.
Ramrod Only moderate, uniform pressure should be applied to the rod by the thumb and fingers, not the palm of the hand. If heavy pressure is required, the bore is probably badly fouled or the ball is oversize. The ball should not be pounded down the bore and the rifle ramrod should not be bounced at the end of the loading stroke. Either may distort the shape of the ball or crush the powder grains. Mark the ramrod at the muzzle to indicate its position in the bore when the load is completely seated. Then refer to this mark each time the gun is loaded to insure that the load is completely seated.
Powder Measure Almost any type of container can be used as long as it throws the charge with consistent accuracy. The powder flask, by far the most versatile, is held upright in one hand with the index finger over the measuring spout. Invert the flask and push the cut-off lever with the thumb to permit the spout to fill. Release the lever, turn the flask upright again, remove the index finger, and pour the powder. For such guns as the rifle-musket, cardboard or plastic cartridge tubes are very useful as they hold a lubricated Minie ball and premeasured powder charge. Pull the ball from the tube (some use their teeth), pour the powder down the bore, and place the ball in the bore. Save that tube as it can be used many times. After the powder is poured into the bore, some shooters slap the gun along side the breech to settle the powder.

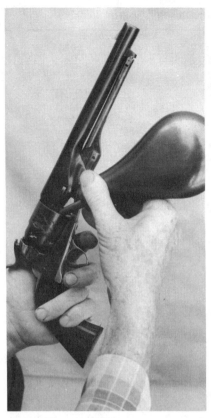

A) After the percussion revolver hammer is set to half-cock, the first loading step is measuring the powder and charging one chamber.

Loading Block A hardwood block drilled with holes of appropriate size to hold pre-cut and lubricated patched balls. It can be quite useful in the field. However, pre-patched balls do not seem to be as accurate as those patched on the spot. Thus this tool is best left to the hunter and casual shooter.
Maintenance Tools These are mandatory in the field if more than a very few shots are to be fired. They should include cleaning patches, bore brush, tooth brush, rags, screwdriver, mallet, nipple wrench, nipple or flash-hole pick, ball screw, and water or other bore cleaner. A pouch is quite useful to carry these tools as well as the balls, powder, and patches. It can be a fancy hunting bag, a military cartridge pouch, or simply a canvas pouch.

The bore should be cleaned regularly, the interval depending on the gun itself, type of powder, type and amount of lubricant, and climate. Periodic cleaning increases accuracy, eases loading, and helps prevent premature powder ignition caused by smoldering patch fragments or powder residue. Target shooting accuracy often requires cleaning after each shot, casual shooting after every 5 shots or so.

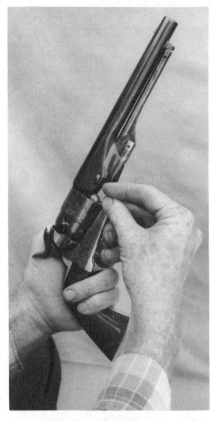

● B) A properly sized ball should seat about one-fourth its diameter into the chamber mouth.
● C) Steady, moderate pressure is applied

Procedure Table

Step by step procedures for loading the various types of muzzleloaders are given in Tables 7 and 8.

This procedure must be modified for revolvers without loading levers. With such revolvers as the Colt Wells Fargo replica, the barrel must be removed and the ball rammed into the cylinder with the cylinder pin or a starter-like rod. The cylinder must also be removed on a Colt Paterson replica, but a special reloading tool is available.

Although some shooters think it is faster to load all chambers with powder and then seat the balls, it is safer to load powder and ball in each chamber in turn. Powder is not as likely to be spilled as the loading lever is operated and the chance of loading a double charge is reduced. However you do it, about 2 minutes is required to load a 6-shot revolver.

With typical service loads, the space between the ball and chamber mouth is filled with grease for both safety and ease of reloading. Grease helps seal the chamber to prevent multifires, helps prevent build-up of hard fouling. Crisco, cup grease, even axle grease, are commonly used.

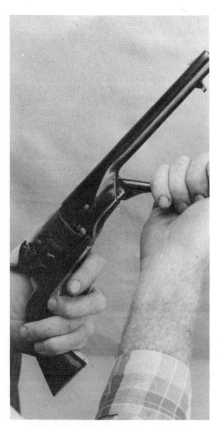
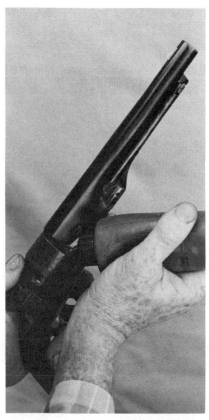
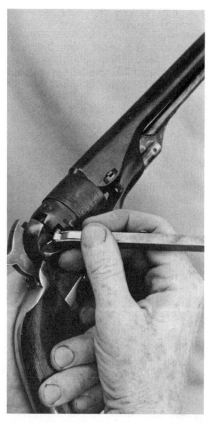

to the ramrod to seat the ball on the powder charge. ● D) Filling the top of the chamber with grease eases subsequent reloading and

increases safety during firing. ● E) Using a capper is the safest and quickest way to seat the percussion caps on the nipples. The open

mouth of the caps may be squeezed out of shape slightly before putting them in the capper to make them hold snugly to the nipples.

Target Rifles

Besides the typical Kentucky and martial muzzleloaders, there are underhammer guns and false-muzzle target rifles. The under hammer guns, such as the modern Hopkins & Allen rifles (and pistols) look and shoot somewhat differently from the typical sidehammer muzzleloader. However, load development and loading procedures are the same.

While there are all types of false-muzzle target rifles, the epitome is the

Table 7   Rifle and Pistol Loading* — Flintlock and Percussion — Round Ball or Minie

1 — Cleaning	Remove all oil from bore before cleaning ignition system. Probe flash hole, dry pan and frizzen, adjust flint or snap a cap or two.
2 — Safety	Put hammer at half-cock and frizzen up or the hammer down on fired cap.
3 — Powder charging	Measure charge and pour down bore; slap breech to settle charge.
4 — Starting	Lube patch and place over muzzle; center ball on patch and push down flush with muzzle; cut off patch flush with muzzle; push ball into bore about 4" with short starter. Fill hollow base of Minie ball with grease; push into bore flush with muzzle.
5 — Seating	Push ball down bore with firm, steady pressure to rest on powder charge.
6 — Fire	Prime pan; lower frizzen; bring hammer to full cock. Or remove spent cap, then re-cap and bring to full cock.

*Muzzle-loading shotguns or pistols are handled the same way except for Steps 4 and 5. Instead, seat over-powder card wad on main charge, followed by lube filler wads; seat both firmly; pour measured shot into bore, then seat over-shot wad firmly and **level**.
When reloading a double barrel shotgun with one barrel still unfired, first remove the percussion cap or empty the pan on the loaded barrel before starting to reload the empty barrel.

Table 8   Percussion Revolver Loading

1 — Cleaning	First, wipe chambers and bore completely free of oil, then snap a cap or two on each nipple.
2 — Safety	Place hammer on half-cock notch.
3 — Loading powder	Load each chamber with measured charge.
4 — Loading filler	Pour in Cream-of-Wheat or seat felt wad, either optional with small powder charges.
5 — Seat ball	Place ball on chamber mouth, sprue up or down, then ram it down on powder with firm stroke of loading lever.
6 — Greasing	Fill chamber between mouth and top of ball with grease. (If greased filler wad is used under ball, this is not needed.)
7 — Priming	Seat percussion caps snugly on nipples.
8 — Safety	Lower hammer to safety notches, studs between chambers, or on uncapped nipple.
9 — Fire	Bring hammer to full cock.

slug rifle used by the most serious of blackpowder shooters. From before 1880 to 1900, slug rifles were the elite of all muzzle-loading arms, and even most breech-loading rifles. They were the blackpowder equivalent of the modern bench rest rifle, and only in recent years have the great groups they made been beaten.

A slug rifle may weigh from 15 to 60 pounds, has a bore over 35 caliber, often 45 or 50, and uses a scope of up to 25 power. The trade-mark of these rifles is their false muzzle, along with the numerous tools required to make and load bullets. Many slug rifles, notably those by Wm. Billinghurst, were underhammer guns.

The design, manufacture, and loading of the bullet makes the slug rifle differ most from the ordinary roundball rifle. A long cylindrical, swaged, usually two-pieced, bullet is used for stability and reduced reaction to wind deflection. Its base is soft to take the rifling while the nose piece is hard to prevent deformation during loading. The nose and base parts are cast separately, then swaged together.

Patches generally are not circular, but strips of bond or banknote paper about .003″ thick, lubricated with sperm oil. Two strips, crossed under the base of the bullet, wrap around it as it is loaded through the false muzzle. Sometimes one-piece, cross patches are used.

The false muzzle, tapered inside from top to bottom, is used to start the bullet uniformly into the bore and protect the rifling from wear by the ramrod. The false muzzle is an absolute necessity on slug rifles as the long, flat based, pointed nose bullet, often nearly groove size, could never be seated uniformly or without damage without it. False muzzles are usually slotted to receive the paper patch strips, and many are used with a mechanical bullet starter which may be attached to the muzzle.

Loading an ordinary false muzzle rifle is much the same as for other muzzle-loading rifles, though more care is usually taken with ball position and ramming. Also more accessories are required, especially for the slug rifle. A typical slug rifle requires false muzzle and bullet starter, loading rod, cleaning rod, two bullet moulds and swages (nose and base) and patch cutter. This is in addition to all the other maintenance accessories plus telescope sight and muzzle or machine rest.

With all these tools and accessories one does not just go out for a casual shoot with a slug rifle. You have to be a lot more serious to take the time and effort required to get the most out of the rifle. However, the results justify the efforts as half-inch groups, or less, are possible at 100 yards and one-inch strings at 200. ●

Bibliography

"Black Powder Pistols." W.A. Carver, GUN DIGEST, 18th ed. 1964, Chicago, Ill.
"Black Powder Replicas." J. Lachuck, GUN DIGEST, 18th ed., 1964, Chicago, Ill.
"Black Powder Rifles in Pennsylvania." E.S. Smith, GUN DIGEST, 5th ed., 1955.
"Cap & Ball Capers." J. Lachuck, Guns and Ammo, July 1961.
Colt Firearms 1836-1954. J.E. Serven, (Foundation Press, Santa Ana, Calif., 1964, 5th ed.
History of The Colt Revolver, A. C.T. Haven and F.A. Belden (Bonanza Books, New York, 1967).
"How to Load and Care For Black Powder Revolvers." R.O. Ackerman, Shooting Times, Jan., 1965.
Kentucky Rifle, The. J.G.W. Dillin (Geo. Shumway, York, Penna., 1967, 5th ed.).
"Making Paper Cartridges." R.E. Colby, The American Rifleman, pp. 28-29, Apr. 1966.
Muzzle Blasts. Journal of the National Muzzle Loading Rifle Assn., Friendship, Ind.
Muzzle-Loading Caplock Rifle, The. N.H. Roberts, Stackpole Co., Harrisburg, Pa. 1958.
Lyman Reloading Handbook, Sec. 7, 44th ed., 1967.
"Muzzle-Loading Pistol Shooting." The American Rifleman, Feb. 1964.
Pennsylvania-Kentucky Rifle, The. H.J. Kauffman, Stackpole Co., Harrisburg, Pa., 1960.
Powder Flask Book, The. R. Riling (Bonanza Books, N.Y., 1953).
"Ramrod Guns, Country Style." E.C. Lenz, GUN DIGEST, 22nd ed., 1968, Chicago, Ill.
Rifled Musket, The. C.E. Fuller (Stackpole Co., Harrisburg, Pa., 1958).
"Slug Rifle, The." P. Autry, The American Rifleman, Dec., 1962.
Small Arms and Ammunition in The United States Service 1776-1865. B.R. Lewis, (Smithsonian Institution, Washington, D.C., 1960) 2nd printing.
"Shoot Today's Black Powder Sixguns." H. French, Guns and Ammo, Nov., 1966.
"Shooting Muzzle-Loading Firearms." L. Olson and B.R. Lewis. The American Rifleman, May, June, 1966.

Cleaning Muzzleloaders

Thorough cleaning of black powder guns is a real must, especially if the piece is to be put away for a time. Black powder residue is highly moisture absorbent, and if you don't get the crud out of your barrel after you're through shooting rust and corrosion will be the result.

Before you pack up your shooting kit, following a session at the range or wherever, run an oily patch or bristle brush down the bore (and into the cylinder chambers if it's a revolver) and then oil the lock, the nipple, the hammer, etc. One of the modern spray cans of oil is a good choice for the lock area, especially one of the water-displacement types such as WD-40, QA-25, LPS, Riel & Fuller's Anti-Rust, etc. Chopie's Black-Solve and Clenzoil are specially formulated for black powder arms, and a cleaning with either as directed will afford protection against rusting for many days.

When you get home, remove the nipple (if it's a rifle or shotgun), scrub the bore briskly with a bristle brush soaked in Hoppe's No. 9 or other powder solvent to remove that oil you put in and as much of the black powder fouling as possible. Use the solvent around the lock area (or one of the spray oils), getting some into the breech via the nipple hole. A toothbrush and a couple of pipe cleaners can be a big help.

Now wipe the bore or chamber dry with cleaning patches, then wet a patch in water, squeeze it out and re-scrub the bore. Water is the best solvent for black powder residue.

Follow up with a re-oiling of the bore or chambers, being sure to get some into the breech area. If the gun is of percussion type, with a removable drum, take the drum off and get oil into it after you've scrubbed it clean of fouling.

A cleaning such as this will be all that's needed if you're going to shoot it again within a week or so—or less—but if the gun is going to be stored for a lengthy time, let me suggest you give the gun the hot water treatment!

First, take the gun apart as much as possible; remove the nipple(s), lock, drum and breech plug. Clean these parts as described above, then put back the nipple(s) of the gun in a rifle or shotgun. Obtain a 2- or 3-foot section of flexible rubber tubing, inside diameter a snug push fit onto the nipple. Automobile windshield washer hose is often just right. Also pick up a funnel that fits inside the muzzle of your gun.

Alternatively, a piece of rubber tubing flexible enough to be stretched over the muzzle serves well; the funnel is inserted into the upper end of this tubing.

Next, get a pail or some other container, attach one end of the hose to the nipple and let the other end lie in the pail. Now, holding the gun upright, funnel in the muzzle, pour hot water—good and hot—into the muzzle. Depending on caliber or gauge, put through a pint or a quart. If the water's hot enough, the heat will dry the bore completely. A revolver cylinder may be boiled in water after removing the cones.

After this treatment, use one of the heavier gun greases (Rig is excellent) to coat the bore and the various component parts, then assemble and put the gun away, by all means in as dry a place as possible.

Do not leave the ramrod in the bore(s) or plug it up in any way. When you want to use the gun again you must, of course, thoroughly remove the heavy grease.

THE TITLE OF this article appears to be a direct self-contradiction; however, it is the stark truth. Those of us who are concerned with the welfare of these United States are ever aware of the importance of our natural resources. We become more observant of these resources when they are in jeopardy. Many are in jeopardy now. Hardly a day passes that we do not read articles, take part in conversations or hear broadcasts relative to the increasing problems of water pollution, air pollution or soil erosion. These are some, but not all, of the problems we face. For hunters, wild animal populations, both big and small, are of prime interest too, and they also are part of our natural resources.

Ironically, the concept of freedom on which this nation was founded and flourished had much to do with the problems mentioned. Apparently blessed with a never-ending abundance of resources, we saw ourselves free to squander them irresponsibly, with little, if any, regard to the future. It must be recognized that in this country's early period sufficient knowledge was not at hand to serve as a basis for long range natural resource planning. Such knowledge is available now and it is to our own immediate interest, as well as to the future's, that we manage our resources intelligently.

Natural resources are of two basic types: nonrenewable and renewable. Nonrenewable resources are those which once used lose their identity as a resource; i.e., burning coal produces heat and ash. A formation of coal once mined does not redevelop for mining next year. Renewable resources are those which once used can replace or renew themselves for use again; i.e., vegetation in a pasture can be used by cattle this summer and replace itself for use again next summer. Wild animal populations are renewable biological resources.

Theodore Roosevelt was one of the early leaders to recognize conservation as "wise use," not "non-use." He felt that non-use of a natural renewable resource was waste. Even though the United States is the world's most wasteful nation, we need not perpetuate this in the management of our renewable natural resources. We must use our wildlife resources wisely, to benefit the greatest number of people now and in the future. This article will explore some of the basic concepts which are the foundation of renewable resource management, specifically wildlife resources.

Carrying Capacity

A certain area of given habitat can support just so many animals without being damaged itself. A rancher

Death has ended this Michigan white-tailed deer's battle with starvation. Note the height to which deer have consumed the browse from the cedars.

Few people know Nature's ruthless game control methods. Fewer still understand the hunter's role in this drama. Read this biologist's study—and pass the word to those who stay home and merely "talk" conservation

by R. J. ROBEL

in the Flint Hills region of Kansas can support 10 steers through the six warm months on 100 acres of good pasture land and still retain the quality of that land. If he introduces 16 steers into his pasture there is less food for each animal and an overgrazing condition results. By overstocking his range, he reduces the quality of his product (beef), as well as the quality of his pasture. If he continues to overgraze the pasture, pasture quality (carrying capacity) will be gradually reduced to the point where it will no longer support even 6 or 8 steers. The cattle rancher is a businessman and is sincerely interested in maintaining his pasture and animals in optimum condition. He therefore keeps his range stocked at or below the carrying capacity. The basic situation in wildlife management is identical to that of the rancher and his cattle.

Instead of a 100-acre pasture, wild animals live in well defined habitat. The principles remain the same. A given amount of habitat can support only so many healthy animals. If animal numbers exceed the habitat's carrying capacity, poor animals and damaged habitat result. In 1906 the Kaibab portion of the Grand Canyon Forest Reserve became the Grand Canyon National Game Preserve. Under the protection from hunters and the elimination of natural predators, the deer herd increased at a rate of approximately 20 per cent per year. It did so at the expense of the habitat. The deer population soon exceeded the carrying capacity of the range. In 1906 the deer herd had been estimated to number about 4,000; by 1924 it was perhaps 100,000. In 1918 the Forest Supervisor reported a decrease in available deer browse, therefore a reduction in the carrying capacity of the range. By 1930 the deer herd was reduced, mainly through starvation and disease, to less than 20,000 animals. A tragic waste of both deer and habitat. Following this overpopulation episode, the region looked as though a swarm of locusts had swept through it and devoured everything except trees, rocks, and thorns. The Kaibab incident was a deplorable example of wasteful management of renewable biological resource through non-use.

Environmental Resistance

The characteristics which determine the carrying capacity of an area are known as "limiting factors." Since these are factors of the environment and seldom act independently, we can look at them collectively as affording resistance to the growth of a population and therefore term them "environmental resistance." Nature is normally in balance, biologically speaking, between the environment and the animals it supports. If the population is increasing too fast and is in danger of exceeding the carrying capacity of its habitat, resistance by the environment increases. If the population level is below the carrying capacity of the habitat, environmental resistance is less intense.

Many factors working together comprise environmental resistance. Predators, lack of food, disease, limited nesting sites, sterility, disproportionate sex ratios, stress, cold, rain, plus many other factors act to control population levels. Normally each of these environmental factors becomes more intense or active as the population increases. Acting together they reduce the rate of population growth. If an environment offers no resistance, a given species will increase to the extent of which it is biologically capable. Let us look for a moment at how fast a population of rice rats in Florida would grow if unchecked by environmental resistance. Beginning with two sexually mature rats on July 1, the population would number about 66 on January 1, and approximately 221 on the following June 30. In only five years the population would exceed 10,000 and in less than ten years the population would surpass 100,000,000 rats. In a matter of just a few years the earth would literally be covered with rice rats. They would eat themselves out of house and home. Nature does not allow populations to go unchecked. She retards or reduces the growth rate to maintain their numbers within the carrying capacity of their environment. This is done in an effective manner: by means of starvation, predators, freezing, etc. Although in human eyes these methods are cruel, the environment must effectively regulate population numbers if it is to retain its balanced integrity.

Population Fluctuations

Any person who has spent time watching or in pursuit of wild animals knows that population levels fluctuate. Since we have stated that each environment has a definte carrying capacity and that animal populations are controlled by environmental resistance, why should a population of animals fluctuate from year to year? Is nature losing its control over populations? Or, are our basic premises erroneous?

Some populations fluctuate in a predictable fashion; with such regularity, in fact, that ecologists have termed them cycles. Well known animals whose population numbers undergo such regular ups and downs are the lemmings and other small rodents of the arctic, the voles (small rodents of open forests and grasslands), the varying hare (snowshoe rabbit) of

Canada and the northern United States, and two species of grouse. In these cycles, there seem to be two definite time periods between the peaks of population numbers: 4-year and 10-year period intervals. The lemmings and voles have population peaks at 4-year intervals, while the varying hares and grouse seem to be more abundant at 10-year intervals. Although much research has been conducted in an effort to solve the mystery of population cycles, no scientist has come up with a cut and dried theory. Some of the more common theories are: cyclic climatic changes, epidemic disease, external and internal parasites, predators, emigration, and inbreeding. *Cyclic fluctuations continue in populations of these species even if they are not subject to hunting pressures. Therefore, closed or very restricted hunting seasons when these populations are low are not based on sound biological facts.*

Although game managers appear unable to explain the causes of regularly occurring cycles, they do a much better job of explaining year-to-year fluctuations of animal numbers. For the most part, these fluctuations result from changes in weather conditions during the breeding and nesting seasons and modifications resulting in a change in the carrying capacity of the environment.

Wet weather coupled with cold temperatures during the spring breeding and nesting season spells disaster for upland game bird populations. Newly hatched pheasants and quail are extremely vulnerable to excess moisture and cold. Sometimes up to 60 per cent of the spring hatch is lost during a cold rainy period of 3 to 6 days. This, of course, appreciably reduces the number of animals available for the sportsmen during the fall months. Likewise, extremely hot and dry weather may also deal a catastrophic blow to an animal population. Even though most upland game birds re-nest if their first nest or brood is destroyed, their second nesting attempt is less productive. Severe rain and hail storms can greatly increase the mortality of juvenile birds during the summer and early fall months. Conversely, when nesting conditions are optimum and survival good during summer months, abnormally high populations result in the fall months.

Even when abnormal weather conditions do not exist to change the reproductive success of the species, populations may be reduced by a change in the carrying capacity of their range. Certain agricultural practices and removal or burning of fence rows and weeds along roadways reduce the amount of nesting habitat available. Drainage of marshes and

sloughs reduces the nesting habitat of waterfowl. No matter how much we manipulate the environment, a population cannot maintain itself and grow without suitable nesting sites.

Seasonal Fluctuations

Seasonal fluctuations of population numbers are directly geared to the carrying capacity of their environment. There are yearly as well as seasonal carrying capacity variations. Normally the carrying capacity of the environment is highest during the summer months and lowest during the winter and early spring months. The period of the year when the carrying capacity is lowest is the ultimate limit for the population. During the summer season, seeds, insects, shelter, and other factors are abundant for wildlife. This is the season Nature chose to produce additional animals. Only when conditions are optimal can young individuals be expected to survive. As the summer ebbs and fall begins, the food supply becomes reduced and shelter is less abundant. During the fall season, mortality exceeds natality and therefore a net loss occurs in the population. This loss continues through the winter. Late winter and early spring are the periods when food is scarc-

This young moose died in early spring from a massive infection and inflammation in both front legs which resulted from foot rot.

est, shelter least abundant, and weather the most severe. This is the period when the environment makes its major cut into population numbers. This is the period when the carrying capacity is lowest. The number and health of the animals surviving the winter determines the reproduction for the following year; *therefore, winter can be considered the critical period for most wild populations.*

Let us look to the normal seasonal fluctuation of a population of bobwhite quail on an Iowa farm. For the sake of simplicity, we'll assume there is food and shelter in the winter habitat sufficient to support 24

THEY MUST DIE!

quail and that all of these birds survive to nest in the spring. Let us assume further that the sex ratio is even, giving us 12 males and 12 females for the nesting season. If these 12 pairs of birds are able to find nesting sites and produce clutches

sult in a Kansas deer population numbering 550,000. If this rate of increase should continue for an additional 5 years (15 years total), the deer population would number over 2,050,000 individuals, far above the carrying capacity of the range. It sounds incredible, but it is true. Nature, however, will not permit the population to reach such astronomical numbers. Through starvation, sterility, disease, parasitism, predation, stress and other natural limiting factors, the population will be held at or near the carrying capacity of the range. As can well be appreciated, a deer herd which is held in check by such natural factors cannot be expected to continually produce the sleek, healthy, vigorous, majestic creatures we normally envision. We believe there is a better method: hunting.

are not aware of the basic biological principles which regulate game populations. In our preceding discussion of a population of bobwhite quail, it was shown that not more than 24 birds could be carried over from fall to spring. If well-meaning sportsmen released an additional 200—or 2,000 —birds in the area in September, there would still be only 24 birds as spring breeding stock. Actually, I'm oversimplifying the situation since the carrying capacity of the winter habitat changes from year to year. In an extremely mild winter, the carrying capacity in our quail example might be 30 birds; however, at the other extreme, in a severe winter with extended periods of low temperatures and deep snows, the carrying capacity might drop to 10 or 12 birds. No matter what, the number of birds which survive the winter is but a small fraction of those entering the fall season. Normally, 6 out of every 10 quail that are alive in the fall of the year will be dead by April 15. This loss will be even greater if more birds are present in the fall months. This occurs whether or not hunting of the population is permitted. The same principle holds true for rabbits, deer, elk, mountain goats, pheasants, partridge, grouse and most all wild game animals. With waterfowl, the shortage of nesting habitat might at times be more limiting than the winter range.

Why hunt to conserve? Remember, conservation is the wise use of our renewable biological resources. Non-use of such a resource is waste. Unless we make use of the animals which are doomed to die and decompose in the field, we are wasting that

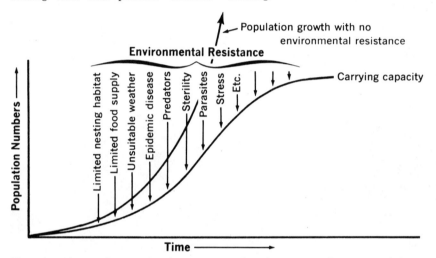
Chart shows how environmental resistance acts against the pressure of game population to exceed its carrying capacity.

of fertile eggs, and if each pair is successful in raising a brood of 8 or 9 young, then a population numbering about 125 would be present during the late summer period. Now recalling that the carrying capacity of the winter range is 24 birds, 101 of these 125 quail must die before the end of winter. The winter range has shelter and food for only 24 birds and no more than 24 birds can survive. No matter how many birds enter the winter on this farm, only 24 will survive to nest the following spring. This principle holds true for any wildlife population.

Right now the State of Kansas is experiencing a deer population explosion and is intelligently attempting to curb the rate of increase and utilize the deer resource by initiating a statewide deer hunting season. Presently the small resident herd numbers about 40,000 healthy deer and for the past several years has been increasing at a rate of 30 per cent per year. This rate of increase, if continued for 10 years, would re-

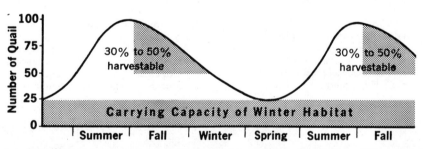
Annual fluctuation of a normal population of bobwhite quail, showing portion which may be harvested. Hunters may take between 30% and 50% of the quail population without diminishing the following year's crop; 75% could be taken (since maximum winter carry over is 25%) if it were certain the 25% would survive. However, some of these birds will die no matter how ideal the conditions — through predation, old age, accidents, etc. — therefore, a harvest of 50% leaves a safety buffer in the population.

Kill to Conserve

How often have you heard the protectionist say, "Close the hunting season for a couple of years and let the animals build up," or "Reduce the bag limit this year so more can survive and breed next spring"? Such people have sincere intentions but

resource. At best we are realizing only the fertilizer value of it. Not hunting upland game birds is similar to a farmer planting corn year after year but never harvesting his crop. Allowing deer to starve can be compared to permitting meat to rot in your refrigerator.

Deep snow, long cold nights, and a lack of food decrease this doe's chances of winter survival.

Wildlife is, indirectly but ultimately, a crop of the land. The land produces more than it can maintain; therefore, the excess can be considered a harvestable surplus. Up to 40 or 50 per cent of the fall quail population can be harvested by hunters without adversely affecting the vitality of the population. Up to 30 per cent of the Kansas deer population can be harvested each year while still maintaining a healthy herd. Under normal conditions, it is almost impossible to overharvest wild populations when incorporating sporting methods. As populations of wild animals decrease, the effort required for a hunter to kill a specimen increases, thus forming a natural check on the percentage harvested by the hunter. Game laws are enacted for two basic reasons: (1) to protect some animals from being overharvested at the wrong time of the year, and (2) to make available the enjoyment of harvesting these animals to the greatest number of people. The second of these objectives is one which few people realize and appreciate. Bag limits and extended seasons work in favor of the hunter and yet do not greatly r e d u c e game population.

Closed seasons don't increase game numbers. A hunter does not work against Nature when he harvests part of the wildlife crop. Rather, he acts as one of Nature's tools by reducing the wild population before the critical winter period. He acts as an artificial predator. Harvesting of surplus g a m e animals by employing sporting methods is wise use of an otherwise wasted resource. The statement, "We must kill to conserve them" is sound and meaningful. •

Hen pheasant frozen in place. Better cover would reduce such losses, but not eliminate them.

It was more than 1000 yards from the loft of the old barn to the sugar maple where his son had been killed, but with the huge, telescope-equipped Horace Warner rifle, the madman was positive he could avenge his son's murder — and he did.

MADMAN of GAYLORD'S CORNER

by LUCIAN CARY

Superstitious New Englanders whispered that the place was haunted, but J. M. Pyne didn't believe in ghosts — even when he heard the roar of a distant gun, and a huge slug from a sharpshooter's Civil War rifle thunked into a tree near his head . . .

This story, first printed over 30 years ago, was one of a series by well-known gun writer Lucian Cary. For our younger readers' information, the character J. M. Pyne is a thinly-disguised H. M. Pope, the late, great barrelmaker.

I T WAS a long time ago. It was a long time ago, when there were no radios and no motor cars and no state police and no newspapers printing photographs brought in by air-

By permission of *The Saturday Evening Post.* © 1935 by the Curtis Publishing Company.

plane from the scene of the crime. It was almost fifty years ago—when J. M. Pyne was young.

J. M. Pyne sat beside the driver of a spring wagon of a summer afternoon with his rifle in a canvas case between his knees. He had hired the wagon to take his trunk and a chest of tools and a box of groceries from the railway station at Winchester four miles up into the New England hills to the place he had rented near Gaylord's Corner. The driver, being a man with a beard, and a native of the region who had returned to it after travels as far west as Indiana, conceived himself as one of wide experience and his passenger as a boy.

He asked a good many questions,

but only now and then paused to hear the answers J. M. Pyne gave him.

He chuckled to himself at odd intervals, as if he possessed some secret source of amusement which he might reveal if he chose. But he made no secret of his astonishment at young Mr. Pyne's purpose in renting the old Barnes place.

"You aim to make gun barrels!" he said.

"Rifle barrels," J. M. Pyne said.

"You figur' to sell 'em to one o' these factories?"

"No," J. M. Pyne said. "I'm going to make them for individual customers."

The driver wagged his head. "I dunno where you expect to git customers way up here in these hills," he said. "You won't have a neighbor 'side of two mile."

Young Mr. Pyne hadn't quit his job in the Hartford bicycle factory without misgivings. He had a wife and a small son to look out for. So far, he had made rifle barrels as an avocation, in the spare time he found after working ten hours a day in the factory. He suspected he was moving to the country because he liked the country. But he had a few dollars in the bank and orders enough to keep him busy for several months. He had sent a small advertisement to Mr. Gould's weekly, *Shooting & Fishing,* in Boston, announcing that he was prepared to make and fit target barrels of superior accuracy. The great George Schalk, of Pottsville, in Pennsylvania, was dead. There was room for a new man. There was always room for a new man if he could make rifles that shot better than other men's.

The old Barnes place had a furnished house, and a good barn, and a shop with water power. It was the sort of one or two man farm and factory that was once to be found every mile or two on every brook in Southern New England. J. M. Pyne had got it for ten dollars a month. His overhead would be but a fraction of what it would be in Hartford.

"Used to be," the driver said, "there was good enough farms hereabouts, and people to farm 'em. But nowadays the meadows are all growin' up to brush. Everybody's gone West. When I was as young as you be, they were all goin' to Californy to dig for gold. They been goin' ever since. When 'tweren't one thing 'twas tother."

They approached a crossroad, with a small church and a cluster of white houses looking on an elm-shaded green. This was Gaylord's Corner. The driver pointed with his whip.

"Yonder, at the store, they got some right good hard cider."

"I'm in a hurry," J. M. Pyne said.

The driver wagged his head sadly. "Just as you say," he said. He turned his horses into the road that led downhill. He flicked the nigh horse with his whip.

"Giddyap," he said.

The plodding animals began to trot, their feet throwing up little spurts of dust that united to form a trailing cloud behind the wagon. They lumbered, after fifteen minutes, across a wooden bridge over a brook and drew up at a small white house built around a central chimney. J. M. Pyne sat a moment gazing at the place. There were lilac bushes as high as the eaves on either side of the front door, and to one side a dozen old apple trees, and on beyond a towering sugar maple, with no branches near the ground. A woodchuck raised himself upright, his head cocked sidewise above the long grass as he looked and

listened. He dropped suddenly and scuttled for his hole.

J. M. Pyne got down from the wagon and unlocked the kitchen door. The place had the musty smell of a house that has long been closed. But it was clean and neat. He stood his rifle in a corner, making sure that it would not fall and bend the delicate windage screw of the front sight, and went out to help the driver get his boxes out of the wagon.

When they had got everything inside, they stood beside the wagon. J. M. Pyne gave the driver the two dollars they had agreed on. The driver put the money in a worn leather pouch with drawstrings. He drew the strings tight and wrapped them round the neck of the pouch and stowed it deep in a back pocket. When he had completed this ceremony, he jerked his thumb at the house.

"Nice place," he said. He added, with meaning, "To look at."

The Ghost of Abel White

The house and the barn and the tall sugar maple were making long shadows on the grass—shadows that reached almost to the brook. The sun was going down. It was warm and still and peaceful. J. M. Pyne looked off across the brook, across the marsh, to the wooded hills half a mile away that rose, tier on tier, to the north.

"I like it," he said.

The driver took out a plug of tobacco and a pocketknife. He cut slivers from the plug and stowed them in his cheek.

"Son," he said sentensiously, "son,

you ain't afraid to sleep here?"

"No," J. M. Pyne said.

"You might be," the driver said. "You might be, if you knew more about this place."

"If I knew what?" J. M. Pyne asked.

"Ain't nobody told you nothin'?" the man demanded.

"No," J. M. Pyne said.

"This place is haunted."

J. M. Pyne smiled. He believed in his micrometer caliper, with which he could so easily do something that none of the old-time rifle makers, not even George Schalk, could do—he could measure to a ten-thousandth of an inch. He did not believe in ghosts.

"That's why there ain't nobody livin' here," the old fellow continued. 'Ain't been for ten year. The ghost of young Abel White druv out every man that's ever tried to live here since."

J. M. Pyne waited impatiently. He wanted the man to get through and be gone.

"You see that big sugar maple yonder? That's where young Barnes shot young Abel White. The coroner's jury called it an accident. But the way I heard it, they was both sweet on the same girl."

"And how," J. M. Pyne asked, "do they know that the ghost is the ghost of young White?"

"Because he's so tall he has to duck to come in the kitchen door. Young Abel was like his father, and old Abel was six feet four."

J. M. was not impressed with this piece of reasoning. But there was no use arguing with a man who believed

J. M. Pyne stooped to pick up a piece of old iron from the grass beneath the sugar maple — and heard the distant roar of a gun, and a bullet's impact with the tree beside him.

in ghosts.

"If I was you," the old fellow said, "I'd find some other place."

"I don't take much stock in ghosts," J. M. Pyne said.

The old fellow put one foot on the hub of a front wheel and climbed up to the seat of the wagon and gathered up the lines.

"Mebbe you don't now," he said. "Mebbe you will before many nights." He backed his team, cramping the wheels so he could turn his wagon around. He got the wagon turned around. The horses pricked up their ears and started out toward home. The driver turned and shouted over his shoulder, "You can't say I didn't warn you!"

A Quiet Evening

J. M. Pyne explored the place as long as the light lasted. He remembered every detail of it from his first visit a month earlier. But he wanted to see it all again. He wanted to make sure he could get a full two hundred yards from the shop window for testing rifles.

He went into the house when it was dark and lit the kerosene lamp in the bracket on the wall and built a fire in the kitchen stove. He had bread and butter and coffee and some thin slices of round steak. He pounded the steak with a hammer and rolled it in flour and fried it in butter with the onions.

When he had eaten, he set the lamp on the table and got out paper and pencil. He had an idea for a rifle action that would combine the strength of the Sharps, with its solid-steel breechblock sliding in a steel mortise, and the camming motion of the Ballard which pushes a cartridge home. He sketched the parts over and over again. He lay awake with the problem for half an hour after he went to bed. He heard the sad monotonous cry of a whippoorwill outside. He heard a patter on the floor overhead. He guessed it was the patter of a chipmunk. He heard the stairs creak, as if

someone were stealing down them. He remembered the old man and his talk of ghosts. He smiled. Old houses did creak when it was quiet enough to hear the sound. Old men and old wives liked to believe in ghosts. He went to sleep.

A Rifle's Roar

J. M. Pyne was up at daylight the next morning. He had a lot of work to do before he sent for Mary and the baby. He worked all day repairing the gate that let the water on the wheel for the shop's power. He scarcely paused, except to eat a couple of sandwiches, for twelve hours. Then he went to the well and drew a fresh bucket of water and drank thirstily. He was aware suddenly of being tired. He walked slowly out toward the big sugar maple, wiping his sweaty face with a big blue-and-white bandanna handkerchief. He stood under the big maple tree, looking at the marsh and the green hills beyond. His foot struck something in the long grass. It was a piece of old iron. He stooped to pick it up and, stooping, saved his life.

As he bent down, he heard the distant roar of a gun, and a bullet struck the tree behind him with a solid thunk.

J. M. Pyle was on the other side of the tree in two strides. He peered around the trunk of the tree, exposing scarcely more than an eyebrow. He could see no sign of the man who had fired the shot. He looked higher. He could see nothing in the green hills beyond the marsh. A gun as loud as that must use a lot of powder, and yet there was no smoke.

J. M. Pyne could only guess where the shot had come from, remembering the sound. He asked himself whether he had heard the shot before he heard the bullet strike. A bullet would start with a velocity of fourteen or fifteen hundred feet a second. That was a good deal faster than sound. But after a couple of hundred yards, the bullet would be going slower than sound. He couldn't remember which he had heard first—the sound of the shot or the thunk of the bullet. But he knew that the sound of the gun had come from a long way off.

It was, of course, an accident that the bullet had come so near to hitting him. Some farm boy a mile away had shot at a hawk high in a tree, not thinking it mattered where his bullet came down in that half-deserted country. But what would a farm boy be doing with a rifle that made so great a noise?

J. M. Pyne kept the tree between himself and the distant hills as he retreated to the house. He got his rifle out of its case and set the windage at zero and the elevation at two hundred yards. It was the first rifle he had made for himself and the only 25 caliber rifle in America. It was a light rifle, weighing less

than ten pounds to conform to the Massachusetts rules for offhand matches, and shot a light charge. But J. M. Pyne loaded it with confidence. He knew what the little rifle would do. He knew you didn't need a heavy charge to stop a man—not if you put the bullet in the right place.

He got back to the shelter of the big sugar maple and watched and waited. He waited till dusk. Then he waited a little longer, until he was sure no one at a distance could see him well enough to shoot at him, before he went around in front of the tree. He found the bullet hole a trifle higher than his heart. It had been made, he saw, by a big bullet. The green wood would have closed around the path of a small bullet. He was able to thrust a wire a full two inches into the hole. He was astonished at the angle. He guessed the angle at more than thirty degrees. That bullet had come a long, long way. It must have come from the wooded hills yonder.

J. M. Pyne got a brace and bit and a chisel. The maple was green and tough. He had to bore several holes and cut away a good deal of wood to get the bullet out without digging into it, but he got it. It was the biggest bullet he had ever seen. It weighed something like a quarter of a pound.

He took the bullet into the kitchen and lit the lamp and got out a magnifying glass and his micrometer caliper. The nose of the bullet was mushroomed. The butt was not much deformed. He measured the diameter of the butt with the micrometer caliper. It measured .6823. He knew, because it had no cannelures for grease, that it had been patched with paper.

Two-Piece Bullet

He saw a hairline around the bullet—the line of a joint. It had been made in two pieces. He picked up the magnifying glass. There was no doubt about it. The bullet had been cast in two parts and swaged together. He tested first the butt and then the forward portion with his fingernail. Even to so rough a test, the butt was softer. The butt had less tin alloyed with the lead than the forward portion.

J. M. Pyne knew the kind of rifle from which that bullet had come. He had never seen such a rifle. But he had heard about such a rifle. And knowing the kind of rifle, he could guess some things about the man who had fired the shot. He wasn't a farm boy shooting at a hawk high in a tree.

The rifle must be of the type that Berdan's sharpshooters had taken into the Civil War. They'd been given something easier to carry a few months after they went in. But they had gone in carrying rifles made for the peculiarly American sport of double-rest shooting. The lightest of their guns weighed twenty pounds and many of them weighed forty pounds, and none of them shot a bullet as big as the one J. M. Pyne held in his hand. The rifle that fired that bullet must be the great-grand-father of double-rest rifles. It must weigh fifty pounds or more. Not even John L. Sullivan could shoot it off-hand. You had to have a rest.

J. M. Pyne got a fire going in the stove and cooked a slice of ham and a couple of eggs. He hardly knew what he was eating. He was thinking too hard. The man who fired that rifle must have known what he was doing. He must have known where his bullet was going. He would be that kind of man. And if he knew where his bullet was going, he was trying to kill J. M. Pyne.

J. M. Pyne was awake before dawn the next morning. He got up and looked out. The stars were still shin-ing. He got into his clothes and cooked himself a solid breakfast of ham and eggs. He made two sand-wiches and put them in the side pocket of his dungaree jacket. He got his compass and five cartridges and picked up his rifle.

He crossed the brook and, skirting the marsh, set out for the hills that began half a mile away. The wire in the bullet hole had pointed slightly east of north. He thought he could find the spot from which that bullet had come. He paused as he entered the woods and changed the elevation of his rear sight to that for seventy-five yards. He knew where to hold, with that setting, for anything be-tween point-blank and a hundred yards. He had carried the little rifle many a mile and shot crows and hawks and woodchucks with it.

The woods were the typical New England sort, of hemlock and beech and oak and birch, and an occasional great chestnut with branches as thick as the trunks of other trees, and an undergrowth of laurel.

J. M. Pyne went slowly, in order to go quietly and to miss nothing, as if he were hunting deer, and paused often to watch his back trail. It was useless to hunt deer in such a forest while the leaves were on the trees. You could see only a few yards ahead in that thicket of greenery, with only an occasional splash of sunlight com-ing through a gap in the foliage aloft. A deer scented you and heard you long before you were near enough to see him. You wouldn't see so much as his white flag as he bounded off. A man, J. M. Pyne reflected, had poor ears and no nose at all. A man was easier to hunt. But unlike any other animal to be found in the New England woods, he might turn and hunt you.

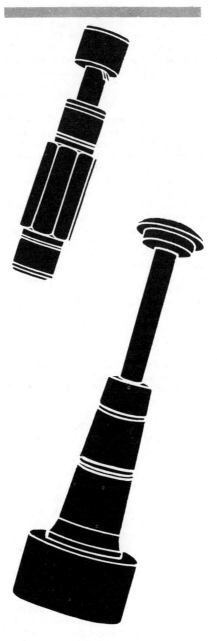

The common bullet swage, top, was of steel, closed at one end. A slightly undersized cast bullet was dropped into the swage, the in-terior of which was cut to form the bullet into the desired shape and dimensions. A ram was inserted behind the bullet, and a quick hammer blow or two "upset" the pro-jectile. Bullet starter, above, guided the bullet into the rifle muzzle with the long axis of the bullet exactly in line with the bore axis.

J. M. Pyne climbed a steep slope with outcropping ledges of granite. He consulted his compass. He must, he guessed, be somewhere near the line of the bullet's flight to the sugar-maple tree. But he could see nothing to the south. He could not see so much as a bit of roof on the old Barnes place.

He turned again north. He went down a little pitch and began to climb the second ridge. The woods were hot, with little clouds of minute insects that got in his eyes.

He paused at the summit to wipe his face with the big blue-and-white bandanna handkerchief. He was, he thought, nearly a mile from the old Barnes place and several hundred feet above it. But he couldn't see it.

He made a circle of a mile or so in diameter, and then a smaller circle, and then a still smaller circle. He came finally to a comparatively open space on a knoll higher than the rest of the ridge. The forest was creeping in. But he saw that the land had once been fenced and cultivated. He found the place where the house had been. The lower part of the big stone chimney was still standing in the middle of a stone-walled cellar with a white birch tree four inches in di-ameter growing beside it. He guessed it must be thirty years since that house had burned down.

He saw, farther on, the old barn. It was much farther away from the house than was common in New England. The wide doors in the mid-dle had come off their hinges and lay on the ground; the mow door above was gone too. But the barn, built of heavy timbers mortised and tenoned together, was little out of square.

J. M. Pyne sat down in the wide doorway and rested. He hadn't had much luck. He hadn't found a place from which a man could have fired that shot. He looked about for a likely tree to climb. He didn't see a likely tree. He stood up. He saw that the ladder to the hayloft, made of heavy rungs let into two posts, was still intact. He laid his rifle down, thought better of it, and carried it in his left hand as he climbed to the loft.

The loft was empty except for an old three-legged bench made of a slab. J. M. Pyne walked to the hay-mow door, looked out and swore softly. He saw a bit of roof in the valley three-quarters of a mile away. He saw a clear space at the foot of the big sugar maple. It must be more than a thousand yards. But he could see clearly the open space in front of the tree where he had been stand-ing late the afternoon before when he had so fortunately stooped to pick up the piece of old iron. He stood now at the place from which that bullet had come.

J. M. Pyne turned and examined the bench. One end was higher than the other. One end was as high as an ordinary table. He explored the shad-ows of the hayloft and found a balk of wood such as would be sawn to split into stove wood. He set the balk of wood on end beside the bench and sat down. He no longer had any doubt.

The Rifle

He walked around the walls of the loft, kicking into a loose bit of old hay here and there. He found nothing. He could just reach the broad top of the plate on which the rafters rested. He walked along the wall, feeling the upper surface of the plate. It was deep in dust and seeds. He felt his way along. He felt a wooden box.

He got the balk of wood and stood on it so he could see. It was a long, heavy box. He raised the lid.

The rifle lay in a compartment of the box made to fit it. It had a full-length telescope sight. J. M. Pyne lit a match and stood staring at the contents of the box. The rifle was as clean and unscarred as the day it was made, and the long octagon barrel was as thick as a man's arm. He saw the false muzzle and the bullet starter and the muzzle brace and patches and caps and bullets and an enormous flask of powder. He picked up the false muzzle and one of the bullets and a patch, and got down from his perch. He stood in the mow door examining the false muzzle and the patch.

He had heard of the cross patch, but he had never seen one before. It was like a Greek cross, cut from tough bank-note paper. The false muzzle was recessed to take the patch. You put the patch on the muzzle, centering it; you centered the bullet on the center of the patch and pushed it part way down with your fingers and adjusted the starter. You hit the starter a hard clip with the heel of your hand and drove it down through the muzzle and pushed it the rest of the way home with a ramrod. The butt of the bullet had to be soft, or you could never have driven it through the false muzzle. The patch was cut so precisely to size that the arms, bending up alongside the bullet, enveloped it without overlapping itself—the edges butted.

J. M. Pyne climbed up on the balk of wood. It took all his strength to lift the rifle out of the case from that position. He guessed the gun weighed well over fifty pounds. He got it down without falling or letting it drop, and laid it on the bench and sat down beside it and looked through the telescope sight. He could see the open space in front of the big sugar maple. The scope was not brilliant. It was too high-powered for so small an objective. But he could quarter the trunk of the maple tree with the cross hairs.

J. M. Pyne carried the rifle out to the haymow door in order to see it in a good light. He knew that it was the work of a fine craftsman. But he could find no maker's name. He stood the rifle up on its butt plate while he thought what he should do. He could disable it easily enough. He could fix it in a few minutes so its owner would never fire it again. But he could not bring himself to ruin so fine a piece. He wanted rather to study it. He wanted to measure the bore, and especially the false muzzle, with soft lead slugs, to find out exactly how the rifling was cut and how much choke it had. He had never made a false muzzle. But he was going to make a false muzzle.

It was harder to get the rifle back in its box than it had been to get it out. But he managed it. He put everything back just as he had found it and picked up his own rifle and climbed down the ladder. He guessed by the sun that it was an hour and a half or so after noon. If the man was coming back to shoot again, he'd wait until late afternoon, until the wind had died down. Even with a bullet that weighed a quarter of a pound, you were at the mercy of the wind at long range.

The Rifleman

J. M. Pyne went down the slope, hunting for a spring or a brook. He found a tiny brook and drank. He sat down on a boulder and ate his sandwiches. Then he went back up the slope and found a place where he could hide, but from which he could keep an eye on the wide doorway of the barn. He sat down to wait. He waited hour after hour. But toward sundown he heard a stick crack. He looked up, as alert as a wild animal. He saw a very tall, gaunt old man striding toward the barn. J. M. Pyne got to his feet, his rifle cradled in his arms.

"Hi," he said.

The old man turned and waited. He had a lean brown face over white chin whiskers. He was dressed more like a townsman than a farmer. He wore a gray suit and a white shirt with a low linen collar and a black tie.

"Who are you?" he asked, with the air of one who had the right to know.

"My name," J. M. Pyne said, "is John Pyne. Am I trespassing?"

"You're on my land," the old man said. "I'm Abel White."

J. M. Pyne stood still and hoped his face gave no sign of his surprise. He did not know what to say. He wasn't going to be driven off. But he hoped he wouldn't have to defy the old man just yet. He wanted to know more than he already knew. He wanted to know why. He saw that Abel White was staring at the rifle he held cradled in his arms. The man was a rifleman. He would want to know about that rifle. He would want to take it in his hands. J. M. Pyne waited.

Abel White broke the silence. "What kind of a gun is that you have?" he asked.

J. M. Pyne opened the breech of his rifle and took out the cartridge and handed the rifle to Abel White.

Side and end views of a false muzzle designed to use cross patches. Ball on top prevented aiming while false muzzle was on gun. Cutter for paper cross-patches, made of hardened steel with sharpened bevel edges.

"Ballard," Abel White said. He held the muzzle up and looked through the barrel. He turned and gave J. M. Pyne a quick, appraising glance. "What caliber is that?"

"Twenty-five caliber," J. M. Pyne said.

"They don't make 25 caliber rifles," Abel White said.

"I make them," J. M. Pyne said.

Abel White gave J. M. Pyne another quick glance. "You made this rifle?"

"I made the barrel," J. M. Pyne said.

Abel White looked through the barrel again. "Eight grooves," he said.

He put the rifle butt down. and J. M. Pyne noticed that, instead of putting the butt directly on the ground, he rested it on his foot, like a careful man who respected rifles.

"The lands are very narrow," Abel White said. "They're little more than knife edges."

"Yes," J. M. Pyne said. "Narrow lands displace less metal and so deform the bullet less."

"You think that is an advantage?"

and a bullet and a patch.

Muzzle-Loaded Bullet

"You talk of deforming the bullet," Abel White said. "The way to deform it least and center it perfectly in the bore is to load it from the muzzle. Nobody ever has, and nobody ever will, get the accuracy from a breech-loaded bullet that can be got from a muzzle-loaded bullet."

He demonstrated deftly the false muzzle, the cross patch and the bullet starter while J. M. Pyne listened. The man seemed to have forgotten everything but the joy of explaining the niceties of fine shooting to a young man who could appreciate them. But he hadn't forgotten everything. He paused in his talk and took a little spyglass out of his pocket and went to the loft door. He trained the spyglass on the old Barnes place.

J. M. Pyne started involuntarily when Abel White turned around. He was no longer the same man. J. M. Pyne had never seen a madman before, but he knew this man was mad. He knew before he spoke again.

yesterday. I almost got him yesterday."

"You missed him?" J. M. Pyne said.

Abel White nodded. "It's two hundred and twenty rods," he said. "I know. I got it by triangulation within six inches. It's easy to miss a man at two hundred and twenty rods. That gun is the best long-range rifle ever made by man. I told Horace Warner that I wanted a rifle that would break them into the same hole at eighty rods, and he made it. But it won't stay on a man's body at two hundred and twenty rods—not quite. And the slightest change of wind is enough to make you miss."

J. M. Pyne nodded. Two hundred and twenty rods was more than twelve hundred yards. A thousand yards was the longest range at which rifle matches were ordinarily shot. The Wimbledon Cup called, originally, for thirty shots at a thousand yards, on a three-foot bulls-eye. No man had ever made the possible score in shooting for the Wimbledon Cup. It took a good rifle to put four bullets out of five in a three-foot bulls-eye at a thousand yards in calm weather. You had no chance to do it in a breeze.

Abel White picked up that fifty or sixty pound rifle and put it back in its box. He put everything back. J. M. Pyne followed him down the ladder. He saw that the man was himself again. His madness was like a nightmare that had passed. J. M. Pyne doubted if he remembered it or how completely he had incriminated himself.

Abel White held out his hand. J. M. Pyne shook his hand.

"Take my advice," Abel White said. "Make muzzle-loaders. Breechloaders are all right for rough-and-ready work like hunting. But you'll never get the finest shooting out of a breech-loaded bullet."

"I'm going to make muzzle-loaders," J. M. Pyne said.

It was after dark when he got home. He sat for an hour after supper trying to find a way out. He was, he felt, perfectly safe as long as he kept away from the space in front of the sugar-maple tree. That space was the only space that Abel White could see. But Abel White had to be stopped.

J. M. Pyne realized suddenly why he had seen no smoke when Abel White shot at him. He had fired from inside the barn loft. The smoke had mostly stayed inside the loft. And by the same token, Abel White had not seen his victim stoop just in time. Abel White had touched the set trigger, and instantly the cloud of smoke from the muzzle of his rifle had obscured his vision. He couldn't see much for a few seconds. It would take the bullet about four seconds to go twelve hundred yards.

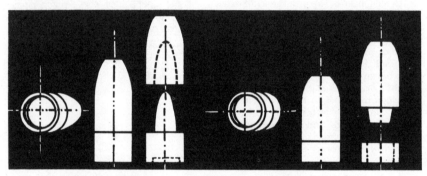

Sketch of typical two-piece bullet. The rear section was of softer lead than the front. The parts were cast separately, then swaged together.

Abel White said.

"It is difficult to control the deformation of a bullet," J. M. Pyne said. "And unless it is deformed the same way every time, you get wide shots. So the less deformation the better."

Abel White stared at J. M. Pyne as if he were a stranger from Mars.

"You know something about rifles," he said.

"Yes," J. M. Pyne said. "I do."

Abel White handed the little rifle back.

J. M. Pyne cradled it in his arms without reloading it.

"Son," Abel White said, "I've got a rifle here that you ought to see. It's one of Horace Warner's double-rest rifles—the biggest one Horace ever made."

He led the way into the barn and up the ladder to the loft. He was so tall he could lift the rifle off the plate without getting up on anything. He laid the rifle on the bench and got out the false muzzle and the starter

"I almost got him yesterday," Abel White said.

J. M. Pyne stood quite still. His rifle wasn't loaded. Abel White was old. But he was powerful. He was eight inches taller and fifty pounds heavier than J. M. Pyne, and he was crazy.

"You almost got him?" J. M. Pyne said softly.

"Young Barnes," Abel White said.

"Why do you want to get young Barnes?" J. M. Pyne said.

"He murdered my son," Abel White said fiercely. "He shot him down in cold blood, and the coroner's jury said it was an accident. Everybody knew he murdered young Abel. But I knew he'd come back, like any other man with the blood guilt on his hands. He came back last summer, and I was waiting here. I put a bullet within a foot of his head. I waited for him every afternoon for two weeks after that. But I must have scared him off. I had to go home to York state. But he's back now. I saw him

Pyne's Preparations

J. M. Pyne got a lantern and went out to the shop to see what he could find. He found some wire. He nailed one end of the wire to the house and stretched it as tightly as he could over a branch of the maple tree. The lowest branch was high, but he tied a piece of iron to a string and threw it over the branch and pulled the wire after it.

He went back to the shop then and made a pulley with a kind of trigger release. He had only odd pieces of metal to work with. He had to bend them cold. But by midnight he had something that worked.

He walked to Gaylord's Corner the next morning and got two balls of twine. He led four lengths of twine from the house to screw eyes in the maple tree and back again. Then he went to work to construct a frame of lath, with joints like a man's knees and elbows. He dressed his framework neatly in an old suit of clothes and tacked a hat on top with the brim turned down to conceal the lack of a face. He had it all done early in the afternoon. He had to wait several hours to try it.

At sundown he hung the scarecrow on the wire and attached his lines. He had one line to each knee and one to the neck and one to the trigger release of the block. He ran the scarecrow out on the wire and tried out his lines. He had, in effect, a puppet. He could make it look very much like a man walking. It would pass for a man at twelve hundred yards, even through a telescopic sight.

The Last Shot

He pulled his creation out into the space in front of the big sugar maple. He let it stand there, within a yard or so of where he had stood two days before when Abel White had shot at him. He waited, his heart pounding. And then he heard the shot. He heard the great rifle roar high up on the hill three-quarters of a mile away and the vicious thunk of the great bullet against the maple tree.

J. M. Pyne made the puppet thrash madly and fall over and lie still in the long grass.

He waited five minutes and made himself wait five minutes more.

Then he gently drew in the puppet. Abel White hadn't missed. The bullet had gone through the middle of the puppet's body.

J. M. Pyne got out his little rifle and loaded it and started for the barn on the knoll. It was only three-quarters of a mile as a bullet flies, but it was a long way around the marsh. It took him twenty minutes. But he made it. Abel White had finished cleaning his rifle and was oiling the bore. He was humming softly to himself as he worked. He looked up at J. M. Pyne.

"I got him," Abel White said. "Three wasn't enough wind to make a ripple in the marsh grass. I held dead on and I got him."

J. M. Pyne helped get the rifle and the case and the tools down from the loft. They put the rifle and all the things that went with it in the case. Abel White stood gazing down at the rifle. It was easy to see he loved it.

"Mr. Pyne," Abel White said, "the rifle has done its work. I shall never shoot it again." He was smiling happily. He looked benignly on J. M. Pyne. "Would you accept it as a gift?"

J. M. Pyne stood there, staring at Abel White.

"I'd like to have it," J. M. Pyne said. "I'd like to see what it would do, and then I'd like to find out why."

"Then," Abel White said, "it's yours. You're the only man I know who'll appreciate it and take care of it."

He shook hands with J. M. Pyne.

"You had better get a horse and wagon," Abel White said. "That gun is heavy."

J. M. Pyne nodded. But he didn't hire a wagon. It cost money to hire horses and a wagon. And the only man he knew in Gaylord's Corner who had horses and a wagon for hire was a garrulous old fellow who talked of ghosts. J. M. Pyne did not believe in ghosts. He got a wheelbarrow. He got that great rifle home by himself. •

Abel White gazed down at the rifle and accessories in their case. "The rifle has done its work," he said. "I shall never shoot it again."

A History of

The GUN DIGEST *is pleased to announce that a new "History of Proof Marks" begins in this, our 22nd edition. The author, Mr. Lee Kennett, is well-qualified to have conducted the new and exhaustive research he engaged in, and we are sure you will find this detailed and comprehensive work instructive, reliable and, not least, interesting and valuable.*

While Mr. Kennett used the framework of the late Baron Engelhardt's "The Story of European Proof Marks" as a structural guide, he has personally visited and talked with Proof House officials in several countries thus far. He will continue to do so until all nations in the survey have been covered. When that time arrives, sometime in 1968, we will publish the complete book.

With this issue we present "Proof Marks in Czechoslovakia." If space permits, we will also present the historical background of proof marks, but that introductory matter will be, of course, an assured part of the finished book.

When the Austro-Hungarian empire collapsed in 1918, Czechoslovakia emerged as one of the successor states. The new republic inherited much of the industry of the old empire, including the arms centers of Vejprty (formerly Weipert) and Brno. It also fell heir to the imperial proof houses at Prague and Vejprty. Both houses continued to operate, using the Austrian proof law of 1891 (for details of this law see under Austria). The old proof marks were also retained, with the exception of the marks for the third, obligatory black powder proof of arms of all categories. New marks, representing the Lion of Bohemia with the numerals "1" and "2" (marks nos. 7 and 8), replaced the marks bearing the Hapsburg double eagle (marks nos. 5 and 6). Since several sources give the old marks as current after 1918, it is probable that the changeover was not completed until sometime in the 1920s.

It was not until 1931 that Czechoslovakia passed a new proof law (Law of 17 December 1931, Supplementary Regulations dated 22 December 1931).

The new law, which took effect on 1 January 1932, reiterated the principle of obligatory proof. Another important provision made smokeless proof compulsory for all arms for which smokeless loads were commercially available. Arms using jacketed bullets had to be proved with them. No factory or other commercial marks could resemble proof marks. The proof rules were as follows:

Shotguns: Barrels in the rough could be submitted to a first, optional black powder proof at a pressure of 15,700 psi. Those which passed were stamped with mark no. 11. Finished, joined barrels of multi-barreled shotguns underwent a second, obligatory black powder proof at 11,400 psi, designated by mark no. 12. The third, compulsory black powder proof was administered to finished guns at 8,800 psi (mark no. 13). The fourth, smokeless proof, compulsory for shotguns, was done with smokeless powder at a pressure of 14,200 psi in guns with 65mm chambers (mark no. 14). Higher pressures were to be used in guns with longer chambers. Automatic shotguns were tested

Proof Marks

Gun Proof in Czechoslovakia

by Lee Kennett

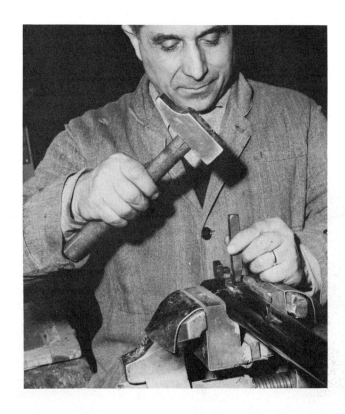

A workman stamps a proof mark on a double gun.

with a proof charge followed by a commercial one.

Rifles: These arms were proved in finished state, usually with smokeless powder. Three smokeless charges were fired; the first two gave 30% excess pressure over the commercial load, the third was a commercial round. Black powder proof required two shots, the first being a proof charge of 30% excess pressure and the second a commercial round. Mark no. 15 was used for smokeless proof; mark no. 13 for black powder.

Handguns: These were also proved in finished state. Automatic pistols were always proved with smokeless powder; the first two charges gave 50% excess pressure and the third was a commercial round (mark no. 15). Smokeless proof of revolvers was done with a proof cartridge generating 50% excess pressure (mark no. 15). Black powder proof was done by filling the case completely with powder and loading it in behind the standard bullet so as to produce at least 30% excess pressure (mark no. 13). In both types of proof a proof round was fired from each chamber.

Small caliber rimfire rifles and shotguns of 9mm or under: These were proved in finished state with black powder loadings similar to those used with revolvers, the proof being designated by mark no. 13. For repeating arms of this category a commercial round was fired following the proof charge.

Though Czechoslovakia did not sign the Brussels Convention, the 1931 law approximated its requirements and Czechoslovakia did sign bilateral agreements on proof marks with Austria and Belgium. Since the new marks were the same for Prague and Vejprty, the latter house used a star as a supplementary mark to indicate proof there (mark no. 16).

In March, 1939, Czechoslovakia was occupied by German troops. Marks nos. 7 and 8 were accordingly changed to meet the new political situation. The substitute marks consisted of the letter "P," signifying *Protektorat*, and the numerals "1" and "2" (marks nos. 17 and 18). Although Baron Engelhardt found evidence that the German proof law of 1939 was applied in Prague after 1940, the

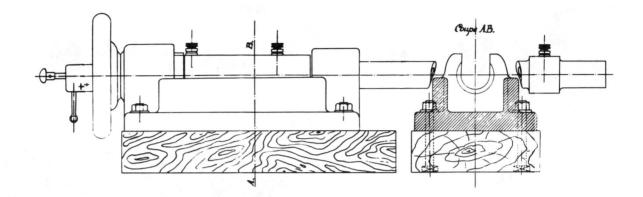

present Czech proof authorities say their regulations of 1931 remained in force. The question is of little practical importance, since few commercial arms would have been produced during the war.

At the end of the war the Vejprty house was closed and proof procedures concentrated at Prague. The law of 1931 remained in force, being modified by a decree of 1955. This decree extended compulsory proof to rivet- and nail-driving guns, compressed air and CO_2 guns, and ammunition for civilian use. Proof of nail- and rivet-driving guns utilized the procedures and proof marks stipulated for rifles. A new mark, no. 19, was introduced to designate proof of air and CO_2 guns.

The 1931 legislation was replaced by the law of 31 May 1962, which is currently in force. The 1962 law simplifies proof procedures considerably. Mark no. 13 is retained for the sole provisional proof of shotgun barrels in the rough. Mark no. 14 is now used for definitive smokeless proof of shotguns and Flobert type arms. Mark no. 15 designates definitive smokeless proof for rifles and handguns. Mark no. 19 is retained for air and CO_2 guns. Mark no. 20 has been introduced for rivet- and nail-driving devices, and mark no. 21 is used to signify proof of ammunition. The proof authorities have their headquarters in Prague, but apparently operate branch installations at Brno and elsewhere. According to the proofmaster, Czechoslovakia now conforms in all respects to the rules of the Brussels convention, though she still is not a signatory. Bilateral agreements have been signed with England and other countries.

Etalon international (pressure gun) adopted by the Brussels Convention, shown in both drawing and photograph. Three crushers are used.

The most recent work on firearms in Czechoslovakia is that of Jaroslav Lugs, available in German translation: *Handfeuerwaffen* (Small Arms), Berlin, 1964, 2 vols.; this work is an excellent treatment of the whole history of firearms in Europe. For relevant legal texts and details of proof in present day Czechoslovakia, the author is indebted to Engineer Edvard Parrizek, Director of the SZU Testing Institute at Brno.

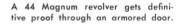

A 44 Magnum revolver gets definitive proof through an armored door.

Czechoslovakian Proof Marks

In this table the mark numbers at left are those assigned by the author, and keyed by him to the text for reference. The 2nd column shows the true form of the proof mark and gives the period of its use. The last column tells of the marks' significance.

No.	Mark / Period	Significance
1	1918-1931	Provisional black powder proof of unfinished barrels at Prague.
2	1918-1931	Same as no. 1, at Vejprty.
3	1918-1931	Black powder proof of joined barrels of multi-barreled shotguns at Prague.
4	1918-1931	Same as no. 3, at Vejprty.
5	1918-?	Definitive black powder proof of arms at Prague.
6	1918-?	Same as no. 5, at Vejprty.
7	1918?-1931	Same as no. 5, which it replaced.
8	1918-1931	Same as no. 6, which it replaced.
9	1918-1931	Optional smokeless powder proof at Prague.
10	1918-1931	Same as no. 9, at Vejprty.
11	1931-1939, 1945-1962	Provisional black powder proof of unfinished barrels. Both houses.
12	1931-1939, 1945-1962	Black powder proof of joined barrels of multi-barreled shotguns. Both houses.
13	1931-	Definitive black powder proof of finished guns. Since 1962, sole provisional proof of unfinished shotgun barrels. Prague; Vejprty house closed 1945-46. See text.
14	1931-	Smokeless proof of shotguns.
15	1931-	Smokeless proof of rifles, revolvers, and automatic pistols.
16	1931-1945	Supplementary mark indicating proof at Vejprty.
17	1939-1945	Replaced no. 11 during German occupation.
18	1939-1945	Replaced no. 12 during German occupation.
19	1955-	Proof of compressed-air and CO_2 guns.
20	1962-	Proof of rivet- and nail-firing devices.
21	1962-	Proof of ammunition and components.

A History of

This new, fully up-to-date "History of Proof Marks" began in our 22nd edition with "Proof Marks in Czechoslovakia." The author, Mr. Lee Kennett, is eminently qualified to have engaged in the fresh and exhaustive research required, and we feel sure this comprehensive and detailed work will be found reliable, instructive, interesting and valuable.

While Mr. Kennett used the framework of the late Baron Engelhardt's "The Story of European Proof Marks" as a structural guide, he personally visited and talked with Proof House officials in several countries thus far. He will continue to do so until all nations in the survey have been covered. When that time arrives, we will publish the complete book.

With this issue we present "Proof in Austria-Hungary—1882-1918," and "Proof in Austria After 1918." Space in this issue does not permit our printing of the author's introductory material, but that will be contained in the finished book.

THE FORMATIVE YEARS
1882 - 1918

ARMS PRODUCTION developed quite early in the domains of the Hapsburg rulers. By the 17th century there were thriving arms centers in Ferlach, Prague, Vienna and Weipert (today Vejprty). Proof was also a widespread custom. Civilian arms were proved by makers or under municipal authority. By the 18th century there was a government proof house for military arms at Prague, and a second one was added at Weipert at the end of the same century.[1]

The first step toward compulsory government supervised proof on a large scale was not taken until 1882. On 12 August of that year the Imperial Minister for Religions and Public Instruction issued a decree authorizing the establishment of public proof houses in the various provinces. The only province to make use of this authorization was Carinthia, which contained the important arms center of Ferlach. The provincial government issued regulations for the Ferlach proof house on 25 November, 1882. In the interest of "avoiding accidents" and "increasing public confidence," the government explained, all imported and domestic arms would be submitted to the proof house, which was attached to the state-run school for gunsmiths.[2]

The regulations called for three separate proofs. The first, provisional proof of unjoined barrels, involved the following steps: visual inspection, verification of caliber, stamping of caliber and proof house control number and, finally, firing proof. The proof charge—equal to two-thirds the weight of the ball—was followed by a thick cardboard wad, a ball of requisite caliber, and a second wad identical to the first. Barrels which passed this proof were stamped with the cipher "EF" (mark no. 1 in Table I). Barrels for double barrel guns were subjected to a second proof after they had been joined. The powder charge for the second proof was equal to two-thirds of the powder charge of the first proof, the

same balls and wadding being used as before. Barrels passing this proof received a mark composed of the Hapsburg double-headed eagle and the letter "F" (mark no. 2). Finished arms were submitted to a third or definitive proof. The proof master was empowered to omit a firing proof and make a simple visual inspection if he deemed firing unnecessary. The powder charge for this third proof was equal to one-half the powder charge of second proof. Shot was substituted for the balls used in first and second proof. The proof master in his inspection was to check particularly for the visibility of earlier marks, reduction in barrel wall strength subsequent to provisional proof, and the tightness and strength of the breech. If there was any doubt about the safety of the arm, firing proof was prescribed. After passing this inspection — and firing proof if warranted — the arms received the stamp of definitive proof, the coat of arms of Carinthia (mark no. 3).

The Ferlach rules provided no special procedures for rifles. Pistols and revolvers underwent both provisional and definitive proof, the latter being simply an inspection at the proof master's discretion. Barrels of double barrel pistols underwent second proof after joining. Powder charges for handguns were one-half those of long arms of the same caliber. Thus every single barreled arm underwent one obligatory and one discretionary proof, and bore marks of first and third proof. Every double barreled arm underwent two obligatory proofs and a third discretionary one, and bore all three marks.

The regulations required only a simple inspection of imported barrels and finished arms if these already bore proof marks recognized by Ferlach (these are not specified). Otherwise they underwent normal proof procedures.

The powder charges for proof at Ferlach were as shown in Table I.

The 1882 rules show considerable influence by the proof practices at Liège; they also embody many features that were later to appear in the

Proof Marks

Gun Proof in Austria-Hungary and Austria After 1918

by Lee Kennett

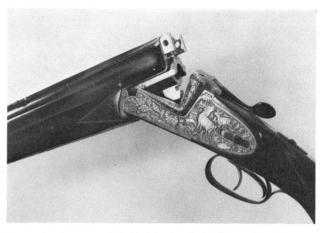

Over-under shotgun made in Ferlach, Austria, by Johann Fanzoj.

regulations of 1891. The rules themselves, however, apparently had little immediate effect. First of all, they applied only to the province of Carinthia, not to the whole Empire. Secondly, though the text indicates a definite obligation to submit to proof, there were no provisions for enforcement. It is doubtful whether compliance was complete. Writers of the era, if they knew about the Ferlach proof at all, regarded it as optional. Friedrich Brandeis, editor of *Der Waffenschmied*, wrote in 1887 that he had tried without success for two years to learn the details of proof in Ferlach.[3]

As early as 1884, the Austrian government had begun preparation of the draft of a new and more general proof law. After two years of work, the drafters sent the proposal to the Austrian parliament. There was an immediate outcry by arms experts and enthusiasts. Although the government had sent an observer to Liège to study proof procedures there, the Austrian draft seemed an unsatisfactory imitation. Most of the criticism was directed at the failure to include a compulsory

TABLE I

Gauge	Bore diameter (in mm.)	Powder charges in grams		
		1st proof	2nd proof	3rd proof
8	19.8	20.6	13.7	6.8
10	19.4	20.2	13.4	6.7
12	18.8	19.6	13.0	6.5
14	18.2	18.9	12.6	6.3
16	17.6	18.0	12.0	6.0
18	17.2	17.8	11.8	5.9
20	16.6	17.2	11.4	5.7
22	16.2	16.8	11.2	5.6
24	15.8	16.4	10.9	5.4
26	15.4	16.0	10.6	5.3
28	14.8	15.4	10.2	5.1
30	14.4	15.0	10.0	5.0
32	14.0	14.5	9.6	4.8
34	13.6	14.1	9.4	4.7
36	13.2	13.8	9.2	4.6
38	12.6	13.1	8.7	4.3
40	12.2	12.6	8.4	4.2
42	11.8	12.2	8.1	4.0
44	11.4	11.8	7.8	3.9
46	11.0	11.4	7.6	3.8
48	10.6	11.0	7.3	3.6
50	10.2	10.6	7.0	3.5

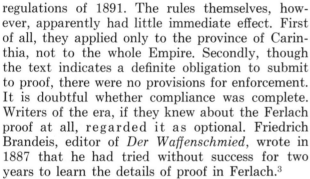

definitive firing proof.[4] While the draft was favorably received by the Austrian parliament, it was not promulgated. Several years of discussion and delay followed. Finally a new law was promulgated on 23 June, 1891, and went into effect 6 months later. The implementing regulations appeared on 9 November, 1891. The new law bore very close resemblance to the original draft.[5]

The law established proof houses at Ferlach, Weipert, Prague, and Vienna. All domestic and foreign arms were to be submitted to proof, except those bearing recognized proof marks — those of the old Ferlach house, Liège, and St.-Etienne were recognized in the law itself. Like the 1882 rules, the new system provided for a first provisional proof for unjoined barrels, a second proof for joined ones, and a definitive proof or inspection, this latter once again left to the proof master's discretion. Powder for all proofs was a fine-grained black powder known as Hunting and Target Powder No. 1, manufactured by the Austrian state powder works at Stein. First and second proof charges were composed of powder, a cardboard wad, a ball to caliber (0.5-mm "windage" or clearance was permitted), and a second cardboard wad. After these proofs barrels were closely inspected. Those showing defects underwent a "ten atmosphere test" with a special pump to reveal cracks. Barrels judged dangerous were sawn in two; those capable of repair were returned to the makers for reworking. Barrels passing first proof received marks 4 to 7. Second proof was designated by marks 9 to 12. The third proof, if warranted, was done with a considerably lighter powder charge than the previous proofs. Third proof or inspection was indicated by marks 14 to 17. However, rifles were loaded with *two* balls, while shotguns had their normal shot charge increased by one-half the weight of a lead ball of their gauge. Pistols and revolver barrels did not undergo provisional proof. Handguns were submitted as finished arms, as were Flobert-type guns. If the proof master ordered proof, the commercial cartridges were used (if such cartridges were not available to the proof house, the customer was obliged to supply them).

For table of powder charges see Table II.[6]

TABLE II

Gauge	Bore diameter (in mm.)	Powder charge in grams			
		1st proof	2nd proof	3rd proof	
8	19.8	21	12	8*	10†
10	19.4	20	11	7	10
12	18.8	20	10	6	10
14	18.2	19	10	5	10
16	17.6	18	10	5	10
18	17.2	18	9	5	9
20	16.6	17	9	4.5	9
22	16.2	17	9	4.5	9
24	15.8	16	9	4.5	9
26	15.4	16	8	4.5	9
28	14.8	15	8	4	9
30	14.4	15	8	4	9
32	14.0	14	8	4	8
34	13.6	14	7	4	8
36	13.2	14	7	4	8
38	12.6	13	7	4	8
40	12.2	13	7	3	8
42	11.8	12	6	3	8
44	11.4	12	6	3	7
46	11.0	11	6	3	7
48	10.6	11	6	3	7
50	10.2	11	6	3	7
various	10.7	10	5	3	7

* Shotguns   † Rifles

Proof charges under the 1891 rules seem to have varied from time to time. Thus the powder charge for definitive proof of a 16-gauge shotgun was given initially (before the law went into effect) as 8 grams. On the table above it is given as 5 grams. In 1911 it was 6.4 grams. This variation probably results from changes in powder composition and the attempt by proof authorities to adjust proof loads to develop specified excess pressures, although this is not mentioned in the initial legislation. First proof was to develop twice the pressure of commercial loads, second proof, 66 2/3% excess pressure, and definitive proof 33 1/3%.

Some other details of the 1891 law were as follows: Each barrel had its bore diameter measured and stamped in millimeters and tenths. In addition, on arrival each barrel or set of barrels was stamped with a proof house control number. Barrels were to be proved in the order of their numbers, apparently so that no single manufacturer would be favored over others by having his barrels proved more quickly. Choke bored barrels were stamped *nicht für Kugel* (not for ball).

Special provisions were made to facilitate the introduction of the new law. Unproved guns in private hands were exempt from proof in most cases. Unproved guns still in the hands of arms merchants and manufacturers had to be submitted to the proof house within one year of the coming into effect of the law. In most cases, however, the proof master would simply inspect them rather than submit them to proof. Such arms were to receive a special mark (no. 19). One valuable feature was the requirement that arms undergoing significant alteration be submitted to proof. This applied notably to shotguns

whose chambers had been lengthened or whose bore diameter had been enlarged. By the same token rifles had to be submitted if the barrel was reworked so as to reduce wall thickness at any point to less than three-fifths of the bore diameter.

Curiously enough, the above law applied only to half of the Empire. The Austro-Hungarian monarchy was, in fact, two countries in one. The ruler wore two crowns, there were two separate legislatures, and two separate governments. Proof in the Hungarian half of the Empire was established by a separate Hungarian law of 17 November, 1891, to go into effect on 18 May, 1892.[7]

As might be expected, the Hungarian law resembles the Austrian one, but is not identical. The Hungarian act is also one of the most vague and confused to be found anywhere. It used the same table of charges as prescribed in the Austrian text, but used them for different purposes. The black powder used was also different, being in this case "Extra Fine Shooting Powder No. 8, type St. P." Moreover, the shot charges were different in definitive proof. In 1911 the shot charge for Hungarian definitive proof of 12 gauge shotguns was 53.1 grams, as against 46.4 grams for the Austrian proof.

One interesting variation from the Austrian law was the stipulation that finished single barrel guns whose barrels had undergone first provisional proof were exempted from definitive proof or inspection. Unjoined barrels underwent proof according to the charges in the Austrian table for first proof, and received mark no. 8. However, both joined barrels *and finished doubles* were tested with the loads for the second provisional proof (marks nos. 13 and 18). No mention is made of the option of simple inspection here. The charges for definitive proof in the Austrian system were reserved in Hungary for (a) finished arms whose barrels had been proved abroad and (b) finished unproved arms in possession of manufacturers and merchants when the law came into effect (stamped with mark no. 20). This proof was optional with the proof master, who could substitute simple inspection.

From all of this it would seem that single barreled guns underwent only first provisional proof, and that double barreled guns of domestic manufacture underwent the same (second) proof twice, once as joined barrels and again when finished. If this is indeed the case, then Hungary, in contrast to Austria, did have a compulsory definitive firing proof for doubles, and with heavier charges than those of the optional Austrian definitive proof. Unfortunately the poor wording of the law defies more definite interpretation. (Speaking of proof of barrels, the law says they may be submitted before attaching of the "wood", when obviously the text should read "breeches.")

Both halves of the Empire adopted an optional smokeless powder proof in 1899 (the Austrian regulation was dated 23 August, 1899). This proof was supposed to develop 50% excess pressure over commercial black powder loads (marks nos. 23 to

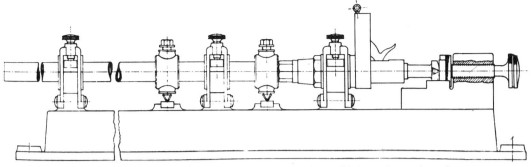

Austrian von Schatzl pressure gun, employing the wedge-shaped blades and zinc plates devised by Rodman. This device utilized four crushers to obtain a reading on the pressure curve.

27). Both halves of the Empire used identical charges and the same powder, "Smokeless Hunting and Shooting Powder No. 1." The proof charge for 12-gauge guns was 3.70 grams of powder and 47.9 grams of shot. For 16 gauge, they were 3.2 and 39 grams respectively. How effective was the proof? The Director of the Military Proof House at Klagenfurt, Herr von Schatzl, calculated the pressure of the 12-bore smokeless proof at 12,800 psi. This figure was obtained, however, on the von Schatzel pressure gun of the Rodmen type. In tests conducted at Liège in 1911, the other gauges then in use gave the pressure as only about 7,000 psi. In light of these figures, one can question the validity of the Austro-Hungarian smokeless proof. There is also room to question the same proof for rifles, also introduced in 1899. Rifles using jacketed bullets were to be proved with the maximum powder charge the case could hold, employing the same powder and projectiles in use commercially. For black powder arms, whose cartridges were commercially loaded with the largest charge possible. This was, of course, no proof at all.

It might be said in conclusion that the Austro-Hungarian legislation of 1891 was in many ways an admirable one, fixing proof charges in terms of excess pressure. Unfortunately, the use of the von Schatzl pressure gun to determine these was less praiseworthy, for the apparatus does not seem to have given very accurate readings. This was the cause for considerable acrimonious debate at the Brussels meeting in 1911, and probably played a role in the adoption of an international pressure gun using crushers.

References

1 Jaroslav Lugs, *Handfeuerwaffen* (Small Arms), Berlin, 1962, II, 147, 202.

2 The text of the 1882 regulations is to be found in Alphonse Polain, *Recherches historiques sur l'épreuve des armes à feu au pays de Liège*, pp. 330-338.

3 Friedrich Brandeis, "Überblick über die Bedeutung des gesetzlichen Beschuss der Handfeuerwaffen", *Der Waffenschmied,* Vol. VII (1887), no. 22, p. 157.

4 These criticisms are found especially in the article by Friedrich Brandeis, cited above. The original draft is to be found in *Der Waffenschmied,* Vol. IV (1884), no. 2, p. 16.

5 The text of the law is to be found in Jules Polain, *Des bancs d'épreuve,* pp. 7-26.

6 These charges are as taken from Polain, *Des bancs d'épreuves,* p. 25, except for the charges for rifles, which are not listed by Polain. These are given, therefore, as found in Georg Koch, *Gesetz betreffend der Prüfung der Läufe und Verschlüsse der Handfeuerwaffen vom 19 mai 1891,* Berlin, 1892, p. 56. As its title implies, this is a study of the German legislation of 1891, but contains valuable information about other proof systems.

7 The texts for the law and implementing regulations are to be found in Jules Polain, *Des bancs d'épreuve,* fascicule 2, pp. 19-29.

Bibliography

In addition to the rather general works already cited in the references, there are two articles dealing specifically with proof in Austria-Hungary which contain considerable information on this subject; neither is signed. They are: "Die Probe der Gewehr- und Pistolenläufe in Osterreich," in *Der Waffenschmied,* Vol. IV (1884), pp. 13-17; "Uber den Beschuss der Handfeuerwaffen in Osterreich," in *Schuss und Waffe,* Vol. IV (1910-1911), pp. 234-236, 250-252.

PROOF IN AUSTRIA AFTER 1918

AFTER ITS EMERGENCE in 1918, the truncated state of Austria retained the old Austrian legislation of 1891 (marks 1-8) as the basis for its proof system (see under Austria-Hungary). It was not until 1929 that a new law, designed to meet new standards, was enacted to replace the older system. The new rules were published on 14 August, 1929, and went into effect one week later. The 1929 legislation is at once an attempt to fulfill the requirements of the Brussels Convention, of which Austria had become a signatory, and to retain certain features of the 1891 system that had become a tradition for Austrian gunmakers and for the two surviving proof houses at Ferlach and Vienna.

For long-barreled guns, two separate proofs were retained. Unjoined barrels underwent first provisional proof, designated now by marks 1 and 2. Proof charges for provisional proof were established on the basis of pressure, but are still retained as elaborate tables. (See Tables A and B below). Second provisional proof was reserved for joined barrels of multi-barreled guns (marks 3-4). The black powder used for these proofs was Extra Fine Hunting and Target Powder No. 1. For unchoked smoothbores and rifles, the projectile was a round-nosed cylinder of lead. Choke bores were proved with shot (Austrian no. 12, approximately U.S. no. 7). Wads for smoothbores were cardboard, 12mm

Austro-Hungarian Proof Marks
1882-1918

In this table the mark numbers at left are those assigned by the author, and keyed by him to the text for reference. The 2nd column shows the true form of the proof mark and gives the period of its use. The last column tells of the marks' significance.

Ferlach Proof House, 1882-1891

1	1882-1891	First provisional proof of unjoined barrels.
2	1882-1891	Second provisional proof of joined barrels.
3	1882-1891	Definitive proof or simple inspection of finished arms.

Austro-Hungarian Proof, 1891-1918

4	1891-1918	Provisional proof of unjoined barrels at Ferlach.
5	1891-1918	Same proof, at Prague.
6	1891-1918	Same proof, at Weipert.
7	1891-1918	Same proof, at Vienna.
8	1892-1918	Same proof, at Budapest.
9	1891-1918	Provisional proof of joined barrels at Ferlach.
10	1891-1918	Same proof, at Prague.
11	1891-1918	Same proof, at Weipert.
12	1891-1918	Same proof, at Vienna.
13	1892-1918	Same proof, at Budapest.
14	1891-1918	Definitive proof or inspection of finished arms at Ferlach.
15	1891-1918	Same proof, at Prague.
16	1891-1918	Same proof, at Weipert.
17	1891-1918	Same proof, at Vienna.
18	1892-1918	Same proof, at Budapest.
19	1891-1918	Proof or inspection of unproved finished arms in stocks of manufacturers and dealers as of 1891, at all four Austrian proof houses.
20	1892-1918	Same as 19, at Budapest.
21	1891-1918	Meaning "not for ball," stamped on choke-bored barrels in Austrian proof houses.
22	1892-1918	Same as 21, at Budapest.
23	1899-1918	Optional smokeless powder proof, at Ferlach.

24	 1899-1918	Same proof, at Prague.	26	1899-1918 Same proof, at Vienna.
25	1899-1918	Same proof, at Weipert.	27	1899-1918 Same proof, at Budapest.

Austrian Proof Marks 1918-1967

1	1918-1940 1945-	Provisional black powder proof of unjoined barrels at Ferlach. After 1951 at 11,400 psi.
2	1918-1940 1945-	Same proof, at Vienna.
3	1918-1945	Second provisional black powder proof of joined barrels at Ferlach. From 1940 to 1945, Ferlach house mark.
4	1918-1945	Same proof, at Vienna.
5	1918-1940	Definitive black powder proof at Ferlach. After 1929 at 8,800 psi for shotguns.
6	1918-1929	Same proof, at Vienna.
7	1918-	Definitive smokeless proof at Ferlach. After 1929 at 12,800-14,200 psi for shotguns.
8	1918-	Same proof, at Vienna.
9	1929-1940	Replaced mark no. 6.
10	1929-	Optional superior definitive smokeless proof at Ferlach or Vienna. After 1962 at 17,000 psi for shotguns.
11	1929-1951?	Definitive proof of foreign guns if without recognized marks.

12	1945-	Replaced mark no. 5. Still used for black powder definitive proof at Ferlach.
13	1945-	Replaced mark no. 9. As for mark 12, but at Vienna.

NOTE: Those periods not showing a closing year indicate continuing use of the mark indicated, up to the time of publication of this book.

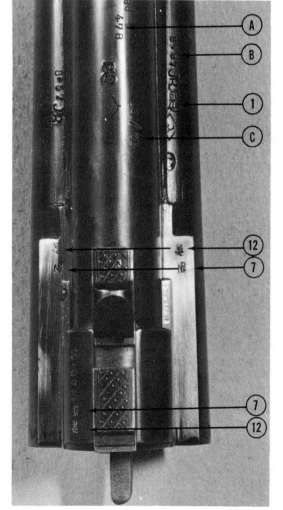

This Austrian-made 3-barrel (drilling) was proofed after 1945. (A) may indicate gun's serial number. (B) is caliber stamp—8.57JR, and (C) shows gauge (28) and chamber length of 70mm. Refer to text for explanation of numbers shown.

thick. For rifles wads equal to bore diameter were prescribed.

Laws of 1929

The 1929 law put an end to the old concept of optional definitive proof. All long arms underwent obligatory black powder definitive proof. For shotguns, the proof charges (Table C) were set to develop pressures of 8,800 psi; for rifles 30% excess pressure was prescribed. This proof was designated by marks 5 through 9. The mark for Vienna was changed slightly, so as to bear the number "2," rather than the old number "4." Since Vienna had in fact become the second proof house in the country, the change seems logical. But Prague, which had been number "2" in the old system of 1891, continued to use this mark after Czech independence. So this mark may, in the period of the late 1920s, indicate Czech or Austrian proof.

Long arms destined for smokeless powder cartridges underwent a second definitive proof, this one with smokeless powder. Proof loads for shotguns of 16 gauge and larger developed 12,800 psi. Those for smaller gauges were to yield pressures of 14,200 psi. Rifles were proved with charges giving 30% excess pressure over commercial smokeless loads (marks 7-8).

Pistols, revolvers, and Flobert-type guns under-

went definitive proof only. Flobert or parlor type arms were proved by filling the longest cartridge the arms would chamber with a full charge of fine black powder and the customary projectile. Other pistols and revolvers received black powder proof and, if called for, smokeless as well. The loads in both cases were 30% excess pressure loads. Revolvers were proved by firing one shot in each chamber. Automatic pistols were proved by firing a series of three shots, to test the working of the action as well as its strength.

Still a third definitive proof was established. This was an optional superior smokeless proof, using heavier loads than ordinary smokeless proof. The mark assigned for this proof was no. 10.

One additional mark was introduced to indicate arms of foreign origin that had undergone definitive proof in Austria. This was mark no. 11. If the barrels of such arms did not bear recognized foreign provisional proof marks, they underwent second provisional proof before definitive proof.

Shotguns received several supplementary marks; these included the bore diameter at muzzle and the word "CHOKE" to replace the old "NOT FOR BALL" stamping. Shotguns whose chambers were longer than 65mm had the length designated, thus 12/70 — a 12-bore gun with 70mm chambers. Shotguns proved for smokeless powder had their barrel weight(s) stamped thereon.

The proof tables under the 1929 rules are as follows:

Table A — Provisional Proof of Shot Barrels

Gauge	Diameter (in mm.)	1st Proof Powder/Shot (grams)	2nd Proof Powder/Shot (grams)
4	20.6-23.2	32.0/192	26.7/160
8	19.0-20.5	20.0/120	16.7/100
10	17.8-18.9	14.0/84	11.7/70
12	17.1-17.7	11.6/70	9.7/58
14	16.5-17.0	10.6/64	8.8/53
16	15.9-16.4	9.6/58	8.0/48
18	15.4-15.8	9.0/54	7.5/45
20	14.5-15.3	8.2/49	6.8/41
24	13.7-14.4	7.2/43	6.0/36
28	13.2-13.6	6.4/38	5.3/32
32	12.8-13.1	6.0/36	5.0/30
36	12.4-12.7	5.6/34	4.7/28
40	12.0-12.3	5.2/31	4.3/26
44	11.5-11.9	4.8/29	4.0/24
50	11.0-11.4	4.4/26	3.7/22

Table B — Provisional Proof for Rifled Barrels

Caliber (in mm.)	Bore Dia. (in mm.)	1st Proof Powder/Shot (grams)	2nd Proof Powder/Shot (grams)
12.4-13.4	11.7-12.8	9.4/42.0	7.1/42.0
11.2-12.2	10.5-11.6	9.0/37.5	6.8/37.5
10.0-11.0	9.3-10.4	8.2/31.5	6.2/31.5
8.8- 9.8	8.1- 9.2	7.0/27.0	5.3/27.0
7.6- 8.6	7.0- 8.0	5.2/21.0	3.9/21.0
6.4- 7.4	5.9- 6.9	3.4/16.5	2.6/16.5

Table C — Definitive Proof for Shot Barrels

Gauge	Case Dia. (mm. inside)	Case Lgth. (in mm.)	Final Proof Powder/Shot (grams)	Service Load Powder/Shot (grams)
4	24.0	101.5	21.3/128.0	16.0/96.0
8	21.2	82.5	12.3/ 80.0	10.0/60.0
10	19.6	70.0	9.3/ 56.0	7.0/42.0
12	18.4	65.0	7.7/ 46.4	5.8/34.8
14	17.6	65.0	7.1/ 42.4	5.3/31.8
16	16.8	65.0	6.4/ 38.4	4.8/28.8
18	16.2	65.0	6.0/ 36.0	4.5/27.0
20	15.6	65.0	5.5/ 32.8	4.1/24.6
24	14.6	65.0	4.8/ 28.8	3.6/21.6
28	13.8	63.5	4.3/ 25.6	3.2/19.2
32	13.2	63.5	4.0/ 24.0	3.0/18.0
36	12.8	63.5	3.7/ 22.4	2.8/16.8
40	12.4	63.5	3.5/ 20.8	2.6/15.6
44	12.0	52.0	3.2/ 19.2	2.4/14.4
50	11.4	52.0	2.9/ 17.6	2.2/13.2

In 1938 Austria was occupied by Hitler's troops, and in a German supervised plebiscite the Austrians voted for incorporation into the Third Reich. This had eventual repercussions on proof. On May 24, 1940, the German proof law of 1939 was declared legal in Austria; the two proof houses at Vienna and Ferlach were to administer German proof and affix German marks, being entitled however to add to these their coats of arms (marks nos. 3 and 4) as a simple house or identification mark. It is doubtful if this wartime change in proof had very great practical effect, for it came at a period of intensive production of military arms in the Reich, to the detriment of civilian production. The association with Germany ended in 1945 and the Austrian government reverted to the proof rules of 1929, with two changes. First, the second provisional proof and the marks representing it were abandoned. Secondly, the mark for definitive black

powder proof was altered. This had been the Hapsburg double-headed eagle; now it became a one-headed eagle bearing in its claws a hammer and sickle (marks 12 and 13).

The Present Proof Law

In 1951 the Austrian government adopted a new proof law. The basic law was adopted on 20 June, 1951; the implementing regulations were issued by the Ministry of Commerce and Reconstruction on 27 October, 1951. These acts, amended by *Verordnungen* or decrees of the same Ministry dated 9 May, 1958 and 12 February, 1962, are the basis for current proof in Austria.

The law requires proof of a wide variety of firearms and explosive devices, including signal guns, gas guns, cattle-killing and nail- and bolt-driving devices actuated by explosive charges. Barrel inserts also fall within this law. Exempted from proof are starter guns (the noise makers used in athletic or other sports events) incapable of firing cartridges other than blanks; mechanisms for scientific use, and firearms whose value is artistic or which are considered collector's items. (The law does not say how old a gun must be to qualify as an antique,

but the general rule in Europe is that guns or models made before 1870 fall into this category and are exempt from most arms legislation). Significantly-altered arms must be submitted for reproof.

Provisional proof has been retained for smoothbore barrels. These are to be proved in sufficiently completed form so that subsequent finishing operations will not weaken them materially. This proof is made with one shot of black powder, the pressure being 11,400 psi (marks 1 and 2). A very unusual innovation has been permitted in provisional proof since 1962; now "non-destructive methods of material testing" may be used. This would seem to mean that electronic scanning, hydraulic pressure setups, or some such technique may be substituted for actual firing proof. It will be interesting to see if this innovation is adopted elsewhere. For the manufacturer, it may well be a less expensive and time-consuming process than proof firing. For the

customer, it will scarcely make any difference, since the definitive proof, and not the provisional one, is his guarantee of safety.

Definitive proof is stipulated for arms of all types. Shotguns for which smokeless powder loads are available are proved with three separate shots — one with black powder and two with smokeless. The black powder proof is at 10,000 psi. The smokeless proof in 16-gauge guns and larger generates a pressure of at least 12,800 psi, and 14,200 psi in smaller gauges. Since 1962 it is possible to prove with smokeless powder only, the proof consisting of one shot with slow-burning powder and one shot with a faster type.

The law provides more rigorous proof for shotguns with chambers longer than 70mm. This would be the case notably with the 76mm or 3-inch magnum. Here proof must generate pressures 1,400 psi greater than ordinary smokeless proof.

Centerfire rifles are proved with two shots of smokeless powder. These must generate a 30% excess pressure over the heaviest commercial loads. In the case of centerfire rifles whose commercial loads generate 47,000 psi or more, the proof cartridges must exceed highest commercial pressures by 14,200 psi.

Arms other than centerfire rifles and shotguns are proved with smokeless or black powder, the former if smokeless commercial cartridges are available. A proof cartridge is fired in each chamber of revolvers, and two consecutive proof shots are fired in automatic pistols.

Firearms may be submitted to an optional superior definitive proof, indicated by mark no. 10. Loads and pressures are apparently set by the proof masters. However, since 1962, any shotgun undergoing this proof must be subjected to a pressure of at least 17,000 psi.

Those who submit rifles to proof are required to submit detailed information regarding the cartridge, commercial loading, gas pressures, etc. The proof house may demand cartridges or cases in order to verify commercial pressures and establish proof loads. (This stipulation refers undoubtedly to the many new rifle cartridges developed in the U.S. since World War II, some of which are still not well known in Europe). In addition, all arms must bear marks indicating their origin or manufacturer, the cartridge for which they are designed, and the composition and quality of steel used.

The 1951 legislation also establishes proof of ammunition. This takes the form of periodical checks of commercial ammunition, particularly for gas pressure, dimensions, and accuracy of descriptive data supplied with the cartridges.

Bibliography

The material in this chapter was drawn from the relevant legal texts and information supplied by the Vienna proof house. The author would like to thank Herr Fachinspektor Oskar Koschaintsch, its director, for his assistance.

A History of

This is the third installment of the new and fully up-to-date series "History of Proof Marks" initiated in our 22nd edition. The author, Mr. Lee Kennett, is highly qualified to have undertaken the definitive research required, and we feel certain his comprehensive and detailed work will prove reliable, interesting, instructive and valuable.

While Mr. Kennett used the framework of the late Baron Engelhardt's "The Story of European Proof Marks" as a structural guide, he personally visited and talked with Proof House officials in many countries in his research. He will continue to do so until all nations in the survey have been covered. When that time arrives, we will publish the complete book.

With this issue we present "Proof Marks in France." The completed and published book will carry a full account of the origins and historical back ground of proof marks.

FRANCE
Origins to 1810

THE CITY OF SAINT-ETIENNE was both one of the earliest and one of the most important arms centers in France; it remains today as the chief seat of arms production. A long tradition credits King Francis I (1515-1547) with starting the serious manufacture of firearms there in 1535. If a similar legend is to be believed, the water at Saint-Etienne possessed mysterious qualities which helped to temper the iron. Unfortunately, records for the 16th century are rare, and it is not until the following century that Saint-Etienne's arms production can be documented. The town's artisans did a particularly lively business supplying the armies of Louis XIV at the end of the 17th century. By 1665 the King had named a royal official to accept delivery and to verify the quality of the arms.

The origins of proof in Saint-Etienne are equally sketchy. According to Gras, gunmakers for the civilian market did their own proving, or delegated one of their number to do it. The proof charge was usually triple the normal one.[1] The practice was well established by 1700. In that year an important change occurred. The Count of Verdun, acting for the royal government, insisted that all civilian

barrels be submitted to proof by royal controllers who proved military arms. Moreover the heavier military proof was administered, requiring a powder charge equal in weight to the ball. Although no law expressly required this, the Count brought pressure to bear on local gunmakers through his power to grant or refuse licenses required to export arms from the town. The gunmakers gave in, but not without strong objections. They argued with some justice that military proof was too strong for the lighter civilian barrels; moreover they argued that the government proof mark was not respected or even known: "No one has confidence in the Saint-Etienne proof mark," said one of their petitions.[2] In truth, the governmental proof marks changed frequently, probably being designed to suit the fancy of each successive government controller. The marks which date from this period are many; they usually contain the controller's initials, in conjunction with a fleur-de-lis, a crown, or crossed palms, part of the Saint-Etienne coat of arms.[3]

From 1700 to 1782 the gunmakers waged a see-saw battle with the crown over rules of proof. In 1726 compulsory government proof for sporting arms was abolished, only to be restored in 1741. Violations were undoubtedly frequent, for gunmakers were reminded of the regulations in 1746 and 1751. A more stringent reminder appeared in

Proof Marks

Gun Proof in France

by Lee Kennett

Careful visual inspection is an integral part of modern proof procedures. Here the inspection is being made by M. Socquet-Clerc, Director of the Paris Proof House.

1764, increasing the penalties for failure to submit to proof. Finally the gunmakers and the government reached an agreement in 1782. A decree of January 17 of that year established a separate, compulsory civilian proof. A less rigorous proof charge was introduced. A charge was set for each gauge, the gauge being based on the number of balls in the French *livre* or pound. There were seven gauges, ranging from 16, with a proof charge of 18 grams of powder, to 28, with a proof charge of 6 grams. The powder was to be wadded separately, followed by the requisite ball and a second wad of folded paper. Upon request barrels could be given a heavier proof. The decree of 1782 also introduced the first regular proof mark for civilian arms, consisting of a pair of crossed palm fronds. The heavier proof was indicated by two of these marks (mark no. 1).

Saint-Etienne had been using its new proof system for only seven years when the French Revolution broke out. The strife and confusion which followed ruined for a time the sporting gun trade. Indeed, the Revolutionary government, at war with most of Europe, banned production of civilian arms in 1792 and turned Saint-Etienne into a vast arsenal.[4] The law of 1782 had become a dead letter. When civilian production began again in the mid 1790s, the gunmakers did their own proving, firing their guns in alleys or even out of open win-

dows; the town fathers replied to this dangerous practice by banning the discharge of any firearm in the city. A solution was reached in 1797, when proof was reestablished under the 1782 rules.

1810-1868

Napoleon brought order to the proof system, as he did to almost every other aspect of French life. His decree of 14 December, 1810, followed the 1782 rules in several matters, but the Napoleonic decree was much more detailed. It even specified the diameter of the proofmaster's ramrod, and the exact size of the wads — a paper 8cm square for the larger calibers and 5cm square for smaller ones. Rationally, proof was according to a scale of calibers or gauges. But the new gauges were unusual in that they were based on the number of balls per kilogram. Thus 32 gauge in this system approximated our 12 gauge. The scale was as follows:

Kilogram gauge	Normal gauge	Powder (grams)
32	12	20
36	14	18
40	16	17
44	18	16
48	20	15
52	22	14
56	24	13

Larger pistols were proved by the pair, with the

A shotgun mounted in the firing cradle ready for definitive proof. The gun is fired from an adjacent room by means of the long cord attached to the trigger. The cradle is lined with foam rubber to prevent damage to the gun's finish.

French Proof Marks
1782-1969

In this table the mark numbers at left are those assigned by the author, and keyed by him to the text for reference. The 2nd column shows the true form of the proof mark and gives the period of its use. The last column tells of the marks' significance.

No.	Mark	Significance
1	1782-1811	Proof of barrels at St.-Etienne (double marks for superior proof).
2	1811-1824	Same as above.
3	1811-?	Same as above, at Charleville.
4	1811-?	Same as above, at Souilhac.
5	1824-1856	Replaced mark no. 2.
6	1856-1869	Replaced mark no. 5.
7	1862-1885	Commercial reproof of reworked surplus military arms.
8	1869-1879	Black powder proof of semi-finished barrels. Double marks indicate superior proof.
9	1879-	Same as above, Since 1924 proof pressure at 14,200 psi.
10	1879-	Superior black powder proof of semi-finished barrels. Since 1924 at 16,500 psi and called double proof.
11	1879-1897	Same as no. 9, but for arms made elsewhere in France than at St.-Etienne.
12	1879-1924?	Same as no. 9, but for foreign-made arms. (Goddard shows a variant without the oval).
13	1886-1893	Black powder proof of finished arms.
14	1893-1897	Same as above.
15	circa 1893	Superior black powder proof of finished arms.
16	1894-1897	Same as above.
17	1892-1962	Provisional proof of barrels in the rough, at 16,500 psi. after 1924.

Saint-Etienne (left) and Paris marks from 1896

No.	Mark	Significance
18	1897-1962	Provisional proof of barrels in the rough at Paris, at 16,500 psi. after 1924. St.-Etienne equivalent is mark no. 17.
19	1897-	Black powder proof of semi-finished barrels at Paris, at 14,200 psi. since 1924. St.-Etienne equivalent is mark no. 9.

| 20 | | Superior black powder proof of semi-finished barrels at Paris, at 16,500 psi. after 1924 and known as double proof. St.-Etienne equivalent is no. 10. |
| | 1897- | |

| 21 | | Black powder proof of finished arms. See text for pressures. |
| | 1897- | |

| 22 | | Superior black powder proof of finished arms (smoothbores) at 11,400 psi. after 1924. |
| | 1897-1962 | |

| 23 | | Proof in finished state of pistols, revolvers, and sub-caliber long arms. See text for details. |
| | 1897- | |

| 24 | NA | Supplementary mark for unjoined barrels. Used with marks 9, 10, 19, 20, 25 and 26. |
| | 1901- | |

| 25 | | Double proof (black powder) of semi-finished barrels at 20,500 psi. until 1924. Presently called triple proof at 18,000 psi. |
| | 1901- | |

| 26 | | Triple black powder proof of semi-finished barrels at 27,000 psi. |
| | 1901-1924 | |

| 27 |  PJ   ☆ PJ | Definitive proof with smokeless powder "J." |
| | 1896-1914 | |

| 28 | PS   ☆ PS | Definitive proof with smokeless powder "S." |
| | 1896-1914 | |

| 29 | PM   ☆ PM | Definitive proof with smokeless powder "M." |
| | 1898-1914 | |

| 30 | PR   ☆ PR | Definitive proof with smokeless powder "R." |
| | 1898-1914 | |

| 31 | PT   ☆ PT | Definitive proof with smokeless powder "T." |
| | 1900- | |

A proof house loading room. Proof cartridges prepared here are frequently checked for pressure by means of the pressure gun.

| 32 | PT   ☆☆ PT | Superior definitive proof with powder "T." See text for pressures. |
| | 1924- | |

| 33 | AR st. etienne   A§R | Definitive proof of rifled shoulder arms at 30% excess pressure. |
| | 1924- | |

| 34 | NORMAL | Supplementary mark to designate a shotgun with 65mm chamber length. |
| | 1924-1962 | |

| 35 | | Supplementary mark for definitive proof in completely finished state. |
| | 1924- | |

| 36 | ARME ETRANGERE / AR.ETR | Supplementary mark for foreign arms submitted to proof. Not used at St.-Etienne since 1962. |
| | 1924- | |

| 37 | R   R | Black powder reproof. |
| | 1960- | |

| 38 | R   ☆ P.T. .R | Smokeless powder reproof. |
| | 1960- | |

| 39 | ☆☆ P. T. R | Superior smokeless powder reproof at Paris. |
| | 1960- | |

NOTE: Those periods not showing a closing year indicate continuing use of the mark indicated, up to the time of publication of this book.

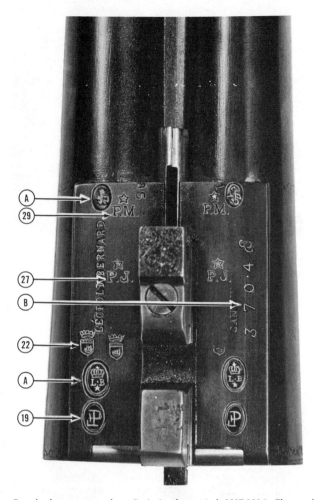

French shotgun proved at Paris in the period 1897-1914. The marks tell an interesting story. Made c. 1880 by Leopold Bernard of Paris and proved by him, using private proof marks (A). Its owner must have been a stickler for safety, as he sent it to the Paris proof house for four separate proofs. (B) Indicates gun's serial number. Refer to text for explanation of numbers shown.

proof charge divided between them. Thus a pair of 44-ga. pistols were proved with 8 grams of powder each. Pocket pistols were proved with 4 grams. All proofs were to be made with wadding over the powder, followed by a lead ball of requisite size and a second wad. Incidentally, the decree reinforced a law of 1799 banning civilian guns of service caliber, then 17.7mm, or within two millimeters of that caliber. This provision, a curious example of restrictive firearms legislation, is still retained in France today.

The decree followed its predecessor in providing for an optional superior proof designated by double proof marks. Superior proof for a 32-ga. barrel was the ordinary proof charge for 44 gauge, superior proof in 36 gauge consisted of the ordinary proof for 48 gauge, etc., these added to the standard proof charge for the gauge. Any barrel failing proof was returned to its maker, who could rework it and submit it again. If it failed a second time, the proofmaster was to break it before returning it.

In the matter of proof marks, Napoleon's law authorized a proof house with distinctive marks in each arms center, and permitted the use of the town's coat of arms for this purpose, though it appears that only Saint-Etienne, Charleville and Souillac devised such marks (nos. 2, 3, and 4). Marks were to be placed at the breech so as to be clearly visible. Barrels were also to be stamped with their caliber at the time of proof, and it was illegal to enlarge the caliber subsequently. This measure was designed to end a practice, common in the 18th century, of submitting barrels to the heavy military proof and then reaming them out afterwards, lightening the gun but reducing the safety margin.

Napoleon's decree remained in force long after his downfall; indeed, it survived, with some modification, until 1868. The proof mark underwent several minor changes. In 1824 a crown was added, probably symbolic of the restoration of the monarchy in 1814 (fig. no. 5). In 1856 the proof house passed under the control of the Saint-Etienne Chamber of Commerce, and the proof mark was enclosed in an oval (fig. no. 6). In 1862 a proof mark was introduced for the proof of reworked military surplus arms (fig. no. 7). By the mid-19th century gunmakers desired more profound changes in the old law. According to Ronchard-Siauve, writing in 1864, the proof charges were excessive. The proof table did not cover many gauges subsequently introduced, so that the proofmasters were obliged to make these up. Finally, the kilogram gauge system had never caught on outside of France. Foreign purchasers were confused by the gauge designations, to the detriment of the French gun trade.[5]

On June 19, 1865, new proof regulations were issued, but instead of being an improvement, they were even worse from the gunmaker's point of view. The proof charges were heavier than before; so high, in fact, that 85 per cent of the barrels submitted failed to pass. The only valuable feature of the new legislation seems to have been a provision granting free entry to foreign arms bearing official proof marks. In any event, the gunmaking trade petitioned, apparently with success, to have the 1865 regulations set aside and to continue under the 1810 system until another law could be drafted. The new law appeared in 1868.

1868-1897

The decree of 22 April, 1868, retained obligatory proof, but overhauled completely the proof charges and bore designations. The Saint-Etienne arms industry had requested a separate proof of finished arms, or definitive proof, but the new regulations only introduced a double proof system for rifled barrels, to be tested before and after rifling. Smoothbores were still submitted to a single proof, administered to the barrel in a rather advanced state of manufacture — completed except for breeching, polishing, and bluing. The proof tables were among the most elaborate ever devised. No longer would the proofmaster be obliged to invent charges for odd calibers. Both smoothbore and rifle tables are given for bore diameters graduated in 2/10mm steps. Table B, for rifled arms, provided 140 separate sets of proof charges, for arms ranging in bore diameter from 9mm to 37mm. Table C, for smoothbores, provided 215 charges for bore diameters from 10.6mm to 53.6mm. This latter diameter — something over two inches — was proved with a half-pound of black powder and five pounds of shot!

The tables, which are far too long to be reproduced here in their entirety, may be found in Polain's *Recherches historiques*, (1891 ed.), pp. 351-358. See Tables B and C for illustrative selections.

Table B — Proof Loads for Rifled Barrels

Caliber in mm	Proof Charge — Grams 1st proof	2nd proof	Diam./Wgt. of Lead Ball mm	grams
9	7.0	4.5	8.5	27.5
10	8.5	6.0	9.5	36.0
11	10.0	6.5	10.5	44.0
12	10.5	7.0	11.5	46.0
13	10.5	7.0	12.5	46.0
14	10.5	7.0	13.5	46.0
15	11.0	7.0	14.5	47.5
20	17.5	12.0	19.5	98.5
25	35.5	23.5	24.5	196.0
30	61.5	41.0	29.5	344.5
35	100.0	66.5	34.5	550.0
37	118.0	78.5	36.5	660.0

Table C — Proof Loads for Shot Barrels

Gauge Nominal	mm	Proof Charges — Grams Powder	Soft #8 Shot
410	10.6	6.0	20.0
32	12.8	7.0	30.0
28	14.0	7.5	35.0
24	14.8	8.0	40.0
20	15.6	8.5	45.0
16	16.8	9.0	50.0
14	17.6	10.0	60.0
12	18.6	11.0	70.0
10	19.6	12.5	85.0
8	21.2	14.0	100.0
4	23.8	20.5	165.0
1 in.	25.4	23.0	190.0
2 in.	50.8	174.0	1700.0
2.2 in.	55.4	218.0	2140.0

Some other features of proof according to the 1868 rules are as follows: Smoothbores of bore diameter of less than 10.6mm were all proved with 3 grams of powder and 20.8 grams of shot. Smoothbore pistols of 10.6mm and less underwent this same proof. In the event that their barrels were too short to contain the charge, they were filled to half their length with powder and the remainder with shot, a wad being placed just inside the muzzle. Pistols with bores of from 10.6mm to 11.4mm, and with barrels under 15cm in length, took a proof charge equal to half of that in Table C. Pistols with a bore diameter of over 11.4mm and/or a barrel length of over 15cm underwent proof as prescribed in Table C. Revolvers were proved once in each chamber, but only with the service load, which seems a curious weakness in an otherwise stringent law. Another feature of the 1868 rules was the inclusion of a table of charges for military muskets, whose manufacture by private enterprise had been permitted in 1860. Finally, the law retained an optional superior proof of smoothbore barrels. The

Darne shotgun of recent manufacture, proved at Saint Etienne. (A) Shows 12.4mm bore diameter. (B) Darne quality stamps; twelve stamps indicate highest quality made except for special order. (C) Chamber length — 70mm. (D) May be gun's serial number. Refer to text for explanation of numbers shown.

superior proof charge contained 50% more powder than that in Table C. As before, this proof was indicated by double proof marks.

It was thought advisable to introduce a new proof mark to reflect the new changes in proof. This was introduced sometime in 1869 (fig. no. 8). In 1879 this mark was abolished, to be replaced by three new ones. One mark contained the palms of Saint-Etienne, a mural crown and the words "St.-Etienne" (fig. nos. 9 and 10), and was reserved for the products made in that locality. The letters A. F., signifying *arme française*, placed in an oval with palms, formed a new mark for arms of other cities in France proved at Saint-Etienne (fig. no. 11). A third mark, composed of palms and the letters "A. E." (*arme étrangère*) in an oval was used for foreign guns (fig. no. 12). Any of these marks stamped twice signified superior proof.

On August 5, 1885, the French parliament passed a law designed to give the arms industry greater freedom to manufacture military arms. The law was badly worded, and a subsequent ruling in 1889 held that the law had abolished compulsory proof of civilian firearms entirely. Although there were many protests, particularly from gunmakers, the government decided in 1895 that proof was official but *voluntary*, a situation that continued for the next 65 years. The results of this accidental end of obligatory proof were actually not very serious, as arms manufacturers generally continued to submit guns to proof. Small caliber rifles, very small bore shotguns, Flobert-type arms and small caliber pistols sometimes were not submitted, and so may not bear proof marks. Finally, one ambitious producer of arms ran his own proof house for a few years. As a general rule, however, any gun generating relatively high pressures was officially proved.

The 1868 law had required only proof of barrels of shotguns and rifles, though in advanced state of manufacture. To supplement this proof — obviously inadequate with breechloaders — a true definitive proof was introduced by a decree of 2 December 1885, put into effect early in 1886. The charges were among the first to be set with the aid of the pressure gun, and were supposed to yield something in the neighborhood of 14,000 psi. The new proof was for shotguns only; some of the charges were as follows:

Gauge	Chamber Length (mm)	Powder (grams) Strong Black #2	Shot (grams) No. 8
20	65	4.50	30
16	65	5.75	31
16	75	5.50	50
12	65	6.75	42
12	70	6.50	55

The proof mark for this proof was the letters "EF" (fig. no. 13). In 1893 the mark was changed slightly (fig. no. 14). The two letters represent the words *épreuve* (proof) and *fini* (finished).

A superior definitive proof followed in 1893, probably to meet the higher pressures of early smokeless powder shotshells then coming into use. This proof was supposed to generate pressures of about 16,000 psi, though the figure is open to doubt, given the problems of accurate pressure readings on the early pressure guns. This pressure was thought to be about 40 per cent in excess of normal operating pressures. Some representative charges are as follows:

Gauge	Chamber Length (mm)	Powder (grams) extra fine black	Shot (grams) No. 8
20	65	6.50	29
16	65	6.50	30
16	75	7.50	40
12	65	7.00	39
12	70	8.75	36

The proof mark was composed of the letters "EF," to which was added an "S" to designate superior proof. There are two variants, of which the first (fig. no. 15) was probably a makeshift used in 1893. By 1894, the second (fig. no. 16) became standard.

In 1892 still another proof was devised to meet the demands of gunmakers for a preliminary proof of barrels *en jambes*, or in the rough, hitherto lacking in the French system. Representative loads for this proof were as follows:

Gauge	Powder (grams) Strong black #2	Shot (grams) No. 8
20	9	50
16	10	60
12	11	70

The proof mark assigned for this proof was a mural crown (fig. no. 17).

So far, we have mentioned proof only at Saint-Etienne. There were of course other arms centers, notably Paris. Did they have proof houses? The answer seems to be that they did not. Most 19th century writers on the subject say quite explicitly that Saint-Etienne had the only proof house. Mangeot, writing in 1856, says that barrels were being

Proof certificate indicating proof at Paris of a 22-cal. rifle.

made in Tulle, Paris, and Chatellerault, but adds: "Only Saint-Etienne possesses a mark of guarantee for its sporting barrels; the barrelmakers of other localities simply put on their barrels a private mark, reserved for their own use." He goes on to say that Paris gunmakers proved on the purchaser's request, their marks being their own initials, in most cases within an oval and accompanied by a crown or a pair of palms.[6] From all of this the logical conclusion is that whatever the law said, proof was compulsory only at Saint-Etienne. That the government was aware of this situation is clear. A directive of 11 August, 1865, ordered arms manufacturers and dealers to take their unproved arms to the local bureau of weights and measures, where they would simply be stamped with the letter "M," in lieu of proof.[7] It was not until 1895 that Paris gunmakers set to work to establish a proof house there, which opened in 1897.

The law of 7 November, 1895, which authorized the establishment of a proof house in Paris, also afforded an opportunity to overhaul once more the much amended rules of 1868. As early as 1892 the Saint-Etienne Chamber of Commerce had created a commission to examine the question. Its report,

Saint Etienne proof certificate for a black powder proved 9mm shotgun.

completed in 1894, was adopted in the new series of rules issued by the Paris and Saint-Etienne houses on 30 July, 1897. The 1868 proof tables for smoothbore barrels were revised in order to lessen charges for bores of 16.6mm and under, judged to be excessive. Thus the proof load in 28 gauge dropped from 7.5 grams of strong black powder #2 and 35 grams of shot to 5 grams and 32 grams respectively. All arms of "small dimensions" were now to be proved in finished state. Pistols of below 11.4mm bore diameter were proved with 2 grams of black powder and 10 of lead; those of larger bore with 3 grams and 20 grams respective-

ly. Revolvers were tested with the service ball loaded in front of sufficient black powder to extend cartridge length to that of the cylinder. The most important changes, however, were in the proof marks. Paris devised a set for its new proof house, while several of the Saint-Etienne marks were changed. Paris adopted a pair of script "Ps" to signify proof of rough barrels (fig. no. 18), an "EP" monogram within an oval (fig. no. 19) for proof of nearly finished barrels, and the same mark twice for superior proof of this type (fig. no. 20). The Saint-Etienne marks for these proofs were unchanged (fig. nos. 9, 10 and 17). Both houses devised new marks for ordinary and superior proof of finished arms. Saint-Etienne used an "F" surmounted by a crown for ordinary proof and Paris used the city coat of arms (fig. no. 21). For superior proof Saint-Etienne introduced a crowned "S" and Paris applied the coat of arms twice (fig. no. 22).

For proof of small bore arms, pistols and revolvers, Paris employed its coat of arms depicting proof of finished arms, while Saint-Etienne used the mural crown followed by the words "St.-Etienne." Both of these were in reduced format (fig. no. 23).

In 1901 three more marks were introduced. The first of these consisted of the letters "N.A.," signifying *non assemblé* or not assembled, to be added to the customary proof mark for finished barrels when these had not yet been joined. A second innovation, and a very confusing one, was the introduction of a "double" and a "triple" proof for finished barrels, to supplement the ordinary and superior proofs already in existence. The ordinary proof was rated in 1900 at 14,200 psi, and the superior at 16,500 psi. The new proofs were much higher. Double proof, indicated by triple marks (fig. no. 25), attained 20,500 psi. Triple proof, which was designated by four marks (fig. no. 26), was rated at 27,000 psi.

So far, all proof charges we have mentioned are with black powder; indeed, the superior proof of finished arms, designed to meet the increased pressures of early smokeless loads, was done with black powder. Since powder production in this country was, and still is, a monopoly of the French government, and the varieties developed were few, the proof houses developed a smokeless proof load for each powder as it was introduced. These were Powder J (and its derivatives, J^1 and J^2) and Powder S in 1896, Powders M, R, and S^2 in 1898, and Powder T in 1900 (fig. nos. 27-31). These represent proofs administered to the finished gun, and they varied considerably in their pressures. Very often the proof charge was stamped on the gun in addition to the proof mark; the practice was more common in Saint-Etienne than in Paris. The basic problem with most of the powders was that pressures were insufficient to meet the 12,000 psi minimum set by the Brussels Convention. As a result, all but Powder T were dropped as proof powders in 1914, though several continued to be available commercially.[8] Powder T is the only one of these early smokeless propellants still being manufactured, and is still by far the most widely used in France today.

Rules of 1928

France was obliged to change her proof system in order to conform to the Brussels Convention; the new rules, known often as the rules of 1928, were initiated by decrees of 18 December, 1923 and 4 June, 1926. Most of the new rules were actually being applied in both proof houses by 1924. The most notable change occurred in provisional proof of finished barrels. Triple proof was abolished; double proof was revised. Neither of these, with their extremely high pressures, had served a very useful purpose. Of the thousands of barrels proved at Saint-Etienne in 1923, only 54 had been given double proof and only 24 triple proof.[9] Considerable confusion arises from the fact that in 1924 the old superior proof (fig. nos. 10 and 20) became double proof, keeping the same marks and pressures. The previous double proof (fig. no. 25) now became triple proof, but with pressures dropped from 20,500 psi to 18,000 psi. About the only clear conclusion that can be drawn from this is that a gun bearing the four marks of triple proof was proved between 1901 and 1924, and is made of a very rare piece of steel indeed.

The 1924 rules retained the proof and marks for barrels in the rough, rated at 16,500 psi. Standard black powder proof of finished shotguns was set at 8,800 psi, and superior black powder proof at 11,400 psi. Marks were not changed. In addition to smokeless proof with Powder T (12,000 psi) a superior proof was offered (fig. no. 32) at 15,600 psi. Rifles and handguns were proved with 30 per cent excess pressure loads, and new marks were introduced for rifles, containing the letters "A.R.," for *arme rayée* or rifled arm (fig. no. 33).

Shotguns were stamped with chamber size and length in millimeters, or with the enclosed word "NORMAL," which signified a shotgun with chambers 65mm long (fig. no. 34). Finally, two sets of supplementary marks were introduced: one designated arms submitted to definitive proof in completely finished state and ready for delivery (fig. no. 35); the other set was used to designate *arme étrangère*, or foreign guns (fig. no. 36).

Present Proof Regulations

Proof in France is today governed by the decree of 12 January, 1960, and by the internal regulations of each proof house drawn up in conformity with it. The most recent Saint-Etienne rules are those dated June, 1962; current Paris rules, virtually identical in wording, were drawn up in June, 1964. The most striking change in the 1962 law is the reestablishment of compulsory proof for all civilian firearms. While there are still only two proof houses, they both operate branches in various arms centers, though the proof practices and marks are identical with those of the parent installations.

A synopsis of the present regulations is as follows: *Category I: Long or Short Barreled Smoothbores.* These must have one of three proofs: black powder proof, ordinary smokeless proof or superior smokeless proof (note that smokeless proof is not obligatory). Two proof cartridges are fired in each barrel; in case of superior smokeless proof, the first cartridge is that for ordinary smokeless proof. Pressure requirements, which are more elaborate than previously, are as follows:

	Chamber length (mm)	Pressure (psi)
Black powder proof	65	8,800
	70	9,200
	75	9,600
Ordinary smokeless proof	65	12,000
	70	12,800
	75	13,500
Superior smokeless proof	65	15,500
	70	17,000
	75	17,000

All arms must be finished, but may be "in the white." Arms completely finished receive the supplementary mark indicating this (fig. no. 35).

All arms are carefully inspected upon reception, and may be refused proof if found defective. If the barrel already bears the mark for optional provisional proof of finished barrels, its caliber must be at least equal to that marked on the barrel at time of provisional proof. Chamber length and chamber and bore diameters must fall within the limits established by the Permanent International Commission on Firearms. After these verifications, each barrel is stamped with chamber length in millimeters, and bore diameter in millimeters and tenths of millimeters. Arms are inspected again after proof. Those judged to have passed are stamped with the requisite mark (fig. nos. 21, 31 or 32) on barrels and breech. A certificate of proof is delivered with each gun, identifying it by factory number and indicating proof type and pressure.

Category II: Long or Short Barreled Rifled Arms. These are proved with two ball cartridges in each barrel, or in the case of revolvers, in each chamber. Proof pressures must be at least 15 per cent in excess of those of maximum commercial loads. For salon type, small caliber arms, the proof cartridge is to be loaded with enough extra fine black powder to obtain the requisite 15 per cent excess pressure when loaded behind the service ball. As with smoothbores, inspection precedes and follows proof. Arms are stamped with marks 23 or 33. Caliber is stamped if it does not already appear.

Category III: Optional Provisional Proof of Barrels. These must bear the mark of the maker, and be in a sufficiently finished state that "their completion after proof will not compromise their solidity, not chambered but with barrel walls polished and dry." After preliminary inspection, bores are calibrated at a point from 15 to 50 centimeters from the breech. Diameter is stamped on the barrel in millimeters and tenths of millimeters. In their subsequent finishing operations, gunmakers may not enlarge the bore diameter by more than 0.2mm. In consequence, on instructions from the maker, barrels may be stamped 0.1mm or 0.2mm larger than they measure, to account for this subsequent enlargement. Barrels may be submitted to one or more of three separate proofs, all of which are made with fine black powder, No. 8 shot and linen paper wads.

Ordinary proof is at 14,200 psi, double proof at 16,500 psi, and triple proof at 18,000 psi. They are then stamped with marks 9, 10, 19, 20 or 25, and with mark 24 if unassembled. Gunmakers may also request higher proofs. In this case the proof charge is indicated on a certificate of proof, but no special mark is used.

Category IV: Reproof of Arms. All imported arms fall into this category, save those from signatory nations of the Brussels Convention and Great Britain. For arms of unusual caliber, proof charges are left to the discretion of the proof master. Guns which have undergone alteration sufficient to compromise their safety must be reproved. Any shot-

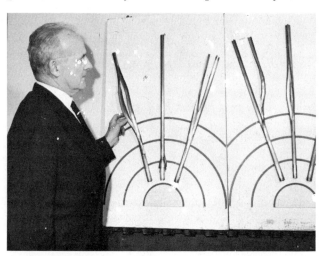

Though such split barrels as these are now less common in European proof houses, they are eloquent testimony of the value of proof.

gun whose bore diameter is enlarged by 0.2mm or whose chamber is lengthened by 5mm or more, or whose barrel has been lightened by 6 per cent of its weight must be reproved.

To indicate reproof five new marks have been devised, all incorporating the letter "R," signifying *rééprouvée* or reproved. Both houses offer a black powder reproof (fig. no. 37) and a smokeless reproof (fig. no. 38). In addition, Paris offers a superior smokeless reproof (fig. no. 39).

The 1960 legislation created no other proof marks. On the other hand, it has dropped certain marks and proofs. Most notable of these was the proof for barrels in the rough. In actual fact, Paris has not proved any of these in a good many years, the barrel making trade having disappeared there. The superior black powder proof of finished shotguns has been dropped, along with its marks. Saint-Etienne no longer applies a special mark to designate foreign guns, though Paris has retained it. One final note on present proof is the substitution of "bars" for kilograms per square centimeter, in

expressing pressure. Thus the certificate of proof for a shotgun with 70mm chambers will show proof pressure of ordinary smokeless proof as 900 bars, rather than 900 kg/cm². The result is, of course, a slight increase in proof pressure, the bar being equal to 1.02 kg/cm². This change was made in 1965.

References

1. J.-L. Gras, *Historique de l'armurerie stéphanoise* (history of the arms trade in Saint-Etienne), St.-Etienne, France, 1905, p. 52.

2. *Ibid.*, p. 34.

3. For these early marks see Stockel, *Haandskydevaabens Bedommelse*, I, 192-193; II, 427-437. For the names of gunprovers before 1782, see Gras, *Historique*, p. 175, who reproduces two lists which are not in complete agreement.

4. Yearly production of military muskets varied from 10,000 to 26,000 before the Revolution. By 1805 production was 45,000 and by 1810 it reached 97,000. These figures make it clear that by Napoleon's time Saint-Etienne had become the unquestioned leader in arms production. Marcel Arbogast, *L'Industrie des armes à Saint-Etienne* (The arms industry in Saint-Etienne), St.-Etienne, 1937, pp. 56-58.

5. According to the same author, the proof charge in 32 gauge (our 12 gauge) was *seven* times the normal hunting charge. M. Ronchard-Siauve, *Traité des canons de fusils* (Treatise on gun barrels), St.-Etienne, 1864, pp. 66ff.

6. H. Mangeot, *Traité du fusil de chasse et des armes de précision* (Treatise on the shotgun and precision arms), 6th ed., Brussels, 1856, p. 198.

7. Gras, *Historique*, p. 163.

8. Information supplied by M. Fiasson, present Director of the Saint-Etienne Proof House.

9. All of the triple proofs and 94 per cent of the double proofs were administered that year for the famous Darne Company, a fact which the company still cites in its catalog of double barreled guns.

Bibliography

R. Dubessy, *Historique de la manufacture d'armes de guerre de Saint-Etienne* (History of the military arms factory of Saint-Etienne), St.-Etienne, 1900.

J.-L. Gras, *Historique de l'armurerie stéphanoise* (History of the arms trade in Saint-Etienne), St.-Etienne, 1905.

Marcel Arbogast, *L'Industrie des Armes à Saint-Etienne* (The arms industry in St.-Etienne), Saint-Etienne, 1937.

Henri Manceau, *La manufacture d'armes de Charleville* (The Charleville arms factory), Charleville, 1962.

Alphonse Polain, *Recherche Historique sur l'eprouve des armes a feu au pays de Liége* (Historical research on the proof of firearms in Liége), Liége, 1891.

Capitaine Languepin, *Histoire de la manufacture d'armes de Tulle* (History of the Tulle arms factory), Tulle, n.d.

M. Ronchard-Siauve, *Traité des canons de fusil* (Treatise on gun barrels), St.-Etienne, 1864.

Report of the proof commission of the Saint-Etienne chamber of commerce, *Etudes sur la differentes poudres employées, sur la résistance des métaux, et sur les charges à adopter pour les épreuves des armes non reglementaires* (Studies of different powders used, of the resistance of metals, and the charges to employ for the proof of non-military arms), St.-Etienne, 1894.

———, "French Nitro Proofs" in *Arms and Explosives,* London, March, 1894, p. 102.

———, "Gun Proving in France" in *Arms and Explosives,* London, September, 1894, pp. 210-212.

Lee Kennett, "Gun Proving in France" in the *American Rifleman,* Washington, D.C., August, 1965, pp. 24-25.

* * *

The author is indebted to M. Socquet-Clerc, Director of the Paris Proof House, and to M. Fiasson, his counterpart in Saint-Etienne, both of whom were extremely helpful, and to Mr. Sealtiel, Proof Master of the London Proof House, who very kindly put his register of foreign proof marks at the author's disposal.

A History of

This is the 4th installment of the new and fully up-to-date series "History of Proof Marks" initiated in our 22nd edition. The author, Mr. Lee Kennett, is highly qualified to have undertaken the definitive research required, and we feel certain his comprehensive and detailed work will prove reliable, interesting, instructive and valuable.

While Mr. Kennett used the framework of the late Baron Engelhardt's "The Story of European Proof Marks" as a structural guide, he personally visited and talked with Proof House officials in many countries in his research. He will continue to do so until all nations in the survey have been covered. When that time arrives, we will publish the complete book.

With this issue we present "Proof Marks in Spain." The completed and published book will carry a full account of the origins and historical back ground of proof marks.

SPAIN
Origins to 1915

BY THE 16th century Spain had taken her place among the arms-producing nations of Europe, Spanish guns being highly regarded and widely exported. Individual makers generally did their own proving, but according to one authority 16th century barrelmakers of Eibar and other centers often had their products tested at the Royal Arsenal at Placencia. Proof remained, however, an individual matter until 1847, when the government authorized the gunmakers of Eibar, the most important arms center, to establish a local proof house. The house was publicly authorized but privately run; it administered voluntary proof only.[1] This arrangement remained in effect until the beginning of the 20th century.

Proof practices and marks remain something of an enigma; many valuable records were destroyed during the Spanish Civil War of 1936-1939, and what is known is rather fragmentary. In the case of shotguns, there were both provisional and definitive proofs designated by marks 1 and 2 respectively. Subsequently, proof was somewhat amplified. All smoothbores underwent provisional proof in the rough (mark no. 1). Finished barrels were tested again and given mark no. 3. This constituted a definitive proof for muzzleloaders, but was only a second provisional proof for breechloaders. After breeching the latter underwent definitive proof, depending upon their breeching system. Those having the locking lever under the trigger guard received mark no. 4. Shotguns having the locking lever incorporated in the fore-end received mark no. 5. These were proofs at moderate pressures, suitable for arms of these systems, often having only one locking lug. Shotguns with two or more locking lugs underwent one of the above proofs and then a heavier definitive proof generating 10,700 psi (mark no. 6). An optional superior definitive proof was also possible, designated by mark no. 7. There were two optional smokeless powder proofs, one at 12,000 psi (mark no. 8), and a superior smokeless with Schultze powder at 12,800 psi (mark no. 9).

By the beginning of the 20th century the privately operated voluntary proof system was no longer adequate. The nature of gunmaking had changed; what had formerly been a craft had now become an industry of sizable proportions. In 1909 Eibar alone produced a half-million guns. The export market had become an important one, but because of *compulsory* proof in other countries Spanish gun exporters were faced with that obstacle. The private proof house at Eibar would hardly do in this situation. First of all, it received no support from the government, but was obliged

Proof Marks

Gun Proof in Spain

by Lee Kennett

to meet expenses from proof fees. Yet these could not be very high or gun makers would not submit arms to its proof. About the only arms submitted were shotguns, but very often makers preferred to prove and stamp their own guns, sometimes with marks that *resembled* foreign proof marks! (This was the source of many complaints in Liége at the beginning of the century). More serious, the Eibar proof house marks were not registered or protected from counterfeiting, with results that can well be imagined.[2]

There was considerable agitation for compulsory official proof at the beginning of the century, but the proposal encountered much opposition from some gunmakers. At a meeting in Eibar in 1907 these makers argued that they operated on a minimal cost basis, and that proof fees would raise their costs too much. Moreover, they feared the delays involved in submission to proof—the Eibar proof facilities being inadequate to handle a large volume of guns.[3] A compromise was reached in 1910, whereby the government took over the direction of the proof facilities and protected the proof marks, though proof remained voluntary. Three new basic proof marks were introduced, undoubtedly to replace former marks that had been fraudulently applied. These were marks 11, 12 and 13. At the same time, a new stamp was introduced to indicate gauge (mark no. 14).

Beginnings of Compulsory Proof

Continual agitation for compulsory proof culminated in a law of 31 January, 1915, establishing this principle. The 1915 law only laid the basis of compulsory proof; subsequent enactments were to bring it into effect. These were slow in forthcoming, perhaps because of continued resistance among some gunmakers. The provisional proof house regulations were not formulated until 1919; even then, compulsory proof did not begin, for new installations had to be prepared. Originally, proof houses were planned at Eibar and Oviedo. Only the former came into existence then, gun proof finally getting under way at Eibar in January, 1923; to give makers even more time to adjust to the new system, proof did not actually become obligatory until April, 1924. A short time later a second proof house was opened in Barcelona, but proving firearms there ceased in 1935. Since that time the only Spanish proof house has been at Eibar.

The new regulations, issued in final form in 1923, conformed to the Brussels' standards, for Spain signed the Convention in that same year. At the same time Spanish laws were changed so as to protect foreign patents from infringement by local gunmakers (the imitation Colt and Smith and Wesson revolvers occasionally seen resulted from this abuse). The establishment of the new system

Spanish Proof Marks

1847-1970

In this table the mark numbers at left are those assigned by the author, and keyed by him to the text for reference. The 2nd column shows the true form of the proof mark and gives the period of its use. The last column tells the marks' significance.

Voluntary Proof System

1847 - 1923

1 Two variant marks for provisional proof. The oval form is thought to be the older.

2 Definitive proof mark; current in the 1880s.

3 Proof of finished barrels; constituted definitive proof for muzzle-loaders and 2nd provisional proof for breechloaders.

4 Definitive proof of shotguns with locking lever under the trigger guard. May also be found on guns with two or more locking lugs.

5 Definitive proof of shotguns with locking lever in the fore-end. May also be found on guns with two or more locking lugs.

6 Black powder definitive proof of shotguns with two or more locking lugs at 10,700 psi.

7 Superior black powder definitive proof.

8 Smokeless definitive proof of shotguns at 12,000 psi.

9 Superior smokeless definitive proof of shotguns at 12,800 psi.

10 **12** Gauge designation.

New Marks Introduced in 1910

11 Replaced mark no. 1.

12 Replaced mark no. 3.

13 Replaced mark no. 5.

14 Replaced mark no. 10.

Compulsory Proof System, 1923 to Date

15 Eibar house mark.

1923-1931

16 Replaced mark no. 15.

1931-

17 Barcelona house mark.

1925?-1931

18 Replaced mark no. 17.

1931-1935

19 Single black powder proof of muzzle-loading single barrel smoothbore at 9000 psi **and** provisional proof of unjoined barrels of muzzle-loading doubles at 13,000 psi until 1929. Thereafter single proof for all muzzle-loading smoothbores at 10,300 psi.

1923-

20 Definitive black powder proof of double barreled muzzle-loading smoothbores.

1923-1929

21	1923-	Provisional proof of breech-loading shotgun barrels at 12,000 psi.
22	1923-1929	Single definitive black powder proof of single barrel breech-loading shotguns.
23	1923?-1929?	Variant form of mark no. 22.
24	1923-	Definitive black powder proof of breech-loading shotguns at 8800 psi.
25	1923-1929	Superior black powder proof of breech-loading shotguns.
26	1923-1929	Optional smokeless powder proof of breech-loading shotguns at 12,000 psi.
27	1929-	Replaced mark no. 26.
28	1923-	Superior smokeless powder proof of breech-loading shotguns at 12,800 psi.
29	1923-	Provisional proof of rifle barrels until 1929; thereafter definitive proof for rifles at 30% excess pressure.
30	1923-1929	Definitive proof of single barreled breech-loading rifles **and** single proof of muzzle-loading rifles.
31	1923-1929	Definitive proof of multi-barreled breech-loading rifles.

32	1923-1929	Definitive proof of military type rifles.
33	1923-	Single definitive proof of parlor guns.
34	1923-1931	Single definitive proof on non-autoloading pistols of one or more barrels.
35	1931-	Replaced mark no. 34.
36	1923-1929	Single definitive proof of autoloading pistols and revolvers.
37	1929-	Replaced mark no. 36 for autoloading pistols.
38	1929-	Replaced mark no. 36 for revolvers.
39	1929-	Indicates proof of foreign arms.
40	1923-1931	Supplementary mark on arms certified by their makers to have standard bore and chamber dimensions.
41	1931-	Replaced mark no. 40.

NOTE: Those periods not showing a closing year indicate continuing use of the mark indicated, up to the time of publication of this book.

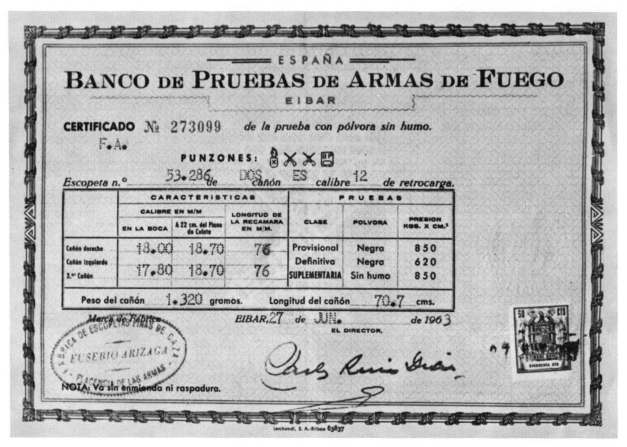

Eibar proof certificate for an Arizaga twelve gauge double barrel shotgun.

brought with it recognition of Spanish proof by Belgium in 1924, and by England in 1927.

There were still complaints abroad about those Spanish gunmakers' marks that resembled foreign proof marks; in addition, the proof authorities in 1924 were accepting the private "proof marks" of such firms as Remington and Winchester as valid.[4] This, of course, was contrary to the Brussels Convention—to which the U.S. had not been a signatory. As a result, a Spanish royal decree of 14 December, 1929, tightened up proof regulations and introduced some new marks. This decree remains the basis of proof in Spain today, though a few marks were altered to remove the royal crown when Spain became a republic in 1931.

All arms must bear, on arrival at the proof house, a factory mark and caliber designation. Bore diameter, measured 22 centimeters from the muzzle, is stamped on the barrel. Each gun accepted for proof receives the house mark (no. 16). Before proof, a visual inspection—viewing—is made of the mechanism and over-all functioning. Cartridges must enter the chambers, fire, and be extracted without difficulty. The regulations state that no arm will be rejected at inspection from "aesthetic" considerations or if its accuracy is questionable.

Muzzle-loading shotguns, single- or multi-barreled, are given a single black powder proof at 10,300 psi after the barrels are finished. They receive mark no. 19 and are stamped with the bore diameter in millimeters and tenths.

Breech-loading shotgun barrels undergo provisional proof in the finished state except for chambering and final polishing at 12,000 psi, receiving mark no. 21 and the bore diameter stamp in millimeters and tenths. When resubmitted for definitive proof, bore diameter must not have been enlarged by more than 0.4mm or the provisional proof is considered invalid. Definitive black powder proof generates 8800 psi, designated by mark no. 24. Definitive bore diameter, chamber length and barrel weight in grams are stamped. Automatic shotguns are proved by firing three magazine-fed cartridges. The first is the ordinary black powder proof charge, or a smokeless one at 12,000 psi if the gun is intended for smokeless powder use. The second and third cartridges are ordinary commercial shotshells. Shotguns may undergo two optional smokeless powder definitive proofs. The first generates 12,000 psi (mark no. 27), the second 12,800 psi (mark no. 28). Proof pressure is stamped in each case.

Rifles, including military types, undergo definitive proof only, with 30% excess pressure loads (mark no. 29). Automatic rifles are fired with two proof cartridges followed by two commercial ones. Saloon (parlor) arms take definitive proof from a case filled with the standard powder loaded behind the regular commercial bullet (mark no. 33).

Non-automatic pistols, of one or more shots, are tested with 30% excess pressure black powder loads (mark no. 35). Autoloading pistols are proved with

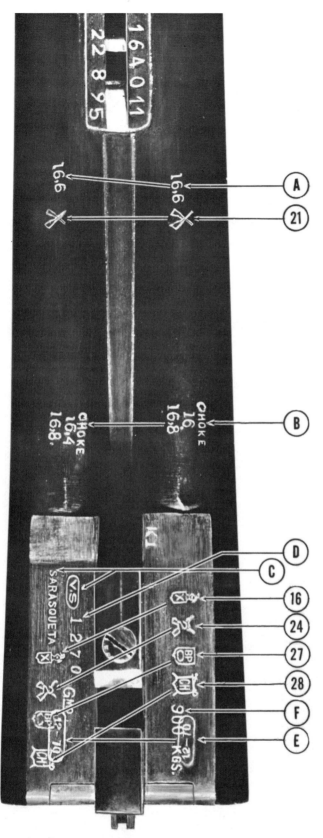

two 30% excess pressure loads followed by two commercial ones (mark no. 37). Revolvers are proved definitively in each chamber (mark no. 38).

Altered or repaired arms are subject to reproof, but no special marks are designated. These arms are to be treated as "new guns." Individuals may submit old arms for proof as well—the ordinary definitive marks being affixed to them if proof was successful. Foreign arms without sanctioned marks undergo definitive proof and bear a special mark (no. 39). Arms certified by their makers as having "standard" chamber and bore dimensions receive mark no. 41.

Shotshell Proof

One of the most interesting aspects of Spanish proof is the voluntary proof of shotshells. Manufacturers may submit these in lots of 1000, along with a sufficient number of rounds to replace those used in testing. Three types of proofs are offered—pressure, velocity, and general serviceability. For the pressure test, the proof authorities pick 20 shells from the lot; 8 are unloaded to verify uniformity in powder and shot charges and wadding. The other 12 are fired in a pressure gun. Shells with 65mm cases and 12 and 16 gauge cases in 70mm, must not generate an average pressure over 8400 psi. For other shells the maximum permissible average pressure is 9100 psi. No single shell may *greatly*(?) exceed these averages.

For velocity tests, 10 cartridges are fired, velocity being measured at 10 meters. Average velocity must conform to specifications of shot weight for each gauge. A general serviceability test is made with 10 cartridges fired from an ordinary shotgun. To pass this test there must be no misfires, ruptured cases or other defects.

Those batches of cartridges which pass these tests are returned to the manufacturer with a proof house certificate attached to each box of shells indicating the proofs they have passed. Should a lot of shells pass the pressure test but fail the others, they are returned to the manufacturer without a certificate. If a lot fails the pressure test, each of the 1000 cartridges must be unloaded in the presence of a proof official! ●

References

[1] Gregorio de Mujica, *Eibar, monografía historica*, 2nd ed., Zarauz, 1956, pp. 77, 89-90.
[2] "Banc d'épreuves des armes à feu d'Eibar," *Armurerie liégeoise*, Liége, February, 1907, p. 947.
[3] "L'Epreuve obligatoire des armes à feu en Espagne," *Armurerie liégeoise*, Liége, October 1907, p. 1009.
[4] "Dans les bancs d'épreuve étrangers," *Armurerie liégeoise*, Liége, June 1924, p. 55.

Bibliography

In addition to the works cited in the references, an excellent work has recently appeared on Spanish arms: J.D. Lavin, *A History of Spanish Firearms*, New York, 1965; it contains several references to proof in the 16th, 17th and 18th centuries, as well as some makers' marks. For information regarding current proof practices, and a copy of the proof house rules, the author is indebted to Lt. Col. Carlos Ruiz Diaz, Director of the Eibar Proof House.

Proof marks on a Sarasqueta 16-gauge double gun made in 1965. The "12-70" stamp at lower left is wrong, the workman having been misled, probably, by the weight—"1270 Gmos." Such errors are not uncommon. (A) Shows bore diameter at provisional proof. (B) Indicates degree of choke and diameter of cylindrical sections. Choke in left barrel has 0.8mm constriction; right has 0.4mm. (C) Makers' name and mark. (D) Weight of barrels in grams. (E) 12-70, gauge and chamber length in millimeters, but should read "16-70." (F) shows maximum definitive proof pressure in kilograms.

FORTY-ROD GUN

by LUCIAN CARY

YOUNG BALLENTYNE didn't know, in the beginning, what J. M. Pyne meant by "a forty-rod gun," or "string measurement," or "the bud." He had never heard of Enoch Worden or Adam Vondersmith. The plan he formed, as J. M. Pyne talked about the old days, was innocent. He did not mean to start a war.

Young Ballentyne went to J. M. Pyne's shop that wintry afternoon as he always did when he got back to the Bridge for a day. He saw a car standing in the snow by the mail-box, and knew that J. M. Pyne had a visitor.

J. M. Pyne opened the door himself. Young Ballentyne saw that J. M. Pyne's white beard was freshly trimmed. It gave his patriarchal head a roguish air. J. M. Pyne introduced young Ballentyne to the visitor.

His name was Walcott and he had something to do with a sportsmen's magazine. Young Ballentyne stood silently by while J. M. Pyne continued his talk with Walcott. You always stood up when you visited J. M. Pyne, because J. M. Pyne was always standing. He was seventy-five, but he had stood at bench and lathe all his life. It never occurred to him to sit down to talk.

Walcott was asking if it was true that modern high-power rifles would shoot better than old-time ones.

"At long range," J. M. Pyne said. "They have more power to buck the wind."

"I've read," young Ballentyne said, "that a Springfield 30-06 will beat an old-time, black powder rifle at any range from fifty feet to a thousand yards."

J. M. Pyne looked at him. "Yes," he said. But young Ballentyne knew from his tone that he didn't mean "Yes." He meant, "So you believe that, do you?"

"Of course," young Ballentyne said, "he didn't mean the Springfield service rifle or the national match. He meant a Springfield with a heavy barrel — a bull gun."

J. M. Pyne went to a cabinet of small shallow drawers and took out three heavy cards about the size of cabinet photographs.

He put one of the cards on the bench and laid a steel rule across the group of bullet holes in the center of it and picked up his magnifying glass. He said the group measured an inch and nine sixty-fourths on centers. The other two groups measured within a quarter of an inch the same. There wasn't a shot in the whole thirty but would have hit a half dollar.

J. M. Pyne picked up the cards in one hand and held them out. "You can't beat

I first read this enjoyable and instructive story over 25 years ago. Published in The Saturday Evening Post for April 18, 1936, it was one of a near-dozen or so pieces written by the famed Lucian Cary, for many years thereafter the gun editor of True magazine.

All had to do with guns and shooting, and I read them all with pleasure. Over the years, in the back of my mind, was the thought that I'd like to bring these stories — or some of them — to the attention of our readers. Here, then, is "Forty Rod Gun" for your reading entertainment — and it shouldn't be too hard to guess that J. M. Pyne and Adam Vondersmith are H. M. Pope and George Schalck, rather thinly disguised. I hope you like it. If you do, I hope you will let us know. We can re-publish more of these stories. JTA

that," he said.

"Those groups," Walcott said, "were shot at two hundred yards?"

"Yes," J. M. Pyne said.

"With a Pyne muzzle-loader?"

"Yes," J. M. Pyne said. He looked at the cards as if it did him good to see again the shooting one of his rifles had done. "John Kelly shot them with a 38 I made for him, with a toggle-joint starter that would put anything down the barrel, and a twenty-power scope." He looked up at Walcott. "That," he said — "that was a gun. I wish I had it now. I tried to get it back when John Kelly died, but somebody else got there first."

"So," young Ballentyne said, "you think a Pyne muzzle-loader would beat a Springfield bull gun up to two hundred yards."

"Up to forty rods," J. M. Pyne said, "shooting double rest, shortest string to count, I'd rather have a gun like the one I made for John Kelly."

"There are men who wouldn't agree with you," Walcott said.

"There are a lot of men who don't know as much about rifles as they think they do," J. M. Pyne said. "In the old days, they would have had to prove their notions in competition. In the old days, men got together and shot double rest at forty rods, and when they got through they knew which gun was best."

J. M. Pyne put the John Kelly targets back in the drawer of the cabinet. Then he stared fiercely at Walcott.

"Where do you think the old-time rifle makers got their reputations? By talk? No. They made their reputations at the target."

"I don't even know who they were," young Ballentyne said.

J. M. Pyne turned on him. "You never heard of Billinghurst or Horace Warner or Norman Brockway?"

"No," young Ballentyne said.

"You ought to have," J. M. Pyne said.

"Were they better than the men who came after?" young Ballentyne asked.

"They didn't know some of the things we found out later," J. M. Pyne said.

"Was any man in your time as good as you were?" Walcott asked.

Young Ballentyne was embarrassed to hear Walcott ask that question. But J. M. Pyne was not embarrassed.

"I am an engineer," he said. "I went to M.I.T. I had the edge on them."

He turned and leaned his back against the bench and took off both pairs of glasses and wiped the lenses carefully.

"There was one man who made me hump myself," he continued. "He was a young German whose father came over in '48 and settled in Pennsylvania. He and I both worked for a while in Enoch Worden's shop in Vermont. He was the most stubborn, pigheaded, obstinate cuss I ever knew. His name was Adam Vondersmith."

J. M. Pyne paused, remembering the past. Young Ballentyne and Walcott waited patiently for him to go on.

"If he hadn't been so pigheaded he would have been as good as I was," J. M. Pyne said. "He wouldn't admit anything. I beat him in a rest match, shooting lubricated bullets against his paper-patched ones. He wouldn't admit that the lubricated bullet was as good. He said I won because I was a better judge of wind than he was. There's nothing you can do with a man that's pigheaded. We had an argument one morning and Vondersmith lost his temper. I was sort of exasperated myself. Enoch Worden fired us both. Vondersmith went his way and I went mine. I never saw him but once after that. We didn't speak. That was fifty years ago."

"Is Vondersmith still making rifles?" young Ballentyne asked.

J. M. Pyne shook his head. "I don't know," he said. "If he's still alive, he must be pretty old. He was a year older than I was."

"Did you know," Walcott asked, "that Enoch Worden is still living?"

J. M. Pyne turned sharply. "No," he said. "He can't be."

"He is," Walcott said. "My grandfather knows him. They used to shoot in the rest matches at Vernon, in Vermont. Worden retired thirty years ago. But he's still living in some little town in Massachusetts."

"Enoch Worden must be nearly a hundred years old," J. M. Pyne said.

"He's ninety-five," Wolcott said, "but he's as smart as ever."

"If he is," J. M. Pyne said, "he's pretty smart."

"We've got to stage a double-rest match at forty rods under the old rules," young Ballentyne said to Walcott, after they left J. M. Pyne. "I'd like to see J. M. Pyne beat some of these birds who think a Springfield bull gun is the last word in accuracy."

"I'm afraid we couldn't stir up much interest in such a match," Walcott said. "The men who shoot bull guns are so sure their rifles are better than black powder guns that they wouldn't bother to come out and prove it."

"Suppose there was money in it. Suppose there was a thousand dollars up."

"That would be different," Walcott admitted.

"I think I can get my father to put up the thousand dollars," young Ballentyne said.

They planned it standing there in the snow outside J. M. Pyne's shop. Walcott said he would start a controversy in his magazine about the relative accuracy of black powder rifles and modern ones, and when the argument got bitter, he would announce the match for the Fourth of July. He was sure his grandfather would bring Enoch Worden to the match. They would make it an event. They would hunt out all the old-time riflemen

who were still alive. They might even find Adam Vondersmith.

Young Ballentyne was starting his car when Walcott called out to him.

"Listen, Ballentyne," he said. "What if J. M. Pyne doesn't win?"

"But he will," young Ballentyne said.

Young Ballentyne drove home, and as he drove he was not so sure. Old men were prone to exaggerate the achievements of the past. J. M. Pyne was an old man now.

* * *

Young Ballentyne learned, after writing a good many letters, that Adam Vondersmith had a shop near Williamsport, in Pennsylvania. Young Ballentyne got up of a morning in spring to drive down there. He came, late that afternoon, to a neat white house with a shop built alongside it. He knocked at the shop entrance and got no answer. He opened the door and walked in. A bell tinkled overhead. He saw a rifling machine, and, on beyond, at a bench under a bank of windows, a tall old man with a white beard.

Young Ballentyne saw that the old man was wearing three pairs of glasses, one in front of the other. He had a graver in his hand, and on the bench was something that looked like a twenty-dollar gold piece.

"It is not, I believe, forbidden by these new laws," the old man said. "I engraved that gold piece thirty years ago to put in the head of a cane I gave an old friend. Now his widow wishes also I should engrave the date of his death and a few words for her son, to whom she gives it."

Young Ballentyne gave the old man a proof of the program for the double-rest matches at forty rods and asked him to read it.

"It is good," he said when he had finished. "It is now many years since I have seen so much prize money offered. In the old time, I have known it to be more. Once my old friend, Will Hays, took the prize money for the *Schützenbundesfest* home in a satchel, so no one could steal it. The satchel was very heavy. The sum was twenty-five thousand dollars, and so much of it was in gold, it was almost more than he could carry."

"Twenty-five thousand d o l l a r s !" young Ballentyne said.

"*Ja*, for one week of matches and maybe one thousand shooters."

Adam Vondersmith gave the program back to young Ballentyne and picked up his graver.

"I came to ask you if you would shoot in our match," young Ballentyne said.

Adam Vondersmith looked up sharply. "*Ach Herrje*," he said, "I do not shoot any more."

"We would like very much to have you," young Ballentyne said.

"No," Adam Vondersmith said. "I

"Yes," said Pyne, "John Kelly shot that 200 yard group with a 38 I made up for him."

vill not shoot."

"I drove all the way from Boston to ask you."

"Today you drive from Boston? You must be tired," he said. He laid down his graver and called out, "Sophy! Sophy!"

A little pink-cheeked old lady appeared at the side door. Adam Vondersmith spoke to her in German.

"*Ach, du lieber Gott!*" she said. She turned to young Ballentyne. "So, you come by Boston already. I have coffee and *Kuchen.*"

Adam Vondersmith took off his apron. "I also will have coffee and *Kuchen,*" he said.

Young Ballentyne followed Mrs. Vondersmith through the side door of the shop, through a kitchen of an amazing neatness, and into the dining room. He sat down at the dining-room table with Adam Vondersmith while his wife ran back and forth, bringing the coffeepot from the kitchen range, and hot milk and slices of cinnamon cake and coffee cake.

She waited on them, refusing to sit down. Young Ballentyne wondered how J. M. Pyne could have contrived to quarrel with a man as gentle as Adam Vondersmith. But it was plain that he was immovable. Young Ballentyne had no hope of persuading him to change his mind and shoot in the match.

"Mr. Vondersmith," he said, "did you ever know a rifle maker named J. M. Pyne?"

Adam Vondersmith leaned forward. "*Ja,*" he said. "I know him — that Johnny Pyne." He turned to his wife and spoke again in German.

Little Mrs. Vondersmith threw up her hands. "*Ach, du lieber Gott!*" she cried. "That man! So hot-tempered! He vas crazy! He vould have killed my husband if Mr. Worden had not stopped him!"

"No," Adam Vondersmith said with sudden violence. "No, he vould not have killed me. I vould have killed him."

"What happened?" young Ballentyne asked.

Adam Vondersmith thrust his chin out at young Ballentyne. "Do you know anything about shooting?" he demanded. "Do you know what a pinhead is?"

"Yes," young Ballentyne said, "it's a tiny bead on a thin stem, used for a front sight."

"So," Adam Vondersmith said. "Do you also know what an aperture front sight is?"

"It is a small ring through which you see the bull's-eye."

"So," A d a m Vondersmith said. "That is how it started. We are talking about sights that morning. Johnny Pyne says he has found out a pinhead is the best of all front sights. I say I do not think so. I tell him I think the aperture is more better." He paused to throw his hands wide. "Which is so — and everybody knows it is so. But you cannot tell Johnny Pyne anything. No matter how I explain to him why the aperture is more better than the pinhead, he says the pinhead is better. Pretty soon he gets crazy mad and curses me for a pigheaded Dutchman, vich I am not. I am High German. So I tell him he is one dumbhead Yankee, vich is the truth. And I see he has a hammer in his hand, and he is so crazy mad he is going to hit me with it, so I pick up my hammer, and just before I hit him we hear a roar behind us, and we turn, and it is Enoch Vorden. He is a small man — Enoch Vorden. But when he is mad he has a voice like an Old Country drill sergeant.

" 'Stop!' he yells. And we stop. Enoch Vorden says he has had enough of us. We are through. But we can only leave separately, and not together, because he will not let us kill each other."

Adam Vondersmith shrugged his shoulders.

"That is vot happens. Me and Johnny Pyne have worked together at the bench for one whole year, but we never speak to each other again. Vot can you do when a man has such a temper? You can do nothing with such a man."

"Wasn't Pyne a good workman?"

young Ballentyne asked.

"Donnerwetter kreuzmillion!" Adam Vondersmith yelled. "Did I say he vas not a good workman?" He leaned forward and fixed young Ballentyne with his blue eyes. "I vill tell you something — that Johnny Pyne is not only good. He vas the best rifle maker in the whole vorld."

"I've always heard that he was good," young Ballentyne said.

"Ach! What you hear people say! What does that mean? *Macht nichts aus!* They know nothing. Nothing. But me, I know. I can put a soft-lead slug in the breech and upset it so it fills the grooves, and push it through the barrel, and tell you how good the man who made it vas. When I have put a slug through a Pyne barrel, I know this is the end — this is as far as man can go."

"Mr. Pyne has promised to shoot in our match," young Ballentyne said.

"But how vould he?" Adam Vondersmith asked. "He is an old man. He is almost as old as I am."

"Just the same," young Ballentyne said, "he has promised to shoot."

"Ach, Herrje!" Adam Vondersmith cried. "You are telling the truth?"

"Yes," young Ballentyne said, "I am telling the truth."

Adam Vondersmith brought his fist down on the table so hard that the coffee cups jumped out of their saucers.

"Then I also vill shoot," he said. "And I vill beat him. I have the rifle to beat him."

"That's the spirit, Mr. Vondersmith," young Ballentyne said.

"My boy," Adam Vondersmith said, "you vill see something. And Johnny Pyne vill see something — something he does not expect."

Young Ballentyne drove back to Boston and M.I.T., and wondered, as he drove, what Adam Vondersmith had in reserve. He seemed so sure he had the gun to beat J. M. Pyne.

* * *

Young Ballentyne stopped for J. M. Pyne before daylight that Fourth of July. He had a hundred miles to drive, and he wanted to be there early.

He and Walcott had spread out the thousand dollars in prize money so it would do the most good. They had allotted two hundred an fifty dollars for each of three ten-shot matches — one hundred dollars for first place, seventy-five dollars for second place, fifty dollars for third place, and twenty-five dollars for fourth place. That left two hundred and fifty dollars. They had agreed to give the two hundred and fifty in one lump sum to the man who made the best score in all three matches.

"I wish," J. M. Pyne said — "I wish I had my John Kelly gun. That toggle-joint starter pushed the bullet down so gently there was no upsettage. There is some upsettage when you hit the starter a blow with the heel of your hand. There's got to be. And it can't always be the same."

Young Ballentyne parked his car at the range and got out J. M. Pyne's rifle and his shooting bag.

J. M. Pyne made a gesture toward the rifle. "I'll carry that," he said.

"I don't mind," Ballentyne said.

"I mind," J. M. Pyne said. "I want to carry my own gun — as I have for fifty years."

Young Ballentyne had to give him the rifle. J. M. Pyne hung the rifle over his shoulder by the strap on the canvas case and trudged toward the shed where the loading stands were and the long line of benches for double-rest shooting. J. M. Pyne did not get far before he was stopped by friends who wanted to shake his hand and wish him well. Young Ballentyne saw that the shed was a l r e a d y crowded. He hurried on. He had to find Walcott and arrange to close the entries at ten o'clock. It seemed to him that every man there had a Springfied bull gun. He saw a dozen marines. He knew how well the marines shot at Camp Perry.

Young Ballentyne was so busy making up lists of shooters and assigning them to relays that he had no chance to see what J. M. Pyne was doing. And then he heard a shout and looked up and saw Adam Vondersmith coming down the line with a rifle in a case over his shoulder.

Young Ballentyne stood up to watch. It was J. M. Pyne who had shouted.

"Why, Adam," J. M. Pyne was saying, "I'm glad to see you."

"I'm glad to see you, Johnny," Adam Vondersmith was saying. "I'd have been glad to see you any day for fifty years."

You knew from the sound of their voices, from the way they continued to shake hands, that they meant what they said. It was touching to see the two old men making friends again.

"Adam," J. M. Pyne was saying, "I never had anything against you. It was foolish for us to quarrel over a thing like that. You know it was foolish, and by this time you know you were dead wrong about a pinhead. You know an aperture is no good except when the light is just right."

"Johnny," Adam Vondersmith cried, "you are wrong; you are wrong."

"Adam," J. M. Payne said earnestly, "you've never used a pinhead that was right. When a pinhead is right, it looks the same size as the bull. You put the top of the pinhead at the bottom of the bull, and the pinhead and the bull make a perfect figure 8, and if you're sighted in, you've got a center

"You pigheaded Dutchman," J. M. Pyne interrupted, "you don't listen to what I'm telling you!"

shot."

"You are yust the same as effer, Johnny!" Adam Vondersmith yelled. "Nobody can tell you anything! You know it all! You think, you *Shafskopf*, that because a pinhead ——"

"Adam," J. M. Pyne broke in, "you're wrong about the simplest principles of optics. You don't know ——"

"Donner und blitzen!" Adam Vondersmith yelled. "I know what everybody knows — that an aperture is the best sight that——"

"You pigheaded Dutchman," J. M. Pyne interrupted; "you don't listen to what I'm telling you!"

Men stood round and listened and marveled at the passion with which they argued. Young Ballentyne thought it would never end. And then he saw a little old man with chin whiskers coming down the line on the arm of a slightly younger man. The little man walked in carpet slippers, with a stick in his free hand. His head was completely bald. His upper lip was clean-shaven. But his lower lip, his chin, his cheeks wore the most luxuriant whiskers young Ballentyne had ever seen. Young Ballentyne knew who he was — who he must be.

Enoch Worden walked straight up to J. M. Pyne and Adam Vondersmith.

"Boys!" Enoch Worden said to those two old men. "Boys!"

They did not hear him.

"You don't understand plain English," J. M. Pyne said, shaking his finger in Adam Vondersmith's face.

"You *Dummkopf*," Adam Vondersmith said. "You always vas crazy."

Enoch Worden's mouth set in a grim line above his chin whiskers. Enoch Worden raised his stick and rapped J. M. Pyne hard across the shins, and almost in the same motion he walloped Adam Vondersmith.

J. M. Pyne and Adam Vondersmith reached for their shins, as any man will when he's struck there. They reached for their shins and forgot each other and saw Enoch Worden, and, seeing him, they were no longer privileged old men. They were boys again in the presence of the boss. They bowed to Enoch Worden. They gave him the deference that courteous youth gives to old age. They shook Enoch Worden's hand; they told him how well he looked; they reminded him of his great past.

But again Enoch Worden shut his mouth in that thin line. He raised his stick. "You've talked enough, you two," he said. "Now get to work." He waved his stick at two marines ensconced at rest benches with Springfield bull guns and telescope sights. "Look at that," Enoch Worden said. "Are you two going to stand here chattering when you've got that to beat?"

A bull gun spoke just then. A bull gun spoke and the hills rattled.

Enoch Worden raised his head. "Are you two going to let a man with a thing like that beat fine rifles?"

Enoch Worden laid a strip of paper across the targets, measuring each shot from the center of the target. Pyne's was the shortest string. The target shown underprinted on page 125 was shot by Harry Pope on April 2, 1912.

"No, sir," J. M. Pyne said meekly.

"Ach, Herrje," Adam Vondersmith exclaimed. "I am again making a fool of myself."

Young Ballentyne took J. M. Pyne's shooting bag to him. J. M. Pyne got his telescope sight out of its cloth bag. Young Ballentyne pulled the 32-40 out of its case. And while J. M. Pyne put the telescope in place and turned up the screws tightly, young Ballentyne laid out the boxes of bullets, the primers, the false muzzle and the starter.

"I guess," he said to J. M. Pyne — "I guess you're ready to fire a fouling shot."

But J. M. Pyne was not listening. He was staring at Adam Vondersmith, three yards away at another loading bench.

"Do you see what he's got?" J. M. Pyne demanded.

Young Ballentyne looked across at Adam Vondersmith. He was fitting a strange implement to the false muzzle of his rifle — an affair with two metal arms opposite each other.

"Don't you know a toggle-joint starter when you see it?" J. M. Pyne said. "The son of a gun has got my John Kelly gun."

"Well," young Ballentyne said, trying to think of something soothing to say to J. M. Pyne, "well ——"

"I waited until John Kelly had been buried a week before I wrote his widow that I wanted to buy back that gun. I thought it was only decent to wait a week. But that Dutchman didn't wait a week."

"At least," young Ballentyne said, "it means he admits a Pyne rifle is better than anything that he can

make."

J. M. Pyne waved his hand at the range. "Look," he said.

The long red silk ribbons that he preferred for wind flags were lifting clear of the posts on which they hung. The long red ribbons were snapping in the gusts.

"He never was a good judge of wind," J. M. Pyne said. "He can't beat me today — not even with my own forty-rod gun."

J. M. Pyne prepared his target. He pasted a long strip of white paper across the top. Then he got out the little steel rule he always carried, and measured off three inches from the center toward the top, and put a black target paster, perhaps three-quarters of an inch square, on that point.

"That's my bud," he said.

"Your aiming point," young Ballentyne said.

J. M. Pyne put a row of target pasters clear across the top of his target, each one inch from the next.

"That's my wind gauge," he said. "If the wind is blowing the bullet three inches to the left, I'll hold on the third paster to the right from the center, and so on."

Young Ballentyne called the first relay and walked down to the butt with the men who were going to shoot. He saw them tack up their targets. He saw that Adam Vondersmith was using a red wafer of the sort that's put on legal papers for a bud. There was a fellow who used four pasters marking the corners of a square. But J. M. Pyne was the only man who had a wind gauge on his target.

Young Ballentyne took up his post behind a big spotting telescope when they got back from the butts. There were sixty men on the line, and J. M. Pyne and Adam Vondersmith were the only ones who were shooting old-time rifles. The relay got impatient waiting for J. M. Pyne and Adam Vondersmith to load. A big marine with a Springfield bull gun sat beside his rest bench and muttered, "Come on. Come on." But he had to wait until Enoch Worden called, "Time."

Rifles cracked all along the line when Enoch Worden gave the signal. Young Ballentyne looked over at J. M. Pyne. He saw that the old man was holding his fire. He was watching the wind flags. Young Ballentyne saw the wind flags stiffen in a gust. J. M. Pyne threw up his head. Enoch Worden called out, "One minute to go." Young Ballentyne wondered if J. M. Pyne would ever shoot. Enoch Worden called out, "Thirty seconds to go." And still J. M. Pyne waited. Enoch Worden called fifteen seconds. And still J. M. Pyne waited. Young Ballentyne saw the wind flags dip. He saw the wind flags drop. And then J. M. Pyne's rifle spoke. It sounded like a 22 after the crashes of the bull guns. It sounded so slow — go bang! How could it ever compete with the power and speed of modern military rifles?

Young Ballentyne looked into the big spotting scope to see where J. M. Pyne's shot had struck. J. M. Pyne's first shot had taken out the center where the diagonals crossed as neatly as if the target had been lying on the bench and he had used a wadcutter. Young Ballentyne swung the scope to look at the other targets. Adam Vondersmith had a shot half an inch from dead center. The big marine had done as well. Not one man in ten was more than two inches from center with his first shot.

There was no way to tell which man had won until they had brought the targets back and Enoch Worden had measured them. Enoch Worden took a clean strip of paper and laid it on a target and measured from the center of it to the center of a shot hole, and made a mark; then he put the mark on the center of the target and measured to the center of another shot hole, and so on, adding automatically the sum of the deviation of the shots from center.

Young Ballentyne hung over Enoch Worden's shoulder to watch him. But he could not stay. He had to get another relay going. He didn't know who had won until he heard somebody shout. He turned and saw them pounding J. M. Pyne on the back, and knew that J. M. Pyne had the shortest string. He saw J. M. Pyne walk back to his loading stand, and went over.

"Who got second?" young Ballentyne asked.

"Vondersmith," J. M. Pyne said. "He should have won that match. His elevation didn't vary half an inch. But he had his shots strung out with the wind. He never was a judge of wind."

"Who got third?" young Ballentyne asked.

J. M. Pyne jerked his thumb at the big marine who had been so impatient while he waited for J. M. Pyne and Adam Vondersmith to load their old-time guns.

"My string was five and three-quarters," J. M. Pyne said. "Vondersmith had six inches. That marine had six and one-eighth inches."

Young Ballentyne learned, late in the afternoon, that J. M. Pyne had won the second ten-shot match. He went over to congratulate J. M. Pyne. But J. M. Pyne was not smiling.

"What's the matter?" young Ballentyne asked.

"Firing pin broke," J. M. Pyne said.

"But surely you can borrow a firing pin."

"There are only two single-shot rifles on this range," J. M. Pyne said. "One is mine and the other is Vondersmith's. You wouldn't find a firing pin that would fit my gun within a hundred miles."

"At least," young Ballentyne said, "you've won two of the three matches."

"I've lost my chance for the third match and for the main prize — for the shortest string in all three matches."

"I'm sorry," young Ballentyne said. "I'm afraid that means a bull gun is going to win."

"No, it doesn't," J. M. Pyne said. "You wait and see."

Young Ballentyne saw him walk slowly over to Adam Vondersmith's loading stand. Young Ballentyne started that way and paused. He was near enough to hear what they said.

"Adam," J. M. Pyne said huskily — "Adam, I'm out of it. I've broken the firing pin of my rifle. It's up to you. The rest is up to you."

"Johnny," Adam Vondersmith said, "I'd give my right arm to win this match."

"You don't have to do that," J. M. Pyne said. "You only have to do what I tell you to do."

"Was ist das?" Adam Vondersmith cried.

"You're a poor judge of wind," J. M. Pyne said. "You always were. What you've got to do in this last match is line up your gun and wait until I touch you on the shoulder. When I touch you — pull."

Adam Vondersmith glared at J. M. Pyne and the veins knotted in his temples.

"Donner und blitzen," he said. "You think you can teach me how to shoot?"

"It wasn't my idea," J. M. Pyne said. "It's what Enoch Worden says."

Adam Vondersmith opened his mouth to speak, and thought better of it and swallowed hard. "So," he said in a low voice — "so it shall be."

Young Ballentyne watched them as they worked together, a little awed by their intensity. Adam Vondersmith loaded the John Kelly gun while J. M. Pyne stood by. Adam Vondersmith laid the John Kelly gun on the rest bench, the muzzle just so, and waited, his eye at the telescope sight. J. M. Pyne stood behind him, watching the wind. After three, four, sometimes almost five minutes, J. M. Pyne was satisfied that the wind was the same as for the last shot. He touched Adam Vondersmith on the shoulder and the John Kelly gun spoke.

They had to score the last targets by lantern light. The sun had gone down and the moon had come up, and still Enoch Worden sat at a table with clean strips of paper and a pencil, measuring string after string. Men stood five deep behind him, watching and waiting. Enoch Worden saved Adam Vondersmith's target till the last. Men who had shot bull guns nudged one another when they saw it, not willing to believe their eyes. Enoch Worden took a silver dollar from his waistcoat pocket and laid it on the target. It covered all the shots. Enoch Worden measured the target with great care. The string came to four and one-quarter inches, meaning that the average deviation of the shots from center was less than half an inch.

Enoch Worden stood up and found his stick and smiled. "Adam Vondersmith has won the third ten-shot match," he said. "He has also won the grand prize for the shortest string in three matches — in the whole thirty shots."

"But for your gun, I could not have done it, Johnny," Adam Vondersmith said to J. M. Pyne. "It is really you who von this match."

"Thank you, Adam," J. M. Pyne said. "If I couldn't win myself, I'd rather see you win."

"I could not have von without your gun," Adam Vondersmith said, "and maybe I could not have von without you there to keep me from shooting on the wrong vind. I never vas a goot judge of vind. I admit it. That is vhy you beat me fifty years ago, shooting your lubricated bullets against my paper-patched ones. That is vhy you make scores with a pinhead that I could not make with the aperture, vich is so much better."

"You pigheaded Dutchman," J. M. Pyne said. "You ——"

He got no farther. Enoch Worden swung his stick sharply — swish, swish! J. M. Pyne reached for his shins, and so did Adam Vondersmith.

"That will do," Enoch Worden said. "Don't you know you've won? Don't you know you've beaten these fellows who thought a bull gun was better than a handmade rifle? Don't you know it took you both to do it? Can't you see it's time to quit and be friends?"

HANDLOADER'S TROUBLES, CURES

*Here's a wealth of valuable tips on how
to overcome the many handloading problems
that can—and do—arise. Required reading
for the beginner, new information for the expert.*

by BOB HAGEL

THERE IS nothing particularly difficult or complicated about loading your own ammunition; in fact it's a lot easier than most uninitiated people seem to think. The beginner can buy one or several of the many loading manuals on today's market, study them with an eye toward digesting what they have to say, and then he (or she) can go right ahead and do a creditable job of brewing up his own personal brand of ammunition. Don't try to take shortcuts: after you have loaded a box or two, don't get the notion that you know more about handloading than the fellows who wrote the manual, and you'll get along OK.

If you are starting out to load your own for the first time, it is a good idea to buy a loading manual* before you start buying tools, that is, unless you have a friend who already knows the ropes, one who will hand you some sage advice. It has always seemed to me that the average guy starting out to roll his own ammo, especially if he's *not* short of cash, is inclined to make the same mistakes as the novice photographer; he goes gadget-happy. True, a gadget bag full of camera accessories is handy to have around, and so is a bench full of assorted loading tools and gadgets for this and that, but it's pretty easy to wind up with a lot of hard-earned dollars invested in certain gadgets you seldom use; dollars that could be used for powder, bullets, primers and more shooting.

Some of my friends manufacturing loading tools may take a dim view of some of the things I'll mention here, comments aimed toward eliminating their gadgets that are not especially essential to loading good ammo. I doubt, however, that it will cut any great holes in their sales, because the handloader who gets serious and loads for several calibers will eventually buy more and better tools anyway.

This is not intended to tell the beginner what tools to buy or not to buy, but to show him a few kinks whereby he can make the most of what tools he has, or show him how to use something he already has available instead of buying something new. At the same time we'll describe some of the many pitfalls even seasoned handloaders fall into, and how to avoid them—how to get the most out of handloading for the best ammunition with the least frustration and cost.

Case Preparation

Chamfering The first thing you must have to load your own ammunition is empty cases, fired or new. Now a case that has never been reloaded has a mouth that is square and flat, often even turned in a little; this is true of a once-fired factory load because it was crimped into the crimping groove on the factory bullet. To make the new bullet start into the mouth of the re-sized case without hanging up and scraping the jacket, the case mouth must be chamfered (inside beveled or angled). There are several tools made especially for this, and they are good, handy and cheap, but I wish I had a dollar for every case I've chamfered with a common pocket knife! Just hold the case in one hand, mouth out, press the thumb of the other hand against the neck or shoulder of the case, insert point of blade at about a 45° angle inside case mouth and rotate around inside case. You'll get perfect chamfers after a little practice.

A lot of handloaders will have a shop with a drill press, or a power hand drill. In this case, using a common countersink chucked in the drill or press, you can chamfer cases as fast as you can pick them up. The drill press should be set at low speed; the hand drill should be put on a stand or otherwise held firmly.

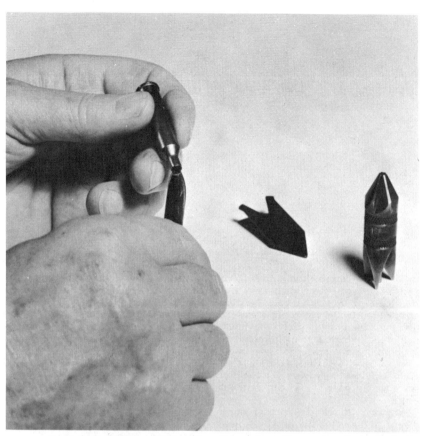

Inside neck chamfering can be done with a pocket knife, too. At right there's the Bonanza Cricket and the RCBS chamfer tool. These last bevel case mouths inside and out.

Shooters Service & Dewey, Clinton Corners, N.Y. 12514, recently developed a primer pocket cleaner that's at once compact, easy-to-use, and works well. This small, hardened-steel tool cleans .175" and .210" pockets, sells for $2.75. SS&D makes other excellent products for the shooter-reloader-benchrester — among them a precision bullet spinner, straight-line bullet seaters, custom-made neck dies, etc. Write for their price list.

Primer Pockets Another item of case preparation is the cleaning of primer pockets on fired cases. It may come as a surprise to some younger reloaders, but there was a time when primer pockets were not nearly as shallow as they are today; for hunting ammunition, where the Nth degree of accuracy was not required, we punched out the old primer and seated a new one in the sizing operation without taking the case from the press to clean the primer pocket. The pockets were then deep enough that you could reprime several times before cleaning was needed, and you never had a "bugged" primer, either. Today this has all changed; primer pockets are so shallow that you're lucky if you can seat some brands of

Primer pocket cleaning can be done with many different tools. That's the RCBS idea at the left, usable for both .175" and .210" pockets. An Allen wrench serves well, too, operated with a swirling motion, as does a screwdriver with the correct-diameter bit. See text for details.

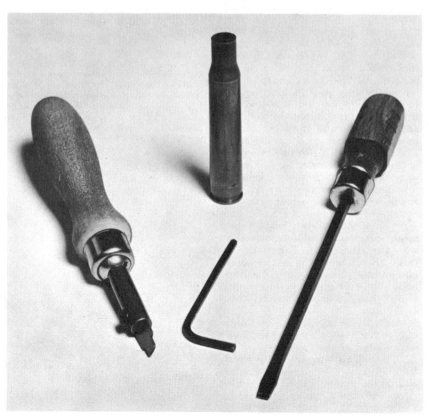

The Herter tool at left quickly and accurately gauges flash-hole diameter within broad limits. The Zenith Primer Mike shown measures protrusion or depression of the seated cap in .001″ increments.

This is Lee Engineering's new low-cost ($2.45) priming tool. Compact and light, it offers sensitive primer seating, comes with both small- and large primer rods. Interchangeable heads—for all popular calibers—are extra at $1.50 each.

primers in certain makes of cases without having them stick up above the base, even if the pockets were scraped perfectly clean. It seems to me that there is entirely too much guff being written that in order to load accurate ammunition you must have a special primer seating tool. Hell, with most new cases you couldn't seat the primer too deep without crushing it.

Anyway, to seat the primer down where it doesn't stick its shiny nose above the face of the case head, you have to clean the bottom of the pocket out right down to the brass. For this they make little steel brushes that fit inside the pocket and are rotated to clean it, blade-like affairs that are also turned in the pocket, etc. There are other tools—not made for the purpose— that are easier to use and work better.

A small, short screwdriver with a shank just smaller than the primer pocket, polished round on the edges that would touch the sides of the pocket, and filed fairly sharp on the bit, works very well. A 222 Remington case with the neck squeezed flat, then filed to the correct width (.170″ or .200″), will also work better than most commercial tools. Many times I've used a small Allen or hex wrench of about 1/16″ diameter, and it works about as well as anything I know of. To use this insert the long end into the pocket, then use a stirring motion around the edges—like stirring flapjacks in a bowl, if you know what I mean—and not a rotating motion as with the other tools. The reason for this is that it cleans the bottom perimeter of the pocket around the flashhole. Which brings up a seldom-mentioned point in using the screwdriver or 222 case.

Check the bottom of a primer pocket and you'll see that it usually has a slight burr around the edge of the flash-hole. This burr keeps a perfectly flat tool from going down to the bottom of the pocket around the outside edge, and that's where your primer really seats. Make your primer pocket

cleaner a little hollow ground or concave so it gets down to the bottom on the edge. That's why most commercial tools fail to do a good job.

An end mill of the correct length, made "dead" on the sides if necessary, would remove burrs around the flash hole inside the case. It would have to be used carefully, with frequent case inspection, to avoid excessive brass removal.

While we're on primers and primer pockets, let's take a look at GI cases with crimped-in in primers. There are many tools available for removing this crimp, which has to be done to seat a new primer. Many of these are reamers of one kind or another, and if you use one you had better be careful how you do it, especially using the type that is tapered. If you ream them just a little too much, or get the tool cocked off a little while you are ream-

Right—Kuharsky Bros.' primer pocket cleaner uses wire brushes (.175″ and .210″) rotated by a crank handle. Pockets are well-cleaned, operation is rapid and effortless. Below—One of the oldest—and best—tool for the handloader is L.E. Wilson's Universal Case Trimmer. Shown standing is the Wilson Neck Reamer, usable with Trimmer, as is Wilson's Primer Pocket Reamer, not illustrated.

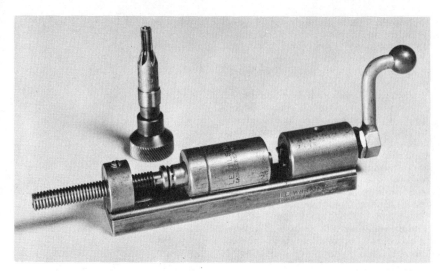

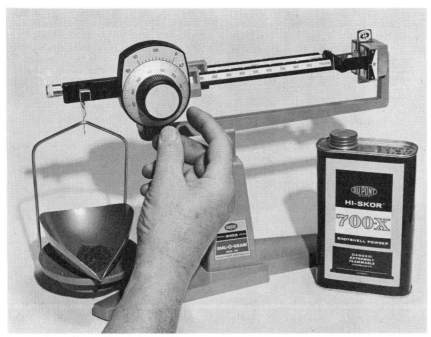

The new and radically different Ohaus Dial-O-Grain scale offers an unusual capacity and a Vernier system for powder charges up to 100-plus grains. Total capacity is 3100-plus grains, not far from a half-pound.

The Texan No. 304 has a desirably heavy base and magnetic damping. Note deep, widely-separated notches for the poises—an excellent feature not found on several other powder scales—and capacity of 510 grains.

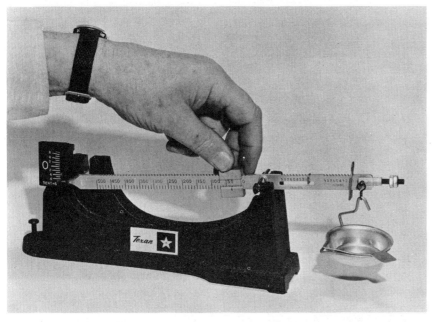

The Belding & Mull powder measure, because of its sliding motion over the charge tube (shown at the rear), maintains a virtually constant "head" of powder in the glass-fronted lower reservoir. Charges thrown are therefore more uniform, and "bridging," or powder hanging up in the drop tube used in conventional measures, is all but impossible. The B&M is a highly popular measure among precision shooters.

ing, you wind up with loose primer pockets. Better to use a swage, which pushes the crimp back where it came from, instead of reaming it out. The L.E. Wilson reamer—and perhaps others—works well and safely if used as directed in the Wilson case trimmer tool. It is then held perfectly in the axis of the primer pocket and, because the reamer is itself chamfered at its bottom edge, it cannot cut into the bottom corner. It is "dead" on the bottom also, so it can't cut the primer pocket bottom.

Neck Lubing When cases are resized, full length or neck only, the inside of the neck should be lubricated lightly so that it will slide over the expanding ball without binding. There are dry powder preparations made for this, but none I've tried works very well because they don't stick to the inside of the neck. Hair or Nylon bristle brushes are also made for this purpose, to be lightly lubricated with case sizing lube, and they work well. But if you don't have one around, just take a bronze bristle bore brush

of the right size, roll it on the lube pad and it does a very good job. It is also stiff enough to help remove powder residue.

If expander buttons were made of tungsten carbide, there'd be no such problems; case necks would ride over carbide buttons smoothly, without effort. I've suggested this to several tool producers but they've contended the extra cost would be prohibitive and the demand thus low.

Powder Scales One thing you must have to reload ammunition is a powder scale. A powder measure is convenient but certainly not a necessity. Incidentally, it's much easier to make a mistake in setting your scale than you might believe. Those beam notches are pretty close together, and it's not hard to set the weight off one way or the other one notch from the one you intend to use. If it's on the one-gr. end it makes little difference, for $\frac{1}{10}$-gr. isn't going to change much, but *watch the other end of the beam!* 5 grains too much powder could cause things to come apart in your face when you touch that one off. It most certainly will if the case is small, the powder fast and the charge you thought you'd set is maximum.

It is also possible for the weight to hang up on top of the peak between the notches, yet appear to be right on the mark. This may happen on either side of the correct notch, and if it falls off the far side you will add 5 grains and plenty of trouble. Don't think this won't happen to you; it will unless you watch it very closely.

Bullets Another pitfall that causes excessive pressures, and an occasional blowup often unaccounted for, is using the wrong bullet weight by mistake with a near-maximum charge for a lighter bullet. *Never have more than*

The Little Dripper, from Shooters' Accessory Supply (SAS), was the first of such small devices (there are now several others made). Designed to trickle a granule of powder or two onto the scale pan, thus bringing to balance the previously measure-thrown sub-weight charge. This technique permits charges to be accurately weighed quite rapidly.

one bullet weight where it is handy to pick it up and seat by mistake.

The closest I ever came to blowing up an action was in loading some experimental 6mm ammunition with a fast ball-powder that was very touchy when you reached the top. I had reached the point where the case showed enough head expansion to back off a grain for the maximum load with that bullet and powder. I loaded up another one with the load cut one grain and took it out and fired it to make sure it was below the point of head expansion. The smoke squirted out around the bolt and I had to kick the bolt handle several times with the heel of my hand to extract the case. The primer pocket was expanded to half again its normal size and the rimless case had a neat little belt where there had been none before. Thanks to the good Remington 700 action, everything held with no damage.

It took me some time to figure out what had happened. I checked the scale; everything right on the nose. There was no other powder on the bench so that wasn't it, the bullets in the box were all 70 grains. Then I remembered that I had just pulled a 100-gr. bullet from a faulty case and laid it beside the press before starting to load; it was no longer there! Picked up by mistake and loaded over the hot load of fast powder intended for the 70-gr., it had all but caused disaster. I had loaded many, many thousands of rounds of ammo, maybe so many that I became careless, but it proves it can happen to novice or veteran if you maybe have your mind on something else.

Never have more than one can of powder on the loading bench while loading, even though you intend to load the same cartridge with different powders at the same time. A charge

of fast powder where a slow powder was intended is likely to spring the seams of the best rifle, and you may lose an eye or a hand in the process.

Another thing to remember about bullets is that all projectiles of the same weight do not necessarily take the same powder charge; the powder charge that works well with one make may be dangerous with another. All bullets of one caliber but by different makers are not always the same diameter. Some will be as much as .001″ larger than those of another make. Then there is a difference in jacket hardness and, perhaps worst of all, the bearing surface is longer on some bullets than on others. The longer the bearing surface the greater the friction, and the greater the friction the higher the pressure with the same bullet weight and powder charge. The worst offender is the bullet with a very long bearing surface; if loaded to the same seating depth as a bullet of the same weight with a short bearing surface, the former will often be jammed up against the lands, kicking pressure up by several thousand pounds per square inch. When changing brands of bullets of the same weight, or even bullets of different shapes of the same brand and weight, try a load or two before corking up a couple of boxes for a hunting trip.*

Actually, in spite of all that has been written about seating depth, and what it should be in a certain cartridge with a certain bullet weight, it is next

*For an important and meaningful treatment of the effect on pressure and velocity that changing only bullets can have, see "Bullet Types and Pressures" by M. D. Waite in *The NRA Handloader's Guide*, p. 96.

to useless information. Not all makes of rifles have throats cut to the same depth, and a certain bullet seated to a suggested seating depth could easily be sticking out too far for a rifle with a short throat. If you don't know what throating your rifle has, stick to over-all factory-loaded cartridge length for that cartridge. This will usually keep you out of trouble because factory-loaded ammo has to be made up to fit any and all makes of rifles.*

If, however, you think the throat in your rifle may be long enough for seating heavy bullets out farther for more case capacity, there is an easy way to tell. Just seat a bullet out to where you want it in a dummy case, then smoke it well with a match or candle. Chamber it and see if it touches the lands, which will leave a good mark on the blackened bullet. If it touches the lands or is pushed back into the case, seat it down a little at a time until it just touches the lands— just a trace. Now seat it down 1/16″ plus the length of the mark left by the lands, and that's the best you can do for that rifle with that particular bul-

*We think it is time for some of the compilers of loading data to throw away their "seating depth" figures, invariably expressed in decimal dimensions. It is a difficult concept to deal with, for one thing. First, the over-all case length must be measured, then the length of the bullet, next these two figures added and the seating deducted to obtain over-all loaded cartridge length. This last dimension is what the handloader really needs, and it ought to be offered.

The handloader has no particular interest in seating depth as such; it offers a means—and a tedious one—of arriving at over-all loaded round length. Why, therefore, shouldn't the bullet makers or anyone else putting load data together, supply the more meaningful, simpler information? ED.

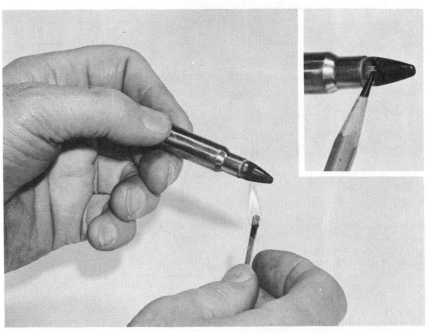

To obtain optimum/maximum over-all cartridge length seat the bullet progressively farther into the case—smoking the bullet nose between trials—until the rifling lands mark the bullet, as in the picture at right. Now seat bullet a bit deeper, allowing bullet to approach within 1/32″ or so of the lands. Note: such seating may or may not permit the cartridge to be fed from the magazine or let loaded rounds be ejected.

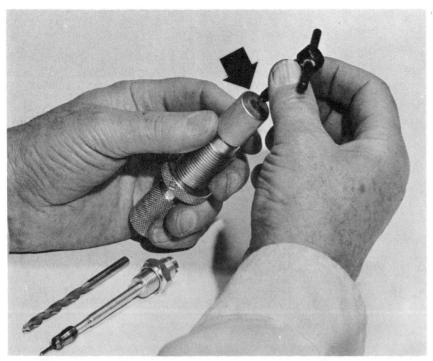

Herter's Stuck Case Remover. To use, the sizing die is removed from the press and the decapping rod unscrewed. The primer pocket is then drilled through and the sleeve (arrow) held against the case head. Next, the T-handled tap is threaded into the drilled hole (through the sleeve) and the stubborn case is pulled out. A valuable outfit when the need arises!

let. This assumes, of course, that the round so-loaded will feed from the magazine and also eject. This seating will help obtain top-rate accuracy and a pressure-velocity relationship about right for that rifle.

(Another means of determining maximum cartridge over-all length [subject to magazine and ejection requirements] can be done like this: close the action and measure to 1/16″ or better the distance from the bolt face to the muzzle. Now open the action and push the bullet being tested into the throat, holding it against the lands by a dowel or stick. Next, measure the bore from muzzle to bullet tip, then subtract this figure from the muzzle to breech face dimension, and the result is your maximum loaded cartridge length. To arrive at optimum over-all cartridge length—with the same bullet—deduct 1/16″ from the remainder found. Example: Muzzle to bolt face is 26½″. Muzzle to tip of bullet X is 23½″. Difference is 3″. Subtract 1/16″ from 3″, leaving 2 15/16″ for optimum loaded cartridge length. ED.)

Dies-Presses There are also a few kinks concerning dies and presses, as well as pitfalls, so let's take a look in that direction.

There is the question of shell holders for the various cases. There are a lot of odd sizes of case heads: some rimmed, some rimless and some belted, but you'd be surprised how many of the oddballs will fit a shell holder intended for another cartridge. It sometimes pays to try that new cartridge in a shell holder you already have before buying a new one, especially if you are not going to load many rounds for it. For instance, both 44 Special and 44 Magnum cases can be loaded using either a shell holder for the 45 Colt or one for the 300 H&H case head. They are not a perfect fit but they work well if the dies are adjusted right. Other cases will do as well with other shell holders, but be sure they fit quite tight if you intend to full length resize, or you may pull a rim off.

Speaking of dies and their adjusting, one of the best things you can do is to remove that lead pellet from the hole under the set-screw in the lock ring as soon as you get the die. I know—it's put there to keep the set-screw from damaging the die thread, but once it is tightened down and squashed out into the thread, you'll have to put the die in a vise and use pliers to loosen the ring. This is damned unhandy when you want to change it in a hurry. Take it out and throw it away; the set screw won't damage the threads if you use a little common sense in tightening it. If you're still worried about hurting the die body threads, a scrap of polyethylene or other soft plastic will work better than the lead shot—and it won't resist releasing.

The split lock rings that Bonanza uses—and sells separately— work very well, and never bind up. A quick ½-turn of their screw releases them right now.

It occasionally happens that you are loading several calibers at one time, that is, one after the other. At such times, especially when you use one press for sizing and another for seating, you may forget to change shell holders when you put in the new die. If the shell holder you're using is, say, for a belted magnum and the second cartridge is of the 30-06 headsize, and you run the '06 case into the full length sizing die, you sure won't be able to pull it out with the magnum shell holder! There's a way to do it, though, that's really simple: remove the shell holder and run the ram up until it is at the right height to let the correct shell holder be inserted *backward* over the cartridge rim and into the slot in the ram at the same time. Pull the handle and out comes the case. This won't work with shell holders that are an integral part of the ram, of course.

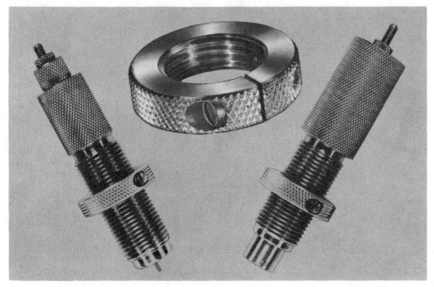

This is the Bonanza Cross Bolt Lock Ring, threaded ⅞-14 for standard reloading dies. A turn of the cross bolt quickly locks the ring on the die body, while loosening the bolt instantly frees the die. A great improvement over conventional lock rings, which lock readily but often strongly resist unlocking.

The L.E. Wilson Cartridge Case Gauge is superbly made, lets the reloader quickly determine correct over-all length and/or head-to-cone length of his cases. Made for many calibers, the latest type shown here is designed for belted cases, permitting the handloader to adjust his sizing die to match his rifle's chamber.

The Bonanza Case Trimmer comprises a sturdy line-bored casting that holds (at left) a sliding and lockable anvil that centers and holds the case against the cutter by means of a stud that enters the primer pocket. The stud on one end is for .175″ primers, the other is for .210″ pockets. A simple, easy-to-use tool, and one that does a good job.

Belted Cases Many handloaders believe that in loading for a belted case they don't have to worry about correct headspace on the shoulder, that is, from belt to cone; don't you believe it, the more so if you want to use those cases very many times and don't want to have head separations! Few makes of dies will allow the shoulder to be set back beyond factory case dimensions, so it may *appear* that everything will work out OK. This ain't necessarily so, because belted cases are generally factory produced to be shorter from belt to shoulder than the chambers they'll be fired in. You can

get away with stretching that case out once, maybe a couple of times, but if you set the shoulder back where it was every time you fire you'll sooner or later extract only the head of the case after a shot.

After the belted case is fired once, *carefully* set the die by trial and error so that it just touches the shoulder, touches it enough so that it can't lengthen out and make the cartridge hard to chamber, just as you would—or should—on a rimless case. This system of die adjustment will let your case headspace on the shoulder as well as the belt, and will eliminate those head separations with belted cases so often bemoaned in print.

I took a crack at gadgets a while back, but L.E. Wilson makes one for belted cases (and for other head types as well) that can't be faulted. This is his regular combination-purpose case gauge, that checks head-to-cone and over-all case dimensions, improved via a movable cone slide for use with belted cases. To use it, simply drop a fired case into the die after loosening the locked cone sleeve, noting that the case base lies between the steps on the headspace end. Now move the cone sleeve up in the gauge body until it lies against the shoulder. Tighten the cone sleeve set-screws, but make sure the head adjustment was not disturbed, and you're all set from now on with that chamber.

Headspace Another thing to remember is that you can also change headspace with the *seating* die. Most seating dies of the non-crimp variety can be set down to where the die shoulder makes contact with the case shoulder enough to set it back and change headspace. Set your seating die on a *fired* case, not a new one, and without a bullet in it. Insert case in press, run it up as far as it will go, screw die down until you feel it hit case, then back it off about a quarter turn and

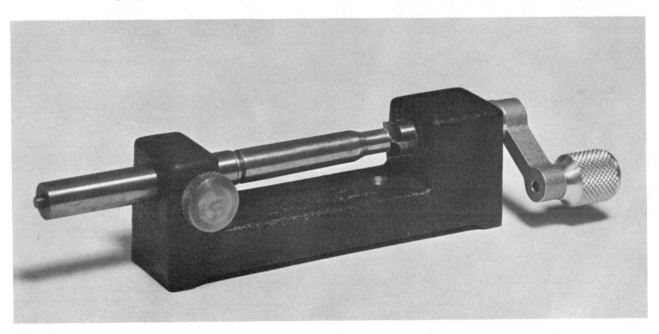

set lockring. Adjust only the seating stem for bullet seating.

Case Lengthening Every now and then I get a letter from someone telling of trouble encountered in chambering cases that have been *neck* sized by using a full length resizing die set so it does not quite full length resize, but gets most of the neck and partially resizes the body. This system will usually work for two or three firings if pressures are fairly low, but with high pressures, where the case is really pushed out into the chamber, you will have trouble closing the bolt on such a cartridge. With this type of so-called neck sizing the brass from the body of the case has to go somewhere when squeezed back to near-original dimensions. It is supposed to go inward, and most of it does, but it also pushes forward and, with no support against the shoulder to hold it, the case lengthens at that point unless the die is set down far enough to prevent the shoulder from pushing forward. Partial sizing of this kind—a resized neck without complete full-length body resizing—will work on cases like the 222 because of a rather long neck and low pressures, but it always leads to trouble with the big cases when used full-throttle.

If you want to read a detailed study of this problem — which also shows that over-all case length grows with partial sizing—see L.E. Wilson's informative article, "Resizing Changes the Case," in *The NRA Handloader's Guide*, p. 52. ED.

If you want to neck size a case and do not have a necking die for that particular case, you may still be able to do it without buying a die. If you happen to have a full length resizing die for a case that is shorter and a wee bit larger in the body, you are in business. As an example, with the 308 Winchester full length sizing die you can neck size 30-06 brass as well with it as you could with a 30-06 neck size die. Just set it up in the press plenty far out so it only starts to size the neck, then screw it in until it just misses the shoulder. Be careful *not to touch the shoulder*, for you could set it back enough to create an excess headspace condition! The 284 Win. will do the same thing for the 7x57 Mauser or the 280 Rem., and the 22-250 will neck size a 220 Swift case.

Case Trimming Some cases are worse than others for stretching of the neck, and all cases will have to be trimmed back if they are fired enough times, especially under high pressures. There are several ways of trimming brass. A number of case trimmers are made for fast trimming, the case being inserted into a collet type shell holder, and the case mouth trimmed by rotating a handle. These are fast but quite expensive if you only load for one or two calibers. There is also the file-trim type used with a loading press, a file used to trim the case off flush with

Case trimming can be done very accurately in the File-Trim die offered by RCBS and others. They're especially valuable when much neck brass must be removed. as in forming cases for one or another configuration.

the hardened top of the die. These work well and are cheaper than the lathe type trimmers. The truth is, if you don't load too much ammo, all you need is the file to cut the case back to the length of a standard new factory case. You may not get the case perfectly square, but it will do for everything except competition or test shooting, and if you look close you'll see that many factory cases are not square either, especially unprimed new cases.

Another question that comes up is how essential is it to ream case necks for accuracy. For extreme accuracy in a rifle that is capable of that kind of tack-driving, it's a good idea, but for average shooting the average handloader doesn't buy too much with it. There are times, however, when it is absolutely necessary.

Case Necks I have seen rifles with chamber necks too tight for the cases of some brands, and a chamber that does not have adequate neck clearance

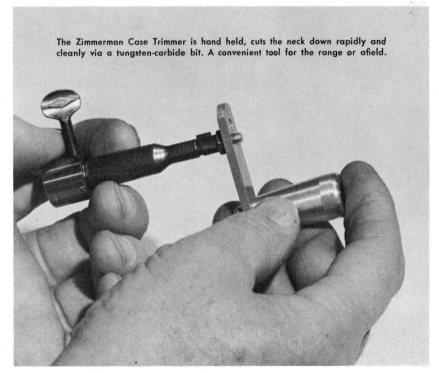

The Zimmerman Case Trimmer is hand held, cuts the neck down rapidly and cleanly via a tungsten-carbide bit. A convenient tool for the range or afield.

The Forster-Appelt Case Trimmer shown is a good investment if you have lots of cases to trim and have access to a drill press. To use, the main body is bolted to the drill press table, centered under the spindle, and the long-arbor cutter is locked into the drill chuck. Cases are then inserted and held by the stepped collet (at lower left), and the spinning cutter brought down. Depth adjustment is made via the drill press stop collars. Collets and the longer arbors required are available to handle all popular calibers.

It is often necessary to ream case necks inside after reducing neck diameter considerably as in necking 22-250 cases from 30-06 brass, or after many firings. Shown is an RCBS Die and Reamer Set, generally part of a set of dies intended for case forming.

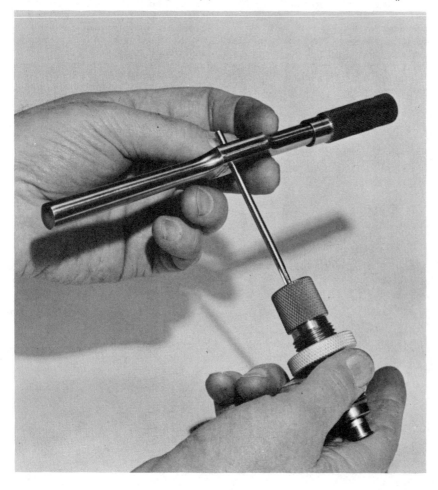

seldom if ever shoots well. This situation is more common in custom rifles, and is more normal in wildcat cartridges than in standard chambering. If you have a rifle that shoots sour for no apparent reason, try sticking a new bullet into the fired case just as it comes from the rifle; if it is tight when inserted with the fingers, the case needs to be reamed or outside turned. Any time a case doesn't show a little smoke around the neck, you'd better check it. If you don't have a neck reamer or outside neck turner you can get by with a drill press or hand drill. Take a drill that just slips inside the case neck, hold case in hand and slip it up and down on the rotating drill. It only takes a little of this to remove enough brass to relieve the case in the chamber. I'll grant you this will not give a perfectly even neck thickness, but I'll also grant you it will make that rifle shoot a lot better than it did with cases with tight necks. I've brought groups down from 4 MOA to as small as 1½" by this method when a reamer was not available. Years ago I found out that being poor is not without advantages; you learn things!

Speaking of accuracy, here's a kink that may save you the embarrassment of beating your wife or using your best musket for a crowbar. Have you ever had a certain batch of pet handloads that consistently shot ½" groups on the 100 yard target with your varmint rifle last summer, then this summer you shot a group to check the sight setting with the same batch of ammo and found they did well to stay in 1½"? It has happened to most of us and we never knew why.

The answer is quite simple once you stumble on to it. When a bullet is seated friction tight in a case neck and left for long periods of time, it seems that some of them stick to the neck of the case and some do not, or maybe it is tension change of individual case necks. Whatever the reason, it happens, and it changes pressures and velocities, raises merry old hell with accuracy. Just put these cartridges back thru the seating die with the seating stem set down just enough to loosen the bullet and, chances are, they'll shoot as well as ever.

One last bit of advice as far as handloads are concerned: before you take off on that long-planned trip to the big game Shangri-La we all look forward to finding someday, run every last one of those handloads through your rifle from magazine to chamber. Don't just try one or two, try them all. It's better to find your mistakes where the loading bench is handy than to find them where there is nothing but the big stillness to echo back your cussing. ●

Artistry in Metal —

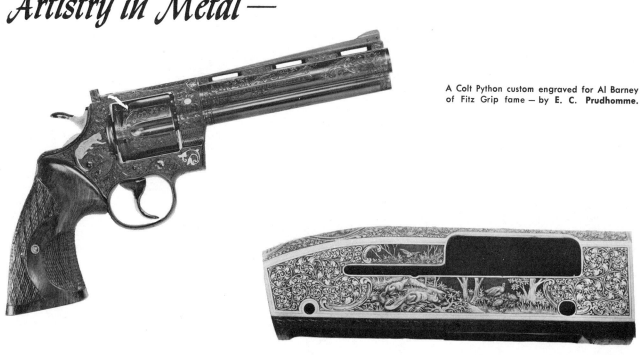

A Colt Python custom engraved for Al Barney of Fitz Grip fame — by **E. C. Prudhomme.**

The master touch and the artistic talents of the engraver are well displayed in this work — by **Arnold Griebel.**

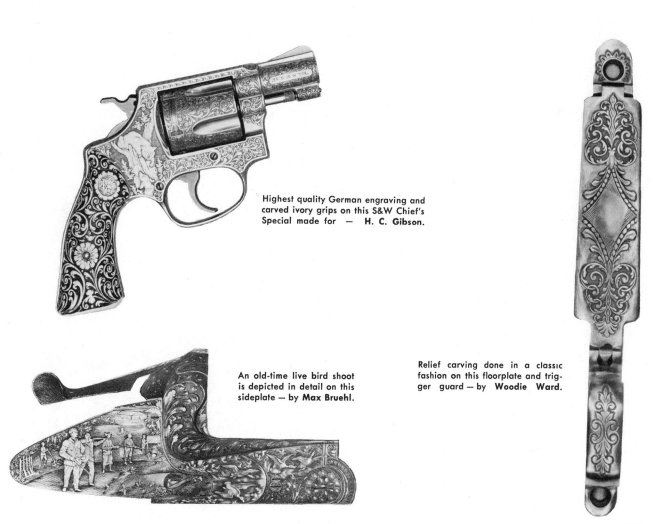

Highest quality German engraving and carved ivory grips on this S&W Chief's Special made for — **H. C. Gibson.**

An old-time live bird shoot is depicted in detail on this sideplate — by **Max Bruehl.**

Relief carving done in a classic fashion on this floorplate and trigger guard — by **Woodie Ward.**

Quiet beauty and meticulous workmanship in both wood and metal of John Amber's custom bench rest rifle — by **John Warren**.

A M12 Winchester receiver with fine leaf pattern engraving and gold ducks inlaid in relief — by **John Rohner**.

This Bergmann auto displays the fine scroll work, excellent high relief game scene and well designed work of **E. C. Prudhomme**.

A deep relief floral pattern frames the gold and silver inlays on this floorplate — by **F. Heym**.

Handsome leaf engraving, animal inlays and carved lever ornament this double — by **Paul Weiss**.

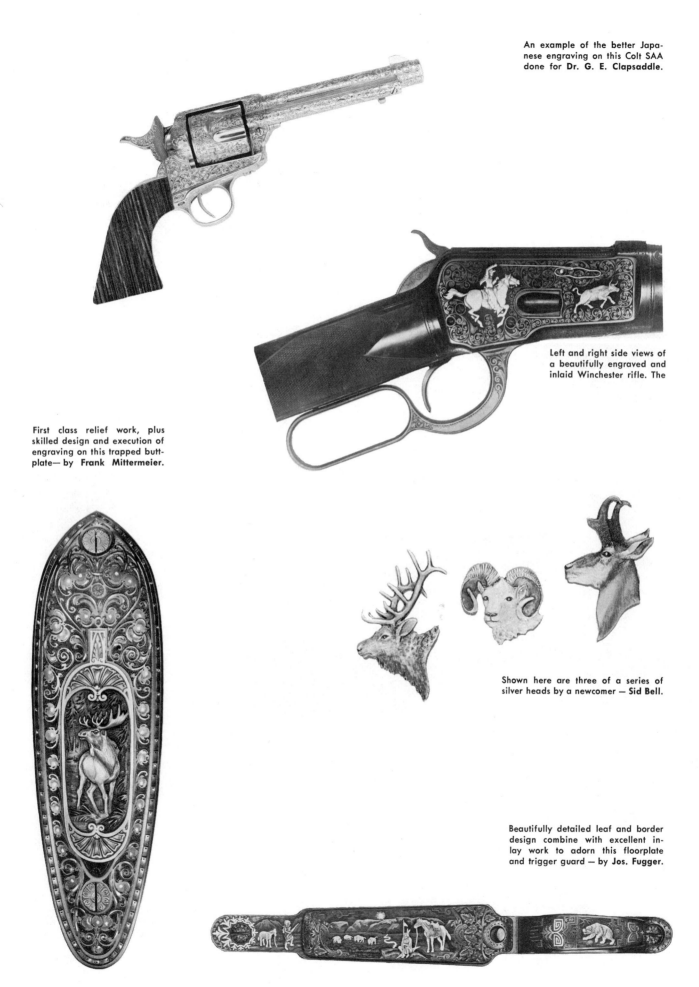

An example of the better Japanese engraving on this Colt SAA done for **Dr. G. E. Clapsaddle.**

Left and right side views of a beautifully engraved and inlaid Winchester rifle. The

First class relief work, plus skilled design and execution of engraving on this trapped buttplate— by **Frank Mittermeier.**

Shown here are three of a series of silver heads by a newcomer — **Sid Bell.**

Beautifully detailed leaf and border design combine with excellent inlay work to adorn this floorplate and trigger guard — by **Jos. Fugger.**

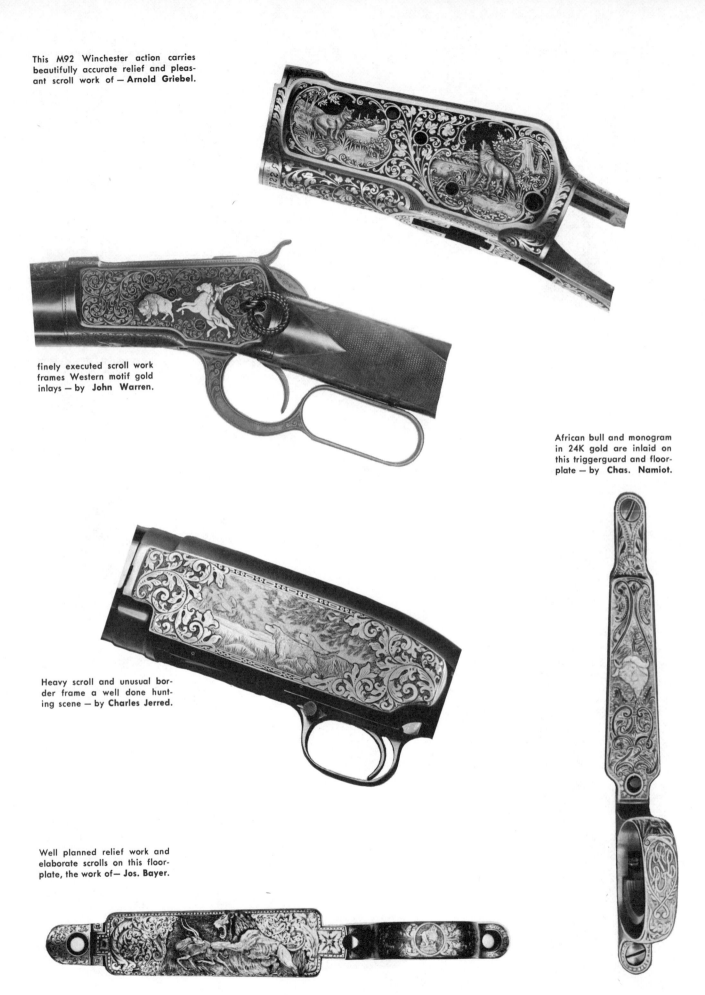

This M92 Winchester action carries beautifully accurate relief and pleasant scroll work of — **Arnold Griebel.**

finely executed scroll work frames Western motif gold inlays — by **John Warren.**

African bull and monogram in 24K gold are inlaid on this triggerguard and floorplate — by **Chas. Namiot.**

Heavy scroll and unusual border frame a well done hunting scene — by **Charles Jerred.**

Well planned relief work and elaborate scrolls on this floorplate, the work of— **Jos. Bayer.**

Art of the Engraver

Arnold Griebel

Robert Swartley

Pachmayr Gun Works

Bill Dyer

Stan Ozias

Robert Kain

Griebel & Prudhomme

Robert Swartley

Arnold Griebel

Bill Dyer

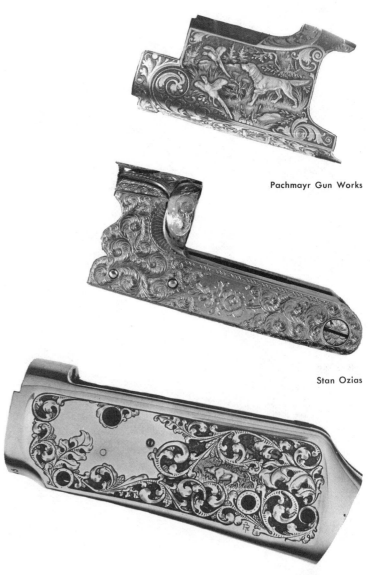

Pachmayr Gun Works

Stan Ozias

Hans Pfeiffer

Robert Kain

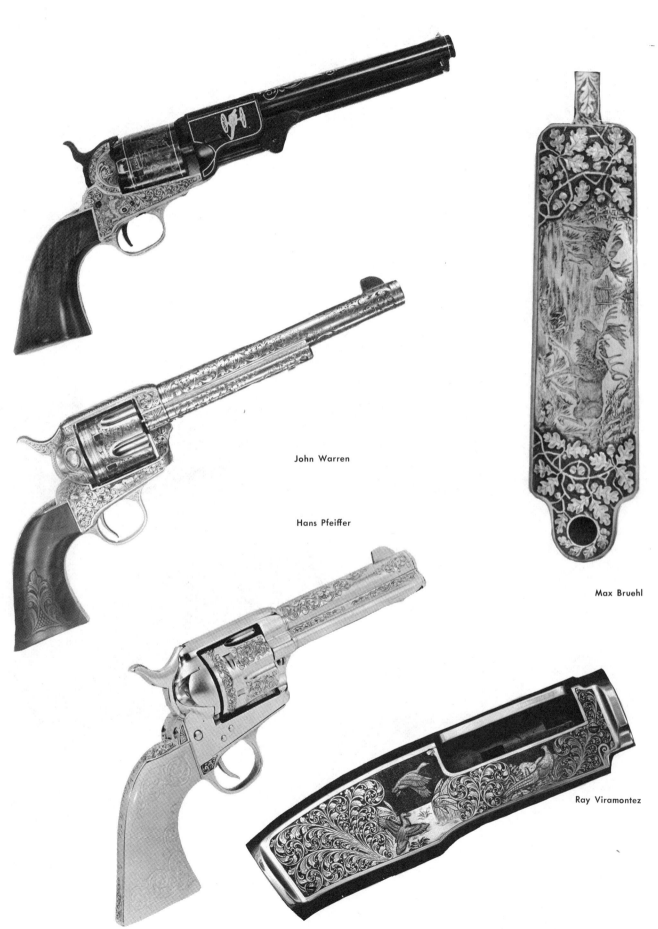

John Warren

Hans Pfeiffer

Max Bruehl

Ray Viramontez

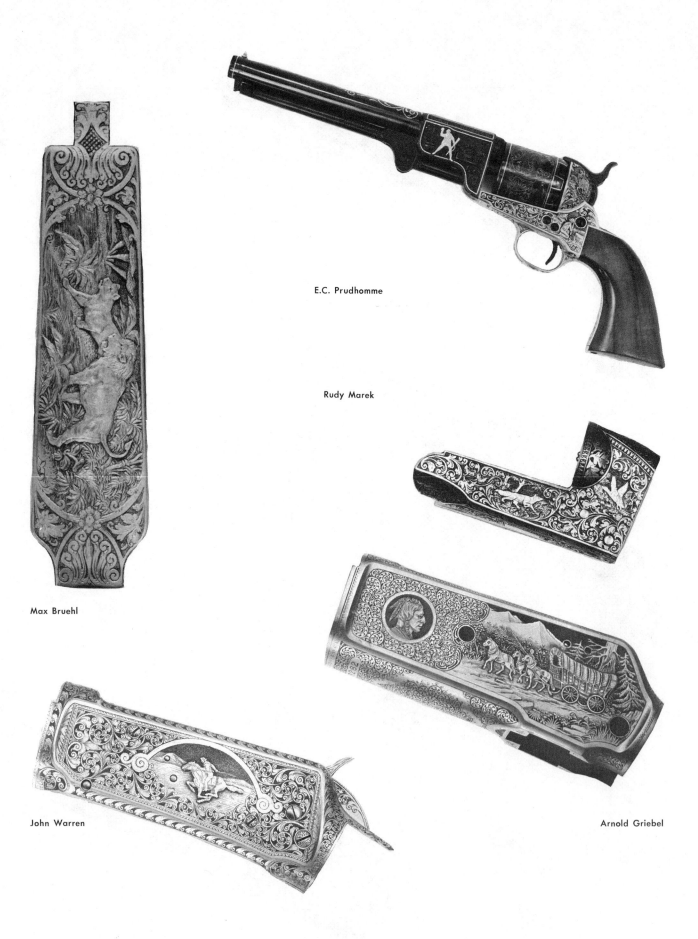

E.C. Prudhomme

Rudy Marek

Max Bruehl

John Warren

Arnold Griebel

Art of the Engraver

Pachmayr Gun Works

Sid Bell

John R. Rohner

John Warren

Arnold Griebel

A. A. White, Inc.

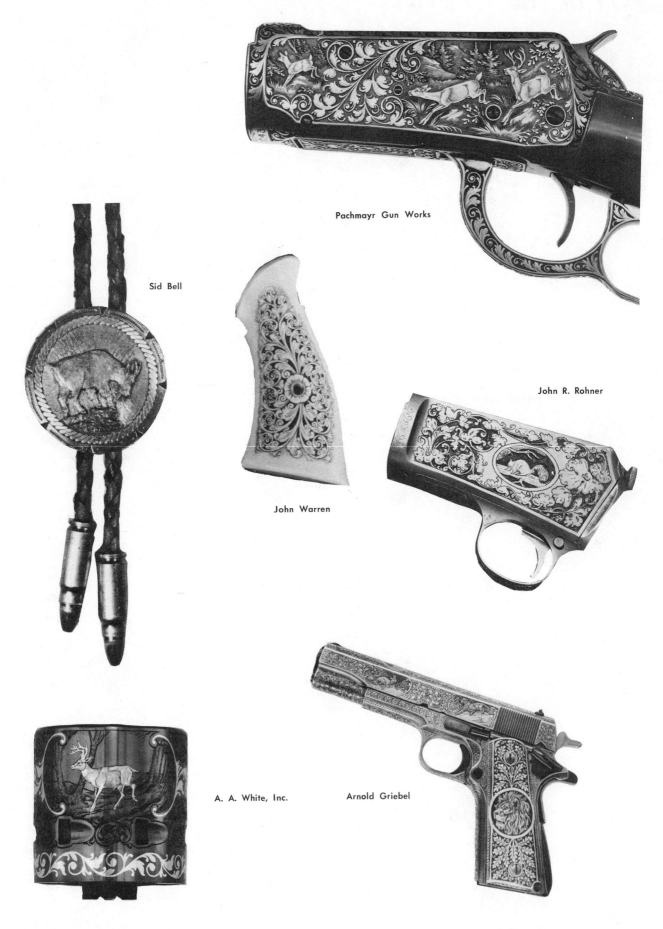

Pachmayr Gun Works

Sid Bell

John Warren

John R. Rohner

A. A. White, Inc.

Arnold Griebel

116

Art of the Engraver

Arnold Griebel

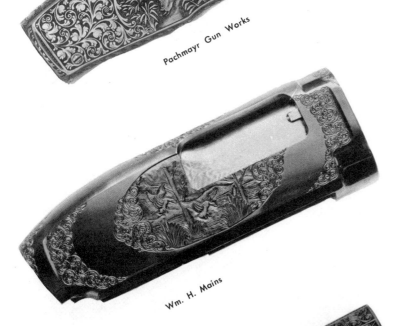

Pachmayr Gun Works

Wm. H. Mains

John Warren

Max Bruehl

K. Jaeger

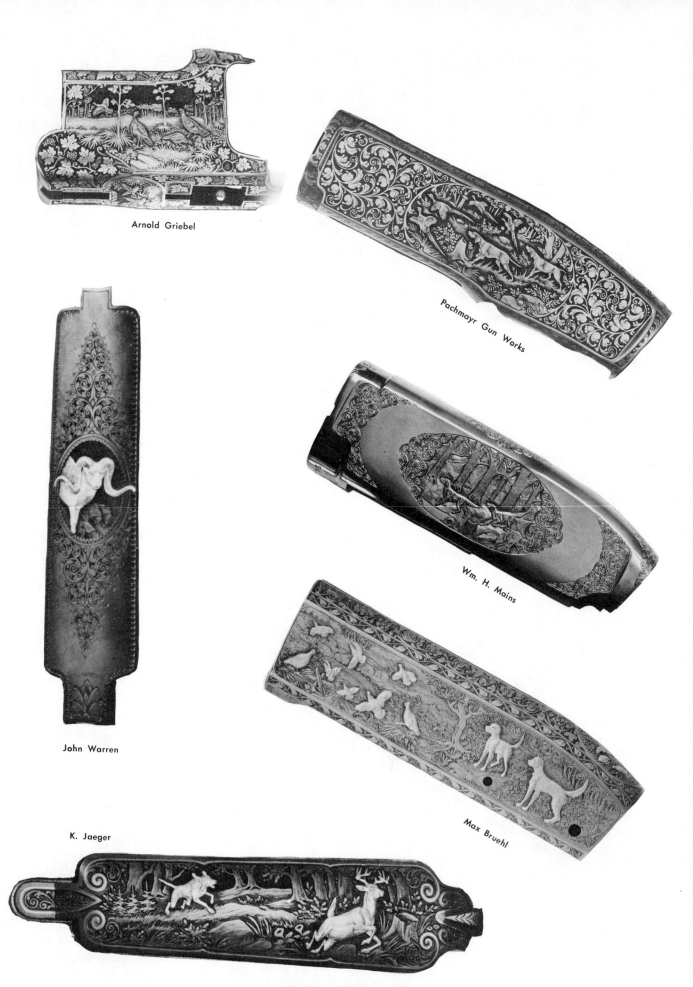

Arnold Griebel

Pachmayr Gun Works

Wm. H. Mains

John Warren

Max Bruehl

K. Jaeger

A. A. White

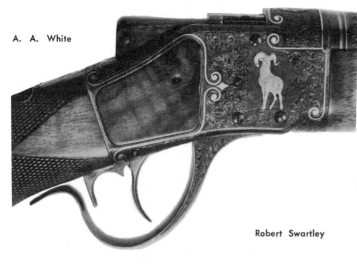

Robert Swartley

Pachmayr Gun Works

Pachmayr Gun Works

Paul Jaeger

A. A. White

Arnold Griebel

Pachmayr Gun Works

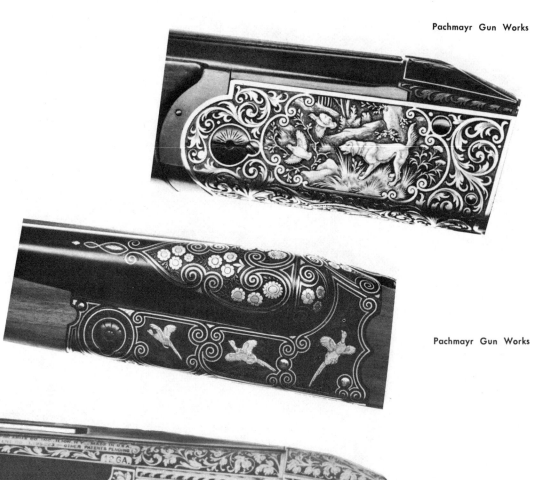

Pachmayr Gun Works

Paul Jaeger

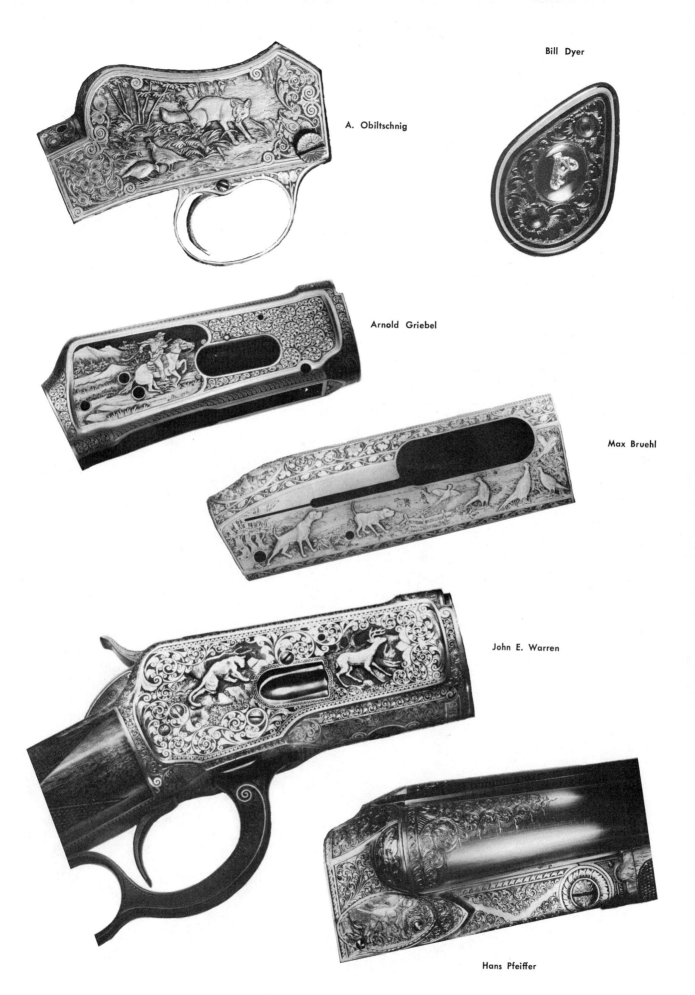

A. Obiltschnig

Bill Dyer

Arnold Griebel

Max Bruehl

John E. Warren

Hans Pfeiffer

121

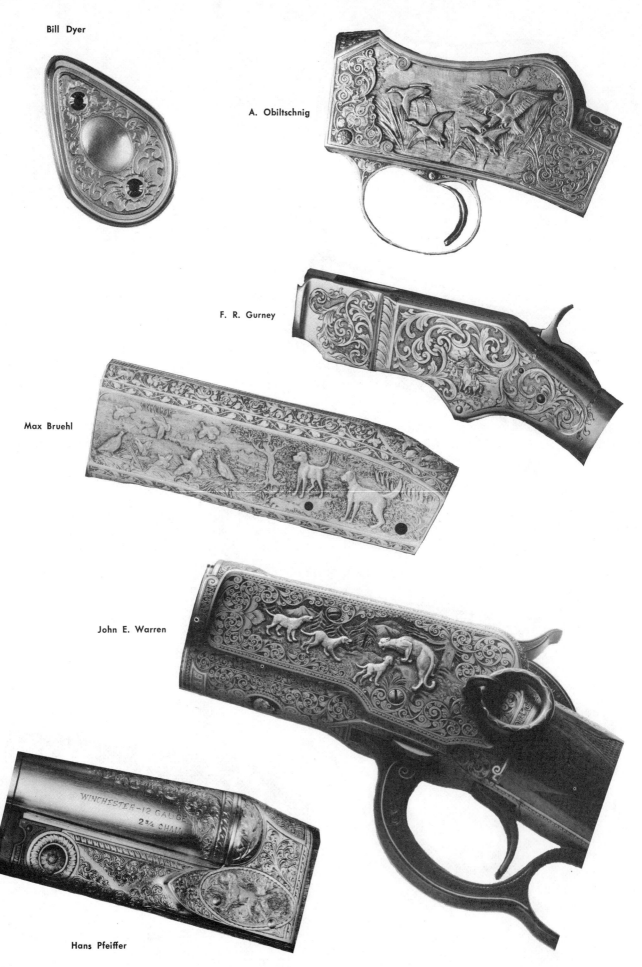

Bill Dyer

A. Obiltschnig

F. R. Gurney

Max Bruehl

John E. Warren

Hans Pfeiffer

122

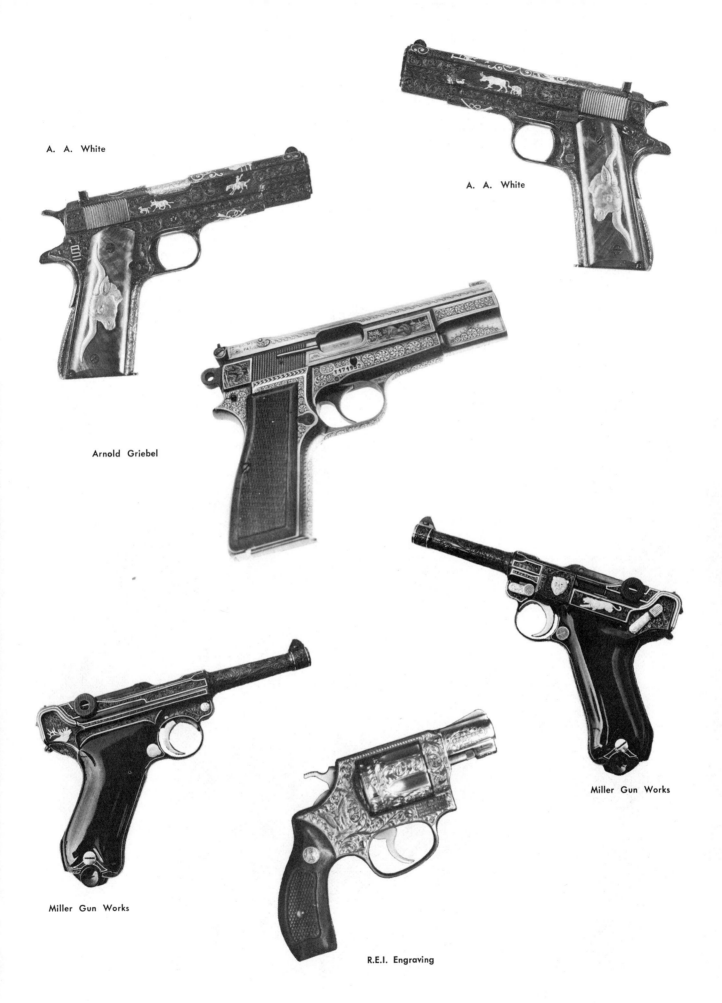

A. A. White

A. A. White

Arnold Griebel

Miller Gun Works

Miller Gun Works

R.E.I. Engraving

123

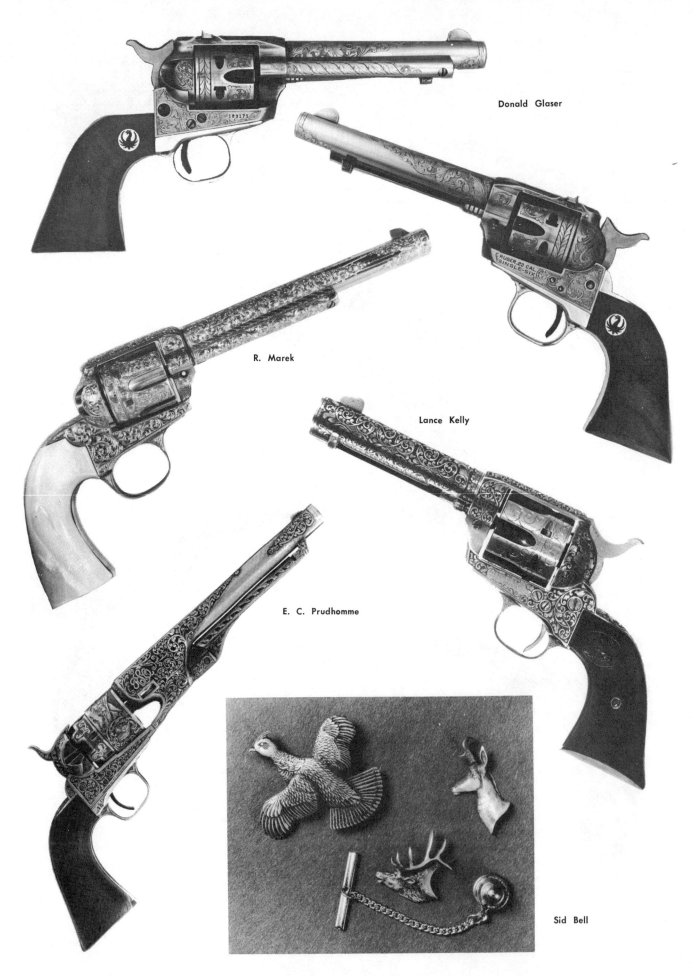

Donald Glaser

R. Marek

Lance Kelly

E. C. Prudhomme

Sid Bell

124

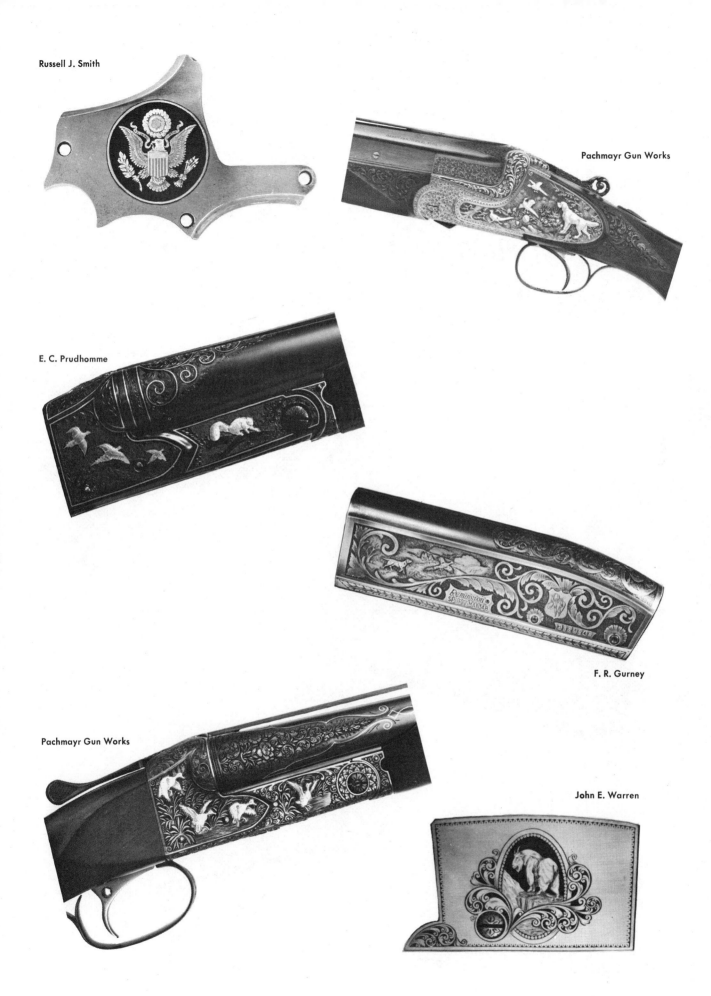

Russell J. Smith

Pachmayr Gun Works

E. C. Prudhomme

F. R. Gurney

Pachmayr Gun Works

John E. Warren

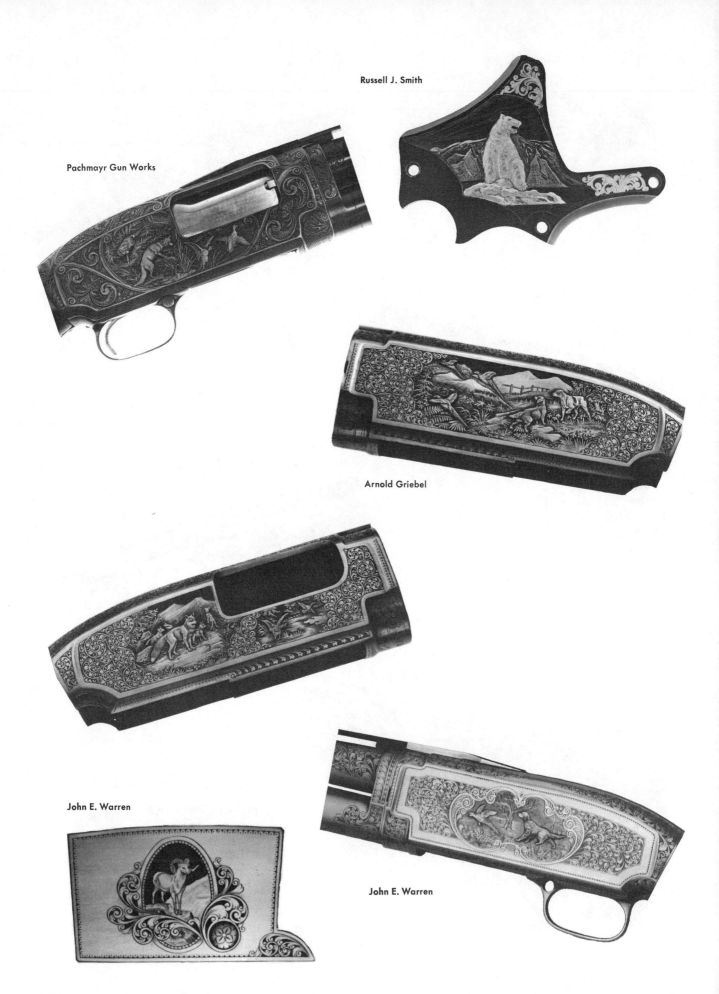

Pachmayr Gun Works

Russell J. Smith

Arnold Griebel

John E. Warren

John E. Warren

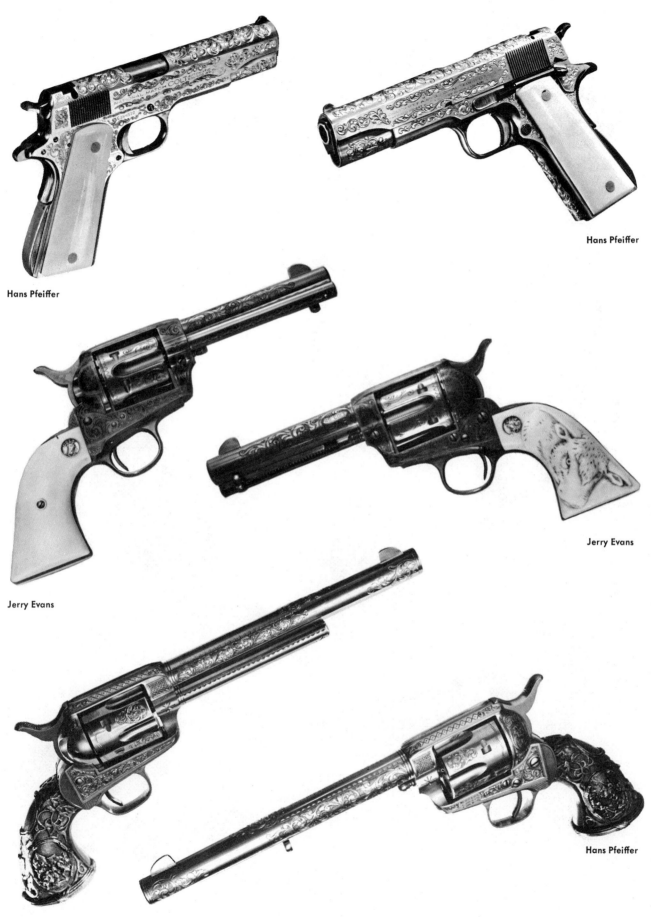

Hans Pfeiffer

Hans Pfeiffer

Jerry Evans

Jerry Evans

Hans Pfeiffer

Hans Pfeiffer

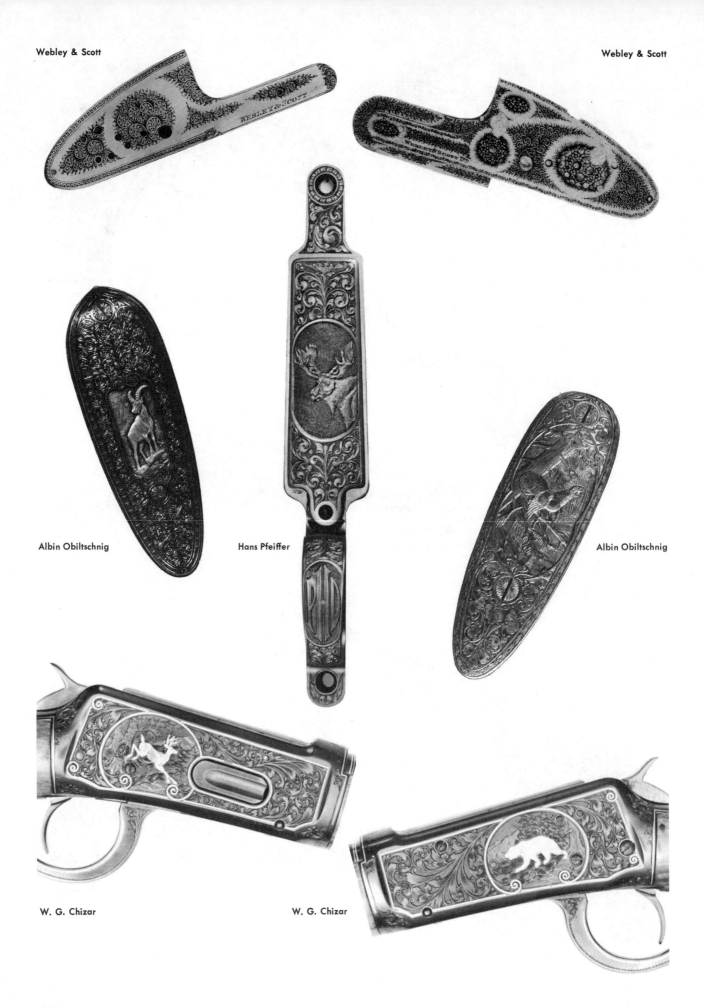

Albin Obiltschnig

Hans Pfeiffer

Albin Obiltschnig

W. G. Chizar

W. G. Chizar

Does your 20-inch rifle — even your 24-incher — give you the ballistics shown in the tables? Does your handgun? Huh-uh! The author tells all.

ballistic bull

Ed HAMCO

by JOHN MAYNARD

AUTOMOBILE advertising is loaded with 'em, those hot-air numbers about power. That Zipmobile V-8 you're interested in — the dealer says it churns up three hundred and eleven horsepower? Amazing. And likewise malarkey. The engineers in the Zipmobile plant ran tests on their V-8? True, but it was mounted not in a car but on a test block. It was tuned to run perfectly at peak horsepower, but rough as a cob at street speeds. The motor turned no fan, spun no generator, whirled no pump to provide power for the steering or the brakes or to slide the windows up and down. It drove no transmission or rear axle. It merely registered ideal and unfettered power against a recording device. If, out of the advertised three hundred and eleven-five straining horses you get much over a couple hundred at the rear wheels of your Zipmobile sedan, you're doing just dandy. The rest have evaporated into Madison Avenue hot air.

Something like that is happening in our numbers about power — which is to say bullet speed and energy — in regard to centerfire rifle and pistol ammunition. If we couple public ignorance of the facts of ballistic life with the blind public belief that printed ballistic tables are near-biblical truth, there exists a golden opportunity for ballistic bamboozlement. That glittering opportunity, it seems, is hardly being let slip by!

As the pure-as-snow politicians would say, let's look at the record.

In 1961 the 264 Winchester Magnum was introduced with a roll of drums and some very fancy ballistic numbers. The 140-grain bullet at 3200, the sheets read, the 100-grain at 3700 feet per second. These magic numbers were arrived at by industry-standardized procedures — these call for shooting under controlled temperatures through barrels rifled to far more precise tolerances than can be expected in usual barrel production; the translation of recorded instrumental velocities into muzzle speeds by calculation and, we may assume, a rounding-off upwards. They were taken with 26-inch barrels as standard. Fair enough? No real quibble, since numbers so arrived at are as near gospel as any in the relatively inexact science of ballistics, the instrumentation employed was tophole, the procedure accepted as normal.

The 264

The first rifle for the 264 cartridge, the Model 70 standard sporter, was likewise made with a 26-inch barrel. Still no quarrel, since more and more members of the shooting public realize, thank Heaven and informed gun-writers, that velocity numbers are so variable among individual barrels (even produced on the same machines) that they are really only index numbers, not absolutes.

But what has since happened? Sako still produces a 26-inch 264 rifle, as does Winchester, but the Remington barrel for the 264 in their new Model 700 series is 24 inches; the Browning sporter measures only 22 inches. Now Winchester has added production of a lighter Model 70 with only a 22½-inch barrel which will almost certainly outsell its longer brother. Yet at no time have these manufacturers mentioned the horrid fact that the original fancy speed numbers no longer apply, that with only 22 inches of barrel in which to burn slow powders the 264 bears a closer resemblance to, say, the 270 than the original copywriters would have cared to admit. Not because it's driving a power steering unit, either.

The basic facts on that one — or at least a clear enough indication as to the facts — have already been

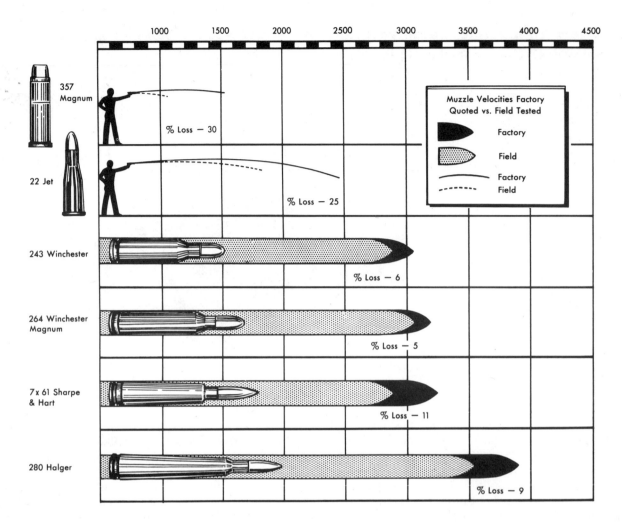

published in the GUN DIGEST, 1961 edition. Editor John Amber's own 264 underwent surgery, two inches of barrel at a time, with results recorded by the reliable and completely disinterested H.P. White Laboratories. The first two inches lost for the 140-grain bullet an average of 56 foot seconds; the next two inches 85. That is some 141 foot seconds for the four-inch cut. We can reasonably expect, therefore, that the muzzle velocity figures for the 264 game-weight bullet from the most recent 700 series Remington rifle (a 24-inch barrel) will average not 3200 but 3145 at best; or that the 22-inch Browning or Winchester will deliver not 3200 but at best 3060. The striking force from the short barrel job is deflated to little more than the muzzle energy for the common or garden variety of 270, is only some 175 foot pounds greater than the 35-year-old 270 out at the 300-yard mark. What price all the fuss and feathers? Could we be living in a dream world of published "horsepower?"

The 243

Or take the 243 which has rapidly risen to great popularity among the newer centerfires. That is likewise the subject of discreet silence where actual performance, what you really buy at the hardware store, is discussed. The original published ballistics on the 243 were based — though it is not a magnum cartridge — on 26-inch barrels, but the rifles widely sold for the 243 are something else again. The popular Model 70 Featherweight is a 22-incher; the Savage lever guns are 24 or, in the more popular model, only 22; the Savage Model 110 is 22; the Winchester 88 is 22; the Sako Forester is 22; the FN is 22; the Browning sporter is 22; the Husqvarna is 22 in the lightweight or 23¾ in a slower-selling style; the Mannlicher is 20 and the Norrahammer is 20¼; Remington's 1962 or 700 series rifles for such calibers are 20 inches in the barrel. As the late Don Marquis used to say, "What the hell, Mehitabel?"

Excepting custom oddballs, the only complete factory-made 243 rifles that carry the 26-inch barrel length (on which all published 243 data was based) are a few Model 70 standard-weight rifles, fewer M70 varminters and Sako varmint-weight jobs. These are hardly popular items. The vast majority of 243's are either 22 inches or 20. Do we get from them all the horsepower we think we get?

Not hardly. The independent laboratories again prove the pudding. From 22-inch barrels of actual rifles the 100-grain hunting bullet is at least 100 foot-seconds (2856) behind the delivery of 26-inch rifle barrels. Even that (2969 in terms of White's 20-foot instrumental velocities) was sub-par in relation to the 3070 that appears in the ballistic tables. The 80-grain picture is parallel and, in at least one expertly chronographed test using a full length pressure barrel of standard dimension, the varmint bullet at 3316 instrumental wasn't coming close to published data

(3500). The 244 Remington, when clocked by the same outfit, was on the button or a little better from 26-inch tubes, but has run into the same complexities in respect to the actual delivery from barrels-in-use. The point of all this is clear. If today's 22-inch 243's are delivering from 100 to 150 foot seconds less than the advertised figures, the muzzle energy figures are off as much as 10%. That's a discount we neither expected nor paid for.

The habit of publishing presumably standardized ballistic numbers based on one length of barrel and then building the vast majority of rifles in a shorter length is not confined to Winchester combinations. In 1962 Remington announced — in answer to public demand for handy and light rifles — the Model 700 line of sporters with 20-inch barrels in such calibers as 243, 270, 280 and 30-06. In the last three named the actual velocity delivered must be at an absolute minimum 100-150 foot seconds below the SAAMI (Sporting Arms and Ammunition Inst.) standards for such calibers, conventionally based on 24-inch tubes. The Remington plant also came out with a new 7mm magnum rifle barreled 24 inches long but accompanied by ballistic dope based on 26 inches. As this is written, disinterested clockings with 24-inch rifles in the 7mm cartridge have not been made,* though they obviously will have been before this article is in print; but it is this observer's guess

---

*A quick check on the editor's range, using the Avtron Model 333 chronograph, gave these results with the new 7mm Remington Magnum:
The 150-grain load gave an average muzzle velocity of 3090 for 10 shots. Highest reading was 3144, lowest was 3068, for a maximum difference of 76.
The average for the 175-grain cartridge was 2910; low reading was 2832, highest was 2944, again for 10 shots. Maximum variation was 162, over twice that for the 150-grain, but one shot clocked unusually slow in relation to the other nine.
Thus the 24-inch barreled M700 Remington in 7mm Magnum caliber shows a loss of some 170 fs from the listed 3260 and shows a 110 fs drop from the catalog figure of 3020 for the 175-grain. Thus, a 55-85 fs loss per inch of barrel, in that the factory figures were obtained in 26-inch barrels.

---

that the "air" in the advertised numbers (3260 for the 150-grain bullet and the 175-grain at 3020) will be at least 75 and more likely 100 foot seconds. And the loss will be even greater, on the order of 150-plus, when 22-inch barreled sporters of various makes go into commercial production, as they inevitably will.

The 7x61mm

A much-discussed example, in modern times, of discrepancy between published and accomplished bullet speeds, as related to barreling, came up with the 7x61 Sharpe & Hart. This was, is, and will be a fine 7mm magnum hunting cartridge of the smaller sort, excellent with bullets in the 140-160 grain categories. The originally announced data, however, contained some ultra-fancy velocity figures — *all based on bull barrels 30 to 31 inches long*. Who carries such barber poles hunting? Ultimately those fancy figures were republished, after firings against the same chronograph with the 26-inch sporters then being marketed. The numbers were de-glamorized by from 140 to well over 300 foot seconds. Quite a difference.

Assorted hassles regarding pressures and other conditions of the firings cloud the picture on the 7 & 61, but if we take the load of 62 grains of 4350 and the 160-grain bullet (a common load for the caliber, and one used by a number of hunters), the picture looks like this: original quoted speed from 30-inch barrel, 1-in-12 twist, 3256 fps; from 26-inch rifle barrel, same twist, 3124, which is just over the figure for Norma-made rounds in the caliber; from the 22-inch barrel, same twist, of the author's Schultz & Larsen-made sporter, 2912.

That difference of at least 200 foot seconds means a loss of some 425 foot pounds in muzzle energy, a full half-foot of added drop at the 400-yard marker. Which, if either, of these is of real importance to you the writer has no way of telling, but any time the baker offers your wife eleven cookies for a dozen she'd let the world know.

Halger Hot Air

You'll have to be wearing some

---

gray in your hair to remember what were probably the greatest hot-air cartridges of all time, the 244 and 280 Halgers. They were featured in Stoeger catalogs, the latter caliber in a fancy rifle on the magnum Mauser action, barrel normally 28 inches long as I recall, in the late 1920's and early '30's — a generation ago. Harold Gerlich† shyly admitted that his 7mm creation would push 100-grain bullets at 3900, 145 grains at 3500, 180 grains at 3043. Wow!! As a kid I can remember going all trembly over that one! I just didn't have the $750 Stoeger wanted for the rifle, not by about $745.

There was almost that much inflation in Herr Halger's ballistics. The case was nothing more or less than the 280 Ross of twenty years earlier — itself no pipsqueak with 146 grains at 3100, 180 at 2800 as claimed. But propellant powders hadn't improved by any three or four hundred foot seconds during those 20 years. They haven't yet, as a matter of fact. Phil Sharpe took the wind out of the Halger balloon when he clocked one of the original rifles, barreled to "… special Halger dimensions … most carefully gauged with Halger barrel gauges and minutely inspected with special optical and magnifying instruments …," and found that 62 grains of Du Pont 4350 gave 160-grain bullets 2965 and 59 grains of this modern powder shoved 180-grain Barnes slugs out at 2770. Pressures prevented any higher speeds. The horrendous Halger was nothing but the 280 Ross plus hot air.

Much the same must of course be said of the 244 Halger, for which was claimed the fancy performance, back between the World Wars, of 87-grain bullets squirted forth at 3770. Since this miracle cartridge used the 7.92x57 case necked to 6mm, and since necking any 57mm rimless case to 6mm will give us the 244 Remington, plus or minus a few thousandths in the neck and shoulder areas, there obviously was

---

†Halger stems from HALbe & GERlich, partners in developing the Halger calibers. See Phil Sharpe's "Halger and His Rifle" in the 7th ed. GUN DIGEST.

perhaps 300 foot seconds of genuine sauerkraut gas in that one, too!

It could be, of course, that Herr Halger took care to have his pressure readings made off one barrel and velocities taken with another, a stunt not unknown at that point and quite possibly not unknown today. More reasonable, however, is the explanation that he just plain lied about the numbers.

It is greatly to the credit of today's riflemaker Roy Weatherby that the cataloged ballistic dope for his line of proprietary cartridges has been revised — and largely downward! Much of the data he supplied earlier was based on individual rifle handloads — the newest figures reflect the conditions of loading of the cartridges now furnished under Weatherby's label. It must have hurt a bit to have in-

tridges, too. The circumstances of the test firing bore little relation to those of actual shooting with available guns. The 22 Remington Jet is a prime example. The original dope sheet on this one shouted of a 40-grain bullet at 2460 feet per second. Super-numbers. Not much was made of the fact that they had been obtained in a close-tolerance pressure barrel *with completely enclosed breech*, though it was clear that an 8⅜ths-inch length of barrel was standard. The 16th ed. GUN DIGEST did report that their chronographing gave an average of only 2000 foot seconds, even that a bit high compared to the later-given H.D. White figures of 1860-odd.

Guns have been and are being made that long, but the original six-gun chambered for the Jet was

8⅜th-inch barrel on an ordinary cylinder gun makes about 2100, some 15% off in velocity and 25% in energy below the figures originally aired. The Jet is still quite a spitfire, but it is not the torpedo we originally read about.

And never forget that any revolver, when loaded to high intensity, as are the 40,000 pounders of today, wastes a great deal of energy in its charge. Don't ever

The specimen shown is taken from *Ballistics on RWS Center Fire Cartridges* (Nurnberg, 1960), a 20-page pamphlet printed in English, and containing complete ballistic data on all RWS centerfire rifle cartridges.

Note that, in addition to the usual velocity and energy figures, RWS reveals the maximum breech pressure, the barrel length (several other barrel lengths are given for other cartridges), the time of flight and, of high importance to the rifleman, the midrange tra-

Symbol	Cartridge	Bullet		Max. permissible breech pressure lbs./sq.in.	Barrel length inch.	Velocity ft./sec.				Energy ft. lbs.			
		Type	Weight grains			Muzzle	100 yds.	200 yds.	300 yds.	Muzzle	100 yds.	200 yds.	300 yds.
153	8x57 JS	Soft Point Round Nose Sharp Shoulder Solid Jacket	196	46 960	23,5	2630	2240	1940	1700	3000	2180	1630	1240

dependent chronographer White peg the 180-grain 300 Weatherby load at 3245 rather than the 3400 that had once caused such a furor, however gratified Weatherby may have been to see his superpotent 460 set at only 25 foot seconds under its original figure, a piffling difference. All his present data, by the way, as is usual with belted-magnum cartridges, is based on 26-inch barrel length. Roy's rifles are made in 24- or 26-inch, with 22-inchers only on custom order. All Norma-published data is based on 24-inch barrels.

The 22 Jet

We have certainly been led at least, if not nudged, down the lane of misunderstanding by certain ballistic situations on handgun car-

the Smith & Wesson Model 53, which at first was made only with a six-inch tube. It is now available with both four and 8⅜ths-inch barrels. Even if there had been some way of closing off (perhaps as in the Nagant line of revolvers) the inevitable opening between cylinder mouth and barrel entrance, the gap between delivered fact and printed fancy would have been considerable.

As numerous independent chronographers quickly discovered the 6-inch barrel was delivering at best some 1860 foot seconds, not 2460, a full 25% under published par. In this instance not so much because of the sub-length barrel as because the gas leakage, inevitable in any cylinder gun, was taking much of the steam out of the load. The

wrap your hand over the front end of the cylinder of a hot number to find out how much. Just rest the frame or the trigger guard on a piece of clean paper and see how much soot firing will deposit on it or how quickly the paper is blast-burned through. The 256 Winchester six-gun load will actually blast-burn holes through leather in half a dozen shots. As this is written, no production revolver has been offered for the 256 — not only because primer extrusion binds the cylinder, but because the six-gun frame actually stretches. What *that* does to the closed-barrel figures that have already been published we wouldn't hazard a guess. Plenty, inevitably. Enough to make closed-breech figures on the super-quick handgun loads interesting reading as fiction.

The 357 Magnum

It took a while for the six-gun clan to find out there was a certain amount of hot air in 357 Magnum dope, too. It was originally introduced at 1510 feet per second for a 158-grain bullet. Colossal. But much trouble. Bad leading, some primer extrusion, certain guns stretching their top straps when

jectories using both iron and scope sights, including figures for 50, 75 and 150 yards.

Surely Winchester-Western and Remington-Peters could easily offer the same comprehensive information. As it is, neither organization even bothers to inform its ammunition buying public whether the published trajectory figures are derived from line-of-bore, line-of-iron sight or line-of-scope sight. Is there any valid reason why such information — readily available, of course — should be withheld?

Too, the power-minded handgunner who buys a short-barreled 357, one with a handy 3½- or 4-inch nose, must remember that he is not buying the knock-em-dead pistola he chose from the ballistic tables because of its some 690 foot pounds of calculated energy. He must end up with some 30% less, since in the various 38-caliber handgun loads the speed loss below the standard barrel (6 inches long for the 38 Special) seems to average about 8% per inch of barrel. Where striking force is concerned, he's buying only a six-inch 38 Special with his stubnosed fighting gun and he won't be buying three times the Special's wallop either. More like only half again as much.

It is admittedly unfortunate that the shooting public so blindly accepts the standardized ballistic fig-

that tell only part of the story in relation to the arms available.

In a conventional table for rifle rounds the cartridge is identified, the bullet weight (and usually point type) is given, plus velocities and energies at the muzzle and relevant yardages out to 300. Finally come midrange trajectory figures, largely useless because they are usually "pure," do not take into account sight heights above the bore. Is there any real reason why the barrel length on which the velocity and energy figures are based cannot be specified in rifle tables as it is in data for handgun cartridges? Is there any real reason — now that the mid-century trend toward short-barrel rifles is obvious to even the most hard-headed — why the courses of experimental firings that are behind the published tables

| | Time of flight sec. | | | Path of bullet above (+) or below (−) line of sight in inches | | | | | | | | | | | |
| | | | | iron sights based on a sight height of 0.8" above line of bore | | | | | | telescopic sights based on a sight height of 2" above line of bore | | | | | |
100 yds.	200 yds.	300 yds.	50 yds.	75 yds.	100 yds.	150 yds.	200 yds.	300 yds.	50 yds.	75 yds.	100 yds.	150 yds.	200 yds.	300 yds.
.124	.269	.433	+ 0.4	+ 0.4	⊕	− 2.0	− 5.9	−21.8	− 0.2	+ 0.1	⊕	− 1.4	− 4.8	−19.4
			+ 1.1	+ 1.3	+ 1.3	⊕	− 3.3	−17.7	+ 0.3	+ 0.7	+ 0.9	⊕	− 2.9	−16.6
			+ 1.9	+ 2.6	+ 3.0	+ 2.5	⊕	−12.8	+ 1.0	+ 1.9	+ 2.4	+ 2.2	⊕	−12.2
			+ 4.0	+ 5.8	+ 7.2	+ 8.9	+ 8.5	⊕	+ 3.1	+ 4.9	+ 6.5	+ 8.3	+ 8.2	⊕

they shouldn't; guns a bit outdated in metallurgy, that probably shouldn't have been chambered for the new round, coming apart with it. The manufacturers started cutting down on the soup. You may recall that one brand was independently clocked (in the interest of handgun-maker Colt) and, from the standard 8⅜-inch tube came 1400, from the 6-inch barrel 200 foot seconds less. If you save handbooks and the free-for-a-post-card ballistic sheets, you'll note that the published specifications dropped first to 1450, then to 1430 and, in recent versions, to 1400. This is reasonably near right, for that long barrel. But the student of handgun numbers — and about a hundred foot seconds — got lost somewhere along the way.

ures, so naively believes that whatever is printed must be right, must apply to all kinds of use of the caliber. But since it is obvious that all of the gun writers and independent chronographers in the country, working in relays, could never educate the great mass of shooters into all the intricacies of ballistic variation, it seems to this writer even more unfortunate that the publishers of the tables, the makers of the ammunition and the guns should, whether by intent or accident, lead that shooting public into further misunderstanding.

This does not need to be. Cartridges intended for leaky cylinder guns need not be tested, their velocity and energy numbers derived, in closed breech guns. Neither do we need to have ballistics tables

cannot be carried one more step, that of cutting a standard-length test barrel back in one- or two-inch increments so that for each caliber a rounded-off figure for approximate velocity loss could be included with the table?

Then the customer, the lamplight student of the tables of numbers, might have some real understanding of what he is getting when he buys the new short-snouted model, or any model for that matter. His understanding would still be no more and no less precise than are the facts of ballistic measurements themselves, perhaps, but it would be vastly more correct than his present ignorant faith. That is placed in numerical gods that are, all too often, made imposing by a bellyful of hot air.

Duelling Pistols

HIGH ATOP the New Jersey Palisades, overlooking the Hudson River and across from New York City, there is a lonely monument. A tablet on this monument does not recite an act of heroism—it has a tragic message. On July 11, 1804, General Alexander Hamilton was mortally wounded on this spot by a ball from the duelling pistol of Col. Aaron Burr. No duel in America created greater public furore.

In 1804 the duel as an arbiter of justice or as a means of proving a man's valor had not given away to the more civilized view that law rather than lead provides more reliable decisions. Less than two years after the Hamilton-Burr duel, on a dreary May morning near the Kentucky-Tennessee line, Andrew Jackson met and put a 70 caliber ball through Charles Dickinson. On March 22, 1820, naval hero Stephen Decatur was killed at Bladensburg, Md., in a duel with James Barron. As late as Sept. 13, 1859, Senator David C. Broderick was killed in a duel with Judge David S. Terry near San Francisco.

All challenged parties in these duels were mortally wounded or instantly killed. The high mortality is not strange when one considers that two of the encounters were fired at ten paces and the other two at only eight paces.

It is not our purpose to delve deeply into the practice of duelling—we shall focus our attention mainly on the pistols used—but a short review of the rise and fall of duelling may help the reader understand why thousands of beautifully matched pairs of pistols were made, and that this trade contributed greatly to the development of firearms.

Back in the early days of our Christian era there evolved in the Celtic nations a barbaric custom of "Trial by Combat," whereby guilt or innocence was supposedly established by the outcome of personal combat. Apparently to be strong and skilled as a fighter was to be always innocent in those days.

Early Duelling

By the early 1300s France had reached greater refinement in such matters and had departed somewhat

Pistols of the duelling type made by Simeon North at Middletown, Conn. They favor the English style. These pistols were presented to Commodore Thomas Macdonough in recognition of his naval victory on Lake Champlain in 1814; they have 9¼" barrels and are 54 caliber smoothbore.

from the old concepts. The duel as a test of right or wrong fell into discard, and it eventually became an institution to settle affairs of honor; a role firmly established in 1527 when King Francis I challenged Emperor Charles V to a personal crossing of swords.

Such examples by personages of great station drew much attention. Soon the duel as a means of settling conflicts of opinion and affronts (real or imagined) spread throughout France and into other countries. At first the sword and poniard were the principal weapons used; France and some other European nations clung to cold steel for duelling weapons long after Great Britain had gone to pistols.

Pistols were considered the more equitable choice of weapons in Great Britain. A strong, skilled swordsman might have a great advantage over a weaker, less agile opponent. On the other hand, most men were familiar with the firearms of the day, normally employing them for hunting and self-defense. Thus duelling with pistols, where the antagonists stood at a distance, gave to each a more equal chance and became a test of bravery and normal skills.

Code Duello

The Irish, always a very proud race of fighting men, record a duel with pistols in 1759. Despite its rather Latin sounding name, the "Code Duello" (26 rules governing the formal duel) was drafted in Ireland at the Clonmell Summer Assizes of 1777. The Code as first adopted covered the various sections of Ireland including Galway; sometimes historians refer to duelling rules as "Galway rules." The Code Duello found favor with the gentry in England and spread to the European continent; soon it was generally adopted by all countries, with minor changes to meet special conditions.

The practice of formal duelling with pistols extended approximately a hundred years from 1777, and the pistols used were first the flintlock and then the caplock. Some breech-loading pistols of duelling pattern were made to accommodate cartridges, but these were few and designed primarily to shoot at targets other than a man's shirt front.

Reasonable men must now agree that duelling was a relic of a barbarous age, yet in the times during which it flourished there were many who defended it. One historian records this view of duelling: "There has been no virtue which has proved half so instrumental to the civilizing of mankind, who, in great societies, would soon degenerate into cruel villains and treacherous slaves, were honour to be removed from them."

Whether duelling helped civilize the world or not, the world did apparently become more civilized by the middle of the 19th century, and an English writer of that period reported, "Duelling is virtually dead in England—the practise may be said to be defunct, *even in the Southern States of America.* And it may be assumed that it is dying a slow but natural death on the Continent of Europe."

It is significant that an English writer referred to duelling in our southern states, for here it was more prevalent there than anywhere in America except in California, where, in the 1859-60 era they preferred for the most part to duel according to the

"Code Californio," using shotguns, rifles, pistols, knives, and even pressure hoses! Western gun duels generally were not troubled with niceties or much polite formality!

Charleston, South Carolina, is said to have had the only American duelling society, members rated by their conquests on the so-called field of honor. South Carolina got around to changing all this, and even today when a governor of that state takes office he must swear that he has not engaged in a duel since 1881 and will not engage in one while in office. The last recorded duel in South Carolina was fought with pistols in 1880. There are now strict laws against duelling in most civilized countries throughout the world. Capt. H. B. C. Pollard contended that such a wide latitude of conduct was permitted in duelling that, "the margin between homicide and duel is extremely confused." This thin line of confusion is today unimportant. There is no recognized "justifiable provocation" for duelling; homicide and duelling are now considered equally reprehensible.

Duelling involved many important political and military men of their time, as well as substantial citizens from various other classes of society; newspaper editors were especially vulnerable to challenges. Right or wrong, good or bad, duelling had a great influence on history. One bibliography I have seen lists over 200 books on the subject. It was a deadly serious business, and in matters so vital the principals demanded the best weapons gunmakers could produce. It is to these handcrafted pistols of duelling type that we shall now turn our attention.

The Duelling Pistol

Duelling pistols as a specific type call for considerable latitude in description. They evolved from the long barreled horsemen's or holster pistols of the early flintlock era. In the late 1700s gunmakers were called on to make pistols with a better grip and balance; surer locks and truer barrels were demanded. For duelling, pairs must be exactly alike, so that no advantage in weapons could be had, and the over-all size and weight must conform to accepted standards. Barrels were seldom under 8″ and more often closer to 10″. Andrew Jackson's duelling pistols were equipped with 9″ barrels.

Great Britain favored smoothbore barrels of rather large caliber, but in France and Germany a somewhat smaller caliber and rifled barrels were prefered. Poly-groove rifling was developed in France and used in French pistols of the flintlock and caplock periods.

Pistols were usually loaded at the duelling ground in the presence of seconds. This was one reason for the practice of putting up the two matched pistols in a hardwood carrying case which would also accommodate the accessories for loading. The custom of casing duelling pistols and accessories has been largely responsible for the excellent preservation of these matched sets and their fittings found in collections today.

English, Scottish, and Irish flintlock duelling pistols conformed to a rather uniform general pattern. They were made with little or no ornamentation, first with a full stock under octagon barrels. Wogdon of London was famous for his graceful pistols of this type, and so many Wogdon pistols were used late in the 18th century that duels were sometimes referred to as "another Wogdon case."

Flintlock pistols of the British Isles reached their greatest perfection in the early 1800s. Their outstanding virtues were sturdiness and dependability; they were a quality product in every part. It has been remarked that the wood was so perfectly inletted for the locks and other hardware that it looked as though it had grown around them. Gradually the fullstock gave away to the halfstock design, and to the fore in pistols of this nature came the inimitable Joseph Manton, without peer in the 1800-1830 era. Joseph Manton's older half-brother John produced fine pistols, too, along with H. Mortimer, Durs Egg, Richards, Nock, Fowler, McDermot, Baker, Probin, Clark, Alley and other craftsmen.

On most of the later flintlock pistols one will find a roller bearing on the frizzen spring, the pan is protected by provisions to make it rainproof, the barrel vent is lined with silver, gold or platinum to prevent corrosion, there is sometimes a safety provision on the hammer, and the barrel is hooked to the stock by a patent breech and held by a barrel key—thus being easy to detach. Barrels, usually octagon, are browned, sometimes in mottled or striped pattern a la Damascus.

Metal parts may be tastefully engraved. The wood stock is usually checked at the grip to assure a good firm hold on the pistol, and the grip is often rounded at the butt—some call this a bag-type grip.

Across the English Channel in France and Belgium, there evolved a different style in matched pistols of duelling standard. Boutet of Versailles, coming into prominence toward the end of the 18th century, led the way in pistol elegance. Few could equal this master armorer in the beauty of his work. Where the English, Irish, and Scots were content to produce plain, sturdy pistols of

...and Duelling Days

by JAMES E. SERVEN

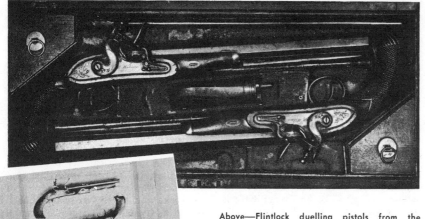

Above—Flintlock duelling pistols from the Fleet Street shop of Harvey Walklate Mortimer, first of the long line of highly regarded London gunmakers of that name. There is good authority for the claim that these pistols were owned, at different times, by Andrew Jackson and by Jackson's friend, General Twigg.

Below—The superb quality of Boutet's work is evident here in one of his plainer sets. Some of his pistols were richly encrusted with gold and silver and are unexcelled masterpieces in the armorer's art. He was the Royal Arquebusier to Louis XVI of France and made presentation arms for Napoleon.

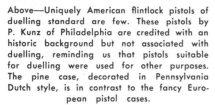

Above—Uniquely American flintlock pistols of duelling standard are few. These pistols by P. Kunz of Philadelphia are credited with an historic background but not associated with duelling, reminding us that pistols suitable for duelling were used for other purposes. The pine case, decorated in Pennsylvania Dutch style, is in contrast to the fancy European pistol cases.

Below—This beautiful pair of French flintlocks is fitted in a polished walnut case lined with green kid leather. Flared rifled barrels are finished in striped pattern and inlaid in gold. On top flat is "LePage a Paris Arqu'er de l'Empereur." A spur on the trigger guard assured a firm grip and a surer touch on the set trigger.

excellent workmanship, the French wanted more decorative treatment. Where the pistols of Great Britain were put up in oak cases, with felt lined partitions to separate the pistols and accessories, the French made their cases of beautifully grained and highly polished woods. Instead of simple partitions, they made the level of their case interiors flush with the top of the base section; the pistols and each accessory were precisely set down into their own individual recesses or "sockets." Collectors call this the French or "flush" style of casing.

Generally speaking, the French flintlock locks differed from the British only in minor style details, but the French octagon barrels were tapered-down toward the muzzle, then made to flare out at the muzzle. Bores were usually grooved by poly-groove rifling. The LePage family (gunmakers to Napoleon) was close to Boutet in the quality of their work; the various members of this prolific gunmaking family have a long and honorable history in their craft. Brunon was another who made fine flintlocks. A feature of pistols made by most French and Belgian gunmakers is the shape of the stock. On both fullstock and halfstock pistols, the grip is more at a right angle to the barrel and differs from the British also in that the butt is usually flat and capped.

Central Europe did not compete very strongly with the British and French in the field of matched and cased flintlock pairs. The Kuchenreuter family of Regensburg (Germany) gave some measure of distinction to Central Europe and was to their country what the LePage family was to France. Their well-made arms were produced through the flintlock and caplock eras. Some of the earliest Kuchenreuter flintlocks have rifled barrels, uncommon at the time. Italy, Spain and other European countries, while producing high quality arms, offered little in the recognized duelling types.

American Duellers

In America, few flintlock pistols were made for the specific purpose of duelling. The gentry among American duellists procured their "field of

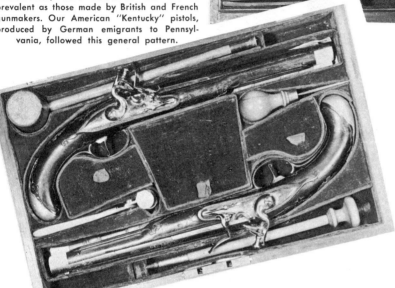

Below—The flintlock duelling pistols of Central Europe, such as these by Johann Andreas Kuchenreuter, were well-made but not as prevalent as those made by British and French gunmakers. Our American "Kentucky" pistols, produced by German emigrants to Pennsylvania, followed this general pattern.

Above—No armsmaker of the flintlock era was more highly praised than Joseph Manton of London, maker of this solidly built pair of duelling pistols. It is claimed that he never made a cheap or low grade weapon.

Below—A very fine pair of American made duelling pistols by J. E. Evans, one of Philadelphia's finest gunsmiths. A silver plate on the opposite side of each pistol is inscribed "Presented to General Edward S. Salomon. Declared by the vote of his fellow citizens as the most popular soldier of Cook County, Sept. 1867." Note the rare "gun stock" powder flask in case.

honor" pistols from abroad. Of course all Americans were not of the gentry. In 1813 Agent Pillet of the Pacific Fur Company had fighting words with one Montour of the Northwest Company. They duelled at six paces, using little flintlock pocket pistols, and with rather comic result. Montour's ball went through Pillet's trouser leg, and Pillet's ball made a neat hole in Montour's coat. A bystander remarked that the "wounds" could be treated better by a tailor than a doctor. When the smoke cleared Pillet and Montour decided they would thereafter refrain from rubbing each other's fur the wrong way.

There are a few exceptions, and some fine flintlock pistols suitable for duelling were made in America; these are primarily the better grade flintlock "Kentucky" style fullstock pistols made in Pennsylvania. The non-sanguinary Jackson-Avery duel was fought with a pair of these pistols. The flintlock "Kentucky" pistols were closest in style to the type produced in Germany and other Central European countries, with bird-head shaped butt. Unusual examples of fine American-made pistols of English pattern may be found in the few deluxe specimens of duelling type made by Simeon North. The majority of North's pistols were plain and rather clumsy big-bore pistols designed for military use,

but his halfstock duellers rated with the best.

Percussion Duellers

Following the practical development of the percussion cap, duelling pistols not only underwent a change in their firing mechanism, but important style changes came along. Bar action locks, wherein the hammer was located near the center of the lock-plate, continued to be popular; but back action locks, with the hammer located toward the front of the lock plate, now made their

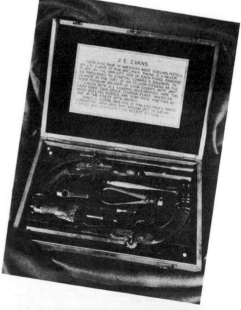

Below—These are pistols of the reknowned armsmaker Wogdon, said to have worked in Dublin and in London. His duelling pistols were second to none in the 1770-1800 period. Duels were sometime called "another Wogdon case."

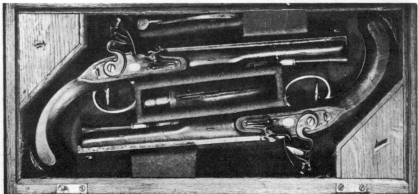

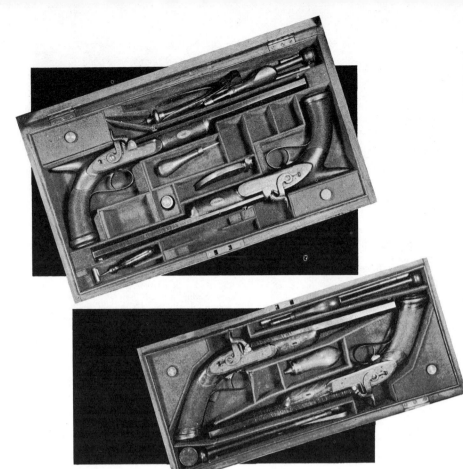

Above—Thomas Baker's saw-handle pistols shown here have unusually long 11½" barrels, caliber 47 smoothbore. These English pistols from 88 Fleet Street, London, were made for the Honorable A. G. Ponsonby of Hatherop Castle.

Below—Samuel Nock of London made these high quality caplock duelling pistols embodying his patented breech. The slanting grip with flat butt is a bit unusual in English pistols.

appearance. Although many English and Irish percussion pistols adhered to the customary rounded bag-type grip, some now turned to a more slanting style with a flat, capped butt. The saw-handle grip, first used in a few flintlocks, now came into greater use. Octagon barrels of about 10" length might be had with smaller bores and with rifling. Single set triggers were more often used.

The use of set triggers in duelling pistols gave rise to rather hot debate. The more experienced duellists claimed set triggers were unreliable and advised younger men against their use. A too-finely set trigger on Senator Broderick's pistol caused the pistol to fire before it was brought up, the bullet hitting the ground in front of Judge Terry; that faulty set trigger may have been responsible for Senator Broderick's death.

By the time the percussion pistol attained full development, the practice of duelling was fast waning. Thus the percussion pistols we class as duelling pistols, because of their general code-conforming pattern, served other purposes as well. It was true, in the flintlock era too, that boxed pistols of duelling style were employed for other services, such as home protection, as travelling pistols, and not infrequently as highly valued presentation awards.

The French must be given high honors in pistols of the percussion era, for some of their work in engraving, inlay, overlay, carving and deluxe casing is high art at its very best. Gauvain, LePage, Devisme, Rennette and a few others stand out in this period. I am fortunate to own a Gauvain set which was presented by the French government to Col. H. T. Siborne (who had been the head of the European Danube Commission). The stocks are of ebony and their surface is completely and intricately carved. The metal finish is silver gray overlaid with gold in two colors. Barrels are fluted and rifled in accordance with the common French custom. The case is of beautifully grained hardwood with a pierced metal plate inset atop the lid bearing the presentation legend. And this hardwood case is contained within a felt-lined leather carrying case. Thus you may see how much more than simple gunmaking went into high quality sets of pistols in the percussion era. The Gauvain pistols were pre-

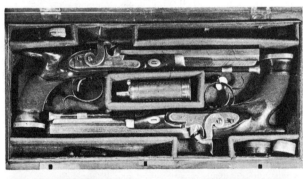

Above — Saw-handled stocks appeared on but few duelling pistols of the flintlock or caplock periods. This sturdy pair is equipped with single set triggers, a feature disliked by experienced duellists.

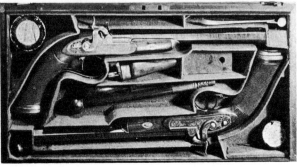

Below — Handsomely crafted English duelling pair stocked with the rather scarce sloping grip and flat capped butt. Barrels show a beautiful striped brown finish favored by the best London armsmakers.

Right—Henry William Herbert, the Frank Forester of writing fame and a great firearms expert, had Kuchenreuter barrels imported from Germany and fitted to these English-made duelling pistols. An unusual feature is the back action form of lock; these locks were often used in small pistols but are seldom seen on duelling pistols.

Left, below—Walnut, ebony, and other hardwoods were usually employed for pistol stocks, but occasionally we find a pair of pistols elegantly stocked in ivory. It is doubtful that pistols endowed with such artistry ever saw service on a duelling ground.

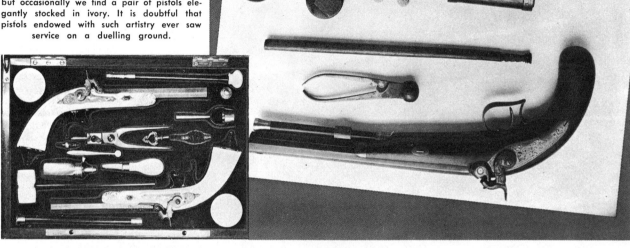

sented in 1879, contradicting the general belief that manufacture and sale of percussion pistols ended with our was between the states.

Gastinne Rennette's Gallery in Paris has maintained facilities from 1838 right up to these modern times for those who wished to practice with or purchase fine percussion duelling pistols—now more properly called target pistols. Famous pistol champions Chevalier Ira Paine and Walter Winans made record scores at the Rennette Gallery.

All pistols of duelling type were not of the high quality described here; some of the French, Belgian and German sets were rather mediocre. The majority of cased duelling sets, though, were so far above contemporary pocket pistols, traveler's pistols, or martial pistols that they were easily the pistol aristocrats of their day.

As the percussion period advanced, Germany made great strides in pistol making. She gave more attention to ornamentation, metal parts being nicely inlaid, engraved or richly chiseled. Her armorers introduced adjustable sights, improved set triggers, better rifling. The barrels of J. Adam Kuchenreuter became famous. They were so well regarded that the distinguished English sportsman Henry William Herbert had Kuchenreuter barrels imported to England and placed on the pair of duelling pistols made up for him by an English gunmaker. Herbert came to America in 1831 and endeared himself to American sports-

men through his many writings under the pseudonym Frank Forester.

Here in America, the making of either flintlock or caplock duelling pistols did not get far off the ground. A few gunmakers in New York and Philadelphia produced some very well-made percussion pairs, usually follow-

ing the English patterns. In fact, it is often somewhat difficult to determine if duelling pistols bearing the names of American gunmakers and gun dealers were made here in toto or whether the locks and barrels and hardware were imported and the pistols stocked here. In some cases it is

Gold mounted duelling pistols with intricately carved ebony stocks. These were presented to Col. H. T. Siborne by the French government as a token of great esteem.

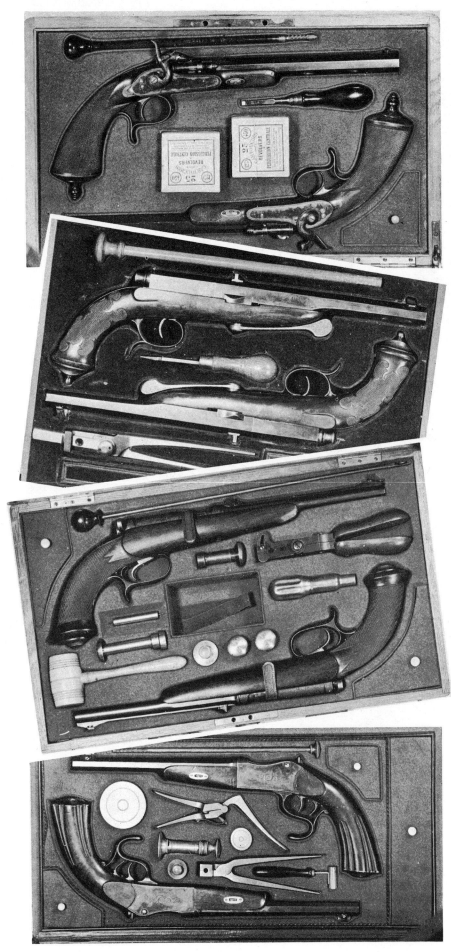

Pair of breech-loading pistols by H. Faure LePage of Paris. The breech cover swings to the side as on the well-known Snider action. A good example of transition period pistols wherein conversion methods from percussion to metallic cartridge were explored.

These pistols illustrate one of the many methods tried in advancing from the muzzle-loader to a breechloader. The hinged barrel is operated by an underlever, very much like system used on some shotguns.

known that pistols made abroad (minus any proof-marks or maker's stamp) were imported and stamped with the name of the American gun-shop which sold them. However, we do know, with equal certainty, that a limited number of fine pistols were completely manufactured here and are credited to craftsmen like Evans, Deringer, Tryon, Constable, Robertson, and a few others. American duelling pistols are quite scarce and highly prized by collectors.

Transition Duellers

Approaching the end of the caplock era, some very interesting transitional arms came off the workbenches. Gastinne Rennette of Paris introduced a breechloading caplock model in which the trigger guard served as a lever to slide the barrel forward for loading the powder and ball at the breech.

Adhering to the general duelling standards of size and outline, several styles of German needle pistols made their appearance, some having a bolt action and others operated by a lever under the forestock. The French made up pistols with a swing-over hinged breech as on Snider patent guns. Pistols with the famous Martini action, operated by the lever trigger-guard, came on the scene. It must be considered that the primary use for these pistols, as well as for many in the late percussion period, was for target shooting or self-defense. A few were even used for hunting, and you will find illustrated a beautiful pair

N. Von Dreyse, inventor of the needle fire system, made these pistols. They are breechloaders, operated by a bolt, and employing the needle fire ammunition.

Breech-loading pistols by German armsmaker Felix Arnd. The action is the Martini type, and something like that used in the Bavarian single shot "Lightning" pistols.

Cased pair of LePage duellers with inter-changeable rifled target barrels. Circa 1835.

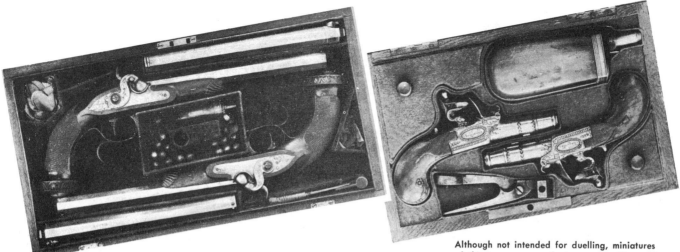

Although not intended for duelling, miniatures of this type were used at some less "formal" meetings. This beautiful pair was made by Boutet, about 1800.

of Kuchenreuter pistols designed to accommodate an attachable shoulder stock, thus making the pistol into a hunting carbine.

Accessories

The accompanying accessories are an interesting feature of cased duelling sets. Uncased pistols usually became separated from their loading implements when they were retired from use, but the duelling sets and their tools and fittings provide an accurate history of these vital elements and components. In covered corner compartments of the English type cases we often find moulded balls, extra flints (or nipples), cleaning patches, and other small items such as an oiler. The partitions usually provide a place in the center between the pistols for a powder flask, and along the sides there are long com-partments for the bullet mould and the cleaning and loading rods—sometimes a nipple wrench for percussion sets.

As you will observe from the illustrations, the flush casing of French sets frequently included such additional items as a wooden mallet to start the bullet, a wad-cutter, lead ladle, spring wise, vent pick, powder measure, screw-driver, and small tapping hammer. These all tell us a story; certainly they make us appreciate the convenience of modern metallic cartridges.

Whatever merit the practice of duelling may have had is irrelevant here; what is important to us is that it was a big factor in driving gun makers to new heights in their art throughout a century of arms making.

Chivalry and valor have ever been highly regarded, but duelling as a demonstration of these virtues has always had its critics. In 1845, "A Society for the Prevention of Duelling" was organized in England. Duelling and duellers were bitterly attacked in America, even though some, like Senator Linn of Missouri, expressed the view that, "duelling is like marrying — the more barriers erected against it, the surer the interested parties are to get together."

The odds of being killed in a duel with pistols were greater than in Russian roulette. During a relatively short period in England 172 duels were fought. A total of 344 men faced death —69 met death and 96 were wounded. Consider the thoughts which might have passed through your mind if you, like Andrew Jackson, had faced a man 24 feet away bent on killing you, awaiting General Overton's words: Ready! Fire! ⊕

"Another Wogdon case" by the famous gun-smith of Dublin and London.

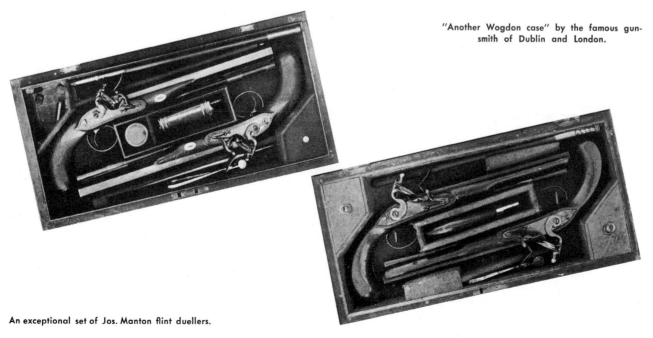

An exceptional set of Jos. Manton flint duellers.

SHOT

Revealing facts about those important little droplets of lead which spell hit or miss in the increasingly popular sport of shotgunning

Typical of American shotmaking plants, the Youle tower was 60 feet across at the base and rose to a height of 175 feet.

by JAMES E. SERVEN

Many People were surprised when a Gallup poll indicated that more shotguns were owned by private citizens than rifles or pistols. This is no phenomenon, nor is it strange that the use of shotguns on ranges and afield is increasing rapidly.

In many areas expanding population has limited rifle ranges. Those who like to shoot often turn to the shotgun, whose relatively short killing range makes trap and skeet shooting quite safe on small acreage. Farmers and ranchers who hesitate to permit the use of high-power rifles on their property are less apprehensive about shotguns—you don't often mistake a cow for a bird or a cottontail!

Today we have come to expect top performance from our shotgun fodder —the powder, primers, hulls, and shot. Each component though, had

quite a climb to get up where it is, and here I would like to give you some background history of the all-important lead shot.

In the very early days of shotgunning there was no dropped shot. Sportsmen in England and on the European continent used "Swan Drops," lead pellets cast in a multi-cavity mould. Usually the cast pellets ran about 200-250 to the pound. Then one day in 1769, it is claimed, one William Watts, a young Bristol gentleman (variously described as a plumber and an engineer) dreamed up the idea of pouring molten lead through a crude sieve and letting the little round droplets that oozed through fall into a trough of water. From here it was relatively quick if high step up to the shot tower.

English sportsmen led the way as

devotees of the shotgun, demanding improvements and publishing interesting treatises such as Col. Hawker's *Instructions to Young Sportsmen.* In company with this active interest among the sportsmen in England and on the Continent gunmakers made great advances, progressing from the muzzle-loading flintlock and the cap-lock to breech-loading guns with fixed ammunition.

I had the pleasure of lunching with Mr. Harry Lawrence of London recently. We discussed the long and distinguished career of the Purdey gunmaking firm which Mr. Lawrence now directs. This firm was founded in the early 1800s. It was somewhat surprising to learn that at Purdey's, where the double barrel gun is still paramount, they adhere to the Old World practice of requiring their

SHOT.

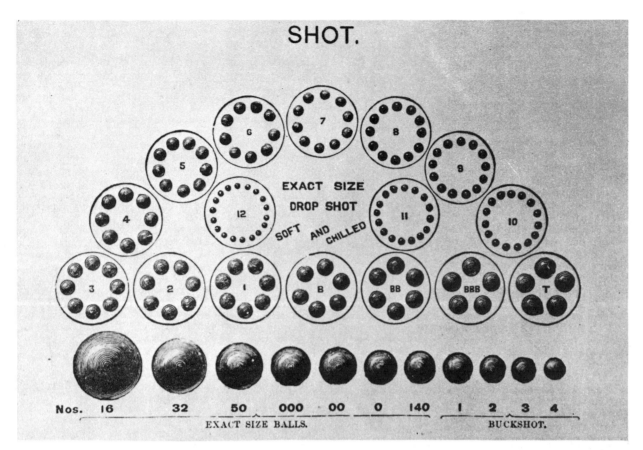

EXACT SIZE DROP SHOT SOFT AND CHILLED

Nos.   16   32   50   000   00   0   140   1   2   3   4

EXACT SIZE BALLS.   BUCKSHOT.

workmen to devote a number of years to apprenticeship before they are permitted to undertake any critical work; such work is entrusted only to those officially accredited as "Master Craftsmen."

As interest in shotgun shooting and the quality of guns increased abroad, so the sport took root here in America. Henry William Herbert, writing under the name of Frank Forester in the 1850s, did much to encourage American field sports. While America lagged behind Europe at that time in the manufacture of fine shotguns, there was great activity and very creditable progress in manufacturing the shooting components. Our gunpowder companies rapidly learned to produce fine grained, clean burning powder, and the production of lead shot became an important business.

One of the interesting landmarks along New York's East River in the 1850s was Youle's Shot Tower. It rose to a height of 175 feet and measured about 60 feet at the base. Just before the day of the shot towers, the means of casting shot had been to run hot lead over a perforated copper plate suspended a few feet over a large kettle or vat of water. The lead drops, in falling so short a distance and being so suddenly cooled and hardened, did not acquire a perfectly globular form. Slower cooling and a perfectly round form were only attained by a long drop, said to have been first tested from the tower of the Church

of St. Mary at Radcliffe, England.

As was customary, the Youle furnaces for melting the lead were located near the top of the tower. This New York tower had a productive capacity of three to four tons of shot per day. Arsenic was mixed with the lead in proportion of forty pounds to the ton to provide the desired alloy.

The molten lead was strained through colanders of uniform design, but of course with varied sizes of perforations for different sizes of shot. Many sizes were produced, from No. 1 swan shot to No. 12 dust shot. The colanders were not always at equal temperature and the size of shot could vary somewhat, and would not always be perfect, requiring a further passing over properly sized sieves before the shot was precisely graded and ready for sale and use. In England they called this "tabling" and the sieves were called "riddles."

Shot Towers in America

As the 1800s proceeded toward their close, the number of American shot manufacturers increased. Prominent in this trade were Thomas Sparks, Tatham Bros., New York Lead Co., LeRoy Co., Merchant's Shot Tower Co., Dubuque Co., and the Montreal Rolling Mills Co. The Merchant's Shot Tower Co. of Baltimore and the Thomas Sparks firm of Philadelphia won commendation at the 1876 U. S. International Exhibition (Centennial) for "Uniformity and

general good finish of pellets."

The Newcastle Chilled Shot Co., Walker-Parker Ltd., and Locke, Blackett & Co. were leading English manufacturers. There were, of course, shot towers in France, Italy, Belgium, Prussia, Austria and elsewhere. The highest tower is said to have been at Villach in Carinthia (southern Austria), being 249 feet high. It should be noted here that a few of the shotmakers (Locke, Blackett & Co. were one) cast their shot down the shaft of a pit rather than from a high tower; others used a plan of part pit-part tower.

There are interesting charts in W. W. Greener's *The Gun and Its Development* which indicate the variety of sizes made by different manufacturers. A rather surprising lack of uniformity is found in the number of pellets to the ounce in the same sizes offered by different manufacturers of that period, especially in the very small sizes. Thus, when using the same measure of shot from different manufacturers it was often difficult to obtain the same patterns.

In Greener's book you will also find considerable information about velocity, pattern and charges. While one of the early and most extensive studies, this is but one of a number of excellent books written on shotgunning by American and English experts in the field. (*The Gun* has long been out of print, unfortunately, but many libraries own copies.)

The nearer to a perfect sphere which each pellet may be, the more accurate will be the flight of the charge. Soft pellets, in receiving the shock of the explosion, in rubbing against one another and the sides of the barrel, may become deformed and fly erratically. It is for this reason that hard or "chilled" shot, though a bit more expensive, found increasing favor. The chilled, hard shot not only was less prone to erratic flight but gave better velocity and deeper penetration.

Among the accompanying illustrations will be found a chart of the American standard shot sizes and data as to dimensions and the number of pellets per ounce. You will also find some of the accessories used by shotgun shooters of an earlier day. For the muzzle-loaders, important pieces of needed equipment were the powder flasks and the shot pouches. These shot containers were put up in several styles; principally they were bag-shaped pouches of hard russet leather, some plain and some embossed with a game scene or other design. The brass or iron tops varied, some shooters preferring the single or double spring "Irish" top which was in effect a removable tubular measuring cup; the majority preferred a lever type which might be adjusted to throw different amounts of shot. These hard leather shot pouches varied in size, too, having capacities of 2½, 3, 4 and up to 5 pounds of shot.

Another shot container for carrying afield was designed in soft leather or canvas and was called a shot belt. It had an elongated shape and was held by shoulder straps; some had compartments for two sizes of shot.

As the shot came from the tower it was put up in canvas bags. Around the turn of the century M. Hartley & Co. advertised "New York shot furnished in all sizes and finishes in 25 pound bags at tower prices ruling at date of shipment." When the shot reached the gun stores, it was found

Shot pouches differed in size, shape, design and type of charger. English flasks tended to be plain, while those made in America often were embossed with game scenes or other designs.

that customers often did not wish to buy large quantities of one size, so the store fixture people of those days designed dealer shot cases. One of the most popular and least expensive was Dunscomb's. This case was designed with eight compartments for different sizes of shot, each holding 35 pounds. A more expensive hardwood "self-weighing" case was also popular, this one divided into ten compartments, each holding 25 pounds of shot. Thus it was made easier for the dealer to measure out the exact size and the desired quantity; those of you who have spilled a few pounds of shot will understand this problem.

Early Shotshells

The evolution from loose powder and shot to the self-contained loads proceeded with the smoothbores after the Civil War as it had with rifled guns. Eley Brothers of London came up with an idea of using "wire loads" — shot contained in thin wire nets

and wrapped in paper. These were presumed to provide longer range and closer pattern. The Roper Company of Amherst, Mass., designed a four-shot smoothbore shotgun which employed a reloadable iron shell, first employing a percussion cap for ignition and later a primer. We soon came to the brass reloadable shell and then the cardboard shell with a brass base. The variety in these was almost endless, loads beginning with 2 drams of powder and ⅝-oz of shot for 28 gauge up to 3¾ drams or more of powder and a fistful of shot for the big 4 gauge. Shotshell length has varied from about 2" to 4". Down the past half-century many theories have been tried and many claims made for combinations of factors to throw the shot most effectively. The history of ballistics is another story, but recommended loads for various game when shotgun shells were loaded with black powder may be of interest.

Game	Powder, drams	Shot ozs.	Shot size
Woodcock	3¼	1	10
Woodcock, Snipe	3¼	1	9
Snipe	3¼	1⅛	9
Quail	3¼	1	8
Quail, Prairie Chickens	3¼	1⅛	8
Prairie Chickens	3½	1⅛	8
Inanimate targets	3¼	1¼	8
Live Pigeons	3½	1¼	8
Ruffed Grouse	3¼	1⅛	7
Ruffed Grouse, Teal	3½	1⅛	7
Prairie Chickens	3¼	1⅛	6
Pintail, Bluebill	3½	1⅛	6
Mallard	3¼	1⅛	5
Mallard, Redhead	3½	1⅛	4
Redhead	3¾	1⅛	4
Canvas Back	3¾	1⅛	3
Turkey	3¾	1⅛	2

This loading chart was designed for 12-gauge shotgun shells. The quantities of powder and shot were reduced somewhat in the smaller gauges. A dram of black powder was equivalent to from 8 grains to 14 grains of the various early smokeless powders, depending on the brand, thus Nitro powders had to be loaded by precise weight or by smaller capacity measures than those used with black powder.

Smoothbore guns were not the only vehicles for the use of shot. Shotshells were made for rifles from 22 to 50-70 caliber and for pistols in the standard calibers. The 22 shells were usually loaded with No. 12 shot, 32 and 38 pistol calibers employed from No. 8 to No. 10, 44 and 45 calibers were loaded with No. 8. Laws restricting the use of shotgun-pistols, and other factors have served to reduce the use of small caliber shot shells except for the 410 and small-bore loads used by ornithologists.

Keeping pace with the factory-loaded shells, the manufacturers of handloading equipment brought forth a variety of tools so that the economy-minded or those who shot often and liked to experiment could load and

No Guns, Foreign or American, Will Outshoot or Outwear the Lefever.

COMPARATIVE SIZES OF DROP SHOT.

Merchants Shot Tower Co., New York.		Tatham & Bros. New York.		New York Lead Co., New York.		The Leroy Shot & Lead Mfg. Co., New York.		Thom. W. Sparks, Phila'phia, Pa.		St. Louis Shot Tower Co., St. Louis, Mo.		Dubuque Shot Mfg. Co, Dubuque, Iowa.		Selby Smelting & Lead Co., San Francisco, Cal.		Chicago Shot Tower Co., Chicago, Ill.	
Sizes.	No. Pell'ts to oz.	Sizes.	No. Pell'ts to oz.	Sizes.	No. Pell'ts to oz.	Sizes.	No. Pell'ts to oz.	Sizes.	No. Pell'ts to oz.	Sizes.	No. Pell'ts to oz.	Sizes.	No. Pell'ts to oz.	Sizes.	No. Pell'ts to oz.	Sizes.	No. Pell'ts to oz.
BBB	39	BBB	42	BBB	44	BBB	44	BBB	48	BBB	46	BBB	46	BBB	46	BBB	46
BB	45	BB	40	BB	49	BB	49	BB	55	BB	53	BB	53	BB	55	BB	53
B	52	B	59	B	58	B	58	B	63	B	63	B	62	B	68	B	62
1	60	1	71	1	69	1	69	1	80	1	79	1	75	1	79	1	75
2	77	2	86	2	82	2	82	2	90	2	98	2	92	2	89	2	92
3	94	3	106	3	98	3	98	3	118	3	116	3	118	3	118	3	118
4	115	4	132	4	121	4	121	4	130	4	167	4	146	4	134	4	146
5	140	5	168	5	149	5	166	5	182	5	181	5	172	5	170	5	172
6	180	6	218	6	209	6	209	6	245	6	252	6	246	6	215	6	246
7	225	7	291	7	278	7	278	7	305	7	306	7	323	7	303	7	323
8	365	8	399	8	375	8	375	8	426	8	426	8	434	8	420	8	434
9	610	9	568	9	560	9	560	9	615	9	584	9	596	9	592	9	596
10	1130	10	848	10	822	10	822	10	950	10	981	10	854	10	874	10	854
11	2200	11	1346	11	982	11	982	11	1660	11	1603	11	1414	11	1401	11	1414
12	3200	12	2326	12	1878	12	1778	12	3416	12	2305	12	2400	12	2080	12	2400
13	12200							Dust	5910								

13

This shot chart was found in an 1893 Lefever Arms Company catalog.

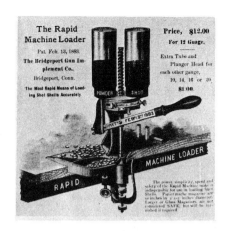

Machine bench loaders for shotgun shells are nothing new; this model was patented over 80 years ago.

reload their shells. The Bridgeport Gun Implement Co. and the Ideal Manufacturing Co. of New Haven were pioneers in this field well before 1900. The Ideal Company later became a part of the Lyman Gun Sight Co. and Ideal loading tools have continued into modern design and current production. Many manufacturers have now entered the loading tool field. There is a great upsurge in powder burning and shot slinging on skeet and trap ranges; reloading clinics are held throughout the country; some of the larger firms who cater to reloaders now buy shot by the carload!

Great interest is generated by the important shotgun tournaments now held throughout the country, and very valuable awards are involved. There is greater national attention devoted to the shotgun sports now than was focussed on the famous series of shotgun matches staged in the 1880s by "Doc" W. F. Carver and International Champion Adam Bogardus. Individual participation has increased tremendously.

Cognizant of today's growing interest, the National Rifle Association has expanded its coverage of the smoothbore sport. From them may be obtained a booklet which provides the NRA rules for "International Type Skeet" and "Modified International Clay Pigeon" shooting. Also available are a booklet devoted to shooting ranges and the big "NRA Illustrated Reloading Handbook." Another publication, the "NRA Firearms & Ammunition Fact Book," contains a wealth of information on ballistics and other important shotgunning factors. Handbooks are also available from some of the loading tool manufacturers, independent publishers, and the manufacturers of guns and ammunition.

In all this enjoyment of a healthful outdoor American sport, those little lead pellets are the indicators of a man's skill. Whether it be a high

shot from a duck blind, the quick aim at flushing quail, a snap shot at a bobbing cottontail, or a swing to the flight of a clay pigeon, the lead pellets you are able to place in your target tell the difference between success or failure.

It is natural for us to ask, "What has the experience of almost 200 years of shotmaking taught us? What steps have been taken to give us more uniform, harder and yet less abrasive shot?"

Improvements in Shot

Many experiments have been undertaken through the years. It was found that slag-lead, although lighter than other lead, was harder and was therefore considered more suitable for shot. Polishing shot by placing it in a drum with a mixture of black lead gave the shot a highly burnished finish pleasant to the eye, but some shooters complained that the black lead caused leading in the bore.

The employment of quicksilver in the shotmaking process produced very excellent shot but the cost proved to be prohibitive and the practice was discontinued. Chilled shot of today is given its proper degree of hardness through the addition of carefully controlled proportions of antimony and arsenic in the molten alloy. Some manufacturers add small amounts of tin to the alloy.

As the business of ammunition-making took on greater proportions, two giants in the field, Winchester and Remington decided to build their own shot towers. The Remington

tower at Bridgeport was completed in 1909 and stands 190 feet tall to the top of the flagpole. It was designed with a campanile exterior so that it would have some architectural merit rather than the appearance of a pregnant smokestack.

Except for mechanization and refinements in some stages the tower shotmaking process is much the same as that followed for a number of years. Electrically heated furnaces have replaced oil burners and earlier heating methods. At the top of the tower at Remington's there are two huge kettles capable of holding 10 tons each of molten lead. Thousands of pounds of lead alloy are brewed here every working day.

Drawn from these huge caldrons at approximately 750° the leaden brew looks like a small stream of water as it is directed over the colanders. The fall of the leaden globules at Remington's tower is 133 feet, and they land in a tank 10 feet deep; the water seethes and boils under this leaden hail.

From the tank the shot is picked up in buckets and carried back up the tower by an endless belt conveyor. An intricate system of sorting follows, after which the shot passes through seven different types of rollers which perform the tasks of cleaning, polishing and applying the finish. Then the shot goes on to storage bins and eventually to loading machines or packaging. It has been estimated that the Remington tower can produce a billion pellets of shot in a working day.

Prior to 1912 Winchester purchased

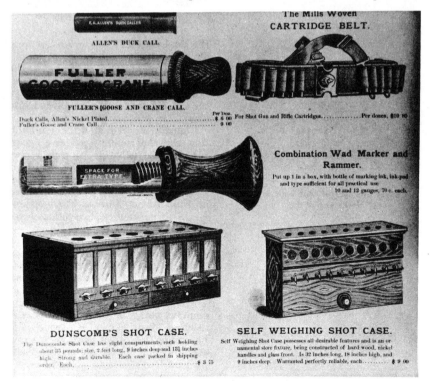

Items long of interest to shotgunners have been game-bird calls, shell belts and vests, and the partitioned cases for dispensing various sizes of shot.

its shot from other concerns, principally the National Lead Company. But when National Lead and the U. S. Cartridge Company (a competitor) became affiliated, Winchester decided it was time to produce its own shot.

Winchester's tower at New Haven was completed in 1912, and the cost was $190,000—a lot of money in those times. This was a very efficient shot factory, however, and those interested in the technicalities can find an informative cross section drawing of this old Winchester tower at New Haven in *Winchester, The Gun That Won The West* by Harold F. Williamson.

The high drop at the Winchester tower measured 154 feet, and the building itself rose to a height of nine floors, each floor employed in the shotmaking process.

On the ground floor the lead and other components were heated, mixed and cast in bars which were lifted by elevator to the eighth and ninth floors. Soft shot was melted and dropped from the ninth floor, chilled shot from the eighth.

From the water well on the ground floor the shot was bucketed to the second floor, drained and lowered to the first floor where it was dried in a steam drum. Now the shot took another conveyor trip up to the sixth floor. Here the first polish was performed and the shot gradually lowered floor by floor to the storage tanks on the ground floor. In this floor by floor trip downward the shot was automatically inspected for roundness, run over thirteen sorting plates, on to a number of revolving screens and given

Above left — Workman feeds a bar of lead alloy into Winchester's caldron high in shot tower.

Above right — Now the molten lead flows in a clear stream over a colander, whence droplets of lead fall many feet into a water tank.

Left — This is what the lead droplets look like as they pass through the colander and start their long drop toward the receiving tank.

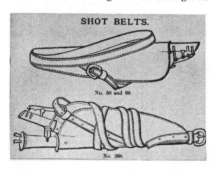

Canvas and leather shot belts as used in an earlier day.

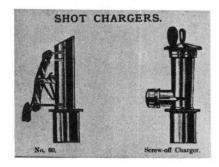

Types of dispensing tops used on shot flasks, usually of brass.

the final polish. These processes were almost entirely automatic. A duplicate set of machinery reduced the chance of any interruption in operations due to breakdowns. About 50 tons of pig lead could be turned into shot in an average working day.

Changes in Winchester's ammunition and shot operations have occurred since Winchester became a part of the Olin Mathieson Chemical Corporation, and the Winchester-Western ammunition division was centralized at East Alton, Illinois. Obviously it would be impractical to produce large quantities of shot in New Haven and ship it to East Alton for loading in shotgun shells, so the New Haven tower is now resting on its laurels and showers of Winchester-Western shot now fall in a plant at East Alton.

The East Alton shotmaking plant employs many of the same processes used at New Haven. Outwardly, it has more the appearance of a grain elevator, and it is built on the "part pit-part tower" design. Rotary screens are used for sorting into size and, based on the mechanical principle that a true sphere will roll straight, sorting for spherical perfection is accomplished by running the shot over four inclined glass plates. These plates are so arranged that any imperfect shot — any that does not roll true — will be discarded.

Most of the shot on the market is now chilled shot, the smaller sizes usually containing a higher percentage of antimony than the larger sizes. Winchester-Western features copper plated Lubaloy shot; some other manufacturers use a nickel coating. In the past, graphite has been extensively used to give the shot a high polish.

New Techniques

By this time it has become obvious to us that shotmaking is and for a number of years has been far from a minor operation; it is indeed an intricate and precise industrial art.

A radical departure from making shot by the traditional shot tower method is now found in the patented process of the Murdock Lead Company of Dallas, Texas. Instead of a drop of many feet the molten lead pellets drop only 3/16th of an inch!

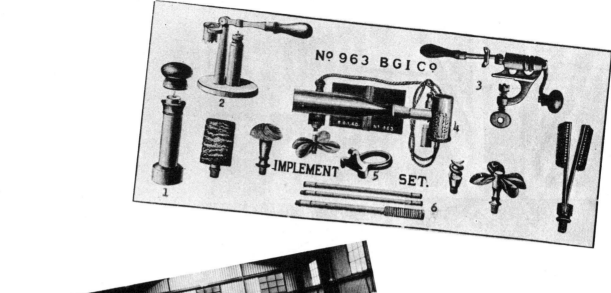

The Murdock Lead Company plant, where shot is made by a revolutionary, patented process. No long fall of the molten lead is required.

The leaden alloy, which contains proportions of tin and antimony to provide hardness, is heated to approximately 700°. It passes along a Z course and finally to a small opening. After the short ³⁄₁₆ths of an inch drop into a water solution kept at approximately 200°, it is claimed that a steam ball forms around the leaden droplets, making them perfectly round. The shot then rolls about two inches, over a special inclined planer board and into the receiving tanks. Thence the shot are screened, prepared, and packaged.

Except for the molten lead feed control the Murdock process is automatically operated. Certainly the space required is less extensive, the working areas more convenient, and the handling less arduous than in the shot towers. We attempt no judgment of the relative quality of shot produced by these varying methods, and no doubt the merits of each will be strongly represented by their proponents.

In concluding this brief history of shotmaking and related accessories, it is quite proper to take notice of the improved vehicles in which the shot are now contained. The cardboard hull replaced the brass shell and now cardboard is being fast replaced by plastic, some of it semi-transparent polyethylene.

Reverting somewhat to the old Eley idea of a "wrapped shot charge," manufacturers now enclose the shot load for special brands within shot-protecting plastic collars or cups, some of which have an integral base which serves as a cushioning wad between the shot and the powder.

Why have men over the years burned midnight oil thinking up ways and means to give us uniform polished or plated shot, better wads, stronger and more durable hulls, more efficient powder and primers, and better all-around shotgun performance? The major efforts have provided: fast, sure, noncorrosive ignition; denser, dependable patterns; greater range;

cleaner kills; no leading; minimum recoil. These goals have been attained to a very commendable degree. Those of you who have enjoyed shotgunning from muzzle-loaders to the old Damascus barrel doubles and on to the pumps and automatics can perhaps best understand the extent of forward strides in shotgun performance.

We go back to this simple truth — no matter how you package it or what you shoot in, the shot is the stuff that puts meat in the pot or shatters the clay birds! It will always be a vitally important component. ●

Instructions to Young Sportsmen, by Col. P. Hawker. London, 1814, 1st ed., London, 1854, 10th ed.

The Gun and Its Development, by W. W. Greener, London, 1881, 1st ed., London, 1910, 10th ed.

Winchester, The Gun That Won The West, by H. F. Williamson. Washington, D. C., 1952.

NRA Reloading Handbook, Washington, D. C., 1961.

NRA Firearms & Ammunition Fact Book, Washington, D. C., 1964.

NRA Illustrated Shotgun Handbook, Washington, D. C., 1964.

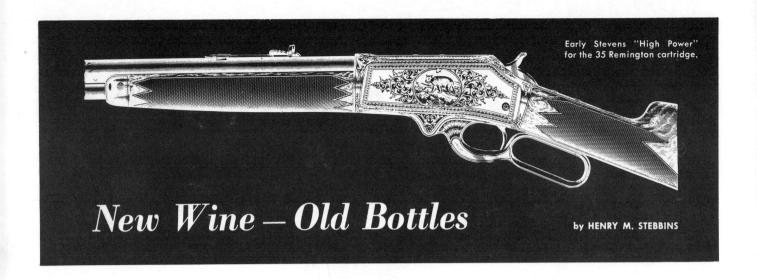
Early Stevens "High Power" for the 35 Remington cartridge.

New Wine — Old Bottles

by HENRY M. STEBBINS

THE SILVERY STUB of what former generations had known as a giant oak stands beside the faint trail. One hollowed limb remains, pointing down the slight grade, and you take the hint. Ten seconds of brush-bending and you stand at the brink of the mushy-banked little stream.

"I've been here before!" you think. "I came in from the other side and a woodcock spiralled up. The 8's dropped him right by that stub."

Most of us have had such an experience afield, and the confirmed guncrank has it again and again as some new piece of equipment comes to market. Quite often it's not so new, indeed!

Peep sights, for instance, weren't new to William Lyman in the late 1870's. Muzzle guns and metallic cartridge rifles had had them, and so had crossbows. Lyman, it's true, popularized the sight for woods hunting by insisting on a large aperture, and still more important, the sense of merely looking through it instead of fixating carefully upon it in the manner of the microscope squinter. The eye caught the center of the peep because the light was strongest there.

But here we're concerned with recent history as it's related to the present, and only with smatterings. A complete listing of gun and ammo reincarnations is out of the question.

Copies and Near-Copies

Later copies or near-copies in gun design are common. The 1898 Mauser with its double-lugged bolt locking close to the cartridge head and its staggered right-left, right-left magazine is well known as being many times a grandfather. The Winchester Model 12 pump shotgun has a number of near-copies, perhaps the earliest being Savage's 12 gauge that appeared soon after World War I. Except for its top tang safety in double-gun style it's almost a dead ringer. Change the digit 3 of Ithaca's Model 37 to 1 and you have the original 17 Remington, a 20-gauge pump that came out of the old Ilion factory for the returning veterans of World War I. Why the Remington folks let this treasure slip through their fingers is one of the mysteries of the trade.

Conversions and "Understudies"

Converting a popular target gun to a sporter, or vice versa, is old stuff. The Winchester 52 and 75 smallbores were designed for gallery and outdoor ranges, but in revised form they go hunting, too. The Savage 19 took hold at once as a range rifle, and three years later, in 1922, appeared a sporter which in various forms was manufactured for a score of years. Just the opposite happened to the Winchester 54 and 70 models, and 'way back in 1918 the Remington Model 12 22 pump was fitted up in "N.R.A. Target" style with a sling, a globe front sight, and a target-disked Lyman rear.

There was nothing new in these conversions. Hadn't the Winchester and Stevens single shots and the Winchester 1895 repeater long before gone into competition as target rifles, the former dressed up with long-pronged Schuetzen buttplates and palm rests for 200 yard offhand, and the '95 with military-type forestock and sights for long-range four-position, prone to standing, shooting.

The Model 30 Remington rifle was no more than a sporting outgrowth of the Model 1917 U.S. rifle commonly called the "Enfield." Thousands of Civil War muskets were converted to shotguns, as was the British Snider musket. Untold numbers of the latter were sold all over the world as the "Zulu."

Understudy arms are nice—a 22 built to resemble a bigbore in almost all respects except recoil and that ever-nagging matter of ammunition cost! The idea is well established in revolvers and auto-pistols currently "made for each other," and the 32-44 S & W on a 44 Russian sixgun frame was familiar 50 years ago, just as interchangeable single-shot rifle barrels had been, still earlier. The 22 M-1 and M-2 Springfields had been the Army's answer to the call for cheap 30-06 practice, but then, hadn't the famous 1873 Winchester been made in 22 short and 22 long a generation earlier?

Sometimes you'd just doctor your bigbore to get cheap practice. The 22 insert barrels for the 7.92mm service Mauser, often seen here since 1945, weren't new. For years Luger pistols had used such a device, firing a tiny bottle-necked cartridge with round bullet of about .15-inch caliber. Heavy Navy ordnance had used 22 rimfires for whisper work, too.

Target Spotters

Modern electronic "guns" spot your shots on a target. They're fun, and pricey, too. Almost any targeteer of the past could afford a Hollifield dotter to slip inside the barrel of his 30-06 1903

Winchester "Extra Light Weight" Model 1886 rifle.

Springfield. It used a little double target set about two inches from the muzzle. You held at six o'clock on the top bull, and if aim and trigger squeeze rated "Expert" a rod tongued out from the barrel and punched a 10 in the lower target. Anyway, you knew where you would have hit with ball ammunition, and after the bull had been shot up you turned the paper upside-down and tried to do better on your second string! The last Hollifield I remember having seen was in 1912, and it was fitted into the barrel and chambers of a Military & Police S & W 38 owned by a keen match shot in Boston. Naturally, targets were printed to accommodate gun models' distance between top of front sight and center of bore.

Combination Guns

The current Savage Model 24 22-410 is the last popularly priced remnant of a long line of rifle-shotgun combinations. Common in muzzle-loader days and down through the later years in rather expensive European cartridge guns, the type always has been tempting in both wilderness and woodlot. Here they have appeared almost entirely in pipsqueak sizes, though a few years back the Marlin over-under 410-and-rifle came in Hornet and Bee as well as in 22 rimfire. The old Marble Game-Getter relied on the bigbore lower barrel for power. It chambered a 44-40 case loaded with a 115-grain round bullet, nearly bore diameter of the true-cylinder barrel. At short range it shot with fair accuracy and delivered punch enough to account for deer and even black bear, on rare occasions. Its long-cased brass shotshell was commonly loaded with 8's, and later the tiny old 2-inch 410's were used in its lengthened chamber.

Lightweights

Featherweight barrels and hollowed stocks for years have kept custom gunsmiths busy, and now we have the 308 Winchester 70. These weight-reducing methods aren't new in American factory-made rifles: witness the 1886 and

1894 "Extra Light Weight" Winchesters and the 1899 Savage "Featherweight" lever actions, weighing 7 lbs. and less.

Taste is a pendulum. Along about 1910, 20-inch rifle barrels were quite the thing. Today some gunsmiths advocate even shorter tubes for arms of far higher intensity. Yet the 18-inch Mannlicher-Schoenauer 6.5mm has been respected all through the years, and some of us remember and have used 14-inch Winchester '92's and '94's.

Some calibers have proved themselves for certain definite uses throughout a generation or more, so much so that early rifles in that size drift out of common remembrance. When the 336 Marlin in 35 Remington came out it was hailed as an entirely new lever-action combination. Well, Stevens repeaters in the rimless Rem sizes are almost collectors' items now, but in the second decade of this century they certainly got around.

Pump Guns

Extension fore-ends for pump shotguns are fairly new. One of the objections to a pump that a short-armed shooter always used to register was that long stretch to the slide handle. The Burgess 12-gauge repeater was, I suppose, a pump gun, though the firing hand did the work, sliding the pistol grip back and forth to reload. The fore-end stayed put, and it didn't rattle, another objection to the standard trombone. But Winchester eliminated this competition with a buy-up, and that may account for later generations of American men being such lithe and long-armed specimens!

A ventilated rib looks nice on today's skeet or trap gun, and it is practical, reducing heat-wave disturbance of the line of aim. Back in 1918 or earlier the Remington Model 11 autoloader could have one, not open and breezy like today's rib, but milled out of the barrel's low, solid rib in short sections. Still, the idea and the effort were there.

The simple bolt-action system has

given us, today, sound and inexpensive scatterguns in single shot and in tubular and box magazine style. This economy in production first was generally known in the Winchester Model 41 single of 1920, a 410 that cost but a fraction of the price of the finely made breakdown Model 20. At about this time the Mauser single-barrels began to come over. They were so cheap that many were sold, and not all of them have blown open yet! Salvaged '98 Army actions made them, with the front bolt lugs shorn off and the breech reamed out. Only the bolt handle was left to hold 12-gauge pressures.

The Remington 760 slide-action rifle boasts the strength of multiple lugs and it corrals 270 backthrust easily. Heavy ordnance has used this system since 'way back when, and it is not quite new in sporting rifles. When Adolph Niedner built himself a personal woodchuck rifle, a high-intensity 25 using necked-down brass from the huge, Krag-proportioned 32-70 the Navy once played with, he studded the front of the bolt with seven pairs of lugs. Some Ross and Newton rifles employed multiple lugs, though not quite so many.

The long tubular magazine of the new Mossberg 146B swallows 30 22 short cartridges under its 26-inch barrel, firepower for the plinker. But a generation ago the Remington Model 12 pump 22 could be had with a full-length, two-foot tube holding 25 shorts, and the butt-stock-housed reservoirs of the old Evans 44's held 30 odd.

Polygroove Rifling

Lately we've all been reading literature on the new multiple-groove rifling in Marlin 22 barrels. A bewildering number of cuts is common in heavy ordnance, and do you remember those bronze, steel-covered barrels of the Hamilton breakdown 22's, and trying to count their grooves? Even before the Hamilton, rifled barrels by H. V. Perry and W. Milton Farrow, both famous shots in the 70's and 80's, carried many grooves: Perry's barrels, generally of 40 caliber, were 16-landed, while Farrow's barrels had as many as 14.

Antique polygrooving, from Sawyer's Our Rifles (Boston, 1920).

Ammunition

Before Kleanbore, corrosion looked hopefully at all gun barrels. Skip the cleaning after a shoot and the barrel never looked the same again. One remedy was the Bohler Anti-Nit or Poldi Anticorro "rustless" steel—and they were practically rustproof. Then came Winchester "Staynless" steel, at a far more reasonable price. One important objection was the difficulty of precisely boring and rifling these hard steels. Not many 52 Winchesters were sold in "Staynless." Now the big enemy is erosion—the burning of steel by high-intensity charges. To combat it we can have new or perfect barrels chrome-plated. It's a different problem and a different remedy, but it sounds awfully familiar, for it's the same old effort, to prolong barrel life.

In the last generation or two, sporting ammunition has stepped right along with general progress. Even shotgun shells have improved, in higher and more uniform velocities. The new wadless, folded crimp over the pellets without doubt made patterns more even in distribution, and the brittle, "frangible" top wads used in some shells helped, too. Since modern smokeless powders are far more condensed than early formulas, the shortening of the shell by the fold crimp still leaves room for plenty of wadding over the powder charge.

Though the wadless crimp is new, a crimpless top wad is old stuff. The solid brass shells sold long ago for handloading with black powder were not meant to be turned over at the mouth. You pressed down the oversize top wad and perhaps ran melted wax over it for stickum. Even so, after firing only one barrel you inspected the loaded shell in the other to make sure that its shot hadn't jolted loose and dribbled out the muzzle. Along toward the end of brass shell days one company did make a few with serrated mouths. You could turn in these fins for a crimp, but you didn't lengthen shell life or improve patterns by doing so.

The 3-inch 20-gauge shells for special long chambers are new. They pack in 1-3/16 ounces of 4's or 1-1/8 of 6 or 7½ sizes and fall just below high velocity 2¾-inch 12-gauge heavies in power. Yet 3-inch 12-, 16-, and 20-gauge shells aren't really new. Sold empty for handloading, they date back half a century, and factory loadings came soon after. The 1914 Winchester 20-gauge single—made on the High Wall frame, for even then single-shot rifle sales were dropping—was regularly chambered for three-inchers.

An old idea that should have caught on—and didn't—was the labeling of shotshell cartons to tell the novice what sort of game the stuff was good for. You may recall "Remington Game Loads" of about 35 years past, the Grouse Load, Squirrel Load, Duck Load, Heavy Duck Load, and so on. If you couldn't read at that age there was still the picture of the bird or beastie to guide you. But this bright thought didn't quite perish. For instance, the label on a 150-grain 308 carton in my glory chest tells the public that this loading is "suitable for deer, antelope, black bear, and similar game."

We have new types of factory-made bullets, yet some are of throwback sort. The jacketed hollow-point, closed with a cap like the Canadian Dominion make's "pneumatic" and some sharp foreigners and Canadian Ross holdovers, or open to the breeze like most current U.S. makes, of course came from the old soft-lead hollow point and Express missiles. Strictly, the Express was a closed-cavity affair. A thin copper tube sealed it, or an empty 22 short would do if you handloaded and didn't loosen up and buy the tubes. The compression of air within the tube was supposed to add to bust-up, and the Hoxeyized bullet went this one further. The Hoxey outfit would take your factory soft-point loads, drill them, and insert a metal tube containing a ball bearing. Sales talk stated that on impact the ball shucked forward, then was driven back hard against the air behind it as the nose caved in. Dubious? Well, the Hoxie folks ran their ads for quite a spell. Business must have been pretty fair.

About the latest thing in the hollow-point game is the Remington Corelokt. The hollow is small because the lead core has swelled up into a little pimple, filling most of the cave. New idea? Ask an old-timer who varied the depth of the hollow-pointing plug in his express mold as he wanted more, or less, prompt expansion of lead.

Today we have superb 22 long-rifle match loads at premium prices, not high when you figure the care and inspection they get. Grandfather too had special long-rifle loads, at standard cost, the uncrimped Krag Armory and Stevens-Pope Armory, and the S & W Long, crimped so that a sixgun's recoil wouldn't loosen bullets. Then came the U. S. Cartridge Company's special Boy Scout shorts, loaded with du Pont's semismokeless Lesmok powder and invitingly packaged, and maybe you remember the USNRA long-rifles in their blue and orange boxes, the first "high-velocity" 22's. They were so much respected for snap that these match loads appeared in hollow-point form for hunting.

The latest Rem-Pete "Match" 22's have smooth bullets, no grease to carry lubrication. Federal Airline 22's got rid of this apparently unnecessary knurling years ago. You don't need much lubrication if the alloy is just right. Over a half century ago many smokeless loadings from BB cap to 22 Automatic and 22 WRF got by with no grease at all. The bullets were hard and wouldn't lead a perfect barrel. But barrels seldom stayed perfect for long when we used the corrosive primed, smokeless 22 ammunition. After the clean stuff came in we saw greaseless bullets again, plated with copper as a lubricant. Now, after much experimentation, we've been given hard wax lubricant that doesn't pick up grit readily.

Wadcutter target revolver bullets are made in 32 S & W Long and 38 Special sizes. There used to be others, 44 Russian, 44 Special, and even 22 long-rifle. About the time of World War I, Remington made this 22 in "flat-end bullet" style. Few were sold. Along in the '30's their Hi-Speed wadcutter came out and perhaps would have lasted if it had been made in standard velocity, too. Fast 22 rimfires just weren't accurate then except in a few arms that seemed to prefer them, and for hunting the wadcutters were no more deadly than hollow points.

Bullet design is endless and it's hard to be new. Lately some handloaders have been trying wire-wound slugs. Shucks, back when the 303 Savage was new, such bullets were commercially made. Folks thought that hard jackets wore out barrels too fast.

The latest, and apparently sound, advice to those who form their own jacketed 22's for close bench-rest competition is to try a short cylindrical or groove-reaching section and a long taper up front to ease the bullet into the rifling. The old sugar-loaf muzzle-loaded bullets had this taper and early lots of 87-grain 250 Savage came close to it.

"Long loading" helps, too, setting the jacketed bullet's ogive right against the start of the rifling. Today's Super-Match and similar 180-grain 30-06 target loads stretch out in this fashion. So did some 180-grain 30 Krag loads that Winchester put up 40 years ago—and definitely stated were not to be run through the magazines of their own 1895 rifles.

Then there's the opposite, the deep loading of handguns' target bullets. Today's 32 and 38 wadcutters are set deep to avoid excessive air space for the light powder charges. Perhaps the first smokeless loading using this idea was the gallery prescription of 32 New Police. It set the standard 100-grain flat-nosed bullet flush with the mouth of the case, but the thought came from black powder times. Then the S & W 32-44 and 38-44 gallery round balls squatted right down on top of the shiny kernels. A little grease was run down the long cases, for lubricant so badly needed.

Back to bullet taper again. The Wotkyns-Morse team set the fashion for spire-point 22 jacketed stuff. Later experimenters rounded off the abrupt corner between bearing section and spire. All this goes back to the "U. M. C. Thomas" 30-40 and 30-06 bullets in 172- and 160-grain metal-cased design. Target stuff, but in Stewart Edward White's Springfield they tipped and cartwheeled and slew African buck about as well as the Army's less stable 150-grainers had on Teddy Roosevelt's trip over there in 1909. Even those UMC spires weren't absolutely new. Remember the 9mm Luger's truncated cone shape? Same thing, minus the sharp point.

We hear of "delayed expansion" bullets now. The Corelokt with its thickened middle jacket is fairly old, and Teutonic, in origin. "Protected points," usually quick to open, may have started some 40-odd years ago with Leslie Taylor's "L. T. Capped Expanding" that he designed for Westley Richards proprietary cartridges. In the 1920's Western tough "Tip-o'-Lead" 220-grain 30 came out, a

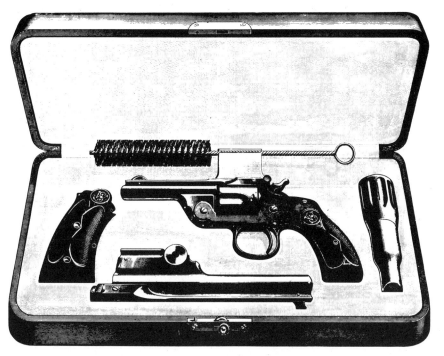

Leather case with combination Model 1891 S & W revolver and single-shot target barrel. The latter was available in 6-, 8-, or 10-inch length, 22 or 38 caliber.

soft point with just a pinhead of lead showing, and a little earlier the Remingtons had jacketed the 45-70-432 grain right up to the point, also their 253 grain for the 40-65 High Power that stepped off at a respectable 1790 f. s. velocity. From the side these two looked like full metal patched jobs.

With the new jacket alloys coming up we hear again the claim of "non-fouling" bullets. There's much truth in this advertising. When almost all loads contained black powder the "non-fouling" claim really pricked up shooters' ears. Pistol targetmen eagerly tried the "self-lubricating" sizes: 32 Short and Long S & W, 38 S & W and Special, and 44 Russian. This curious and rather expensive bullet had a deep hollow base filled with grease backed by a plunger. Up front, holes led to the taper just above the bore-bearing section. Squish-and-shoot-clean was the idea, and the type was marketed for about 20 years. Then, after World War I, hardly anyone monkeyed with black powder. But we had surplus 30-06's with cupro-nickel jackets to fire and clean up after. You may remember using Mobilubricant—about as soft as melting butter—to cut down fouling, or finishing a day with five 'hind-side-before bullets pushed out by cut powder charges.

The handloader always has been tinkering, and it's hard to come up with

something new. Grease wad disks behind jacketed bullets have their admirers and detractors. But when you used paper-patched bullets in your black-powder target rifle you set a cardboard wad, then a disk of Japan wax, down below your bullet—or you learned to, next time.

Powder

Duplex loading or the use of two granulations of smokeless in the high-power rifle case is well established. It's a matter of ignition and proper combustion rate that bothered muzzle-loading rifle shots until they learned to light off the coarse stuff with a pinch of fine-grained priming powder—FFFG to start FG, and so on. When smokeless powder and hotter primers went into cartridges, handloaders eventually found that a priming of black under the smokeless took practically all the "inevitable corrosion" curse out of nitro powders in handy little small-bore, close-to-town rifles. Later they found that reversing the process made black powder burn with amazing cleanliness. "It leaves the barrel as slick as a whistle," they say now. My unvoiced comment on some recent priming charges is that it's fortunate that they still leave an assembled barrel and action in their hands.

Then there was Pyro, du Pont No. 20, that was World War I's 30-06 pro-

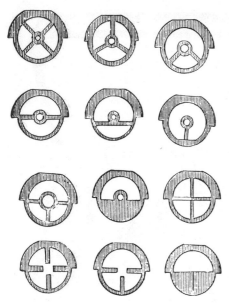

12 of 16 different apertures offered the Creedmoor shooter in 1880. From a Sharps Rifle Co. catalog of that date.

pellant. Excess stocks of it were sold off cheaply, and so freely that 20 years later we found the stuff wasn't so good any more. But not all had gone sour—some was only sluggish—and about three grains of black powder sifted through an 06 charge would make the old stuff talk again, and not too violently, either.

Also in that pyrocellulose series of powders was du Pont No. 10. Today we hear a lot about 4350, coarse-grained stuff that's super-efficient in big cases using heavy bullets—rather light bullets, too, as we later found out. Well, in a way that 4350 takes the place of No. 10. It's better, of course, and far more flexible. But both are really at their best in sizeable cases with steep bottle-necks. Today it's blown-out Magnum brass; then it was the once-famous 280 Ross and the almost-forgotten 276, 280, 30, 33 and 35 Newton, magnums in their own right, regardless of date.

Sights & Scopes

Today's iron-sight target shooter has a flock of front-sight inserts to worry about. Which size of aperture is best for prevailing light conditions, or shall he switch to a post or try the pretty little brown polaroid disk? Though the old-timer generally had a pinhead and a "globe" (thin-rimmed aperture), the rifle nut of those days had plenty of apertures to choose from. Also, at an extra cost, he could get a target front with a spirit level built in. Then he could enjoy all of today's frustration, as well as trying hard to keep the little

bubble of air centered exactly under his front sight.

For hunting we have the combination ivory and black steel post. Take your pick for the background you expect to find. This old Lyman tipup design stems, apparently, from the Beach front sight. It carried an open post and a hooded pinhead, one for game, the other for target.

The modern Redfield Sourdough gold-tipped post front sight has earned its assured place. Slanted forward, the gold picks up all the light that the sky grants it. Old-timers chuckle a bit at it, though, for years ago they sneaked into Mamma's boudoir and used her nail-file to put a lean on their reliable Marble, King, Lyman, Redfield, or what have you.

Some modern experimenters have tried peep rear sights on pistols, and it's been stated in print that dried not so long ago that factory-fresh handguns never carried them. Again, some of the mossbacks are amused, remembering the little old Stevens Diamond Model

Windgauge sight, with spirit level and 3 apertures, $4.00 in 1897. Dozens of different apertures could be had.

single shots. Made for trappers, with weight kept down to 12 ounces, the Diamond 22 came with either open or peep rear sight. No, this wasn't the "pocket rifle," with butt drilled for a skeleton steel stock, but a pistol. The peep sight's aperture was tiny, and to use it you held the gun in both hands, close to your eye. Naturally it was handy and effective for close-range work on the winter trapline.

Lately we've had offset scope mounts for Winchester lever guns and Remington autoloaders that eject their brass more or less straight up. Forty years or more ago, target scope mounts like the Winchester were on hand with "offset adapters." Like the modern devices, they set the glass to the left, exactly wrong for a right-handed shooter. Mounted to the right, they'd make him force his face against the stock comb, and he could hold more steadily. Remember, these old glasses rode so high that with central mounting only the

hunter's unshaven jaw rested on the comb.

In later years, double crosshairs in the big game hunting scope's reticle have proved their worth afield. You use the lower one for longer shots, and the space between these two horizontal hairs will serve as a sort of range-finder, too. Perhaps this idea stemmed from the double hairs available in old target scopes. Vertical as well as horizontal were double, and you ordered them to frame a certain size of bulls-eye at some definite range. There were even triangular reticles, composed of three hairs. Useless gadgets, were they? Perhaps.

Odds and Ends

But we guncranks have so many practical ideas—among the rest—that many an odd trick, for a time forgotten, enjoys reincarnation. Sometimes it's badly needed, like the clips that made Colt and S & W 1917 six-shooters so fast to reload under stress. As most of us know, these little half-moons of steel grip rimless 45 Auto hulls in clumps of three. That makes two drops, not six, to recharge the cylinder. It looked like a new development, but it wasn't. Long before, in England, the system had been used, though these clips were wire and the gun's cylinder had to be counterbored to receive them.

Now we have several makes of auxiliary shotgun barrels, short inserts that you drop into a 12-, 16-, or 20-gauge bore when you want quiet, inexpensive practice with 22 shot cartridges or short 410's, or even with small rifle loads like the Hornet. Do you remember the full-length inserts, usually 30-30 or 38-55, that were slid into one barrel of a double 12, come deer season? The re-

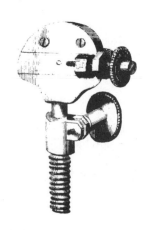

Windage and elevation adjustments in 1808. From *Scloppetaria* (London, 1808), the first book in English on rifled arms.

sult was a heavy, ill-balanced gun, but if the range was too long for buckshot you had a bullet to try. They were meant for business, not practice!

Quite often a shotgun-type tang safety is gunsmithed into a bolt action, or into a Savage Model 99 lever action, for that matter. They're quick and handy, especially under a scope. Remember the Savage 1920, their first bolt gun in the high-power bracket? You still see them around; so look for that sliding safe, and admire it. I always do.

The latest Mannlicher-Schoenauer has two safeties, an excellent idea. The usual flop-over wing safety at the rear of the bolt is handy enough when you use iron sights, but it hides under a low mounted glass. Then the extra safety comes in, down at the right of the receiver, just where your thumb would jab for it. A gunsmith job standardized, sure, but have you seen those little Stevens bolt guns, 22 repeaters, and 22 and 25 single shots, that also had two safeties? Transitional stage in production, no doubt, for the early pull-back-and-twist bolthead safety was there, also the new sliding lock at the right of the receiver, still used on the Savage.

Set triggers aren't new, but only coming back. The cross-bow had them, even the muzzle loaders as far back as the wheellock were fitted with them; then single-shot cartridge rifles of several makes, and Winchester tubular magazine lever guns and old Mausers and Mannlicher-Schoenauers. So the expert use of them never became a lost art—not quite.

Trap-door buttplates can save the day, and they're popular on modern custom jobs. Maybe they came from the patchbox in the side of the muzzle-

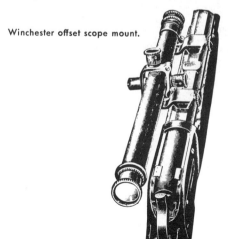

Winchester offset scope mount.

loading rifle's stock, though now they make a convenient, forget-proof warehouse for a pull-through cleaner, oil, and so on, or a couple of extra cartridges. Winchester 1873 38-40's and 44-40's with curved "rifle" buttplates carried jointed steel cleaning rods under that plate as regular equipment, and other models had this feature on order.

Cleaning

In those days it paid to clean your gun and be sure of it. It still does, sometimes, and a Borescope is a handy gadget for bolt actions or any solid-frame or takedown guns that don't give you a close-up peek into throat and bore when the action is opened. You set this small prismatic spyglass into the

Schuetzen Double Set triggers, from an 1897 Winchester catalog.

breech and see right down the barrel. For bench-rest accuracy in the hot-shot 22's, at least, the throat or leed of the rifling must be close to 100% perfect if groups are to stay small. Fine idea, the Borescope, and it came from the old Winchester barrel reflector, a simple mirror set at a 45° angle. They were made in styles and sizes to fit opened actions from the 1903 22 automatic to the yawn of the 1886 and 1895 big game rifles.

RIG came out maybe 20 or 30 years ago, when corrosive primers still were used a lot. The claim stated that a full smearing of this applesauce-like grease kept an uncleaned barrel from rusting. Evidently it did, but long before this the Birmingham Small Arms people in England had their Safetipaste for the same purpose, and it too was good.

Handloading

Though handloading is fun, some people look on it as work or else do so

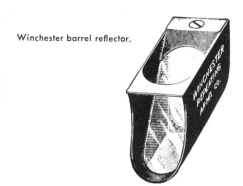

Winchester barrel reflector.

much of it that it becomes work. Some have pretty elaborate loading machines, even power-operated. But in 1899 the Ideal folks put out their quantity loader for shotgun addicts. It had reservoirs for both powder and shot and a rammer for seating wads. About that time, possibly a little later, there was the Beecher loader, quite similar. However, in modern style it had huge reservoirs for powder and pellets, easy to check, for they were of glass.

Even a few methods persist, or are reborn, in the shooting game. Take shooting sticks. No, I don't mean those canes that fired a light rifle or shot cartridge, but sticks used to support the weapon and make steady holding easier. They go back before the days of rifled barrels, to bull-with-a-snowshovel accuracy, when a bell-mouthed scatter-gun of firelock or flint persuasion was almost too heavy to hold if it slung enough slugs to be effective. In buffalo-hunting days they were revived for the superbly accurate use of heavy-barreled Sharps or Remington long-range 44's, 45's, and 50's, and now we see them again in the woodchuck hunter's kit.

On ranges like the one at Creedmoor, Long Island, it was common practice to clean the black-powder Remington, Sharps, and other target rifles after each shot. Paper-patched lead bullets weren't meant to be fired through a dirty bore. In those days even the shotgun was cleaned after each round at trap, for black-powder buildup is fast. Smokeless came along and let us devote the odd moments in a match to autopsy and wishful reconstruction of the immediate past. But no, we can't rest. Only recently one of the top benchers discovered, at least to his own satisfaction, that groups hold up better during a day's competition if the close-printing rifle is cleaned after reach string.

Really quite hard to find something completely new, isn't it, even if we go no farther back than 50 or 100 years?

The Ones That Shoot Back

" . . . there was a bellow of rage . . . and, out of the trees burst a great silvertip. He was down at the third shot, but I was five years older." An unforgettable experience for O'Connor and one of many told here about the world's most dangerous game.

by JACK O'CONNOR

MY GUIDE and I had seen the big grizzly from the top of a hill. He was about 1500 feet below us and was earnestly engaged in turning over rotten logs for the grubs and mice he found beneath them. Quickly we appraised the situation. A strong wind was blowing directly from us toward the bear. It looked as if we might get up to him if we stayed about 200 yards to one side, worked past him, and then approached up wind. Not far from where he was feeding was a dead fir, the last tree standing of what had once been a heavy forest. But many years before a fire had swept through the woods and all the trees had been killed. Now only this gaunt gray skeleton stood in the midst of the second growth with its patches of muskeg, its yellow grass, its crisscrossed half-decayed trunks, its low berry bushes, its scarlet kinnikinik, and its scattering of pale yellow willows. The big snag would make a fine marker to work back to when we were to hunt up the grizzly.

Scent of Grizzly

When we saw the bear we were above timberline. We ran and slid down a long steep shoulder of the mountain until we came to the flat. We worked beyond the dead tree until we had the wind on the bear. Then keeping the direction of the tree in mind we began to work cautiously up wind.

Presently we found the place where the bear had been working when we first saw him. A log had been torn asunder and his big tracks were fresh in the soft soil where it had rested. I could almost smell bear. The guide plucked a piece of dry grass, tossed it into the air. Down there in the timber the wind was not so strong as it had been on top, but it was still steady, still blowing the way it had been. We sneaked furtively along, putting every foot down with the greatest of care, taking precautions not to put our hobnail boots down on a dry twig or a stone that might move.

As we worked along up wind the tension mounted, and my thumping heart bounced around in my chest so noisily that I felt the bear must surely hear. I felt an insane desire to cough and I knew that the palms of my hands were sweating. I reflected gloomily that when we saw the bear it would be close and that because of an idiotic Canadian law which forbade a guide to carry a rifle, it was just me and the bear. My clumsy foot broke a half-rotten stick then. It sounded like a rifle shot and my guide turned around to glare at me.

A moment later and about fifty or sixty yards away, I saw something move in a patch of thick, young timber ahead of me. The guide had not seen it. I stopped, raised my binocular to my eyes. Whatever it was had long, dark, silver-tipped hair. It could only be the grizzly. I put down the glass, raised my rifle. I tried to decide just what part of the bear I was looking at. Then my excited imagination drew outlines. That patch of hair I could see through the opening, I convinced myself, was the chest area. Through the scope I simply *knew* it was the chest area. By this time the guide had seen the bear, too, and he watched as I threw off the safety and raised the old 30-06. Afterwards he told me he could see no more than I could. From my actions he assumed I knew what I was doing.

Near Disaster

For a moment the post reticle wobbled around on the patch of hair, but then it settled down, and I squeezed the trigger. The crash of the shot down there in that dark, dank, and lonely forest sounded like a crack of doom. For seconds afterwards I could hear it echo and re-echo from the surrounding hills.

Then from the patch of little trees came a mad and terrible bawling. For a moment it was accompanied by the sound of movement as if something was threshing around. Then there was silence — or almost silence, as I thought

I could hear a hoarse and labored breathing.

"You got the sonofabitch," my guide said.

"I'm not sure," I whispered, moving quietly over toward him, as if his presence would shield me from the wrath of a hurt and vengeful grizzly.

"Where'd you hit him?" he asked.

"I thought in the lungs, but I'm not sure."

"Damn it," he jerked. "Never shoot at a grizzly unless you've got him with his pants down."

"I'm sorry," I said humbly.

For two or three minutes we stood there silent. My legs were still weak and trembly. I still wanted to cough.

My guide was getting impatient.

"He's dead," he finally announced. "I didn't hear him run and he quit roaring."

"Let's wait a while." I still thought I could hear an animal's labored breathing.

"Oh, hell . . . he's dead. Look, I'll go over here to the side and see if I can see him."

So he circled around to my left trying to find an opening in the trees that would give him a look at the bear.

Suddenly there was a bellow of rage. The guide whirled and ran at right angles to me and out of the trees burst a great silvertip that to my startled eyes looked as tall as a moose and as heavy as a rhino. I don't think I have ever worked a bolt half so fast in my life. He was down at the third shot, but I was five years older. I'll never be quite the same again. My guide was a bit wrought up, too. He grabbed my rifle from my hand and emptied it into the carcass of the bear and while he did so he was making remarks about grizzlies in general and this one in particular. As I had feared, my first shot had been too far back, had gone through the big bear at an angle and had lightly touched one lung.

From that snafu and near disaster I learned a little lesson that if applied will keep hunters of dangerous game living a long time: *Never shoot at an unwounded head of dangerous game unless you are sure you can kill him or render him helpless.*

It is a good maxim to follow. Generally I have done so. Since that time I have killed eight grizzlies and a couple of Alaskan brown bears. I have never even come close to getting et. I haven't always followed that rule with other stuff and I cannot remember a single time that I have violated it but what I got into trouble.

I also learned something else that day, and that was that the danger associated with a game animal is compounded of two ingredients — himself and the country in which you find him. Before that day I had collaborated on one grizzly. A pal and I found it across a canyon and above timberline in the open. We had accurate scope-sighted rifles and were reasonably good shots. Killing that bear was like shooting fish in a barrel. But taking on a grizzly 200 yards away above timberline and getting in a fight with one at 50 yards or less in timber and muskeg are two different things.

The hunting of dangerous game gives a thrill that nothing else in sport quite equals, and many men are eternally fascinated by it, some to the extent that they find the hunting of anything else a waste of time. I suppose that this is the same impulse that leads men to climb high and dangerous mountains, to drive too fast, to fight bulls, to dally with chorus girls, or otherwise run grave risks. A friend of mine who hunted in Africa recently was left cold by the rare and beautiful antelope such as sable and kudu. What really sent him was the big tough stuff. He managed to get charged by a rhino and chased by a few elephants and when a wounded buffalo came tearing out of the reeds at him with death in his eyes he was delighted.

Buffs and Lions

There are almost as many notions as to which are the world's most dangerous animals as there are animals that can be called dangerous. When I was in Africa I made it a point to pump all the white hunters I ran into as to their choice of the No. 1 tough guy. I have also tried to winnow the opinions of others from books they have written. The only conclusion I could reach is that the individual choice depends almost entirely on the hunter's experience.

Syd Downey, the white hunter's white hunter, is inclined to put the Cape buffalo in first place as a bad actor. He has been run over and tossed by buffalo, as has Myles Turner, another famous African white hunter. Don Ker, who had never had a close shave with a buffalo, but has had trouble with elephants, votes for the tusker. John Hunter, veteran white hunter who wrote the book *Hunter,* thinks the sly and agile leopard is the most dangerous of all. The rhino ranks pretty low on most people's list of bad actors, but Bwana Charles Cottar, the Oklahoma frontiersman who became a famous African guide and ivory hunter, was killed by one.

From what I have heard and read, I am inclined to think the lion is the most dangerous of the African game animals and that lions kill more armed white men than do any other animals. Compared to the thick-skinned rhino and buffalo he is soft of skin, tender, and frail. But the lion can conceal himself in very little cover, and when he charges he comes on like a flash, so close to the ground that it is easy to shoot over him. Unlike the elephant he charges determinedly, and to stop

him you have to kill him. A lion does not have to be wounded to be dangerous. He'll charge if he is followed or annoyed.

In his definitive work, *The Book of the Lion,* Sir Alfred Pease places the lion in the top spot. He says there are records of men who have shot hundreds of buffalo without getting into trouble, and he says if they had shot half that number of lions they would have had a good many narrow escapes. Certainly more white men have been killed in Kenya colony by lions than by anything else. When I was hunting there a planter went out to shoot a lion that had killed a cow. He wounded the lion with his first barrel, missed with his second when the lion came for him. He was mauled so badly that he died in a Nairobi hospital. Of the long list of professional hunters who have lost their lives in the bush, the lion has accounted for far more than any other.

Leopard, Tiger, Gaur

If the vicious, crafty, and vindictive leopard were as large as a lion, he'd be the world's most dangerous animal. He charges without a warning growl, and he is cunning and determined. But he is a small animal, so small that he can be stopped with buckshot. My friend, Herb Klein, killed an exceedingly large one when we were in Africa, but I doubt if it weighed 150 pounds. There are records of several men, including Carl Akeley, the sculptor-taxidermist, who have killed wounded leopards with their bare hands.

That world's largest cat, the Indian tiger, has killed and eaten enormous numbers of men, but few of his victims have been armed white men. Most tigers are shot from the safety of machans in trees or even from the backs of elephants. Usually the hunter has a good chance to place his bullet, and if by chance the tiger is wounded he can generally get the help of elephants or of many natives. Those enormous wild cattle, the fairly common gaur and the rare wild water buffalo of India are dangerous, but their reputations are less fearsome than that of the African Cape buffalo.

Rhino and Elephant

The rhino is formidable largely because of his chronic ill temper and his unpredictability. He is an exception to the general rule that animals are dan-

gerous only when annoyed and wounded. The rhino has a grudge against the world and a low boiling point. Many people have been tossed or pounded by rhinos when they were going about their business and had no idea there was a rhino in the country. But the menace of the rhino is lessened by the facts that he is almost blind and not to difficult to dodge and likewise that a shot will generally turn his charge. The rhino is not difficult to kill either — or at least that is what those with a lot of rhino hunting experience tell me.

The great wild cattle of Asia and Africa — the Cape buffalo of Africa, the wild water buffalo, the gaur, and the sladang of India and other parts of Asia, seldom pick a fight. But when they are wounded they are among the most dangerous and vindictive of enemies. The buffalo of Africa is the only animal that would vie with the lion as the most dangerous animal and many put him in the No. 1 place. But he can conceal himself less easily than the lion and he is a larger mark.

Most hunters of wide experience in Africa do not rank the great elephant as nearly as dangerous as either the lion or the buffalo. When a lion makes up his mind to stand his ground and fight only death will stop him, they say. The same thing is generally true of a wounded Cape buffalo. But a heavy bullet slammed almost anywhere into the head of an elephant will turn him. I am also told that it is impossible for an elephant to move with a broken leg or shoulder.

Every member of the African Big Five — lion, rhino, elephant, buffalo, and leopard — can be considered a formidable opponent, but because of the ease with which he can conceal himself, his determination, and the speed of his charge, the lion probably deserves the No. 1 spot.

The only North American animals that can be counted as dangerous are the grizzly and brown bears — and some of them can be tough indeed. The late Ned Frost, famous Wyoming sheep and grizzly guide, felt that when the number of grizzlies and the number of hunter casualties were taken into consideration, the grizzly was a more dangerous animal than the African lion. Ralph Young, the famed brown bear guide of Southeast Alaska, is convinced that under the right (or wrong) set of circumstances the big Alaskan brown bear is the most dangerous animal in the world.

Big Bears

The grizzly and the brown bear are close relatives and there isn't any doubt but they can be bad actors. When white men first encountered grizzlies, the big bears didn't have the least fear of them because they were used to poorly armed Indians. Many a pioneer hunter and trapper was mauled and killed by grizzlies. Even today in true wilderness areas where grizzlies are not familiar with men and rifles they display little fear.

An exceedingly large grizzly will weigh as much as 900 pounds, but the average male will weigh about 500 or 600. The largest of the big browns will weigh as much as 1500 pounds. An African lion that will weigh over 400 pounds is a very large one and a tiger that will weigh over 500 is likewise very large. Since as a general rule the larger an animal is the more difficult it is to kill, the grizzly should be somewhat harder to stop than either a lion or a tiger, and the big brown should be enormously more difficult to pile up.

Those who argue that the grizzlies and the browns are the world's most dangerous animals have much to back them up. Back in the days when I was hunting in the Canadian Rockies and the Yukon every fall and writing a good deal about grizzlies, correspondents used to send me many newspaper clippings and other accounts of killings and maulings by grizzlies. From them I estimated that about a dozen

people were killed or mauled by the big bears every year in Canada between the American border and the Alaska line. In Portuguese East Africa a few years ago, one pride of lions killed and devoured literally hundreds of natives and depopulated a whole district. Several hundred Indians are killed annually by tigers. However, African and Indian natives are not often armed, whereas the victims of the grizzlies most often are.

But no matter which of the world's dangerous animals you vote for, any of them can cause trouble if they are poorly handled, and most of the killings and maulings are done by wounded animals. In the fall of 1956 a pair of Montana sportsmen wounded a grizzly and followed it up. One of them was killed. In Alaska in the spring of 1956 a grizzly killed not only the armed hunter but his armed guide — an astounding feat! An account of a terrible mauling in Alaska by another grizzly has recently appeared in OUTDOOR LIFE, and I have on occasion written of the shocking experience of my old Yukon Indian friend and guide, Field Johnson, who was with me when I shot a couple of grizzlies in 1945 and one in 1949. Field was the victim of an unprovoked charge when he was hunting moose near the little Yukon village of Champagne. The grizzly beat him up and buried him. When Field thought the bear had gone, he tried to get out of his grave. But the bear had lain quiet nearby and when he saw Field get up, he mauled him again, dragged him by the feet more than a mile, and buried him once more. When Field regained consciousness the bear was gone and the sun was almost down. Field managed to stagger to the Alaskan Highway and modern antibiotics saved his life. He will never completely recover from the terrible experience.

The placement of that first shot on any game is of great importance, but when the game is dangerous the placement may mean the difference between a clean, easy kill and tragedy. A few years ago an American hunting in India took a shot at a tiger moving through tall grass. Whether his bullet was deflected or whether he did not lead the spot he wanted to hit enough I do not know. The bullet hit the tiger in the abdomen. The great cat went down, got up roaring, charged into the line of beaters. He got one beater down and was mauling him. The

hunter fired again, but this time in the melee he hit the beater in the leg. The high velocity bullet so mangled it that the leg had to be amputated. A few days later the tiger was found dead and half devoured by vultures. The hunter will carry a sense of guilt to his grave.

When I was in India I violated my own rule of never firing a shot unless I was sure the bullet would kill the animal or break it down. A few days before, when I was hunting spotted Axis deer (chital) by spotlight, we had seen a tiger about 80 or 100 yards off the road in high grass. The spotlight was not too good and the big cat was pretty well concealed. I could not tell which end of the tiger was which. I had only a 270 with me and I refused to shoot.

The Indian shikari, who had previously seen me down a flying peacock and several running chital stags with the same rifle, was disgusted. The *burra sahib* (that old man — namely, me) was a good shot, he told our outfitter, but when he encountered a tiger he was definitely chicken.

Tiger in Darkness

I still remembered that crack some nights later when this same shikari was with me in a machan high in a tree over a tiger bait. Not long after sundown we heard the tiger calling up the canyon, but it grew dark and the tiger did not come. Stretched out in the machan, with a sweater draped over me and my 375 Magnum with a cartridge in the chamber and on safe beside me, I counted sheep for a while and then began to doze.

I was awakened by a crunching of bones on the bait. I managed to sit up without making a sound.

"Shere (tiger)?" I whispered to the shikari.

"Shere," he said in confirmation.

I had told the English-speaking outfitter that afternoon when we went to the machan to instruct the shikari that when I punched him twice with my elbow he was to turn on the 5-cell flashlight by which I was to do the shooting. I switched off the safety, trained the big rifle on the bait, and then gave my two punches.

I had seen dozens of drawings of sahibs shooting tigers on baits from machans. Always they show the tiger in plain view. But when the light went on I couldn't see a thing. The bait was

lying by a bush and the tiger had approached from behind the bush and had drawn the rear end of the carcass into the bush before he started to feed. In the glare of the light the shadows of the limbs and twigs on the tiger's stripes made perfect camouflage.

"Shere," the boy whispered. *"Chute!"*

Taking it for granted that he had enough sense to center the bright spot in the middle of the beam on the portion of the tiger I was to hit, I put the crosswires of the scope right in the middle of the bright spot and touched one off. The tiger let out a startled roar and took off like a drunken buffalo bull.

Tiger Jumped

At dawn the next morning I shinnied down a rope to the ground and quickly found a little blood. Until late that afternoon we tracked the tiger. We finally came onto it by a little water seep high in a rocky canyon. He saw me just as I saw him and he had to make one jump to be out of sight in the bordering jungle. I could plainly see that he had only a flesh wound in his cheek. All that day he

had lain by the little seep, drinking now and then and soothing his wound by lying with his cheek against the cool, damp sand. If the bullet had been a few inches to the left I would have got that tiger, but I was not justified in shooting.

The tiger I got later was galloping through tall grass ahead of an elephant drive, but I reasoned that I could kill him before he got to cover. I did.

The one African lion I have shot was in contrast a very neat operation. Don Ker and I were out to look at our baits in the gray of dawn. There was a maned lion on our first bait, but Don thought we could do better, so we sneaked off. Baits 2, 3, and 4 were blanks. A lion had been on bait No. 5, so we parked the car and hunted on foot.

Suddenly our Dorobo tracker grabbed my arm and whispered that magic word: *"Simba!"* I followed his pointing finger and could see the head and neck of a fine maned lion about 200 yards away in the grass. He hadn't seen us and was looking back toward the bait.

About 75 yards from the lion was a big termite hill and Don and I crouched and sneaked rapidly toward it, keeping it between us and the lion. Once behind it, I poked my head around the side. The big cat hadn't moved. I laid my left hand against the hill and rested the 375 against it. The sight of the crosswires sharp and black against the lion's neck steadied me. I squeezed the trigger carefully and the lion was down, threshing about, roaring horribly. Another shot finished it.

The Best First Shot

The best place for that first shot on most dangerous game is through the shoulder. The crash of a heavy bullet against the shoulder blade seems to transmit shock throughout the system and almost always knocks the animal flat. If the penetration is sufficient and the angle correct, both shoulders are broken and the animal is helpless. That is my favorite shot on a grizzly. It is also a fine shot on a buffalo or a rhino and one that will knock a charging animal head over teakettle. It will even anchor an elephant.

With the same old 375 in my hands

I lay in the rain on a lonely beach on Admiralty Island in the spring of 1956 while a big brown bear rolled along directly toward me. I had made up my mind that when he got to a certain piece of driftwood, I'd let him have it. When he reached that point, I broke his downhill shoulder and tipped him over. I then jumped up and let him have a couple through the lungs. That was it.

The classic shot on elephants is into the brain, with aim taken between the orifice of the ear and the eye, from a broadside position or at an angle to reach the same objective. An elephant so hit will fall as if a rug had been jerked out from under him. However, if the brain is missed a head-shot elephant, I am told, will travel forever. For that reason many white hunters prefer to have their clients shoot for the lungs and then wait until the elephant drowns in his own blood and falls. Some like the shoulder or heart shot, but whatever it is the shot should be taken with the greatest of care. An angry and wounded tusker is bad business.

Head and Neck Shots

As a general thing head shots are not a good idea. The brain is a small mark, and unless the angle is right the bullet can be deflected by bone. The history of Indian hunting, for example, is full of rhubarbs that came about because some sahib tried to poke a bullet into a tiger's brain and only succeeded in wounding him. A dangerous animal with the side of its face shot off, its nose shot off, or its jaw broken can still do a lot of damage.

The often-used neck shot is a dandy if the bullet breaks the spinal column, but no good if it doesn't. In Africa I once decided to break the neck of a topi, an antelope about the size of a mule deer. We wanted it for camp meat for the crew. I rested my left hand against a tree trunk, then laid the scope-sighted 375 across my wrist. At the shot the topi flattened. The boys shouted in glee, rushed over to *halal* it — cut its throat so it would be official eating for Mohammedans. Suddenly the topi decided it didn't like what was going on, jumped to its feet, and ran for almost 200 yards before it toppled over.

On the other hand the animal with both shoulders broken will be helpless and the one with one shoulder gone will be knocked flat and put out of action for a time. Large heavy animals cannot navigate on three legs.

The type of country an animal is hunted in has much to do with the degree of danger it presents. A grizzly shot in the fall in a big open basin above timberline presents far fewer hazards than the same bear shot in the willow jungle along a salmon stream. If I could take them in the open above timberline I'd shoot any grizzly that ever lived with a 257, but if I had to hunt them in heavy cover I'd want a 375.

Generally speaking, dangerous stuff, particularly in brush, is best hunted with rifles using heavy bullets at moderate velocity. Such bullets are less deflected by brush or turned from their course by bone and they have the momentum to knock down an animal in case of a charge. Syd Downey says that in the case of an unwounded lion the 270-gr. bullet of the 375 Magnum is the world's finest lion medicine, but when a lion is charging he wants the 500-gr. soft point bullet in his double 470. Given a side shot at a grizzly, it is no trick to slip a 130-gr. 270 bullet through his ribs and knock him for a loop. In willows and alders I'd rather have a heavier bullet for a frontal or shoulder shot. Favorite tiger medicine in India is the 450-400, which uses a 400-gr. 40 caliber bullet at 2200 f.p.s., but the 375 Magnum with its 300-gr. bullet at 2450 f.p.s. is gaining on it. For elephant, rhino, and buffalo in Africa the standard cartridge is the 470 Nitro Express with a 500-gr. bullet at 2125 and about 5,000 foot pounds of energy — an exact ballistic duplicate of the new Winchester 458. For American grizzly and brown bear, the hunter should take at least a 30-06 or 300 Magnum with the 220-gr. bullets or better still the 375 with the 270 or 300-gr. bullets.

Proper armament is part of handling dangerous game, but the most important ingredient is what lies in the hunter's head. If he is calm, experienced, cool, he'll take his time and he'll place the bullet just where he wants it. If the animal is moving rapidly or is concealed by brush which may deflect the bullet he'll either postpone shooting or pass up the shot altogether.

I think it is entirely normal for anyone going after his first head of any dangerous game to be somewhat spooky, but if he remembers not to fire until he is *sure* where the bullet is going to land he won't get into trouble.

Just so the hunter is *sure* of that first shot, he doesn't have to get too close. Much of the philosophy of the British white hunter was evolved in the days of black powder and open sights, and many pros try to get their clients far too close. Often this is a mistake. A client that is reasonably calm when he is 125 yards from a rhino, may be jumping right out of his pants if his guide sneaks him up to within 25 yds. Any competent woodchuck hunter should be able to kill a grizzly with neatness and dispatch at 200 yards if he takes his time, gets into a good position, and waits for the bear to co-operate. But if his guide hauls him up to within spitting distance he may come unglued. That has happened many times. It is far better to take a good shot at some distance than to work closer and gamble on having to shoot at a running animal or on the hunter's getting jittery.

Right Spot, Right Shot

Whether it is at 30 feet or 250 yards, that first shot simply must go into the right spot. If it does all is rosy, because a modern rifle with the right bullet makes puny man more than a match for the roughest and toughest animal that walks the face of the earth.

But if it doesn't, then there's trouble.

It's a nerve wracking business — this following up a wounded animal that may launch a charge at any moment. Sometimes the hunter is so jittery and unnerved when the charge comes that he is paralyzed. In the spring of 1955 a New Delhi business man hunting in Northern India's terai country didn't even lift his rifle while a wounded tiger charged fifty yards to maul and kill him.

Once a wounded animal is located in a ravine or a patch of long grass every effort should be made to pin point it by making it move or growl. Sometimes the grass is fired. Often the animal can be got to move by firing rifles or shotguns into a suspected location. In India men are put up trees to pelt brush patches with stones. Sometimes the patch is driven by elephants or a herd of tame buffalo.

But the best thing is never to let an animal be wounded. That first shot is the one that counts!

THIS ARTICLE is written in the fervent hope that it will dispel some of the confusion which plagues transactions between the custom stockmaker and the custom stock buyer. Having been a stockmaker all of my adult life, I have many times run afoul of this confusion. I am speaking primarily of the buyer's inability to give the stocker a clear picture of what he wants. The hodge podge of ideas that the

the one you built for Joe Blow ten years ago." This last request afflicts the stocker with mental contortions, trying to remember what that stock looked like. The buyer is by no means entirely to blame for this confusion. He reads and hears so many conflicting claims that it would be surprising if he were not in a dilemma. It will be very gratifying if this article does a little to alleviate the situation.

my remarks, not at the wealthy connoisseur or collector who has his own favorite stocker and is able to pay for some idiosyncrosies, but rather at the average "Joe Shooter," who has saved his nickels for many days toward the purchase of that one fine "custom built" gun. This man should welcome some counseling before making such an investment.

Before getting into the mechanics

The classically simple rifle at its best —a 30-06 Mauser, with French walnut stock, made for C. R. Hiatt.

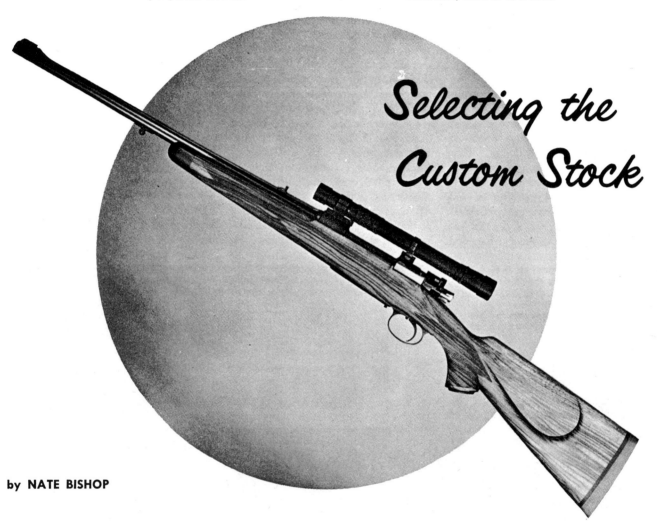

Selecting the Custom Stock

by NATE BISHOP

buyer comes up with are at times downright comical. An exaggerated example is the shooter who comes in and says, "I want a stock made of that rare breed of exotic Circassian mahogany, with fore-end shaped like Weatherby's, a schnobble like Shelhamer's, a pistol grip like Holmes's, a cheekpiece and Monte Carlo comb like Keith's, and checkering like Kennedy's." Or perhaps he says, "I want a stock exactly like

The word "Custom" has been much misused as it applies to gunstocks. It has been used to advertise and describe stocks on which the only variable dimensions are comb height and length of pull. For the purposes of this article I use the word "Custom" in referring to stocks made entirely to order. That is, no limitations of any kind. Naturally, this rules out the production type stocks. I am directing

of selecting a custom stock, it would perhaps be wise to say a few words on how to go about judging the quality of such a stock. It is surprising indeed how few individuals are capable of determining whether a finished stock is good or bad, insofar as the workmanship is concerned. I have been disillusioned at times by the person who upon examining my work, says in a sneering manner, "How in the hell do you get these prices? I've got a buddy who makes stocks just as good or better for one-fourth the price of yours." This man is perhaps overly blunt, but completely honest in his convictions. He simply cannot see the difference. You possibly could throw a cat between the wood and metal of his friend's stocks, yet Mr. Blunt is probably totally unaware of this sloppy workmanship. Sad though it may be, this failing is not confined to the laymen. Many professional gun people will casually glance at stock work and pronounce it good or bad. Fifty per cent of the time they are wrong. On the other hand, nothing pleases a dedicated stocker more than very close scrutiny of his work. Pick up a magnifying glass and he will positively glow!

Let us proceed with a step by step examination of a custom stock. First, take a look at the finish – if possible under reflected light. The finish should be *absolutely* smooth. A pebbly appearance is an indication of insufficient rubbing or too much build-up. There are numerous prepared finishes now on the market which can be applied with the fingers. This ease of application entices one to apply too much. Second, look under the finish for sanding or rasp marks. Pay particular attention to those hard to reach places, such as the point of the comb and behind the pistol grip. Of course, there should be no visible marks at all under the finish. Third, examine the contour lines of the cheekpiece and comb flutes, the transition lines along top and bottom of stock. These lines should be sharp and distinct. Any rounding off indicates insufficient care in sanding. Fourth, closely scrutinize the fit of wood and metal. There should be no visible openings between gun and stock at any point. And, by all that's Holy, do not condone glass or other bedding compounds as a cure-all for 'Gaposis.' These bedding aids are a boon to the amateur, who is handicapped by inexperience and improper tools, but the professional stocker should have no need of them. Fifth and last, give the checkering a thorough going over. All diamonds should be perfectly peaked. A precise check on parallelism of lines can be accomplished by sighting across the pattern and noting if the peaks of the diamonds are in a straight line flowing around the stock. If peaks are staggered, lines are not parallel. Check the borders for run-overs, a cardinal sin with first class workmen.

So, with a little practice, you will be able to recognize quality. One word of caution: do not be distracted by a beautifully grained piece of wood. You should be concerned only with workmanship.

Choosing the Stockmaker

In choosing the maker of your custom stock, let the aforementioned examination be your guide. A point that may come as a surprise to many is the fact that there are fewer than a dozen men in the United States capable of passing this examination without a downgrade.

As with any other fine handicraft, quality stock work commands a price, a price that perhaps seems high to the prospective buyer. Let me try to justify this "exorbitant" figure. An average price for a finished stock, by one of the above mentioned stockers, would be in the

Smooth, clean inletting cuts indicate the care taken by the stocker.

Below—Arrow indicates direction of predominating grain. For optimum strength, grain should always run thusly.

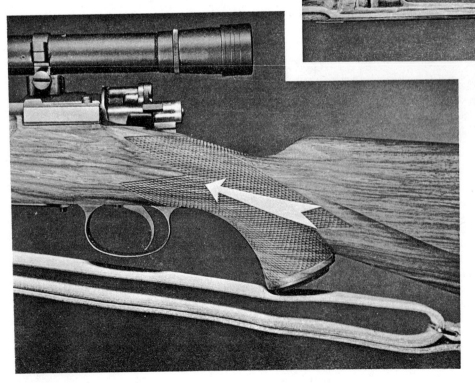

neighborhood of $200. Consider that these craftsmen spend approximately seventy hours at hard, tedious labor on each stock, and a little division will show that they are paid $2.85 per hour. This amounts to ditch-diggers wages for an almost immeasurable degree of skill, a skill which took many years to perfect.

Most assuredly your pocketbook is a determining factor in choosing the maker of your stock, and if you want the best you must be willing and able to pay. If your purse is limited, I hope my remarks will help you get the most for your money.

Elsewhere in this book there are many examples (pictures) of the custom stockmaker's art. These are

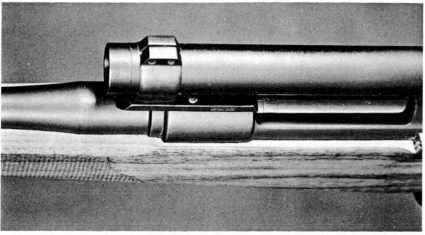

representative, for the most part, of the captioned stockmaker's favorite work. They vary greatly in design. This latter fact should make it easy for any individual to select a stock with lines pleasing to his personal tastes. Note the name of the maker below the picture of your selected stock and make every effort to see, in the flesh, so to speak, some examples of his work. If this physical examination is not possible, then you must take your chances on the question of quality. Most reputable stockmakers guarantee satisfaction, so your risk would not be too great.

There are two reasons why I suggest choosing your stockmaker via his designs. One) as mentioned previously, all custom stockers have favorite patterns and designs on which they naturally do their best work. It follows that it is to the buyers advantage to stick with these established designs. Two) I am trying to prevent you from committing the unpardonable sin of showing your chosen stockmaker a picture or example of another man's work, and saying, "Please copy." Not only does this insult, but it perhaps

would be like asking Ford to build you a Cadillac, or vice versa.

Assuming that you have now chosen your stockmaker, we are ready to start on the pertinent information you'll want to impart to him.

Selecting the Wood

Personal tastes play a large part in the selection of wood for a custom stock. In view of this, I can only generalize. First, let us divide stock woods into two groups: dark and light. (There are some tropical or exotic woods which fit into neither group, but their use is so limited that we won't consider them here.) The "darks" consist of American walnut, French walnut, Circassian walnut and Claro walnut. The "lights" comprise maple, myrtle, mesquite and cherry. Since the stockmaker's art is, to a large degree, only as good as the material with which he works, it is imperative that he work with the best wood available. It is for this reason that some stockmakers work only with French or Circassian walnut, undoubtedly the finest woods procurable. Their refusal to work with other woods is not motivated by greed, as some would suppose, but rather because these dense, high tensile-strength woods allow them margins they wouldn't have with other species. To be more specific, the stocker is able to produce twenty-four-line or finer checkering, reduce the size of stock to minimum dimension without undue fear of breakage or splitting, and because of French and Circassian walnuts' inherent stability, there is less chance of warping. Another wood which should not be overlooked is the English walnut being marketed in California. Actually, since this wood is a transplant from the same geographical area in which French and Circassian are grown, they can be loosely grouped together. Mr. Joseph M. Oakley, of Oakley & Merkley,* has recently discovered a limited number of trees in California which he calls "California Black English Walnut." These trees are original plantings of softshelled English walnut. As near as Mr. Oakley can determine by ring count they are 80 to 90 years old. The wood from these trees has the same density, strength, and working qualities as the finest French or Circassian, and is fabulously beautiful in appearance. A supply of Black English in my stock bins would make me a mighty happy man. (Also worthy of consideration is the fact that your chosen stockmaker will charge you just as much – and perhaps more – for working on a poor piece of wood. Certainly, this $100–$200 labor charge should not be wasted on

———

inferior wood.) As to quality, other woods fall into categories below French, Circassian and Black English walnut. For obvious reasons, I cannot list them in order. I might mention a strange phenomenon, in my judgement, concerning a choice between dark and light stocks. Upon acquiring, a stock of light wood may be a highly prized possession, but as time goes by it has a peculiar tendency to become tiresome. With dark woods the opposite holds true. Finally, a comment concerning figure or fancy grain in a stock blank. From the standpoint of appearance, figure or fancy grain is highly desirable. However, bear the following facts in mind; fancy wood does not ordinarily have the strength or stability of straight grained wood, and is generally somewhat heavier. So, if you are planning an extremely light sporter, forego the fancy grain in favor of strength and light weight. If you are planning a target rifle, forego the fancy grain because of warpage danger.

Bedding

Since there are only two common methods of bedding a rifle into wood, we should be able to cover the subject with few words. The action portion of the rifle should always be bedded with as much bottom contact as possible (sides of action should be fitted tightly but without any wedging), and all rearward facing vertical surfaces, with the exception of the recoil lug, should be slightly relieved. Recoil lug must be fitted with total contact on rear face. So, actually, the two methods pertain only to the barrel—these are the "pressure-point system" and the "free-floating system." Which is best is a question open to much argument. Some sick rifles can be cured by changing the bedding from pressure-point to free-floating and vice versa. I think your choice should be determined, to some extent, by the area in which you live and hunt. If you live in a place of extreme atmospheric changes, the free-floated job would perhaps be best, since these atmospheric changes can slightly alter the shape of the stock. This circumstance happening to a pressure-point bedded stock would affect point of impact and, quite possibly, accuracy. If you are in doubt as to which method you prefer discuss the matter with your chosen stock-maker. He can advise which is best for your particular rifle.

Fittings

Fittings consist of fore-end cap, pistol grip cap, buttplate or recoil pad, and swivels. Here again personal tastes enter the picture. It is possible to produce a highly presentable stock by using all, any part, or none of these fittings. Let's start with the fore-end cap. Although the majority seems to favor contrasting wood caps, an attractive job can be turned out with

plain rounded fore-end, or a well designed schnobble. If you choose contrasting wood for your stock fittings, be sure it is not so gaudy as to distract from the stock itself. Most commonly used woods for fore-end caps are ebony and rosewood, neither of which is unduly gaudy. As with the fore-end, pistol grips can be made attractive without using a cap. Naturally, if you choose a contrasting wood cap, it

should match the fore-end cap. Other than contrasting wood, blued steel is really the only suitable material for grip caps on fine custom stocks. The most popular combination in stock fitting is: ebony fore-end cap, checkered steel grip cap, and checkered steel Niedner-type buttplate. If you're willing to pay the costs, you may have a trap buttplate fitted; these have a

hinged door which opens into a hollowed-out receptacle in the stock, suitable for a spare cartridge or two, a cleaning pull-through, etc. If you are susceptible to recoil, you will no doubt want a rubber pad installed. Although there are many brands available, the only pad worthy of consideration is the solid type found on Winchester magnum rifles and shotguns. This type of pad does a much

Arrow indicates downward direction of predominating grain. A stock with such grain is only suitable for installation on a shotgun, using a draw-bolt.

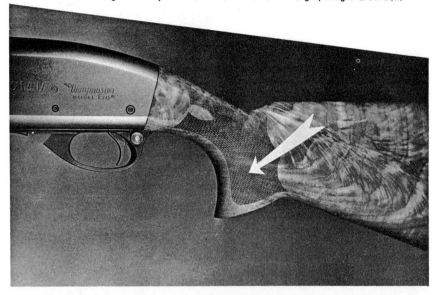

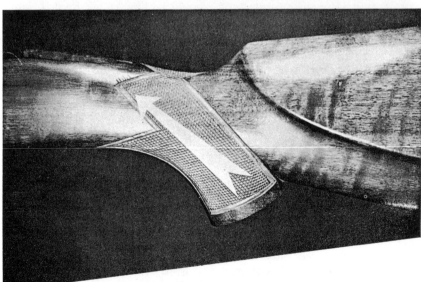

Several indications of sloppy workmanship. Note pebbly appearance of finish, coarse sanding and rasp marks under cheekpiece, and the rounding of cheekpiece contour line or edge. Arrow points out checkering run-overs. The checkering pattern itself is basically wrong. Instead of diamonds, it is made up of squares.

better job of absorbing recoil than those dirt catching, honeycomb styles, and is much more pleasing in appearance. The final addition in fittings are sling swivels, a must on a modern hunting rifle. The best position for the front swivel is immediately ahead of the fore-end cap, mounted directly to the barrel. It has been argued in the past that a swivel mounted on the barrel will cause a change in bullet point of impact when a tight sling is used in shooting, but how many so-use a sling in the field? On the other hand, this barrel mounted swivel will be a boon in getting through brush or thick timber, for the muzzle of the barrel will be lower on the shoulder. Keep this fact in mind if your custom rifle is being built from the ground up. Ask your gunsmith to braze a permanent base in this position, or an encircling band to take the swivel. As to type of swivel, I would suggest the "quick detachable." A weather beaten sling hurts the appearance of your rifle. Q.D. swivels will enable you to easily remove the sling while the rifle is on display in your rack.

Another point I should make here concerns the sequence to follow when building your custom rifle. First, of course, have all metal work done, barrel fitted and chambered, all alteration completed, sights fitted, polishing, etc. Then, while the gun is still in the "white," send it to your stockmaker. If engraving is desired, this should be done after completion of the stock. The final step is the blue job.

Finish

Although his choice is limited, the stock buyer should certainly indicate his preference in finishes. As mentioned earlier, there are many prepared finishes now on the market. These can be roughly grouped into epoxies, resins, oil, and lacquer base finishes. Before you conclude that I am contradicting myself, please be informed that most stockmakers concentrate on one finish; two at the most. In other words, though there are many types of finishes available, your choice from an individual stockmaker is narrowed down. One finish that cannot be grouped with the four types above is called French polish. Since this finish is composed of almost equal parts of shellac and boiled linseed oil, it stands by itself. These two ingredients are incompatible, that is, they will not mix in the bottle. The secret of French polish is in the application, which is accomplished by using a double layer wiping pad of well-washed lintless flannel or cheesecloth. The inner layer is plain cotton flannel. The inside portion of the pad is soaked in liquid shellac, the outer layer in boiled linseed oil, or the oil may be applied from an oilcan while working. A practiced continuous motion will mix the oil and shellac as it is being applied to the stock. The resulting finish is quite impervious to moisture, and is durable. However, unless dulled by rubbing with steel wool, or by reducing the shellac quantity, French polish is quite glossy.

I would estimate that seventy-five per cent of the top stockmakers in the nation turn out their finest work with oil finishes. The rest turn out equally good work with other finishes.

Not being a chemist, I cannot give

you an analysis of various finishes, or their exact resistance to moisture, but I've experimented with most and have reached some definite conclusions. Some are very good, some are very bad, but in my opinion you cannot go wrong if you specify a *good* oil finish. Although another finish would, perhaps, be superior for one specific purpose, oil is undoubtedly the best all-round finish. I should perhaps elaborate some on this

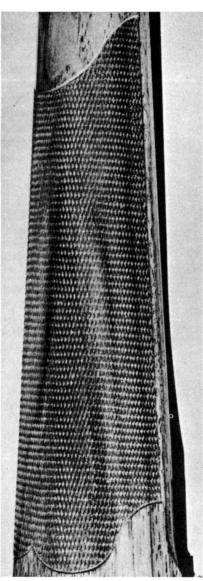

Diamond peaks flowing in straight lines around the stock indicate a well-planned layout, perfect parallel cuts. Good checkering.

last statement. I do not mean to imply that I am in favor of the promiscuous use of just any kind of oil. The old raw and/or boiled linseed oil finishes are now passé. The use of these oils involved a method of application which went something like this: apply once a day for a week, once a week for a month, once a month for a year, and once a year for the rest of your life.

Even then your heirs were left with something less than a perfect finish. Raw and boiled linseed oil are by nature quite thin and are too readily absorbed by some woods. Too much absorption can destroy all contrast in a beautiful stock, and finally result in actually decaying the wood itself.

I believe I am correct in assuming that practically all stockmakers today who specialize in oil finishes use a highly refined product with additives. This refining and these additives retard absorption and give linseed oil a better body. The trade name of one such product is G. B. Linspeed, which I consider the finest of oil base finishes. With this finish, a highly satisfactory job can be turned out in less than a month.

Checkering

The final thing to be talked over between stock buyer and stockmaker concerns checkering.

Here also pocketbook and personal tastes enter the picture. The overall size of the pattern and the spacing of lines (wood permitting) generally determine price: the larger the pattern and the finer the lines the more the cost. Your personal tastes control the design or ornateness of the pattern.

Some shooters feel that checkering should be merely functional, providing only a rough surface for grasping. I believe, however, that the larger group feels that checkering should be both decorative and functional, and that a stock without checkering is like a cake without frosting. As stated, the size and shape of your chosen checkering pattern is determined by your bankroll and your sensibilities. However, the line spacing should be determined by the evaluation of several factors. If your gun is to be a fancy showpiece, by all means indulge in fine line (24 and finer) checkering. If you are building a hunting rifle, I would suggest 18 or 20 line work, since finer line checkering mars and fills with dirt too easily. A final consideration: French and Circassion walnut are the only woods which can safely be checkered 24 lines or finer.

Summary

In addition to the opinions offered here, you may procure more specific information from your chosen stockmaker. In any case, after digesting all this data, you should be able to approach your stockmaker and order your stock with clear and precise particulars.

A true, well made custom built rifle is many things to many men—a conversation piece, a decoration, a useful tool, and a constant source of pride and joy.

Regardless of which category you would place yours in, I hope you will soon become the proud owner of a custom built rifle.

165

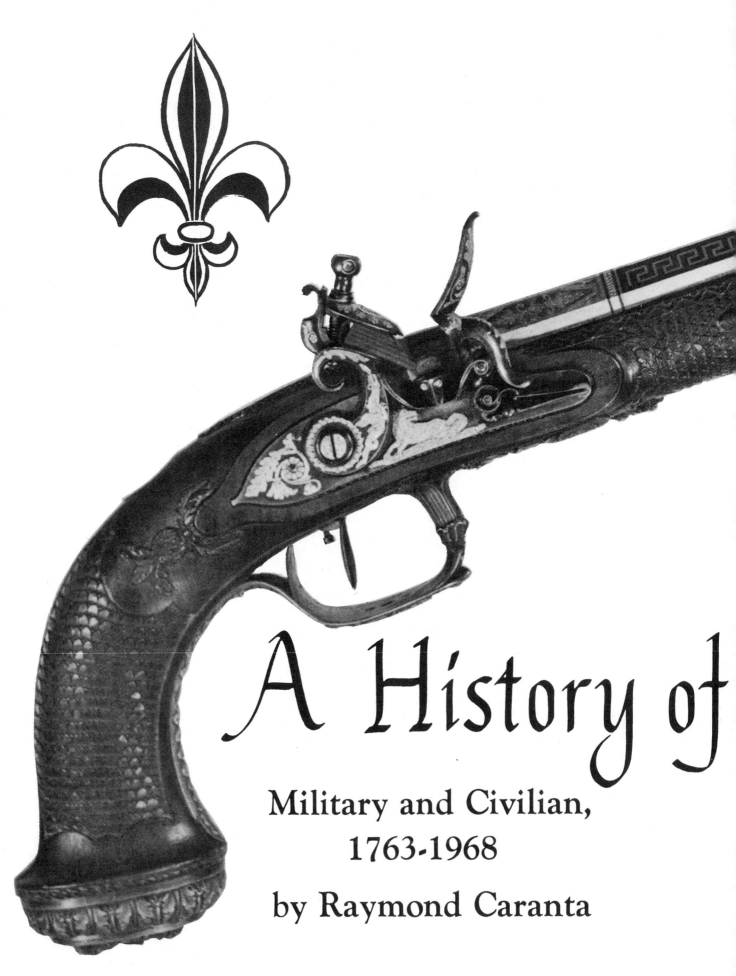

A History of

Military and Civilian, 1763-1968

by Raymond Caranta

Superb flintlock pistol by Nicolas-Noel Boutet

French Handguns...

A profusely illustrated review of French pistols and revolvers that covers
the earliest official cavalry and constabulary flintlocks, the wide variety of side-
arms made during the French revolution, the elaborate and magnificent pistols
made by Boutet and Lepage during the Napoleonic era, the great array of
percussion handguns, and on through the cartridge revolvers and pistols of the
20th century — a presentation without precedent.

ALTHOUGH THE USE of the pistol was widespread in France during the 16th century, 1763 is an important date in French military handgun history. Before that year, there was no official service handgun in the French army; choice of pistols was left to the discretion of the various commanding officers.* The first national system of firearms, which did not include handguns, was adopted in 1717 and these long guns were manufactured in the newly created Royal Manufactories of Charleville, Saint-Etienne, Maubeuge and Klingenthal. Pistols were not included, since this type of arm was considered mainly a personal defense weapon which did not meet any specific tactical requirement. The Royal Household (*Maison du Roy*), was the only exception to these rules, according to the following abstracts of the *Milice Française,* quoted in the famous monograph of Capt. Maurice Bottet.[1]

"The Royal Household Light Cavalry was armed with sabers of standard type and pistols. The pistols did not have to be standard. Everyone followed his individual fancy until 1714, when the Duke of Chaulnes had 230 pairs of flintlock pistols of the same model, marked with three fleurs-di-lis, made for him and distributed without cost to the light cavalry.

"The King's carabineers in 1720 were furnished with sabers of the same length and blade width; with standard rifled carbines and loading equipment, with two sizes of bullets, some to be forced into the rifled bore with a hammer and steel rammer, the others smaller for fast reloading in case of emergency; with the best pistols available of 15 *pouces* (French approximate equivalent of an inch) over-all length (from the King's instructions concerning his carabineer regiment, given on its foundation in 1693)."

When the necessity for equipping the French army with flintlock pistols was recognized under the 1763 regulation, the two following basic models were manufactured.

1763 Cavalry model. 230mm (9.05") round barrel and 1763 service musket lock. The caliber was 17.1mm (0.67"), slightly under the 17.5mm (0.68") bore of the musket, the musket's allowance for fouling being deemed unnecessary for a weapon which was to be used only occasionally. The grip was much more slanted than on later models.

1763 Constabulary (Gendarmerie) model. 128mm (5") barrel and 15.2mm (0.59") caliber.

Later, the famous 1777 boxlock flintlock pistol, called *à la Mandrin,* from the name of the famous French smuggler, was manufactured in the standard 17.1mm service caliber. This gun was carried by naval officers and the troops of La Fayette and Rochambeau. The U.S. Model 1799, the first U.S. government contract pistol manufactured by North & Cheney, resembles this early French pistol.[2] This gun was characterized by its huge round brass frame with arsenal marking and the inverted direction of the frizzen spring.

Along with 1763 pistols fitted with special brass furniture, the French navy used the 1786 Navy pistol and special small size pistols, most of which were manufactured in Tulle. They had brass or steel furniture and left- or right-hand locks. These guns, mostly from Duche, were well made and so popular among navy officers that many were later converted to percussion. They are easily identified by their butt end, shaped as a dolphin head.

Before the French revolution, the officers, mostly aristocrats, paid for their guns from personal funds, and many finely finished pistols were made by master gunmakers such as Laroche, Boutet, Lepage, Desainte and Lamotte. Others of a much lower grade were also manufactured, mainly in the provinces, by minor craftsmen for less wealthy officers and, it must be said, for actual use! The pocket pistols of the time were mostly smaller versions of the conventional sidelock belt or horse models.

During the French revolution, many fine pistols seized from aristocrats or from the enemy were presented to republican officers or even, as in a case known to the author, given as rewards for gallantry. This custom was largely discontinued after the institution of the Legion of Honor in 1802.

During that period, the pocket pistol evolved into boxlock designs, known in French as *pistolets à l'écossaise.* They were less bulky than their sidelock counterparts, the latter popular in Great Britain at that time.

Later, the famous *An IX* (year nine of the French revolutionary calendar beginning on September 22, 1792) pistols, that served in all the Consulat and Empire wars, were manufactured in tremendous quantities.

Because of this period's importance in French history, the following data is given on the features of these two pistols:

The Year IX (1801) cavalry model had a 201mm (7.91") pentagon-round barrel of 17.1mm (0.67") caliber. Over-all length was 370mm (14.56"). A steel rammer and brass furniture were featured. On Messidor 2, year XII (1804), a lanyard ring was added to the brass butt cap.

The Year IX Gendarme or infantry officer's model had the same caliber and general configuration but was of reduced size with a 128mm (5") barrel and iron furniture.

Both models used the standard lock of the Year IX service musket. Its strong mainspring gave them relatively great reliability. Later they were modified to the Year XIII pattern by shortening their fore-ends and fore-end bands.

While not outstanding samples of workmanship, these guns were sturdy service pistols within the limits for which they were intended according to 1st Empire military regulations; i.e., for providing great stopping power at a practical combat range of 10 feet or so, by firing the regular service ball backed by half of the musket powder charge. These guns were improved in 1816 and 1822.

The first service pistols specifically designed for French general officers were made by Boutet at the Manufacture de Versailles under the specification regulations of the 1st Vendémiaire, year XII, which read as follows:

Generals — Service caliber (17.1mm) pistols, blued barrel and iron furniture with silver butt cap ornamented with a Medusa head.

General staff officers, General-adjutants, adjutants and aides-de-camp — Service caliber pistols with blued iron furniture plain silver butt cap.

Space does not permit exhaustive examination of all styles of handguns made during the two-century period considered here; therefore, emphasis has been concentrated on the martial and commercial models most likely to be encountered by the average collector or history student.

For their assistance during the preparations of this article, the author wishes to thank these friends: Jean Renaux, Pierre Cantegrit, Louis Boinet, Gabriel Jean Sumeire, Roger Huillet, Jean Jordanoglou, Marcel Colas and René Allovon.

Also the leading French manufacturers, including the Ingènieur Militaire en Chef Dufoux, form the Manufacture Nationale d'Armes de Saint-Etienne, M. Joseph Uria, General Manager of the Manufacture d'Armes des Pyrenees Françaises, and the M.A.C., M.A.B., Bergeron, Manufrance and Manurhin managements.

---

*1763 was the year of introduction of the first official French service pistol. The existence of a 1718 flintlock service pistol is highly controversial and if it is true that such pistols exist, it is nevertheless difficult to determine whether they are true martial pistols because of the lack of official military markings.

Typical pocket flintlock pistol of the first half of the 18th century. Made during the reign of King Louis XV, this pocket pistol is typical of the small size flintlocks of that time. Most expensive were the elaborately engraved types, with gold and silver inlays.

Early 18th century horse pistol.

Over-under flintlock horse pistol of the French revolutionary period.

Model 1777 military flintlock pistol. This box-lock arm called à la Mandrin, was widely distributed among LaFayette's troops. This model is easily identified by its brass frame and peculiar barrel mounting, the gun illustrated was made in 1793 in the French St.-Etienne arsenal.

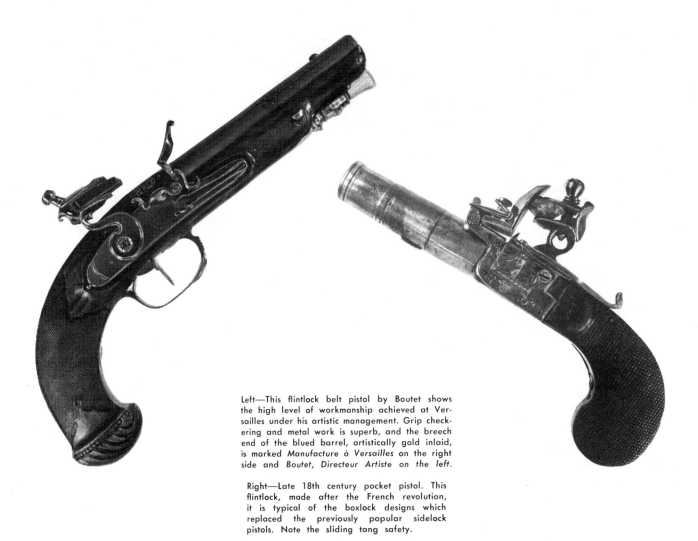

Left—This flintlock belt pistol by Boutet shows the high level of workmanship achieved at Versailles under his artistic management. Grip checkering and metal work is superb, and the breech end of the blued barrel, artistically gold inlaid, is marked *Manufacture à Versailles* on the right side and *Boutet, Directeur Artiste* on the left.

Right—Late 18th century pocket pistol. This flintlock, made after the French revolution, it is typical of the boxlock designs which replaced the previously popular sidelock pistols. Note the sliding tang safety.

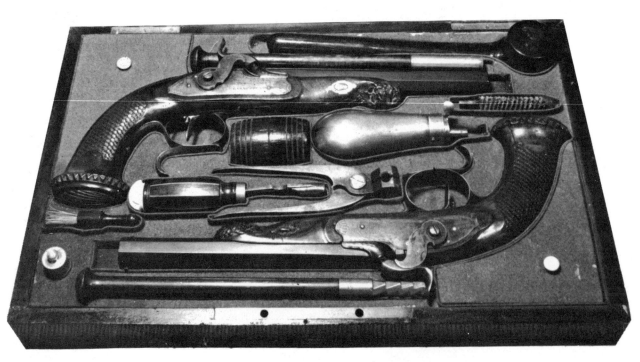

This cased pair of percussion duelling pistols was made during the 1830s by *Brezol-Robin* at Charleville. They have hair-rifled 14mm (55-cal.) barrels and set triggers. Front sights are adjustable for windage and rear sights for elevation. A family of gunsmiths named Brezol worked at Sedan in the mid-19th century.

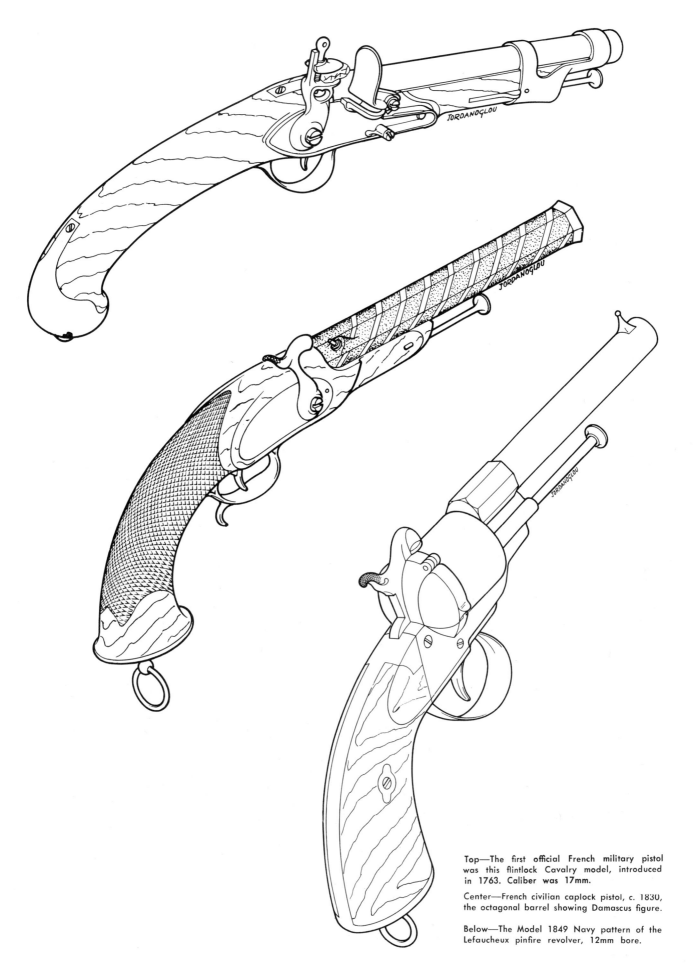

Top—The first official French military pistol was this flintlock Cavalry model, introduced in 1763. Caliber was 17mm.

Center—French civilian caplock pistol, c. 1830, the octagonal barrel showing Damascus figure.

Below—The Model 1849 Navy pattern of the Lefaucheux pinfire revolver, 12mm bore.

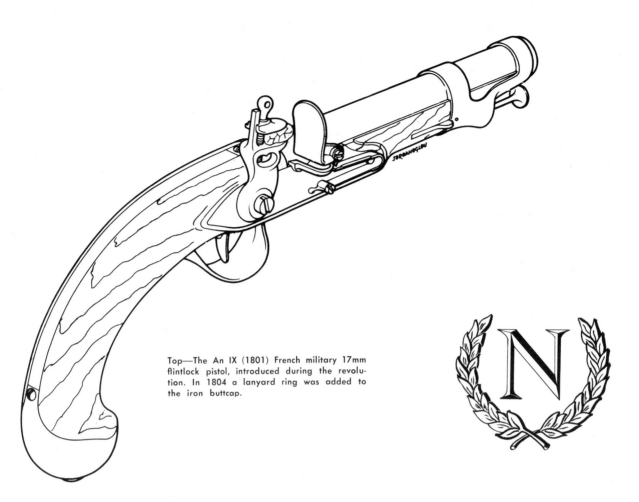

Top—The An IX (1801) French military 17mm flintlock pistol, introduced during the revolution. In 1804 a lanyard ring was added to the iron buttcap.

Above—According to Empire regulations, the pistol was to be used only at very close ranges, such as in this action in the Battle of Wagram, where a French cavalryman captures an Austrian flag.

Engineer Corps officers, Inspectors, Commissionaires and Quartermasters — Same regulations.

Fortress staff officers — Service caliber pistols with blued iron furniture.

The same regulations were adopted for the Navy officers on Prairial 7, year XIII, of the French Republic. Before that date, the only requirement for army officer's service pistols was that they be of service caliber.

Light smoothbore belt pistols and rifled horse pistols were also manufactured at Versailles, for the imperial guard Mamelukes. Only 502 pistols of these two types were manufactured. A special pistol was also made for the imperial guard Dragoon officers. This pistol was fitted with a silver butt cap decorated with the Emperor's monogram "N" topped by a crown and surrounded by crossed oak and laurel branches.

Many returning emigrés used English-made pistols.

With the return of the Bourbon family, new pistols, such as the King's bodyguard model, were designed for officers. They were made in the styles of 1814 (with blued barrel bearing the inscription GARDES DU CORPS DU ROY and the butt cap decorated with the royal escutcheon) and 1816 (blued barrel without inscription and butt cap decorated only with three fleurs-de-lis); the constabulary (*Gendarme*) model bearing the same inscription; the light cavalry (*Cheveaux-léger*) model, with fleur-de-lis engraved on the barrel and brass butt cap; the musketeer (*Mousquetaire*) model, with bronze or silver furniture and special marking on the barrel; the horse grenadiers (*Grenadiers à cheval*) model, of the same pattern octagonal barrel bearing the related marking, and the king's eldest brother (*Guard de Monsieur*) model.

The last service flintlock pistols to be made were of the 1816 and 1822 systems, embodying slight improvements over the Year XIII models. Most were made, like the preceding service pistols, in the cavalry and constabulary sizes, but officers' models were also provided. Later the cavalry officer's models were converted to percussion and the word *transformè* (converted) was added to their nomenclature. Two outstanding gunmakers emerged from that era, Boutet and Lepage.

Nicolas-Noël Boutet was born on August 31, 1761, son of Noël Boutet, gunsmith to the King's light cavalry regiment. In 1788, he married the daughter of the well known M. Desainte, *Arquebusier ordinaire du Roy,* who made him his charge. On August 23, 1792, the Republican Convention government entrusted to him the artistic management of the newly created Versailles manufactory. From 1794 until his death in 1833, Boutet produced some of the best made and most elaborately ornamented pistols ever assembled. His work is so important that it is not possible to cover it, even briefly, in the space of this article. The author recommends rather reference to such specialized books as the authoritative *The Art of the Gunmaker*[3] and to the catalogs of the world's leading gun collections.

Even after the termination of his last contract, in 1818, after the invasion by the Allies, Boutet continued to assemble fine guns in Paris until his death.

Boutet's story is well told in Capt. Bottet's *History of the Versailles Manufactory.*[4] However, less is known about Lepage, *Arquebusier de l'Empereur.* He was born of a family of gunmakers, and a child's gun, made for the young

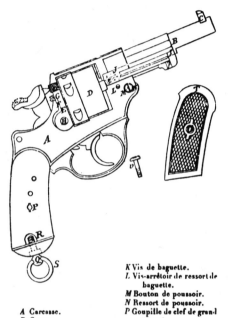

A Carcasse.
B Canon.
C Guidon.
D Barillet.
E Porte.
F Ressort de porte.
G Vis de ressort de porte.
H Pivot de porte.
I Clef.
J Ressort de baguette.

K Vis de baguette.
L Vis-arrêtoir de ressort de baguette.
M Bouton de poussoir.
N Ressort de poussoir.
P Goupille de clef de grand ressort.
Q Pivot d'anneau de calotte.
R Vis de pivot d'anneau de calotte.
S Anneau de calotte.
T Plaquette de droite.
U Rosette de monture.
V Vis de rosette de monture.

M1873 cavalry revolver.

Duke of Orléans about 1760, bears his signature. He worked in a more classical style than Boutet and, during the Empire, his production was more devoted to the building of Napoleon's rifles and shotguns. In 1829 Lepage made the last wheel-lock pistol manufactured in France.[5] His descendents continued to make guns during at least the first half of the 19th century, according to the many percussion guns bearing Lepage signatures.

THE PERCUSSION PISTOL

By the end of the Empire, many percussion pistols were being sold commercially, but a military version did not make its appearance until 1833. The first hair-rifled percussion service pistol, called the *Pistolet d'Officier Modèle 1833,* was adopted this year, these distinguished by their very shallow multi-groove rifling. Designed for cavalry officers, this gun, like the 1836 Gendarmerie officer's model, used the back-action lock (*à la Pontcharra* in French, from the name of Col. Pontcharra) typical of the French service percussion guns. This interesting service model (many pistols of the same general pattern were widely distributed by the Belgian manufacturers) featured an octagonal barrel with 48 grooves and a butt-recess containing a powder measure and spare nipples. The butt cap was held by two screws. This pistol was much better balanced than the previous flintlock models and was as accurate as a dueling pistol.

The Gendarmerie officer's model was made in two barrel lengths, the resulting over-all lengths being 245mm (9.6") and 270mm (10.6"). Both look like big derringers and have 38-groove rifled barrels reinforced with five flats at the breech. The 1855 staff officer's model over-under pistol and an obscure 1855 officer's model were the last percussion pistols designed for the French service.

For the troops, the Year IX, Year XIII, 1816 and 1822 models were converted to percussion. These models were later modified by addition of rifled barrels under the systems of 1854 and 1857. A Gendarme model featuring a conventional back-action lock was designed in 1842 and modified in 1848. Special Navy models (*Pistolets de Marine Modèles 1837 et 1849*), were issued to replace the obsolete flintlock models. These have little importance, because they were soon replaced by Lefaucheux pinfire revolvers of a much more efficient design.

Meanwhile, multi-shot pepperboxes, such as the Belgian Mariette, appeared and gained popularity for home defense, close-quarter military use and even for pocket use. French craftsmen turned out, principally in Saint-Etienne, great quantities of cheap boxlock pocket pistols with a single or side-by-side barrels.

French gunmakers, mostly in Paris, continued to assemble fine dueling and target pistols from about 1850-60, but most component parts came from outlying areas or even from Belgium, which by that time produced many cheap copies of the most prized guns on the market. Gastinne-Renette was the most famous gunmaker of that era. The Belgians' strong position was due to their low-prices, a result of high production, and to their excellent workmanship on more expensive pieces. They were, however, never able to match the best French and English gunmakers for top quality pistols.

Second Empire duelling pistol, one of a pair by *Devisme à Paris*. Beautifully made, this pistol represents the mid-19th century French style immortalized by Gastinne-Renette. The ornamentation is restrained but of first quality throughout, while the excellent lock provides a crisp trigger pull. It would be difficult indeed today to achieve the high over-all workmanship of the Paris gunmakers of that brilliant epoch.

Duelling pistols by *Brier à Paris*, a cased pair typical of the Second Empire duelling sets. These remained in use up to the end of the 19th century.

This side-by-side, 7mm pinfire derringer was manufactured during the Second Empire by *Devisme à Paris*. Numbered 222, it is marked *Devisme Brevetè SGDG*, and the functional lines of this little gun make it a natural pointer. The selective trigger button operates each hammer in turn.

Typical percussion pocket pistol. This type started to gain popularity about 1830 and became the most widely distributed style of percussion hand-gun. The specimen illustrated features an ivory stock and silver furniture.

This early 14mm (55-cal.) folding-barrel percussion duelling pistol, one of a pair, was manufactured in the early 1830s by *Lefaucheux*. The gun is gold inlaid on the barrel: 2. *Inv^R. Lefaucheux Brevetè à Paris*. The address *Rue de la Bourse* is engraved on the lockplate. This breech-loading pistol, transitional between the plain percussion and the pinfire system, used a metallic case with a small hole in it to transmit fire from the cap.

M1892 8mm, 6-shot service revolver has swing-out cylinder, can be fired single or double action. Length over-all, 9.43"; barrel is 4.6" long, has 4 grooves, a left-hand twist of one turn in 9.44"; weight, 30 oz.

Lefaucheux 7mm pinfire 7-shot revolver, typical of his 19th century work. Marked *E. Lefaucheux Brevete, Paris* on the folding trigger. Engraving is good quality scroll, and workmanship is excellent, but unfortunately these are better known through the cheap French or Belgian copies, made for export to African or South American markets.

French 11mm (.433"), 6-shot service revolver, Model 1873, the original cavalry version of the *Chamelot-Delvigne*, used in the French service. These 42-030 bright-finish guns are very rugged. The 4.35" barrel has 4-groove rifling with a L.H. twist, one turn in 13.8".

Typical Flobert BB cap *salon* or parlor pistol, the first popular cartridge handguns. These did much to develop target shooting in the last century, and hundreds of "Flobertist" clubs were formed in France. Floberts were made until WW I.

THE EARLY CARTRIDGE HANDGUN

About 1845 Flobert invented the bulleted breech cap and guns to handle it, forerunners of the later rimfire arms, while Eugene Lefaucheux, son of the pinfire cartridge inventor, manufactured his first pinfire revolvers in 1854, shortly before Smith & Wesson introduced the first U.S.-made fixed ammunition, the 22 Short. These guns immediately became popular in France and were soon copied in Belgium.

Before the success of the Lefaucheux revolvers, several French inventors, such as the Parisian gunsmith Lenormand (for years erroneously credited in France with being the inventor of the modern revolver, because in 1815 he made a handgun featuring a fixed barrel and five rotating chambers), had failed in their attempts to develop an efficient revolving handgun. Several years after Lenormand, the Belgian Herman improved this handgun design, but it was nevertheless unsuccessful. Comblain, Mangeot, Loron, Devisme and Perrin patented several revolvers, none of which attained wide distribution.

The Loron design replaced the conventional powder with a special fulminate, and the Devisme single action revolver, while well-made, had a break-open device with a weak latch which prohibited the use of heavy powder loads. The double action pinfire Perrin used its cylinder pin as a rod ejector and, though exported to the U.S. during the Civil War, never became popular in its own country. The wierd Lemat percussion and pinfire revolvers (using both ball or shot) were designed by a New Orleans doctor and made primarily for export to the Confederacy.

From 1850, the Colt 31 pocket percussion revolvers were sold in France but they were soon replaced by the then new and more efficient pinfire designs. Among American manufacturers, only Smith & Wesson seemed to have been successful in France, principally because their guns used fixed ammunition, while other U.S. revolvers were of the percussion type. The percussion system was advantageous in wild countries such as the American West or Africa, since it permitted shooting heavier loads than the weak copper cartridge cases did, and eliminated most ammunition supply problems. However, it seemed obsolete on the Continent almost from the very beginning because of the different conditions of use.

Nevertheless, for years the pistol was not considered an important piece of armament, and many officers relied primarily on their swords. The author has examined hundreds of battle scenes drawn by contemporary artists and was interested to see that most officers were shown holding only their sabers. When an officer was armed with a handgun, it was held in his left hand, the right grasping his sword. Capt. Gerard, who cleared Algeria of its lions, wrote that he went there with a brace of pistols but soon discarded them as useless. According to this famous hunter, even the service musket ball often ricocheted from a lion's frontal bone.[6]

During the 1870-71 Franco-Prussian war, French officers used a hodgepodge of previously described percussion pistols, plus the Smith & Wesson No. 2, Lefaucheux pinfire, Adams and other British revolvers, together with centerfire designs by Devisme and Galand. After the fall of Sedan, National Guard officers soon recognized the

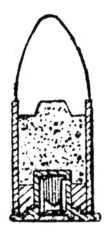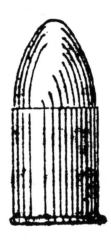

Centerfire revolver cartridge for Model 1873 revolver. The charge is 10 grains of very fine black powder. The pure lead, hollow-base .460″ diameter bullet weighs 178 grains.

revolver's importance as a service weapon and the new French Republican government imported huge quantities of American Colt, Remington and Starr percussion revolvers, while Smith & Wesson hurried into new production their No. 2 32-cal. rimfire tip-up models.[7, 8] Webley and Adams revolvers were also imported. By that time, the French navy was extensively using Lefaucheux revolvers of various designs. In particular, the 1870 model prefigured the famous 1873 government pattern. The first Lefaucheux revolver was adopted on March 4, 1859, by the French navy as the *pistolet-revolver modèle 1858*.[9] Later, the Lefaucheux revolvers were adopted by the Italian, Russian, German, Swedish and Egyptian navies.

French navy revolvers were made in two basic models, the 1858 and 1870 revolving pistols, but may be found in these five different versions:

> *Original 1858 model.* 10.7mm (0.421″) caliber, 6 shot, single action. Wt., 1090 gr. (38½ oz.).
>
> *1858 N model.* The 1858 revolving pistol modified in 1862 by the elimination of several screws, introduction of a new cylinder stop and replacement of the original iron ejection rod by a steel one.
>
> *1858 T model.* The 1858 or 1858 N revolving pistols modified in 1873 by the introduction of a double action lock and reworked to shoot the new service centerfire cartridges.
>
> *1870 model.* 11.1mm (0.437″) centerfire caliber, 6 shot, single or double action. Solid frame, weight, 1035 gr. (36½ oz.).
>
> *1870 N model.* Plain 1870 model modified by reinforcement of cylinder pin attachment and enlargement of frame cut out in 1873.

The 1858 and 1858 N pinfire handguns used a 13.5-gram (207-gr.) lead bullet backed by 0.63 grams (10 grains) of fine black powder, while the 1858 T and 1870 revolvers fired a more powerful centerfire cartridge featuring a 12.8 gram (181-gr.) bullet propelled by 0.80 grams (12.3 grains) of the same black powder.

After the war the French government adopted the Chamelot-Delvigne revolver as modified by a board of officers. A cavalry version having a long, non-fluted cylinder was called the 1873 model, while the one for infantry use had a light, shorter, fluted cylinder and was called the 1874 model. Both versions were 11mm (0.433″) caliber.

The board rejected models by Lefaucheux, Latouche-Gunther and Galand. The Lefaucheux was the basic 1870 solid frame model modified to meet the commission's requirements, while the Galand, which was available for commercial sale, had been specifically altered for military use. The Galand differed widely from this inventor's conventional simultaneous-ejection models, and was known as the *Galand de guerre.* (Galand war model.) The number of lock components was reduced to eight (against 14 in the conventional Chamelot-Delvigne model). While highly praised in a contemporary issue of the Belgian *Spectateur militaire* magazine and in the "Revolver" section of the 19th century Larousse encyclopedia, this revolver failed before the commission, as did the Latouche-Gunther, a close adaptation of the British Deane-Adams. (It might be noted here that Galand manufactured centerfire revolvers, featuring simultaneous ejection of fired cases in 1868, a full year before the appearance of the S & W No. 3 revolver, the first U.S.-made model having this feature.)

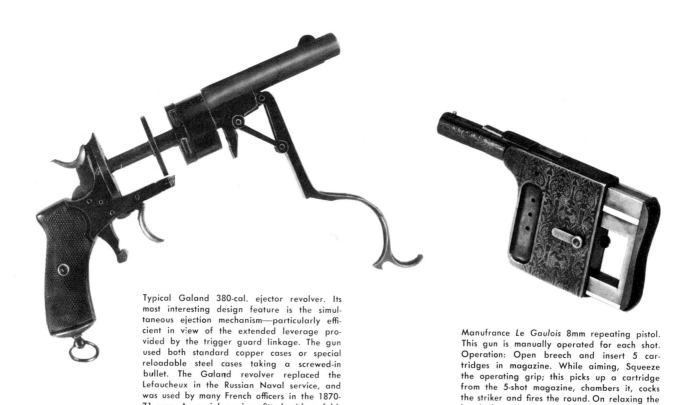

Typical Galand 380-cal. ejector revolver. Its most interesting design feature is the simultaneous ejection mechanism—particularly efficient in view of the extended leverage provided by the trigger guard linkage. The gun used both standard copper cases or special reloadable steel cases taking a screwed-in bullet. The Galand revolver replaced the Lefaucheux in the Russian Naval service, and was used by many French officers in the 1870-71 war. A special version, fitted with a folding-wire stock, was called the "Sportsman."

Manufrance Le Gaulois 8mm repeating pistol. This gun is manually operated for each shot. Operation: Open breech and insert 5 cartridges in magazine. While aiming, Squeeze the operating grip; this picks up a cartridge from the 5-shot magazine, chambers it, cocks the striker and fires the round. On relaxing the hand, the spring-loaded operating grip returns to rest position and ejects the empty case.

Steel dummy adaptor case and round ball for short range practice with the M1892 revolver. A similar adaptor, not shown, was made for the 11mm M1873 French service revolver, these propelling a grooved and greased cylindrical bullet.

Manufrance Populaire bolt action pistol, cal. 6mm Bosquette. Weight, 32 oz.; length 17.3". Intended for gallery shooting.

French 6-shot pepperbox on the Mariette pattern, marked on the tang: *Perfectionné par Dessagne à St. Etienne.*

THE MODERN HANDGUN

The 1873 and 1874 double action revolvers were very rugged and served during most of France's colonial conquests. They were also widely used in both World Wars as substitute service pistols. The author has experimented extensively with these handguns and except for some trigger return-spring failures, was always amazed by their reliability, even with an 1873 specimen rechambered for the 45 ACP cartridge. This rechambering practice is, nevertheless, not to be recommended, since these guns are intended for black powder only. The 1873 and 1874 revolvers were designed to meet the following specific requirements using the language of the day:

"1. The gun shall not be of the simultaneous-ejection type.

2. The gun shall be homogenous and sturdy. It shall be designed so that it will be impossible to catch, bend, loosen or lose any part in normal use.

3. The cylinder shall be easily removable for maintenance; nevertheless it should be positively retained in place by the cylinder pin. The cylinder pin should be easily removable but a system should be provided to prevent its loss.

4. The gate shall be simple, sturdy and easily operated. It should be designed so that it will be impossible to open it inadvertently. It should be located so that the shooter can determine immediately if he has forgotten to close it.

5. The ejection rod shall be sturdy and easily operated; it shall slide freely in its housing. At rest, it should be securely fastened by unsophisticated sturdy components. It should include no projection, not be liable to bend or to fracture and be efficiently protected against corrosion.

6. The barrel shall be rifled so as to provide accurate point-blank shooting at 25 meters without requiring the use of an unusually high front sight which is likely to catch. The trajectory should be sufficiently flat to maintain this shooting condition up to 50 meters and to permit shooting at ranges above 100 meters without undue deviation.

7. The gun shall be of the center-fire system.

8. A postive safety notch shall be provided.

9. The gun shall be capable of single and double action operation.

10. The lockwork shall be simple, sturdy and suitable for military use. It should permit easy inspection and lubrication everywhere and under all conditions. The disassembly and reassembly procedures shall be absolutely foolproof and carried out without tools in such a manner that it will be impossible to lose any lock component. The use of screws with the main components shall be unnecessary; springs shall be strong and sturdy but capable of smooth operation. The lockwork should be as simple as practicable; its operation should be easily understood by unskilled personnel and its components sturdy enough to permit repair and replacement by an average gunsmith."

The workmanship of these guns was excellent and their

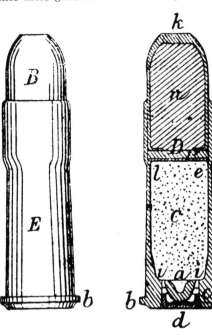

M1892 8mm revolver cartridge. Rimmed brass case holds a copper-jacketed bullet with lead core. The load is 11.5 grains of black powder, behind a 120-gr. copper-jacketed bullet. Despite its relatively small caliber, this flat-point bullet proved a good manstopper during the days of the Third Republic colonial empire and in the trenches of World War I. Note apparent reverse necking of what is, actually, a quite straight case. Artistic license, doubtless; this illustration is from an 1894 French miltary manual.

design met the rigid requirements. All component parts bore the serial number and the lock was finished like a fine watch. Their only drawback was the cartridge which, like most European ammunition of this period, was low-powered compared with American cartridges of similar caliber, such as the 44 Russian, the 44 WCF or the 45 Colt.

Nineteen years later, the French government adopted the Model 1892 swing-out revolver, manufactured principally in the Manufacture d'Armes de Saint-Etiénne until 1924 in a special 8mm caliber. This six-shot revolver fired a flat-point full-jacketed bullet weighing 8 grams (102 grains) propelled by 0.73 grams (11.23 grains) of special black powder. Smokeless cartridges were also manufactured. This gun was a masterpiece of design from the military viewpoint. The lockwork was reduced to four main components: trigger, hammer, hand and mainspring. The strut was made part of the hammer. A sturdy roller replaced the conventional hammer stirrup, one of the weakest components of most double action revolvers. The lockwork is readily inspected by unscrewing the sideplate retaining screw (a coin can be used) located on the right side of the frame above the grip, and swinging out the sideplate-trigger guard unit. The left-hand stock is then easily removed and the action fully exposed.

This revolver had a special cylinder release catch that, when moved to the rear with the cylinder in firing position, permitted loading the cylinder, chamber by chamber, in total darkness. The gun was light (840 grams—30 oz.) and handy with its standard 117mm (4½″) barrel. As for accuracy, it still holds a French record set by Martin at 20 meters which would be difficult to beat, even with a modern standard service revolver.

The major drawback of this revolver also lay in its cartridge, which was considered not powerful enough by modern standards. Nevertheless, this ammunition should not be dismissed lightly. It gained a grim reputation in all corners of the French colonial empire and during World War I.

As a result of the success of German autoloading pistols in WW I, the French army pressed into service many 32-cal. Spanish autoloading pistols bearing the Ruby (*Gabilondo y Cia-Elgoibar*) and Star (*B. Echeverria*) trademarks; also many Spanish copies of Colt and Smith & Wesson swing-out revolvers, chambered for the 8mm service ammunition.

By the end of the last century, great quantities of cheap pocket revolvers had been manufactured in France and Belgium for the commercial market. Most were on the Bull Dog (for centerfire smokeless and black powder cartridges) and Lefaucheux (for black powder pinfire cartridges) patterns. The most common black powder calibers were the 22 Long, 320, 380 and 450, while smokeless powder cartridges included the 6mm Velo Dog and 1892 8mm. In the pinfire series were the 5mm, 7mm, 9mm, 12mm and 15mm Lefaucheux. A similar series of centerfire black powder cartridges was also created but never became popular, at least not internationally. Copies of the

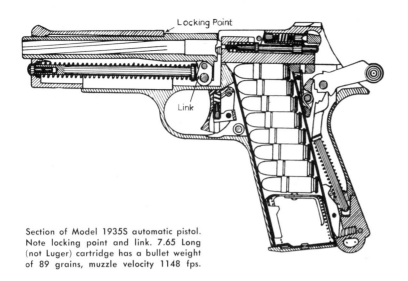

Section of Model 1935S automatic pistol. Note locking point and link. 7.65 Long (not Luger) cartridge has a bullet weight of 89 grains, muzzle velocity 1148 fps.

This Unique Model L 22 LR pistol, the basis of the popular Combo carbine/pistol, is also made in 32 ACP and 380 ACP. Straight-blow-back, single action operation.

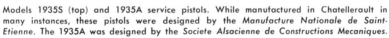

Models 1935S (top) and 1935A service pistols. While manufactured in Chatellerault in many instances, these pistols were designed by the *Manufacture Nationale de Saint-Etienne*. The 1935A was designed by the *Societe Alsacienne de Constructions Mecaniques*.

Model 1950 pistol in 9mm Luger caliber, the current French service sidearm. Capacity, 9. Operation is of the short recoil, single action.

Manufrance Le Francias 7.65mm (32ACP). Capacity, 9 cartridges. Straight blow-back, double action only.

French Ordnance Revolver Model 1892

Historical Notes

Erroneously referred to as a Lebel (Lt. Col. Nicolas Lebel, chief designer of the 1886 Lebel rifle, died in 1891), it was designed by a French ordnance commission, and was intended for officer issue to replace the old black powder 1874 officer's revolver. However, World War I logistics forced one standard pistol and cartridge. (WW I armies, in fact, never had enough of any one arm, and rear area troops might be armed with just about anything.) It was the standard French sidearm until 1935 when it was replaced by the MAS 1935A and 1935S automatics. Police units continued using them until after World War II.

The 1892 revolver fires a low-powered 8mm cartridge, comparable to our 32 S&W Long, that Americans do not consider a military cartridge; however, it was designed in an era of flamboyant heroics when many officers went into battle waving a "swagger stick." These colorful officers never intended to shoot anyone; their job was to direct the fire of their command. Many European armies share this same view.

Modern smokeless powder, non-corrosive cartridges (8mm Lebel, 1892) have been imported and are generally available. Do not confuse this pistol cartridge with the 8mm Lebel rifle cartridge.

Disassembly

Make sure revolver is unloaded. Turn disassembly screw (5). This will release the sideplate (3) allowing it to be swung forward and exposing the entire working mechanism. Remove left grip (28). With your fingers, squeeze mainspring (7), at the same time lifting it up and out. This is not difficult. The hammer (8) may now be removed. Push back the pawl (12) so it clears its recess in the frame, and it can be removed, followed by the trigger (13). Note that the mainspring, hammer, pawl, and trigger are numbered 1, 2, 3, and 4; the order of their removal. Unscrewing the strut screw (10) allows removal of strut (9) and strut spring (11). Remove right grip (26) and sideplate (3) by unscrewing their respective screws (27 and 4).

To remove the cylinder gate (23) open the cylinder, then reclose the gate. This will release pressure on the cylinder spring (24) and allow it to be pried out from the bottom. The cylinder gate (23) and cylinder catch (25) can then be removed.

If necessary, though it is not recommended, the cylinder and crane assemblies can be removed by first removing the crane screw (15), then with a punch, gently tap forward on rear of crane spring (16) exposed on inside of frame until the spring and crane are free of the frame. Unscrew extractor-knob screw (20) then unscrew knob (19). Crane (14), extractor bearing (21) and extractor spring (22) will come forward and off of extractor. Extractor (18) can be pushed out of rear of cylinder.

This revolver is well designed and has several outstanding features: (1) easy access to mechanism; (2) it cannot be fired with the cylinder gate open; and (3) the chambers may be loaded or checked without breaking open the cylinder by opening the gate and squeezing the trigger, thereby rotating the cylinder.

The date of manufacture is stamped on the right side of the barrel, i.e., S (series)—1893.

Parts List

1. Barrel
2. Frame
3. Sideplate
4. Sideplate Screw
5. Disassembly Screw
6. Disassembly Set Screw
7. Mainspring
8. Hammer
9. Strut
10. Strut Screw
11. Strut Spring
12. Pawl
13. Trigger
14. Crane
15. Crane Screw
16. Crane Spring
17. Cylinder
18. Extractor
19. Extractor Knob
20. Extractor-Knob Screw
21. Extractor Bearing
22. Extractor Spring
23. Cylinder Gate
24. Cylinder-Gate Spring
25. Cylinder Catch
26. Right Grip
27. Right Grip Screw
28. Left Grip
29. Lanyard Ring
30. Lanyard Ring Plate

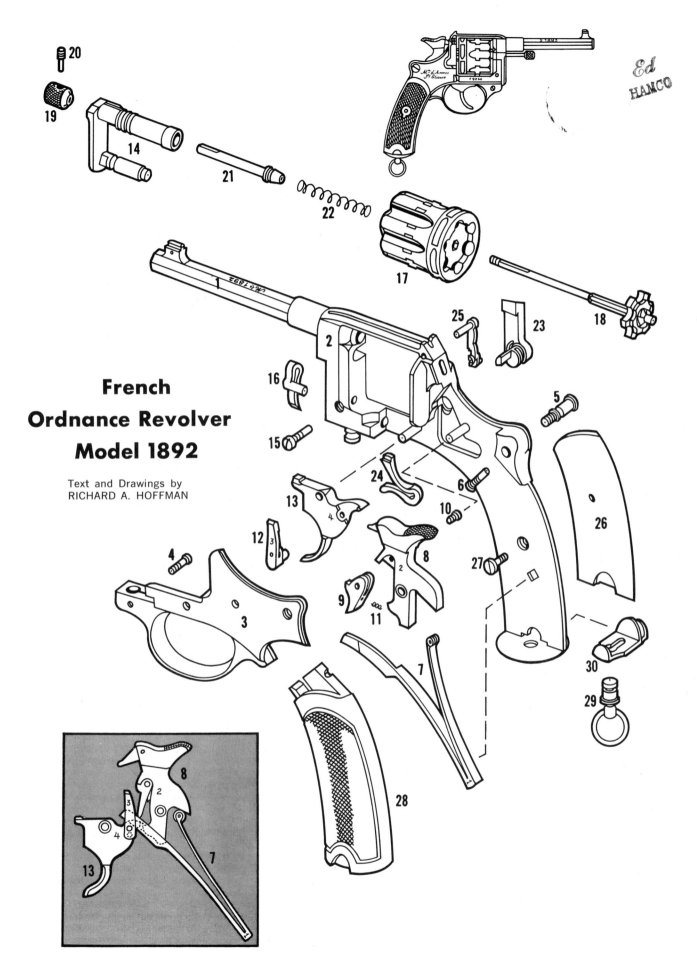

French
Ordnance Revolver
Model 1892

Text and Drawings by
RICHARD A. HOFFMAN

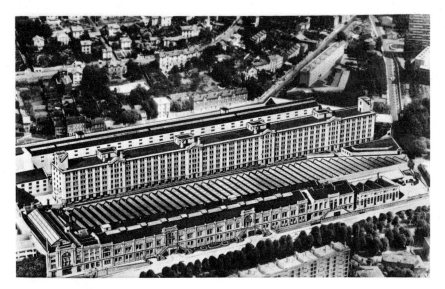
A view of the Manufrance factory in Saint-Etienne (Loire).

break-open Smith & Wesson revolvers were also manufactured, principally in Belgium. Some of these evolved into freak hammerless or two-barreled (over-under) weapons having two sets of chambers in the cylinder, the outside set firing through the upper barrel, the inside set through the lower. These were intended primarily for the African market. In the 1890s, freak pistols, such as the Manufacture d'Armes et Cycles de Saint-Etienne 8mm *Le Gaulois,* appeared, but met only with moderate success.

French-made 25- and 32-cal. automatic pistols, mostly on the Ruby and Browning patterns, such as the Peugeot, Monobloc, Union, Unique, MAB, etc., flooded the market after WW I; the Le Francais double action autoloading pistols had been first manufactured in 1908.

TARGET SHOOTING

The sport of target shooting was greatly developed by that time, both with the rifle and pistol.

Pistol shooting had evolved from the custom of dueling and was practiced in Paris shooting galleries such as the celebrated one managed by Gastinne-Renette. Following the visits around 1880 of some famous American shooters, including the Chevalier Ira Paine, the Smith & Wesson New Model single action 44 became famous as a target arm among the top French shooters.

Most early French target shooting had been at 12 meters with Flobert pistols. Following the foundation in the mid-1880s of the Patriots League, which evolved into the Union des Societes de Tir, 50-meter shooting developed. An interest in revolver target shooting also arose in the army, and the 1892 model became increasingly popular as a big bore target revolver.

On September 15, 1894, the following shooting program with the service revolver (1873 or 1892 model) was set up for French cavalrymen: [10]

12 shots single action at 15 meters; 12 shots single action at 30 meters, and 12 shots double action at 15 meters, each phase to be fired in two 6-shot strings. All shots were fired on 200mm (approximately 8″) or 400mm targets, each hit counting one point. A score of 24 brought a first-class marksman rating, 12 a second-class rating.

In 1900, the Union Internationale de Tir created the free pistol class of shooting. The first world championship was held in Paris and won by the Swiss champion Roderer with a 503x600. (He would have been 23rd at Strasbourg in 1965 with this score.)

In 1935, the French government adopted two versions of a Petter patented locked-breech autoloading pistol chambered for the 7.65 MAS cartridge. The Model 35-A featured a two-link barrel support and arched grip, while the less sophisticated 35-S had a conventional one-link

barrel support and straight grip. The locks of these two pistols were removable as a block. The government's intention was to replace the WW I 32 ACP substitute automatic pistols with more powerful handguns of modern design. Unfortunately the cartridge used was not as well-designed as the guns themselves and jams were relatively frequent in normal service. Furthermore, the increase in power was negligible.

After WW II, this handgun evolved into the Model 50, the current French army pistol, chambered for the 9mm Luger cartridge. It is widely used by all government services and gives full satisfaction for all practical purposes.

In the post-war period, due to severe regulations on firearms, the number of French commercial pistol manufacturers was reduced to these five:

Manufrance This company is a direct descendant of the famous Manufacture Francaise d'Armes et Cycles de Saint-Etienne, which was founded in 1885 by Etiénne Mimard and Pierre Blachon. A total of some 80,000 shotguns, rifles and handguns are produced here annually, along with 30,000 sewing machines, many thousands of bicycles and numerous other items. More than 3000 persons are employed by Manufrance, the home plant on Cours Fauriel in Saint-Etienne occupying 2 million-plus square feet. They distribute over 700,000 copies of their catalog, called the *Tarif-Album,* the latest edition of which contains 680 pages. Among their interesting firearms are double action autoloading pistols in 25 and 32 ACP, called Le Francais, and a bolt action target pistol for gallery practice.

Bergeron Also located in Saint-Etienne, this company was founded in 1903 by Louis Bergeron. Its main interest is the development and manufacture of high quality target guns. The only handgun in current production is the Federal bolt action free pistol in 22 LR and 6mm. This gun, a new model of which is in the planning stage, has won many national honors.

MAB Located in Bayonne, MAB was founded in 1921 by the late M. Barthe. This company specializes in the manufacture of autoloading pistols. Today's production includes their new 9mm automatic pistols. These are made with 15-shot (two-column) and 8-shot (single-column) magazines as the P-15 and P-8 models. MAB also manufactures their conventional Model D 32 ACP 9-shot pistol, formerly used by the French Surete Nationale, their Model A 25 ACP, and an inexpensive but very good 22 LR target autoloader, the Model R-22. Some ten years ago, the French shooter Molle won the Olympic rapid fire pistol championship of France using this model in 22 Short.

Manufacture d'Armes des Pyrenees Francaises Located at Hendaye, near the Spanish border, this organization was founded in 1923 by its present manager, M. Joseph Uria. It's trademark is "Unique." Originally located in Behobie, the factory was moved to its present site in 1928. This company produced only 25, 32 and 380 ACP autoloading pistols until 1937, when they created the first French-made 22 LR self-loading rifle. In 1948, they developed their Model Rr, the first French-made 22 LR autoloading pistol. In 1962 the Combo, a pistol-carbine combination, was brought out, and in 1964 a fine bolt action rifle chambered for the 22 WRF and 22 LR cartridges was added to their line. Their dependable Rf-51 autoloader, a 9-shot pistol handling the 32 ACP cartridge, is used by police in France and West Germany.

Unique also manufactures the Fr-51 380 ACP autoloader, the Mikros palm-gun in 22 Short and 25 ACP, their popular 22 LR Model L (basis of the Combo) and a full line of inexpensive but reliable fixed-barrel 22 LR

Above—Reduced-charge practice shooting. This sketch, from the 1914 Manufrance catalog, humorously illustrates the *vie de caserne* (barracks life) before the 1914-1918 war.

Below left—Another good reflection of the period is this shooting lady practicing with a BB pistol. The most popular gallery caliber was the 6mm Bosquette, a reinforced BB cap firing a conical lead bullet. Under French rules this class of shooting was done at 12 meters.

Below right—Shooting session at the *Prefecture de Police*. This sketch from the 1914 Manufrance catalog reflects the atmosphere of the *belle epoque* better than a long description. At the beginning of this century, the 1892, 1874, Municipal and other service revolvers enforced the law against the Bull Dog guns of the underworld Apaches.

(D series) and 22 Short (E series) autoloading pistols. Accuracy of these guns is warranted by a test target fired at 10 meters.

Manurhin This organization controls factories located in Mulhouse, Bitchswiller-Les-Thann, Essonnes-Corbeil and Eckbolsheim in France, in Luxembourg and in Sarrebruck in Saar. Their production includes machine tools as well as military equipment, flexible hoses, inspection equipment, ammunition, and electronic equipment. Handgun production is a small — but for shooters, important — part of their activity, as this company manufactures under exclusive license the Walther line of double action pocket pistols and the Walther Sport 22 LR target autoloader.

Manufacture Nationale d'Armes de Châtellerault This is the only government arsenal manufacturing the French army service pistol. It was created by a royal ordnance on July 14, 1819, for the purpose of concentrating beyond the Loire river, the Klingenthal, Maubeuge, Charleville and Mutzig manufactories. In 1828 the production of cold steel weapons was begun, and in 1865 production of firearms started in Châtellerault. Later, two inspectors from this factory, Close and Verdin, developed the repeating mechanism and the saber-bayonet of the famous Lebel military rifle. On September 19, 1891, an order was placed by the Russian government for the manufacture of 500,000 Mossin military rifles. This contract was fulfilled on April 19, 1895. In 1924 the factory began manufacture of the Model 1924 automatic rifle. After WW II production of the Model 50 pistol, designed in Saint-Etiénne, began and is still going strong.

If recent trends continue it seems possible that the commercial pistol market will decrease somewhat, due to the increase of restrictive legislation in many countries; nevertheless, the position of these French handgun manufacturers looks sound because they have consistently improved the quality of their position in their own country and are building up a good reputation in the export business. ●

References and Works Consulted

1. *Monographies de l'Arme Blanche et de l'Arme à feu portative*, Capt. Maurice Bottet (Paris, 1959).
2. *Gun Collector's Handbook of Values*, 3rd ed., Charles Edward Chapel (New York, 1955).
3. *The Art of the Gunmaker*, J. F. Hayward (New York City, 1962-64).
4. *La Manufacture d'Armes de Versailles, Boutet, Directeur Artiste*, Capt. Maurice Bottet (Paris, 1903).
5. *The Treasury of the Gun*, Harold L. Peterson (New York, 1962).
6. *Les Chasses d'Afrique*, Jules Gérard (Paris, circa 1850).
7. *Remington Handguns*, Charles Lee Karr, Jr., and Carroll Robbins Karr (Harrisburg, Pa., 1960).
8. *Smith & Wesson Revolvers*, John E. Parsons (New York, 1957).
9. *Les pistolet revolvers de Marine, système Lefaucheux*, G. Demaison and M. Moy (from "Les Arequebusiers de France" Bulletin No. 6, 1964).
10. *Réglement sur l'instruction du Tir des Troupes de cavalerie* (Paris, 1894).
— *Maximes, Conseils et Instructions sur l'Art de la Guerre*. Revision of an 1815 manual (Paris, 1855).
— *Manuel du cavalier*. 15ème Régiment de Chasseurs (Belfort, 1876).
— *Larousse du XIXème siècle* (Encyclopedia). Revolver item.
— *Mémorial du chasseur Français*. Volume 7, 1895 (Le Gaulois pistol).
— *Tarif-Album*. Manufrance catalogs, 1900 and 1914 editions (detail drawings).

Manurhin-Walther Sport-C, a 22 LR target version of the PP belt models. In September, 1964, at Pontarlier the Marseilles shooter Yves Couderq won France's national smallbore pistol title (ISU standard regulation) using this handgun fitted with a 6" barrel. His score was 564/600.

Manurhin-Walther Model PP pistol. Cal. 32 ACP of 380 ACP.

Current MAB military pistol of short recoil design with locked breech and rotating barrel.

Ibex in Iberia

Cabra Montes—the long-horned goat
that is unique to Spain—travels the
wind-swept ridges of the high and rocky
Sierra de Gredos. Finding a big one
in three days was the challenge.

by JOHN T. AMBER

T HE NINTH WINCHESTER Seminar for writers and editors was held in Europe in December of 1967 (see GUN DIGEST, 23rd ed., p. 30), and during our week's stay in Spain for red-legged partridge shooting there were a few evening entertainments—despite the fact that we never got back to Madrid from the shooting area near Toledo until 9 or 10 o'clock. From then to midnight is the fashionable time for dinner in Spain, however, so we didn't really miss much—after shedding our hunting clothes, followed by a quick bath and an equally quick drink or two, we'd be ready for whatever the agenda offered.

One of these affairs was a cocktail party given by Herb Jerosch—then manager of the Castellana Hilton in Madrid — followed by a great dinner in the grand manner in that famous hotel. The cocktail party was well attended—in addition to our small group of Jack O'Connor, Pete Barrett, Bill Talley, Bob Petersen, et al, there were many figures from the world of sport and Spanish government present, among them his excellency Don Manuel Fraga Iribarne, the Minister for Touring and Sport.

Senor Iribarne is a great enthusiast for sports in general, and for hunting in particular, we soon learned after being introduced to him. With the welcome help of Senor Max Borrell—who speaks English fluently—acting as an interpreter, we were deep in gun and shooting talk with Don Manuel. The upshot was that Jack O'Connor and I were invited to visit Spain in the fall of 1968 to hunt the famed Spanish ibex — *Capra hispanica* — in the Cote de Gredos some hundred miles west of Madrid. Sometime before the hunting season opened in September we'd receive the formal invitation, we were told, a choice of dates in September and October would be offered and, having selected a suitable time, we'd receive by mail the hunting license itself.

The Spanish ibex (locally, Cabra Montes) has been held by Abel Chapman* to be an animal found only on the Iberian peninsula, and nowhere else. He wrote "To this splendid game-animal, the Spanish ibex, we allot place of honour in our list [of game available in Spain] not only be-

*The Gun at Home and Abroad, Vol. III (London, 1914).

cause he represents the supreme prize in Spain to the cragsman-hunter, but also by virtue of the species being peculiar to the Peninsula. . . . The ibex of Spain stands out clean cut and distinct from all of his congeners (family) the world over, as a lion differs from a leopard, or a grouse from a blackcock."

Cabra Montes

The Spanish ibex is a small animal, about 30-34 inches at the shoulders, average weight some 70-80 pounds. In summer the back shows brownish-grey, shading off down the flanks and legs into tannish-white. There is the usual beard, typical of the goat family, long and thin in an old ibex.

The horns are quite different from other ibex; the triangular-section horns start upward and outward from the head, then go backward and, at the tips, inward, thus performing a half-spiral. The front surface of the horns is divided into ridges, but nothing like the prominent knobiness of other ibex.

At the turn of the century the Spanish ibex was almost extinct. In

Early morning at the Parador de Gredos.

the Sierra de Gredos a mere 15 animals were known to exist in 1905. At that dire stage, the large landholders relinquished their shooting rights to King Alfonso XIII, who immediately shut down all ibex shooting for several years, and a serious effort was made to stop the wanton killing of ibex by the numerous sheepherders. By 1910 an official count of the Gredos ibex alone showed well over 400 animals—a miracle of recovery.

Since that time ibex hunting has been carefully controlled, and I am sure that a census taken today would reveal many hundreds of ibex living in the Gredos. Several other mountainous areas of Spain contain ibex— the Pyrenees, the Sierras de Cazonia y Segura and de la Serrania de Ronda, et al.

For the reader who might like to do some hunting in Spain, let me point out that the invitational procedure I've touched on earlier is the preferred way of going about it. True, organized partridge shooting—which can be arranged through Winchester's World Wide Adventures—and other hunting can be arranged after one's landing in Spain, but to bring a gun in without having an invitation means visiting a Spanish consulate or embassy here, describing the gun in detail, getting a special firearms entry permit, and the applicant must show his State hunting license as well.

Spain, like most European countries, keeps firearms under strict control, which perhaps explains why those entering Spain carrying firearms should have an invitation to show the police and customs agents on arrival.

In due course I received my invitation and list of dates to choose from, so I selected October 3d to 5th. Jack O'Connor received his invitation also, and we were planning on hunting the Gredos together. Unfortunately, Jack had to forego the ibex hunt, but I left London for Madrid on September 30th, and I'll give you an idea now of what the problems would have been if I hadn't possessed that all-important invitation from Sr. Iribarne.

I'd brought my Model 77 Ruger bolt action to Europe, which 308 I eventually carried on the ibex hunt. After spending a short time in Italy, I flew to Frankfurt, the rifle still with me (I'd left it in bond at Milan's airport), but I then decided to send the M77 to Madrid by air freight. I didn't want to lug it all over the rest of Europe.

I wrote on the shipping tag that I would be reaching Madrid a few weeks later, that I was coming to Spain at the express invitation of Sr. Fraga Iribarne, and that I'd collect the gun on my arrival.

Trouble at the Pass

Despite these precautions, it took me almost 2 hours to obtain the rifle, and I was aided by the secretary of a Madrid friend, a girl fluent in English and Spanish. We had to talk to the police and customs men—pay a few small fees—before I got that rifle. It would have gone faster, I learned, had I carried the rifle with me.

I'm not complaining, I'm just telling it like it was—when in Rome and so on, of course, and U.S. frontier agents can put just as many obstacles in the way of the foreigner entering this country, to mention not the troubles a returning citizen sometimes has.

So—with my Ruger rifle and my cartridges at last in my hands — I set off for Madrid. I planned to spend a couple of days there, get settled in at the hotel, shop for a couple of last-minute things I wanted for the hunt, then make the drive to the Gredos mountains.

I'd been warned that the Gredos were rough and rocky in the extreme —no cover of any kind, the scattered vegetation thin and low—so I wanted to get a pair of moderately heavy work gloves, preferably of leather, and perhaps a pair of lightweight leather chaps. There'd be a lot of scrambling up and down the boulder-strewn slopes, and plenty of crawling about on my hands and knees, I'd heard.

Maybe I went to the wrong stores, but I could not find one glove shop that had the kind I wanted! Never heard of 'em, I was told, so maybe the Spanish laborer does his stuff barehanded. In any case, I bought a pair of pigskin dress gloves—for which I was thankful later—but passed up the only *chaparejos* I saw; thin, too-dressy types and all quite short. I could have brought the right kind of gloves with me, of course, but I'd thought Spain—famous for leather goods, and justly so — would have work gloves!

On October 2nd I rented one of the little 850 Fiats—a 2-door coupe with a rear engine, 4 on the floor and no guts. Matter of fact, it was fun to drive, though the gearbox was in constant use—it handled well, no power steering needed, and on the last 50 miles or so of winding, twisting gravel roads that led upward toward the Gredos, I found it cornered nicely, too. The heavy rear end was a little twitchy on the loose-gravel bends once in a while, but there wasn't enough power in hand to break it loose—and lose it.

Parador de Gredos

I reached the Parador de Gredos late in the evening. Spain's secondary or country roads aren't any better marked then some of ours, and I made a miscue a couple of times. These paradors—or tourist hotels— are scattered over much of Spain now, invariably at or close to some national park or other attraction for the visitor. The parador at Gredos is a long structure of weathered grey stone, two stories high, with a long and inviting verandah open to the sun. From this southern exposure the valley drops away, then gradually rises, first gently, then steeply into the immensity of rocks and boulders great and small that make up the Cote de Gredos. It's a grand view at any hour. For those who appreciate a quiet, restful holiday, basking in the sun or walking through the countryside, the Parador de Gredos offers a charming and soothing environment. There is, thankfully, no radio or television in the rooms—nor in the library or lounges—no entertainment of any kind. The service is excellent, though, the food and wines very good indeed. The rooms are ample and delightful, the furnishings simple but adequate, with much handsome wood panelling.

I was to enjoy my too-brief stay here, but now to bed for I'd be getting up at about 6 in the morning. I had been expected, of course, so even though I got there too late for the regular dinner period, some food was made available through the gracious help of a waitress and the cook.

The next morning, under a brilliant blue sky, I drove about 10 miles to my meeting place with the *guardas* who were going to find me an ibex. My lunch and theirs, stowed in huge saddlebags, had been handed to me

at the parador, and included was a full liter of local red wine—*tinto*—for each of us.

Two of these deeply-tanned, weather-beaten men were to be my guides, the third one acting as horse wrangler. Our mounts were already saddled, and in a moment we'd left this end-of-the-road rendezvous—already well up into the foothills of the mountains—and were on our way. It was a beautiful day, my new companions were friendly and jovial fellows, and I was looking forward, keyed up and e x c i t e d, to my first glimpse of Cabra Montes — I felt great.

I'd been briefed in Madrid by a man who'd been hunting in the Gredos recently, so I already knew what the general strategy would be. In good weather we'd climb the horses a few thousand feet, then dismount and make our way to the top of the ridges. There we would be in a position to glass the rocky slopes below, to clamber down on foot if ibex were spotted far below or descend also to see if any bucks were lying up underneath the overhanging cliffs.

By 8 o'clock we had reached the first mountain top, eroded away to

a fairly broad, roughly rounded area, broken here and there as we moved forward by great, jagged masses of solid rock jutting up into the sky. These formed good vantage points for scanning the country below, but were usually impossible to get around without our scrambling several hundred feet down to easier, shale-covered slopes. Here we could skirt the base of the great rocks, then climb back up again to the tops.

Sierra de Gredos

The Gredos peaks there are not extremely high, some 7000-8000 feet or so, but I suppose we must have climbed up and down their steep and boulder-strewn slopes a score or more times during that day's hunt. Getting down was much harder work usually, leaps having to be made of 5 or 6 feet onto the next big rock below, but the climb back up was almost as bad. I was soon puffing and blowing, but I'd at last make the ridge again. I was to lose 12 pounds in that short time, and I became so dehydrated that I drank water endlessly at the end of the day—or so it seemed.

About 10 o'clock that first morning, after we'd gone down the rock

The guardas of the Sierra de Gredos are rugged, hard working men, good at their job and fond of it.

face for the 5th or 6th time, my two guides had moved in behind a huge boulder to glass the area underneath it and to see the section to the left as well—ibex could be concealed here, asleep or lying up, which we couldn't have located from the top.

Suddenly they began whispering excitedly, and I knew they'd found ibex. Both men were stretched up on tiptoe, peering over the rounded mass of rocks at a steep angle, for the ibex were lying asleep on a ledge almost vertically below them. All this I sensed instantly, of course, but I'd learned long ago that in European hunting you generally wait for a signal

and during the next couple of ibex sightings.

Sleeping Ibex

I had never seen an ibex before, of course, and I had no real idea of what they would look like. Not until I saw the 3 running did I realize how beautifully their brown-tan-white coloration blended in with the rocks and brown soil we were on. Those 3, too, had been lying asleep, Paco told me finally, but I hadn't known that earlier.

I now tried to explain that because I was unfamiliar with the game, that because I'd have trouble again, no

a cold, clear spring close by. I was, of course, kicking myself a bit for not having got a shot at the first trio—two of them had good horns, I'd thought, and Paco agreed—but the hunt wasn't over yet. The meal break was welcome, and I had my fill of water, wine and thick cheese sandwiches. It was good to be up in the mountains again.

Evening came, and while we saw several bands of ibex through the rest of the afternoon, none had horns I was going to settle for this early in the game. I was hopeful of taking a gold medal goat, a record-book ibex—which my ticket permitted—though

The horses were tired at the end of our first long day, and so was I.

from the guide before moving up for the shot. I stood there, wondering what was going on for what seemed like several minutes but was doubtless much less, when Paco motioned me forward, indicating by gestures that I was to shoot.

I squeezed in between them, my glasses ready to locate the ibex below me, but I'll be damned if I could find them. Frantically I swung the binoculars, trying to see almost straight down and everywhere else, but not until they moved did I see that there were three ibex, running at top speed out of there. My rifle was propped up against the rocks! In another movement, some hundred yards away, a band of 16 or 17 ibex jumped up and ran. The first 3 had been lying some 200 yards from us.

This larger bunch the guides had not mentioned, indicating to me by their raised hands only the 3 first seen, but there was the usual frustrating language problem. I've got only a smattering of Spanish, so perhaps they had seen the others and said so, but that wasn't what bugged me then

doubt, in spotting any ibex located, that I wanted to get my glasses working as soon as their's were onto an animal.

I didn't get the message over, I could see that, for on the next couple of times that ibex were located, the same damned thing happened—I'd be called into position at the last moment, just before the ibex moved out, it seemed, for my own locating of them. True, I was finding them now a lot more rapidly, but I still wasn't all set to shoot. Fortunately, on these first several small bands, I saw nothing worth shooting, and the guides agreed.

Still, I was getting in some good practice at identifying ibex—which was to prove invaluable later—and I was now shoving my way up to the lookout point just as soon as I could see that ibex had been located. If a good head did show, I was going to be a lot better prepared than I had been.

The day wore on, sunny but nicely cool, and about 2 o'clock the guides, the wrangler and I sat down to eat,

I might change my mind about that on the third and last day if I'd been unsuccessful.

It was a long haul back to the meeting place, much of the ride in darkness. I was bone-weary, again extremely thirsty, and glad that my poor old horse knew the way home without strong guidance from me.

I reached the parador about 8 o'clock, changed and showered, then sat down in the pleasant dining room to a good dinner—over which I almost fell asleep.

Hundreds of Ibex

I got to the guide's corral next morning, not quite as full of energy as I had been the day before. I had got a good night's sleep, but yesterday had been tough—too tough maybe—but I was still keyed up about finding a really big ibex, and the whole day stretched before me.

That entire day was pretty much the same as the day just passed—we climbed up and down interminably, we got back on the horses now and then to move to another range, and we saw, I suppose, at least a hundred ibex—mostly females and youngsters, with none of the bucks presenting a first class rack. In the two days we must have looked over some 200 ibex, I think.

At about 5:30 or so we were toiling back up to where the horses stood. The three of us had dropped down into a steep-sided narrow canyon, one that stretched downward and away at about 90 degrees to our main ridge. The western edge of this canyon rose high and sharp-edged, its other side sloping away to a broad valley far below. We had been unable to see anything of that offside slope, so we'd descended into the canyon floor, then scaled the wall to peer through the vertical cracks and openings in it hoping to find game somewhere on the other side. Nothing—we three looked through our glasses slowly and carefully, handicapped at this hour by the sinking sun at our backs. The broken, jagged rocks below our eyes were filling with shadow, growing more inpenetrable by the moment. Nothing moved.

Ernesto and I scrambled down to the canyon's floor, then started climbing back up among the stones, headed for our main ridge and the horses. The hunt was over for the day. Paco, however, had not descended to the bottom of the canyon; instead, still searching for an ibex, he'd continued to move along the steep canyon wall, stopping to use his glasses as he went. Then, as Ernesto and I were well up the mountain—and well away from Paco at an angle—he whistled softly. I didn't hear him, but Ernesto did, and because he was in front of me I could see him motioning to me to turn around. Paco was beckoning to me urgently. Quartering my way to him as fast as I could over the tangle of rocks, my rifle loaded and safe, he pointed steeply down as I reached his side. Far below, just inside the shadow line stood a big ibex in a narrow cleft in the rocks. Only his back and fore-quarters were visible, his magnificent horns looming over his withers as he fed, head down.

Muerte!

Leaning way out from the opening in the rock, I raised the rifle and fired, remembering as I did to hold low on the animal's shoulder. At the report Paco shouted *"Muerte, muerte,"* clapping me on the back and pumping my hand in congratulation. By this time Ernesto had reached us, and we began a 3-man celebration. The ibex was indeed dead — Paco said he'd never moved after the shot — but now came the job of getting to him. I'd made the shot at about 200 yards, but the open valley floor was far below that, the course up to the dead ibex filled with great rocks—and steep. Night, too, would be on us in a half-hour or so.

By this time our wrangler had

started toward us, leading one horse for me, but the guides waved him off, shouting that he was to bring the horses down the other side of the ridge and around to the valley floor below our ibex.

I'm willing to confess that I sat and rested where I was. I wasn't about to scramble down to that ibex —he wouldn't go away—then have to climb back up again, perhaps. I'd had

just about all of that I could handle in two days, and the successful *cazadore* has some privileges, no?

The men soon reached the ibex, dressed him out and tied him behind a saddle as I watched. I'd changed my mind, of course, and after resting a few minutes I'd also made my way down to the ibex. His horns measured just 77 centimeters each (30.3 inches), neither one damaged or

broomed, and I was pretty damned well pleased with myself and my very good ibex. No, not a gold medal trophy, but at the time I made the shot I'd have settled for an ibex showing a lot less horn! I'd about had it.

We had hunted a range this day much farther off than before, and the ride back took nearly four hours. Happy hours, though, riding under a brilliant moon, singing and laughing—I

The horns of this Capra hispanica measured 77 centimeters, well above average.

was sorry to have it come to an end as we reached my little car.

I drove back the next morning to collect my horns and make a few pictures—it had been too dark at the time I'd shot—and said goodbye to my guides. Hard-working, game-wise, competent and friendly *companeros*, and if it had not been for those last-moment efforts of Paco's I might well have left for Madrid empty-handed. ●

THE
WHITWORTH

Fig. 1. Military Match Rifle, cased in oak and complete. The first commercially available Whitworth, which appeared in 1859, this is the pattern given as prizes by the National Rifle Association of Great Britain in 1860, 1861 and 1862. This type was also given as a prize by many Volunteer units and civic organizations during those years. Note that the case is unlined. The round capbox, the lock and breech design, the smooth-headed ramrod and stock design are characteristic of this model. *Courtesy E. J. Burton.*

The first comprehensive and critical review of a famous rifle, the result of the author's deep and diligent research. Fully illustrated.

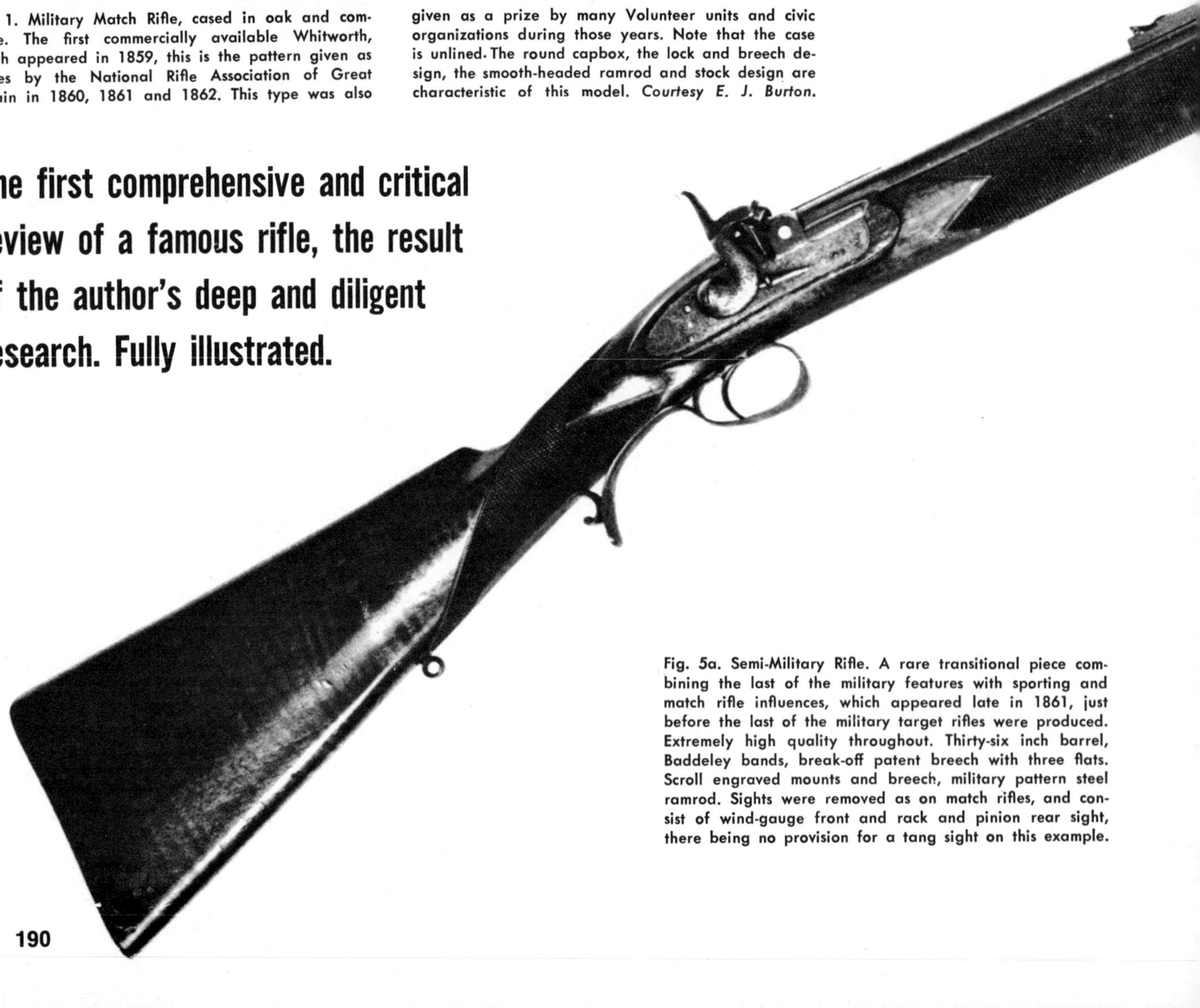

Fig. 5a. Semi-Military Rifle. A rare transitional piece combining the last of the military features with sporting and match rifle influences, which appeared late in 1861, just before the last of the military target rifles were produced. Extremely high quality throughout. Thirty-six inch barrel, Baddeley bands, break-off patent breech with three flats. Scroll engraved mounts and breech, military pattern steel ramrod. Sights were removed as on match rifles, and consist of wind-gauge front and rack and pinion rear sight, there being no provision for a tang sight on this example.

by DeWITT BAILEY II

RIFLE

a great milestone in rifle history

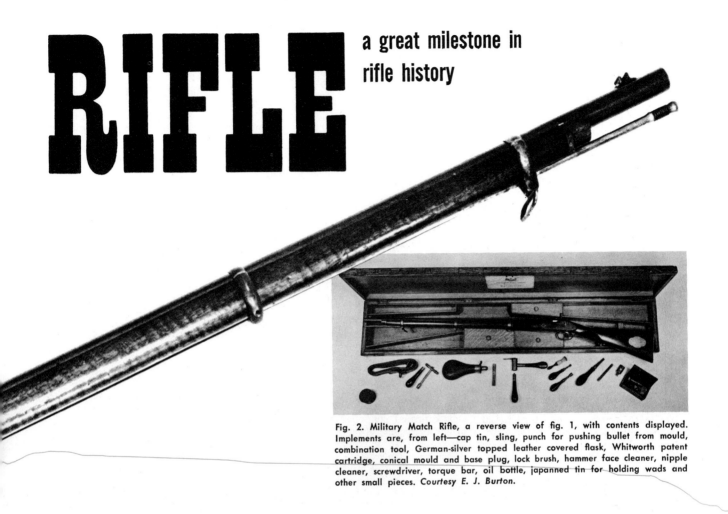

Fig. 2. Military Match Rifle, a reverse view of fig. 1, with contents displayed. Implements are, from left—cap tin, sling, punch for pushing bullet from mould, combination tool, German-silver topped leather covered flask, Whitworth patent cartridge, conical mould and base plug, lock brush, hammer face cleaner, nipple cleaner, screwdriver, torque bar, oil bottle, japanned tin for holding wads and other small pieces. *Courtesy E. J. Burton.*

JOSEPH WHITWORTH began his career as a toolmaker in Manchester in 1833. He died in January, 1887, with a world-wide reputation as the most eminent producer and designer of precision machine tools. The standards set by his machines are still current today. His standardization of screw threads, dating from the 1840s, still stands.

Problems with the production and performance of the Pattern 1853 Enfield rifle musket, the absence of standardization of tools and gauges, the problem of supply in the face of the Crimean War and its extraordinary demands, led the British government to call upon Whitworth in 1854 to suggest remedies to existing difficulties. Whitworth's exhibits at the Great Exhibition of 1851 had won his international acclaim, and as the nation's most outstanding engineer and machine tool manufacturer it was natural that he should be selected to investigate the standardization and mass-production possibilites of the Enfield works.

In 1854 Joseph Whitworth was not well acquainted with the manufacture of small arms, and in order to familiarize himself with the processes and practices involved he visited most of England's leading gunmakers. His basic conclusion from these visits was that gunmakers proceeded upon little if any actual proven theories, but rather from hit-and-miss experiments and methods learned during their apprenticeships. From this it followed that there was no rational explanation for the irregularities in the performance of the Pattern 1853 Enfield; before Whitworth would undertake to criticize this particular weapon he felt it necessary to establish in his own mind just what the perfect form of rifled small arm should be. From the experiments he conducted to find the answer to this question came the Whitworth rifle and the heavy ordnance so well known, at least in name, to arms collectors today.

It appeared to Whitworth that both the caliber and barrel dimensions of the Pattern 1953 Enfield had been chosen by arbitrary and unscientific methods. It was obvious to him as well that the problems encountered in its performance were due to inaccuracies in the interior of the barrels, possibly even in their basic construction. Whitworth explained his views to the government and offered, if the government would pay his expenses, to conduct a series of tests to determine the best form of small arm for military service. He refused to accept any salary for his work.

In the early stages of his work, Whitworth experimented with a wide variety of rifling twists, calibers, barrel lengths and metals, reaching such extremes as a 20-inch barrel with a twist of one turn in one inch. Whitworth had apparently not examined any other than the standard Enfield 577-caliber barrels, but had seen a polygonally-rifled barrel designed by Isabard Brunel and constructed by Westley Richards. Richards and Whitworth worked closely together during the early stages of Whitworth's work, and much of Dhitworth's knowledge of

Fig. 3. Military Target Rifle, breech closeup. Note the Enfield style snail, with underside overhanging lockplate, Whitworth trademark on tail of plate, sliding safety bolt and typical WHITWORTH marking above bolt. The rear sight is an early pattern before the rack-and-pinion type was adopted; many of this model are found refitted with a rack-and-pinion sight of an early type. Hammer, trigger guard and trigger, checkering pattern and form of breech (note patent breech but absence of hook breech) are typical of this model. *Courtesy E.J. Burton.*

the firearms trade must have been gained from Westley Richards. It was not until the end of 1856 that Whitworth appears to have settled on a design for his rifle; its first official tests came in April, 1857. From this time onwards, the now-familiar hexagonal bore, with a twist of one turn in 20 inches, seems to have been the standard in Whitworth rifles. The tests of 1857 and 1858 proved the far superior accuracy of Whitworth's system against that of the 577 Enfield (which were rifled with three lands and grooves having a twist of one turn in 78 inches, with the depth of rifling gradually decreasing from the breech to the muzzle), but as accuracy was but one of the criteria to be considered in the acceptance of any system for military use, the basic issues were far from solved. Such questions as fouling, tendency to miss-fire, ease of handling, manufacture of ammunition suitable for military conditions, costs of manufacturing—all seemed to create some doubts in the minds of the investigating committee members. In addition, a small-bore Enfield had performed very nearly as well as the Whitworth rifle, and there was some question whether Whitworth's system might be the only answer.

The Crimean War had been weathered, the national emergency was over, and thoughts of economy were again uppermost in the minds of the government. By 1859 the whole project had been narrowed down to two basic problems. First, would other manufacturers be able to produce the standard of precision required to manufacture Whitworth rifles in some future emergency, if they were to be produced on a large scale? Secondly, Whitworth still asked £10 per rifle for 1,000 or 1,200 rifles, while the Pattern

1853 rifle musket cost £3.5.1 from contractors or £1.19.8 from Enfield ($48.00 for the Whitworth as against $15.44 and $8.48 for the Pattern 1853 Enfield). Economy won the day and the question of Whitworth vs. Enfield was dropped. It was at this point that Whitworth turned his energies to heavy ordnance rifled upon his hexagonal principle. During the next 5 years a nationwide controversy developed as to the comparative merits of the Whitworth and Armstrong systems. During the Civil War the Confederacy purchased a number of Whitworth field guns and naval cannons in breech-loading and muzzle-loading styles; the Confederate ironclad ram *Stonewall* was armed with two of Whitworth's heavy naval guns.

Concurrently with the military experiments being conducted on behalf of the government, an increased interest in rifle shooting was developing among civilians, culminating in what was termed the "Volunteer Movement." The political friction between England and France present in the 1850s had increased after the conclusion of the Crimean War (in which the two countries had been allied) largely because of the expansionist tendencies of Napoleon III, and the discovery that the Orsini bomb plot against Napoleon had been planned and developed in England. The always invasion-conscious British public, egged on by a ubiquitous and inflammatory press, increasingly clamored for protective measures against possible French invasion.

In 1859 the parliamentary act authorizing the raising and equipping of volunteer corps to fight on English soil, in case of invasion—which had been passed in the Napoleonic Wars period—was regenerated. A rapid rise

in the number of rifle companies throughout England resulted. As of January 1st, 1860, one hundred per cent of such troops would be equipped at government expense if the necessary conditions were met. It soon became obvious that a national organization devoted to the development of accurate rifle shooting was highly desirable, and the National Rifle Association of Great Britain came into being in November, 1859. The first meeting was held at the beginning of July, 1860.

First Whitworths

At this meeting Queen Victoria fired the opening shot with a Whitworth rifle mounted on a rest. For the next 8 years the Whitworth rifle, in various models, was always among the top contenders for honors at British rifle matches.

Aside from the rifles themselves, the initiative of Joseph Whitworth in creating a superbly accurate rifle (for its time) spurred other gunmakers and inventors into action. The result was a profusion of rifling systems, mostly based on the basic Whitworth principles of a 451-caliber bore with a twist of one turn in 20 inches, firing a 530-gr. bullet. The fact that a number of these systems ultimately succeeded in out-shooting the Whitworth in competition does not detract from the significance of Whitworth's contribution in establishing the basic knowledge, and in taking the first positive steps towards a formerly unthought of degree of both range and accuracy in military and civilian marksmanship.

In the spring of 1860 experimental rifles were again ordered from Whitworth, but the trials were not actually held until mid-1861. Further trials were held in 1862, and both proved beyond any doubt the superiority of "small bore" (.451" as opposed to .577") weapons so far as accuracy was concerned. Other small bore rifles were tested during these trials, but Whitworth's proved the best of the lot. The Ordnance Select Committee, in charge of the trials, had stressed the importance of putting the rifles into the hands of troops to determine their performance under field conditions. It was with this factor in mind that 1,000 rifles were ordered in May, 1862. As these rifles gave no initial indications of the problems which later developed, a further 8,000 rifles of a slightly different pattern were ordered in 1863. These were issued on a trial basis to a number of British Army units in England and on foreign duty. Despite the official adoption of the Snider breech-loading system in 1865, many of these Whitworth muzzleloaders were still in the hands of troops as late as 1867. Whitworth rifles continued to be used in the firing for the Queen's Prize at Winmbledon through 1870.

To bring his rifling system to the

broader attention of the general shooting public, Whitworth entered the commercial market in mid-1859, hoping that success among sportsmen and Volunteers would induce the government to take up the matter of his rifles again. The advent of the National Rifle Association was a Godsend to Whitworth insofar as his civilian market was concerned, for the majority of the prize rifles awarded at N.R.A. meetings for the remainder of the muzzle-loading era were Whitworths.

In 1860 a retailing company known as the Whitworth Rifle Company set up offices at 51, Sackville Street, Manchester. Shortly after receiving the order for 1,000 rifles in May, 1862 (it turned out that only a part of these rifles were produced by Whitworth, aside from the barrels), the firm name was changed to the Manchester Ordnance & Rifle Company, an obvious indication that Whitworth was now actively engaged in the production of cannon. By 1865 the addresses of the Manchester Ordnance & Rifle Company and Joseph Whitworth & Company are combined, indicating that the market in both rifles and heavy ordnance was sufficiently diminished that the operation could be combined under one roof. There is, in fact, considerable doubt that the small arms made with Whitworth's rifling were actually fabricated at any Whitworth works. The barrels were probably the only part of the rifles actually made by the Whitworth firm. In the case of the Pattern 1863 Short Rifles Whitworth made but 1,803 of the 8,203 barrels supplied.

The Various Models

The rapid rise of the Volunteer movement and Whitworth's desire to keep his rifling system before the eyes of military men brought about the introduction of what was to become the most common of non-military Whitworths—the *military target rifle*. The earliest form of this rifle made its appearance in the summer of 1859, but it would seem that by the time of the formation of the National Rifle Association, and its first meeting in July of 1860, certain modifications and improvements had taken place to produce the rifle in its best-known form (figs. 1, 2 and 3). This is the rifle used in most small bore competitions at Wimbledon, and the rifle which was presented to Queen's Prize winners and numerous runners-up, as well as for other competitions. Many were presented by various organizations, both civil and military, to members of Volunteer units who had won local or regional competitions. Whitworth thus received a large measure of "free" advertising through the Kingdom.

In basic outline the military target rifle resembles the Pattern 1853 Enfield, but the refinements are legion and the contours more elegant. Some early examples have 33-inch barrels, presumably to conform more closely to the Pattern 1860 Short Rifle, then the standard issue for rifle companies and for sergeants of line regiments. Three barrel bands of normal Enfield clamping pattern hold the barrel to the full length forearm. The steel ramrod is similar to the Enfield, having a slotted head but lacking the concentric rings of the Enfield. Most rifles have a patent breech, but there is no false breech; the tang screw must be removed to take the barrel from the stock. The patent breech is recessed on the left in the manner of contemporary sporting arms, but the tang and snail closely resemble the Enfield; the snail slightly overhangs the lockplate, and generally has borderline engraving (fig. 3). The lockplate is of Enfield pattern but smaller, and the hammer is a compromise between the heavy military and lighter sporting patterns, generally having Enfield-pattern border engraving. There is a sliding safety bolt forward of the hammer, and two lock screws hold the lock to the stock; Enfield pattern screw cups support the screws on the left of the stock.

The stock is of dark walnut, some examples having fine contrasting colors. It is fitted with steel furniture throughout, consisting of a forearm cap of Enfield pattern, trigger guard similar to the Enfield, round capbox, and Enfield-pattern buttplate. Sling swivels are mounted on the upper barrel band and through the rear of the trigger guard strap. The wrist and forearm are checkered, the diamonds large and coarse compared to later models, but quite typical of contemporary Volunteer rifles. The furniture, excepting the color case-hardened capbox, is heat-blued.

The sights of the military target rifle present something of a confusing study to the arms collector. As they went from the works the sights were relatively plain, but because they were the "first of the breed" they later underwent, in many cases, considerable alteration at the hands of not only gunsmith and individual owners, but from the Whitworth firm itself. The original rear sight consisted of a long leaf with platinum-lined notch and slide, graduated to 4° on the left side and 1,000 yards on the right side, both on the bottom of the leaf. There were a number of minor variations in the sight bed; some were virtually flat, or with very slight elevators on either side, while others have one or two distinct steps to the elevators. The front sight was a windage-adjustable blade, a small screw in the center of the front face of the sight base allowing for adjustment.

Fig. 4. Typical Whitworth accessories found with military target rifles. Left to right—wooden knob (above) screws onto steel ramrod to aid in loading; base plug for conical bronze one-piece bullet mould; bullet mould with typical Whitworth markings; octagonal steel oil bottle; nipple cleaner; hammer face cleaner; torque bar which fits through slot in head of rod to give a better grip when cleaning or extracting a ball; military Whitworth cartridge; Whitworth's Patent "trap door" cartridge, with military load of 70 grains of black powder and a 530-gr. bullet. Horizontal item at bottom center is hollow bore protector, used when loading and cleaning. Courtesy E.J. Burton.

The great popularity of the Whitworth rifle and its extensive use at N.R.A. meetings led shortly to a refinement of the sighting equipment, and a hooded front sight with pin-ball post replacing the earlier blade. The famous "rack & pinion" rear sight so often seen on Whitworth rifles was patented by Whitworth and Hulse on August 2, 1861, along with a hooded front sight and a combination tool. Whether the sights were actually being produced before the patent was taken out is questionable, but by 1862 the Whitworth Rifle Company was notifying dealers that they would re-equip any of their rifles with the new "Patent Sights," re-finish the barrel,

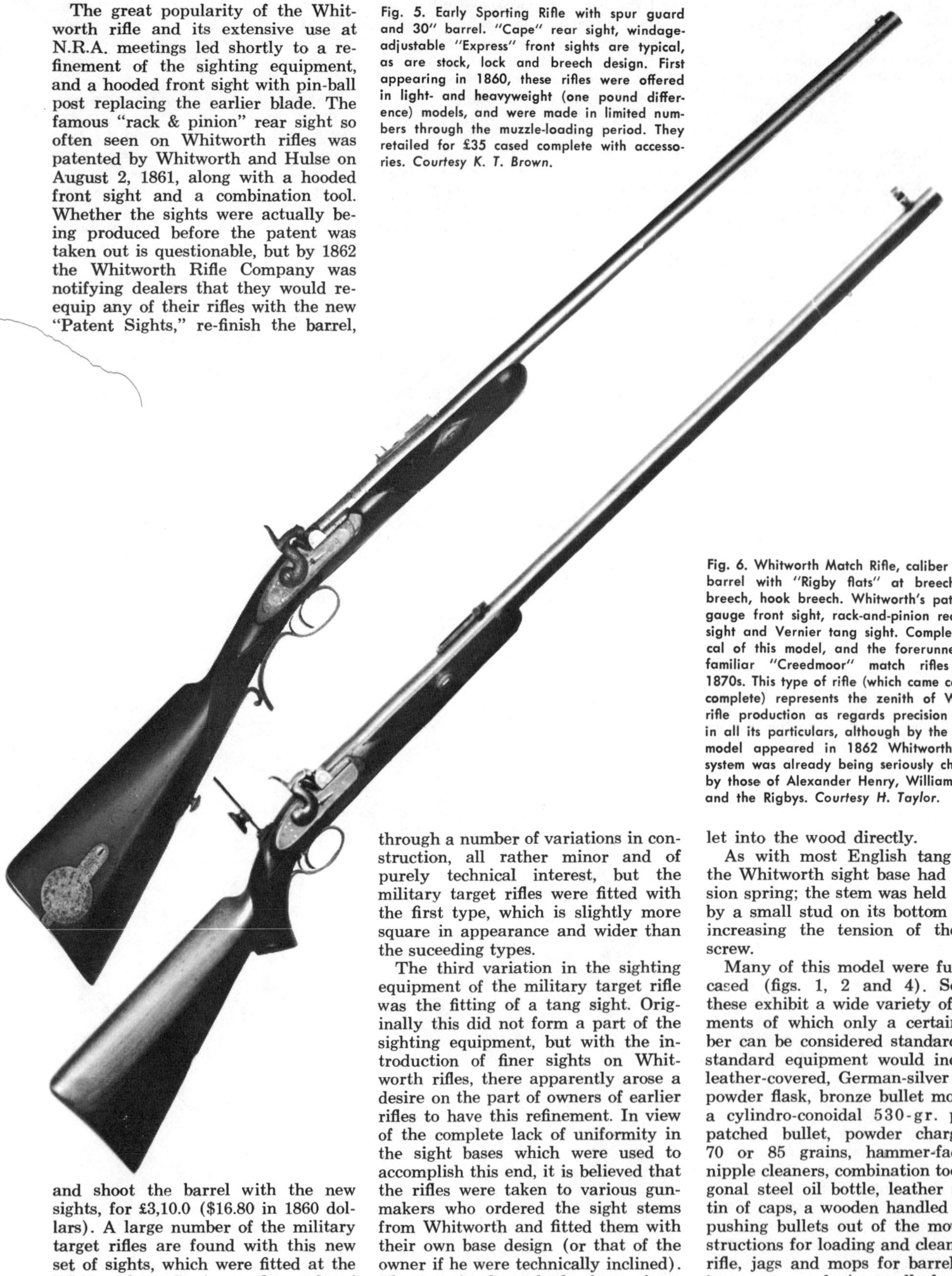

Fig. 5. Early Sporting Rifle with spur guard and 30" barrel. "Cape" rear sight, windage-adjustable "Express" front sights are typical, as are stock, lock and breech design. First appearing in 1860, these rifles were offered in light- and heavyweight (one pound difference) models, and were made in limited numbers through the muzzle-loading period. They retailed for £35 cased complete with accessories. Courtesy K. T. Brown.

Fig. 6. Whitworth Match Rifle, caliber 451, 36" barrel with "Rigby flats" at breech. Patent breech, hook breech. Whitworth's patent wind gauge front sight, rack-and-pinion rear barrel sight and Vernier tang sight. Completely typical of this model, and the forerunner of the familiar "Creedmoor" match rifles of the 1870s. This type of rifle (which came cased and complete) represents the zenith of Whitworth rifle production as regards precision shooting in all its particulars, although by the time this model appeared in 1862 Whitworth's rifling system was already being seriously challenged by those of Alexander Henry, William Metford and the Rigbys. Courtesy H. Taylor.

and shoot the barrel with the new sights, for £3,10.0 ($16.80 in 1860 dollars). A large number of the military target rifles are found with this new set of sights, which were fitted at the Whitworth works (or at the works of some gunmakers hired by Whitworth to do the work) in 1862. The first form of hooded windgauge front sight did not have interchangeable discs, but was fitted with the pin-ball post only. The rack & pinion rear sight went

through a number of variations in construction, all rather minor and of purely technical interest, but the military target rifles were fitted with the first type, which is slightly more square in appearance and wider than the suceeding types.

The third variation in the sighting equipment of the military target rifle was the fitting of a tang sight. Originally this did not form a part of the sighting equipment, but with the introduction of finer sights on Whitworth rifles, there apparently arose a desire on the part of owners of earlier rifles to have this refinement. In view of the complete lack of uniformity in the sight bases which were used to accomplish this end, it is believed that the rifles were taken to various gunmakers who ordered the sight stems from Whitworth and fitted them with their own base design (or that of the owner if he were technically inclined). These variously took the form of extended flat planes made of wood; of extensions of the tang strap which were dovetailed to receive the small base and stem, and windage adjustable by means of a drift and mallet; and various designs of bases being

let into the wood directly.

As with most English tang sights, the Whitworth sight base had no tension spring; the stem was held upright by a small stud on its bottom and by increasing the tension of the pivot screw.

Many of this model were furnished cased (figs. 1, 2 and 4). Some of these exhibit a wide variety of implements of which only a certain number can be considered standard. Such standard equipment would include a leather-covered, German-silver topped powder flask, bronze bullet mould for a cylindro-conoidal 530-gr. paper-patched bullet, powder charger for 70 or 85 grains, hammer-face and nipple cleaners, combination tool, octagonal steel oil bottle, leather sling, a tin of caps, a wooden handled rod for pushing bullets out of the mould, instructions for loading and cleaning the rifle, jags and mops for barrel cleaning, grease wads (generally hexagonal in form), and a wooden knob with threaded brass center which screwed onto the end of the ramrod to aid in loading, spare platinum-lined nipples and a screwdriver. Items which may be considered as optional in Whitworth cased sets of this and other models would include a bullet swage, a lock brush, packets of hexagonal bullets, a brass muzzle protector for use in loading; a torque bar which fitted through the slotted head of the ramrod to aid in cleaning the barrel, removing bullets when they had been seated without powder, "bad" loads, and so forth; powder chargers which screw on the end of the ramrod to place the entire charge in the breech, patch paper, patent cartridges, mainspring vise, a ball puller and a tompion or muzzle stopper. Sporting and purely target models also included loading rods and short starters, and a double-ended rod having at one end a Whitworth hexagonal scraper and at the other a brass charger to breech-position the entire powder charge.

The military target rifle sold for £20 ($96 in 1860 dollars) or £25 ($120 in 1860 dollars) cased complete. The cases were of oak, with varnished finish in natural color, and were unlined (figs. 1 and 2).

Concurrently with the introduction of the military target rifle, Withworth made his bid for the deer-stalking market with the introduction of a Sporting Rifle in the summer of 1859. They appear to have enjoyed but limited sale right through to 1866, judging from a study of serial numbers and markings. Despite the relatively long period of production—so far as Whitworth rifles are concerned—these sporting rifles are among the rarest of Whitworths (aside from the experimental models), since Whitworth production seems to have been very largely taken up with military and semi-military style rifles. This emphasis is, of course, quite natural, since it was the military authorities that

Whitworth was primarily interested in impressing.

Whitworth's sporting rifles were very similar to the usual British sporting rifles of the mid-19th century except that they were made only with full round barrels rather than the normal octagon type. They are fitted with a hook or break-off breech, a patent breech design internally, and the snail has a platinum plug. The barrels are blued, the patent breech color case-hardened. The early sporters have 30″ barrels, while later rifles have varying lengths down to 28½ inches; 30 inches appears to have been the standard. Another feature typical of the early sporting rifles is the use of a spur trigger guard (fig. 5) rather than a pistol grip stock; the latter feature is found on a few of the later sporting rifles. The furniture, of blued steel, is of typical shotgun pattern, and finally engraved with scroll work and animals. The round capbox is typical. Stocks were of highly polished fine-grained walnut often showing beautiful color contrasts.

The sights of the sporting rifle as they left the works consisted of a long bead "express" front sight which was windage adjustable, and a "Cape" style leaf rear sight having separate leaves folding into the base for 100 and 200 yards, plus a long leaf, with a slide hinged forward of the short leaves, for 300, 400 and 500 yards.

Sporting rifles appear to have been sold only as complete cased sets, as there is no provision for a ramrod on the production model. This item was included in the set and carried by the gentleman-sportsman's keeper or bearer. The rifles were offered in "heavy" and "light" weights, 7½ and 6½ pounds respectively. A complete

cased outfit consisting of the rifle, "mahogany case, with leather covering...bullet mould, powder flask, 300 rounds of ammunition and a full set of apparatus," sold for £35 ($168 in 1860 U.S. dollars) in either weight.

The continuing growth in popularity of rifle shooting, and the expanding program of the National Rifle Association encouraged Whitworth to further refine and upgrade the appearance of his military target rifles, and the result was the semi-military rifle (fig. 5a), combination of military and sporting features, designed for long range target shooting.

These were first marketed in the late fall of 1861; they appear from the first to have been but a transitional piece. In terms of serial numbers these rifles occur for a brief period just prior to the appearance of the military target rifles with 36″ barrels and Baddeley bands. They ceased to be produced about the time the Match Rifle was introduced in the spring of 1862. In point of sales, however, it appears that the supply of military target rifles continued to be sold concurrently with the semi-military rifle. All of the latter type thus far noted are highly finished arms, all having at least some scroll and floral engraving on the locks and mounts, and very fine checkering. Although obviously intended as presentation-grade weapons, only a very few of them carry inscriptions or plaques.

The barrel of the semi-military rifle, 36 inches long rather than the 33 inches of the earlier model, is fitted with a sporting pattern breech having three "Rigby" flats and a hook breech. The side of the snail has a platinum plug, and the left side of the patent breech is recessed deeply as on other

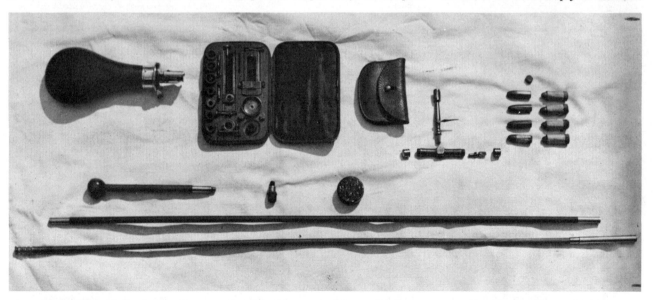

Fig. 7. Whitworth Match Rifle accessories. From left—Patent-top leather covered flask calibrated for two brands of powder; sight case holding wind gauge front, rack-and-pinion rear, and Vernier tang sights, with 8 interchangeable front sight discs, sight-adjusting key, two peep cups (one missing); wallet for small spare parts; combination tool, disassembled; Whitworth hexagonal bullets in various stages from naked to fully cased with wads attached; short starter; hexagonal bore mop; cap tin; loading-cleaning rod; double-ended rod with Whitworth hexagonal scraper on left and charger for placing powder in breech of barrel on right. *Courtesy H. Taylor.*

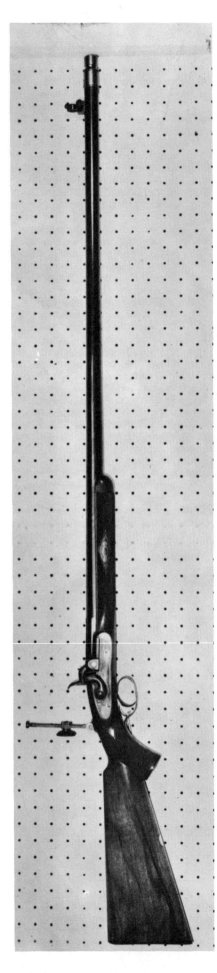

high-grade sporting arms of the period. The barrel is held to the full length stock with three barrel bands of the type patented by Major J.F.L. Baddeley, R.A., on May 10th, 1861. These bands have smooth outer contours with the screw heads recessed into the band to avoid catching on clothing. The military form of steel ramrod is retained, but of the usual Enfield pattern having both a slotted head and concentric rings, reduced in size to fit 45 caliber. The stock tip remains of the Enfield pattern, but here the military features of the rifle end; the remainder are of a sporting design.

The lock of the semi-military rifle is of the same pattern as the sporting rifle (fig. 5a), but the engraving is not quite as lavish on most examples known. The sliding safety bolt is forward of the hammer, and there is only one lock screw, having a plain circular cup supporting it on the left side of the stock. The tumbler is detented, and rifle rather than musket nipples are used. Those examples known bear the mark WITHWORTH RIFLE CO MANCHESTER on the lower edge of the plate.

The stock is of fine-grained walnut with a lighter color and better contrast than previous models, with a highly polished oil-varnish finish. The checkering is of fine quality and execution. The fore-end is longer between the lock and lover barrel band and displays a greater expanse of checkering. The furniture is heat-blued throughout and, excepting the stock tip, is of the type found on sporting rifles of the period. The trigger guard has a long checkered spur which acts as a pistol grip, the forward finial being in the form of a round pineapple. The buttplate has a short ornamental top tang, but the two screws securing it to the stock are both on the face of the plate. The capbox is omitted on this model, as on the majority of 36-inch barreled military target rifles.

The sights of this model are virtually identical with those of the match rifle which succeeded it, except that not all semi-military rifles are fitted for tang sights. The front sight, of the Whitworth patent variety, was furnished with at least 8 interchangeable discs of varying types. It was adjustable for windage, a thumb screw entering from the right side. One variation has the discs removable by the use of another thumb screw, while the other makes use of a square key fitting into a flush screw. The windage adjustment screw is also found in these two styles. The rear sight is of rack and pinion style. When a tang sight is present it is of the standard type found on the match rifle (fig. 6).

Judging from the serial numbers there were probably less than 100 of the semi-military rifles produced before Whitworth, in the spring of 1862, abandoned the military style with the introduction of his match rifle. The style of this rifle is what is generally known in the United States as a "Creedmoor" rifle, as it is identical in profile to the Rigby rifles used by the Irish teams at the International Matches held at Creedmoor, New York, beginning in 1874.

The match rifle has a 36-inch full round barrel, with the same patent breech design and lock as on the semi-military rifle (fig. 6). There is no provision for a ramrod, and the barrel is held to the half-stock by a single wedge or key surrounded by oval

Fig. 8. Probably made in the mid- or late 1860s, the 36" round barrel having the three barrel flats usually found on Rigby target rifles. The center or top flat is engraved METFORD'S PATENT 948. GEORGE GIBBS, 29, CORN STREET, BRISTOL. is engraved ahead of the Metford markings, on the top center of the barrel. The case-colored lockplate is marked GEORGE GIBBS also. The nipple boss carries a platinum plug. ● The Gibbs serial number, 9764, appears on the trigger guard rear tang. ● The Vernier tang sight is calibrated to 4 degrees, in increments of 10 minutes, with **Rad. 37.8** (for the distance between this sight and the front sight) hand engraved on a strip of platinum inlaid into one side of the staff. The front sight is adjustable for windage, takes various discs. ● The hard rubber grip cap is fluted in a sunburst design, the hard rubber buttplate grooved crosswise. The fore-end tip is of buffalo horn. ● The muzzle has a small pin at its top to take the bayonet-locking slot of the 1¾" long false muzzle. The false muzzle, not common on British match rifles, is rifled with 5 lands, these about ⅔ the width of the grooves, right hand twist of about one in 30". This is not Metford's celebrated segmental rifling, but rather his first patented system. It looks much like modern rifling—aside from land width. ● The rifle weighs an even 9 lbs. without false muzzle. John Amber's coll.

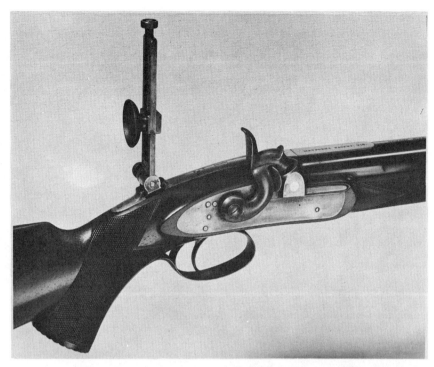

steel escutcheons on both sides of the stock. The stock tip is of black horn, as is the grip cap. There is no capbox. The stock is of full pistol grip type, with finely checkered wrist and fore-end. There is an initial plate set into the stock to the rear of the pistol grip. The wood used on match rifles is dark and straight-grained, as was typical on target arms to avoid possible warping.

The sights (fig. 7) consist of the Whitworth patent windgauge front sight, on many rifles the rack and pinion rear barrel sight, and the Whitworth Vernier tang sight. A rear barrel sight is not present on all rifles of this model.

Match rifles were furnished fully cased with loading and cleaning accessories and ammunition. Figs. 6 and 7 show an unusually complete outfit in superb condition. It should be noted that such articles as powder flasks and combination tools and, in fact, all accessories save the bullet moulds (which were not included in target outfits since extruded bullets were considered necessary to first-class accuracy at long range), were not made by Whitworths but were purchased from various contractors in such implements. The great majority are very similar to one another and it is obvious that these tools were purchased in quantity batches, and that the same contractors were patronized for succeeding purchases; it is not correct, however, to expect one set of implements to be identical to those in another similar cased set. Target Rifles are the only sets in which packets of patched hexagonal bullets should be considered standard rather than optional equipment.

Fig. 8 shows a fine match rifle made by one of Whitworth's chief rivals in the later period. The Gibbs-Metford rifle pictured is described in detail in the caption accompanying it.

At this point in the chronological examination of the various Whitworth models we turn from the best quality target rifle and revert to an issue military rifle: the *Pattern 1862 Whitworth Rifle*. It was for this rifle that an order of 1,000 stand was placed in May, 1862, but from existing examples it is clear that Whitworth did not manufacture anything close to the total numbers, he may not even have supplied all of the barrels. This rifle is, in fact, correctly termed an *Enfield-Whitworth*, as they were set up at the Royal Small Arms Factory at Enfield Lock. There are, however, a number of examples known with commercial markings, (fig. 9) which differ from the issue piece in minor aspects.

The *Pattern 1862 Whitworth* has a 36-inch iron barrel of the usual 451-caliber and rifling characteristics, the barrel being secured by three Baddeley-pattern barrel bands. As it was made at Enfield, all parts are interchangeable, and in addition all parts excepting the ramrod, stock tip and two forward barrel bands will interchange with the *Pattern 1860 Short Rifle* (so far as lock and furniture are concerned. The Pattern 1862 was intended to conform as closely as possible to the issue *Pattern 1853 Rifle Musket*, and the barrel takes the same bayonet. The front sight is of similar design, while the rear sight is basically similar but adapted for the use of either cylindrical or hexagonal bullets, the latter graduations extending for another 100 yards.

These rifles apparently met with considerable approval upon being is-sued to various regiments, and it was decided to equip a larger number of troops with the small bore rifle for extensive trials. The result was the *Pattern 1863 Whitworth Short Rifle*. It was decided to use steel rather than iron for the barrels of this model, and in order to keep the weight within limits the barrel length was reduced to 33 inches, thus making it officially a "Short Rifle" even though it was fitted with three barrel bands rather than the normal two. The sword bayonet fastens to the upper barrel band rather than to a standard on the barrel, as it was considered too difficult to weld a sword bar to a steel barrel. This same welding problem caused the snail to be made integral with the barrel, rather than separately as was the normal practice when using iron barrels.

The *Pattern 1863 Whitworth Short Rifle* (fig. 10) is again an "Enfield-Whitworth" even though Whitworth actually finished up 100 of these rifles at Manchester. The steel barrels were obtained from four different contractors, including Whitworth, who supplied 1,497 barrels which bore normal Whitworth serial numbers beneath the barrel as well as the date of setting up. The rear sight differed from that of the *Pattern 1862 Withworth* in having the elevators inside the sight leaf rather than outside; the graduations for conical and hexagonal bullets were unchanged. It will be remembered that, in 1859, Whitworth had quoted a figure of £10 per rifle; the Enfield cost was just over £2.10.0—or $48 as opposed to $12 in 1860 U.S. dollars. Over 8,200 of this model were produced, of which something over 1,700 appear to have been issued for trials initially. Presumably there were

Fig. 9. Pattern 1862 Whitworth military rifle, a prototype made at Manchester with commercial markings and non-standard trigger guard. The issue model, of which 1,000 were made at Enfield, has normal Enfield trigger guard and lock markings. Standard Enfield pattern ramrod. 36" barrel with three Baddeley barrel bands. *Tower of London collection, British Crown copyright.*

Fig. 10. Pattern 1863 Short Rifle and sword bayonet. 33" barrel, to Baddeley barrel bands and special pin-fastened upper band with bayonet lug on right side. Lock is marked ENFIELD, the stock also. Note special "H" and "C" rear sight, and over-all close resemblance to standard Enfield rifle. *Courtesy E.J. Burton.*

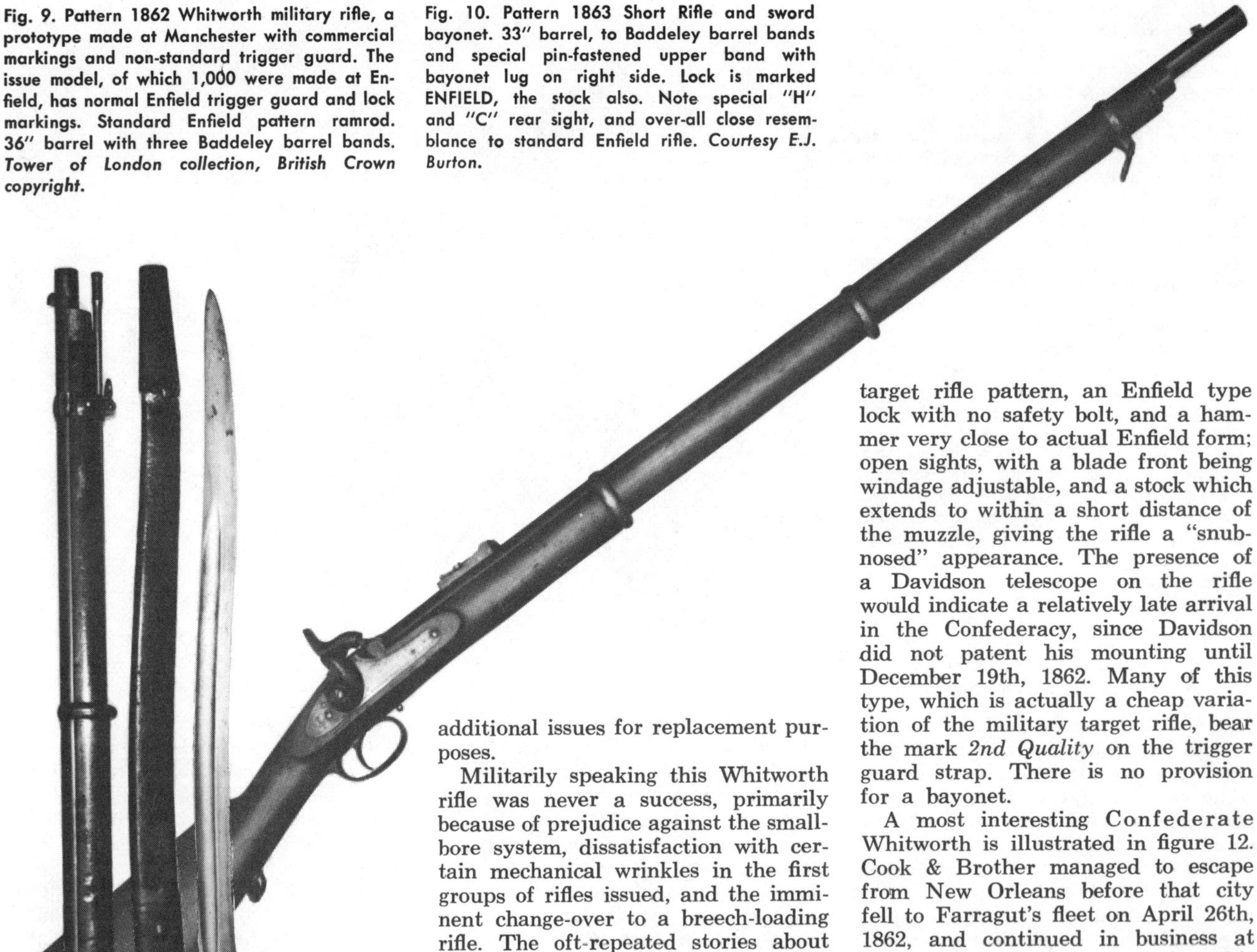

additional issues for replacement purposes.

Militarily speaking this Whitworth rifle was never a success, primarily because of prejudice against the small-bore system, dissatisfaction with certain mechanical wrinkles in the first groups of rifles issued, and the imminent change-over to a breech-loading rifle. The oft-repeated stories about fouling problems and loading difficulties are not borne out by the official reports on the trials of these rifles. Aside from obviously prejudiced exceptions the rifles were highly praised on these points from such unlikely areas as India and South Africa. It does not appear that hexagonal ammunition was ever issued in quantity with the military rifles, and in general the troops got on well with them. However, their marksmanship does not appear to have markedly improved over that obtaining with the 577 Enfields, which is rather surprising.

The Confederate Whitworth

The actual *extent* to which Whitworth rifles were used by Confederate troops during the Civil War is still conjectural, but examination of those rifles known to have been used or at least owned by Confederate personnel, and consideration of their serial numbers, has led to the conclusion that (with the possible exception of some individual pieces brought through the blockade by private persons), the Whitworth rifles used by Confederate troops were all of one basic type as shown in fig. 11. The only significant variation is the absence of checkering on one or two examples. Typical features of the type are a 33-inch barrel, two Enfield pattern barrel bands, iron mounts of the military

target rifle pattern, an Enfield type lock with no safety bolt, and a hammer very close to actual Enfield form; open sights, with a blade front being windage adjustable, and a stock which extends to within a short distance of the muzzle, giving the rifle a "snub-nosed" appearance. The presence of a Davidson telescope on the rifle would indicate a relatively late arrival in the Confederacy, since Davidson did not patent his mounting until December 19th, 1862. Many of this type, which is actually a cheap variation of the military target rifle, bear the mark *2nd Quality* on the trigger guard strap. There is no provision for a bayonet.

A most interesting Confederate Whitworth is illustrated in figure 12. Cook & Brother managed to escape from New Orleans before that city fell to Farragut's fleet on April 26th, 1862, and continued in business at Athens, Georgia. The fact that this rifle bears the New Orleans address would indicate that it was produced and purchased prior to the fall of New Orleans to Federal forces; this, coupled with the high serial number for the Confederate type (C575) indicates that most of the Whitworth rifles used by the Confederates were manufactured prior to the spring of 1862—which coincides neatly with already established serial ranges and dates. The rifle itself is typical of the type, but it lacks the checkering found on the majority of this pattern.

Later Production

Taken as a whole, civilian Whitworth rifle production tapered off sharply after 1862; while a steady trickle of match rifles and sporting rifles appears to have been turned out during the period 1862-1865, the major part of Whitworth's efforts during this period seems to have been devoted to the production of heavy ordnance, government trials of his rifling system in both ordnance and small arms, and his machine-tool business. Small arms production as such seems to have been secondary to those other considerations. It is, however, during this later period that some of the most interesting of Whitworth's rifles, including the 30-caliber sporting rifle, 568-caliber semi-military rifle, and double-barreled sporting rifle were made, all on a very limited basis which might reasonably be called—with the possible exception of the double barreled rifles —experimental production.

The single barreled sporting rifles produced in this later period generally have full pistol grip stocks, as opposed to the earlier rifles with spur trigger guards, and some of the later rifles lack capboxes.

The double-barreled sporting rifles generally have barrels varying from 24 inches to 28 inches, the majority being about 26 inches long. The barrel group is one piece of steel, into which both bores have been drilled, a feature which Whitworth patented in June, 1857. The half-length stocks have a full pistol grip, two pipes for the ramrod, no capbox, and a black horn cap on the pistol grip. The low bead express front sights have windage adjustment, while the rear sights use a series of flip-up leaves for 100 to 500 yards. The locks have sliding safety bolts forward of the hammers.

ing period proceeded on a regular chronological basis. Having commenced with the number 1, the initial series continued through to 1,000, and then re-commenced with a letter prefix and proceeded through a series of these prefixes as follows:

1—1000 : first production, 1857 through mid-1860.

B1—B999 : mid-1860 through late 1861.

C1—C999 : late 1861 through mid-1862. If gaps exist it will be in this series.

D1—D999 : spring 1862 to early 1863.

E1—E999 : early 1863 into mid-1864, primarily Pattern 1863 Military Rifles.

F1—F700 : mid-1864 through 1865; after F700 some breechloaders appear in regular numerical order. BSA-marked rifles also occur in this series.

Although there are still some unanswered questions regarding the connections between the Whitworth firm

but as most of these include a date on the lockplate, the problem is greatly simplified. There are some individual instances, however, where the date is misleadingly late for the rest of the rifle. Lockplates on these early rifles generally bear the mark WHITWORTH PATENT, plus the serial number and Birmingham proof marks. The lockplate is marked, forward of the hammer and above the safety bolt, WITHWORTH 1860 in two lines, or simply WHITWORTH. To the rear of the hammer appears the Whitworth crest (a crowned wheatsheaf), a W sometimes appearing beneath the wheatsheaf. The great majority of locks used on Whitworth rifles, even some of the plain military rifles, were made by Joseph Brazier of Wolverhampton; this is shown in some form generally on the inside of the lockplate. This may be his initials—*JB* or *IB*—to the most elaborate form noted so far: *JOSEPH BRAZIER ASHES,* the latter word being the name of Brazier's works.

Fig. 11. A Confederate Whitworth with 33" barrel. Except for the Davidson telescope, in typical side mount, the rifle seems a standard Confederate Whitworth in all features. Some are without checkering. Note snub-nosed appearance, two Enfield barrel bands, and early-pattern adjustable open sights. Enfield-pattern lock. *Courtesy Tennessee State Museum.*

Whitworth Production and Serial Numbers

If it is accepted that there are no significant gaps in the indicated serial number ranges of Whitworth rifles, the total number produced with commercial markings would be about 5,000 of all styles, including the early rifles and BSA-marked rifles with Whitworth-serialed barrels, but excluding the greater part of 1,000 *Pattern 1862 Military Rifles* and all but 1,600 of the 8,200 *Pattern 1863 Short Rifles;* both of these were assembled at Enfield and bear Enfield marks. If these last are included, a grand total of approximately 13,400 Whitworth muzzle loading rifles were produced from all sources. Those rifles produced under license from Whitworth by such makers as Bissell, Beasley Brothers, and McCririck—which did purport to be honest imitations of Whitworth's rifling—are not included, and would increase the total somewhat.

From a study of existing rifles and fragmentary records, it appears that the serial numbering of Whitworth rifles from their first production in 1857 through the end of the muzzle-loading era and into the breech-load-

and the Birmingham Small Arms Company, it is clear that Whitworth offered to supply the gun trade with their barrels, in either finished or semi-finished state, the latter being rifled only. In 1866 B.S.A. had used Whitworth barrels on their rifles for the N.R.A. and other standard Short Rifle patterns are known with B.S.A. markings and Whitworth serial-numbered barrels; in addition several match rifles of Whitworth profile and rifling have been reported with B.S.A. markings. It is obvious that B.S.A. purchased a batch of barrels from Whitworth in various states of completion and applied them to a small group of rifles of the several popular styles, in the 1865-66 period.

Whitworth Markings

With the conspicuous exception of those experimental rifles made throughout the entire production period of Whitworth muzzle-loading rifles, a study of the markings on the rifles relates directly to the serial numbers, and makes the assignment of a production date relatively easy. The early Whitworth rifles, made prior to 1860, bear a variety of non-standard marks,

At the very end of the production period for military target rifles (during which time the "Second Quality" rifles of this type were being made), the lock markings change to WHITWORTH RIFLE Co. MANCHESTER, with the Whitworth crest behind the hammer. This mark continues in use, along with the WHITWORTH PATENT marking on the breech of the barrel, through the period of the semi-military rifle and the early production of the match rifle.

Shortly before the conclusion of the C-prefix serial number range, the lock marks change to MANCHESTER ORDNANCE & RIFLE Co.; and this marking continues through the D- and E- or F-prefix serial ranges, being found almost entirely on Pattern 1862 and 1863 military rifles, and on match rifles. The WHITWORTH PATENT mark on the breech of the barrel is retained, as is the Whitworth crest to the rear of the hammer, with and without the W beneath.

The Pattern 1862 Rifle and the Pattern 1863 Short Rifles made at Enfield bear standard Enfield markings for the period; the date is

The long Vernier-system folding tang sight is engraved on the rear of the staff, T. MURCOTT GUNMAKER (on one side), with 68 HAYMARKET LONDON N° 509 on the other.

The picture of the muzzle area shows the deep chamfering of the hexagonal rifling and the form of the slotted steel ramrod.

The 33" barrel is full round, shows double Birmingham proof marks, the serial number 937, and is marked WHITWORTH PATENT at the top rear.

The walnut stock shows good figure, and is coarsely checkered at wrist and ahead of the lockplate. Weight of the Whitworth rifle shown is 9½ pounds. John Amber's collection.

This 451 caliber Whitworth rifle was probably made in mid-1860 in view of the style of markings on the lockplate—WHITWORTH RIFLE C° MANCHESTER—and the serial number 937, without letter prefix, on the barrel. The rear barrel sight is of the Vernier type (double pinions and pinion bar are missing); the front sight dove-tail base once held a globe or hooded sight container with windage control knob, these sights were added later, perhaps, by Whitworth, using the style patented by Whitworth and Hulse in late 1861. The right side of the rear barrel sight base is marked WHITWORTH/RIFLE Co. PATENT, while the top of the folding leaf is graduated on the right side 1 through 12 for 100 to 1200 yards; the left side is marked 10, 20, 30 and 40 for minutes of angle.

200

stamped over ENFIELD forward of the hammer, and a crowned *VR* on the tail of the lockplate. The barrel breeches of both military models bear the mark WHITWORTH PATENT. Where the barrels were supplied by the Whitworth firm a normal D-, E- or F- prefix serial number will appear on the underside of the barrel, generally accompanied by a figure such as 6/63, indicating that the rifle was set up in June, 1863.

In the later production period there was considerable mixing of markings, particularly on sights and sight parts. It is not uncommon that a rifle bearing MANCHESTER ORDNANCE & RIFLE CO. markings on the lock will have WHITWORTH RIFLE Co. on the sight base of the rear barrel sight and the stem of the Vernier tang sight. Similarly, a few rifles bearing THE WHITWORTH COMPANY LIMITED on the lockplate will have MANCHESTER ORDNANCE & RIFLE CO. on the abovementioned sight parts.

In the final production period of Whitworth muzzle-loading rifles, the lock and barrel markings change almost entirely. The Whitworth crest is the only hold-over from previous patterns. The lock markings in the very high E-prefix serial range and throughout the F-prefix range read THE WHITWORTH COMPANY LIMITED, while the markings on the barrel are changed to WHITWORTH MANCHESTER in a circle or oval form. Some of the very last Whitworth muzzleloaders have J. WHITWORTH & Co. Manchester on the lockplate. As this was the firm name of Whitworth's machine tool business, this would seem to indicate nearly the end of Whitworth's production of firearms. An early breech-loading double rifle by Whitworth is marked in a similar manner, with the trade label of the case reading "JOSEPH WHITWORTH & COMPANY Patentees and Manufacturers of WHITWORTH RIFLED ORDNANCE, SMALL ARMS & SPORTING GUNS. General Machine and Tool Manufacturers. Works, Chorlton Street, Manchester, London Office, 28, Pall Mall, S.W." This rifle follows closely upon the serial number of the last muzzleloaders, and there is no evidence at present known to prove that production of breechloaders was long continued.

Whitworth's essay into the field of small arms seems never to have gone beyond the scientific and theoretical stage in his own mind. Commercially speaking very little was done by Whitworth to advance the sales of his rifles. Contemporary literature on the topic is noticeable by its scarcity, advertising nil. The success of this rifling system and the presentation of so many of his earlier rifles as prizes went far towards advertising, but quite clearly the rifles themselves were

only a vehicle for his system, and a bid for government work. It is curious that while Whitworth's reputation for the introduction of standardization in mechanical and industrial processes is so great, his rifles were no better in construction than any other eminent gunmaker of the time: the parts will not interchange in any respect. Some sights will, by pure luck, fit more than one rifle, but lock parts and furniture all exhibit minor variations to a degree precluding interchangeability. Those military rifles made at Enfield upon Whitworth's system will, of course, interchange to conform to government standard, as will other Enfield rifles

Fig. 12. Confederate-marked Whitworth, possibly unique. Made for Cook & Brother before they evacuated New Orleans in April, 1862. The crowned wheatsheaf on the lockplate's tail is a Whitworth trademark. *Courtesy Weller & Dufty Ltd.*

made after 1858. All major parts appear to have been obtained through the gun trade, Whitworth manufacturing the barrels only (even this point remains controversial), and the rifles were set up at one point following the normal procedures of the time. Although Whitworth took out several patents dealing with small arms and their appurtenances between 1854 and 1865, very few of the items covered appear to have been produced or used. Even implements peculiar to Whitworth rifles (such as the patent combination tool and hexagonal wad punches appear to have been made in lots by more than one contractor, and there are consequently very few accessories which can positively be labelled as "Whitworth tools," as will be noted in the illustrations.

The place of the Whitworth rifle in the history of rifled longarms and ballistic history is of paramount importance. Sir Joseph Whitworth (he was made a baronet in 1869), through analytical study which had never before been applied to the science of firearms design, demonstrated what could be done with elongated projectiles and precision machining; so well did he succeed in his efforts that he spurred the entire British gun trade into a period of experimental production the likes of which had not been previously witnessed. As a result of the standards for accuracy set by Whitworth's rifles, other gunmakers tried system after system—there were at least two dozen, all primarily variations of the basic Whitworth system of 45-caliber barrels with a twist of one turn in 20 inches and polygonal rifling—to equal or excel the Whitworth. This led to the ultimate development of such systems as those of William Metford and Alexander Henry, which led the world not only in civilian shooting but in military marksmanship and long range accuracy well into the 20th century. ●

The writer wishes to express his sincere gratitude to Dr. C. H. Roads for permission to use certain facts and figures concerning the experimental and military Whitworth rifles, contained in his superb volume, *The British Soldier's Firearm, 1850-1864*, and to those gentlemen who kindly furnished photographs of rifles in their collections.

Astra 900, cal. 7.63mm Mauser, No. 5155. One of the early models, this has a small-ring hammer and only one line of inscription on the left side. (Later versions of the 900, and all 901, 902, 903, and 903E models, have large ring hammers and a second line of inscription, thus: Patented July 12, 1928.)

The 901 is the same as the 900 except that it has a lever on the right side which may be set for either semi-automatic or full-automatic firing.

ASTRA AUTOMATICS —SERIES 900

IN THE DECADE following World War I numerous copies of the German 7.63mm Mauser pistol began appearing on the European markets. The majority of these copies came from Spain; they resembled the Mauser in appearance, but differed in mechanical design.

Although other copies did precede it, the Astra 900, which appeared near the end of 1928, is probably the best known of the Mauser imitations. Externally it resembles the Mauser, but a closer examination reveals the differences. The Astra has a sliding plate on the left side of the action body which, when removed, exposes the internal mechanism for removal. In the Mauser design the sides of the action body are solid and the internal mechanism is removed from the rear of the action as a unit. The Astra barrel and extension are two separate pieces, instead of one piece as in the Mauser design. The Mauser barrel extension is removed from the action body by sliding it rearward along milled guides. The Astra guides are cut away at intervals to allow the barrel extension to be lifted off the action body, instead of being slid off. The type of breech locking — prop-up — is the same for both designs, but the methods of achieving it are quite different. The Astra design necessitates a separate barrel return spring not found in the Mauser automatic pistols.

The Mauser design is a beautiful example of the use of interlocking parts. To lower manufacturing costs the Astra design does away with these interlocking parts, pinning the various members of the action and lock to the frame of the action body and barrel extension. This type of construction is quite strong, and allows manufacture without the need of so many expensive machine tools and jigs.

Shortly after the introduction of the 900 model, Unceta & Company, manufacturers of the Astra pistols, brought out the 901 and 902 models. These are simply full-automatic versions of the 900, with the 902 having a longer barrel and a larger magazine capacity. The later Mauser design of this type has a selector lever, or switch, on the left side of the action body, while the Astra selector lever is on the right side of the action. When the lever is pushed into its upward position a small cam holds the trigger bar out of engagement with the sear, allowing full-automatic fire, as long as the trigger is not released or until the magazine is empty. This mechanism differs in design from that of the Mauser, but the manner of functioning is the same. Although the 900 and the 902 are the best known of the Astra models, there are four other models in the 900 series. Of this total of

six, only one model is marked with the model designation — the Modelo F — standard sidearm of the Spanish Civil Guard.

With the exception of the 900, all models are capable of full-automatic fire, a feature not entirely practical on a weapon of this type. The Astra actually preceded the Mauser in this regard, since both the Astra 901 (10-shot) and the 902 (20-shot) appeared on the market before the Mauser M1932 *Schnellfeuer* (rapid fire) Pistol. The later Astra 903, 903E, and Modelo F, with detachable magazines, came after the Mauser M1932.

All models of the Astra may be loaded from the top using 10-round stripper clips. The models 903, 903E, and Modelo F may also be loaded by inserting the already charged detachable magazines.

The safety on the Astra 900 series is not the Mauser universal safety-lock type, which allows the hammer to be released when on safe. When the safety lever on the Astra is upward a small S appears, indicating that both the hammer and bolt are fixed in position, and that the weapon is thus safe. When the lever is turned downward the hammer and bolt are released and a small F appears, indicating the arm is ready for firing.

The Astra also differs from the Mauser in the graduation of the tangent rear sight.

Astra 902, cal. 7.63mm Mauser, made with non-detachable 20-round magazine. It is actually the same as the 901 except for having a longer barrel and the additional 10-round magazine dove-tailed onto the regular magazine housing. With the lever, on the right side, turned to "20," as shown, the weapon delivers full-automatic fire; rotated to the "1" position the weapon fires semi-automatically.

The Astra 903, cal./7.63mm Mauser with 20-round detachable magazine in position and 10-round magazine alongside, as seen on the cover of a factory brochure. This model has a selector lever also, but has a shorter barrel than the 902. The third line of inscription illustrated here on the factory drawing has never, as far as the author knows, appeared on an actual weapon, other than the Modelo F.

The 903E is the same as the 903, except for having a slightly different magazine catch, loading platform, and may be semi-automatic only.

The 903 is standardized in cal. 7.63mm Mauser, although a factory catalog states that it would be furnished, on request, in 9mm Parabellum (Luger), 38 Colt (Super) and 9mm Bergmann. The other models were available in 7.63mm Mauser only, except for the Modelo F.

ASTRA 903 AUTOMATIC PISTOL

CAL. 7.63 m/m (.300) WITH INTERCHANGEABLE 10 AND 20 ROUND MAGAZINE AND DETACHABLE STOCK. — 160 m/m BARREL (6,3")

by LARRY S. STERETT

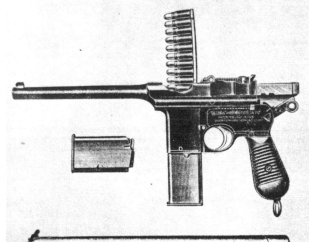

The pistol ready for loading from top per clip, with the 20 round magazine placed and the 10 round magazine separated.

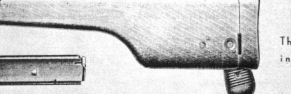

The pistol resting in holster-stock

Mauser pistol sights vary from a top graduation of 500 meters up to 1000 meters, depending on caliber and model. One model even has a fixed rear sight. All models of the Astra, regardless of caliber, are graduated to 1000 meters (1094 yds.).

The disassembly of the Astra models differs radically from that of the Mauser. The following procedure should be used:

1. Cock the hammer and place the lower edge of the safety lever in line with the groove on the sliding cover. Placing the barrel against something solid, push it backwards, or grip the barrel in the left hand and push it rearward. Using the right forefinger, push the rear bolt, located above the caliber mark, through from the right side.

2. The cover may now be slid backward with a slight pressure of the left thumb, exposing the interior mechanism for inspection.

3. Place the safety lever in firing position, push the barrel backwards, and push out the round headed bolt in the center of the frame, from right to left. Be careful when removing this bolt as the pressure of the stop spring will now cause the frame and barrel to separate. Remove the safety lever.

To assemble, reverse the above operations.

EXCELLENT FIREARM FOR ALL MILITARY AND POLICE SERVICE AND FOR PROTECTION OF PUBLIC INSTITUTIONS, BANKS, ETC., AND ALSO FOR BIG GAME HUNTING

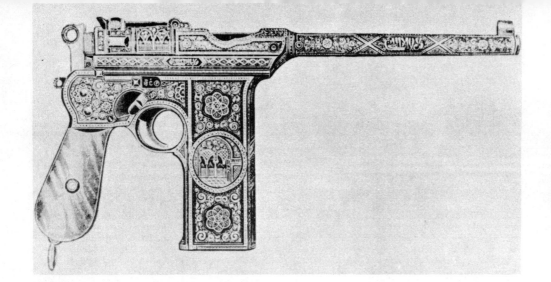

Deluxe Astra 902, covered with gold inlaying and engraving in the "Toledo" style, as seen in a factory illustration.

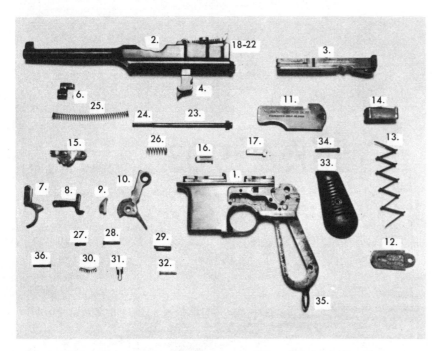

Not shown in the above view are the following parts, which are still in position: the bolt lock axle and pin holding the bolt lock in the receiver; the extractor on top of the bolt; the magazine plunger and spring, which is used to hold the magazine floorplate in place, and the main spring and hammer spring bolt located in the rear part of the grip.

Component parts of the Model 900 Astra pistol
1. Frame
2. Barrel and extension (receiver)
3. Bolt
4. Bolt lock
6. Bolt spring top
7. Trigger
8. Sear
9. Hammer locking lever
10. Hammer
11. Sliding cover
12. Magazine floorplate
13. Magazine spring
14. Magazine follower
15. Safety
16. Round-head bolt
17. Square-head bolt
18. Sight
19. Sight slide
20. Sight spring
21. Sight catch
22. Sight catch spring
23. Firing pin (striker)
24. Striker spring
25. Bolt spring
26. Barrel stop spring
27. Sear axle
28. Hammer release bolt
29. Hammer axle
30. Trigger spring
31. Hammer locking lever spring
32. Hammer stop
33. Grip stock
34. Grip stock screw
35. Hold ring
36. Trigger axle

Astra Modelo F with a 10-round magazine in place. Chambered for the 9mm Long (38 Bergmann), it is the standard sidearm of the Spanish Civil Guard. It has a selector lever for single and full-automatic fire and a special retarder mechanism. The lever is located directly above the grip on the right side (note that the pin above the grip does not appear on the other models) instead of above and forward of the grip as on the 901, 902, 903, and 903E models. The lever positions are marked differently also, with an "A" for *Ametrallador* (full-automatic or machine fire), and a "T" for *Tiro a Tiro* (single shot or semi-automatic fire), instead of the "1" and "20" found on the other models having selector levers.

The Modelo F not only has a different inscription on the left side, but is the only one of the 900 series having the actual model marked on it. Anyone unfamiliar with Astras would have to consult a catalog to determine what model he might have.

Pista Ametra ASTRA modo F de 9mm (38)
Unceta y Compañía GUERNICA (España)

Translated this means "Machine Pistol ASTRA Model F, Unceta & Co., Guernica, Spain."

The grip stocks on the Modelo F may vary slightly from those of the other models, and the magazine catch does not show on the left side, as it does on the 903.

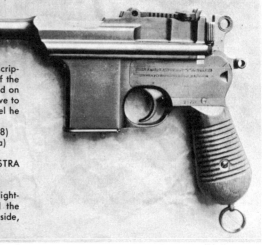

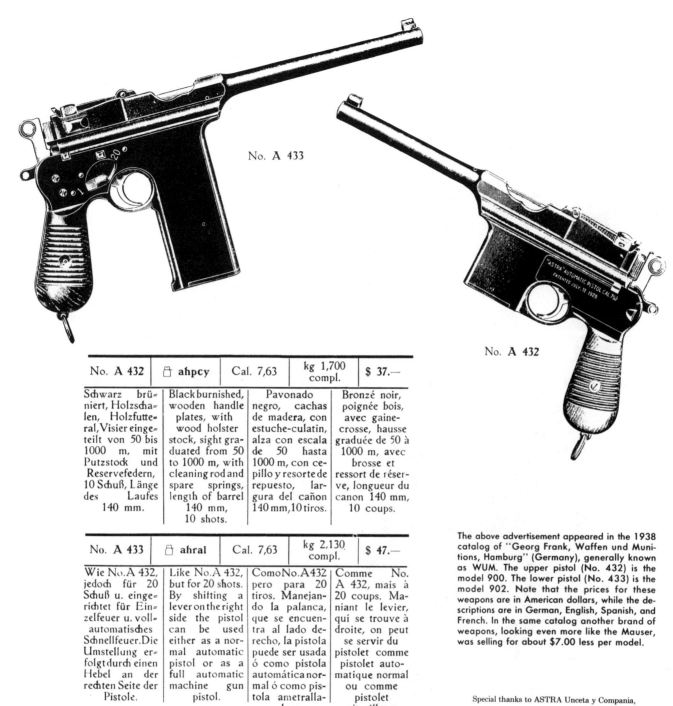

No. A 433

No. A 432

No. A 432	⊟ ahpcy	Cal. 7,63	kg 1,700 compl.	$ 37.—
Schwarz brü=niert, Holzscha=len, Holzfutte=ral,Visier einge=teilt von 50 bis 1000 m, mit Putzstock und Reservefedern, 10 Schuß, Länge des Laufes 140 mm.	Black burnished, wooden handle plates, with wood holster stock, sight gra=duated from 50 to 1000 m, with cleaning rod and spare springs, length of barrel 140 mm, 10 shots.	Pavonado negro, cachas de madera, con estuche-culatin, alza con escala de 50 hasta 1000 m, con ce=pillo y resorte de repuesto, lar=gura del cañon 140 mm, 10 tiros.	Bronzé noir, poignée bois, avec gaine-crosse, hausse graduée de 50 à 1000 m, avec brosse et ressort de réser=ve, longueur du canon 140 mm, 10 coups.

No. A 433	⊟ ahral	Cal. 7,63	kg 2,130 compl.	$ 47.—
Wie No. A 432, jedoch für 20 Schuß u. einge=richtet für Ein=zelfeuer u. voll=automatisches Schnellfeuer.Die Umstellung er=folgt durch einen Hebel an der rechten Seite der Pistole.	Like No. A 432, but for 20 shots. By shifting a lever on the right side the pistol can be used either as a nor=mal automatic pistol or as a full automatic machine gun pistol.	Como No. A 432 pero para 20 tiros. Manejan=do la palanca, que se encuen=tra al lado de=recho, la pistola puede ser usada ó como pistola automática nor=mal ó como pis=tola ametralla=dora.	Comme No. A 432, mais à 20 coups. Ma=niant le levier, qui se trouve à droite, on peut se servir du pistolet comme pistolet auto=matique normal ou comme pistolet mitrailleuse.

The above advertisement appeared in the 1938 catalog of "Georg Frank, Waffen und Muni-tions, Hamburg" (Germany), generally known as WUM. The upper pistol (No. 432) is the model 900. The lower pistol (No. 433) is the model 902. Note that the prices for these weapons are in American dollars, while the de-scriptions are in German, English, Spanish, and French. In the same catalog another brand of weapons, looking even more like the Mauser, was selling for about $7.00 less per model.

Special thanks to ASTRA Unceta y Compania, S.A., for their kind assistance.

Astra Automatic Pistol Data

	900	902	903	Mod. F
Caliber	7.63mm	7.63mm	7.63mm	9mm Long
Length with holster	25.5"	28.75"	27.00"	27.9"
Length w/o holster	11.5"	13.00"	12.1"	12.4"
Thickness	1.25"	1.25"	1.25"	1.25"
Height	6.00"	6.00"	5.9"	5.9"
Weight, empty magazine	2.75 lb.	3.38 lb.	2.81 lb.	2.98 lb.
Weight, 10-rd magazine			3.38 oz.	3.66 oz.
Weight, 20-rd magazine			5.17 oz.	5.84 oz.
Barrel length	5.5"	7.25"	6.3"	6.3"
Weight, holster stock	15.5 oz.	1.33 lb.	1.38 lb.	1.22 lb.
Magazine capacity	10	20	10 or 20	10 or 20
Magazine type	fixed	fixed	detach.	detach.
Cyclic rate		300/min.		260/min.

handloading

by Frank C. Barnes

THE HANDLOADING of military cartridges is a firmly established phase of the loading game. It is a matter of interest to a substantial number of shooters. Obsolete, surplus military rifles of varying caliber and diverse origin have been sold in copious quantities since the end of World War II. There was a modest sell-off following World War I, but this was of limited scope because the major powers retained their pre-war models and calibers. World War II saw a shift to semi-auto and full automatic weapons accompanied by changes in caliber or cartridge type. Consequently, there has been a virtual avalanche of phased-out military hardware on the world markets. Some of this went to arm "underdeveloped" countries, and much has appeared in the U. S.

Up to the end of World War II, only four military cartridges were handloaded to any extent here. These were the 45-70, 30-40 Krag, 30-06 and the 303 British. Presently there are about 20 smokeless and four or five black powder military cartridges enjoying various degrees of popularity.

Although these surplus weapons are obsolete from the military point of view, there is nothing to prevent their adaptation to sporting purposes. Handloading is, in fact, an essential element of this use conversion, even if for no reason other than to provide sporting type bullets. Military ammunition, with its full jacketed bullets, is not suitable for anything except target

The 30 calibers, l to r: 7.5mm Swiss, 7.5mm French MAS, 30 U.S. Carbine, 30-06, 30-40 Krag, 7.62mm NATO, 7.62mm Russian.

the military calibers

A detailed and comprehensive rundown on the popular military cartridges, and how to load for them. Ballistics, vital dimensions and load tables are supplied, plus data on case forming or procurement.

practice or varmint shooting. Even here, it must be used with caution because of the dangers of ricochets.

The performance of most military cartridges is subject to improvement through handloading with sporting components. However, in a few instances this is limited by designed working pressures. In other words, the cartridge can only be improved safely by firing it in a stronger action than the one for which it was designed.

European military and sporting ammunition is usually loaded with the Berdan type primer. This has an integral anvil, in the bottom of the primer pocket, and is more trouble to decap and reprime than the Boxer type used by U.S. manufacturers. This latter type is completely self-contained, with the anvil as part of the primer. However, in recent years many of the British and European ammunition companies have turned out Boxer-primed cases for the American market. Norma of Sweden exports Boxer ammunition and cases in popular metric sporting and military calibers. These are much easier to work with if available.

The military cartridge of a nation is usually also a popular sporting round, at least in the country of origin. Therefore, many military rounds have been highly developed for sporting purposes. The 6.5 x 55 Norwegian, 303 British, 8mm Mauser and our own 30-06 are prime examples of this. Military cartridges are developed to fill

certain use requirements and represent the end result of considerable engineering and design effort. All make potentially good hunting rounds, although some are more flexible than others. With the exception of the 30 U.S. Carbine, any of the military calibers discussed are adequate for deer-sized animals, but not all are a good choice for larger game.

Although the American Civil War was fought mostly with muzzle-loading arms, by the time it ended the breech-loader was firmly established. The decade between 1865 and 1875 was one of experimentation and change in the military arms field as the major powers moved towards the breech-loader as their military weapon. The original caliber was usually a reflection of the muzzle-loading bore in use at the time. Most countries first adapted a conversion mechanism so they wouldn't have to junk all the muzzleloaders in stock.

Consequently, military calibers were initially rather large, ranging from 50 to 60. It developed that, with the self-contained cartridge, smaller calibers were more efficient and effective for military use. As the result, there was a gradual reduction of caliber, first to 43 or 45, and later even smaller.

By 1886 the French carried this so far they adopted an 8mm cartridge with a bullet diameter of .323″. This, the 8mm Lebel, was the first smallbore smokeless powder military cartridge and was quite revolutionary for

the time. Unfortunately, it appears to have exhausted French inventive genius as they haven't come up with anything new or startling in the small arms field since. The other powers followed suit and within a few years all had designed and adopted new military cartridges ranging from 6.5mm (.263″ to .265″) up to 8mm. The British introduced their 303 and the U.S. settled on the 30 caliber.

Almost all the surplus military weapons being sold today are based on designs and cartridges that actually date back to the period between the late 1800s and World War I. The few exceptions are semi-auto weapons developed just prior to or after World War II.

The 6.5s

As a group, the various 6.5mm military rifles and cartridges are among the most useful for sporting purposes, or at least from the view point of North American hunting. With the heavier bullets of around 140 to 150 grains, they are all excellent antelope, deer and black bear cartridges. In the hands of an experienced hunter they will also do quite well on larger animals. With proper bullets, any of these 6.5s is far more effective than the 30-30.

With light bullets of 80 to 100 grains the 6.5s make very good long range varmint rifles. Recoil is moderate and most shooters do better with the 6.5s

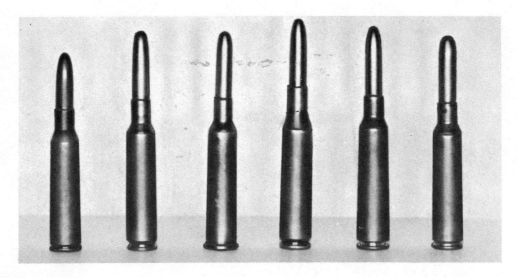

The 6.5s, l to r: 6.5mm Jap., 6.5x54 Mann.-Sch., 6.5x53 Mann., 6.5x58 Vergueiro, 6.5x55 Mauser, 6.5x55 Carcano.

than with larger calibers. Lyman offers a number of moulds for 6.5 cast bullets. The bore diameter of 6.5mm military rifles is subject to rather wide variation and it is advisable to measure the bore before ordering sizing dies. Proper cast bullet diameter may vary from .263″ to .268″.

6.5 X 50 Japanese

This cartridge is also found listed as the 6.5 Arisaka or 6.5 Muratta. The case is semi-rimmed and difficult to duplicate from other brass. This is the cartridge for the Japanese Model 38 (1905) bolt action rifle. The cartridge was actually developed in 1897.

Although practically unknown until World War II, many thousands of 6.5 Japanese rifles are now in use, brought back by returning service men or sold through surplus dealers. Ammunition was once a problem. However, Boxer-primed sporting ammunition and empty cases are made by Norma and available through most dealers. Extreme caution should be used in working up maximum loads for these rifles because of the considerable variation in bore diameter.

6.5 X 52 Italian

Italian military cartridge adopted in 1891 for their bolt action rifle which combines a Mannlicher receiver and magazine with a solid, Mauser type bolt. It is usually listed as the 6.5 Mannlicher-Carcano or occasionally the 6.5 Paravicino-Carcano. This is the cartridge that figured prominently in the assassination of President Kennedy.

Although similar to the 6.5 Mannlicher-Schoenauer, the two are not interchangeable. However, 6.5 Carcano cases can be made from 6.5 X 54 Mannlicher brass. Cases should first be trimmed to 2.05″, then reformed in full-length 6.5 Carcano dies. Design working pressure of the 1891 Italian

Mannlicher-Carcano rifle is approximately 38,000 psi. Maximum loads should be kept at or under this level. Norma Boxer-primed cases and sporting ammunition with a 156-gr. soft point bullet are available.

6.5 X 54 Mannlicher-Schoenauer

Cartridge for the Model 1903 Greek-Mannlicher bolt action rifle, but actually developed about 1900. It is also a popular European sporting round and was loaded in the U.S. up to 1940-42. Sporting ammunition is currently loaded by British, European and Canadian companies. Boxer-primed cases and ammunition are made by Norma, RWS and Canadian Industries (Dominion).

6.5mm Mannlicher cases can be formed from 30-06 brass, although this is a lot of trouble. It involves swaging the head, turning down the rim, reaming the neck, full length sizing, trimming to proper length, etc. It is easier and cheaper to buy commercial cases.

The 6.5 Mannlicher is fairly sensitive to slight variations in powder charge, both from the standpoint of accuracy and pressure. A change of one, or even one-half, grain can make a difference, and maximum charges should be approached with caution. Excess headspace has been reported in many military rifles of this caliber and it is a good idea to have a gunsmith check this.

6.5 X 53R Roumanian and Dutch

In a sense this is a rimmed version of the 6.5 Mannlicher since the only difference is in the rim. However, it predates the rimless 6.5 Mannlicher by several years. This cartridge was introduced for the Model 1892 Roumanian-Mannlicher rifle and adopted by the Dutch in a similar rifle in 1895. Performance, loading data, etc., is practically identical to the 6.5 Mannlicher.

Sporting ammunition of this caliber has been loaded in Britain and Europe. However, Eley-Kynoch appears to be the only one which lists it at the present time. It is possible to make 6.5 X 53 Rimmed cases from 30-40 Krag brass, but again, this is a hell of a lot of trouble. The rim must be turned down to .525″, thinned to .049″; case full-length sized, trimmed back to 2.1″, neck reamed, etc.

To those readers who want to make up cases for odd calibers I recommend the book, *Cartridge Conversions*, by Geo. C. Nonte, Jr., The Stackpole Co., 1966, rev. ed.

6.5 X 55 Swedish & Norwegian

Cartridge for the 1894 model Swedish-Mauser and Norwegian-Krag rifles. This is another number all but unknown here until after World War II. It is a very popular sporting round in the Scandinavian countries and has picked up quite a following in the U.S. as the result of the surplus military rifles sold here.

The 6.5 X 55 is one of the most flexible and useful of the 6.5mm military cartridges. Husqvarna sporting rifles are chambered for this round and imported by U.S. dealers. Ammunition to be fired in military rifle actions is standardized at approximately 45,000 psi, but handloads for the Husqvarna sporting rifles can be loaded to somewhat higher pressure levels.

Norma offers a good selection of Boxer-primed sporting ammunition with bullets of 77, 93, 139 and 156 grains or empty cases.

6.5 X 58 Portuguese Vergueiro

This round was used in the 1904 model Portuguese military rifle, a basic Mauser type, but with such Mannlicher features as the split-bridge receiver. In 1937 Portugal adopted the Model 98 Mauser rifle and the 8mm Mauser cartridge. Most of the older rifles were then converted to the new caliber. For that reason, military rifles of this caliber have been rare on the surplus market.

On the other hand, the 6.5 X 58 achieved a degree of popularity as a sporting round. Eley-Kynoch and DWM load sporting ammunition of this caliber. All I have seen had the Berdan type primer. The 6.5 X 58 is often confused with the 6.5 X 57 Mauser, and although the two are very similar they are not the same.

Cases can be made by full-length sizing and trimming 30-06 brass.

7 X 57 Mauser

Although designed as a military cartridge, the 7mm Mauser is a very popular sporting round all over the world. It was first introduced in 1892, but was not adopted on a large scale until 1893. The improved Model 93 Mauser rifle adopted by Spain started the ball rolling and later Mexico and many Latin-American countries adopted the 7mm.

Ammunition is loaded in the U.S. and at one time American sporting rifles were chambered for the round. American companies load only the 175-gr. bullet, but Norma provides 110- and 150-gr. loads in addition to the 175-gr. CIL loads a 139-gr. bullet that is quite popular. Ballistically the 7mm is only slightly less powerful than the 270 Win. or 280 Rem. It is considered adequate for any North American big game but is on the light side for the big brown bears. Recoil of 7mm Mauser rifles is relatively moderate and it is a good caliber choice for a boy's or woman's rifle. There is a good selection of jacketed or cast bullet types and weights available to the handloader.

There is considerable variation in thickness and capacity of 7mm Mauser cases and caution should be exercised in working up maximum loads. Remington and Norma cases are heavier than Winchester-Western and tend to give higher pressures with the same charge and bullet. There is also rather wide variation in the bore diameter of 7mm military rifles; check this when ordering sizing dies for cast bullets. Standard jacketed bullet diameter is .284″. Cast bullet diameter may vary from .284″ to .287″, for best results.

7.35mm Italian

Usually listed as the 7.35mm Mannlicher-Carcano, this cartridge was adopted by Italy in 1938 to replace the 6.5mm round. The Model 38 service rifle differs only in minor details from the 1891 type. The action is practically identical.

No sporting version of the 7.35mm round has been loaded, but dealers often replace the military bullet with a similar soft point and sell these for deer hunting. The odd bullet diameter of .298″ poses something of a problem

in reloading. However, jacketed bullets of 128 and 150 grains are available and Lyman's 300136 (150-gr.) is the proper size for cast bullets.

The 7.35mm Carcano is designed for the same working pressures (38,000 psi) as the 6.5mm rifle. In a strong action the 7.35mm cartridge could be improved rather markedly. However, it is not safe practice to do this in the Italian military rifle.

As it stands, the 7.35mm delivers performance between the 30-30 and the 300 Savage. It is an effective deer and black bear number. Cases can be made by neck-expanding and reforming 6.5mm Mannlicher brass.

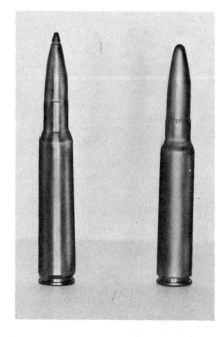

The 7mm Mauser (left) and 7.35mm Carcano.

7.5 X 54 Swiss Model 1911

The original version of this cartridge was introduced in 1889, the present slightly altered round in 1911. It is used in the Swiss Schmidt-Rubin straight-pull rifle.

The modern (1911) cartridge is a true 30 caliber and uses .308″ diameter bullets. Older rifles have a .304″ groove diameter and care must be exercised not to use the larger bullet in the pre-1911 model weapons. Carbine and rifle models designated as Model 11, 96/11 and 31 are intended for the 1911 round. If in doubt, have a gunsmith measure the bore of your rifle.

Golden State Arms Corp. (Pasadena, Calif., but now out of business) marketed Boxer-primed (.210″) 7.5mm Swiss cases. There is no similar case from which it is practical to form this brass. In power it is in the same class as the 308 Winchester.

7.5 X 54 French MAS

This is a rimless cartridge adopted by France in 1936 to replace the older

rimmed 8mm Lebel. Both the cartridge and the French Model 36 bolt action rifle have been relatively scarce items on the surplus market.

.308″ bullets can be used for loading. No sporting or Boxer-primed cases are presently available. Dealers replace the military bullet with a 150-gr. soft point and the reader can do the same thing to make up hunting ammo. There isn't any similar round that can be used to make up 7.5 X 54 MAS cases. All in all, this is one of the least useful of the surplus military cartridges. Power is similar to the 30-40 Krag or 303 British.

30 U.S. Carbine

Adopted by the U.S. Army in 1942 as a possible replacement for the 45 auto-pistol. The M1 carbine and its cartridge have become quite popular in recent years for sporting use. However, the 30 carbine cartridge is strictly a small game and varmint number. Sporting ammunition with soft point bullets is loaded by American companies and Norma.

Considerable data has been published on this cartridge and the 30 M1 carbine. The *Speer Manual* and Lyman's *Handbook* include much information on loading American military calibers. There is no point in repeating this here.

30-06

U.S. military cartridge adopted in 1906 for the Springfield (Mauser type) bolt action rifle. The 30-06 cartridge has subsequently become, possibly, the most popular sporting round ever developed. Entire books have been written on this cartridge and so much data is available on loading it that there is little point in rehashing the same material here.

30-40 Krag

This is the first small bore smokeless powder cartridge adopted by the U.S. Army. It was used in the American modified Krag-Jorgensen bolt action rifle of 1892. The Remington-Lee, Remington Rolling-Block, Winchester single-shot and Model 95 lever action were sporting rifles once available in 30-40 caliber.

Sporting ammunition is loaded by American companies and handloading is not a problem. The 30-40 cartridge is adequate for practically all North American big game. Again, this is a common and well-known American cartridge, amply covered in the handloading manuals.

7.62mm NATO / 308 Winchester

This is the official U.S. military caliber at the present time. Commercial designation is 308 Winchester. The cartridge was adopted by the military in 1954, but Winchester introduced their sporting version in 1952. Both sporting and military ammunition with Boxer type primers are readily available. The 308 Win. is a popular sporting round and load detailing here would be largely repetition.

7.62 X 54R Russian

Cartridge for the Russian Model 1891 Mosin-Nagant bolt action rifle. Modest quantities of these rifles, manufactured by the New England Westinghouse Co., were sold off after WW I. These were rather well-made rifles in spite of the clumsy design. Those sold after WW II and the Korean War are mostly klunkers.

Groove diameter of these rifles varies from .309″ to .311″, although .308″ jacketed bullets are usually the proper size. For best accuracy with cast bullets, .310″ bullets seem to work in most rifles.

Remington used to load 7.62mm Russian sporting ammunition, but discontinued it some years ago. Norma Boxer-primed cases and ammunition are currently available. The 7.62mm Russian performs similarly to the 30-40 Krag, and it is adequate for most North American big game, provided one uses the proper bullet.

7.65 X 53 Mauser

This cartridge originated for the Model 1889 Belgian Mauser rifle and was used later in the 1891 Argentine Mauser. Both have similar actions. It was originally designated as the 7.65mm Belgian Mauser and loaded by American companies. Both Remington and Winchester chambered sporting rifles for it, but it has been obsolete here since about 1936.

After WW II large quantities of the Argentine Model 91 Mauser were sold as surplus and the cartridge returned with a new name, 7.65mm Argentine-Mauser. A number of other nations have also used this cartridge as a military round. Norma very quickly introduced sporting ammunition and Boxer-primed cases and this is a fairly useful sporting number. Performance is close to the 308 Winchester.

Groove diameter of 7.65mm Argentine rifles will vary from .311″ to .313″. Measure the bore and pick the bullet that most closely fits since jacketed bullets of .311″, .312″ and .313″ are available. Working pressure of these rifles is about 40,000 psi and handloads should be kept at or near that level.

303 British

The 303 British must be considered one of the most successful of the military cartridges. Adopted in 1888, it remained in use with only minor changes until 1957. The Lee-designed bolt action rifle it was fired in spanned the same period and, like the cartridge, was an effective design. During the same period the U.S. used the 45-70 Springfield single-shot, 30-40 Krag, 30-06 Springfield the and 30-06 Garand (plus the 30 M1 carbine).

303 sporting ammo has been loaded in the U.S. for many years. The Winchester single-shot and Model 95 lever action were made in 303 caliber, as was the Remington-Lee bolt action and No. 5 single-shot. No American rifles have been so chambered since 1936.

The 303 is a popular hunting round in Canada, Africa and throughout the British Commonwealth. As loaded in the U.S. it is in the same class as the 30-40 Krag, but the British (Eley-Kynoch) produce much heavier loadings that are pretty close to the 30-06. Regardless, it is adequate for practically any North American big game. Late model Enfield rifles can stand working pressures of around 50,000 psi. Early models are usually limited to the 45,000 to 48,000 psi range. Although the cartridge is very similar in type, shape and powder capacity to the 30-40 Krag, it can be loaded to higher pressures and therefore is potentially more powerful.

Proper jacketed bullet diameter is .311 to .312 inches. There is, however, considerable variation in groove diameter of 303 military rifles. There is a good selection of 303 jacketed and cast bullets to choose from.

7.7 X 58 Japanese Arisaka

The Japanese military adopted the 7.7mm cartridge in 1939 to replace the older 6.5mm round. It is intended for the Model 99 Arisaka rifle, a bolt action only slightly modified from the Model 38 type.

The cartridge uses the same .311″ diameter bullet as the 303 British. In fact, it is a sort of rimless 303, the British cartridge having influenced its design. Norma Boxer-primed cases and sporting ammunition are available. It is possible to make 7.7mm Japanese cases from 30-06 brass even though the '06 has a smaller base or head diameter. Cases made in this way should be fire-formed with a moderate charge before loading full charges.

Nominal working pressure of Japanese 7.7mm rifles is about 42,000 psi, although they will stand somewhat more than that. The better-made actions are quite stout, but some of the Japanese actions turned out during the war lacked the refinement of pre-war models. Therefore, it is best to stick to moderate loads. The 7.7mm cartridge is in about the same class as the 30-40 Krag and the 303 British.

8mm Mauser

The 8mm Mauser is one of the outstanding military cartridges of the world. The original version was adopted in 1888 and had a .318″ diameter bullet. In 1905 an improved spitzer bullet with a larger diameter of .323″ was introduced. This has been a source of confusion in many quarters ever since.

The original cartridge and .318″ bullet is designated by a "J" for *Jnfanterie* (8X57J). The later .323″ version is designated by an "S" or "JS" (8X57S or 8X57JS). This is really of no concern to those using Model 98 pattern Mauser military actions because they all fire the larger .323″ or "S" type bullet. Early models were altered to the new round and any firing the original bullet would be as scarce as hair on an egg. However, some sporting rifles are chambered for the older .318″ round and one should be aware of this. If in doubt, have a gunsmith measure the bore. The 8mm Mauser is also listed as the 7.9X57JS.

The 8mm Mauser has been loaded in the U.S. for 60 years or so, and at one time it was one of the standard calibers for the Winchester Model 54 sporting rifle. However, it has not been very popular here, despite the fact that it is an excellent sporting round. The influx of surplus 8mm Mauser military rifles has changed all this and it is now fairly common among big game hunters.

If loaded to full capability the 8mm Mauser is in the same class as the 30-06 and will handle any North American big game. American sporting ammunition is underloaded, but Norma, DWM and RWS turn out livelier loads. Good Model 98 Mauser actions will stand working pressures of 50,000 to 55,000 psi. Bullet diameter is .323″ and there is a good selection of jacketed and cast bullets available.

8mm Lebel

The 8mm Lebel was the first small bore smokeless powder military cartridge adopted by any power. The French introduced it in 1886 along with the Lebel bolt action rifle. It was replaced in 1936 by a rimless 7.5mm round. However, 8mm Lebel rifles saw service in WW II.

Remington-manufactured Lebel rifles were sold as surplus after WW I, and Remington also turned out sporting ammunition. Only modest numbers of these rifles have appeared since WW II and Remington no longer loads their sporting round.

Ammunition for 8mm Lebel rifles is something of a problem in many areas. Remington sporting ammo can still be found in dealers stocks, but is not readily available in many locations. Cases can be made from 348 Winchester brass by reforming in an 8mm Lebel sizing die, trimming to 1.98″ and fire-forming. Proper bullet diameter is .323″.

In performance, the 8mm Lebel is similar to the 30-40 Krag and is effective on most American big game. Working pressure of Lebel rifles is about 45,000 to 48,000 psi.

8 X 58R Danish Krag

Cartridge for the Model 1889 Danish Krag rifle. A quantity of these rifles showed up in Surplus stores a few years back, but the cartridge is not widely used here. Single-shot rifles based on the Remington rolling-block action are used in Denmark and occasionally appear here. Performance in the sporting version is somewhat greater than the 30-40 Krag.

Bullet diameter is .322″ to .323″. Military ammunition has the Berdan primer. However, Norma sporting ammunition and Boxer-primed cases have been available. Working pressure of the Danish-made Krag rifles is considered somewhat higher than the American-made model, about 45,000 psi maximum.

The 303 calibers, from top to bottom: 7.7mm Jap., 303 British and the 7.65mm Mauser.

Conclusion

The military rifle cartridges covered herein are by no means complete as to total numbers, but, they do represent those more commonly encountered here. Black powder military cartridges were covered in the 3rd edition of the *Handloader's Digest*. See, "Black Powder Guns" in that issue, by the author, if you are interested in that handloading category.

The handloading of military cartridges is not only interesting, but quite necessary in some calibers as a means of obtaining good sporting ammunition. If restrictive legislation does not cut off the flow and sale of surplus military arms the practice will probably continue to grow. Loading dies and components are available for practically all the cartridges listed. ●

LOADING TABLES FOR MILITARY CARTRIDGES

Cartridge	Bullet/grs.	Powder/grs.	MV/fps	Remarks
6.5mm Japanese	120	4064/36	2775	
	139	N203/32	2365	
	140	4350/39	2630	
	156	4064/28	2050	
6.5x53R Mannlicher	139	3031/34	2558	
	156	4320/35	2145	
6.5x54 MS	87	3031/40	2980	
	120	4320/38	2576	
	139	3031/34	2563	
	156	4320/35	2170	
6.5x58 Vergueiro (Mauser-P)	120	4831/47	2615	
	139	4831/45	2463	
	156	4831/44	2395	Near Max.
6.5x55 Mauser	87	HV-2/43	3300	
	120	4831/52	2771	
	139	4831/50	2680	Near Max.
	156	4350/42	2450	
6.5x52 Carcano	87	3031/34	2562	
	120	3031/33	2450	
	140	4320/35	2320	
	156	4320/33	2157	
7x57 Mauser	130	4320/44	2863	Speer
	150	4831/52	2770	Norma
	160	4350/47	2665	Speer
	175	4064/42	2450	
7.35mm Italian	128	4198/34	2650	
	150	4320/42	2622	Speer
	150	H380/42	2527	Speer
7.5x54 Swiss (Schmidt-Rubin M-1911)	150	3031/45	2750	
	165	4064/43	2632	
	180	4064/45	2483	
7.5x54 French MAS	150	4064/44	2665	Sierra Bullet
	180	3031/38	2370	Speer Bullet
30 U.S. Carbine	110	H-110/14	2030	Speer
	110	2400/14	1991	Speer
30-06	110	4064/56	3297	Speer
	130	4320/55	3149	Speer
	150	4350/59	2950	Speer
	165	4320/51	2842	Speer
	180	4320/49	2655	
	200	4831/56	2466	Speer
	220	4350/52	2447	
30-40 Krag	110	HV-2/41	3029	Speer
	150	4895/44	2654	Speer
	180	3031/37	2272	
	220	HV-2/35	2156	
7.62mm NATO (308 Win.)	110	RL11/46	3208	Speer
	150	RL11/42	2709	Speer
	180	RL11/38	2417	Speer
	200	4895/40	2348	Speer
7.62x54R Russian	150	HV-2/44	2752	
	180	HV-2/42	2412	
	200	HV-2/41	2345	
7.7mm Japanese	150	4320/44	2625	Speer
	180	4320/41	2434	Speer
	215	4064/43	2300	Norma
303 British	115	HV-2/38	2732	32-20 Bullet
	130	4198/37	2725	Norma
	150	4064/43	2700	
	180	HV-2/36	2338	Speer
	215	4064/38	2205	Norma
7.65mm Mauser (Belgium, Argentina)	150	HV-2/40	2815	
	180	HV-2/36	2402	
8x50R Lebel	150	HV-2/44	2700	Sierra Bullet
	170	HV-2/42	2325	Speer Bullet
	196	HV-2/40	2268	Norma Bullet
8mm Mauser (8x57JS)	125	3031/49	3067	Speer
	150	HV-2/46	2888	Speer
	170	HV-2/44	2669	Speer
	225	4350/54	2431	Speer
8x58R Danish-Krag	150	3031/52	2850	
	196	HV-2/52	2600	Norma Bullet

Note: Loads listed in the above table should be safe in any military or sporting rifle in good condition provided the proper bullet is used for the bore diameter of the rifle. Loads have been selected more for efficiency than maximum velocity.

When reloading the military calibers for game hunting, it is advisable to use soft point expanding bullets. The illustration at the left shows the Remington "Core-Lokt" bullet, its construction in cross section and an expanded bullet as it expanded in animal flesh at 100 yd.

DIMENSIONS OF MILITARY RIFLE CARTRIDGES

Cartridge	Case type	Diameter					Length		Twist	Primer Boxer	Dia. Berdan
		Bullet	Neck	Shld.	Base	Rim	Case	Cart.			
* 6.5x50 Japanese	G	.263	.293	.425	.455	.471	2.00	2.98	7.9	.210	.199
6.5x53R Mannlicher	A	.263	.297	.423	.450	.526	2.10	3.03	9.8	—	.199
* 6.5x54 Mann.-Schoen.	C	.263	.287	.424	.447	.450	2.09	3.02	7.8	.210	.199
6.5x58 Vergueiro	C	.264	.293	.426	.468	.465	2.28	3.22	7.8	—	.216
* 6.5x55 Mauser	C	.264	.294	.420	.480	.480	2.16	3.15	7.9	.210	.199-.216
* 6.5x52 Carcano	C	.265	.295	.430	.445	.448	2.05	3.02		.210	.199
* 7x57 Mauser	C	.284	.320	.420	.470	.474	2.23	3.06	9	.210	.216
7.35x51 Carcano	C	.298	.323	.420	.445	.449	2.01	2.98	10	—	.199
* 7.5x54 Swiss	C	.308	.334	.452	.494	.496	2.18	3.05	10.5	.210	.216-.217
7.5x54 French MAS	C	.308	.340	.441	.480	.482	2.11	2.99	10	—	.199
* 30 U.S. Carbine	D	.308	.331	—	.354	.354	1.29	1.67	10	.175	—
* 30-06 U.S.	C	.308	.340	.441	.470	.473	2.50	3.34	10	.210	.217
* 30-40 U.S. Krag	A	.308	.338	.415	.457	.540	2.31	3.10	10	.210	—
* 7.62x51 NATO (308 Win.)	C	.308	.338	.447	.466	.470	2.01	2.75	12	.210	.217
* 7.62x54R Russian	A	.310	.332	.453	.484	.564	2.11	3.02	9.5	.210	.254
* 7.7x58 Japanese	C	.311	.338	.431	.472	.474	2.28	3.13	9.8	.210	.199-.216
* 303 British	A	.312	.337	.402	.458	.530	2.21	3.05	10	.210	.250
* 7.65x53 Mauser	C	.313	.338	.429	.468	.470	2.09	2.95	10	.210	.216-.217
* 8x50R Lebel	A	.323	.347	.483	.536	.621	1.98	2.75	9.5	.210	.199-.216
* 8x57JS Mauser	C	.323	.353	.443	.469	.473	2.24	3.17	10	.210	.217
* 8x58R Danish-Krag	A	.323	.355	.460	.500	.575	2.28	3.20	12	.210	.216-.217

A=rim bottleneck C=rimless bottleneck D=rimless straight -G=semi-rimmed bottle neck. All dimensions are in inches. Twist is given as inches of bbl. required for one revolution. * Indicates sporting loads and/or cases with U.S. Boxer primers available.

AVERAGE BALLISTICS OF MILITARY RIFLE CARTRIDGES

Cartridge	Bullet/grs.	MV/fps	ME/fp	Remarks
6.5mm Japanese	139	2500	1930	Japan
6.5x53R Mannlicher	156	2433	2085	Roumania, Netherlands
6.5x54 Mann.-Schoen.	159	2223	1740	Greece
6.5x58 Vergueiro	139	2775	2372	Portugal
6.5x55 Mauser	156	2395	1993	Norway, Sweden
6.5x52 Carcano	162	2296	1902	Italy
7x57 Mauser	173	2300	2031	Spain, Mexico, et al.
7.35x51 Carcano	128	2483	1749	Italy
7.5x54 Swiss	174	2720	2859	Switzerland (1911)
7.5x54 French MAS	149	2674	2359	France (1936)
30 U.S. Carbine	110	1900	900	U.S. (1941)
30-06 U.S. Springfield	152	2805	2665	U.S. (1906)
30-40 Krag	220	2000	1950	U.S. (1892)
7.62mm NATO (308 Win.)	150	2805	2665	U.S., NATO
7.62x54R Russian	147	2886	2727	Russia
7.7x58 Japanese	175	2400	2237	Japan
303 British	174	2440	2300	Britain, U.K.
7.65mm Mauser	185	2500	2568	Belgium, Argentina
8x50R Lebel	198	2380	2481	France (1886)
8mm Mauser	154	2882	2837	Germany, et al
8x58R Danish-Krag	237	1968	2041	Denmark

Bullet weight and ballistics above are for the most commonly encountered military round. Where more than one country used the same cartridge, they often had different loadings. In some instances, the same nation used variations in loading at different times.

The 8mm Lebel (left) and 8mm Mauser.

Hunting jaguar in the Nayarit region of Mexico, Askins for 10 days lugged a 44-40 "El Tigre" carbine, never got to shoot it — just as well, for it wouldn't group in a foot circle at 40 yards!

Ed
HAMCO

GAME FIELD GOOFS

by Colonel CHARLES ASKINS

A few lucky men spend their lives hunting. They roam from Alaska to Mexico to Africa to New Zealand — wherever game awaits. Deadly are their rifles, tremendous their trophies. Unlike you and I (if printed reports are true), they never seem to miss. Never? Well, hardly ever . . .

THE OTHER DAY I dropped a 280 cartridge into a 7mm Magnum chamber and fired it. It was unintentional, the end result of a piece of damfool stupidity. Mine. It did not take the rifle apart but I don't know why. The casing was split from end to end and hot gas spewed out into the action and jetted back into my face. Fortunately for me, the musket was one of the strongest, the Remington M700. Had it been any lesser gun, I reckon I'd have had a lot of iron to comb out of my whiskers.

That piece of knucklebrained fumblebum stuff set me to counting the number of guns and hunting booboos I've pulled over the years. When I finished the tally I felt myself over real careful-like to see if I was still all in one piece. Surprisingly, I was.

They say the Lord looks after fools and drunks, so that must account for my luck, as there have been times when I could qualify on both scores. Let me describe a few of them.

Before I took to fighting wars I was a U.S. Border Patrolman, stationed about 20 miles west of El Paso, Texas. Just at daylight one morning I was tracking a couple of *contrabandista* through a little waterstop on the north line of the Southern Pacific. The pueblo was called Strauss. It is in New Mexico and about 6 miles from the International boundary. It was raining, a rare happening on the desert, and I was in a half-run to keep the tracks in sight before the shower puddled them out.

I loped through the tiny settlement hot on the spoor. The pair quit the railroad tracks above the two-bit hamlet and struck out across the desert. I followed them not more than a quarter-mile and found them sacked out under a rag of a tarp.

Sixgun in hand, I Injuned forward, intending to snatch the tarp off the pair and have them cold turkey. As I leaned forward to grab the tarp, the renegade on the far side reared up on his elbows, a carbine in his hands. I let drive at him with the New Service 44-40 I was packing—and missed. The bullet cut the dirt at his shoulder.

The smuggler did not fire and I let the one shot suffice. It was a good thing I did. The pair were not *contrabandista* at all. They were two old willies and the "carbine" was a pick handle. I'd had my narrowest escape from committing manslaughter.

In Vietnam, one day, I wheeled my battered old jeep up to a Chinaman's little farm and looked the place over. Beside his flimsy corral lay a dead heifer. The farmer was a Nung Chinese. The Nung are soldiers who

The writer, looking slightly goggle-eyed after finding he has bashed a second waterbuck, twin to the one below, but has a license for only one.

This Vietnamese tiger didn't get away, but another — posing in the moonlight at a mere 60 feet — did, to Askins' discomfiture.

elected to come south out of the border country between North Vietnam and Red China, and fight the Commies beside the South Vietnamese. This particular Nung had grown too old for the wars and had commenced to farm the land.

He told me a tiger had killed the cow the night before. I wanted to sit up over the bovine and give the cat his lumps that night, but the farmer would have none of that. The cow, he explained, belonged to his landlord and he would have to skin and butcher the critter and peddle the meat to the Third Nung Division which was encamped some 4 miles away, near the village of Song Mao.

I couldn't let this little inconvenience keep me from that cat. I scouted around and purchased a goat and, come the evening, tethered the blatting nanny on a nearby terrace hard by the creek which an inspection during daylight hours had showed the huge feline was using. When the sun went down, I put my back to a mighty Dao tree and felt pretty certain Old Stripes would be along sooner or later.

Directly after sundown two things came out. The mosquitoes and a big fat yellow moon which came boiling up out of the South China Sea. It was almost as light as day. I could see my goat some 50 feet below me. With some premonition that she was on an

exposed flank, the goat blatted incessantly. I liked that. The tiger should be back for the heifer but he knew all about nanny goats, too.

At about 9:30 I looked over at the trail coming up out of the nullah and it was bare in the moonlight. At 9:31 I glanced over there again, impelled by the sudden taut silence of my bait. There stood the biggest, most handsome tiger in the jungle! He was simply magnificent there in the moon's brilliant glow, the black stripes on his tawny hide so distinct I could have counted every one of them.

Stripes, Stripes, Stripes——

I was in a sitting position, my elbows on my knees, my rifle in my hands. The shooting iron was a mite on the light side for Asia's toughest carnivore, but I reckoned it would do. Especially at 60 feet. I had a 1x scope on the rifle—a scope with a lot of field, no magnification, and unhappily blessed with these infernally worthless crosshairs. I swung the glass over on the tiger—he seemed in no hurry—and what I saw made me the unhappiest GI in all Vietnam.

All the scope showed at the 20-yard distance was stripes. Stripes in the top of the glass, the bottom, and on all sides. I just could not see the crosswires. But time was a'wastin' and I didn't know how long he'd stay. I squared the cat's shoulder off in the glass and worked on the trigger.

On the shot, the animal reared straight up and fell over backward in the nullah. I went forward with a torch and shined it into the tules, looking for my prize. He had done a lot of thrashing around after he fell and I wasn't exactly surprised not to find him. But there would be a lot of blood. Buckets of it. A good spoor to follow and I was positive he could not go far.

When daylight came, I set out to track down my Mr. Stripes. Well, not only was there no blood, there was no tiger. As a matter of fact, the tiger had gone a mile across the paddy and raided another Chinese farmer, taking off a 2-year old buffalo. I had missed that tiger, big as a Missouri mule, or so he seemed there in the moonlight, at the ignominious distance of 60 feet! I'll never live that one down.

In Africa a few years ago to give the 338 Magnum a wring-out test before it was placed on the market, I got into a band of Grant's gazelle. I had Capt. Allen Pope, our leading soldier of fortune, with me, and we had a little pow-wow as to who would shoot first. "Aw, go ahead," Pope said magnanimously, "I'll take the next one."

Tony Dyer, one of the better white hunters in Africa, motioned and I came up beside him and we commenced to stalk the animals. We moved up for a half-mile and finally could get no closer. The shot was a long one. Too far for a poor hitter like me, but there was no help for it. The Granti were getting fidgety and would take it on the lam any minute. I'd have to shoot. I did.

The buck Dyer had picked out for me dropped. But it was up again and off, limping, immediately. "You've hit him fair enough, but I think too far back," Dyer commented. "I'll go back and get the safari car. You follow him up."

A Grant to Spare

I found the blood-flecked spoor—not easy, what with the tracks of others in and over it—and took it through a patch of thorn. When I broke out on the other side, there stood my Grant, not more than 80 yards distant. We saw each other at the same time and he decided he still had some go left in him. On my second shot he did a cartwheel.

I went up to him and had a look at the horns. This wasn't my buck. Certainly not the trophy Dyer and I had selected from the band. Those horns had been in the record class, these were quite ordinary. About this time Dyer tooled the old Willys safari wagon around the bush and had a look.

"Hell's blood!" he exploded, "You've done it! You've bashed in two Grant." Not more than 60 yards away we found the first buck, piled up and deader than Farouk. The horns were good for the Rowland Ward record book. Some 31¼ inches. Tony took the second buck on his license and I took a ribbing for a piece of typical dumb dude shooting.

You'd think these kind of booboos would sink in, but not on old Askins. On another safari, Bill Jenvey, white hunter from Down Under, and I were scouting for buffalo. This was along the Uaso Nyero River of the Northern Frontier and I had taken a bull but he wasn't much for horn. Returning to camp in the dusk of the evening, we bumped into a gaggle of waterbuck. I had only the 458 Winchester with me and no cartridges save full metal patch. Nothing daunted, we fell out of the safari car and in the gathering gloom minced forward.

At fully 300 yards I let drive at the biggest bull in the band. The slug struck the ground at the critter's feet. I held over his back and on the third shot I got blood. The bull fell, arighted himself, and limped off slowly,

weaving like a drunken Sam Salt. He went over a slight rise and out of sight. "Follow him." Jenvey directed. "I'll go back and bring the safari car forward. There are several more buck over that rise. Don't shoot unless you see your buck limping." I nodded, already in a run.

I galloped up the hill, peeked over the crest and there stood my water-buck. He was a handsome rascal and although I knew he was badly hit he had his head up and looked quite alert. I knifed 500 grains of hard metal into his brisket and he went down like he'd been struck by nuclear reaction.

The distance was about 90 yards and in the thickening gloom I had trouble threading my way forward. I had scarcely gone 40 yards before I stumbled onto a waterbuck stone dead. It was my first one.

Tardily, I remembered Jenvey's admonition, "Don't shoot unless you see him limping." I had two water-buck and the limit was one. I gave my second prize to a hunting mate who had licensed for the game but hadn't had the luck to see one. What Bill Jenvey told me when he arrived with the safari car and discovered we had two buck instead of the regular quota cannot be published, not even in a book with the liberal unexpunged editorial policy of this one!

One spring I took one of the hot new 300 Magnums to Alaska with me. It was a conversion from the standard right hand bolt action to the port side. I am a southpaw and while I can reach over the bridge pretty well and grab the bolt, I would rather have it mounted on the handy side. Especially when I am going to be hubbing up against the biggest of our bears. The conversion of the action had been done by a reputable guns-tinker and I was satisfied with it.

When I checked the rifle out for zero on the ice in front of guide Nelson Walker's quarters in Kotzebue, sometimes it would fire and other times it would not. I attributed this to a drop or two of oil. The mercury was hanging around minus 35 degrees and this causes some gun oils to solidify. I sloshed the bolt around in a can of airplane gas and reassembled it. There was the same off-again on-again routine. I took the rifle over to Al Guthrie, who is a good amateur gunsmith, and Al put in a driving spring from Walker's old Model 70. That fixed it. I belted a whale of a big white bear, a record book stud, and came away for a go at walrus down on St. Lawrence Island.

The fall following, I was out on the Alaska Peninsula with John Swiss. John is a ring-tailed tooter on hunting the giant Alaska brown bear, and on moose, too. I had shot a lot of the bruin so I went out with Swiss for a big moose.

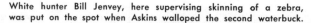

White hunter Bill Jenvey, here supervising skinning of a zebra, was put on the spot when Askins walloped the second waterbuck.

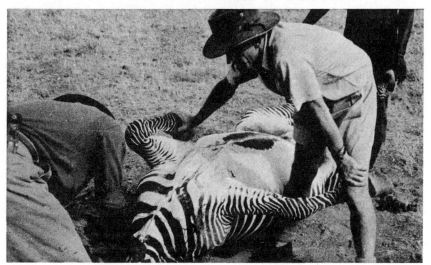

Askins' big Alaskan moose, bagged despite a rifle which fired only twice in four attempts.

We found him all right. And the stalk was a good one. We got up to 60 yards. The first shot was a killing one, but these old lunker bulls like you find out on the peninsula can pack a lot of lead. The bull went down but he got right up again and started off. The second shot was a misfire. So, too, was the third. I finally got the fourth to go bang. It decked the game. "I thought you had fixed that dam' rifle last spring." Swiss growled. "We'd have sure been in a helluva fix if that moose had been a 10-foot brownie." And so we would, for John was packing only a six-gun, his 338 left back in the boat a couple of miles to the rear. The moose went 70½ inches.

When I got back to home base, I gave that musket a real going over. The conversion was strictly a Rube Goldberg. Sometimes the striker would fall freely, other times it was partially caught by the bolt. Anyone with the acumen of a 10-year-old would have checked out these possibilities before going out to joust with the biggest game on the continent, but not me!

During 10 years in the Border Patrol I got into quite a few gunfights with the *contrabandista* along the Tex-Mex frontier. These powder-flecked fisticuffs resulted in a pretty high casualty rate. In fact, it seemed like more of the opposition cashed in their chips than ever regained their health. As a result of this, I got so I seldom ventured out unless all gussied up with a sixgun in my pants.

Trigger Trouble

One fine spring evening I was jogging up Mesa Street, in El Paso, and had along not only my best girlfriend but her mama as well. I was packing a gun in a half-breed rig. It was, of all things, a 22 automatic, and although it might look like middlin' poor ordnance for self-defense, these little stingers shoot 11 times quick-like and point better than any other handgun made.

This was a real special gun. I had sent it to Berdon, who in those days was the gee-whiz guns tinker, and he'd put one of his go-to-hell triggers on it. This trigger was a new development, designed to break clean as glass, with no backlash, and pulled at about 2 pounds. As I say, I had this 4-inch cutter in a shoulder rig and I sorta slapped my arm against the gun to move it into a more comfortable position. The slap was enough for that hair trigger Berdon had whumped up. The gun fired. I was driving at the time and the hollow-point high-speed slug went boring down through my hip.

It was only a few blocks to the hospital so I drove over there, found I could walk okay and so bounced up to the desk and announced I had shot myself. This sort of shook up the reception committee but the gal recovered and soon had me shunted in and ready for first aid.

Doc Gallagher, who I had known for a long time, soaked a pull-through in iodine and swabbed out the bullet channel. The slug had missed the hipbone and gone out through the buttock. About 7 inches of penetration, which I thought was pretty good for a 22. When that wound channel got well filled with iodine it felt a hell of a lot worse than the bullet did boring its way downward, I'll tell you!

I took the gun apart next day and had a look at the Berdon masterpiece. His bearing surfaces between sear nose and notch were so infinitesimally small that any sudden jar could set the gun off, safety or no safety. These are the kind of things a feller should explore before he gets to shooting holes in the seat of his pants.

Another time, hunting jaguar in Nayarit, I whipped into Mazatlan and sat around a couple of days waiting for my guides. They eventually showed up and we pushed off for the hunting camp, 150 miles to the south. It is a bloody nuisance to carry a shooting iron into Mexico so I had permitted my head guide to talk me into coming down gunless. He'd have a good rifle for me, he said. I had with me my old hunting partner, Earl "Tex" Jones of Abilene. He would need some kind of a powder burner, too.

Jonesy was sort of my guest on this one. I had talked him into the hunt, so when it came to a selection of the rifles I gave him a good-looking Springfield. It had been sporterized, made into a Mannlicher style actually, and had an excellent set of Williams sights. It was an Improved '06 and was more than adequate for the biggest *tigre* south of the Rio Grande. My cat-killer was something else again!

It was a Spanish-made 44-40, built before the Spanish Civil War by Garate Anitua y Cia, Eibar. Dubbed the "El Tigre," it was the spitting image of the old Winchester 1892 carbine. I glanced through the barrel. It looked like the inside of a rusty length of sewer pipe. I shot the little snapper. Of the 10 rounds fired, 7 went through the target as keyholes. The group measured 14 inches at 40 yards.

Now, shooting jaguar is a serious business of plunking the great cat spang through the heart. If he is in a tree you absolutely must drop him cold turkey. If he tumbles out with any life remaining in him he is dangerously apt to disembowel a dog or two. It does not take any great degree of shooting skill to slice his heart in two—that is, provided you have a decent gun. With my venerable 44-40 and its tumbling slugs, I wondered if maybe like Sasha Kemal I should just make a spear and go for the feline with that.

We hunted 10 days and never started a jaguar. It wasn't for lack of hard work. But as it turned out I did not have to turn my thoroughly worn old clunk on one of the monster cats. Some good came of that, for all its lack of action. I learned right there never to go into the gamefields without my own ordnance. Regardless of what the outfitter may tell me about his for-hire artillery, hereafter I'll just fetch along a gun I know is capable of pitching all the slugs through the target point foremost.

* * *

These confessionals are seldom related by gents like me who go knocking around the gamelands across the world. Mostly we just keep our boo-boos top secret. There ought to be a moral to this saga somewhere. The least, I reckon, I can say is that having gotten this account of these utterly stupid dumbcluck stunts off my chest, I'll hold up my hand and solemnly affirm I ain't gonna do 'em anymore. I'd like to say that, but in all honesty I am not so sure. ●

THE NATIONAL RIFLE CLUB

The story of an 1886 shoot between the last of the great muzzle-loading marksmen and the breech-loading upstarts from Walnut Hill.

Introduction and notes by John T. Amber

W. Milton Farrow
From an old cut

WE ARE particularly pleased to reprint this account of a great event in shooting history from the 1886 pages of **Forest & Stream.** It was the occasion, apparently, of the first shoulder-to-shoulder contest between the die-hard advocates of the muzzle-loading rest rifle and several noted marksmen using the newfangled breechloaders (these last had only been in use generally for some dozen years).

Mr. Murray Leyde of Painesville, Ohio, an old friend, was kind enough to send me a photo copy of the old account. In it I learned exactly how string measurements were made in that period, clearly and without question—as you will learn in your reading of the report. It had been assumed that the technique was pretty much as the anonymous correspondent has it, but here is the exact methodology outlined. Briefly, each shot in the string was measured from the intersection of the diagonal lines to the bullet hole, then the 10 measurements were simply added together.

It is difficult to compare these old string scores with today's targets—most commonly measured from center to center of the bullet holes farthest apart—unless a reproduction to a known scale of the old target is available for measuring. In the present instance we have two of them to assess.

Fletcher's first string measures 2⅝" center to center, the string total 9⁷⁄₁₆" as the table shows. Brown's third string measures 3³⁄₁₆"—almost a full inch greater than Fletcher's—but Brown's string score on his ten shots is 9¹³⁄₁₆", or only ⅜" worse. Fletcher's group is quite obviously a better one than Brown's, but simply reading the string measurements would not have revealed the graphic difference.

Another nice bit of source data given in this 1886 report is the quite exact load information put down for most of the contestants, to say nothing of the drawing that depicts, to scale, the variety of bullets used by 15 of the marksmen.

Further comments will appear in the text, set inside brackets.

VERNON, Vt., May 27, 1886. — A dozen sedate looking gentlemen squatted along on low stools, clad in work-a-day clothes, each looking with a pre-occupied air out through the low shutter opening of the house in which they sat. Then a lull in the blowing gale and away banged a dozen rifles with the noise and effect of small pieces of ordnance. This was the scene which greeted your correspondent on his arrival at this quiet Green Mountain hamlet yesterday morning.

It was the annual spring meet of the National Club, and the men were shooting with the old style muzzleloaders at the old-fashioned targets, and scoring according to the old mode of string measure. They were a sort of Rip Van Winkle gathering, and one felt prompted to ask where they had taken the long nap and where they had kept the weapons from

rusting all the time. The club itself had grown into one of the institutions of the country. Its record runs back long befo' de wah, and far back in the fifties and forties the charter members tell of gatherings where there was *some* shooting, plenty of rivalry and no end of a good social time. The weapons of those days were indeed massive affairs, and the printed notices of the meetings with the list of allowances which the 40-lb. barrels are to make to the 15-lb. pigmies shows what at one time were the classes of rifles in the meetings.

The club has been a progressive affair though, and now such a thing as a 40-pound barrel would be a rarity. Members recall such, but they were handicapped out of existence and nobody seems particularly sorry that they have gone. The club is rather an aggregation of atoms

than a complete entity. There are officers elected at the fall meeting. Then a programme is made up. It is always the same. Three strings of 10 shots each. Shot on two days. Each one shooting hands $5 to the secretary. This fund pays the trifling expenses of the meeting and the remainder is divided in a sweepstake fashion. Those who enter become members for the nonce and when the meeting breaks up and the shooters take courtly adieus one of another the society exists only in the secretary's note-book until the next gathering. There are no disputes, no expensive machinery, no eating up of funds in managerial waste. Simple shoot and good fellowship, what could be more truly rural, more idyllic, more sportsman-like.

The oldest member shook his head, thought a while, thought some more, and finally said that he reckoned the first steps were taken in 1854 or '55 toward making the gatherings more formal than they had been. Before that time they had met and shot, but after a surprise party fashion, nobody being quite sure when he started for the rendezvous whether he would have a solitary bit of practice or whether he would form one of a jolly company. All in all the club is a unique sort of an institution. The one great aim of its members is to secure the greatest accuracy. Such a trifling fact as the utter impracticability of lugging the arm about in any useful fashion for hunting or general target work, does not seem to bother the National members at all. Once convinced that they can gain a quarter-inch on a string of 10 shots by adding half a dozen pounds of metal to the barrel and the added weight is put on without a question.

[Ned Roberts wrote *(The Muzzle-Loading Cap Lock Rifle)* that the National Club was organized on June 16 of 1858. The first matches were held at Waltham, Mass., with the matches at Vernon, Vt., beginning in 1868, said Roberts. See his book for further data on the match rules, etc.]

This particular spring meet was to become an episode in the history of the club. Much correspondence had been indulged in with the Walnut Hill marksmen, and these capital shooters of the modern school had promised to come up Vermontward and try conclusions with their antediluvian prototypes. The old fellows were delighted with the prospect of a good lively set-to, for the spirit of fight is strong within them, and there had been so much talk on the seemingly everlasting theme of Muzzle vs. Breechloader that everybody was charmed at the prospect of having the two classes of arms brought side by side, each in the hands of enthusiastic experts and each shooting under the same weather conditions. So when the 12 o'clock train came up from the southward at yester noon, and out of it tumbled Hinman and Rabbeth, Frye, Ellsworth and Maynard, each with rifle and shooting traps, it was generally agreed that the spring meeting of 1886 was to be a big success. The chroniclers were there too, ready with pen and pencil to picture in word and line the doings of this novel rifle meet. Mr. Gould came down from Boston, that *The Rifle* might know all that occurred, and with convenient camera caught the various doings of the riflemen.

[The Walnut Hill club at Woburn, near Boston, has been a world-famous institution since 1875, the year of its incorporation. Harry Pope, Adolph Niedner, Franklin W. Mann—in addition to those mentioned in the account here—and many other shooters renowned in their day were members of Walnut Hill. ● Arthur C. Gould (1850-1903) was the editor of *The Rifle* (1885-1888), its successor *Shooting & Fishing* (1888-1906) until his death. He also wrote two excellent books, especially worth studying by those in-

Wm. V. Lowe at his machine rest in Vernon, Vermont. After a photograph.

terested in shooting lore of the past—one was *Modern American Rifles,* the other *Modern American Pistols and Revolvers.* Both were long unavailable until reprinted by Tom Samworth in the 1940s. Unfortunately, both are again out of print.

A. C. Gould, who also wrote as Ralph Greenwood, exerted a strong influence on rifle and handgun shooting in his time. He had a vast enthusiasm for shooting, he wrote well and with full knowledge of his field.]

The newcomers were greeted in the most kindly spirit. There was the range 40 rods away from that little outhouse sort of a shooting box. Across yonder bit of low-lying water-covered meadow to the face of the low hill, where a temporary fence of slab boards sufficed to hold the paper targets. Sticks here and there held all manner of streamers, for each marksman carried his own private wind signals, and stuck them up as his fancy dictated. Some used long whip-lash streamers of silk, slightly weighted at the tip. Others again preferred the bag-like bits of muslin and these stood out like great bleached bolognas. One had contrived a wee wind signal, a model on a quarter-inch scale of the big dial at Creedmoor. It was a picturesque range, but the main interest was at the firing point. Here was the house we have mentioned, about 20 ft. long; on the side facing the targets away to the westward, shutters lifted up, really opening the house side. They were low and one was compelled to stoop or sit down on the low stools if a view of the targets was desired. Pushed up against this opening ranged in line were the rests on which the muzzleloaders were placed. They were of the saw-horse pattern, securely fastened to stakes driven into the soil and so arranged that when placed upon them the gun muzzle would be about 2 ft. from the ground. Along the other side of

the shooting house was the loading table, an ordinary workbench with notches along its front edge, and here the members do the manual work of the shooting, the cleaning and swabbing, patching and loading, with all that care and deliberation which characterizes the typical muzzle-man.

Let us take our friends in order, beginning in that far away corner where a portly gentlemen whose clear eyes in a measure belie the slight tinge of gray in his hair. He is Mr. R.C. Cressy of Brattleboro, Vt. His arm is of Brockway make, with an octagonal barrel, and comes just within the 15 lbs. standard 28 in. barrel. It has a caliber of 39, with an even twist of 1 turn in 16 inches, 8 grooves. The bullet is of Brockway make, forced out cold under a 40-ton pressure into long rods, then cut off in lengths and again swaged to shape. They have a uniform composition of 1 tin to 20 lead. The powder which Mr. Cressy uses is Hazard FFg. A bullet picked up from his box weighed 338½ grains, while a powder charge weighed 84½ grains. He uses a greased paper patch laid in two pieces across the gun muzzle. Like the majority of the other weapons, his arm is slightly choke bored, a point upon which some of the marksmen lay a great deal of stress. His method of attaching the weapon to the rest is very simple. The crosspiece attached to the barrel has in it a V-shaped notch (in front), and this goes to a screw fastened in the rest top. In the rear there are the usual thumbscrews, one below lifting the rear of the piece, and one on either side giving the brass notched piece in which the barrel rests a lateral motion.

Next to Mr. Cressy sits D.A. Brown, of Boston. He has a round barrel arm made by Warner, of Syracuse. It falls within the 15 lbs. standard, has a uniform twist of rifling with one turn in 20 in., 8 grooves, of 45 caliber. The barrel is 30 in. long, and is slightly larger at the muzzle than the breech, the purpose of this disposition of weight of metal being to stiffen this outer end of the barrel and prevent in a measure the springing of the barrel. Mr. Brown uses a Warner made bullet with a hard point built up of a 1 to 1 antimony and tin composition, while the rear end of the bullet is of pure lead. The two parts are closely swaged together and the taking of the rifling by the pure lead heel is the point aimed at in this composite missile. He uses powder of the Dead Shot brand, American Powder Company make. The bullet, weighed by your correspondent, as all the other powder and bullet weights in this report were taken, showed a weight of 671 grains, while a single powder charge showed 142½ grains. In loading, Mr. Brown uses a linen shellacked and then greased, two narrow strips laid crossways of the muzzle in order that the 8 grooves might be taken uniformly. His shooting stand resembles exactly a miniature gun carriage. There are two long ways on either side on which the cross head forward rests and slides, while at the rear there are two side and bottom screws. Mr. Brown is deliberation and good nature itself. His every motion is cyphered down to a system, and it is almost amusing to see him pour the powder in and then with moistened rod at once look for it. Yet in this way he avoids that constant menace of the absent-minded muzzle marksman, a bullet in the barrel and no powder behind it.

Next in line came Farrow—W. Milton Farrow, known on every rifle range from California to Constantinople. He is now a Brattleboro resident, making rifles, and it was one of his own make that he was shooting. He had secured a rest and had elbowed his way in among the old timers. His weapon was the pigmy one of the meeting. It weighed complete but 9 lbs., had a 34 in. barrel of 32-cal. and had 7 grooves of 1 turn in 16 in. The rifling was peculiar with a ratchet cut and one on which Mr. Farrow pinned his faith. The powder charge—American Co. FF. make—weighed 45 grs. and the bullet 163½ grs. The last was a 1 to 20 composition, hot drawn. In loading, Mr. Farrow, after carefully cleaning, inserted the patched bullet, and after pushing it home with a gauged wooden rod, from the rear inserted the freshly loaded cartridge shell behind it. Mr. Farrow had all the advantages of the dead rest, the long sight and the sliding when the recoil came. He had clamped a crosspiece to his barrel near the muzzle and this enabled him to use the wooden rest he had secured.

[Farrow was probably the best rifleman of his long day—about 1878 to 1898. Not only did he win numerous matches in the U.S., he went to Europe where he literally beat everybody. He won top awards in military style shooting, as well as in offhand or schuetzen shooting. See his own book, *How I Became a Crack Shot,*

and Roberts and Waters' book, *The Breech-Loading Single-Shot Match Rifle* for details of his life and feats.]

Mr. L. Park, of Greenfield, Mass., was next in the line of closely-crowded shooters. He was the funny fellow of the company and sandwiched his shots with rallies of wit. He had come up to have a good time, and his advice to those about him on shooting topics would have filled a manual on the subject. He strongly urged a member who had missed the foot-square target to take the rifle down and introduce the weapon to the target, while his sly jokes at the men who knew it all were often keen and to the point. He had an octagonal 15 lbs. barrel, 38-cal., 1 to 16 even twist, 8 grooves. The bullets were of uniform composition, 1 tin to 20 lead, and the powder used was Hazard's FFg. The barrel was 30 in. long, and was made by Brockway. A charge taken showed 82½ grains of powder to 356 grains of lead. In loading he used paper patches; while on the rest a very complete brass cast rear device for elevating and swinging the rifle butt. The big, booming piece did not look out of place in Mr. Park's big, brawny clutch. He handled it like a toy pistol, but a puny National Guardsman would have found it a stiff burden.

Mr. F. Fenn is one of the younger members of the club. He resides at Dover Plains, N.Y., but generally manages to get up and enjoy the shoots. He uses a gun made by Phillips, of New York, and in this meeting was in very bad luck, owing, he thought to the use of some special cartridge he had made. These were of the composite type with a hard point made by putting 2 ounces of antimony in a pound of lead, while the bullet heels were of pure lead. The weapon was of 45-caliber, having 8 grooves of gain-twist rifling starting in at one turn in 72 inches and finishing with one turn in 24 inches. The barrel was 27 inches long, of octagonal form, and into it he poured Hazard's FFg powder. One charge weighed showed 128 grains, while one of the bullets turned the scale at 572 grains. A stout wooden block (plank) held the gun while the entire block was moved on its bed from (the) center pin forward by the three rear screws. It was a simple, strong, though somewhat clumsy device. A paper patch was used in loading.

[Edwin Phillips of New York City was a riflemaker of the highest attainments as well as a fine shooter. Little is known of his life or his rifles, but at least one beautiful rifle by Phillips may be seen in detail in *George Schoyen — Riflemaker Extraordinary,* by John Dutcher in this 25th GUN DIGEST. Phillips is listed in Swinney's *New York State Gunmakers* and in *American Gun Makers,* but only just.]

Mr. E.B. Stephenson followed along the line with his big muzzle-loader. It shook a small section of the State when it went off. It was a 50-caliber weapon with a 30 in. 15 lbs. octagonal barrel made by Ferris. There were 9 grooves,

necessitating in loading three paper patch slips. The rifling grooves were concentric with the bore of the barrel and had a gain twist increasing from 1 in 72 to 1 in 24 in. The bullet was worthy of special attention. It was of the composite order, with a soft heel, a soft point and a hard inner section, this gave that close grip on the rifling when the upsetting came which was particularly striven for in this make of bullet. A paper patch was used and Hazard's FFg powder. A charge taken and weighed showed 603 grains of lead and 118½ of powder. The rest device was the simplest in the house. Two bent strips on either side forward preventing any jumping up of the muzzle, while aft the barrel rested on a broad tongue, the upturned edges of which afforded place for the screws used in side adjustments.

Veteran L.C. Smith was next in the line, a patriarch among patriarchs, he knows the history of the club since its formation. He was a charter member and has never missed a meeting. He is yet full of shoot and is always deep in some experiment to settle some point in the science of rifle shooting. The consequence is that as a prize winner his name does not appear as often as it otherwise would. His gun has a 28-inch octagon barrel. To name its maker would be difficult, since it has been cut and re-cut so frequently. It is of 46-cal. with a uniform twist of 1 in 18. The bullet is of similar make to that used by Mr. Brown, and comes from the works of Warner, at Syracuse. Behind it he puts Fg powder of Hazard make. A sample charge weighed 113 grains in powder and 649 grains in bullet. He uses a cut paper patch, made in the form of a Greek cross, so that the paper is not doubled below the heel of the bullet. His rest in shooting is a very complete one with a pair of guiding ways forward, while the shifting of the trigger end is done with great throttle valve wheels. This, as many of the other guns, has the double nipple. In place of using the ordinary percussion cap, a flat primer is placed over the nipple paper (proper?), and over it a false nipple with a striking pin is screwed. This pin when struck by the falling hammer starts the primer and the charge is ignited without any loss of powder or spitting from the touch-hole.

D.S. Cox, of Neperan, Westchester Co., N.Y., has a 38-cal. gun having a 28 in. octagonal barrel, with 8 grooves and a steady twist of 1 in 16. His bullet is 1 to 20 uniform composition, and the powder FFg Hazard. The loss of one hand puts him to some disadvantage but not to any material extent, and he is always ready on time for his shot in the string. He uses stout parchment paper patch cut very narrow. His rest has a narrow iron guiding way forward, while a brass resting block, near the breech, enables quick adjustment to be made, as the cross hair lines of the telescope demand. A sample load showed 305½ grains of lead and 69 grains of powder.

Norman S. Brockway has the solemnity

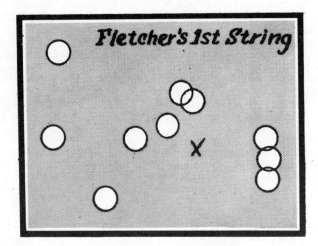

Fletcher's 1st String

of an owl, and carries about with him the responsibilities of the whole match. He is a rifle maker at Bellows Falls, and knows all about this style of rifle. He is the secretary of the club, and seems to have a life lease on the position. He goes to work in his methodical way, not only in his official labor, but in his shooting as well. He uses one of his own make of rifles, an octagonal barrel, 28 in. long, 42-cal., with 8 grooves twisting evenly 1 in 16 inches, and the powder used is Hazard's FFg, and the patch strips are of the usual parchment paper sort. A V on the rifle cross head pushed home close on the screw projecting from the rest bed, and the rifle is ready for shooting, guided by the stout compact directing rest at the rear. One charge showed that the cold pressed bullet of 1 in 20 composition weighed 417 grains while the powder showed 99 grains.

C.F. Fletcher, of Bellows Falls, Vt., is another of the young men in the ranks. He uses a Brockway made gun and has a 38-cal. rifle with a 28 inch octagon barrel. There are six grooves of 1 in 16 twist, and the bullet is of the cold pressed type and of 1 in 20 composition. The powder is of Hazard FFg make, a charge taken weighed 339½ grains of lead with 82½ grains of powder. He uses a paper cross patch, and in loading is most careful in every movement, being specially careful about the cleaning out of the rifle before inserting a fresh charge of powder. His rest is of a simple sort, a V notch forward and a block with three screws aft completing the fixtures.

Wm. V. Lowe is a Fitchburg, Mass., citizen, and comes up to the match with what he styles a mongrel gun, that is

several makers and remakers have tried to make it better and with varying success. It has a 28-inch octagon barrel, 45-caliber with uniform-twist rifling 1 turn in 20 inches and 8 grooves. He uses a combination bullet, lead butt and hard joint, and employs Fg Hazard powder, one charge taken and weighed showed 108 grains of powder to 585½ of lead. His patch is a thin parchment paper one cut in Greek cross fashion and with an abundance of grease. His rest had a double base, the upper one on which the rifle was placed being movable at the rear and so admitting a vertical and lateral adjustment.

Outside of the shooting house the breechloader visitors from Boston were accommodated. A rest was improvised by driving two stakes in the ground, placing a cross head and then a long plank with a notched block at the end enabled the Bostonians to sit comfortably on chairs and draw their rifles carefully and exactly.

Mr. Hinman used a 35-cal. Maynard and into this he put the patched bullet and the freshly loaded shell, charged with Laflin and Rand musket powder; a sample charge of powder weighed 61½ grains, while the bullet of 1 to 20 composition weighed 258 grains.

F.J. Rabbeth had a Remington-Hepburn rifle of 38 cal. It had a round barrel and aperture front sight, as did the arms of his associates—Messrs. Hinman, Frye and Ellsworth. He had the regular 330-gr. Remington patched bullet, as shown, of 1 to 20 composition. It was loaded with Laflin and Rand powder. A sample charge showed, powder 67½ grs.; bullet 330 grs.

Mr. Frye used a Ballard 38-cal. rifle of the ordinary make. His patched bullets were the 330-gr. Remington make and the powder, Hazard's FFg, a sample charge weighing 55½ grs. in powder and 330 grs. in lead.

Mr. Ellsworth, jolly and fat, capital at off-hand work, as his Manchester score of the week preceding showed, not so good at the strange rests provided, was provided with a 30 in. long barrel Ballard of 38-cal. loaded with a homemade bullet of 1 to 30 composition. The rifle was in all respects like that of Mr. Frye, with the full Rigby barrel. The powder used was Oriental Fg and a pattern charge showed 48 grs. of powder to 293 grs. of lead.

The plan of shooting is a very simple one: On the morning of the first day each man devotes his time to fixing up his shooting stand. There is a small trunk full of tools—oil bottle, rags, ammunition and knick-knacks of every kind—to be unpacked; then the gun itself and the telescope and the rest fixture, all are unpacked, and the various parts put in place. This is no small job. Each man takes a cardboard about a foot square, tacks it upon the low fence against which the shooting is done, and then the small black patch or "budd" is banged away at until the marksman has everything down fine. He watches the flags, makes

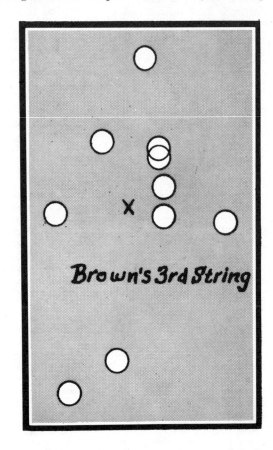

Brown's 3rd String

due allowance for wind, finally determines just where the aiming budd is to be placed in order to get the shots aimed about the spot where the lines drawn from opposite angles of the piece of cardboard cross in the center. So it may happen that each of a dozen men may be aiming at a dozen different points and all striving to get their shots bunched at the same point. When each man has got his piece in good working order there is a pause for luncheon, and then comes the counting string. It is shot on a time limit; that is, a timekeeper with watch in hand waits until all are loaded and then the call of "Time" is made. Five minutes elapse, and in that period of time the shot must be fired. Each rifle is in place with hammer raised; "click," and the hair triggers are set. Then in silence each waits for those flags to be a trifle less frisky; for that fishtail wind to swing about to the other side of the center before touching off. Each is, in fact, waiting for that precise wind which prevailed when he fired his last trial shot, the record of which he knew and was satisfied with. Often in a temporary lull the line of rifles will go off in a volley. While again, some unlucky one who waited for a better chance is compelled, when he hears the voice of the timer call out "Four and three-quarters," to shoot in whatever wind may be blowing at the time. As the rifle recoils, the right hand is ready to check it; but from first to last there is no sighting beyond a glance through the telescope to see that the cross hairs have not been directed to another point.

[At this period metallic sights and telescopes lacked the precision adjustments common enough today, and "clicking over" to counteract a wind change couldn't be done. It appears to have been a better system to allow for a certain wind velocity and direction, placing the aiming budd as indicated. ● In the style of shooting described in the last paragraph above, the shooter sat facing the long axis of the rifle. He squeezed or pinched the rear of the trigger guard and the trigger between his left thumb and forefinger.]

For loading another five minutes is allowed, and there is need of it. First the muzzle end of the barrel is wiped off, then the false muzzle is carefully fixed and linked down; then comes the pumping and the cleaning. One after another the patches are adjusted to the wiping rod and passed down. There are patches wet with saliva and others saturated with oil. Finally come the cleaner bits of rag, and then perhaps another final patch, fixed just right. Each man has his own style of swabbing out, and the expression of serious concern on the faces of some as they keep their eyes on the rafters as the stick goes up and down almost suggests that a silent prayer goes up as the stick goes down. The barrel clean, the loading is in order. The powder is poured from the flask with just such a tap and no other to the measuring tubes. Then down the funnel at the barrel mouth, and if the shooter be particularly careful he carries his method to the point of sending a stick down to see that the powder is really there, and the light stick resting on the granules gives them just the proper amount of packing. Then the patch, in some of the false muzzles, is inserted in side slits until they cross directly over the bore; or perhaps if the patch is already cut out, it is placed in

FIRST STRING

	1	2	3	4	5	6	7	8	9	10		Total
Fletcher	1 3/16	3/4	1 11/16	1 7/8	7/16	5/8	9/16	3/4	3/4	13/16		=9 7/16
Rabbeth	4	3 1/4	1 11/16	1 5/8	2 1/2	13/16	15/16	13/16	1 7/8	5/8	=18 1/8	=12 5/16
Brown	1 3/16	1/2	7/8	2	2 5/16	1/2	1/4	2 11/16	2 1/2	1/2		=13 5/16
Lowe	7/8	7/8	2 13/16	1 1/2	2 13/16	7/8	3/8	5/8	1 7/8	1 1/16		=13 11/16
Cox	2 1/2	2 3/8	1 1/8	1 7/16	2 5/8	1 1/16	1	1/8	7/8	1 11/16		=14 1/4
Brockway	3 1/2	1 15/16	1 1/4	1 13/16	1 13/16	1 11/16	3/16	1/2	1 3/4	2 3/8		=15 3/16
Hinman	2 1/8	2 5/16	1 13/16	2 5/8	4 1/8	2 3/8	2 1/8	1 1/4	1 5/16	4 1/4	=24 5/16	=16 15/16
Park	2 15/16	1 15/16	1 15/16	1 7/16	1 7/16	15/16	3/16	1 1/16	1 1/16	3 3/4		=17 1/16
Farrow	2 3/8	2 3/8	2 7/8	3 11/16	1 7/8	2 11/16	3 3/16	2 1/16	2 3/8	1 9/16	=25 1/16	=19 5/16
Ellsworth	2 3/4	3 5/8	1 3/8	2 3/4	5 3/16	1 1/8	3 7/16	4 1/2	3 1/4	4	=23	=22 15/16
Stephenson	6	4 7/8	3 1/8	1	1	1 5/8	2 13/16	1 3/4	2 5/8	3		=25 3/16

SECOND STRING

	1	2	3	4	5	6	7	8	9	10		Total
Hinman	2	3/4	2 9/16	1 5/16	1 9/16	3/4	1 1/2	3	1 7/16	1 13/16	=16 5/8	=10 1/2
Rabbeth	9/16	13/16	2 9/16	1 13/16	2 3/16	1 1/2	9/16	3 1/16	1 1/2	3 11/16	=17 7/8	=11 5/16
Park	3 1/16	7/8	15/16	9/16	3/8	1 5/8	2 1/4	11/16	11/16	15/16		=12 3/8
Brown	15/16	1 7/8	1 3/4	1 3/4	1 1/4	1/2	3/8	1/4	1 13/16	1 5/8		=12 1/2
Smith	1 7/8	2 1/16	15/16	1 3/8	1 1/2	1 13/16	2 5/8	1 11/16	3/4	1 1/2		=16 1/8
Fletcher	3/4	9/16	2 3/4	11/16	3	1 13/16	2 3/8	1 11/16	1 1/4	2 7/16		=16 11/16
Brockway	1 9/16	5/16	2 7/16	4	15/16	5/16	1 11/16	1 5/8	1 13/16	3 3/4		=17 7/16
Frye	2 1/4	3 1/2	1 3/16	2 1/8	1 7/8	2	2 1/8	3 5/8	4 1/4	3 1/2	=26 11/16	=18 1/8
Stephenson	5 11/16	3 3/8	2 3/8	2	1 1/8	3/8	15/16	13/16	1	2 1/8		=19 13/16
Ellsworth	3	1 1/8	1 1/8	3 7/16	2 1/16	2 1/8	3 3/8	4 15/16	4 3/8	3 1/16		=21 1/16
Lowe	1 1/4	2 7/8	4 9/16	3 5/16	2 1/16	3/8	15/16	1 5/8	3	3 1/4		=23 1/4
Cox	4 3/16	4 1/4	4 5/16	3 1/4	4 3/4	2	3 3/4	1 9/16	7/16	1/4		=28 3/4

THIRD STRING

	1	2	3	4	5	6	7	8	9	10		Total
Brown	2	1 9/16	1 1/16	3/8	3/8	11/16	11/16	1 9/16	3/4	3/4		=9 13/16
Fletcher	2 3/4	1 1/2	9/16	15/16	1	1 5/16	1 1/4	7/16	2 3/16	2 1/8		=14 1/16
Lowe	1 1/16	1 7/8	3/4	13/16	3/8	1/4	2 15/16	3 1/4	1 5/8	1 9/16		=14 1/4
Frye	2 15/16	2 1/16	3 3/8	2 11/16	2 5/8	3/16	1 11/16	1 7/16	1 13/16	4 1/8	=22 5/16	=15 1/8
Brockway	2	1 3/8	1 15/16	1 13/16	2 1/8	7/8	3/4	3/8	2 7/8			=16 1/4
Rabbeth	3 1/4	1 5/8	3 1/16	4 1/16	2 9/16	7/8	1 15/16	2 1/2	2 1/4	2	=24 1/8	=16 5/8
Park	2 7/8	1 3/8	3 1/2	5/8	3/4	2 1/16	1 7/16	7/16	1 1/16	2 9/16		=16 11/16
Hinman	3 1/4	3 5/16	1 7/8	2 5/8	1 7/16	2 3/4	1 13/16	2 1/4	2	3 1/8	=24 5/16	=16 3/4
Cressy	1 13/16	2 1/4	2 9/16	1 13/16	7/16	2 1/8	1 1/2	1/2	1 1/2	2 1/16		=18 3/16
Ellsworth	1 3/16	1	2	1 3/8	4 5/16	5 9/16	2 1/8	1 5/16	4 3/16	3 1/8	=26 3/16	=18 5/16
Smith	1 11/16	5 1/4	2 3/4	1 1/2	1	1 1/2	2 1/2	2 1/16	1 3/4	1 5/8		=21 5/8
Stephenson	7/8	1 1/2	1 9/16	4 11/16	7/16	3	2 1/4	5/8	7/8	6		=21 13/16
Farrow	2 1/16	3/4	5 3/4	3 15/16	1 3/8	6 1/4	9/16	1 13/16	4 1/4	2	=28 3/4	=22 7/8
Cox	3 1/4	3 11/16	3 3/16	2	2 3/4	4 1/16	1 1/2	1 7/8	2 1/16	1 11/16		=26 1/4

a depression cut across the top of the false muzzle. Now the bullet just given a turn in the greasy finger or perhaps wiped carefully with a oily rag and then placed upon the patch. The ball starter now comes in and assists in pressing the bullet well down into the barrel, a collar fitting over the barrel end, a piston in it whose hollow end just fits over the bullet point, and with several sharp blows from the lump of leather-bound lead at hand, the bullet, patched with exactitude, is pushed down out of sight. Then the rod comes in again, and down the bullet is propelled, now very easily, until it rests with a fixed pressure upon the top of the powder. The capping is another operation, and with gun on rest the wrench comes in, the false nipple is unscrewed, the old cap picked off with point of penknife, and when a new primer has been inserted and the nipple rescrewed, the piece is ready for the timer's call for the second shot.

Meantime a lad has patched each bullet-hole with a narrow strip of paper, a second shot comes, it may cut the patch, if so there is no dispute as might very readily arise when such close shooting is done. So on through the series of the shots consuming an hour and a half perhaps, for each man, when time is called, looks and waits for the wind to suit him, and the loading is a matter not to be slurred over by any means.

The question of a proper allowance to be made the smaller rifles was the first one considered after the Bostonians had unlimbered and prepared for work. "Make your own proposition and we will agree to it," was the generous proffer of the home guard of muzzle shooters. So the visitors thought that ten per cent for telescopic sights should be allowed, then an additional ten per cent for the fixed rest and finally three inches off the string for the difference in the weight of weapons. Under these conditions of difference the men shot, and the complete scores of the several strings will show how the handicap worked.

The first string was shot on the afternoon of the 26th. The weather was chilly, far past the point of comfort, while a wind flickering and shifting in fishtail fashion from about 12 o'clock point, made the shooting very "onsartin" indeed. The breech men soon found out where the advantages of the rest system was, for where they with eye down to peep sight were unable to catch any fluctuations of the wind, and often pulled trigger just as the gust followed the lull, the muzzle shooters sat with eyes wide open watching the streamer, and when the right second came a slight pressure of the finger on the hair trigger and off the piece of ordnance went. It will be seen that the light guns held their own, and Rabbeth, quick to catch the conditions of the difficult new range, had won a place among the three prize winners at the head of the column. Fletcher made a very creditable target indeed, especially under the conditions. The shooting over, there was a general pilgrimage to the tar-

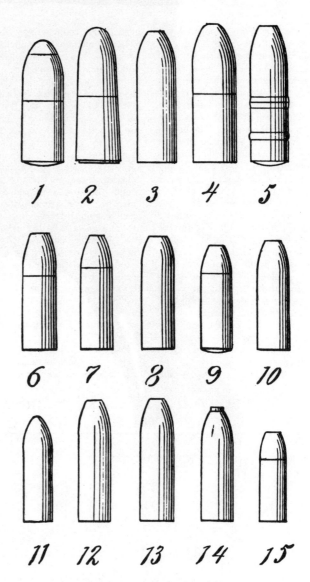

THE BULLETS—FULL SIZE

	Grains		Grains		Grains
1. Stephenson	603	6. Brockway	417	11. Hinman	258
2. Brown	671	7. Cressy	338½	12. Rabbeth	330
3. Lowe	585½	8. Park	356	13. Frye	330
4. Smith	649	9. Cox	305½	14. Ellsworth	293
5. Fenn	572	10. Fletcher	339½	15. Farrow	163½

gets, and as Secretary Brockway drew the tacks the probabilities of place were canvassed. On the back of each bit of pasteboard the shooter's name was written, so that when the scorer having thrust a pin into the exact center and having attached the measuring rod, did not know the marksmen as he read off the shots in inches, eights and sixteenths.

An evening spent in rifle chat, in talk of trajectories and deflection, of initial velocity and windage and all the other topics of interest to marksmen, and all hands retired to an early couch to sleep sound till early morn, then up for a double string. The wind had moderated in a great measure, and again the marksmen were at it bright and early to get windage before the tune was called on the first string. The breechmen had caught the bearing of things in better

shape, worked together with more harmony, and the counting up found two of them leading the score. This was somewhat of a surprise to the host club men, but they were satisfied that the score had been made in direct rivalry, and were more than pleased with the fact that the breechloaders could do so well. The target of honor in this match belongs to Mr. Hinman. It is unfortunate that the antiquated style of marking does not admit of numbering the shots, but such as the target is we present it, in full size, and remembering that it was shot at 220 yards, it is good work even from the sort of rest provided for the day.

With a sky threatening rain, there was no recess between the second and third strings of the meeting. The wind had died down some, and the strange rifle range sight was presented of men waiting for a bit more breeze to come up to waft them on the target. This was the position of those men who had sighted during the morning when the wind was fresher and could not afford to do any trial shooting in the midst of their string. There were at the finish of this string fewer men who carried off their targets rather than have their scores go upon the record. None of the breech men appear in the place of the winners, though Mr. Frye just falls without it. Mr. Farrow, who had not the 10 per cent for fixed rest deducted from his string, was not in good luck. He was busy at his perpetual experimenting, and was not in the best of form. The big Warner gun of Mr. Brown came to the front in good style, and a string of less than 10 inches was deserving of special credit when the rather tricky wind is considered. In addition to the 50, 30 and 20 per cent division to first second and third in each string there was a silver medal presented by Mr. L.C. Smith for the best aggregate string of the meeting. This went to Mr. Brown on a total of 35⅝ inches for 30 shots. Very close, even with the arm used.

The meeting, on the whole, had been a capital success; so thought the old National Rifle Club, for though it is old in years it is full of the true youthful sportsman's feeling; so thought the visitors, for they had been most kindly treated and carried away with them only the most pleasant recollections of the quiet little Vermont village just over the Massachusetts line. To our readers we present the whole story, with figures and picture. The targets are taken from the original cards. The scores are from the official record, while the weight of powder and lead where given are from the samples taken by your correspondent (and weighed by an expert in the Fairbanks Scale Co. on a Fairbanks scale.—Ed. F. and S.). There were regrets for absent ones; for Williamson, the club president, away at his home at Comack, L.I.; for Gardner of Scranton, Romer of Peekskill, Warner of Syracuse, Tyler and Col. Rice of Vermont, Wm. Wetmore of New Hampshire, D.C. Pearl of Meriden, Conn., and W.B. Farrington of Boston, while the standard conundrum was where Phillips, the gunmaker, had hidden himself in the Far West. The adieus were given, with an accompanying hope that the next meeting of the club would see a large delegation of the modern school of marksmen, those who think with your correspondent, that accuracy of the very highest degree may be secured without the accompanying discomfits of the heavy ordnance style of weapon. W.

Forest and Stream, June 3, 1886.

SUMMARY

	1st String	2nd String	3rd String	Total
Brown	13 5/16	12½	9 13/16	35⅝
Fletcher	9 7/16	16 11/16	14 1/16	40 3/16
Rabbeth	12 5/16	11 5/16	16⅝	40¼
Hinman	16 15/16	10½	16¼	44 3/16
Park	17 1/16	12⅜	16 11/16	46⅛
Brockway	15 3/16	17 7/16	16¼	48⅞
Lowe	13 11/16	23¼	14¼	51 3/16
Ellsworth	22 15/16	21 7/16	18 5/16	62 11/16
Stephenson	25 3/16	19 13/16	21 13/16	66 13/16
Cox	14¼	28¾	26¼	69¼
Frye	.....	18 11/16	15⅛	33 13/16
Smith	.....	16⅛	21⅝	37¾
Farrow	19 9/16	.....	22⅞	42 7/16
Cressy	.....	.....	18 3/16	18 3/16
Fenn	.....	.....	.....	.....

Bibliography

American Gun Makers, by Col. Arcadi Gluckman and L. D. Satterlee. The Stackpole Co., Harrisburg, Pa. 1953.

The Breech-Loading Single-Shot Match Rifle, by Major Ned Roberts and Ken Waters. D. Van Nostrand Co., Inc., Princeton, N.J. 1967.

How I Became A Crack Shot, by W. Milton Farrow, Newport, R.I. 1882.

The Modern American Pistol and Revolver, by A. C. Gould. Boston, 1888 (reprint of 2nd ed. Plantersville, So. Car. 1946).

Modern American Rifles, by A. C. Gould. Boston, 1982 (reprinted 1946, Plantersville, S.C.)

The Muzzle-Loading Cap Lock Rifle, by Ned H. Roberts. Manchester, N.H. 1944, and later eds.

New York State Gunmakers, A Partial Checklist, by Holman J. Swinney. Cooperstown, N.Y. 1951.

Detachable Aiming Points

by GUY LAUTARD

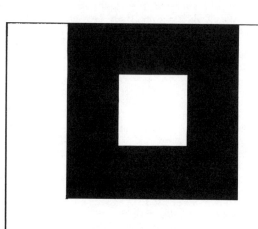

HAVE YOU EVER noticed how the crosshairs of a telescopic sight can disappear in the center of the standard bullseye target? Here is what I did to gain a better aiming point and, at the same time, a record-keeping system that is among the simplest.

From a piece of white cardboard I cut a 5″ square and drew in a border 1½″ wide on all four sides. Using black water colors I painted this border an intense, flat black. Several coats were needed to give the desired color. Drying between coats was expedited by placing the 5″ square on top of the shade of a wall-hung reading lamp, which took about 5 minutes. The result is a black square (5″x5″) with a 2″x2″ white square in the center.

A hole was punched along the middle of one side of the aiming point. In use, a plain white sheet of paper is tacked up on the target frame just as would be a normal target. The aiming point is hung from a nail in the target frame at the center of the top edge of the white sheet.

I have used this aiming point with a 22 Hornet and a Lyman 6x Wolverine scope at 100 yards, but it's usable, of course with any caliber. The rifle is sighted-in to put the point of impact 6″ low at this range. After firing a group, all pertinent information is written on the white sheet of paper hung up with the aiming point. The point of aim should be marked on this sheet through a small hole punched in the center of the little white square. This allows me to keep load data and the resulting group together for future reference. The aiming point never gets shot up and can be used indefinitely.

A larger aiming point might be desirable if using a scope of lower power and/or when longer ranges are the order of the day.

Don't forget that when you go out in the field with your rifle you'll have to zero it to place the point of impact several inches higher, but having done it once you can easily switch from one elevation setting to the other thereafter if you have noted the number of clicks involved. This will instruct you, I think, in the actual click values of your scope—not all of them respond as advertised! ●

COLT

SINGLE

Longitudinal section of
Colt's Army revolver, showing
the essential parts of the mechanism.

Ounce FOR OUNCE there probably has been more unadulterated baloney written, published, and otherwise disseminated about the Single Action Colt revolver than any other handgun ever manufactured. The reason for all this ballyhoo is simple: the old "thumb-buster" was — and still is — one of the finest handguns ever made. It's few disadvantages are often far outweighed by its pure romantic appeal alone.

The Single Action Colt, as we know it, is a development of the first Colt patent of 1836, and the lock mechanism of today's Single Action Colt is virtually identical to that of the Walker model Colt, first manufactured in 1847! The design of the Walker and Dragoon models was further refined in the 1851 Navy and 1860 Army models. The Single Action design, the first large-caliber revolver made by Colt for metallic cartridges, was the logical development from these earlier models.

The Rollin White patent of 1855, which covered bored-through cylinders to take metallic cartridges and which was held by Smith & Wesson, delayed the development of cartridge revolvers by other manufacturers until its expiration in 1869. During this period many systems for employing metallic cartridges and evasions of the White patent were marketed by other arms manufacturers. The Thuer and Richards conversions of the 1851 Navy and 1860 Army models were the Colt company's notable attempts

to adapt their revolvers for metallic cartridges yet not infringe the White patent.

It was not until 1872 that Colt could introduce their first large-caliber, conventional-cartridge revolver; this, the 44 rimfire revolver (popularly called the open-top Frontier), was a true transition model, not merely a conversion of an earlier percussion gun.

Single Action Introduction

The Single Action Army revolver, based on the Charles B. Richards patent of July 25, 1871, was introduced in 1873. Later William Mason patents in 1872 and 1875 covered minor improvements in the basic design. Originally designated as Model "P" at the Colt factory, following its adoption by the War Department, the first commercial designation of the new model was the "Peacemaker." It was marketed under this name in 45 Colt caliber by B. Kittredge & Company, the Colt agent in Cincinnati, Ohio and by other Colt dealers. It was not until some time later that the designation "Single Action Army" was applied.

In 1878 the Single Action Colt in 44-40 caliber was introduced as the "Frontier Six Shooter" and it was soon thereafter marketed in additional calibers. Between 1875 and 1880, about 1900 Single Action Colts in 44 rimfire Henry caliber were manufactured. These were serially numbered separately from other Sin-

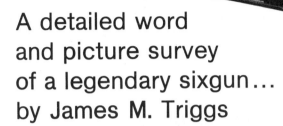

A detailed word
and picture survey
of a legendary sixgun...
by James M. Triggs

ACTIONS

gle Action models, including the Bisley.

The Single Action Colt was continually manufactured from 1873 until 1941. The highest recorded serial number is 357,859 — a production record for any single action revolver ever made, including percussion models. Following is a list of calibers in which the Single Action Army was made.

Rimfires —

22 Short, Long, Long Rifle	32
22 WRF	44

Centerfires —

32 Colt	41 Long Colt
32 S&W	44 German
32-20	44 Russian
32 44	44 S&W
38 Short Colt	44 S&W Spl.
38 Long Colt	44-40
38 S&W	45 Colt
38-44	45 ACP,
38 Spl.	450 Boxer
357 Mag.	450 Eley
380 Eley	455 Eley
38-40	476 Eley
41 Short Colt	

Single Action Variations

Many variations of the Single Action Colt have been made over the years, by both the factory and individual gunsmiths. Only the principal mechanical variations of importance to the shooter and collector will be discussed here.

As originally manufactured, the Single Action Colt was designed for black powder loads. After about number 165,000 (1896) the space for the cartridge head between the rear of the cylinder and the face of the recoil shield (headspace) of the frame was reduced to .060″ to prevent primers from backing out because of pressure. Improvement in heat treatment processes and the use of better steel resulted in greater frame strength capable of handling the increased pressures of smokeless powder loads. The original frames were made of wrought iron; about 1883 soft steel was adopted for this part. Modern cartridges should not be used in SA revolvers bearing serial numbers below 165,000.

In the earliest Single Actions, the base pin was secured by a screw which entered the front of the frame at an upward angle. The Mason patent for a tranverse, spring-loaded base pin latch, through the side of the frame, was included in the design at about serial number 150,000 (1893).

Several minor changes to the original Model P were made in the ensuing years. The original ejector rod head had been a disk-shaped button. This was changed to a curved knob which conformed more closely with the under-contour of the barrel and ejector tube. Also, the front sight blade was slightly enlarged, and a small change in rifling design was made at about serial number 273,000.

All the basic Single Action models are detailed in Fig. 2.

The initial acceptance of the Single Action Colt and its continued popularity, particularly on the fron-

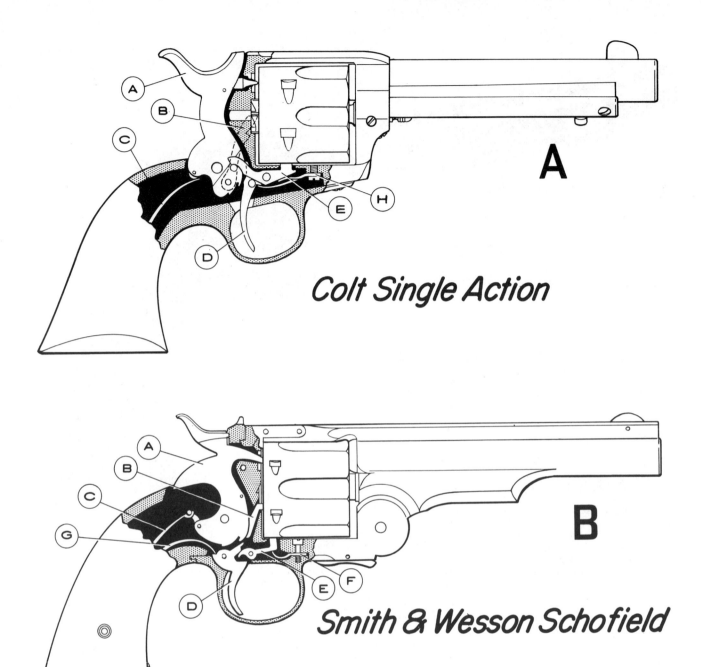

Colt Single Action

Smith & Wesson Schofield

tier, were probably results of its ruggedness, mechanical simplicity and dependability. A number of other single action, large-caliber cartridge revolvers were contemporary with the Colt, but none compared with it where these factors were considered. Smith & Wesson's American and Schofield models were break-top types and, while they offered faster reloading, their delicate lock and joint parts would not stand up to the kind of handling demanded. The Forehand & Wadsworth and Merwin & Hulbert revolvers also employed delicate or complicated mechanisms which were subject to malfunction or breakage in hard usage. The sturdy Remington 1875 single action revolver, which

closely followed the Colt design, was never made in sufficient quantities to displace the Colt. Shown herewith, for comparison, are cross-section drawings of the Colt, Smith & Wesson, and Remington revolvers (Figs. 1A, B, C, D), as well as the modern Ruger Blackhawk. Other illustrations show all of the basic Single Action Colt revolvers in a graphic form.

Production of the Single Action Colt was discontinued in 1941. After World War II, Colt closed for about nine months for reorganization and,

Fig. 1 — These cross-section drawings on this and the next page show the Single Action Colt, Smith & Wesson Schofield, Remington Model 1875, and the Ruger Blackhawk for comparison. All are drawn to the same scale. Note the similarity of the Remington and Colt designs and simplification by the use of coil springs in the modern Ruger. Note the comparative complexity

after reopening, announced that this model would no longer be manufactured. Many of the tools, jigs, and fixtures used to produce it, some purportedly dating back to Civil War time, had been placed in storage at some time during the war and could not be found afterwards.

In the late 1940s and early 1950s came a terrific resurgence of interest in the old single action handguns, due in large part to the popularity of Western television shows and the birth of quick-draw competitions. Colt

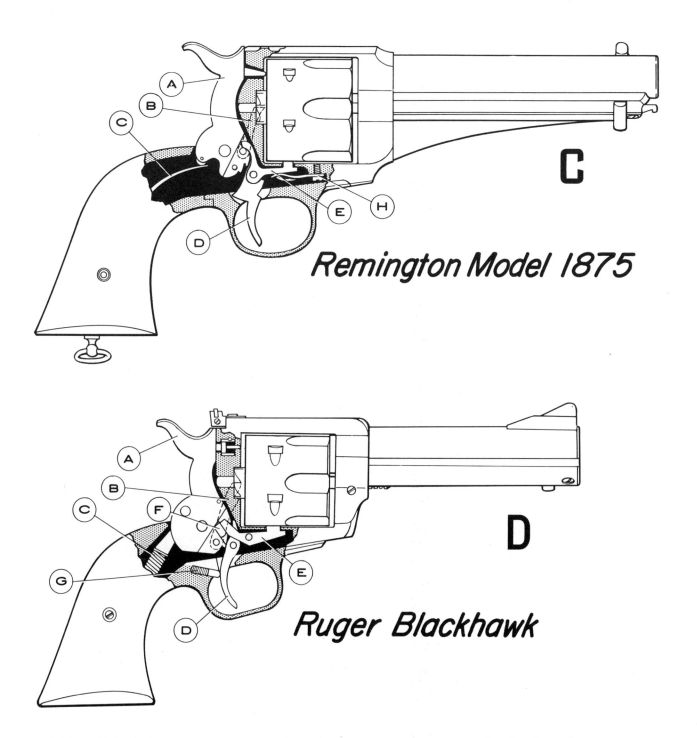

C

Remington Model 1875

D

Ruger Blackhawk

and delicacy of the Smith & Wesson as compared to the Single Action Colt.

Parts key: A, Hammer; B, Hand (cylinder pawl); C, Mainspring; D, Trigger; E, Cylinder locking bolt; F, Locking bolt spring; G, Trigger spring; H, Bolt & trigger spring (combined).

declined to put the Single Action Army back into production, but other manufacturers were busy.

The Great Western Gun Co. introduced about 1955 and sold for a few years a near-duplicate of the Model P. Differing only in using a frame-mounted floating firing pin, these Hy Hunter-made sixguns were of generally inferior quality, and the company did not prosper. Toward the end of the venture, Great Western gun kits were marketed, at a reduced price, but these were hard to as-

semble in a satisfacory, shootable manner.

It seems likely that the Sturm, Ruger Co.'s greater success was based on their famous Single-Six design. Though their first offering was an excellently designed 22 autoloader, it was not until they began producing a line of single actions that the company really flourished. The Single-Six was patterned after the original Colt Single Action, but incorporated some radical changes for the better, such as a one-piece grip/frame and modern

coil springs intsead of flat ones.

New-Old Colts

In late 1947 Colt decided to use the Single Action parts remaining in stock to assemble as many finished SA revolvers as possible. About 300 of these pre-war/post-war guns were produced. They were assigned numbers in serial number gaps in the *original* series.

Colt neither advertised these guns nor offered them for sale. It is a matter of speculation just what did happen to them, but apparently a number found their way into the hands of various persons, either as "gifts" or presentations from the company. It would be impossible to tell if any

Fig. 2 — Major Colt Single Action Army Models

Types	Frame	Barrel	Sights	Stocks	Finish	Calibers†		Barrel Lengths (ins.)
Standard Army	A	ST	M	E	J	45 Colt		Q — 2½ to 4
Standard Civilian	A	RST	M	EFGH	JL	45 Colt, 44-40, 38-40, 32-20, 41 Long Colt		R — 4¾
Short Bbl. Models	D	Q	M	EFGH	JL	45 Colt		T — 5½
Standard Target	BD	RST	NO	GHI	KL	38 Colt, 45 Colt, 22, 41 Long Colt, 450 Eley		S — 7½
Long Bbl. Models	ACD	V	MNO	EG	J	45 Colt		U — 12 (standard)
Standard Bisley	AD	QRST	M	FGI	JL	32-20, 38-40, 45 Colt, 44-40, 41 Long Colt		V — 8 to 16
Target Bisley	BD	RST	NO	FG	JKL	455 Eley, 32-20, 38-40, 45 Colt		W — 3 (standard)
Standard (1955)	A	RSTU	M	FG	JK	45 Colt, 38 Spl., 357, 44 Spl.		
Short Bbl. (1960)	D	W	M	F	J	45 Colt		
Target (1963)	B*	RSTU	P	F	J	45 Colt, 38 Spl., 357, 44 Spl.		

Frame Types
A — Standard
B — Target flat top (Fig. 6, No. 2)
B* — Target flat top (Fig. 6, No. 4)
C — Milled flat top (Fig. 6. No. 3)
D — Without ejector

Sights
M — Fixed square blade front, groove rear
N — Removable square blade front; notch rear, adj. in dovetail
O — Bead front, adj. leaf rear
P — Quick draw ramp front, micro., adj. rear

Finish
J — Casehardened frame, gate, & hammer, remainder blued
K — Over-all blue
L — Nickel or silver-plated

Stocks
E — 1-piece wood
F — 2-piece wood
G — 2-piece rubber
H — 2-piece rubber, oversize
I — 2-piece ivory or pearl

† Calibers are listed in the order of their popularity. Only the most common are given here; see the text for the others, such as the 32 rimfire, 32-44, 32 S&W, 380 Eley and 45 ACP. See **The Peacemaker and Its Rivals,** John E. Parsons (New York, 1950), for a detailed survey on this point.

Note: Throughout the life of the Model P many minor variations were available, usually on special order. These included slight differences in barrel lengths from catalog listings, non-standard combinations of finishes, etc. Also, since some changes were easy to make by owners, they are often seen now, such as different front sight blades in the target models.

given high-numbered Single Action were one of these 1947 models, since the workmanship and finish are identical to that of earlier revolvers. Accompanying documents which indicated a shipping date after 1947 might mean the gun had been one of these.

Because of increasing demand, Colt resumed manufacture of the Model P in 1955. Calibers were 45 Colt and 38 Special, with the 357 Magnum added in 1960 and the 44 Special in 1962, which was also the introduction date for the new flat-top Frontier. Barrel lengths were 4¾″, 5½″ and 7½″. A 12″ model in 45 caliber only was offered as the "Buntline Special," a concession to the television popularity of Wyatt Earp at that time! Regular stocks were checkered hard rubber, as on older models, but two-piece hardwood stocks were also available. In 1960, a version with a 3″ barrel was introduced as the Sheriff's Model, to be sold exclusively by one

American firearms dealer.

In 1962, a modernized version of the flat-top target models was introduced. Almost identical to the old target guns, the new Single Action has a quick-draw ramp front sight and micro adjustable rear sight.

A 125th Anniversary model was also introduced. It came in 45 caliber only with 7½″ barrel, over-all blue finish with the revolver highly polished. Two-piece hardwood grips with the Colt medallion were fitted. Trigger guard and backstrap were gold plated. This revolver was available with a fitted presentation case.

In 1960 Colt had introduced a smaller version of the Single Action design in 22 and 22 Magnum rimfire calibers. Called the Frontier Scout, this gun had a 4¾″ barrel. The trigger guard and backstrap were combined in one casting, similar to the Ruger single actions. Blued over-all or nickel-plated, the Frontier Scout has been offered in many fancy presenta-

tion models commemorating various events. While this little single action closely resembles the old Model P, it cannot be properly included as a Single Action Army model for the purpose of this discussion.

Single Action Mechanics

The design and interior mechanism of the Single Action Colt are simple and follow that of the earlier Colt percussion models. The one-piece frame encloses the cylinder, and the barrel is screwed into the frame. The cylinder and cylinder bushing revolve on a base pin, which runs through the frame lengthwise.

The basic lock mechanism of the Single Action design is shown in Fig. 4. As the hammer (A) is cocked, the hand (B), which is pivoted to the hammer at its lower end, rises through a slot in the frame and engages the ratchet teeth at the rear of the cylinder. The lower point of the hand engages one of the cylinder

Sam Colt, the boy, whittling out the first version of the handgun which was destined to be produced longer than any other model.

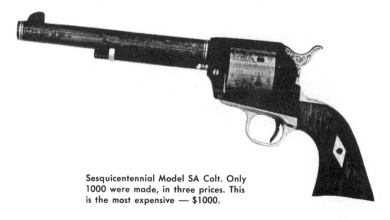

Sesquicentennial Model SA Colt. Only 1000 were made, in three prices. This is the most expensive — $1000.

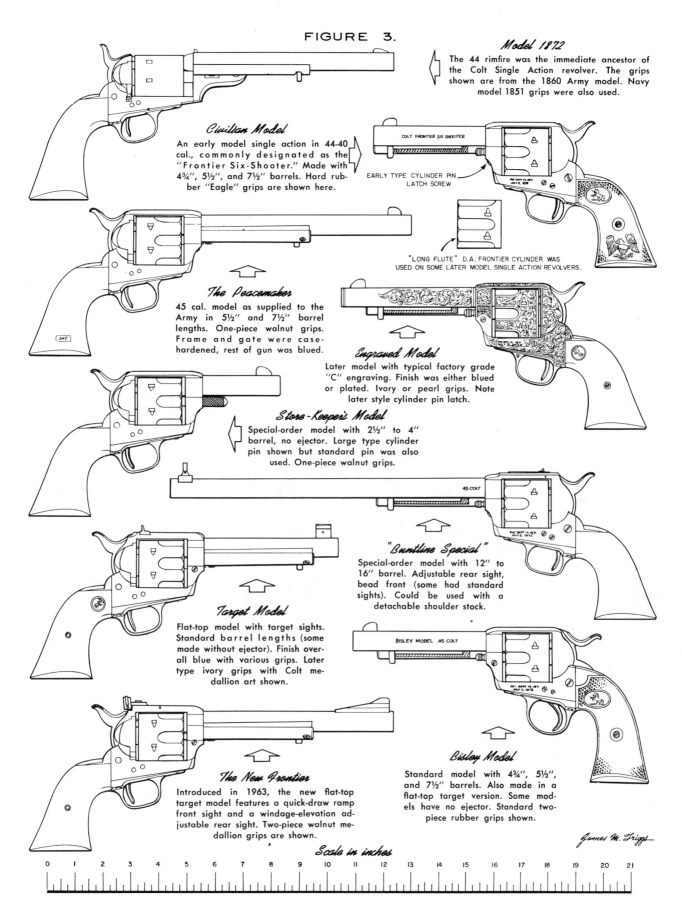

FIGURE 3.

Model 1872

The 44 rimfire was the immediate ancestor of the Colt Single Action revolver. The grips shown are from the 1860 Army model. Navy model 1851 grips were also used.

Civilian Model

An early model single action in 44-40 cal., commonly designated as the "Frontier Six-Shooter." Made with 4¾", 5½", and 7½" barrels. Hard rubber "Eagle" grips are shown here.

COLT FRONTIER SIX SHOOTER

EARLY TYPE CYLINDER PIN LATCH SCREW

"LONG FLUTE" D.A. FRONTIER CYLINDER WAS USED ON SOME LATER MODEL SINGLE ACTION REVOLVERS.

The Peacemaker

45 cal. model as supplied to the Army in 5½" and 7½" barrel lengths. One-piece walnut grips. Frame and gate were case-hardened, rest of gun was blued.

Engraved Model

Later model with typical factory grade "C" engraving. Finish was either blued or plated. Ivory or pearl grips. Note later style cylinder pin latch.

Store-Keeper's Model

Special-order model with 2½" to 4" barrel, no ejector. Large type cylinder pin shown but standard pin was also used. One-piece walnut grips.

45 COLT

"Buntline Special"

Special-order model with 12" to 16" barrel. Adjustable rear sight, bead front (some had standard sights). Could be used with a detachable shoulder stock.

Target Model

Flat-top model with target sights. Standard barrel lengths (some made without ejector). Finish overall blue with various grips. Later type ivory grips with Colt medallion art shown.

BISLEY MODEL .45 COLT

Bisley Model

Standard model with 4¾", 5½", and 7½" barrels. Also made in a flat-top target version. Some models have no ejector. Standard two-piece rubber grips shown.

The New Frontier

Introduced in 1963, the new flat-top target model features a quick-draw ramp front sight and a windage-elevation adjustable rear sight. Two-piece walnut medallion grips are shown.

James M. Triggs

Scale in inches

0 1 2 3 4 5 6 7 8 9 10 11 12 13 14 15 16 17 18 19 20 21

ratchet teeth just as the revolution of the cylinder has carried the preceeding tooth from the upper part of the hand.

The bolt (E) engages the stop notches in the cylinder to lock it in position for firing. As the hammer is cocked, a small hammer cam (AA), permanently staked into the lower right-hand side of the hammer, rises, pressing up the rear end of the bolt and pulling the head of the bolt down and out of the cylinder stop notch. When the revolution of the cylinder is about complete, the beveled lower surface of the hammer cam (AA) comes to the split rear end of the bolt, which slips off the cam, allowing the head of the bolt to snap back against the clyinder wall and slide into the stop notch as the cylinder completes the last few degrees of revolution. The bolt and trigger spring (F) acts both to press the bolt into the stop notch and to keep the trigger (D) forward with its sear end against the hammer.

Single Action Takedown

Figures 5, 6 and 7 show detailed exploded views of the various parts of the revolver. (See illustration captions for identification of parts.) Disassembly of the Single Action Colt is simple. The cylinder is removed by opening the loading gate and pressing in on the left-hand end of the base pin

catch, withdrawing the base pin toward the muzzle of the revolver. With the hammer in half-cock position, the cylinder can be dropped out of the frame. On older models, the base pin is removed by unscrewing the base pin screw from the front of the frame.

Remove the stock screw and stocks. On models with one-piece wood stocks, the backstrap must be removed first with the stock attached. Unscrew the backstrap screws and butt screw to remove backstrap. Remove the mainspring screw and mainspring from the rear leg of the trigger guard. Remove front and rear trigger guard screws and pull trigger guard off bottom of frame. Unscrew trigger and bolt spring screw and drop out the spring. Remove the trigger and bolt screws and drop out trigger and bolt. Remove hammer screw and remove hammer to rear of frame, drawing the attached hand and spring out of its slot in the frame. Hand can then be lifted out of hammer. Unscrew gate catch screw and drop gate catch and spring out bottom of frame. Draw gate out of frame toward front. Unscrew base pin latch screw from nut and draw out of frame with spring.

Remove ejector tube screw and lift front of ejector tube clear of stud in barrel. Pull entire ejector assembly out of frame to front. Ejector rod and spring can be drawn out of

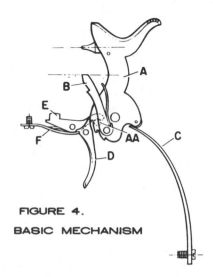

FIGURE 4.

BASIC MECHANISM

Fig. 4 — The basic lock mechanism of the Single Action Army revolver is shown here in profile. Parts key: A, Hammer; B, Hand (with hand spring); C, Mainspring; D, Trigger; E, Bolt; F, Cylinder and bolt spring; AA, Hammer/Bolt cam.

ejector tube to rear. Note that the ejector head is screwed tightly to the forward end of the ejector rod and care should be exercised in removing the head.

Reassembly of the revolver is accomplished in reverse order.

The basic stripping procedure has been outlined; however, there are several other steps for complete disassembly which necessitate some degree of skill and special tools. Removal of the barrel requires a suitable wooden clamp to hold the barrel in a vise and a metal block to fit around the front of the frame, for turning the frame off the barrel. Care should be taken to avoid damaging the ejector tube stud at the forward end of the barrel. The threads in this stud are not standard and they are difficult to repair if the stud is damaged. Initial turning of the barrel from the frame is often quite difficult because of the extremely tight fit.

Accurate fitting of a new barrel requires a metal lathe to turn the rear barrel shoulder so that the barrel can be seated tightly with the front sight properly aligned and ejector tube stud the correct distance from the front face of the frame. This is not a job for an amateur and would be best left to the professional gunsmith or to the factory. Likewise, the installation of a new cylinder often requires precise machine work. Both operations are beyond the scope of this article. If in doubt about replacing these parts, return the gun to the Colt factory where the work can be best accomplished.

The recoil plate set around the firing pin hole in the rear of the frame is a semi-permanent part. To remove it, a proper size punch must

Tuning the Single Action Colt

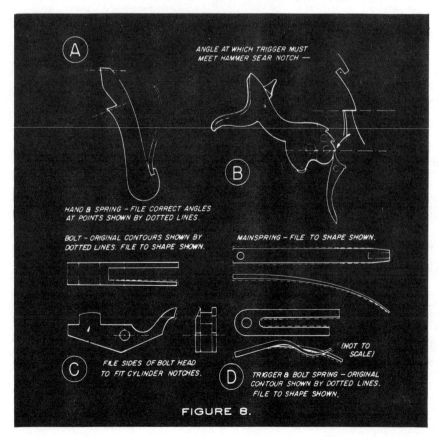

ANGLE AT WHICH TRIGGER MUST MEET HAMMER SEAR NOTCH —

HAND & SPRING – FILE CORRECT ANGLES AT POINTS SHOWN BY DOTTED LINES.

BOLT – ORIGINAL CONTOURS SHOWN BY DOTTED LINES. FILE TO SHAPE SHOWN.

MAINSPRING – FILE TO SHAPE SHOWN.

FILE SIDES OF BOLT HEAD TO FIT CYLINDER NOTCHES.

(NOT TO SCALE)

TRIGGER & BOLT SPRING – ORIGINAL CONTOUR SHOWN BY DOTTED LINES. FILE TO SHAPE SHOWN.

FIGURE 8.

be used to drive the plate out through the frame. The new or replacement recoil plate should then be seated in place and staked or punched into place. The factory uses a small, circular edge punch to do this job, but a small center punch can be used, securing the plate in the frame with a circular ring of punch marks. After punching, the front surface of the recoil plate and its surrounding frame area should be filed and polished smooth.

Tuning Up the Action

The Single Action is an excellent design, but its successful functioning depends in large part on the quality of the steel used in its manufacture and in the precision fitting of its working parts. Modern machine production methods have in large measure eliminated the careful hand fitting of years past and leave something to be desired so far as the shooter is concerned. Following are some things the home gunsmith can accomplish to slick up the action of this model on a do-it-yourself basis:

The Hand: The hand, or cylinder pawl, is pivoted to the lower end of the hammer. It is most often damaged or broken by hard cocking. Fanning the Single Action Colt — that is, driving the hammer back with the heel of one hand while the trigger is held back with the other, and allowing the hammer to fall at the end of its rearward travel — is the most frequent instance of hard cocking. The hammer should be stopped in its rearward motion by the slot in the backstrap, *not* by the gun's hand ramming again the clinder ratchet after the cylinder has been locked in its firing position by the bolt. A small amount of metal, carefully filed from the two faces of the hand as shown in Fig. 8 (A) will allow the hammer to stop against the backstrap if the hand is too long. Care should be taken not to remove too much metal — it's easy to correct a hand that is to long but impossible to fix one that's too short, unless you resort to welding on more metal.

Hammer and Trigger: Careless or hard cocking, such as "fanning" the Single Action, will also damage the trigger sear and the hammer notches. The only way to repair a cracked or broken hammer notch or sear is to weld on additional metal.

The angle at which the trigger nose or sear meets the full-cock notch of the hammer is critical. Most modern-made guns have a full-cock notch a little too deep for a real crisp trigger-pull. On the other hand, older guns will often have a notch and trigger nose which are badly worn, possibly dangerously. A trigger nose or sear which does not fit the hammer notch correctly will result in either a very hard trigger pull or, what's more dangerous, in having the trigger meet the hammer notch at an open angle which might allow the hammer

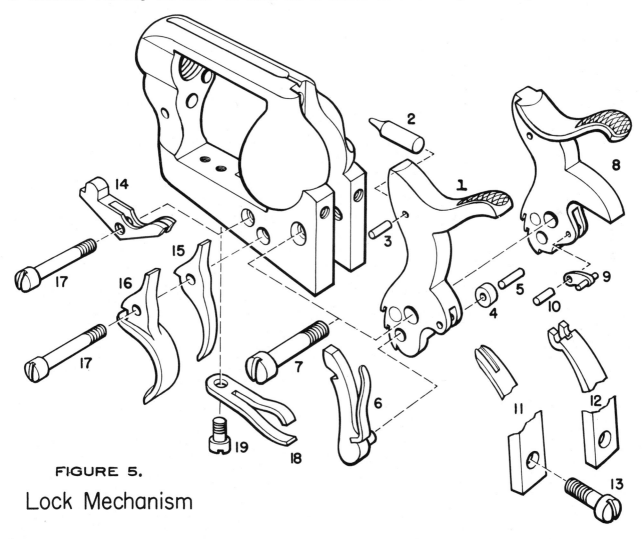

FIGURE 5.

Lock Mechanism

Parts List

1. Hammer, standard	5. Hammer roll pin	8. Hammer, Bisley model	14. Bolt
2. Firing pin	6. Hand (with spring)	9. Stirrup, Bisley model	15. Trigger, standard
3. Firing pin rivet	7. Hammer screw (Note: Elongated screw used on models designed for use with detachable shoulder stocks)	10. Stirrup pin, Bisley model	16. Trigger, Bisley model
4. Hammer roll		11. Mainspring, standard	17. Trigger & bolt screws (2)
		12. Mainspring, Bisley model	18. Trigger & bolt spring
		13. Mainspring screw	19. Trigger & bolt spring screw

FIGURE 6.
Mainframe Components

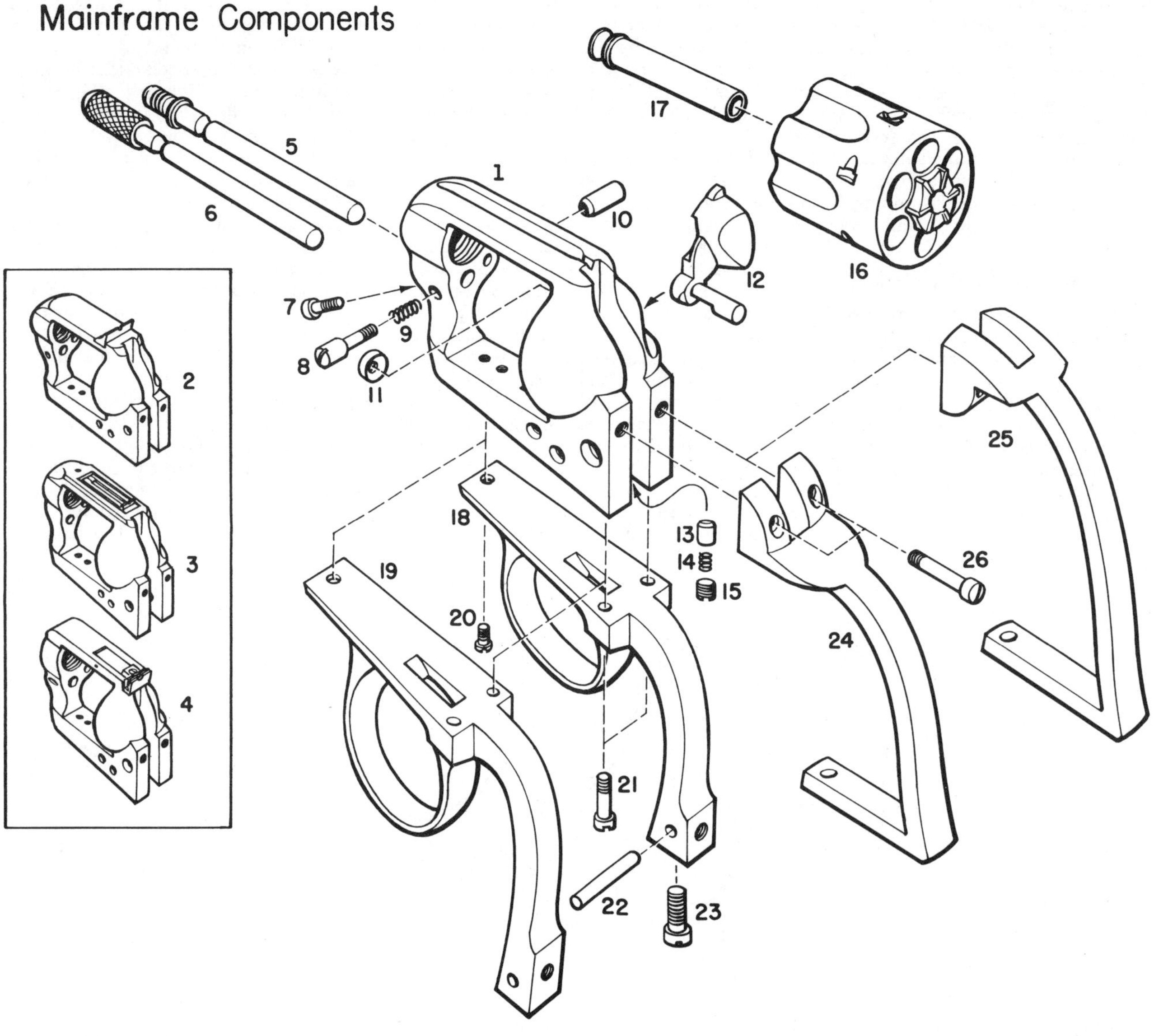

Parts List

1. Mainframe, standard
2. Mainframe, standard target with rear sight; flat top, Fig. 1B.
3. Mainframe, long barrel models; milled flat top, Fig. 1C.
4. Mainframe, 1963 target model, w. and e. adj.
5. Base pin, standard
6. Base pin, knurled
7. Base pin screw (older models, enters front of frame)
8. Base pin catch screw
9. Base pin catch spring
10. Base pin catch nut
11. Recoil plate
12. Gate
13. Gate catch
14. Gate catch spring
15. Gate catch screw
16. Cylinder, standard
17. Base pin bushing
18. Trigger guard, standard
19. Trigger guard, Bisley model
20. Front trigger guard screw
21. Rear trigger guard screws (2)
22. Stock pin (used on models with two-piece grips only)
23. Butt screw
24. Backstrap, standard
25. Backstrap, Bisley model
26. Backstrap screws (2)
Note: (Stocks are not shown. All two-piece stocks provided with inlet escutcheons and transverse grip screw.)

to slip off of the full-cock position. The correct angle for the trigger and hammer notch is shown in Fig. 8 (B). The trigger nose and hammer notch can be filed carefully to this angle, finished with fine emery paper and polished. It might be necessary to use a stone on the hammer, as it is casehardened. After fitting these parts, have the worked-on areas lightly casehardened by a good gunsmith.

The Bolt: Bolts on many older guns fit quite loosely in the cylinder locking notches and may not engage the hammer cam properly because of wear. Usually it is best to replace the bolt. Since new bolts are made somewhat oversize, careful fitting will be in order.

File the sides of the bolt head to fit into the cylinder notches properly. Note that the contour of the top of the bolt head must also be changed to an angle which will correspond with the cylinder notches. The height of the bolt head is adjusted by filing the lower part of the rear end of the bolt where it rests on the hammer cam. File a bevel on the left-hand rear tip of the bolt as shown in Fig. 8 (C) to allow it to slip over the hammer cam easily. This spring-like rear end of the bolt can also be thinned slightly for smoothness of bolt opera-

tion. Do not caseharden the bolt after finishing.

The Springs: The action of the revolver can be smoothed and lightened appreciably by carefully reshaping both the mainspring and bolt and trigger spring as shown in Fig. 8 (D). Do not attempt to grind the springs as this will remove the temper of the metal; rather, use a small stone and fine emery cloth. Although not critical, the hand spring can also be thinned slightly and polished to cut down on friction as it slides in its channel in the frame.

Tuning other single action revolvers of modern manufacture is basically

the same as that described above. With revolvers like the Ruger, the action can be smoothed a great deal by reducing the power of the coil springs employed. This is accomplished by clipping a turn or two off of the spring until it seems about right. Don't take off too much!

Customizing the SA Colt

While custom rifle makers, both amateur and professional, have been able to find many varied military and commercial long arms that lend themselves admirably to a number of conversions, handgun enthusiasts have found few such readily convertible arms — with the exception of the

Single Action Colt. Its bad points notwithstanding, the fact remains that no other model offers the handgun crank such a wide variety of possibilities for custom alteration as does the reliable old Colt.

The Single Action and Bisley model Colts have one of the strongest revolver frames ever made. This strength lies in the fact that a generous amount of steel has been used throughout. Such beefy construction, free from the weakening cutouts of many more modern revolvers with swing-out cylinders, provides an excellent foundation for a customized handgun. Furthermore, the quality of the metal makes it easy to anneal and to shape. The frame's thickness permits case hardening without risk of ruining it, which is not true of some more modern revolvers.

The Single Action and Bisley models are basically the same gun. Only the hammer, trigger, mainspring, backstrap, and trigger guard are not interchangeable between the two models. All that is necessary to convert the Bisley frame for use with conventional Single Action grips is to alter the height of the rear face of the frame slightly. Some typical conversions and custom alterations of both the Single Action and Bisley models are shown in Fig. 9.

Both the Single Action and Bisley models offer fine grips, and each lends itself well to changes according to the whim of the individual shoter. A close look at the Bisley reveals features which are much in demand today for target revolvers, such as the wide-spur hammer and wide trigger. These came "built-in"

Samuel Colt

on the Bisley with its introduction in 1895. Technical discussions aside, what other handgun offers these — as well as a built-in bottle opener? The Bisley hammer will do this job very well!

With the combination of a rugged frame and easily disassembled component parts, which make most conversions relatively simple, the desires of the shooter with respect to caliber can be indulged with almost limitless abandon. The Single Action Colt can be converted to virtually every handgun cartridge ever manufactured and can be used with some rifle cartridges as well, such as the 22 Hornet and 30 Carbine cartridges. These latter will necessitate the use of a specially made cylinder to accommodate the long cartridge cases.

New cylinders and barrels in the

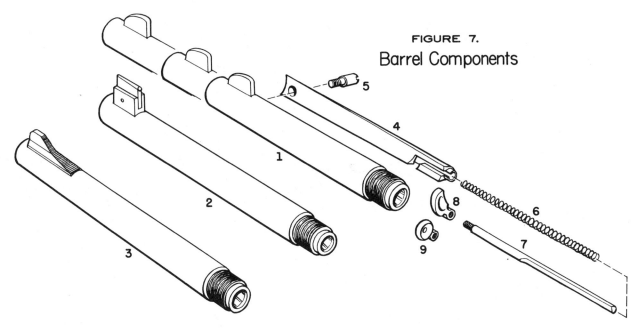

FIGURE 7.
Barrel Components

Parts List
1. Standard barrel, 4¾", 5½", 7½", fixed blade sight
2. Target barrel, bead sight
3. 1963 Model target barrel, quick draw ramp front sight
4. Ejector tube
5. Ejector tube screw
6. Ejector spring
7. Ejector rod
8. Ejector rod head (new style)
9. Ejector rod head (old style)

Note: (Ejector tube stud is factory-installed in barrel, hence is not listed as a separate component.)

233

three standard lengths (4¾", 5½", 7½") are available in a variety of calibers, either from the Colt company or from custom gunsmiths such as Christy and others. Many calibers not presently available can be easily made up by having a cylinder of smaller caliber rechambered to take the desired cartridge. Special or extra-long barrels in the desired caliber can be made up from a wide selection of rifle barrels available at reasonable prices from various arms dealers specializing in old or surplus parts.

Hard Hammer Fall

One of the complaints about the Single Action Colt is the hard hammer fall, which invariably jars even the best shooter slightly off target. The solution to this problem is to have a gunsmith shorten the hammer fall, but since this short action conversion is a tricky and expensive job at best, a good alternative is to "skeletonize" the hammer by drilling holes in it. This operation, combined with lightening the mainspring, as shown in Fig. 8 (D), will considerably lessen the jar of the hammer's fall. This kind of alteration would be considered a sacrilege by the serious collector but it does improve the action of the revolver.

The Single Action hammer can be

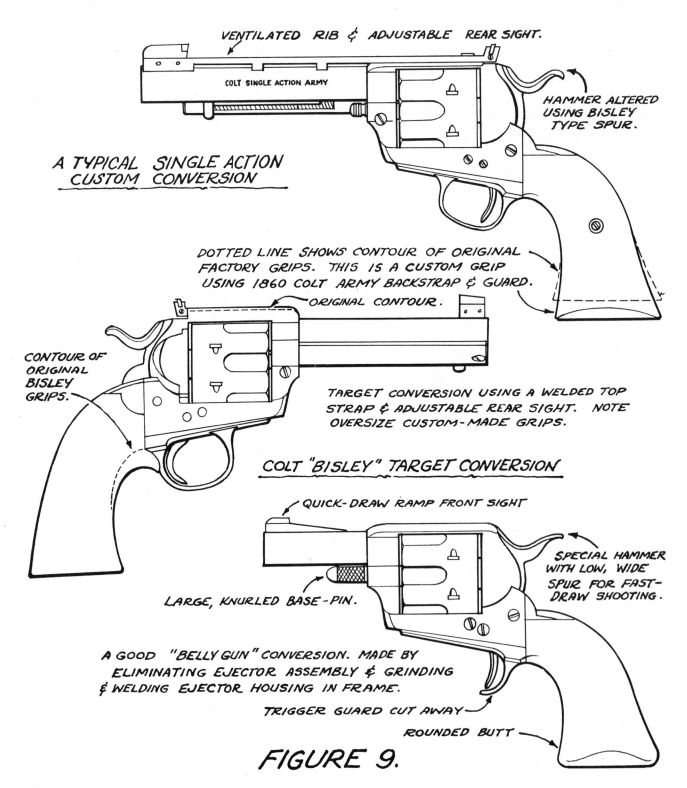

VENTILATED RIB & ADJUSTABLE REAR SIGHT.

COLT SINGLE ACTION ARMY

HAMMER ALTERED USING BISLEY TYPE SPUR.

A TYPICAL SINGLE ACTION CUSTOM CONVERSION

DOTTED LINE SHOWS CONTOUR OF ORIGINAL FACTORY GRIPS. THIS IS A CUSTOM GRIP USING 1860 COLT ARMY BACKSTRAP & GUARD.

ORIGINAL CONTOUR.

CONTOUR OF ORIGINAL BISLEY GRIPS.

TARGET CONVERSION USING A WELDED TOP STRAP & ADJUSTABLE REAR SIGHT. NOTE OVERSIZE CUSTOM-MADE GRIPS.

COLT "BISLEY" TARGET CONVERSION

QUICK-DRAW RAMP FRONT SIGHT

SPECIAL HAMMER WITH LOW, WIDE SPUR FOR FAST-DRAW SHOOTING.

LARGE, KNURLED BASE-PIN.

A GOOD "BELLY GUN" CONVERSION. MADE BY ELIMINATING EJECTOR ASSEMBLY & GRINDING & WELDING EJECTOR HOUSING IN FRAME.

TRIGGER GUARD CUT AWAY

ROUNDED BUTT

FIGURE 9.

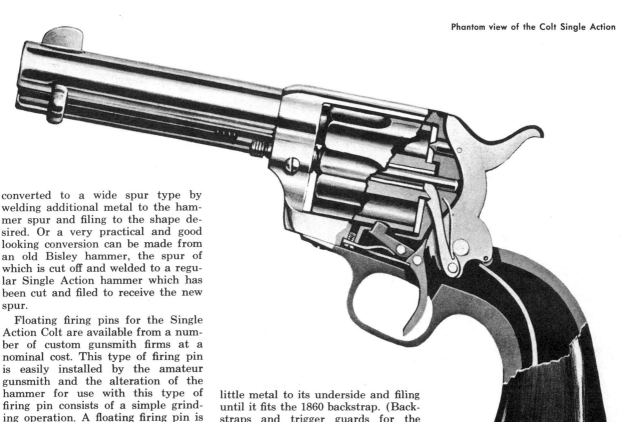

converted to a wide spur type by welding additional metal to the hammer spur and filing to the shape desired. Or a very practical and good looking conversion can be made from an old Bisley hammer, the spur of which is cut off and welded to a regular Single Action hammer which has been cut and filed to receive the new spur.

Floating firing pins for the Single Action Colt are available from a number of custom gunsmith firms at a nominal cost. This type of firing pin is easily installed by the amateur gunsmith and the alteration of the hammer for use with this type of firing pin consists of a simple grinding operation. A floating firing pin is definitely recommended for use with all rimfire cartridges as well as all high pressure loads.

The Single Action grips offer many possibilities for alteration to fit the hand of the individual shooter. One of the easiest and most practical changes, thought by many to be an improvement over the standard grips, is to install an 1860 Army model Colt trigger guard, backstrap, and grips. This results in a grip which is about ½" longer than standard and provides plenty room for the little finger. These man-size grips are especially desirable when shooting high powered cartridges. The 1860 Army trigger guard is made of brass and the regular iron Single Action trigger guard can be substituted for it by welding a

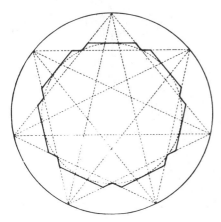

This form of rifling was the design of Alexander Henry, Scottish gunmaker. It is found in his rifles, also in Peabody-Martini rifles and was used in Colt Single Actions for a time.

little metal to its underside and filing until it fits the 1860 backstrap. (Backstraps and trigger guards for the models 1851 Navy, 1860 Army, and Single Action Colt are all interchangeable on the Single Action frame.)

These parts for the older percussion Colts are usually available from the many dealers in antique arms and parts. Since most of the original old parts are from unused arsenal stock, they are usually in excellent shape. In addition to these, many dealers are offering modern-made replacement parts for these older revolvers. If other changes in the shape of grips are desired, the trigger guards and backstraps are easily altered fy forging, or by welding on additional metal which can be filed to shape by hand.

In any conversion or custom job, after the gun has been fitted and polished, the frame, gate and hammer should be re-casehardened, especially when the gun is to be used with one of the more powerful cartridges. While it is possible for the home gunsmith to do this work, it is much better (and much easier) to send the frame back to the factory or to a competent heat-treating plant. They are better equipped to do the job, and incidentally, to bring out the desirable coloring associated with good casehardening. The small cost of having this work done by a professional does not justify the sweat and aggravation the amateur will undergo when he attempts to do it himself.

Exotic Alterations

For the shooter who is never quite satisfied with a run-of-the-mill conversion, there are countless changes that can be made in the old hogleg to put the gun into the "exotic" class.

Such a novel change would be the installation of an octagonal barrel, a stunt guaranteed to raise the eyebrows of even the most jaded gunbug! The Sheriff's Model type of Single Action can be made up easily by grinding off the socketed boss that holds the ejector tube on the right-hand side of the frame and welding to match the original contours. A long cylinder pin can be turned on the lathe and knurled appropriately. The home gunsmith should take care, however, in any such operation that he does not attempt to duplicate exactly a rare original model. This practice would most certainly be looked upon as counterfeiting by the serious antique arms collectors. Remember that the purpose of customizing your Single Action Colt is to have an *improved* gun which is unique and suits your personal taste — not to re-create an existing model.

The original Single Action sights can be left as is or various adjustable target-type sights can either be purchased or made up and installed. Full-length ventilated ribs, semi-ribs, etc., can also be installed. Any of these improved, modern sights will usually make quite a difference in your hitting capabilities with the gun and will improve its appearance as well.

E. C. Prudhomme did the engraving and gold inlaying on both these SA's — the basic 5½" model, below, and the Buntline, right.

Fitting an adjustable rear sight to the Single Action frame is another one of those jobs which would be better left to a professional gunsmith. This operation usually requires drilling and tapping, either of which can ruin the frame if the job is bungled. (Note: such drilling and tapping should be done *before* any re-case-hardening is accomplished).

The last item in customizing the gun, and the most important operation where appearance is concerned, is the finish. Regardless of the finish desired — blued, plated or whatever — the quality and appearance of the final product will depend almost 100% on the care with which the gun first was *polished*. All of the hours spent in customizing a good gun can be canceled by hasty polishing. Over-zealous buffing on a power wheel results in numbers and markings becoming indistinct or lost altogether; sharp edges become rounded and ugly. The best technique is to use progressively finer abrasives, emery paper, and crocus cloths until a high polish is achieved; *on flat surfaces use these abrasives with a flat piece of metal such as a file.* If a power buffing wheel must be used, *go easy!* Final buffing *can* be done very nicely by hand, using soft cloths. Good results are achieved through lots of patience and painstaking workmanship. Even though the process takes a lot of time and hard work, it is worthwhile in the end.

The Final Touch

As the final touch you might want the gun engraved. All kinds of engravings are available in qualities that vary from excellent to terrible. As a rule, you get just what you pay for. Generally, it is a lot better to pay what it costs to have a first-class job done by a well-known, reputable maker than to spend less money on a poor job. A finely engraved handgun is always a pleasure to own and increases in value in proportion to the quality of the work. Money spent on a bad job is just money thrown away, as it actually decreases the gun's worth.

When the job is all finished and you have stopped admiring your handiwork, take the gun out and shoot it, correcting any minor faults in sighting, grips, etc. Many custom handgun makers do this after completing all alterations but before the finish or engraving is applied. The more you use a customized or tuned gun the more you will come to appreciate it, especially if you have done a good workmanlike job. Even if you are using a standard, factory-made, unaltered, simon pure Single Action Colt, the more you shoot it the more you will appreciate its rugged dependability. It is truly one gun that is here to stay. •

EVER SIT down and give serious thought to those shots that looked like a lead-pipe cinch but produced a clean miss? The ones that should have smashed the bullet into a vital spot but only wounded the animal? Ever wonder why the bullet didn't land where it should have, when everything seemed perfect to put it exactly where you wanted it? There are plenty of reasons why we miss and a good many of them are never suspected or analyzed. There is always a reason for a miss and it isn't always the fault of the rifle, the sights, or ammo or the fact that you didn't hold when you squeezed the trigger, though any of these things can raise merry old hell with your shooting.

To make consistent hits, of course, the rifle must be accurate; if it isn't, the sooner you find it out the better, and there is only one way to be sure; check it on a paper target. But most riflemen will check this out in sighting in, so we will assume that the rifle is correctly sighted in and the hunter knows exactly where it shoots at various ranges. But here is where one of the gremlins that cause unaccountable misses goes to work.

A lot of hunters seem to feel that all they have to do is sight old Betsy in with a cartridge that fits, check it at various ranges — or more likely take someone else's word for drop figures — and every cartridge they can shove down the spout will put its bullet in the same place. Far from it. Even if your rifle shoots two or more weights of bullets to the same point of impact at 100 yards, they won't land in the same place at longer ranges. The heavier bullet will gradually drop below the lighter one, provided they both have fairly good bullet coefficient, and at the 400 yard mark you would either overshoot with the lighter bullet if holding for the drop of the heavier one, or undershoot with the heavy bullet if holding right for the lighter, faster slug.

Bullet Shapes and Weight

Even the shape of the bullet can throw you off enough out at long range to cause a miss or to only

MYSTERY
?
MISSES

by BOB HAGEL

Light colored game like the pronghorn, seen in bright light of flat, open country, may seem much closer than they actually are; shots often go low by misjudging range.

cripple. A round nose bullet loses velocity much faster than a spitzer and, therefore, the drop is greater as range increases. For example, a 180-grain 30 caliber spitzer bullet with a muzzle velocity of 2700 fps will drop 7″ less at 400 yards than will the 180-grain round nose bullet. That's enough to miss a pronghorn buck if you were sighted for the wrong bullet.

Now here's the other side of that coin! It seems to be a general consensus among hunters that if a rifle is sighted in with a heavy bullet, say a 220-grain 30 at 100 yards, it is sure to shoot a 180-grain high at that range. If you take this for granted and switch loads in the field, as a lot of fellows do, and stick in a 180-grain for the long shot, you may get another miss you can't account for. While it is true that most rifles do shoot a heavier bullet low at 100 yards when sighted with a lighter one, *not all do*. I have had at least two rifles that kicked the heavy bullets high. The first one was an old Krag that put a 220-grain some 8 inches up when sighted at 100 with a 180-grain. I now have a fine, very accurate 285 O.K.H. that lands the 175-grain Nosler 1½ inches above the 160-grain at 100 yards. This could cause you plenty of unexplained misses on yonder canyon side.

While it may seem of minor importance, the canting of a rifle, or a scope rolled over slightly in the mount rings (which causes you to cant the rifle to keep the reticle vertical) will send your bullet wide at long range. Even when sighted correctly at 100 yards, a canted rifle will gradually pull the bullets to the side as range increases, while bullet drop helps to multiply this error. This can cause a miss at small targets, or wound game at extreme range.

All such causes of mysterious misses can be foreseen and eliminated by the well-informed shooter, but there are others that are not so tangible, that are usually learned the hard way — lying awake nights trying to figure out what went wrong!

Optical Snares

Perhaps more well-held shots are

missed at longer ranges by misjudging distance than for any other reason and, if everything is right, the range need not be particularly great. Take the black bear I wounded and lost many years ago because the range was not what it looked.

This particular bear was not especially large but was one of those blacks that shine like a new pair of patent leather shoes, with hair so long it rippled as he moved. It was late afternoon and the low mid-April sun was very bright on the open ridge where he fed. The range appeared to be some 300 yards, with a wide canyon between us. I dropped onto my belly, snugged into the sling — holding was no problem. The 172-grain bullet in my 30 Newton, traveling at over 3000 fps, was dead on at 300. Quartering his shoulder with the crosshair, I squeezed one off. The big rifle bucked and the bear turned a complete back-flip, running, rolling, running through the heavy timber to the bottom of a brush-filled side canyon. A small opening let me miss clean at twice the original range, let me also see a front leg flopping loose at the elbow. With little blood plus a solid matt of needles I finally lost his trail. I wished I had missed him clean.

Long before this I knew why that bullet had not gone where the crosshairs centered. The range was close to 400 yards instead of the 300 estimated. Why had I guessed wrong? Because while I was in shadow the low, bright sun had illuminated the bear on the open ridge, thus making him look closer than he would have in normal light.

The same thing can apply equally as well in reverse. When you are in bright sun and the game on the far side of some canyon is in shadow, it will appear to be much farther away than it actually is. There is no way of being sure just how much this kind of lighting will throw you off, but here's something that will help: when an animal is in bright sun and you are in shadow, and the range is such that you're forced to hold a bit high for a center hit, hold somewhat higher than you would for the distance the animal appears to be. If he is in deep shadow and you sit in the sun, watch the tempta-

tion to hold too high; he won't be as far as he seems.

If you don't believe this, try watching game feeding across a canyon sometime when they are under the shadow of a heavy cloud, then, when it lifts and the sun hits them, notice how much plainer they stand out, how much closer they look.

Quartering Shots

Shots fired at animals that are standing at acute angles to or away from the hunter cause plenty of trouble. These shots are more likely to wound than to miss completely. What fools you is that the animal that appears to be nearly broadside is often quartering to such a degree that the bullet intended to reach a vital area may not do so.

A few years ago I eased up in sight of three spike bull elk feeding on an open face at around 150 yards. The one I wanted was quartering toward me and, although I waited for some time, he did not change position; a gusty wind made it unwise to wait longer. Not wanting to ruin the front quarter, I held just behind the front leg thinking the bullet would pass through the lungs in front of the paunch. When the 250-grain 333 bullet landed he just stiffened, put his nose high in the air and stood without moving. Then he slowly turned presenting exactly the same shot from the other side. The other elk were getting nervous and I knew if they started to go I would be hard put to tell one spike bull from the other, so I gave him another one.

Animals usually loom big against snow, but these rams in shadow on the far side of a canyon may fool you into thinking they are much farther than they are, causing a miss from too much holdover.

This time he went down. Both of those bullets had landed in the same spot on opposite sides, crossed and made exit in the paunch, but missed all except the extreme rear part of the lungs. Had I been using a small light bullet I might never have known what happened, why the bullet did not land where intended.

Likewise, a quartering shot taken from the rear can land in the paunch, never reach the boiler room, when you swear you held for the lungs. The clearer, brighter light of western skies has a bearing in this connection, too — the easterner especially should remember that here in the West he'll frequently see game, sharp and clear, illuminated by brilliant sun shining through a near-hazeless atmosphere! Under these conditions, that antelope or deer may be a lot farther away than he looks to be.

This same "optical illusion" will make an animal standing in a narrow opening in the trees in flat country seem much farther away than it actually is. Again, animals seen thru fog, rain or falling snow, will seem to be much farther than they really are. Oppositely, an animal seen on bright snow, especially a dark animal, will seem much closer than he proves to be when your bullet lands low. A pure white mountain goat will appear much closer against dark rock than would a bighorn sheep in the same spot, causing a low miss or a broken leg.

Uphill — Downhill

There are perhaps more shots missed when shooting downhill in mountain country, shots that leave the hunter shaking his head, than any other type of shooting. Most hunters seem to think that if the bullet is traveling downward, the drop from line of bore will be seriously affected. Actually, as far as practical bullet drop within hunting ranges is concerned, drop that would materially change your hold, you will never notice it unless you are shooting at very steep angles — angles of from 45 to 90 degrees. Of course if you fired straight down — or straight up, for that matter — your bullet would have no trajectory, therefore it would certainly shoot above the normal point of impact, but you will have to be pretty fast to figure out how much and still have time for a shot. The fact is that you don't often shoot at angles of over 45 degrees, either up or downhill; here you can pretty well forget about change in bullet drop.

What really occurs that causes you to overshoot an animal is another optical illusion, more or less.

Bears can fool you badly as to both range and size. If seen in low brush a small bear may seem enormous; large bears in high brush seem small. This makes distance hard to judge.

You don't see what you think you see. Here's what happens: when you look down a 40-degree slope (and that's damned steep) and see an animal standing broadside, you see not only his side but his back as well. When you think you're holding in the center of his ribs you are, in reality, holding near the top of his back. While a sheep may present some 20 inches from back to belly on the level, that expanse is cut down greatly when viewed from above at a steep angle; you do see a full width view of his back, so you are inclined to center your sight much too high. If you happen to be shooting about mid-range of the distance you're sighted in for, your bullet may be above the line of sight from three to five inches. You'll overshoot and may never know exactly why.

This same thing will happen when shooting up a slope at the same angles. Your trajectory does not flatten enough more to make any difference, but you are seeing less of the side, more of the belly, actually holding lower than you think, therefore you get a low hit.

These, then, are some of the reasons for those "mysterious misses" we can't explain, those misses that baffle us until we forget them. What I've put down won't cure all of your missitis pains, but if you'll remember them they may help make a solid hit instead of blowing dust in a buck's face or breaking his leg. Good hunting.

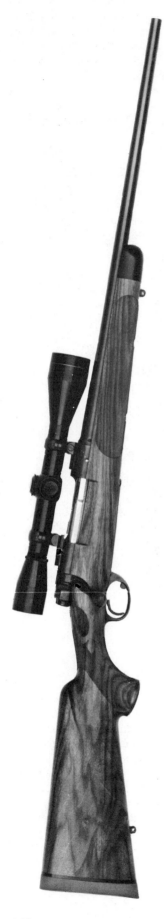

Rx

FOR THE MADE-TO-

The rifle stock is, at worst, a gun
a superb combination of material, design and
approaches perfection. Here, the Old Irish

THE STOCK FOR the sporting rifle should above all assist the man using the rifle to shoot it fast and accurately. If, in addition, the man who lays out the scratch for the stock considers it a thing of beauty, that is so much gravy.

I am talking now about rifles made to be used. As odd as this may seem, hundreds of rifles are cunningly and expensively put together and then never used in the field. Some are never even fired. There are collectors of rifles just as there are collectors of match folders, postage stamps, butterflies, Persian rugs, and autographs of the great and of the notorious. I once knew a very wealthy man whose hobby was having fine custom rifles made up by the world's most skillful craftsmen. He would select the wood, the action, the scope, the mount, and draw up detailed specifications. Then when at last the rifle was delivered, he would sight it in and put it in his gun rack. When he died he left behind about $100,000 worth of fine rifles, almost all in brand new condition. Since this chap didn't use his rifles, his primary consideration was that they look good in the rack.

I am a sucker for a handsome rifle (or at least what I think is a handsome rifle) but I think the first thing a rifle stock should be judged by is its utility. The various parts of a rifle stock evolved because they were useful. If their presence and their proportions enhance the looks of the stock so much the better.

The pistol grip is standard on modern stocks for hunting rifles because it enables the shooter to hold the rifle more firmly and to control the trigger better. The cheekpiece is found on most sporter stocks because a properly designed cheekpiece helps in quick mounting and steady holding, since it gives the face a greater area of sup-

port. The fore-end has two functions— to assist the rifleman in controlling his piece as in a quick running shot and to keep the left hand away from the hot barrel. The Monte Carlo comb on rifle stocks was designed to put the eye in line with the scope for quicker and steadier aiming. On bolt action rifles such combs generally slope upward toward the rear, so the cheek is supported but the forward portion of the comb is low enough to permit withdrawal of the bolt. The point of the comb drops off to the grip so that the shooter can put his right thumb around the small of the stock at the pistol grip and yet not get smacked in the nose when he shoots a rifle of considerable recoil. The dimensions of the stock should be such that the shooter can mount his rifle quickly, hold it steady, aim speedily and shoot accurately. Checkering on the rifle stock is primarily to afford a good, sure grip for the hands, and secondarily it is a form of decoration.

It is when we start discussing such subjective matters as the beauty of the rifle stock that we get into arguments. What is my dish of tea is not necessarily anyone else's. Notions as to the beauty of gun and rifle stocks are as variable as notions as to the beauty of women. We all know that ideals of feminine beauty vary with the race, with the country, with the class, and with the era.

De Gustibus . . .

Photographs of many of the famous beauties of the 1890s and early 1900s — women over whom kings lost their thrones and on whom rich men squandered fortunes, women who made strong men tear out their hair by handfuls—depict gals who would be considered horse-faced, overweight and ordinary today.

I once spent part of an interesting evening many years ago discussing feminine beauty with a well-to-do and sophisticated Chinese, who has probably long since been shot by the Com-

M70 30-06 stocked in French walnut by Jerry Fisher. Style is pure classic, from the solid rubber buttplate to the horn fore-end tip installed with right-angle joint.

by **JACK O'CONNOR**

Gun Editor, Outdoor Life

MEASURE GUNSTOCK

handle, a club; at best, a work of art —

workmanship which, taken as a whole,

man gives his pungent views on the subject

munists. He told me that one of the most depressing aspects of travel in the United States and Europe was the staggering number of downright home-ly women one encountered. He would travel for weeks, he told me, without seeing a woman he did not consider exceedingly ill favored.

This statement intrigued me no end, since I had been in both China and Japan in my youth, and I felt much the same way about Oriental lovelies as he did about European types. I showed him the picture in a magazine of an American motion picture actress who at the time was considered the beauty by whom other beauties were judged. All over the United States and Western Europe, girls tried to look exactly like her and wistful young men dreamed of her at night.

My Chinese friend thought her downright ugly. Her eyes, he said, were too round, and the fact that they were blue gave him the creeps. Her delicately modeled, slightly tip-tilted nose he found grotesquely large, her fair hair freakish. Her face, he told me, was too long, too thin. Her shoulders were too square and her legs so long as to appear deformed. To him feminine beauty meant a flat-nosed, sloe-eyed, moon-faced Chinese gal built solid and close to the ground.

And so it is with rifle stocks. One man may like dark French walnut, classic lines, conservative design. Another may dote on light-colored wood, inlays in mother-of-pearl and various colored woods, carvings of cavorting nymphs, carousing satyrs, and bounding bruins.

Stock Design Influences

Many influences have been operating on sporter stock design of recent years. Very close, full pistol grips have their utility on target stocks, but are out of place on a sporting rifle. The target shot has plenty of time to get set and get his hand just so, but the game shot often has to mount his

rifle and fire almost instantaneously. Then the extra close pistol grip is both slow and awkward. There is probably some utility to the thumb-hole stock on a target rifle, but it is both awkward and out of place on a sporter. The fore-end of the bench rest rifle is quite properly flat so it will lie motionless on a rest with no tendency to cant. However, the fore-end that is flat on the bottom has no place on a rifle to be used in the field. The palm of the partially closed human hand that must grasp the fore-end is not flat.

As farfetched as it may seem, the design of automobile bodies has had considerable effect on that of rifle stocks. One stockmaker of note puts a sharp ridge along his fore-ends from the receiver ring forward, the exact counterpart of similar ridges on auto-mobile bodies. The pressed-in curves and convolutions of automobile bodies that are put in to give a switcheroo and a new look to the latest models have their counterpart in stock design. The blobs and strips of chrome known to the trade as "jewelry" and with which many automobile bodies were formerly plastered have their counter-parts in the carving and inlays one often sees on rifle stocks.

The tendency to go to extremes one sees in the design of both men's and women's clothes can also be seen in rifle stocks. If good tailors make men's trousers somewhat narrower than was common a few years back, some makers of clothing turn out trousers so narrow it is difficult to get the feet into them. If men's suit jackets be-come somewhat longer, numerous cus-tomers will demand coats still longer. Women's dresses have been getting shorter in recent years and some women are now actually wearing their skirts above their knees.

Just a touch of California influence shows in the fore-end tip of this claro walnut stock by Gale Bartlett; however, Monte Carlo comb is very graceful and cheekpiece blends beau-tifully into pistol grip.

241

The smooth-flowing lines — almost a trademark of Keith Stegall — are perhaps the dominant feature of this fine stock, but the traditional-pattern checkering and lack of fore-end tip should not be missed.

Built by Mashburn Arms, Co., this 7mm Magnum with its conservative Monte Carlo comb comes close to being today's classic design, though the whiteline spacers are a jarring note to O'Connor.

This Len Brownell-stocked 7mm Magnum looks almost alive, an effect created by his checkering pattern, combined with similar angles of fore-end tip, bolt handle and rear of Monte Carlo comb.

High, almost-horizontal comb line is Dale Goens' solution to the scope problem. The crotch-burl claro walnut blank is gorgeous, but almost overshadowed by the perfection of Goens' checkering.

Though the European influence is obvious in this stock by Paul Jaeger, basic lines are close to those favored by many American hunters.

Holland & Holland's version of the classic stock has a low comb and considerable drop at heel for use strictly with iron sights from the offhand position.

Fore-end on this 300 Magnum is completely classic, as are pistol grip and steel buttplate area, but Tom Shelhamer added cheekpiece of his own style to accommodate the scope's higher line of sight.

Thumbhole stock, such as this one by Peterson on left-hand Weatherby Mark V, isn't particularly favored by the writer on a sporter, though OK on target rifle.

This stock by Stag reflects the California influence which leaves Jack cold. Though of highest workmanship and execution, the "applied" look of cheekpiece and fore-end section is distracting, says the author.

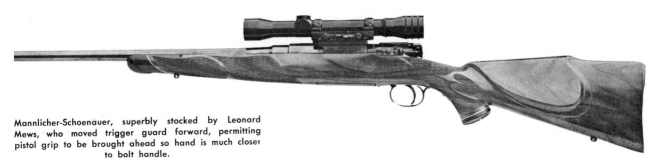

Mannlicher-Schoenauer, superbly stocked by Leonard Mews, who moved trigger guard forward, permitting pistol grip to be brought ahead so hand is much closer to bolt handle.

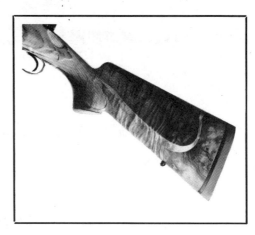

Compare classic treatment of pistol grip, comb, cheekpiece and checkering on Prince Abdorreza Pahlavi's M70 by Al Biesen, right photo, with extreme style of Winslow stock, at left. Jack believes the exaggerated pistol grip serves no function.

Extremes in styles and extremes in rifle stocks often go hand in hand. A chap I know is a connoisseur of both rifle stocks and girlfriends and his choices in both have many points in common. His rifle stocks are extreme in shape, off-beat in color, and marvelously inlaid, carved, and checkered. I once had dinner with him and one of his doxies. This gal was as flashy as one of his stocks. Her hair had been bleached and then dyed gray. She wore false eyelashes about 1½ inches long. The heels of her shoes were so high that she walked on her toes and I was afraid she was going to pitch forward on her face at any moment. Her fingernails were so long and so red that they looked as if she had just manually disemboweled a greater kudu. She could have used her earrings as spinners to catch steelhead trout and she wore her dress about three inches above her shapely knees. She was an intriguing little dish but a bit exotic for my reactionary tastes. As far as taste goes in women and rifle stocks, I am a bit of a square.

If a functional pistol grip flares a bit at the bottom to give the hand a better grip, why do some stockers make it unusually long and give it an extreme flare? If the fore-end should be slightly flattened for better gripping, why must some stockers make it 4″ wide and as flat as a pancake?

Monte Carlo Combs

I am pretty skeptical as to whether a Monte Carlo comb ever improved the looks of a rifle stock, but it is getting so that the Monte Carlo is in fashion and it is difficult to peddle even a single shot 22 without one. Actually, the Monte Carlo originated in Europe for pigeon shooting, a sport in which a lot of scratch often rides on a single bird. The shotgun Monte Carlo comb is parallel to the rib of the barrel, so that the eye will always see the barrel in the same way, no matter where it is placed on the comb. Then the elevation will be uniform and the shooter will know where his shot charge is going. Obviously if a stock has much drop, the placement of the cheek at various points along

the comb will affect the elevation of the shot charge.

As we have seen, the best Monte Carlo combs for rifles slant upward toward the rear. This keeps the point of the comb low enough so that it will clear the bolt and yet give more support to the cheek unless the shooter crawls the stock clear to the point of the comb. In addition the comb slides away from the cheekbone as the rifle comes back in recoil.

A stock designer must take care when he turns out a Monte Carlo. A very high proportion are ugly, do not cut down on recoil or support the face, and make the buttstock look like the business end of a canoe paddle. Why any rifle designed to be used with iron sights should have a Monte Carlo is more than I can fathom. Often a Monte Carlo is combined with considerable drop at the heel of the stock. A high comb with excessive drop is the conbination which makes a rifle a real kicker.

The best Monte Carlo on an American factory stock is, I believe, that on the Remington 700. It is handsome, graceful, and useful. I have no idea who designed that stock, but whoever he was had a sense of utility and an eye for line.

Sometimes Monte Carlo combs are combined with a curious feature called a "roll over" comb. The cheekpiece is like a limp pancake draped over the comb. The stock is undercut on the off side to help achieve this effect. To me it looks ghastly and has no utility whatsoever.

I am somewhat dubious as to the general utility of any Monte Carlo. The same effect can be achieved by a thick, well-rounded comb and the same drop at heel as at comb. Actually such a stock gives less recoil effect than any other, as the recoil comes back as almost a straight push. If there is much drop at comb, the stock recoils upward to bang into the cheek. The worst kicker of all is the stock with a high, sharp comb combined with considerable drop at heel. Incidentally the greater the area of the butt, the less the recoil effect, as it distributes the recoil over a greater

surface. A rifle of heavy recoil like the 458, the 375, or the 416 kicks less if it has a large, wide butt, the same drop at heel as at comb, and a bit of cast-on, so the stock is pushed away from the face by the recoil.

Classic vs. Rococo

In general, two types of rifle stocks are being produced at the present time in this country and in Europe. One is the "classic" stock which has been a matter of slow evolution since the first bolt-action sporting rifles were produced in England and in Germany about 75 years ago. The best classic stocks are conservative in design and effective in the field. The good ones depend for their class on careful and graceful shaping, meticulous inletting, well-chosen wood, and clean, precise checkering. A classic stock turned out today looks much like a similar stock made 40 years ago, but a careful examination would show that the design has been adapted to the higher sight line of the scope and greater recoil of popular magnum cartridges. Today's classic stock has less drop at heel, a thicker comb, probably a somewhat thicker fore-end, and possibly a conservative Monte Carlo.

The other type might be called the "rococo," a four-bit word meaning something characterized by a florid style of shape and ornamentation. Designers of rococo stocks seem to feel that anything that is new and different is good. They go in for bizarre shapes, gaudy ornamentation, showy checkering and carving and numerous white spacers. They like pistol grip caps and fore-end tips of odd and bizarre shape. The grip cap of the classic stock is a plain oval, usually of blued steel, sometimes checkered or lightly engraved. The classic fore-end is put on at a right angle to the barrel and is of East Indian buffalo horn or black wood like ebony.

The difference between the classic and the rococo stocks is that between clean, functional, simple lines, with restrained and elegant ornamentation, as compared to gaudy decoration and off-beat shape. The classic stock can be compared to the New England

M70 30-06 stocked in French walnut by Len Brownell for Eleanor O'Connor, celebrated lady tiger hunter, left; above, somewhat bizarre comb design by Reinhart Fajen might let shooter's thumb hit his nose on recoil. "Hooked" pistol grip is not viewed with favor by author.

colonial or the Georgian house, which have looked good for generations. The rococo stocks are like the late Victorian mansions and the later "bungalows." The same difference is seen in woman's dresses. I have a wife and a couple of good-looking daughters. I like to go along with them occasionally when they shop for clothes. Almost invariably the fussy, over-ornamented, extremely styled dresses dabbed with useless bows and frills are the cheaper ones—those on the $35 rack, let us say. Since my gals like clean lines and elegant simplicity, they wind up (sob!) at the more expensive racks.

Not long ago, I heard a dealer in fine gunstock wood giving advice to a talented young stockmaker who wanted to make the production of fine stocks his life work. "Learn to make the classic stock," he told the lad. "By the time a man can afford to pay top prices for stock work, he is generally conservative enough in his tastes to want the classic style." This may be, but I have seen plenty of well-heeled characters with rococo stocks.

California Stocks

I have heard rococo stocks referred to as "California stocks" and it is true that many stocks turned out in California are pretty far out in left field, but many exceedingly fine classic stocks are likewise turned out there. Some very fine classic stocks have come out of the gunsmithing department of Kerr Sport Shop in Beverly Hills, Pachmayr Gun Works, Los Angeles, or G. & S. Bartlett of San Fernando.

However, some pretty wild looking stocks have originated in southern California. Many consumers have liked them, and as modified, advertised, and distributed by Roy Weatherby, the somewhat rococo stocks have had considerable effect on stock design in other parts of the world. A couple of years ago I was walking down a street in the West End of London when I spied a gunshop. In the window on display was a rifle stocked with a British version of the

Weatherby stock. I like to swallowed my upper plate. I wouldn't have been more astonished if I had seen a photo of the queen in a bikini. Actually the standard Weatherby stocks are a cross between the classic and the rococo. Some of the newer outfits turn out stocks that make a Weatherby look as if it had been designed for Edward VII by Holland & Holland.

The less a consumer knows about stock design and workmanship, the more enthusiastic he is apt to be about the rococo stock, and the showier it is the better he likes it. A couple of years ago, a sporting goods dealer I know put in his window two rifles he was trying to peddle for the modest commission there was in it. One was of the rococo type. It was stocked with some light-colored wood, so light it was almost yellow. It was covered with inlays of ivory and various colored woods. The floorplate, trigger guard, and receiver were covered with poorly executed and very large scroll engraving that looked as if it had been done by an intoxicated saddle maker. Also on the floorplate was the portrait of an animal I took to be a gut-shot elk. The checkering was coarse, indifferently executed, and of the French skip line variety. There were white spacers between stock and fore-end tip and between pistol grip and cap. Receiver, floorplate, trigger guard, and bolt handle were gold-plated. On an area where there was no inlay there was a carved scene of a tiger having a death battle with a python.

In the same window was another rifle which had been owned by a gun nut and big game hunter who had passed to his reward. It was a 30-06 on a square-bridge Mauser Werke action with a hinged floorplate and release button in the trigger guard. It wore the now obsolete 2¼x Zeiss Zielklein scope on the old Redfield Sr. mount. It had been stocked back in the '30s by the late Alvin Linden, an eccentric old Swede genius who had a shop in Bryant, Wis., and was one of the best stockers who ever lived. The wood was very hard, glowing French walnut with long dark lines in the buttstock. The checker-

ing ran about 26 lines to the inch and was absolutely perfect. Fit of metal to wood was flawless.

Until the two rifles were sold a week or so later, there was always a crowd around the window. Which rifle had stopped them? You guessed it—the rococo job.

Each of the citizens who bought a rifle thought he had a bargain. The chap with the gold-plated, carved, and inlaid job has a conversation piece. He loves it. The one who bought the old Linden job likewise thinks he got a rare bargain. He marvels at that wonderful checkering with every diamond exactly like every other diamond. He gets an artistic satisfaction out of the graceful pistol grip, the smooth curve of the comb. He wouldn't be caught dead with the other guy's showy rifle, and the other guy wouldn't give three books of trading stamps and a secondhand lawn mower for the mousy Linden job.

Both of these citizens are right. If a rifle handles fast and shoots accurately, the shape and the decoration are the business of the person who buys it. He has as much right to his taste in rifle stocks as my Chinese friend had to his taste in feminine beauty. If he thought my gals had noses that were too long and too prominent and he disliked their round and ghastly blue eyes and didn't dig light-brown hair, that was his perfect right. It was likewise my right to think his Far Eastern maidens were built too close to the ground and had profiles like Easter eggs.

I must admit that as far as stock design and decoration go, I string along with the classic school. I am not bowled over by pictures carved on rifle stocks or tattooed on women. I can take French skip line checkering or leave it alone. White spacers leave me cold and gold plating gives me a seizure. If there is any engraving on a rifle I want it neatly executed and inconspicuous. I'd rather spend my hard earned shillings on hard, fine-grained wood with good color and figure, good shaping, precise inletting, and plenty of perfectly executed checkering. •

Mrs. O'Connor, her gentleman shikari Prince Abdul Kyum, and a large tigress. Eleanor shot two tigers with a 30-06. In India those who have never used anything smaller say the 375 Magnum and the 450/400 should be used.

The Killing Power Controversy

by JACK O'CONNOR

Paper No. 1,319 in that old, old argument, with Jack insisting, rightly enough, that where you put it, not what you put in it, makes the big difference. True, yet it's better to be a bit over-gunned than not, right? Sure, but even the 22 Hornet has killed . . .

I HAVE BEEN following gun and shooting literature for many years and I have probably read many hundreds of articles on the subject of killing power. Some writers swear by lightning-fast bullets. Others whoop it up for large heavy missiles at moderate velocity.

There was a time when I read them all with starry-eyed innocence, but I must confess that in my declining years I find some of them difficult to follow.

One of the principal troubles with most of these articles is that they are based on testimonial evidence, and much testimonial evidence has a way of being pretty unreliable. When two amorous young men who have dated Susie Jones and who have spent many hours gazing rapturously into her luminous eyes cannot agree as to whether they are blue, green, gray, or hazel, what chance has the poor hunter to make a clear and objective report?

Not much! He is excited, untrained as an observer, prone to tall tales and alibis. Generally he is prejudiced. He is quick to jump at conclusions, and he almost never blames his own poor shooting instead of his rifle and his cartridge. Furthermore, even if a hunter with limited experience is a good observer, his conclusions aren't worth too much. Animals often react in different ways to the same placement of shots with the same bullets of the same caliber. Now and then animals are knocked flat with superficial wounds and occasionally they'll travel for considerable distance with hits that should have done them in.

As an example I once shot a very large buck mule deer squarely through the lungs with a 150-gr. 30-06 bullet. The buck ran around 300 yards and was still alive when I got to it. In this case the bullet had not opened up. If I had shot only one deer I might have thought the 30-06 a poor killer on mule deer. A few years later, with the same cartridge and exactly the same bullet, I shot another mule deer, running and perhaps 225-250 yards away. The buck went down so hard I expected to find it stone dead, but when I got up to him he got to his feet and started to wobble off. My shot had gone through one front knee. If that had been the only deer I had ever shot I might have thought it possible to hit a deer just about anywhere with a 30-06 bullet and knock it down. This last experience was genuinely cockeyed. My only explanation is that the buck may have had all of his weight on one leg. When the bullet hit it he may have fallen so hard he was stunned. Both of these are extreme cases but they happened!

In many years of hunting I have seen several hundreds of head of what passes for "big game" shot, and I have knocked off a bit myself. I have been in on the last moments of animals as small as the dik-dik, a tiny

antelope about the size of large jack-rabbits, and as large as elephants, which are the size of small houses. I am not quite as quick with my answer about killing power as I used to be.

Experience is a great teacher, and experience has often proved my notions wrong. Because of my poor shooting I once wounded a deer with a 30-30. The result was a long chase and for a time I looked down my nose at the 30-30. Then the occasion arose when I had to hunt with a 30WCF or not shoot. I killed three bucks with three shots and none of them went over 50 yards. Those three bucks don't make me an authority on the 30-30, but they did teach me that if a man owns a 30-30, knows its limita-

anyway. They shot half of them with their powerhouse 35, half with a 7mm Magnum. They found one cartridge killed just as well as the other. They decided there was no crying need for the 35 and so shelved it. An American bison is heavier than the African Cape buffalo and almost as large as the Indian gaur. Would a 7mm Magnum kill these two just as neatly? Probably.

Not long ago I was talking to an old sourdough who for years shot moose, caribou, and sheep for the market in the free and easy days of the post-gold rush Alaska. He told me that articles listing proper calibers for this and that and giving figures of how many foot pounds of energy one needed to kill animals of various

Ed Quinn, former Chrysler Corporation executive, killed this large East African leopard with one shot from a 7mm Remington Magnum. Kenya and Tanzania regulations say that for all dangerous game, including leopard, a 375 or larger should be used. The 7mm Magnum was more than plenty.

tions, and can shoot it, he'll get himself plenty of venison; if it wounds only it is probably his fault and not that of the cartridge.

Magnum Malarkey

Much of the stuff written about suitable calibers for various big-game animals is, alas, malarkey of the purest ray serene. I sadly suspect that most of it is about as sound as the old notion that strong liquor made strong men. Some years ago a manufacturer was thinking seriously of bringing out a powerful 35 magnum cartridge for heavy American and foreign game. As an experiment some of the hired hands made a deal with a chap who owned a private buffalo herd to shoot 20 animals he was going to knock off

weights at various distances really threw him. He couldn't read one, he said, without becoming short of breath, breaking out in hives, and seeing spots before his eyes.

To save money this old boy used to cast lead bullets and load them to a velocity of about 1800 fps. He shot no end of caribou, moose, and sheep with these pip-squeak 30-30 loads, he said, and couldn't remember losing an animal he had hit well. He also told me of an Eskimo pal of his who used a 22 Hornet to feed a whole village with caribou and moose meat. This simple, untutored savage told this sourdough friend of mine that from the time he got a Model 54 Winchester in 22 Hornet until he had worn it out 20 years later, he had lost

416 Rigby rifle owned by Jack O'Connor. Metal work by Tom Burgess, Spokane, Wash., stock by Bob Johnson, also of Spokane. Brevex Magnum Mauser action, 24-inch barrel, ramp front sight, adjustable express rear. Weaver K2.5 scope on special Burgess bases with Redfield rings, Canjar trigger, special Burgess safety, front swivel base sweated to barrel. This 10½-lb. rifle is used with 416 cases made from 378 and 460 Weatherby cases with the belts turned off. Load is the 400-gr. Barnes bullet in front of 105 grains of 4831, velocity 2500 fps and energy is 5,652 ft. pounds.

exactly one animal hit with it—a grizzly.

I certainly wouldn't select a 22 Hornet for hunting deer, much less grizzly, but there is no doubt that a good shot with a 22 Hornet can keep himself in meat. Once in the course of a Mexican hunt, I left my 270 in camp and was out potting the big antelope jackrabbits with which the country abounded. I was armed with a single-shot rifle for the 2-R 22-3000 cartridge, a then popular wildcat with about the power of the 222. Suddenly I became aware that a very juicy buck mule deer had trotted out of an arroyo and was standing broadside about 200 yards away. The temptation was too much for me. I held the intersection of the crosswires for a high lung shot and squeezed off. The buck took one convulsive leap and piled up.

On an African trip a companion of mine brought along a rifle for the 222 Remington cartridge. We used it not only for varmints but likewise often for meat and bait animals like Grant's gazelle and topi (which are on the order of deer in size), and hartebeest, which are a bit larger, about the size of the smaller caribou. Mostly we used high lung shots. We never fired at an animal at over 200 yards and never pressed the trigger unless we knew where the bullet was going to strike. Almost every animal we shot at was dead within 10 ft.

Once when I was much younger and more sanguine I took a pop at a very large bull elk at a distance (measured not guessed) that left the 130-gr. 270 about as much remaining energy as a 25-35 bullet would have at 200 yards. The bullet went right through both lungs and I found it

later under the hide on the far side. The bull wobbled around for 5 to 10 seconds on rubber legs and fell.

KPD Disputed

Actually I think differences in killing power between various comparable cartridges using bullets of similar construction lie largely in the imagination. I am often asked which is a better killer, a 270 or a 30-06, a 264 or a 7mm Magnum. The answer is that any of them is adequate with well-placed shots and inadequate with poorly-placed shots. In the spring of 1963 I saw a friend shoot a large Alaska brown bear with a 7mm Remington Magnum. The range was, as near as we could estimate, a bit short of 300 yards. A large Alaska brown bear weighs twice as much as a lion or a tiger and can be very dangerous when wounded. Generally the cartridge recommended for brownies is the 375 Magnum, and some have gone so far as to recommend elephant cartridges like the British 450/400 or the 458 Winchester. The 175-gr. bullet from the 7mm Magnum went through both of the bear's shoulders and was found under the hide on the far side. The bear didn't move out of his tracks. A 458 or even a 37mm anti-tank gun could not have done a better job.

My friend the bear slayer had previously been convinced that one needed at least a 375 for the big bruins. He had taken the 7mm along for black bears and seals and was in fact out after seals when we ran into the brownie.

The results radically re-oriented his thinking. Later he asked me just how far down the line could one go in the choice of brown bear cartridges.

I could only say that I'd be darned if I knew.

I suspect, though, that caliber, velocity, foot pounds of energy, and all the other hocus-pocus that we rifle nuts set so much store by is far less important than many of us think. Pioneer woodsmen and homesteaders killed off the deer, black bear, and elk east of the Mississippi with smallbore muzzle-loading rifles. Powder and lead were expensive so the boys were pretty sparing with it. As a consequence the rifles they used had about the power of the now just about obsolete 32-20 — and anyone tackling black bear or elk with a 32-20 today would by many be considered halfwitted. I doubt seriously if these animals are any tougher today than they were 150-200 years ago. If Daniel Boone could knock off a big black bear or a whitetail buck with a Kentucky rifle firing a 78-gr. bullet at a velocity of 2000 fps and turning up 690 ft. pounds of energy at the muzzle, I see no reason why someone today couldn't do the same thing with the 80-gr. 32-20 bullet at 2100 with 780 ft. pounds. The pioneers didn't think they needed more power until they crossed the Mississippi and encountered the buffalo and the grizzly. Then they went to bigger calibers and heavier bullets.

A generation ago I sat in on a session of the Arizona game commission that set the minimum calibers for Arizona's big game. It was decided that the mildest caliber that would be allowed on deer was the old 25-35 with its 117-gr. bullet at 2300 with 1370 ft. pounds of energy and the lightest bullet legal on deer would be the 87-gr. bullet of the 250-3000 Savage. Elk, if I remember correctly, were to be taken with no bullet weighing less than 150 grains and with less than the power of the 30-40. The 30-30 at that time was outlawed on elk, as a great many elk had just been wounded by poor shooting with 30-30s during Arizona's first legal elk season.

This rare and handsome Mozambique nyala was a one-shot kill with Eleanor's 7x57.

Minimum Calibers & Bullets

Probably this business of specifying minimum calibers is a good idea, as there is no doubt that a 30-06 (all things being equal) will make a more severe and extensive wound than a 30-30, and a 7mm Magnum will make a more severe wound, let us say, than a 243. I also believe that the setting of minimum bullet weights is a good idea, as, all things being equal, it is much less difficult to construct a reasonably heavy bullet that will get deep inside an animal than a lighter bullet.

A young engineer of my acquaintance is a long-gone gun nut but he is a naive type and has had scant hunting experience. Delving deep into the mysterious mumbo-jumbo of his trade, he has compiled an elaborate chart showing exactly at what range it is possible to kill certain game animals with various calibers. An elk is a dead duck, let us say, at a maximum range of 326 yards with the 130-gr. 270 bullet; at 411 yards with the 7mm Remington Magnum, and 506 yards with the 300 Weatherby Magnum.

If we follow this chap literally, the 270 would kill the elk at 326 yards but wound it with a hit in the same place at 327, while the 7mm Magnum would kill at 411 yards and wound a few yards farther — all with bullets of the same construction and the same placement.

Such stuff is, of course, the worst kind of nonsense. Animals are killed cleanly by putting properly-constructed bullets into vital areas and not by energy figures, fancy rifle stocks, gold plating on bullets, or anything else. If a bullet gets well inside an animal and ruptures both lungs the animal quickly dies. If the bullet goes through the heart, the animal quickly dies. If the brain is struck or the spine broken ahead of the shoulders the animal dies instantly. If the liver or kidneys are ruptured the animal seldom lives long.

But if an animal is shot in the guts, has a broken leg, a muscle wound anywhere, it doesn't make much difference what he is hit with. The result is a wounded animal.

Nor have I ever been able to convince myself that the size of the hole in the end of a rifle barrel had much to do with how well a weapon kills. I believe this notion that large calibers kill better than small is (like many other gun notions) a hold-over from the days of muzzle loaders shooting black powder and spherical lead bullets. In those days there wasn't too much difference in velocity

Eleanor O'Connor, famed lady hunter, knocked off this good Tanzania sable with a 7x57 Mauser.

with any of the muzzle loaders and since all bullets were round and made of soft lead, the only way it was possible to get more killing power was to increase the diameter and the weight of the bullet.

Today a bullet can be made to blow up quickly and violently, to expand to .35″, .40″, .45″ or .50″ and drive in deep. It can be made not to expand at all. Consequently I doubt if there is much magic in the initial caliber of the bullet.

Elk Hunting

I once read that a group of Idaho elk guides made the statement that when their hunters used rifles of 30 caliber or under they wounded on the average of three elk for every one they brought to bag. I have my doubts as to whether any large and representative group of Idaho elk guides ever made such a statement. The Idaho elk guides I know sing another tune. Most of them tell me that it doesn't make too much difference what their dudes shoot elk with just so they hit them right.

Many people have shot more elk than I have, but I have killed enough of the big deer so that I am not completely ignorant. If I can count right I have brought back 18 shot with the 270, mostly with the 130-gr. bullet. I have wounded one with the 270 — a gut shot. The bull lay down and I wouldn't have lost it except that my companion ran ahead of me, started smoking it up with a revolver, and got it traveling. Night came on and we had to give up the trail. Most of the elk I've shot haven't moved 25 yards after they were hit. One of the last elk I saw shot was killed with a

280 Remington and the 140-gr. bullet. Hit in the lungs, it collapsed at the shot, and rolled downhill. The last elk I killed was a big 7-pointer. Hit with the 150-gr. factory bullet of the 7mm Remington Magnum, he didn't move out of his tracks. Without exception the elk I have seen that went off wounded for any distance did so because they were hit in nonvital areas.

There are no pat answers to this business of making clean kills on big game, and it is of course better to be somewhat overgunned than undergunned. However, the two most important factors in getting quick and humane kills are the proper placement of the shot and the use of a bullet which is strongly enough constructed to get inside an animal, to break bones if necessary, and which will yet expand sufficiently to lacerate flesh and rupture blood vessels.

If a well-designed bullet is properly placed, it doesn't seem to make too much difference within limits what caliber is used. A well-placed 6mm bullet will do a much better job of bringing down a deer or an elk than a poorly placed 458 bullet. Likewise a well-placed 30-30 bullet of good construction is a better killer than a poorly placed bullet from a 300 Magnum.

Little Rifles

In 1962 my wife and I made safaris in Mozambique and in Angola. Between the two countries for trophies, bait, and meat we shot quite a bit of game. She used a little 7x57 Mauser for the most part and I the much more powerful 7mm Remington Magnum. The magnum shoots flatter, hits

harder, develops much more energy. The shots were not difficult and almost all were well placed. The difference as far as results went didn't amount to much. The 7mm Magnum knocked some animals down in their tracks that might have gone 20 or 30 yards if hit with the 7x57. With the flat-shooting magnum and the fast-stepping 150-gr. bullets I felt justified in taking some shots at longer ranges than my wife did. I flattened a couple of bull kudu (antelope about as large as elk) with one shot each, but my wife with her less powerful rifle used two shots on one kudu and three on another. However, in either case the animal was vitally hit and probably would not have gone more than 100 yards after the first shot.

The most important factor in killing power then is a man behind the gun who can place his shot and the next most important factor is the use of a properly constructed bullet. If the hunter can shoot and if he uses a bullet which gets in deep enough and expands properly, he has no need of a cannon.

On a tiger hunt in India in the spring of 1965 my wife, who is allergic to recoil and not afraid to admit it, used a 30-06 with the 180-gr. bullet. Our professional hunter carried a double 450/400, which drives a 400-gr bullet at about 2150. He was badly shaken when he saw the small hole in the end of that 30-06 barrel. He had more respect for what he called the "little rifle" when she killed her first tiger so dead with her first shot that it didn't have time to growl.

W. D. M. "Karamojo" Bell shot well over 1000 elephants and no end of lions, leopards, buffalo, and antelope with the 7x57 Mauser, generally using the 175-gr. full metal-jacketed (solid) bullet. Charles Sheldon, the first man to collect all four varieties of North American wild sheep, not only shot dozens of rams and caribou but large moose, grizzlies, and Alaska brown bear with the 6.5 Mannlicher using a 160-gr. bullet at not much more velocity than that of a 30-30. He almost never used more than one shot on an animal, and if he had any close calls with brown bears or grizzlies he does not mention them in any of his books.

Animals may have got tougher than when **Daniel Boone was knocking off** black bears and whitetails with his Kentucky pea-shooters, and in the decades that have passed since Sheldon quit rolling over grizzlies and brownies with his 6.5. But I doubt it!

It has been my experience that if I hit an animal right with a good bullet from any reasonably adequate cartridge, he's almost always quickly in the bag. If I don't hit him right I am generally in trouble, no matter what I am using.

The longer I hunt and shoot the more I agree with the old Indian guide who said "Any gun good shootum good!" ●

George Schoyen—from a photo made about 1900.

RIFLEMAKER EXTRAORDINARY

A fully detailed and thoroughly documented account of the great Denver craftsman and his long years at the bench. Profusely illustrated with numerous specimens of his superb work.

by John T. Dutcher

Top—Schoyen-Ballard 32-40 schuetzen rifle equipped with an A.W. Peterson telescope. The wood, action modification, and barrel are by Schoyen. *Dallas Bray coll.*

The lower portion of this Ballard receiver has been cut away to make a closer and more aesthetic pistol grip stock—a feature often found on better-grade Schoyen-Ballard rifles. Note the close inletting of wood to metal. *Dallas Bray coll.*

F INE GUNWORK of every description," read the advertisement of George Christian Schoyen, considered to have been one of the best rifle barrelmakers of all time. Schoyen barrels were the choice of many of the best marksmen of the Schuetzen era. Noted offhand riflemen such as Dr. W.G. Hudson, Dean W. King, Jr., and C.W. Rowland, the great rest shooter, used Schoyen barrels.

Schoyen was born in Norway in 1845. He immigrated to the United States shortly after the Civil War, first settling in Chicago. Disaster struck on October 8, 1871, when the Chicago fire burned Schoyen out. Undaunted, Schoyen, his wife, and first daughter moved to Denver, Colorado. There he went to work for Carlos C. Gove, a well-known maker of percussion muzzle-loading target and sporting rifles. Gove also made under-lever conversions of the Remington rolling-block rifle; it is possible that Schoyen performed many of the modifications on these rolling blocks, plus other alterations and general gun repair.

Schoyen, who had spent 7 years learning the gunmakers' trade in Norway, proved an accomplished and prolific workman. It is no wonder, then, working in an environment such as Gove's Denver Armory, that Schoyen

should have added to his knowledge of riflemaking. Word spread quickly of the Norwegian gunsmith's talents. Before long, the gunshop in the back of Gove's Denver Armory, located on the banks of Cherry Creek at 340½ Blake Street, was filled with orders for Schoyen barrels. Most of those early barrels were fitted to Sharps, Ballard and Remington buffalo rifles, replacing the original worn barrels. Orders soon came in for target rifle barrels which were fitted to the currently popular single-shot, breech-loading actions and a few percussion rifles.

Gove and Schoyen were correspondents and disciples of William Billinghurst, of Rochester, New York, one of the better known makers of caplock muzzle-loading rifles. These three gunsmiths often followed similar lines of thought and experiment.

During 1884, Gove, who was aging and involved with political and real estate ventures, sold his Denver Armory to Schoyen and D.W. Butt. The Denver City Directory of 1885 carried an advertisement listing Schoyen and Butt as successors to Carlos Gove, and offering to sell all types of sporting goods and firearms. This firm dissolved two years later, and Schoyen formed a new partnership in 1887 with Fred A. Burgen, moving to 1420 Blake Street, next to the Elephant Corral. One product of this partnership is described in the August 1, 1888, *Sports Afield* magazine as "a fancy 40 caliber Sharps hunting rifle equipped with a fine pistol grip stock of Tunisian walnut and a Remington barrel made for big game hunter, Dr. H.A. Lemen." There is no evidence that either Butt or Burgen (sometimes spelled Bergen) were gunmakers.

As the railroads developed through the West, word of Schoyen's skill spread beyond the Rocky Mountain region, and he began getting orders for high-grade hunting rifles from many celebrities, European as well as American. Lord Lennox, Earl of Dunraven, and Col. Vivian both used and endorsed Schoyen barrels. For Lord Ogilvie, Schoyen made a fine set of double-barreled guns (one a rifle and the other a shotgun) said to have cost $250 each. William F. "Buffalo Bill" Cody and Annie Oakley had Schoyen repair their firearms, and Schoyen's grandson recalls reloading rifle ammunition with shot for them. These cartridges were undoubtedly used for aerial shooting. (God help the Indian holding the cigar in his mouth if Bill or Annie forgot they still had shot loads in their guns!). Today, Schoyen hunting arms are rarities, and in all probability they were never common.

Schoyen is best remembered for rebarreling and altering fine target rifles. He may have been directed in this area by C.W. Rowland, of Boulder, Colo., who thought very highly of Schoyen. Carlos Gove, too, was a dyed-in-the-wool target shooter, and he undoubtedly influenced Schoyen to devote his talents in this direction. In his later years, Gove used a 35-caliber muzzle-loading Schoyen-Ballard for target shooting. For many years a dispute has raged as to which was the best barrelmaker: H.M. Pope, A.O. Zischang or George Schoyen. All three were master craftsmen, and this question will probably never be resolved. L.R. Wallack, in his book, *Modern Accuracy*, quotes a letter written by Har-

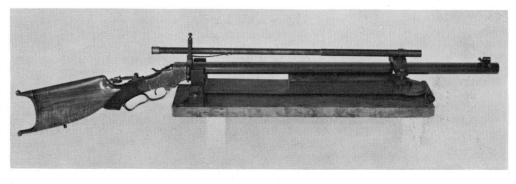

Schoyen-built machine rest, with telescope, used in testing Schoyen rifles at the old Denver Rifle Club Range. The rest is fully adjustable for windage and elevation. The Stevens rifle, clamped in the V-mounts, recoils to the rear on the leaf spring below it. *George Kane coll.*

The Denver Rifle Club in 1905. George Schoyen is shown lying down at the far right side; J.P. Lower is sitting in the middle. Original photo by Dr. W. G. Hudson.

vey A. Donaldson regarding Charles W. Rowland's opinion of Schoyen barrels. "Rowland really had a warm spot in his heart for the famous Denver (Colorado) gunsmith George C. Schoyen. He told me he believed Schoyen made the finest barrels that he ever used. He said of course Pope made a good barrel, but that all of Schoyen's barrels were good, and that he never made a poor shooting barrel. I have correspondence from Rowland wherein he states that it had been necessary to return more than one barrel to Pope for additional lapping, etc., or whatever it was Pope did to it, before it performed properly."

Rowland, a famous bench rest shooter, is credited with many feats, notably the shooting of a 10-shot group measuring .725-inch—10 shots in one hole at 200 yards! To quote again from Wallack's *Modern Accuracy:* "On May 26th, 1931, Mr. Rowland completed a string of 40 consecutive shots at 100 yards with a 32-40 Schoyen rifle. The 40 shots were not all fired in one day, as a lot of time was required to get all conditions right before getting off a shot. For example, the last 10 shots fired took from 12 noon to 5:00 P.M. The day was a bit windy and the shooting was only done during lulls. Rowland's equipment was a 32-40 Schoyen rifle, breech-loaded, using a Peters shell, 9½ Remington primer (NM) 12 grains of DuPont shotgun powder and a blotter wad with 1-pound pressure. The sight used was a 20x Stevens scope. The bullet was of 200 grains, base-pour and cutoff (type), cast 1/20. A Pope machine rest was employed. The 40 consecutive shots measure ½ x ½ center to center of widest shots."

Keep in mind that Rowland was a man in his seventies when he did this shooting! This is certainly a tribute to Rowland and Schoyen as well. However, as mentioned earlier,

the discussion over who made the most accurate barrels will never end, for Rowland used a Pope 32-40 in shooting the .725-inch group which was the standard of accuracy for half a century at 200 yards.

One of Rowland's favorite rifles had a 39-caliber bore chambered for the 38-55 case. This barrel was unearthed during the excavation of a foundation for a large building near Boulder Creek, at Boulder, Colorado.

Mr. Rowland was on hand and thought he heard the ring of fine steel. He called to the workmen and asked for, and was given, the old relic which he took to George Schoyen for reboring. When it was finished Schoyen said, "Yah, it is so, dat is the finest piece of steel effer I saw!" With this barrel Rowland later shot several 10-shot groups at 200 yards from a bench rest that measured ⅞-inch extreme spread.

At the offhand rifle matches, Schoyen rifles also proved to be superbly accurate. At Cheyenne, Wyoming, on May 21, 1899, Peter Bergerson equaled the world record with a Schoyen-Ballard rifle. His 32-40 was loaded with 42 grains of FFFg DuPont powder and a 216-gr. bullet muzzle-loaded. Oddly, Bergerson was also a custom barrelmaker. Today, little is known of him, although William L. Bruce, former member of the U.S. International Rifle team remembers him as being a fine gunsmith. Bergerson was competing for the first prize—a new Stevens No. 54 Schuetzen rifle—when he shot this group, narrowly defeating the runner-up, who was using a 35 caliber Schoyen-Winchester rifle.

On August 16, 1903, D.W. King, Jr., began shooting regularly each weekend at the Denver Rifle Club. His goal was the world record, then held by H.M. Pope. Early in January, 1904, he climaxed a run of 3040 consecutive shots using his Schoyen-Ballard rifle with a score of 917 out of a possible

1000. King shot 27 straight 10s (centers). He had the world record, and in doing so shot the highest average for the number of shots fired that had been attained. King manufactured early Schuetzen shooting accessories, such as a clever duplex powder measure, and gunsights, first in Denver and later in San Francisco, California. As the March, 1904, issue of *Outdoor Life* stated: "This shows the ability of Mr. King and the Schoyen rifle."

Late in 1905, Dr. Walter G. Hudson visited Denver and had Schoyen rebore his 33-caliber Remington underlever Schuetzen rifle to 38-55 at a cost of $6.00. Although this was the most economical means of attaining a Schoyen rifled barrel, it shot well, as the many records and meets that Hudson won indicate. At the American Record Match, February 22, 1910, held at Greenville, New Jersey, Hudson scored a 99 out of a possible 100. Earlier, he broke the world record with a 922 out of a possible 1000 using the same rifle.

Another Schuetzen rifleman, W.A. Kuntz, shooting offhand at 200 yards, hit a silver dollar 5 times straight with his 14½-lb. Schoyen-Ballard rifle. The list of users of Schoyen's work is endless and includes William S. Green, Tom D. East, Tom Blunt, Jim Ricker, Dr. Asquith, and J.P. Lower, the early-day Denver gun dealer.

Schoyen built both ornate and utilitarian rifles. One of J.P. Lower's sons, Joe, had Schoyen build a fine Sharps-Borchardt Schuetzen rifle with a diamond set into the engraved action. Later, the Colorado National Guard ordered fifty 22 caliber barrels that were bored off-center, so the firing pins in the Krag actions to which they were fitted could be used. If you want one of those Krags, you had better look diligently, since nearly all of them were converted back to their original calibers many years later by A.W. Peterson. Harry Pope did this job also.

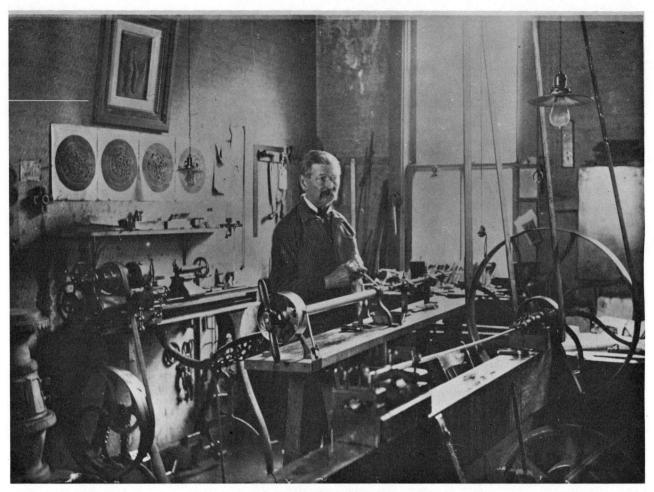

George Schoyen in his shop shortly after the turn of the century.

Schoyen's Barrels

The demand for Schoyen barrels, action modifications, custom stocks, and reloading accessories, had grown so great that by 1903 Schoyen formed another partnership. On October 1st, he was joined by Axel W. Peterson under the firm name of Schoyen and Peterson, located at 1417 Lawrence Street, Denver. A.W. Peterson had made quite a name for himself as an expert offhand rifle shot and gunsmith. He also had an inventive mind, and had recently developed one of the first rifle telescopes with internal adjustments. This partnership proved to be an advantageous combination as Peterson, who had not previously made barrels, quickly learned the skill of making the Schoyen barrel. As Peterson said of Schoyen in 1944, "His name vas on our barrels vether he made them or me. Ve both made the Schoyen barrels. He vas a very fine workman." Peterson was considered to be one of the best marksmen in the country, and traveled to many matches competing with a Schoyen-barreled Sharps-Borchardt rifle. In late 1906 Peterson scored a 98 out of a possible 100 with his muzzle-loading 38-55.

Schoyen's barrels were of the wide-groove and narrow-land type. The 22

and 25 calibers had 6 lands and grooves; the 28, 32 and 33 calibers had 7 grooves; the 38, 39, 40 and larger calibers had 9. Typically, these barrels had a right-hand twist and were generally not choked. The lands were about .03-inch wide, the grooves averaged .12-inch wide and .0025 to .003-inch deep. As Schoyen was a custom maker, deviations from the average barrel will be found. There are several larger caliber Schoyen rifles with both

6 and 8 rather than 9 grooves, and at least one rifle was made with a left-hand twist. The twist per inch varied somewhat in Schoyen's barrels. For example, Dr. John May owns a 38-55 Schoyen with one turn in 18 inches, and I have a Schoyen rifle in the same caliber with one turn in 16 inches. Until approximately 1900, these barrels were bored with a foot-operated treadle lathe and then rifled by hand. However, after Schoyen added power

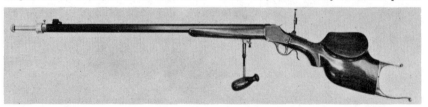

Winchester single shot rifle with Schoyen false muzzle barrel, stock, and action modifications. This perchbelly stock is the type most commonly found on Schoyen rifles. See text for details. *John Dutcher coll.*

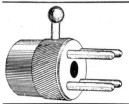

A Schoyen advertisement from the November, 1902, issue of *Outdoor Life.*

Schoyen false muzzle and bullet starter, the latter commonly made of aluminum. *John Dutcher coll.*

This point-pour bullet mould is the style typically made by Schoyen. Of 32 caliber, the mould is brass lined and the sprue cutter works on the bullet nose. *Claude Roderick coll.*

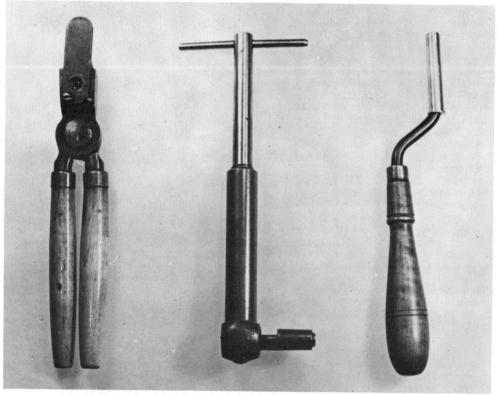

Schoyen bullet mould, bullet lubricating pump, and bullet breech-seating tool. Mould from *Claude Roderick coll.*, pump and seating tool from *John Dutcher coll.*

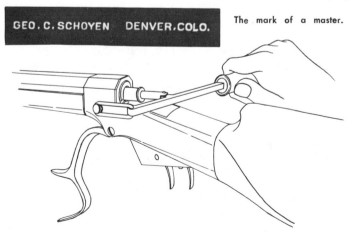

GEO. C. SCHOYEN   DENVER.COLO.

The mark of a master.

One method of breech-seating a bullet in the bore's throat and a Schoyen-made side-anchored lever. Drawing by John Dutcher.

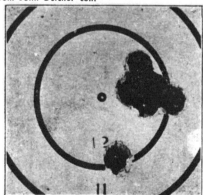

Ten shots at 200 yards, fired in April, 1903, by C.W. Rowland of Boulder, Colo. He used a Schoyen 32-40 rifle owned by John Barter of Boulder. As the July, 1903, *Outdoor Life* said: "It is rumored that Mr. Barter is now sitting up nights guarding his treasure, as there are a number of rifle cranks in Boulder."

equipment, he still continued to rifle his fine barrels by hand. Col. Frank H. Mayer, the old buffalo hunter, recalled that in the late 1890s he lost a quart of "Old Monogram" betting Dean King and Old Man Gilbert that they could not kick out a bore of 30 inches in two hours on Schoyen's treadle lathe. It is said that normally it took Schoyen nearly two days to make a complete rifle barrel. For a more detailed description on rifling these barrels, see L.L. Baker's article.

Schoyen shimmed the cutting head of his rifling machine with cigarette paper and made very light cuts. This operation was repeated until the desired bore dimensions were reached. He did little lapping or polishing, and occasionally when a barrel turns up that has been fired very little, slight traces of tool cuts are found in them. Most of these barrels were made of soft steel, and they'll polish up nicely with a little shooting. Each Schoyen barrel of 32 caliber or larger size was tested and guaranteed to shoot a 2½-inch or smaller 10-shot group at 200 yards. Schoyen, or one of his assistants, would ride the Denver & Intermountain Railroad to the Denver Rifle Club grounds at Golden, and test these barrels in an adjustable machine rest that he had built. This rest includes a telescope sight of Schoyen's manufacture.

In a recent survey of 67 different Schoyen rifles, nearly one-half of them were chambered for the 32-40 cartridge, 12 were made for the 38-55 and 8 for the 22 rimfire. The rest—many of them single specimens—were comprised of the following calibers: 40-70 Sharps straight, 33-40, 25-21, 28-30, 39-55, 40-70 Ballard, 25 rimfire, and 32- and 45-caliber caplock rifles. Undoubtedly, this is only a partial list. One third of these rifles were equipped with false muzzles and bullet starters of several styles. The false muzzle generally had 4 aligning pins. A few were equipped with locking levers made to fit lugs attached to the side of the barrel. One rifle has turned up with a 2-piece false muzzle. A few rifles were made for paper-patched bullets. Most barrels are octagonal, but part-octagon and round barrels are also found. Schoyen applied a rich chestnut-brown finish to many of his barrels. A formula for what is said to be this finish is found in Ned Roberts' book, *The Muzzle-loading Cap Lock Rifle.* His charge for "re-blacking" a rifle barrel was $1.50. An interesting copy of Schoyen & Peterson's price list reveals figures that will make you weep, my friends! However, as an old friend and single shot rifle fan, J.V.K. Wagar, has pointed out: "While prices were low in those years, so were wages."

Schoyen Tools

To assist the riflemen, Schoyen, together with Peterson, designed a full

The fine rifle seen here shows to good advantage the craftsmanship of Edwin Phillips, gunmaker in New York City circa 1860-1890. The oval gold plate set into the cheekpiece reads: Presented by the/HELVETIA RIFLE CLUB OF NEW YORK/to the/Third Union Shooting Festival/New York, July, 1868 in 5 lines. The schuetzen match in question was held near Jones Beach on Long Island—later to become the famous Creedmoor range. The various matches took a week to complete, and gross income was $30,000! Re-entry match fee was a nickel, but to compete in the American Match cost $10—a handsome sum in 1868.

All of the metal is fully and beautifully engraved—including the heavy steel buttplate, which is also silver inlaid—to patterns found in the L.D. Nimschke pattern book published by John J. Malloy.

When this Phillips rifle was made it had, most probably, a barrel of at least 45 caliber, perhaps even larger. At some time in the past, perhaps in the 1880s or so, George Schoyen fitted the muzzle-loading barrel now on the rifle. He matched the original engraving (or someone did) that shows on the breech flats to a quite good degree, but a close look reveals that the later work is not by Nimschke.

The caliber is 32-40, in effect, for the tools that came with the rifle—mould, false muzzle, piston starter, and so on—are identical with those that Schoyen furnished with his breech-loading offhand or bench rifles.

The 5 visible flats of the breech are engraved, the three flats of the breech and barrel being inlaid with gold lines. The back-action lockplate, the hammer, the steel buttplate, the barrel muzzle and both tangs are also engraved. On the left side of the action Columbia is seen seated, surrounded by a group of flags, while a golden-eyed fish is shown locked in combat with a snake.

The extension of the standing breech is marked L.D.N. over ENG.—For L. D. Nimschke, the engraver.

This Phillips-Schoyen rifle weighs 17 pounds without its false muzzle, but including the nearly 31-inch unmarked telescope sight. The barrel without false muzzle is 31¾-inch long. A steel cross-foot is attached to the underside of the barrel for rest shooting.

The name EMIL BERGER is engraved into a silver inlay on the left side of the buttplate. Berger was, presumably, the winner of the rifle of the 1868 shoot, but I've been unable to trace him. The cased rifle came to me from Iowa—the home state of many schuetzen shooters for many decades—and there was a family of marksmen named Berg in that area. Perhaps there was a connection.

line of loading tools and accessories: at least two styles of re- and decappers, both single- and duplex-cavity powder measures, bullet lubricating pumps made in two sizes (both of which had interchangeable dies), buttplates, palm rests, bullet moulds, custom buttstocks, and fore-ends. He also did repair work of all kinds and complete refinishing. Schoyen built many specialized tools, one of which was a grease-gun-type lubricating pump that ejected thin, uniform strips of olio lubricant from which Mr. Rowland made wads for his meticulous shooting.

Typically, the Schoyen mould is a brass-lined Ideal or Winchester mould altered to a point cut-off type, and casting a tapered bullet similar to the Pope. A few hand-made moulds were made in different styles. Mr. Schoyen's grandson has a beautifully crafted example, a double-cavity type with a point sprue cutter.

The custom buttstocks and fore-ends found on Schoyen rifles were generally made by A.W. Peterson or Henry Simmons; occasionally Schoyen did stock work also. Simmons worked for Schoyen prior to Peterson's entering the business, and stayed on during the partnership doing general gun repair.

Often the buttstocks are of the large perch-belly type, well-adapted to offhand shooting, though not always understood by today's riflemen and collectors. "Too large, too ungainly looking," or "It's ugly" are comments often heard. But they have a purpose. The large high cheekrest was fitted to hold the shooter's cheek, while the deep perch-belly lower part was designed to rest on the shooter's chest muscles, giving him maximum support of the rifle. They were not made to look at, but to use and, given time, one finds they have a purposeful beauty of their own. Each was made to the individual shooter's specifications. Of course, as Schoyen and Peterson's brochure stated: "We also make other shapes to order." A number of rifles have turned up with stocks that don't have the common characteristics attributed to Schoyen and Peterson, namely—shape, checkering styles and workmanship. For example, I've examined several with stocks by O.A. Bremer. These were custom rifles, so, I'm sure many other deviations and combinations of several gunsmiths' work will turn up from time to time. In examining Schuetzens, one will find a few "improved" home-horror-and-multilation type alterations that have been perpetrated on these rifles through the years. Such frustrating examples should not be blamed on the original gunsmith. It's all part of the game and should be expected if you have a fondness for this type of rifle.

Schoyen's inventive abilities are found in the fine double-set trigger modifications that are occasionally

George Schoyen in 1912. The poster on the wall behind Schoyen advertises a Schuetzenfest held in Frankfurt, Germany that same year.

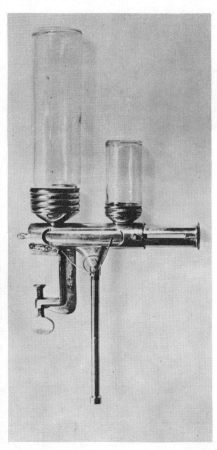

The Schoyen-Peterson duplex powder measure sold for $5.00. The smaller jar held the priming charge, while the larger jar metered the main charge of black powder. *Claude Roderick coll.*

seen on his rifles in addition to a clever barrel take-down system for the Ballard and other single shot actions. A taper pin is fitted through the action immediately below the barrel shank area. This pin passes through a groove milled in the bottom of the barrel shank. By tapping the small end of the pin, it is easily removed; and the barrel, which has coarse, easy threads, is screwed out by hand. When the pin is in place, the barrel is as tight as one could desire. A more refined version of this take-down system has a small button fitted to the left side of the action, it is pressed to dis-engage the barrel, then screwed out in the same manner as described above. This taper pin sometimes serves a dual purpose. It may also be used as an anchor pin to attach a lever type breech-seating tool that assists in pushing bullets into the barrel's throat. It is believed that Schoyen was the first to develop the side-anchored breech-seating tool.

Schoyen, along with Peterson, built many of the machines and tools they used, including a lathe. Being frugal Scandinavians, they used the old forge that Carlos Gove brought across the Great Plains from Iowa in 1860. This forge was still in use until the closing of the Peterson Gun Shop, shortly after World War II.

In the survey above of 67 Schoyen rifles, nearly half have Ballard actions, followed in order of numbers, by the Winchester Hi-Wall, Stevens 44 and 44½, and Sharps-Borchardt. A few Sharps side-hammer, Remington rolling block, Remington Hepburn, and two Remington-Schuetzen (underlever) actions are also found, along with several percussion-lock rifles. It is not believed that Schoyen produced cap-lock rifles in their entirety, but altered those made by other makers. If one were to describe the typical Schoyen rifle, as taken from the survey, it would be a 32-40 caliber offhand target rifle built on a double-set-trigger Ballard action, equipped with a full octagon No. 4 weight barrel. It may or may not be equipped with a false muzzle, and bullet starter. The barrel finish would be brown and the action case-hardened in color. It would have one of the large perch-belly Schuetzen buttstocks so typical of Schoyen's work. It would weigh between 13 and 14 pounds and, most importantly, it would be extremely accurate.

Yes, I know many are not that way —I own several without the above mentioned characteristics—but what

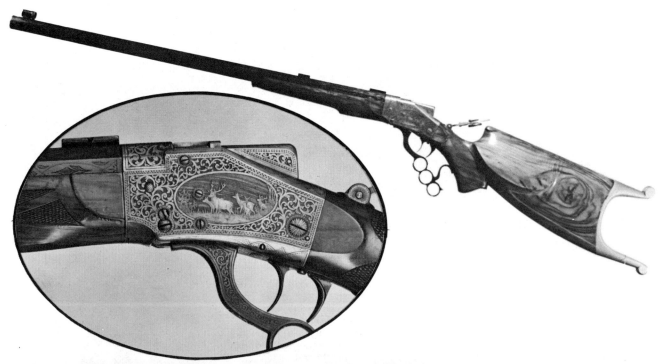

Fancy Schoyen Sharps-Borchardt 38-55 Schuetzen rifle. This rifle has Schoyen's triggers, barrel, finger lever and wood work. The close-up shows the excellent and unusual engraving, which covers the receiver, barrel breech flats, lever, etc. Rather oddly, the scroll work is less well done than the animal figure—the detailing and anatomy of these is superb. All of this engraving lies well above the background.

The Denver Rifle Club Team, winner of the Coors Championship Cup, July, 1898. Rear row, from left—D.W. King, J.A. Ricker and George C. Schoyen. Front row, from left—O.E. Adamson, Harry Willis and A.W. Peterson. Adamson holds a Maynard rifle, Willis a Remington-Hepburn, while Peterson's rifle is a Sharp-Borchardt with panelled receiver. Regrettably, the other rifles can't be seen.

I've described is the type found most frequently in the survey.

What kind of a man was this master craftsman? Schoyen is said to have been of average size, with brown hair and blue eyes, who dressed neatly in a suit and tie, even while at work making those fine rifle barrels. He is known to have had the happy faculty for making and keeping friends. A lady I talked with recently recalls Schoyen as a good family man who raised 5 daughters with the help of his Australian wife, whom he met in Chicago. She calls him "the kindest man I ever knew." He enjoyed his grandchildren, who spent much time in the shop and took turns helping Grandpa work his kick-operated treadle lathe. He also sent them out to look for old discarded shoes which, it is claimed, were used as charred leather in color-pack hardening rifle actions. A grandson, George Kane, has a diminutive Schuetzen rifle built on a Remington No. 2 action, which his grandfather built for George when he was a small boy. Schoyen was an officer in the Pioneer Rifle Club, a member of the Denver Rifle Club, and a member of the Sons of Colorado. In earlier years he was considered a consistent rifle shot, and as late as 1898 he was a member of the Denver Rifle

Henry Simmons (left) and George Schoyen, in the back ground, at his rifling machine. Photo taken in the 1890s.

Club team that won the Colorado State Championship. The Schoyen gun shop is remembered as a popular meeting place for gun enthusiasts of the day, and was often used for meetings of the Colorado Rifle Association.

By 1915, Mr. Schoyen and one of his sons-in-law had acquired a ranch south of Ralston Creek, near Golden, Colorado. Schoyen, who worked hard to attain the American dream, was thinking of retiring—but not completely. Although 70 years old, he was still capable of putting in a day's work, and there were so many old customers who insisted on a genuine Schoyen barrel. He decided to dissolve the partnership with A.W. Peterson and move his shop to the Ralston Creek ranch. But time had taken its toll, and Schoyen never made the move. He died on Saturday, January 23, 1916, at the County Hospital, shortly after midnight. He had suffered a stroke Friday morning while making a 22 caliber barrel.

The *Rocky Mountain News* carried word of Schoyen's death. In that story, J.P. Lower, the famous Denver outfitter during the frontier days, said of Schoyen: "That man was an artist, an artist. He was the best gunmaker in the country. You couldn't beat him anywhere. And a fine man, too. A fine gunmaker and a fine man was George Schoyen." ●

One of two styles of re-de cappers made by the firm of Schoyen & Peterson. *John Dutcher coll.*

RIFLE BARRELS

New muzzle loading barrels with loading outfit................$25.00

Outfit consists of false muzzle, bullet starter, special bullet mould to run from point, lubricating pump, and ramrod.

Old barrels bored, re-rifled, and fitted with false muzzle, with loading outfit complete, same as new barrels, $20.00

Bore and re-rifle muzzle loading barrels $10.00

If new bullet moulds are necessary, they will be extra.

New breech loading barrels.$12.00

Bore and re-rifle old breech loading barrels $6.00

We do not re-bore repeating rifles.

We will fit your sights, extractor and forearm to our new barrels, but if new ones are required they will be extra.

Our barrels are fully guaranteed for accuracy, quality and workmanship. A 32-calibre and larger sizes, will make 2½ inch group or better at 200 yards from machine rest if weather and conditions are right.

We consider a 30 inch barrel, 32-calibre or larger, the best, but will furnish 32 inch at the same price. For smaller calibres we think 28 inch the best.

Barrels smaller than 32-calibre and over 28 inches long, $2.00 extra.

Weight of No. 4 barrels is about 7½ to 8 pounds; heavier barrels will be $1.00 a pound extra.

Special bullet mould to run from point	$3.50
Lubricating pump	2.50
Extra disc	.75
Palm rests, our own make	3.50
Finger grips fitted to levers same as on our make of rifles	
Polishing and case hardening actions	3.00
Re-black rifle barrel	1.50
Re-black double barrel	3.00
Re-stocking shot guns and rifles according to shape and quality of wood used	$6.00 to $25.00
Forearms for rifles from $1.50 to $5.00	

PRICES NET

In ordering stocks give length from forward trigger to center of butt plate, and drop from level top of barrel to top of butt plate and comb.

We also make a specialty of rifle stocks of our own design, that are made to order to fit the person and allowing the shooter to stand and hold in a perfectly natural position.

The records that have been made with our special target rifles speak for themselves.

Read it and weep! An early Schoyen & Peterson price list.

Bibliography
Books
Ripley's *Believe It or Not.*
Roberts, Major Ned and Kenneth L. Waters. *The Breech Loading Single Shot Match Rifle.* Princeton, N. J., 1967.
Wallack, L. R. *Modern Accuracy.* New York, N. Y., 1950.
Periodicals
"A Good Combination," *The Sporting Goods Dealer,* IX, No. 2 (November, 1903), 47.
Baker, Leighton L. "How Peterson Barrels Were Made," *The American Rifleman,* CVIII, No. 8 (August, 1960), 26.
Beise, Charles J. "Rifleman Extraordinary," *Western Sportsman,* IV, Nos. 2 and 3 (December, 1940 and January, 1941).
Denver City Directories, 1884 through 1916.
Leopold, E. A. "The Schoyen Rifle," *Shooting and Fishing* (November 14, 1901).
Outdoor Life (November, 1902).
——— (July, 1903), 492.
——— (December, 1903), 870.
——— (March, 1904), 188.
——— XVII-XVIII (April, 1906), 407.
——— (January, 1907), 98.
Rocky Mountain News (January 24, 1916).
Sports Afield (August 1, 1888).
Tedmon, Allyn. "That Man Peterson," *The American Rifleman,* XCII, No. 1 (January, 1944), 22.
"The American Record Match," *Arms and The Man,* XLVII, No. 22 (February, 1910), 460.
The Denver Post (January 24, 1916).
"The Genesis of the American Rifle," *The American Rifleman,* LXXXIV, No. 3 (March, 1936), 12.
"Trap and Target," *Outdoor Life* (June, 1899 and February, 1900).
Other Sources
Personal interviews with William L. Bruce, Norman Ghen, Mr. and Mrs. George Kane, Mrs. Minne Kirk, Floyd Redding.

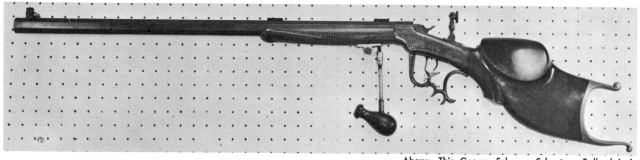

Above—This George Schoyen Schuetzen Ballard is in John Amber's collection. There are three barrels—one in 22 Long Rifle caliber, another in 38-55, and the 30¼-inch 32-40 barrel is pictured. Only the latter has a false muzzle. As pictured, the rifle weighs 15½ pounds. Because the breech take-down screw goes through the front of the action, the serial number has lost two digits, reads 3xx92 ● Left—the tang sight on the Schoyen Ballard is the Pope double-capstan type, the adjusting pin shown inserted into one of the several holes ● Below—The 32-40 bullet mould with the Schoyen Ballard is marked BY H. M. POPE, HARTFORD, CONN. Most other Pope moulds seen are unmarked.

Accessories for the Schoyen Ballard rifle. From left—false muzzle, H.M. Pope mould, bullet starter for false muzzle and breech-type bullet starter. Palm rest at top.

Blunder Busts !

by WALTER F. ROPER

WHEN ONE considers that in the different kinds of fire-arms can be found practically every kind of mechanical motion, it isn't any wonder that guns provide a most interesting subject for study for anyone at all "mechanically minded." Add to this the fact that guns provide a means for men to deliver a tremendously powerful blow, accurately and at long and even at extraordinary distances, and it is easy to understand the fascination they have for most men and boys as well as for a great number of women.

One of the fundamental instincts of an American is the desire to improve things, and when this instinct leads to the changing of guns by those who are not completely familiar with all the factors involved, trouble frequently results—and often serious injury to the shooter.

In the hope of preventing trouble and injuries, let's consider some of the things that should *not* be done to guns. *All of them HAVE been done,* as the repair departments of any of the firearms manufacturing concerns can testify.

Without doubt the most usual bit of gunsmithing attempted by shooters is the lightening or sharpening of the trigger let-off by stoning the parts. As this can be extremely dangerous with any kind of gun, let's give it some careful thought. Each of the three usual kinds of guns, because of the different treatment each can receive, calls for individual consideration. These three types of guns are: (1) revolvers, (2) automatic pistols, rifles, and shotguns, and (3) single- and double-barrel shotguns and pump-action rifles and shotguns.

1. DON'T CHANGE SEAR ANGLES.

First let's put down this fact as basic. With any simple action—that is, one that does not work on the set trigger principle—it is absolutely necessary to have a certain minimum engagement of sear and hammer for safety. There is too much chance for wear to round over the edge of either the sear point or hammer notch to depend upon the edge of either for the engagement that will provide a safe, uniform support for the hammer at full cock. There should always be a certain amount of flat engaging surfaces. This means that the notch in the hammer must have real depth. The second fundamental requirement is that the trigger must cause at least a slight backward motion of the hammer when it is moved out of the hammer notch. If this does not occur, even a very slight jar can cause the trigger to slip out of the notch and cause an accidental discharge.

With a revolver, the two-pound trigger pull allowed by the rules of the National Rifle Association and the U.S. Revolver

Association is the very minimum that should be attempted. Even so, since much of this amount can be due to the trigger and main springs, great care must be taken to make sure that the engagement of the trigger point (sear) and the hammer notch is sufficiently deep and at such an angle that the pressure of the main spring tends to force the trigger into full engagement in the hammer notch. To produce such a pull and meet the other requirements is not a job for anyone who has not had real experience. *Better have a competent gunsmith do it.*

In an effort to lighten the trigger pull, shooters often try lightening the main or trigger springs of a revolver, either by shortening a strain screw or grinding or shortening the spring. Not only can this cause misfiring but in some makes of revolvers it can affect the operation of the safety mechanism. *It should never be done.*

The second class of guns—automatic pistols, rifles, and shotguns—calls for even greater consideration before any work is done on the trigger mechanism. In these guns the trigger (or sear) must engage the hammer almost instantly, as the motion of the slide (or bolt) which forces the hammer to full cock is extremely rapid. In addition the inertia of the rapidly moving hammer, and in some cases the trigger also, can cause over-motion which can affect the immediate and complete engagement of the parts. Not only should the engagement be greater in guns of this type, but the angle of the engaging surfaces must be such that the trigger cannot possibly slip or rebound out of the hammer notch.

With automatic rifles and shotguns, another factor makes deep engagement of sear and hammer absolutely necessary. Guns of this kind are often allowed to slip through the fingers while held in a vertical position until the butt strikes the ground. The jar given the parts of the gun when this happens can easily make an improperly made trigger-hammer mechanism disengage and cause an accidental discharge.

This possibility must be kept in mind when the trigger pull of a single- or double-barrel or slide-action shotgun is worked upon. Making a trigger pull is therefore not simply a matter of stoning the parts until a certain weight of pull is obtained. All of the things that are affected by the trigger pull must be understood and kept in mind by the gunsmith.

2. DON'T CHANGE THE BALANCE OF PARTS IN A GUN.

The letter that accompanied the bolt-action shotgun returned to the factory stated that the owner had been killed by the gun going off when he allowed it to drop a few inches while the barrel was vertical, until the butt struck the ground. It was immediately thought that the trigger or ham-

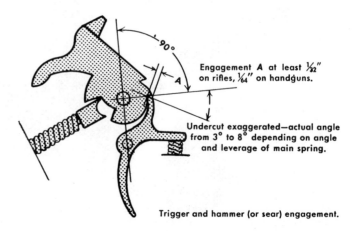

Engagement A at least 1/32" on rifles, 1/64" on handguns.

Undercut exaggerated—actual angle from 3° to 8° depending on angle and leverage of main spring.

Trigger and hammer (or sear) engagement.

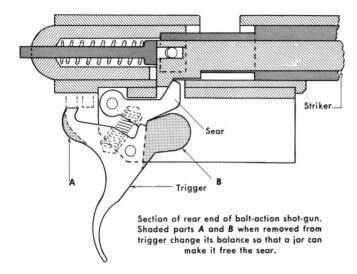

Section of rear end of bolt-action shot-gun. Shaded parts *A* and *B* when removed from trigger change its balance so that a jar can make it free the sear.

mer, or both, had been stoned in an attempt to lighten the trigger pull, or had become worn, and the jar the gun had received had made the trigger slip out of the hammer notch.

Examination of these parts, however, showed that the engagement was ample for safety and that something else had caused the gun to fire. The cause was soon found—a large section of the trigger located above the pivot had been cut away—for what reason could never be determined, for the owner of the gun was dead. His death was directly due to the change he had made in the balance of the trigger.

The inertia of the parts of a gun is one of the seldom-mentioned factors that gun designers have to consider carefully, and changes in the balance of parts of a gun should never be made. In the gun referred to, the metal that had been taken from above the pivot of the trigger had been put there by the manufacturer for a very important reason—i.e., it caused the trigger to press more firmly into the notch in the hammer if the gun received a blow on the butt. When that weight above the center was removed, inertia caused the heavier lower part of the trigger to move backward and caused the trigger to slip out of the hammer notch when the gun received a blow on the butt.

Every moving part of a gun is affected by inertia brought into action when the recoil makes the gun move rapidly. The parts have been proportioned so that they will not move out of the proper relationship with other parts, so the removal of metal from a part can, and usually does, affect the operation of the gun and can cause accidental discharge. *Don't do it.*

3. HOMEMADE DEER LOADS.

Every fall when the deer season comes around, manufacturers of shotguns are sure to receive guns with burst barrels. Some, of course, will have been ruined by such obstructions as snow, mud, a twig, or similar things, but others will have burst barrels caused by the shooter using deer slug loads he has made by replacing the shot in a shell with a deer slug.

Most deer slugs are of such a size that they will fall through the barrel, but a slight deformation of the slug can prevent it from doing so, and if it happens to be jarred out of the shell it can cause an obstruction that will cause a bad bulge and usually a burst barrel.

The slug of one of these homemade deer loads won't move instantly when a shot is fired in the other barrel of a double gun. Its inertia keeps it stationary. The crimp of the shell, weakened by being unfolded, spreads; and the shell moves

back with the recoil, leaving the slug in the barrel. If this happens, and it has many times, the slug may be overlooked, and a fresh shell put in behind it. If that shell is fired, the result will be a ruined gun, and possible serious injury to the shooter. *It's too dangerous—don't do it.*

There is another type of homemade deer load that is certain to ruin a shotgun barrel, and often so weaken it that the barrel actually bursts. This is the substitution of steel balls from an old ball bearing for the shot in a shell intended for bird shooting. Whether done in the hope of obtaining greater penetration, or just because the needed buck shot loads were not on hand when needed, the result will be a badly gouged barrel, the hard balls actually rolling grooves in the bore. If several of these loads are fired, the metal of the barrel can be so reduced in thickness in spots that it is not strong enough to withstand the pressure and a split or burst barrel results. Even if the burst does not occur, the gouged barrel will mean that a new barrel will be required. *Don't do it.*

4. DON'T WEAKEN THE FIRING PIN RETRACTOR SPRING OR ALTER THE RETRACTOR STUD.

The shooter who had the following experience didn't deliberately do either of the things noted above. In his case the part just broke, but the same thing could be made to happen by changing the firing pin spring or the retractor stud in a gun. Both are put there by the manufacturer to prevent the firing pin from being thrown forward and striking the primer. Often the blow delivered when an action is closed fast is enough to fire the cartridge or shell. This shooter's pump-action shotgun jammed, and he took it apart to see what was causing the trouble. It was a little piece of steel about 1/4″ in diameter and 1/2″ long which he thought had probably fallen into the action in some way. When he had removed it, the gun seemed to work all right and he considered he had done a first-class job and saved time and the cost of sending the gun back to the manufacturer.

The next week-end he went to the Skeet Club. He was one of the careful shooters who load only a single shell for the single targets, so everything went fine until he loaded for doubles, then when he reloaded fast for the second target, the gun fired as he closed it. That ruined his score, but he continued, and again when he reloaded fast for the second target of the doubles, the gun fired. That ended his shooting for the day. That little piece of steel he had removed had been the

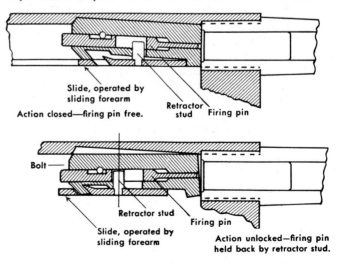

Slide, operated by sliding forearm

Action closed—firing pin free.

Retractor stud Firing pin

Bolt

Retractor stud

Slide, operated by sliding forearm

Firing pin

Action unlocked—firing pin held back by retractor stud.

Tipping bolt, slide-action shotgun.

retractor stud. When it broke off, there was nothing to prevent the firing pin from throwing ahead when the action was closed fast and inertia made the firing pin keep on going when the bolt stopped. It struck the primer hard enough to fire the shell.

Some guns depend upon a spring around the firing pin to prevent the inertia from throwing the pin forward. In such guns the strength of the firing pin spring is most important; so if a spring has to be replaced, it is vital that it have the proper strength. In guns having a retractor stud this part should never be altered, and if you find a small piece of steel in the action, *don't just remove it.* It may be the retractor stud and the part should be replaced before an accidental discharge can occur. It might easily be more serious than simply the loss of a clay target.

5. DON'T TRY TO REDUCE THE PULL OF AN S & W REVOLVER BY WEAKENING THE TRIGGER SPRING.

A gun designer who can make a single spring or part do the work that otherwise would call for two springs or pieces, is smart; but a shooter who reduces the strength of a spring to get a certain result without considering the effect of doing so upon all the parts of the gun, is taking chances—to say the least. Take the fine S & W revolver action, for instance. In it the trigger spring also operates the rebound slide that cams the hammer back from the primer of the shell after discharge. Weakening that spring will of course make the trigger pull lighter, but it is downright criminal to make such a change, for it can make the gun completely unsafe. Just consider it for a moment. If that spring is weakened, it may not push the hammer back far enough for the flat part of the rebound slide to come under the flat surface of the hammer. If that happens, a blow on the hammer can drive it forward and strike the primer of a loaded cartridge and fire it. *The gun may be pointing at your body or that of someone else. Don't do it. Don't alter a gun in any way until you understand everything that can be affected by a change.*

6. LOOK OUT FOR 20-GAUGE SHOT SHELLS IF YOU SHOOT BOTH A "12" AND A "20."

A lot of shooters agree with me that there isn't any sweeter gun for field shooting than a really fine double "20," but when it comes to ducks or pheasant the "12" is needed. That combination, while perfect for the shotgun man, can also be poison.

It so happens that the rim of the 20-gauge shell is just exactly right in size to wedge firmly in the forcing cone of a 12-gauge gun if the 20-gauge shell is dropped into the chamber of the larger bore gun. Usually it wedges so firmly into the forcing cone that it won't drop out even when the gun is opened and the breech lowered. Sometimes even a bump on the gun butt won't free it. When no shell is seen in the chamber when the gun is opened, it is easy for a shooter to conclude that the shell was ejected and fell into the grass and was lost. So he loads again, this time with a 12-gauge shell! When he fires, he has at least (if he is lucky) a ruined gun. If unlucky, he may have lost a hand or perhaps his life. The 20-gauge shell will explode more often than not and when it does a section of the barrel will be blown out. Not just split, a piece will be torn away and that piece can cause a terrible wound.

The moral is simple — *don't let* 20-gauge and 12-gauge shells become mixed. Turn your pockets inside out after a day afield. A 20-gauge shell can get caught in a corner of a pocket and remain there and be picked up accidentally instead of the 12-gauge shells you thought you were getting. *Watch those 20-gauge shells.*

7. DON'T STONE PARTS JUST BECAUSE THEY SHOW THEY RUB ON SOMETHING.

This is another case where a knowledge of *all* the functions of a part is necessary before changes are made. Let's consider a revolver now. Perfect alignment of the cylinder chambers with the bore is vital for accuracy, of course. That is so obvious that there is no need to go into a proof of it, and all fine guns are designed to produce that alignment. Some guns have a cylinder latch that is fitted to engage notches in the cylinder with a minimum of play and hold the cylinder from rotating in either direction, while other guns are so made that the cylinder is held over against the cylinder latch by the hand that rotates the cylinder, pressing against the flatted side of the cylinder ratchet after the cylinder has been turned the correct amount. In guns that operate on this latter principle, the hand is fitted so it will press against the flat portion of the ratchet tooth, and will show a bright surface due to the rubbing it receives. Many a shooter, thinking that that rubbing will make the trigger pull harder, has stoned that hand of his gun and spoiled the alignment and the accuracy of his gun. *Don't stone that bright spot. If you do, you will affect the alignment of the cylinder and bore.*

8. SMOKELESS AMMO IN EARLY S & W's.

The following recommendation is made with reluctance, as it may discourage someone from taking up my favorite handgun sport—i.e., single shot pistol shooting. However, it is a warning that should be given. *Don't shoot any of the modern smokeless 22 Long Rifle cartridges in either the Model 91 or Perfected Model single shot pistols until the breech of the barrel and the extractor have been built out to surround the head of the shell.*

With the black powder or even the early Lesmok 22 Long Rifle ammunition, shell heads seldom if ever burst when fired

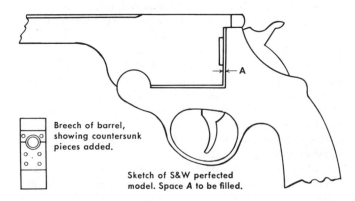

Breech of barrel, showing countersunk pieces added.

Sketch of S&W perfected model. Space A to be filled.

in these guns even though the rim of the shell was not surrounded by metal, but things were different when the new ammunition came along. Shell heads of this modern ammunition must be supported or they will blow out and an injured hand usually results.

Have a flat piece of steel fitted to the breech of the barrel, thick enough to just fill the space between the back surface of the barrel and the frame. This piece will reach to the top surface of the extractor, and be recessed for half the shell head. Another piece must be fastened to the back surface of the extractor and recessed for the bottom half of the shell head.

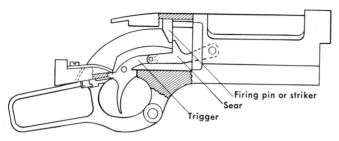

Firing pin or striker
Sear
Trigger

Savage Model 99 (Action closed).

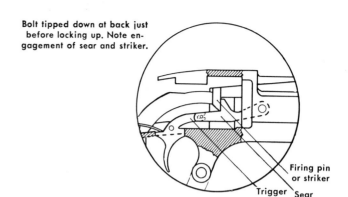

Firing pin or striker
Trigger Sear

Savage Model 99 (Action open).

Don't take a chance. A piece of copper from a shell driven deep into your thumb can cause a serious and extremely painful wound.

9. A SPECIAL DON'T.

While on the subject of the single shot pistol, here's an emphatic *Don't.* If you happen to get hold of an S & W Single Shot Pistol chambered for the 38 S & W cartridge, *don't use it.* Especially if you find it will take the 38 *Special* cartridge. (Yes, there were a few of them made.) There was always a question about the strength of those barrels that were made to shoot the S & W 38 regular cartridge, but even the 38 Special black powder load was considered unsafe by those who tried it. With any modern smokeless cartridge the barrel simply isn't strong enough. An effort was made to obtain and destroy all of the experimental 38 Special barrels that were made, but there are probably a few of them in existence, so look out. *Don't fool with one of them.*

10. THE S & W 38-44 AND MAGNUM.

Built on the same frame and apparently otherwise very much alike, owners of the S & W 38-44 Outdoorsman Revolver often see no reason why they cannot have their gun chambered for the slightly longer Magnum cartridge, and have the most powerful handgun ever built as well as a fine target gun.

Again there are other factors that must be considered besides just the matter of making the cylinder take the slightly longer cartridge. The truth is that while the 38-44 cartridge can be fired safely in a gun having a cylinder in which the cartridge heads are not encased in steel, the Magnum cartridge, which develops much more pressure, *must* have the head encased to make certain that none will be burst. So, when the factory tells you that the Outdoorsman cannot be chambered for the Magnum cartridge, *don't have some gunsmith chamber the cylinder a little deeper so it will take the longer Magnum cartridge. Don't do it.*

11. THE 455 AND 45 AUTOMATIC CARTRIDGES.

Have you one of those fine S & W guns that were chambered for the 455 English cartridge? Have you been thinking that if you could have it fitted with a cylinder that was chambered for the 45 Automatic cartridge you would have a gun you could use more? *Don't consider it.* Here again there is something else to be considered, in this case the depth of the rifling. The 455 cartridge uses a lead bullet and the barrel of the guns made for that ammunition had deeper rifling grooves than is proper for the metal patched automatic bullet. It just isn't safe to shoot those hard-jacketed bullets in the deeply rifled 455 barrel. Those 455-caliber guns are fine but are not right for anything but lead bullets.

12. THE SAVAGE MODEL 99.

If the shooter who made the change I'm going to describe now in his Model 99 Savage rifle had ever seen a cut-away model of the gun and had seen how the parts worked, he never would have reduced the engagement of the hammer and the sear as he did, and he would not have had the experience of having the gun fire before it was locked up. His intention, when he took the rifle apart to give it a thorough cleaning, was fine. Guns should be cleaned like any piece of machinery. The trouble was he didn't understand how the action worked and when he saw that the hammer showed by the long brightened surface that it engaged the sear a great distance, he figured that by shortening that engagement he would improve the trigger pull.

What he didn't realize was that to lock up, the rear end of the bolt rises, so, although before the lock-up occurs, the hammer does engage the sear a considerable amount (a mighty good feature too), when the bolt rises into the locked-up position, the engagement is reduced to no more than in the usual type of hammer and trigger action.

He didn't reduce the engagement much, but it was enough so that the hammer slipped off the sear just before full lock-up took place. The action blew open and the repairs were decidedly expensive. Fortunately, he wasn't injured, that was just good luck. *Again, don't change parts in a gun until you fully understand what they do. They are made as they are for some good reason — usually to prevent you from ever being hurt.*

13. FIRING PINS ARE IMPORTANT.

There is no question about it, firing pins do break. In fact, that is probably the most common cause of a gun being put out of action. Most firing pins look like a simple piece to make, and when, after a struggle a shooter manages to get the pin out, he decides to have his friend at the garage turn one up and save time, rather than sending the gun back to the maker to be put into shape. Did you ever see a rifle or shotgun go off when the action was closed? Ever see what can happen when a primer is punctured? If you have, you will know two good reasons for having someone fit a new firing pin who *knows* what he's doing. It's not just a matter of getting the pin the right size and the cross cut for the retaining pin in the right place. The length of the pin as well as the right length of the retaining pin cut are of vital importance. If the pin protrudes through the bolt just a little too much, the gun may fire when the bolt is closed; or if it doesn't do that, the pin may puncture the primer. Both are dangerous. *Don't try to do jobs on guns until you know all the requirements—it's safer.*

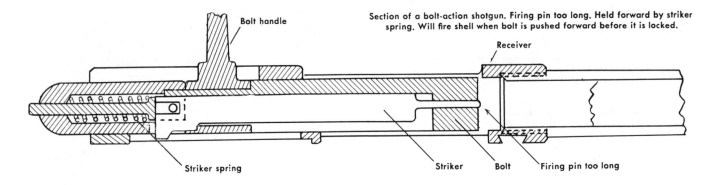

Bolt handle

Section of a bolt-action shotgun. Firing pin too long. Held forward by striker spring. Will fire shell when bolt is pushed forward before it is locked.

Receiver

Striker spring

Striker | Bolt | Firing pin too long

14. DON'T WEAKEN THE TOP STRAP OF A REVOLVER.

The victim of this bit of gunsmithing was one of the most admired handguns ever built—the S & W Triple Lock or New Century Model. It was just luck that the shooter wasn't seriously injured. With light target loads for the 44 Special cartridge, this shooter did remarkable shooting, and with the high-power loads he had developed he had shot several deer and a lot of smaller game. His only criticism of the gun was that the old-fashioned half round, thin front sight and very small rear notch didn't make sighting any too easy. He wanted a large gold bead front sight and a rear sight that he could adjust, and with a proper size notch for the new front sight.

He didn't accept his gunsmith's recommendation that he leave the gun alone and decided to install the new rear sight he had purchased, himself. He did a good job too, being careful to make the dovetail cut in the top strap a nice fit for the base of the new sight. The results he obtained in his target shooting were better than he had hoped for, for now he could sight at exactly six o'clock and make center tens because he could set that new rear sight just as needed.

Then came the time to get ready for his annual deer hunt. He felt sure that now he would be able to set the sights so he could hold on the spot he wanted to hit instead of the over-hold he had to use with the old sights. His first few shots in his effort to sight the gun for the longer range went all right and he loaded up to shoot a five-shot group. That's when it happened. On his third shot the top strap ruptured and the gun was ruined. The dovetail slot he had cut into the top strap had reduced its strength fully 50% and it just couldn't stand the strain of the heavy loads.

Many shooters, remembering that some of the old Colt guns had no top strap, have wrongly concluded that the top strap of a revolver doesn't bear much of the stress of the discharge. Don't you believe it. A stress diagram of a revolver will show that the top strap is under a heavy strain. Weakening it by cutting a dovetail slot in it for a rear sight is dangerous—especially if you ever want to shoot a heavy load. *Don't do it.*

15. DOUBLE ACTION SHOOTING.

Back in the days when a misfire was a basis for claiming an alibi, I once saw a shooter get four alibi runs before the range officer took a hand. That shooter was a double action artist and a good one too. He had done everything he could think of to make his gun work as easily as possible. One of his "adjustments" was to shorten the strain screw of his S & W revolver. That of course lightened the pressure of the main spring. Evidently he had obtained some ammunition with harder primers, or some that were less sensitive, for he never would have attempted to compete with a gun that would fail as often as his did in that match.

Weakening the main spring in order to make double action shooting easier not only can cause misfiring, it can ruin the accuracy also. Manufacturers have found that even if the hammer blow is not light enough to actually cause misfires, the poor ignition resulting from too light a blow will change a highly accurate arm into one that no one would care to shoot.

The shooter referred to had also made another "adjustment." To make the action as easy as possible, he had lightened the trigger spring also. His claim was that the lighter the trigger spring, the faster he could cock the gun double action. What he didn't take into consideration was that as he lightened that trigger spring he lengthened the time taken for the trigger to return to its forward position, so while he may have gained a little because of his faster firing pull, he probably lost just as much, and maybe more, because of the longer time required for the trigger to be ready for the next shot. *Take everything into consideration before you make changes in a gun.*

16. IF YOU MAKE A SET OF STOCKS FOR YOUR HANDGUN.

Many shooters are having the fun of making their own hand-fitting stocks, and in the hope of helping them get really fine results, the following "don'ts" are offered.

First of all, don't make your stocks too big. The tendency is always to go to the other extreme after trying to hold a gun easily with the undersize grips supplied on most factory guns. Try to keep the palm side of your stocks of such a thickness that the second knuckle of your second finger is directly under the center of the trigger guard. This is easily possible with a revolver, but cannot usually be done on stocks for an automatic pistol due to the size of the frame. On these guns get as close to that condition as possible. Next, don't make the "filler" between the trigger guard and the front strap too narrow. Keep it wide. The larger the surface that rests upon your second finger, the less you will feel the

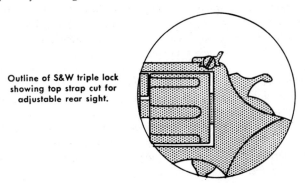

Outline of S&W triple lock showing top strap cut for adjustable rear sight.

weight of the gun. Also, slope the bottom surface of that filler downward from the palm side of the stocks to the finger side. *Don't make it straight across,* your finger slopes downward to the left and you don't want an edge bearing on that finger—it will make it sore in a short time.

One more "don't." Of course you will bulge the palm side of your stocks to fill the hollow of your hand. *Put that bulge in the proper place, not in the center of the stock.* The place for it is right up against the back strap. That is where the hollow of your palm comes when you close your hand on the stocks. When you have your stocks all made just as you want them, *don't,* unless you know how to do it, try to checker them yourself. Better have a real expert do it—it's too easy to spoil a good set of stocks by messing up the checkering job.

17. DON'T FORGET TO CLEAN THE EXTRACTOR OF AN AUTO-MATIC PISTOL. IT CAN BE DANGEROUS IF LEFT DIRTY.

No matter what other cleaning utensils you have, or even if you have given up cleaning the barrel since non-corrosive ammunition became available, *don't neglect the extractor of any automatic using greased ammunition.*

Here is what happened when one shooter neglected to attend to that most important part of cleaning. In the middle of a string on the 50-yard range, he was called to the club-house telephone. He took the magazine out of his 22 automatic, then pulled the slide back to extract the shell that had been put into the chamber when he fired his last shot. Then he laid the gun on the firing line table. When he returned, he prepared to leave, as he had been called home. Just before he put the gun into his shooting box, he pressed the trigger to relieve the tension of the main spring. Fortunately the gun was pointing at the ground, but even then when it suddenly fired, the bullet struck the shooter standing next to him in the foot.

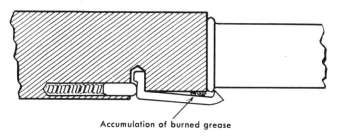

Accumulation of burned grease

Investigation showed that the extractor was held up from its proper way-down position by an accumulation of burned grease. When the slide worked fast when the gun was fired, the extractor was held down a little harder than the spring pressure by the inertia developed, and would just pull the fired shell out of the chamber. When the slide was worked by hand, however, inertia was not developed and the extractor would slide over the rim of the cartridge that was in the chamber and leave it there. The shooter had done everything required to make the gun completely empty and safe, but that dirty extractor had set the stage for what might have been a fatal accident. As it was, a fellow shooter was painfully injured.

A good stiff-bristled toothbrush is a good tool to use in cleaning the extractor, but however you do it, *don't forget that extractor.*

Study your guns, find out how they work, what each part does and what will be affected by the change you have in mind. A lot of thought has been put into the design of every gun. There is a good reason why it is made as it is. *Understand that reason.*

There is always a chance to improve any mechanism, but really know what you are doing before taking a chance. Things happen too quickly when the trigger is pulled, and there isn't any time to correct a mistake.

PRACTICE NECESSARY FOR GOOD SHOOTING

How accurate is your "shooting eye" this season? Chances are you missed a lot of easy shots in the first open days and you still may be fussing and fuming about your poor marksmanship. There is usually a very definite reason for this, and that is lack of practice.

"A good many sportsmen," says Henry P. Davis, public relations manager, Remington Arms Company, Inc., "make the mistake of stowing their favorite gun away at the end of the open season and never paying any attention to it until upland birds and waterfowl are fair game again. Then they wonder why they miss the usually fairly easy shots offered during the early part of the open season.

Shooting is just like anything else. You've got to keep at it to be really proficient. I don't mean one has to practice with conscientious regularity to maintain a fair degree of marksmanship once he has acquired the knack of handling a sporting firearm effectively. But I do mean that consistent practice pays off in game fairly and cleanly bagged, and any man's shooting ability gets pretty rusty if he neglects it.

It has been said that once a person learns to swim or ride a bicycle, he never loses the knack. That may be true, but he is surely not as proficient a swimmer or cyclist as he once

was if he gives these sports only an occasional fling. Shooting is much the same. Once the gunner has acquired the knack of breaking clay targets, registering bulls-eyes or handling his gun effectively in the game fields, he can usually be counted on to do a fairly good job without regular practice. He should hardly be expected to step up to the traps and break a straight without a bit of brushing up, but he at least knows enough to keep his head down on the stock, to follow through on his swing and to shoot ahead of angling flying targets.

But practice is the one thing that can keep a gunner's marksmanship up to par. And it is not difficult to maintain. There are skeet and trapshooting facilities available in almost every community. And rifle clubs are located all over the country. But even if organized shooting facilities are not conveniently available, handtrap shooting is always easily accessible. And shooting "clay" targets thrown from a Remington handtrap is about the finest wing-shooting practice the gunner can obtain. With this small, light and easy-to-handle trap, the gunner can throw his own targets if he so desires, or have a companion dish up for him **an almost duplicate of any game shot in the books.** Targets simulating an exceedingly wide range of angles, heights and distances can

easily be offered with a minimum of effort. These could vary from high-over-head passing duck shots to low, skimming "grass cutters" in imitation of running rabbits.

It's just a whale of a lot of fun to shoot targets thrown from a handtrap because of the high versatility of this sport. Almost any type of competitive shooting game can be originated and thoroughly enjoyed. "Surprise" angles can be sprung and the thrown targets may be made as easy or as difficult as desired.

This type of shooting is of particular value in familiarizing the gunner with different shooting distances, how to gauge them and how much lead is necessary at each. Markers may be placed at known distances and targets thrown over them at various angles. This is a quick and very effective method of determining how much to lead various game birds at different distances. Even the speed of the target can be regulated by the thrower.

All a shooter needs to keep his trigger finger sensitive and his "shooting eye" keen is an open space where it is safe to shoot, a quantity of "clay" saucers and his favorite gun and shells. A simple little handtrap completes the accouterments and puts him in business. Not only will he have a fine afternoon of sport, but he'll be correcting his shooting errors and pointing toward better success in the hunting field."

READERS of the third edition of the HANDLOADER'S DIGEST may recall that this writer did a piece on reloading our more recently developed rifle cartridges, entitled "Loading the New Ones." Judging from letters received, this feature met with a favorable response, and one reader, S/Sgt. Donald R. Boyd of the United States Air Force, proposed that several of the more popular older cartridges be given a similar treatment.

Following that suggestion, the writer has selected four old and two not-so-old cartridges to discuss and talk about loading, in the hope that the information given will be interesting as well as helpful, especially to owners of rifles in these calibers.

rifles of adequate strength. For these cartridges especially, such a survey of reloading possibilities can have even greater significance.

The Not-So-Old

The first pair of cartridges to be scrutinized are not really old, yet they are obsolete. That is they simply failed to make the grade in the popularity department, so that although only 30 years old, no rifles in either caliber have been factory produced for some time now.

I'm talking about the 218 Bee and 219 Zipper—two dandy little varmint cartridges introduced by Winchester in 1938 and 1937 respectively, almost certainly as a result of the 22 center-

should have been placed on the absence of good telescope sights for top-ejecting Winchester lever actions. Varmint shooting, being a game involving small neutral-colored targets at medium-to-long ranges, demands more "seeability" and aiming precision than can be obtained with any kind of iron sights, so that no matter how inherently accurate a rifle may be, it is severely handicapped for this use unless fitted with a good scope sight.

Bad publicity, like a poor play review, is another thing that can damage a cartridge's chances for popular acceptance. I recall, for example, how two decades ago, some gun writers were saying that the Hornet was a more accurate round than the Bee,

Modern powders and bullets have given new life to old cartridges. Here is full detailed data for . . .

LOADING THE OLD ONES

TESTFIRE
GD
REPORT

...and some not so old

by KEN WATERS

Ours is a big country and the well-made rifles chambering these 6 cartridges are proving slow in wearing out. Countless thousands are still in use, many actively afield each year, continuing to bag game for their owners, and rifles are still being produced overseas for one of them. But whether the object of their shots be game, paper targets or just tin cans, they continue to deliver enjoyable outdoor recreation which, after all, is a primary function of sporting arms.

That enjoyment can be doubled and tripled, in both quantity and intensity, by reloading these cartridges. Thus, our objective is to show how this may be done, not only safely but with accuracy that equals or betters their original factory loadings. One of them is no longer commercially loaded, and two others can be handloaded to give considerably more power in certain

fire craze spawned by the famous 22 Hornet, which had shown varmint shooters what could be done with light, fast-stepping and quick-opening jacketed bullets. The Bee and Zipper were both attempts to make the same sort of ballistics available to those preferring lever action rifles; oddly enough, both are better cartridges (in this writer's opinion) than the Hornet despite the way in which they have been allowed to languish into obscurity.

The reason usually advanced for this is that the light barreled Model 65 and 64 lever action rifles in which they were chambered lacked the fine accuracy required of a varmint rifle; to a certain extent this was probably true. However, having owned a Winchester 65 in 218 Bee and a Marlin 336 in 219 Zipper, it is my impression that the biggest share of the blame

that being the era when all sorts of virtues, good and bad, were attributed to case shape. Doubting it even then, I purchased one of the inexpensive little Winchester 43 bolt actions in 218 Bee caliber and mounted a scope on it. Just as I had thought, accuracy proved fully as good as that delivered by 22 Hornet rifles of equal weight and barrel stiffness. For that matter, however, even my Model 65 lever action did as well, out to about 125 yards, as would most Hornets if iron sighted.

The Zipper, because it was expected to perform at still longer ranges and because it was factory loaded with a bullet of indifferent accuracy, suffered even more by comparison with scope sighted bolt action rifles. Substitute a known-accurate 50, 52, 53 or 55-gr. bullet of current manufacture for that old 56-gr. Winchester hollow-point, and your Zipper will shoot much tighter groups. Better still, fire them in a Marlin lever action or bolt gun with a scope sight, and you'll find it hard to believe you have the same cartridge.

Our approach to better accuracy in these two calibers can therefore be made along two or possibly three lines:

(1) Select the best suitable bullets available.

(2) Experiment with various powders and loads until the one best adapted to your individual rifle is found.

(3) If at all possible, mount a good scope sight.

Shooters lost no time in comparing it with the 22 Hornet, and they liked the almost 200 fs greater velocity which the Bee had at its muzzle, many failing to notice how this advantage dwindled to 100 fs superiority out at 200 yards. Nevertheless, there's no getting around the fact that the Bee delivers some 15% more bullet energy at that range than does the 22 Hornet and, but for the early (and mistaken) claims of better Hornet cartridge accuracy, the Bee might have won the popularity race. Both were rather prematurely killed off by the 222 Remington.

Once-fired 218 Bee cases of Winchester make have a capacity of 14.8

ingly. At the very least, do not mix Winchester-Western brass with Remington-Peters.

As with practically all such small capacity cases, fast burning powders are indicated simply because they won't hold enough of the slower burning propellants to attain desired velocities. A corollary of this fact, of course, is that they are therefore quite sensitive to small increases of powder. Only ½-gr. more of 4227 or 2400, in some instances, will result in a gain of as much as 100 fs velocity. In the normal loading ranges, this may involve only a slight difference in pressure, but when working at or close to top psi levels, pressures may rise rath-

218 Bee

Essentially a necked-down 25-20 with straighter body, longer 15-degree shoulder slope and shorter neck, the Bee is a small capacity, bottle-necked, rimmed cartridge intended for varmint shooting inside 200 yards. Because of its short case length of 1.345″ and its rimmed form to control headspace, it is ideally suited for lever action rifles with short receivers, such as the Winchester Model 65 in which it was introduced, as well as rebarreled single shot rifles. In one of the latter, or in a suitable bolt action, it can be handloaded to give increased ballistic performance, but even its standard factory load of 46-gr. hollow-point bullet at 2860 fps MV the Bee offers a trajectory of 200 yards almost identical to that of the 300 Savage with the 180-gr. Silvertip factory load.

grains of water when filled to the base of case necks or, in other words, to the bases of seated bullets. By comparison, early thin-walled lots of Hornet brass averaged about 13 grains water capacity, while more recent and heavier Hornet cases hold only some 11.4 grains. This larger powder space is what accounts for the Bee's higher velocity, and it uses that limited capacity very well when it is noted that the 222, with room for 23.8 grains of water—or 60% more powder space—achieves only 12% higher velocity. Before leaving this subject of case capacity, however, it might be well to note that 218 Bee Remington brass—in some lots, at least — has an even greater capacity, which will have a direct bearing on developed pressures. Before making up any maximum loads, check the capacity of the cases to be used and adjust charges accord-

er suddenly. Reasonable caution is therefore indicated.

Factory loads in the 218 Bee develop about 44,000 psi, and I would advise that this level *not* be exceeded when loading for either the Model 65 lever action or the light Model 43 Winchester bolt action. Incidentally, these factory rounds chronograph at an actual 2760 fps in 24″ barrels, or 2821 in a 26″ length.

Du Pont 4227 and Hercules 2400 are the powders usually listed for reloading the 218 Bee, and they are probably the best for most purposes in this cartridge. However, there are at least two others which are useful under certain conditions. Hercules Unique has been found to give fine accuracy with cast bullets in light loads, and 4198 responds well in close to capacity loads with bullets of 50 grains or more weight, delivering good velocities at lower pressures. I am of the opinion though, that factory load velocities cannot be exceeded, if indeed they can be equaled, with powders available to the handloader and still stay within our pressure limitation of 44,000 psi. To the best of my knowledge, none of the loads listed in our table exceed that figure, although I was unable to test them for pressure.

Any standard small rifle primer may be used with these loads, there being no need for a magnum primer with such fast burning powders in a small case like this. If pockets stretch so that primers fit loosely, color-code

A better alternative would be to use a lever action as a two-shot rifle, loading one round only in the magazine, and the other directly into the chamber. In this way, both rounds could have spitzer bullets without danger, and the shooter would be assured of the same striking point for each.

The Sierra 40- and 45-gr. Hornet bullets expand well because of their thin jackets, and have sufficiently blunt soft points for use in the Model 65 lever action; also, I believe the 50-gr. Norma (No. 608) would be all right insofar as point shape is concerned. However, it should be borne in mind that unless case necks are tightly sized for a close friction grip on bullets, it will be necessary to select those having a cannelure for crimping. Also, the cannelure must not be positioned so as to cause too much of the bullet to project outside the case,

be trimmed back to 1.335″ or thereabouts. Be uniform in this, especially if they are to be crimped, and again let me remind you to sort and segregate cases by make. Cases for the lever action may have to be full-length resized after every shot. My Model 65 was tolerant in this respect, neck-sizing being sufficient for about three loads.

Handled properly, there is absolutely no reason why a 218 Bee shouldn't be just as accurate and deadly as a 22 Hornet, given a barrel and bullets of equal accuracy and an equivalent sighting arrangement. This means that it will take all of the smaller varmints to about 200 yards, and the larger ones such as fox to around 150 or 160 yards. I once shot a very large hawk that was in the process of killing a chicken. The range was approximately 90 yards, and when

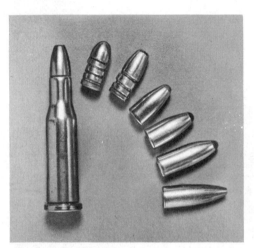

218 Bee Loads, Bullets and Factory Round

Bullet	Powder/grs.	MV	Remarks
43 Cast GC 225438	Unique/4.0	1750	Small game.
43 Cast GC 225438	2400/9.0	2192	
43 Cast GC 225438	4227/10.0	2227	Fast cast load.
48 Cast GC 225415	2400/8.5	2026	
48 Cast GC 225415	4227/9.5	2072	
40 Sierra Hornet	4227/13.4	2913	Accurate HS load.
40 Sierra Hornet	2400/12.0	2889	
45 Sierra Hornet	4227/12.0	2572	
45 Sierra Hornet	4227/12.7	2698	Accurate.
45 Sierra Hornet	2400/11.5	2673	
50 Speer SP	2400/11.0	2570	Good load.
50 Speer SP	4227/12.4	2653	Accurate
50 Speer SP	4198/14.5	2600	
52 Speer HP	2400/10.5	2490	
52 Speer HP	4227/11.7	2500	
52 Speer HP	4198/14.0	2516	Good load.

those cases and save them for very light loads only, or if too loose, discard them entirely—and reduce that load a little.

If your 218 Bee happens to be a bolt action or single shot, a really broad selection of bullets in all weights from 40 to 55 grains is available. Owners of lever action rifles with tubular magazines will have to be content with fairly blunt, round-nose bullets, either soft- or hollow-point, unless they are willing to use their rifle single-shot, loading cartridges with spitzer bullets directly into the chamber. Because of the jarring shock of recoil, rounds with sharp pointed bullets should never be placed in a tubular magazine where they bear against the primer of the round ahead of them.

One alternative would be to load a cartridge with a spitzer bullet into the chamber for the "shot that counts," then fill the magazine with blunt nose bullets. Before this is done, however, shooters should test both types on targets to ascertain whether the change in bullet shape will result in a different point of impact. If so, I would not consider this a good practice.

making for too long an over-all cartridge length.

The Remington 46-gr. hollow-point is perhaps the best choice from this standpoint, although I personally prefer to use soft points and a heavy friction fit rather than crimping. Unfortunately, the lever action user doesn't have much to choose from in weights above 46 grains.

Standard specifications for the 218 Bee call for a barrel with .224″-.2245″ groove diameter, and a twist of 1-in-16″. Accordingly, jacketed bullets should be .224″, and cast bullets sized .225″. A good feature of the Bee was that barrels were not bored undersize as were many Hornets. I would not advise using bullets heavier than 53 grains though, partly because velocities will be lower, but mostly because the 1-in-16″ rifling twist then becomes marginal. If 55-gr. or heavier slugs are to be used, a steeper twist of 1-in-14″ would be preferable.

No particular trouble should be experienced in reloading the 218 Bee. Cases may stretch some if heavy loads are used or fired in a sloppy chamber and, when found to be in excess of the 1.345″ maximum length, they should

the Bee cracked that hawk leaped about a dozen feet in the air and fell stone dead. Both wing butts had been shattered and a large exit hole caused instantaneous death. That was with the old 50-gr. Wotkyns-Morse bullet driven by 12 grains 4227, sighting with a Winchester No. 98 peep sight mounted on the rear of the Model 65's bolt. Best of all, the chicken survived!

I always had an affection for the 218 Bee, and wish I'd never been foolish enough to part with that fine little Model 65 rifle.

Here are some 218 Bee loads from my files:

219 Zipper

Rimmed case—long sloping 12 degree shoulder—.224″ groove diameter —1-in-16″ rifling twist—and a reputation that belied its fine accuracy potential; all these things the 219 Zipper shares in some degree with the 218 Bee. But there are important differences too. Case capacity, averaging 33 grains (water) to base of neck, is more than twice that of the Bee, permitting the use of slower burning powders for higher velocities at reasonable pressures. Also, heavier bullets of greater sectional density suit this cartridge for work at longer range.

Most recent factory ballistics called for a 56-gr. hollow-point bullet with an MV of 3110 fps and ME of 1200 fp. Detractors will sneer that its 1550 fps remaining velocity at 300 yards is a full 200 fs less than that of a 50-grain soft point from the much smaller 222 Remington, but such derogatory comparisons ignore the true capabilities of the 219 Zipper cartridge when freed of its lever action restrictions. In a good bolt action or single-shot rifle, Hornady's 55-gr. spire-point bullet can be started out at 3400 fps and will still be traveling over 2000 fps out at 300 yards! This is not only better than anything the 222 can do—it is every bit as good as the 222 Magnum with its hottest handloads.

The Zipper must therefore be prop-

either, despite the fact that Winchester rifles in 219 caliber were not dropped until after World War II, while Marlin chambered rifles for the Zipper up to 1961.

True, the 219 Zipper was based upon the old and still manufactured 25-35 case, necked down; and, with the proper dies, cases for the 219 can be formed from 25-35 brass. They can also, with a bit more effort, be formed from 30-30 and 32 Winchester Special brass, but non-reloaders and beginners are hardly up to this task, and I remain convinced that there is at least an implied obligation to produce ammunition and/or empty cases for a reasonable number of years after the last American-made rifle in a standard commercial caliber is discontinued.

Rim diameter and thickness are identical to those of the other car-

table for our best loads to date, as well as a poor one for comparison). The Marlin 336 has an extremely stiff barrel, which may well account for much of its reliable accuracy performance. 4895 and 4320 produce about the best velocity/pressure ratios. At the same time, powders as fast burning as 4198 and Reloder 7 can be effectively used if desired, especially for lighter loads. The 219 Zipper is a flexible cartridge for reloading.

Primers indicated are the standard large rifle type, none of the above-listed powders requiring magnum priming. The bullet story, however, is an exact repeat of that told in connection with the 218 Bee. For lever actions with tubular magazines you'll need blunt nose projectiles — either soft- or hollow-points, unless they are to be single loaded or with not more than one in the magazine. Single-shot

219 Zipper Loads, Bullets and Factory Round

Bullet	Powder/grs.	MV	Remarks
43 Cast GC 225438	2400/10.5	2010	
43 Cast GC 225438	4227/11.5	2022	
48 Cast GC 225415	2400/11.0	2070	
48 Cast GC 225415	4227/12.5	2150	
48 Cast GC 225415	4198/15.0	2200	
45 Sierra Hornet	Re #11/26.5	3570	Very accurate. Under MOA
45 Sierra Hornet	3031/27.5	3560	
50 Sierra SP	3031/25.5	3350	Accurate. Good load.
50 Sierra SP	Re #11/26.0	3444	
50 Sierra SP	Re #7/22.0	3300	
50 Sierra SP	4895/28.5	3428	
52 Speer HP	3031/25.0	3295	
52 Speer Silver Match	4064/28.0	3345	Most accurate load tested.
54 Gardiner HP	4895/25.5	3055	Accurate load.
55 Hornady SP	4895/25.0	3000	Average accuracy.
55 Norma SP	3031/25.0	3186	
60 Hornady SP	4895/24.5	2867	Good load in wind.
63 Sierra Semi-Ptd.	4064/26.0	3000	Poor load; see text.

erly thought of, almost, as two separate cartridges—one with blunt nose bullets for use in lever action rifles at working pressures in the 40,000 psi class, and the other free to use ballistically superior pointed bullets at considerably higher pressures. It is only natural, therefore, that results should be drastically different. Not the least of possible improvements is a halving of deflection due to cross-winds. For these reasons, plus the fact that it is highly accurate in stiff barrels, tightly breeched and scope sighted, the 219 Zipper should not have been permitted to die a premature death.

The writer seldom presumes to take a great and respected manufacturer to task, but in this one instance I have always felt that Winchester displayed an unusual lack of consideration for shooters'—including recent customers'—interests when they abruptly discontinued production of this cartridge in 1962 without prior notice to allow stocking up (to my knowledge, anyway). Still worse, empty unprimed cases have not been made available

tridges named; case body varies by less than a thousandth at the base, body taper is very close, especially in the case of the 25-35, and the Zipper has the shortest case length, hence any of the others can be trimmed to 1.93" following forming. Most reference sources specify 1.938" as the case length of 219 Zippers, but the new Hornady Handbook gives 1.875". I therefore measured new Winchester and Remington cases of late lots and found them to be 1.936". Our trim-to-length of 1.930" is thus correct.

Awhile back we mentioned the suitability of slower burning powders for this round. The writer has tried 3031, 4064, 4895, 4320, and all three powders of Hercules' Reloder series with bullets weighing from 45 to 63 grains in his 219 caliber Marlin Model 336. Excellent accuracy—less than minute-of-angle groups—was obtained with 4064, Reloder 11, 4895 and 3031 in the order listed. Actually any difference between these four has been minuscule and you wouldn't go wrong with any of them. (See the included

and bolt action rifles, however, free the handloader to use just about any .224" diameter bullet.

My own experience with this cartridge verifies the findings of other experimenters in years past that the old 46- and 56-grain factory hollowpoints are not too accurate, particularly the former. However, the 45-gr. Sierra Hornet round nose soft-point bullet gave us splendid accuracy when fired off by 26.5 grains of Reloder 11.

Speer's recently introduced 52-gr. Silver Match proved to be the most accurate of all bullets in my Marlin, and even the relatively heavy 60-gr. Hornady went into an inch for 5 shots. When the still heavier 63-gr. Sierra was tried, though, groups spread wide with evidence of bullet tipping on the targets. Evidently—and not surprisingly—this is just too much bullet for a 1-in-16" twist, and if I were having a custom rifle made up in this caliber, intending to use 55-grain and heavier bullets, I'd specify a rifling twist of 1-in-14".

Firing factory loads in the Marlin

LOADING THE OLD ONES

336 produced an initial base expansion of .0025″, following which, successive reloads further increased case expansion by an additional .001″—.003″. Ordinarily, I would consider any expansion of more than .0015″ subsequent to the initial firing as excessive, and admittedly some of our loads do seem maximum in this rifle. But it should be remembered that we were working with a lever action rifle and only neck-sizing cases between firings. Cases did not suffer as a result, re-entering the chamber readily. Thus, it would appear that, to a degree anyhow, the measured expansion was cumulative, occurring over a succession of shots. Accordingly, while I do not feel that any of our loads were excessive, I would consider the heaviest of them as being maximum in lever action rifles.

If there were such a thing as a varmint rifle match limited to lever action rifles, I'd use this Marlin 336 in 219 Zipper with handloads and a Weaver V-8 scope, and feel not in the least handicapped. The same goes for shooting live varmints of fox and coyote size in the field. It's a combination I trust and one that I wish was still available for today's varminters.

For our second pair of old cartridges, we turn back the calendar to 1892—the year both were introduced. They've been a fighting pair, literally, both starting life as military rounds and participating in more than one war, plus a rebellion and an insurrection or two. In the beginning they were even on opposite sides—that was the Spanish-American War of 1898—

but that didn't take long to end, and about the same time sportsmen over a substantial portion of the globe became aware of their possibilities as big game hunting calibers.

Of course I'm referring to the 7x57-mm, often termed the "Spanish Mauser" in those early days, and the 30-40 Krag or 30 U.S. Army. Each is too well known to require our delving into their histories here, except to note that both were—and are—extremely well-balanced cartridges, and as such performed for their respective countries with an efficiency that might have been expected.

Two points in particular however, deserve noting. The Winchester High Wall single-shot rifle in 30-40 caliber was the first smokeless powder sporting combination produced in the U.S., dating from 1893 and thus preceding the 30-30 by a year or two. The 7mm Mauser is one of the oldest military and sporting calibers for which both rifles and ammunition are still being made (although only cartridges are made for it in this country). New rifles chambered for the 7x57 must be imported.

For all their 75 years of age, both the 30-40 and 7mm Mauser continue to serve shooters in America, especially those hunters who demand adequate killing power while shunning the newer magnums as excessively powerful. Present day ballistics of each are much improved over those of the 1900 era, modern powders making it possible to develop higher velocities without increasing pressures. Let's look at them individually.

The 30-40 Krag

Selected from over 50 different rifles extensively tested by a U.S. Army Ordnance Board, the Krag-Jorgensen was adopted as our new service rifle in 1892. With it came a new cartridge known as the "30 U.S. Army," and

popularly referred since as the 30-40 Krag.

This was a drastic change for the military to make, previous service rifles having been of 45 caliber and larger, and reflected the changes brought about by the introduction of smokeless powder. Another "first" for the Krag was its use of metal jacketed bullets. That first 30-40 cartridge contained approximately 38 grains of an early issue smokeless, and a 220-gr. round nose bullet with cupro-nickel full metal jacket. Muzzle velocity ran from 1990 to 2005 fps, and effective range was considered to be about 600 yards.

Younger shooters may think it strange that this cartridge, specially designed for a bolt action military rifle, should have been given a rimmed case, but of course this was because the Krag did not employ a clip-type magazine. With a case length of 2.314″, the 30-40 is both shorter and slightly smaller in diameter than a 30-06, resulting in an internal capacity (measured to base of case neck) averaging 22½% less. For today's denser smokeless powders, this is more of an asset than a detriment, and taken in conjunction with a case neck that is almost one-half inch long, it is practically ideal for reloading.

Over the intervening years, 30-40 loadings have undergone several changes of importance to today's owners. Adoption for sporting use brought soft nose bullets suitable for hunting big game, and along with the original 220-gr. weight, a sharp-pointed 180-gr. put in its appearance. Muzzle velocity for the Remington-UMC 180-gr. factory load in 1915 was given as 2320 fps. Still later, a 150-gr. loading with 2660 fps MV showed up. Peters offered a 225-gr. "Belted" for the biggest game, and there was even a special Short Range Winchester cartridge with 100-gr. bullet.

So much for background history.

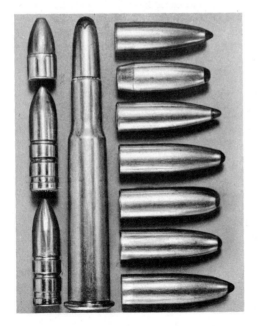

30-40 Krag Loads, Bullets and Factory Round

Bullet	Powder/grs.	MV (26″ Bbl.)	Remarks
160 Cast GC 311375	4198/21.5	1790	Very accurate.
165 Cast GC 311413	4227/14.5	1374	Very accurate.
165 Cast GC 311413	4895/35.0	2108	Accurate.
100 Hornady S/J	3031/44.0	3000	Short range varmint.
150 Sierra Sptz.	HiVel #2/37.5	2543	
150 Sierra Sptz.	H-414/44.0	2455	
150 Sierra Sptz.	4895/44.0	2622	Vertical stringing.
150 Sierra Sptz.	4064/43.0	2588	Vertical stringing.
150 Sierra Sptz.	4350/49.0	2522	Vertical stringing.
150 Norma Match B.T.	4895/35.5	2269	Very accurate.
165 Speer sp.	4895/41.0	2433	
165 Speer sp.	4064/41.0	2472	Accurate.
165 Speer sp.	4350/47.0	2413	Best all-round load.
180 Sierra sp.	Re #11/36.0	2346	
180 Sierra sp.	4320/39.0	2243	Accurate.
180 Sierra sp.	Re #21/40.0	2177	
180 Sierra sp.	H 414/40.0	2240	
180 Sierra R.N.	HiVel #2/36.0	2363	Max. (42,000 psi).
180 Speer R.N.	4064/40.0	2359	Vertical stringing.
180 Speer R.N.	4350/45.0	2354	Most accurate load tested.
200 Speer sp.	4350/44.0	2230	Good load. (38,500 psi).

Today's 30-40 factory cartridges, while of decreased variety, offer increased performance. Winchester-Western lists their 220-gr. Silvertip at 2200 fps and a choice of either Silvertip or Power-Point in 180-gr. at 2470 fps Remington has only 180-gr. weights, but offers both a round nose and the pointed Core-Lokt traveling 2470 fps at muzzle. Canada's Dominion brand includes a single 180-gr. round nose number, likewise at 2470 fps. Unfortunately, there is no longer a factory 150-gr. loading. The 30-40 is thus a close competitor of the 303 British and 300 Savage, and not so far behind the 308 that any animal fairly hit would ever know the difference.

The most important point concerning the 30-40 Krag cartridge to be noted by handloaders is its pressure limitation, made necessary by many of the old rifles in which it was chambered. Loads in the 32,000 to 40,000 psi bracket are most common and to be preferred, but under no circumstances should they ever be allowed to exceed 44,000 pounds per square inch (psi). Consider 40,000 psi as normal max.

This is where that smaller case capacity averaging 47.5 grains (water) will be appreciated, it being possible to use charges that come close to filling the case without having so much that pressures climb above the established limits. The far more pleasant recoil of the 30-40 as compared to a 30-06 of equal weight, is also attributable to this lighter loading.

Optimum canister powders appear to be IMR 4064, and Hercules Reloder 11, which latter replaced the old and excellent HiVel 2. 4350 is likewise an excellent choice with 165-gr. and heavier bullets. With continued testing, it may develop that Reloder 21, Hodgdon's newest H-414 and Herter's No. 100 are also suited to use with heavy bullets. Vertical stringing of shots with 4895 would indicate a lack of uniformity in pressures, making it less desirable even though safe in recommended loads.

Considering both accuracy and power, 4350 has been outstanding in the writer's test rifles—an original military Krag with 30″ barrel, and a Model 1895 Winchester with slender 26″ barrel. Our two favorite loads to date have been: (1) The 180-gr. Speer RN with 45/4350, and (2) 165-gr. Speer spitzers and 47/4350. IMR 4198 is a good choice when cast bullets are to be used in moderate loads.

Being a true 30 caliber—that is, with bore and groove dimensions of .300″ and .308″ respectively — one would normally not anticipate any problem of bullets. However, there are a couple of things that should be pointed out in this connection, the first of which is that some of the early 30-40 caliber rifles—Krags especially—varied considerably in their groove diameters, running both under- and oversize (from .307″ to .313″). This could easily affect pressure development as well as accuracy, hence I suggest that handloaders slug and mike their barrels, thereafter selecting bullets which provide the best fit. Several bullets intended for 30-30s measure .307″ rather than .308″, and these would be practical for reloading a 30-40 with tighter-than-normal bore.

Secondly, it should be remembered that original 30-40 barrels were chambered with long throats to accommodate the old blunt-nose 220-gr. bullets. In such barrels, it is entirely possible that trouble may be experienced in getting lighter and shorter spitzer bullets to shoot accurately because they must jump across what is, in effect, a section of free-boring. It's common to blame the rifling twist for being too steep and over-stabilizing the bullet. Correct in theory, but seldom true in actuality!

The rifling twist of most 30-40 caliber rifles is 1-in-10″, as it must be to handle 220-gr. bullets, and by ample experience in a number of rifles, this is not at all too steep for even 150-gr. bullets. All that's necessary is to seat those lighter bullets as far out of the case as can be done and still permit them to function through the magazine and chamber properly. If you're content to single load, seat the bullet out to just miss the rifling.

It would be hard to find an easier cartridge to reload than the 30-40. That long neck helps in seating bullets correctly and holding them firmly without any need for crimping. Often cases can be reloaded time after time with only their necks being sized, and usually trimming won't need to be done too often. When it is, trim to 2.304″. Either standard or magnum large rifle primers may be used; personally, I seat magnums only when using 4350 powder.

Cast bullets perform especially well in most 30-40s, perhaps because of that generous throat which readily accepts the larger .311″ diameter often found, but partly also, I think, due to the long case neck that makes it unnecessary for bullet bases to project down into the powder space. If you have a Krag or other 30-40 rifle with a clean and not too worn barrel, cast bullets with gas check and long full-diameter bearing shank, such as Lyman's Loverin-designed 311466 and 311467, may well surprise you with their accuracy.

I'll not plug this oldie as "best" for any purpose, but I will say that an awful lot of fun can be had with it. Plenty accurate in a good barrel for big bore target shooting, it is also a game killing cartridge that was once hailed for its power, even on elk and moose. There's no reason it can't still deliver the goods as well or better than ever.

The 7mm Mauser

The Spanish-American War taught us the merits of the 7x57mm as a military cartridge, but the round was not a wartime surprise as has sometimes been intimated. Not only did we know of it beforehand, but it had actually been manufactured in this country from about 1896, or two years before the war.

Original specifications called for a round-nosed full-metal-jacketed bullet weighing 172.8 grains with a muzzle velocity (presumably taken in a 29″ barrel) of 2296 fps. Berdan primers and a charge of from 37 to 38 grains of a European smokeless powder created chamber pressures of just under 45,000 psi. Bore diameter was (and still is) .276″ with .284″ between opposing grooves. Four land rifling having a twist rate of 1-in-8.6″ were employed to stabilize this long bullet.

Several writers have referred to the 7mm Mauser as being much superior ballistically to the 30-40 Krag, but it is difficult to see this in their early loadings, especially when the Krag was used with 180-gr. Remington spitzer bullets. Comparable mid-range trajectory heights when shooting at 500 yards were:

30-40	220-grain	49.98″
30-40	180-grain	29.68″
7mm	175-grain	40.85″

They were, in fact, quite evenly matched, with most of the 7mms alleged superiority properly attributable to the Mauser's clip-loading feature, which enabled soldiers to reload faster.

Right now we're interested in the cartridge, however, and although the early sporting loads in the 7mm—which were virtually the military round with a blunt soft nose bullet replacing the FMJ—established an enviable record around the world for deep penetration, subsequent factory offerings were to make it a far more flexible hunting round.

Today, despite the unfortunate fact that Winchester and Remington only produce the 7mm Mauser in a single 175-gr. RNSP loading at 2490 fps, Federal has added a 139-gr. round whose MV is given as 2680 fps, Norma offers additionally a 150-gr. semi-pointed boat-tail at 2756 fps and a 110-gr. varmint load at a surprising 3067 fps, while Dominion lists both a 160-gr. at 2650 fps, and a 139-gr. at 2800.

Not having had an opportunity to try all of these factory loads, I can't help wondering whether they are actually capable of making those speeds in 22″ and 24″ sporting rifle barrels, but rather doubt it. Speer's laboratory tests in a 22″ tube revealed that while the Federal 139-gr. and Remington 175-gr. loads came very close to their claimed speeds, the Norma 150-gr. failed by almost 200 fs to make its published 2756 fps, and both Winchester and Federal 175-gr. loads were off by a substantial 110 to 235 fs. I

LOADING THE OLD ONES

can't seem to find any published ballistics for Sako's 155-gr. 7mm ammo, but in our 24" barrel Mauser it chronographed at an average 2456 fps.

Based upon these results, as well as our own tests and the reports of other reliable chronographings, it is the writer's feeling that reloaders shouldn't expect more than about 2770 fps with 139- or 140-gr. bullets, 2650 with 150-154 gr., 2600 with 160-gr., and 2420 fps with 175-gr. slugs. If these muzzle speeds are exceeded, pressures are almost certain to exceed the standard 45,000 psi.

The 7x57 Mauser has a conventional and quite modern appearing rimless case with very little more taper than a 270, and a shoulder slope that is some 3 degrees steeper. Best of all, from a handloader's standpoint, is its generously long neck—almost 3/8"—ideal for holding the long bullets of this caliber.

Case capacity averages about 53 grains (water), which is close to 7% more than most 308s, and 12% above most 30-40 cases. You're likely wondering then how come muzzle velocities aren't higher! Three reasons. Most important is that sectional densities of 7mm bullets are greater than those of 30-caliber bullets (under 180-gr.), while the area of a 7mm bullet's base upon which powder gases have to push, is smaller. A 154-gr. Hornady 7mm spire point, for example, has a sectional density of .273 compared to the .247 of a 165-gr. Hornady 30-caliber, and the 30-caliber bullet, like a

larger piston, has approximately 17% larger base area.

Lastly, remember that 45,000 psi pressure limitation. With allowable pressures some 5000 psi higher in a 308, this is bound to have an effect on velocities. Reduce pressure in a 308 to 45,000 psi, and 180-gr. bullets will only be given some 2450-2475 fps—not too much more than the 2400 fps of a 175-gr. 7mm slug. Hence, these velocities are entirely reasonable. Then too, I fail to see any reason why loads up to 50,000 psi couldn't safely be used in a good commercial Mauser of recent vintage, or to Remington 30 and Winchester 70 rifles.

There's little doubt in my mind but that the medium-slow and slow burning powders are best in this case with bullets heavier than 150 or 154 grains. As will be seen from our table, Reloder 21, 4895, 4350 and even maximum loads of 4831 did very well, both as to accuracy and velocity. Somewhat contradictory to previously published reports, however, the same powders also performed excellently with bullets as light as 139 grains. Biggest surprise of all was our compressed load of 53/4831 behind 139-gr. Hornady bullets. While not as consistently accurate as 49 grains of 4350 or 42/4895, it did give slightly higher velocities, and grouping that couldn't be called poor.

If I were asked to name my favorite 7mm load, however, I'd have to say the 160-gr. spitzer with 52 grains of 4831. Averaging some 2700 fps with good bullet weight and superb accuracy, this seems an ideal combination of power and long range hitting ability. At reasonable ranges, there should be enough punch left in this load to down most species of game to be found in the original 48 states and Canada, assuming of course, that the

shooter does his part.

Bullets and primers present no problem. Any .284" or .283" bullet can be used, and with a choice of weights from 110 to 175 grains, it's fairly obvious that the 7x57 is a versatile and highly useful cartridge. Standard large rifle primers will fire any of the powders named in this medium capacity case, but I prefer magnum caps when loading with 4350 or 4831.

I can't think of any particular problems connected with reloading the 7mm; it's almost a "natural" for this purpose. Barrel groove diameters will be found to vary some, especially in foreign made rifles, but in most instances this is readily taken care of by a judicious bullet selection from the size and weight variations offered. If a bore is extremely tight, it would be wise to reduce loads for that particular rifle, but this is a problem of individual rifles rather than criticism of the cartridge itself. In this connection, I would also warn that the heavier loads should *not* be used in the old Remington rolling-block single shot rifles. Loads shown are for bolt action rifles.

When case length goes beyond 2.235", trim to 2.225", and do not let over-all length of loaded cartridges exceed 3 1/16". Neck or partial resizing of cases should be sufficient, since these are mostly all bolt action rifles, unless cases from other 7mms are allowed to become mixed with yours. If that happens, it's best to play safe and full length size all empties.

As a final note, I suggest to those planning on using cast bullets, that they *not* choose any of the handsome spitzer shapes with long tapering noses and one or two grease grooves near the base. While pretty to look at, I've been disappointed in the way they shoot in this caliber. These long 7mms

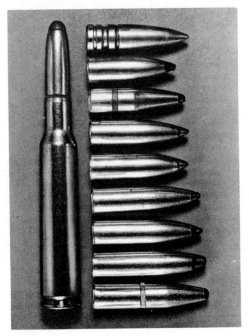

7mm Mauser Loads, Bullets and Factory Round

Bullet	Powder/grs.	MV	Remarks
150 Cast GC 287405	4227/19.0	1830	Accurate.
150 Cast GC 287405	4198/21.0	1722	Accurate.
120 Sierra spitzer	N-201/42.0	2814	Good load.
120 Sierra spitzer	4895/44.0	2921	Somewhat erratic.
139 Hornady	HP-101/42.5	2585	Accurate.
139 Hornady	Re #21/45.0	2694	Erratic.
139 Hornady	4831/53.0	2790	Compressed. (Max.).
140 Sierra spitzer	4350/49.0	2772	Excellent.
140 Sierra spitzer	4895/42.0	2687	Excellent.
145 Speer spitzer	4895/41.5	2602	Excellent.
145 Speer spitzer	4350/48.0	2708	Excellent.
150 Winchester P-P	Re #21/44.0	2570	Accurate.
160 Curry spitzer	Re #21/43.5	2480	
160 Curry spitzer	4895/41.0	2594	Some flyers (Max.).
160 Curry spitzer	4831/51.0	2646	
160 Curry spitzer	4831/52.0	2704	Most accurate. Compressed. (Max.).
160 Speer spitzer	4350/46.0	2569	Excellent.
175 Speer magnum	4895/40.0	2427	Excellent. Accurate (Max.).
175 Hornady	HP-101/41.0	2385	Very accurate.
175 Hornady	Re #21/42.0	2388	
175 Hornady	4350/44.0	2365	Excellent. Very accurate.
175 Hornady	4831/48.0	2460	

32-40 Loads, Bullets and Factory Round

Bullet	Powder/grs.	MV (26" Bbl.)	Remarks
(A) Target Loads (Low Pressure)			
181 Cast GC 321297	2400/13.0	1450	Very accurate.
181 Cast GC 321297	4227/14.0	1403	
181 Cast GC 321297	4198/17.0	1450	Good target load.
181 Cast GC 321297	HiVel 2/18.3	1295	Outstanding accuracy.
181 Cast GC 321297	HiVel 2/20.0	1430	
181 Cast GC 321297	Unique/7.7	1210	Short range target load.
170 Hornady .321" SP	Re 11/18.7	1334	Very accurate; low pressure.
(B) Medium Loads			
170 Hornady .321" SP	HiVel 2/22.0	1560	Approx. 20,000 psi.
170 Hornady .321" SP	Re 7/21.0	1583	
170 Hornady .321" SP	3031/23.0	1585	
(C) Heavier Loads for Strong Action Rifles Only			
170 Hornady .321" SP	3031/25.0	1721	
170 Hornady .321" SP	3031/28.0	1925	Max.—Best accuracy.
170 Hornady .321" SP	4895/29.0	1886	Good load.
170 Hornady .321" SP	Re 11/27.0	1923	
170 Hornady .321" SP	Re 7/25.0	1868	
170 Hornady .321" SP	4198/20.0	1718	

need to be stabilized, and a blunt nose gas check slug with full-diameter bearing section over most of its length, containing multiple grease grooves, such as Lyman's 287405 and 287448, designed by Guy Loverin, will generally be found to give far better accuracy. Our table gives a couple of starting points which, with a little luck, may result in a good practice and small-game load right off.

32-40 & 38-55

Our final pair of old cartridges go back still farther—to about 1884, in fact—yet many readers will be familiar with them even today since they are still with us, in certain makes at least.

Chances are, if you've ever fired a 32-40 or 38-55, it's been in a Winchester Model 1894, Marlin Model 1893 or Savage 99 lever action repeater. They're the rifles that seem to be around in the most numbers, but are in fact only a few of the many types and models that were produced in these calibers. Originally, both were Marlin-Ballard cartridges, introduced for their fine single shot match rifles, and were primarily intended for 200 and 220-yard off-hand target or Schuetzen shooting.

In this field they were eminently successful, both proving to be extremely accurate when properly loaded, while delivering mild recoil at the butt end. Understandably, it wasn't long before several folks got the idea that they should also make good deer hunting loads, and the late 1880s being the era when lever action repeaters were burgeoning, these two rounds found ready acceptance from a number of rifle manufacturers.

Some of these actions—particularly the early single shots and repeaters—were relatively weak, while others were quite strong. This is the reason background history can be important to reloaders. When we set out to refill 32-40 or 38-55 empties today, we must first know what rifles they are to be used in. Because the cartridge makers don't know which one that will be, this is precisely the reason once-available "high power" and "high velocity" smokeless loadings were dropped years ago, leaving only the mild-as-punch commercial offerings currently produced in this country.

So greatly different are the strengths of the various rifles available at one time or another in these calibers, that I decided the only safe approach to their reloading would be along the lines wisely adopted by Lyman for the 45-70 cartridge in the 42nd edition of their *Reloader's Handbook*. In that booklet, loads for the comparatively weak-action 1873 Springfield were kept separate from those for the strong Model 1886 Winchester. It made so much sense that I've done much the same thing here for the 32-40 and 38-55.

Naturally, any such listing as this is bound to be somewhat arbitrary, but dividing lines must be drawn somewhere so I've classified them as follows:

Strong Action
Winchester 1894 Lever Action
Marlin 1893 Lever Action
Savage Model 99 Lever Action
Remington-Lee Bolt Action
Remington-Hepburn S.S.
Stevens Model 44½ S.S.
Winchester High Wall S.S.

Medium Strong Action
Marlin 1881 Lever Action
Bullard Lever Action
Bullard Single Shots

Weak Action
Ballard Single Shots
Stevens 44 S.S.
Stevens Tip-Up S.S.
Maynard 1882 S.S.

Please note that we don't list every make and model ever chambered for the 32-40 or 38-55, but only those more likely to be encountered. Fortunately, those rated as having strong actions are the most commonly seen (with two exceptions) and, if in good sound condition with proper headspacing, are quite capable of handling pressures in the 35,000 psi bracket. Both cartridges use the same basic brass case as the 30-30 and 32 Winchester Special, so there is no reason why they shouldn't be able to. Indeed, with the 38-55 in particular, the greater expansion ratio provided by that large and generally long bore, causes pressures to drop rapidly once the bullet is in motion.

So that there is no chance of our being misunderstood, let me state unequivocally that if your 32-40 or 38-55 is *not* one of those rifles listed in our first column as having a strong action, you should stick with the light-to-medium loads listed in published tables, loads which do not exceed factory cartridge ballistics. If, on the other hand, you have a Winchester 1894, Marlin 1893, or one of the other strong ones, you can, by judicious handloading, turn that old rifle into a far surer killer of deer and black bear.

LOADING THE OLD ONES

The 32-40

First, a quick look at vital statistics. This is a rimmed case 2.130″ long, with .424″ and .506″ base and rim diameters, and straight-tapered sides to bottom of neck. Water capacity averages just under 34 grains to base of seated bullets, and standard U.S. factory ballistics call for a 165-gr. jacketed soft point bullet leaving the muzzle at 1440 fps. Canada's Dominion 32-40s are listed as giving a 170-gr. bullet some 1540 fps. Velocities for this caliber are commonly taken from 26″ barrels, and you'll probably be using this length or longer.

Winchester barrels in 32-40 have groove diameters from .320″ to .321″, while Marlins generally run .319″-.320″. Either will accept bullets from .319″ to .322″; in my tests I have used mostly .321″ jacketed and .3225″ cast gas check (G.C.) slugs. The standard rifling twist is 1-in-16″.

If a sufficiently hard alloy—say, 1-to-16 or harder—is used, plain cast bullets are entirely practicable at even the highest velocities reasonable in this cartridge. Above 1500 fps however, I have a distinct preference for those with gas checks to protect their bases and, despite the fact that cast bullet accuracy is excellent in 32-40s with clean, un-worn barrels, even at respectably high speeds, I always recommend the use of jacketed soft points for hunting reloads. This is because cast bullets alloyed hard enough to stand the higher velocities do not give as reliable expansion as soft points.

There will be many who disagree with me on this point, but after almost three decades of experimenting, I've come to prefer jacketed bullets when after big game, even including whitetail deer. This accounts for the lighter loads shown with cast bullets in our tables, but should *not* be taken to mean that cast slugs are less accurate. On the contrary, they make fine barrel-saving loads for target shooting in the 32-40s slow rifling twist, but may not open up on game unless bone is struck. Hollow-points help in this respect, but are by no means sure-fire when hard cast. 165- and 170-gr. flatnose soft points as produced by Winchester, Remington, Hornady and Speer in diameters of .320″ and .321″, are top choice when heading into hunting country. Don't worry about barrel life. You won't fire enough shots at game to wear out one of these barrels in a lifetime.

Back in 1914, Winchester listed a high velocity loading for the 32-40 with 165-gr. jacketed bullet at 1752 fps. By 1941, the speed of this load had been upped to 1950 fps. I wanted to see if I could duplicate those loads and yet, realizing they were much too potent for rifles with weaker actions, it was also desired to develop combinations which approximate present factory velocities while giving even finer accuracy.

In all, some nine different powders were tried, the fastest burning being Unique, and the slowest 4895. Charges were tailored to bullet type and acceptable pressure/velocity ratios, and experiments continued until the desired combinations of accuracy and bullet speed had been achieved.

For target loads with cast bullets in the 20,000 psi and under range, fast burning powders such as Unique, 2400, 4227 and 4198 appear to work well, and nothing slower burning than the old Hi-Vel 2 was used. Resulting velocities varied from 1200 to 1450 fps, and this first group proved to be OK, even in old Ballard and Stevens 44 rifles. Shooters wishing to accasionally use jacketed bullets in the older rifles—and they shouldn't be used as a steady diet—will find our load of 18.7 grains of Reloder 11 with Hornady 170-gr. flat-nose soft points, highly and consistently accurate with low pressures.

A second group, which might be referred to as "medium loads," were based upon these same 170-gr. .321″ Hornady bullets at moderate velocities of 1500-1600 fps. With these, I stepped down a notch in powder burning rates to 3031, also trying the recently developed Reloder Nos. 7 and 11. Actually, the loads in this bracket, as shown by our table, are very similar in performance to the Dominion factory rounds, and are good choices where something more powerful than U.S. factory loads is desired. They are *not* recommended for 32-40s with weak actions, however.

The third and final group stepped out at from 1700 to over 1900 fps, two of these loads coming close to duplicating the H.V. factory rounds of 30 years ago. Had we used 165-gr. rather than 170-gr. bullets, they should have been fully as fast. Although I do not have measured pressure figures on these heavier loads, they are conservatively estimated at not more than 35,000 psi. This is partially attested to by the fact that case expansion in the vital base area did not exceed .001″-.0015″ over miked diameters taken after initial firing of factory rounds in the same chamber. Case lengths remained exactly the same, a further good sign. Accuracy, while in most instances not quite as good as with the lighter target loads, was still of a high order once the load best suited to the individual rifle had been determined. 28 grains of 3031 with Remington 9½ primers and the 170-gr. Hornady bullets gave especially fine accuracy. I believe the average 32-40 rifle, if the bore is good, will be found to group better than most 30-30s.

Standard large rifle primers give entirely adequate ignition with any of the powders suited to the 32-40 and, as a matter of fact, for the lighter cast bullet and target loads I prefer those primers of a milder nature as giving still finer accuracy. For example, the writer has carefully saved his remaining supply of the discontinued Winchester 115 primers, which were less violent than the standard 120s and long known for their superior performance with light target loads. Today's Federal 210 and Remington 9½ primers have been proving good for such use.

Reloading the 32-40 is easy, but consists of two quite different procedures, depending upon the rifle being loaded for. In the case of lever action rifles, full-length resizing of cases is always called for to assure certain and uniform chambering, and to avoid unnecessary strain on the extractor. With a single-shot rifle, however, it is only necessary to neck-size cases, assuming no mix-up of cases from other rifles is allowed to happen. More than that, accuracy will be a bit better and cases last a little longer if only necks are sized.

For lever action rifles, bullets must be seated deep enough to keep overall cartridge length from exceeding the specified 2.50″, again to provide sure feeding and chambering. The seating die should be adjusted to turn a firm crimp of case mouth into the bullet's cannelure or crimping groove. In the single shots, I have obtained best accuracy by seating bullets out just short of touching the rifling lands, with nothing more than a uniform friction grip of case necks to hold bullets. Do *not* crimp when loading for single-shot rifles.

Finally, select only round or flatnose bullets, regardless of rifle type. Pointed bullets are dangerous in tubular-magazine lever action rifles (if placed in the magazine), and although quite safe in single shots, give greatly inferior accuracy due to their longer length in proportion to weight, making it more difficult to stabilize them with the slower twist rifling and at the lower velocities common to this caliber.

Recoil of the 32-40 is most pleasant, and barrel life will be long, especially if cast, lubricated bullets are used in the older single shots with their soft steel barrels. There's no reason why jacketed bullets shouldn't be loaded in the later repeating rifles. however.

If carefully loaded as explained, with due caution and attention to details, your 32-40 can be made to deliver either better accuracy or increased game killing power—possibly both—depending only upon rifle strength and condition.

Lyman's Ideal lubricant has always performed well for me at reasonable cast-bullet velocities, but more recently I have been trying the new Javelina

38-55 Loads, Bullets and Factory Round

Bullet	Powder/grs.	MV (26" Bbl.)	Remarks
(A) Target Loads (Low Pressure)			
250 Cast PB 375248	2400/15.0	1357	
250 Cast PB 375248	4227/17.0	1330	
265 Cast GC 375296	4198/20.0	1350	
265 Cast GC 375296	HiVel 2/23.0	1355	
(B) Medium Loads			
255 Winchester S.P.	HiVel 2/26.0	1455	
255 Winchester S.P.	4895/29.0	1415	Very accurate; mild pressure.
255 Winchester S.P.	4895/32.0	1560	Very accurate.
255 Winchester S.P.	3031/30.0	1601	
(C) Heavier Loads for Strong Action Rifles Only			
255 Winchester S.P.	3031/33.0	1760	
255 Winchester S.P.	3031/35.0	1866	Max.; powerful and accurate.
255 Winchester S.P.	Re 7/30.0	1684	
255 Winchester S.P.	Re 7/32.0	1796	Very accurate; best heavy load.
255 Winchester S.P.	Re 7/33.0	1852	Max.; powerful and accurate.

lubricant, a blend of 50% Alox 2138F and 50% pure yellow beeswax. This comes in brown colored "sticks" for use in lubricating pumps, but may be applied directly by hand, and is proving very effective in withstanding the higher temperatures of increased velocities.

The 38-55

Much that has just been said concerning the 32-40 applies equally to the 38-55, particularly our comments as to reloading procedures and techniques. This is because the 38-55 is not only the same type of rimmed, straight-walled case, but is even the same basic brass and has very nearly the same powder capacity. Too, both cartridges are used in precisely the same types and models of rifles. Fundamentally, only the caliber and bullet weights are different.

It should not be assumed from this, however, that there are no additional considerations. Merely increasing the bore diameter from 32 to 38 produces substantial changes in the expansion ratio and bullet-base area, thus inevitably affecting such things as powder burning characteristics, developed pressure, and the ratio of change-to-bullet weight. These factors influence both the choice of powder and charge weights and, in the 38-55 with its relatively high expansion ratio of 14 and low ratio of charge-to-bullet weight, medium and medium-fast burning powders in fairly small charges are indicated.

Thus, we find 3031, the old HiVel 2, and Hercules new Reloder 7 among the best propellants for full-power loads in this cartridge. Slower burning powders such as 4895 and Re 11 can be used, of course, but velocities will be lower in proportion to charge weight, and combustion will probably be incomplete. Going in the other di-

rection, small amounts of fast burning powders, including 4198, 4227 and 2400 may be used with excellent accuracy in light target loads, but here it is imperative to guard against the possibility of getting in a double charge! If this happens with a powder such as 2400, the result will almost certainly be a blown-up rifle.

Note carefully the way in which the loads in our table have again been grouped in three different categories, and be guided accordingly. American factory loaded 38-55s develop only 1320 fps with 255-gr. jacketed soft point bullet, by way of comparison, while Dominion factory rounds are listed at 1600 fps, making these latter the most powerful commercially loaded 38-55s available. As will be seen, either of these are readily duplicated with handloads but again, as with the 32-40, the determining consideration must be the rifles strength and condition. If there is any doubt, play it safe, and *always* start below listed loads, working up gradually. Remember, the higher the velocity or the faster burning the powder is, the higher pressures will be.

Case capacity of the 38-55 averages about 37½ or 38 grains (water), and I consider 35 grains of 3031 or 33 Reloder 7 to be a maximum charge for *use in the best and strongest rifles only.* These loads are both powerful and accurate, driving the 255-gr. soft point bullet at better than 1850 fps for a muzzle energy of close to 2000 fp. Inside a hundred yards, the 38-55 with its heavier and larger diameter bullet is therefore a better game killing load than the 30-30 or 32 Special. Recoil, while heavier than that of a 32-40, is still quite mild—certainly not enough to induce flinching or other poor shooting habits.

The writer's favorite high power hunting load in a strong action 38-55

consists of 32 grains Reloder 7 with Remington 9½ primers and the Winchester 255-gr. soft point bullet. Accuracy with this load has been far better than with any other heavy combination; at almost 1800 fps we have an excellent woods hunting cartridge for deer and black bear. No hot loads with 4198 have been listed because pressures tend to mount rapidly and I found them inaccurate also.

Pertinent dimensions for the 38-55 cartridge consist of a case length of 2.128", which should be kept trimmed to a uniform measurement of about 2.118". Maximum over-all loaded cartridge length for repeating rifles is 2.44". Barrels in 38-55 caliber may vary, depending upon the maker, from .376" to .379" groove diameter, so it behooves reloaders to determine the actual diameter of ther rifle's bore before selecting a bullet.

Winchester factory soft points mike .376" and have given me splendid accuracy in several different 38-55s, but Lyman moulds can be obtained casting bullets of various dimensions from .377" to .382", so if your barrel has a groove diameter of more than .377", a better fit will be obtained with one of these. My own preference with cast bullets is for a .002" oversize slug that will positively fill out the rifling grooves and seal off the bore, preventing gas leakage past the bullet.

Cast bullet accuracy is especially good in this big bore with its slow 1-in-18" rifling twist, and I particularly recommend them for the fine old single-shot rifles whose soft steel barrels were never intended for jacketed bullets. With the right fit of bullet to bore, a good lubricant such as the new Alox-containing Javelina, and loads tailored to your individual rifle, I'm betting you'll be pleasantly surprised at the performance of a 38-55 or 32-40, either in the woods or on the range. ●

INDIAN GUNS

Contrary to popular opinion, the Plains Indians were "Good shots, good riders and the best fighters the sun ever shone on," said General Benteen. Here is the story of their firearms and their shooting ability.

by Norman B. Wiltsey

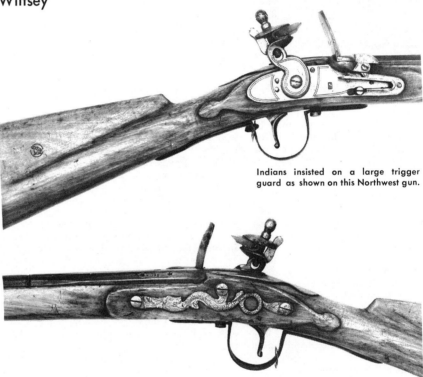

Indians insisted on a large trigger guard as shown on this Northwest gun.

Hudson's Bay trade gun in flintlock form. Percussion versions are nearly identical.

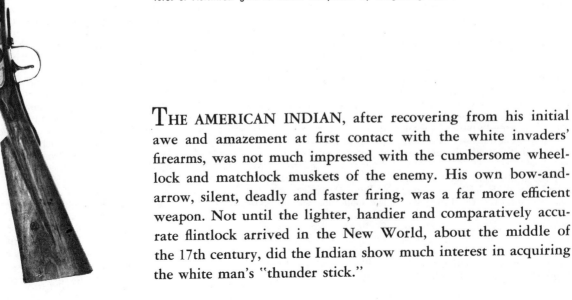

The serpent side-plate and proof marks on the barrel were required features of Northwest guns to assure acceptance by bargaining Indians.

THE AMERICAN INDIAN, after recovering from his initial awe and amazement at first contact with the white invaders' firearms, was not much impressed with the cumbersome wheellock and matchlock muskets of the enemy. His own bow-and-arrow, silent, deadly and faster firing, was a far more efficient weapon. Not until the lighter, handier and comparatively accurate flintlock arrived in the New World, about the middle of the 17th century, did the Indian show much interest in acquiring the white man's "thunder stick."

& GUNFIGHTERS

The first Indians to obtain the new flintlocks in appreciable quantities were the Huron and Algonquin allies of the French in New France — the Canada of today. The powerful Iroquois Confederacy, implacable foes of the French since 1609 — when Samuel de Champlain, accompanying a war party of Algonquin, Huron and Montagnais braves, killed two of their chiefs with his arquebus near what is now Ticonderoga — countered by trading beaver skins for flintlocks with the Dutch at Fort Orange (Albany, N.Y.) and Rensselaerwyck on the Hudson. The canny Dutchmen received 20 prime beaver pelts for one gun and a correspondingly high price for gunpowder. Later the price for both coveted items was sharply reduced by order of the Dutch government as a necessary measure to retain the friendship of the Iroquois and prevent, if possible, their trading with the French.

The guns sold to Indians by both French and Dutch traders were short, light snaphances known as *fusils,* the term later corrupted to *fusees.* When the English took over New Amsterdam from Peter Stuyvesant in August of 1664, they quickly found that the Iroquois expected them to continue the fair trade practices belatedly established by the Dutch. The latter continued in business for many years after the English take-over and gradually became assimilated with the conquerors. Stuyvesant's Dutch province became the property of the Duke of York and his beloved New Amsterdam became New York.

The haughty Iroquois could not have cared less about all these territorial shifts by the whites. Ruling the great forests from Canada to Tennessee and from Maine to Lake Michigan, they were the balance of power between the rival French and English and they never let either faction forget it. They hated the French, but would trade with them if trade suited their purpose. They distrusted the English, but cynically allied with them to keep the French and their Indian allies north of Lake Champlain. Heavily armed, with flintlocks supplementing their bows and tomahawks, the warlike Iroquois (the Five Nations) had crushed in turn the mighty Huron Confederacy—themselves comprised of tribes of Iroquoian people—and the People of the Panther, the hard-fighting Erie. The major battle of the last campaign, in 1654, saw less than 2,000 Iroquois opposed against nearly 4,000 of the Erie.

In 1666 the French mounted a full-scale military invasion of Iroquois territory, burning towns and crops, ruthlessly dealing what they believed to be a death-blow to the Five Nations. Further decimated by a deadly epidemic, the tenacious Iroquois grimly met a new challenge from the Susquehanna to the south. Defeated in the first battle of this new war, the beleagured Iroquois Confederacy received unexpected assistance when an epidemic similar to the plague that had ravaged their own ranks struck the Susquehanna. European settlers along the borders of the Maryland and Virginia colonies helped out by banding together and attacking the weakened Susquehanna. The appreciative Iroquois, moving in, mopped up almost without opposition.

This, the last of the major Indian-against-Indian wars on the Eastern frontier, left the Iroquois holding the future destiny of the nation in their hands. They were ideally situated to capitalize on their favorable position, and astute enough to do so. The adroitness of Iroquois statesmanship is amply illustrated by the remarks of La Grande Gueule (Big Mouth), noted Onondaga orator, to a French governor in 1684: "We Iroquois will go where we wish, allow passage through our country only those who seem to us good, and will buy and sell with whom we please."

So the Great League flourished for nearly a century more. The Five Nations became Six Nations with the addition of the Tuscarora around 1720. Four of the six—the Mohawk, Onondaga, Cayuga and Seneca—sided with the English in the Revolutionary War; the Tuscarora and the Oneida decided to aid the Colonists. Thus the Great League, after more than 300 years of existence, came to an end.

We get a glimpse of the type of arms furnished by the British to their Indian allies in Carl P. Russell's carefully documented book *Guns of the Early Frontiers.* Russell cites a request from the English governor Benjamin Fletcher, to the British Committee of Trade in London in 1693 for "200 light fuzees from their Majesties to the Five Nations of Indians; they will not carry the heavy firelocks I did bring over with me, being accustomed to light, small fuzees in their hunting."

Fletcher received more than the 200 "fuzees" requested, as the wealthy Lords of Trade in London knew well the economic importance of keeping on friendly terms with the Iroquois.

Geronimo, War Chief of the Apaches, shown with a Sharps rifle in this famous photograph by A. Frank Randall which is now in the collection of the Smithsonian Institution.

These weapons were undoubtedly the short, lightweight flintlocks in use by European cavalrymen of the period, commonly called musketoons or carbines. After 1675 practically all guns in the New World were of the true flintlock variety, but in the loose terminology of the times these continued to be designated as snaphances. Musketoon, carbine and fusee—or "fuzee"—derive from the French *mousqueton, carabine* and *fusil-court,* as the French short, light musket preceded the English version.

Effectively blocked from direct southern expansion down Lake Champlain and the Hudson River by the English and their Iroquois allies, the French moved westward from New France into present-day Michigan, Wisconsin, Minnesota, Indiana and Illinois. Traders went right along with the intrepid *coureurs de bois,* seeking to strengthen the ties with their own Indian allies with guns, powder and ball, pots, kettles, vermillion, hatchets,

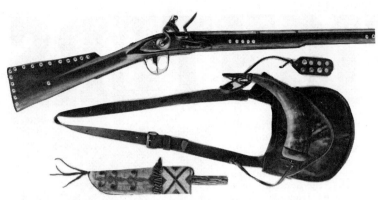

The Northwest flintlock was popular as a trade item throughout western Canada and the American West; it was made and used for a hundred years or more.

knives, beads and mirrors. Russell states: "In the last decade of the 17th century, French muskets were in use by natives everywhere from Lake Winnipeg to Lake Champlain and south to the mouth of the Mississippi."

The French weapons, so liberally distributed to the Indians, were inferior to English arms. Many warriors were killed or injured when a fusee burst upon firing. Most of these accidents were doubtless caused by

and Iroquois for control of the New World. About 80,000 French military muskets were supplied to the Colonists during the Revolution. Many of these arms may be found in American collections today, but hardly a trace remains of the thousands of French trade-guns sold to the Indians. What happened to them is one of the fascinating mysteries in the history of firearms.

Swedish colonists, who settled in

the Spanish in Florida, following a formal declaration of war by England in 1739. In 1763, Spain ceded Florida to England.

In the Southwest, encroaching French traders bartered their inferior flintlocks in New Mexico and Texas early in the 18th century. Hard-riding Comanches, armed with French fusils, conducted raid after raid upon Spanish settlements until, by 1759, all of north Texas was abandoned by Spanish soldiers, settlers and missionaries. With the rout of the enemy from northern Texas, the insatiable Comanches turned to harrying the New Mexico towns.

Rated by early frontiersmen as the greatest horsemen of all the Plains tribes, the Comanches were trained in warfare from childhood. One trick of horsemanship, which few white men were ever able to master, was the spectacular stunt of swinging over the "off" side of a mount, using the horse's body as a shield. By hooking a leg over the horse's back, and hanging in a rope loop attached to his saddle or plaited into his horse's mane, the warrior had both hands free to use gun or bow, or to pick up a wounded comrade. When using a muzzle-loader on horse-

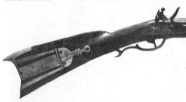

Good specimen of the Kentucky long-barreled flintlock rifle.

overcharging, since at first the naive red man operated on the theory that if a little powder and one musket ball was effective, then two balls and a double charge of powder would do twice as well.

Raid and counter raids between the hostile factions finally resolved into the six-year French and Indian War, beginning May, 1754, and ending in September of 1759. New France officially ceased to exist one year later when the Governor de Vaudreuil surrendered Montreal and all of Canada to the English general, Amherst.

Russell estimates that 200,000 muskets had come from the French factories during France's more than a century of struggle against the English

what is now Delaware and southeastern Pennsylvania from 1638 to 1655, evidently used Dutch or English guns for their trading with the local Delaware, Susquehanna and Mahican Indians, for no guns of Swedish manufacture have been traced to that period.

The Spanish invasion of the New World contributed little to the acquisition of firearms by the Indians; all gun trading was outlawed.

Whatever guns the sullen tribesmen in New Spain acquired were received from French and English traders. Creek, Chickasaw, and Cherokee braves, armed with French and English guns, assisted the English colonists in a bitter four years' war against

back, these early-day pirates of the prairie carried a powder horn and a mouthful of balls. The powder charge was poured by guess at full gallop, a wet bullet spat into the muzzle and the ball settled by a thump of the hand against the butt. The trick was to fire the gun when the barrel was level, but before the ball rolled out.

The English Hudson's Bay Company, attempting to take over all trading with the Indians of the Northwest after the fall of New France, discovered that the French traders were still much in evidence. Nine different French companies had combined by 1784 to form the North West Company in direct competition with HBC. Grace Lee Nute writes in *The Voyageur* that she found 2,431 voyageurs represented in the government licenses issued at Montreal and Detroit for the year of 1777. These rugged adventurers, other traders already afield, plus the employees of the Hudson's Bay Company and the American traders from the new United States, brought the total of traders to "5000 men sprinkled from Montreal to the Rocky Mountains and from Hudson Bay to the Gulf of Mexico." Guns and ammunition provided the best trading bait to swap for furs with the more than 300,000 Indians roaming this vast territory.

Short, light fusils continued to be the favorite arm of the red men. Not

Indians often cut down the barrels of their guns for easier handling when hunting buffalo. Caplock gun, shown at right, was made in fewer numbers and in later years of production.

until around 1805 was this type of weapon generally recognized as the "Hudson's Bay fuke," the "Northwest gun," or the "Mackinaw gun." Russell describes it as: ". . . light in weight, often short of barrel, and cheaply constructed. Commonly it was gauged to shoot a one-ounce ball; that is, it was 16-gauge, or about 66 caliber, although some were smaller. The trigger guard was clumsy in appearance and was large enough to permit access to the trigger even though the trigger finger was enclosed in glove or mitten."

Many of these distinctive Northwest guns were made by Barnett or Bond, British gunmakers. Most, if not all, carried a brass dragon-pattern sideplate on the left of the stock. Many such guns traded by the Hudson's Bay Company were further distinguished by the figure of a seated fox superposed on the initials TB or EB on lockplate and barrel. The fox is still part of the company crest.

W. Chance and Son; J. Hollis and Son; Ketland; Lacy and Company; Parker Field and Company; Robbins and Martin; Sargent Brothers; and Wilson, all British firms, contributed guns for use in America, in addition to Barnett and Bond.

Leman of Lancaster; Deringer of Philadelphia; Henry of Philadelphia and Boulton, Pennsylvania and the C.H. & S. Co. of New York are among the American gunmakers known to have turned out facsimiles of the Northwest gun for the Indian trade. The U.S. government got into the field by building over 1,200 "Indian muskets" during the years 1807-1810. Most Indians rejected these substitutes for the Northwest Gun, and in 1848 nearly 700 of the guns were still in storage at the Springfield Armory where they had been manufactured.

In the middle 1820s the redmen became aware of the superior accuracy of the rifle over the smoothbore, and began to demand them in exchange for furs at the annual rendezvous of the American Fur Company. Deringer, Henry, and Tryon of Philadelphia all made rifles for the Indian trade; some used the new caplock ignition system, but many warriors still preferred the tried-and-true flintlock. The famed Goulcher family of gunsmiths — the name was also spelled Golcher — made both flintlocks, percussion locks and rifle barrels in their shops in New York City and Philadelphia for the Indian trade.

During the early 1800s the Plains Indian enjoyed a transitory reign of glory as the "Noble Red Hunter of the Prairies"—the perfect "Child of Nature," according to the Eastern press. But the telltale signs pointing to his down-grading to the status of "ruthless savage" were beginning to appear. The vast territory west of the Missouri, despite Lewis and Clark's expedition to the Pacific in 1805-07, was still designated on most maps as

"The Great American Desert," but already the greedy white man was beginning to covet the Indian's virgin lands. Under the terms of the Indian Removal Act, signed into law by President Andrew Jackson in 1830, all tribes east of the Mississippi River were to cede their lands in exchange for territory in the West. It goes without saying that the land to which they were banished was arid, infertile terrain which the whites did not want for themselves. The Choctaw, the

Sitting Bull, shown in ceremonial dress, is holding his later favorite weapon, an 1873 Winchester. Probably one of the few, if any, 73s used in the Custer fight.

Chickasaw and the Creeks were the first to be forced from their ancestral home-land; the Cherokee the last of the four great southeastern tribes to leave. In the spring of 1838 the sad migration known as the "Trail of Tears" cost the lives of 4,000 of the 13,000 Cherokees on the fearful journey west to what is now Oklahoma.

The Seminoles of Florida, operating under the brilliant leadership of Osceola, defied the removal order and battled the Army to a standstill in a war (1835-1842) that cost the lives of 1,500 soldiers and $20,000,000 in military expenses. Only after Osceola had been captured and imprisoned through treachery did the war peter out. Most

Seminoles eventually moved west to Indian Territory, but a few bands moved deep into the shadowy Everglades, and easily eluded the Army's clumsy efforts to root them out. The descendants of these dauntless ones live there today, still as independent as ever, and proud of the fact that they have never signed any form of peace treaty with the government of the United States.

War between the Indian and the white man on the Great Plains became inevitable with the virtual disappearance of the beaver trade, the consequent acceleration in the slaughter of the buffaloes for hides, and the appearance of the settlers' wagon trains west of the Missouri. The Plains Indian had welcomed the fur traders who brought the guns and ammunition he wanted and the trinkets craved by his women-folk; he had tolerated the mountain men who were hunters and wanderers like himself; but the hide hunters who destroyed the buffalo, and the settler who fenced off land and called it his, were entirely a different proposition. Clashes inevitably occurred between Indians and the Forty-niners and the pioneers heading

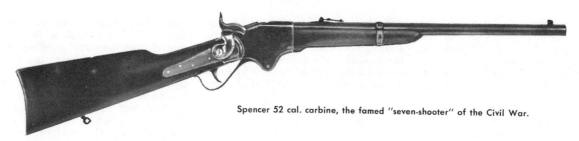

Spencer 52 cal. carbine, the famed "seven-shooter" of the Civil War.

west over the Oregon Trail, yet—in the curious manner of Indian warfare—the tribesmen lost no opportunity to trade for guns with the whites. The warriors were avid for modern rifles to replace their ancient trade guns; not for hunting game but for killing white men.

George Bird Grinnell, noted recorder of Indian history, in his book *The Fighting Cheyennes,* observes: "American Horse (a Cheyenne chief) has told me that the emigrants passing up the South Platte River to the mines between 1858 and 1865 were largely armed with the Sharps military rifles, and the Indians secured many of them in trade from these travelers. They were useful arms. The Indians also had some old-fashioned cap six-shooters, and during the year 1875 (the year before the Custer debacle on the Little Bighorn) there was a good deal of trading done for improved rifles.

"The method by which the Indians kept themselves supplied with ammunition for firearms, not only loose ammunition but also fiixed, has always been more or less mysterious, but they explain that in those war days they were constantly purchasing powder, lead, primers, and also outfits for reloading cartridges. They carried with them as part of their most prized possessions sacks of balls they had molded and cans of powder. So far as possible, they saved all the metal cartridge shells they used or found, and no doubt became expert reloaders of shells."

The late Stanley Vestal, University of Oklahoma professor, famed Western historian and close friend, before his death in 1957, of the Sioux, compiled a box score of 12 major engagements

between redman and white, including the Custer fight. In these engagements a total of 10,356 Indians fought 5,249 whites. The results: Indians, 69 killed, 28 wounded; whites, 383 dead, 102 wounded.

The list appeared in an article Vestal—who was actually Professor Walter S. Campbell—wrote in *Guns Magazine* for December, 1956. "Other than the astonishingly low number of casualties on either side," Vestal said, the battles, "reveal an important trait of the Sioux campaigns. The Indians, like Napoleon, fought as a rule only when they had the advantage of numbers. . . . They did this with hardly half enough guns to go around under the best conditions, and with no cannon at all."

Today's Western television fan stubbornly believes that the average Indian warrior was a lousy shot compared to the average U.S. Cavalry trooper. This, too, is part of the glamorous mystique of the Old West, for when we turn to the men who actually traded shots with hostile braves we find that, gun for gun, the Indian was more than a match for the soldier. More than that—and this, also, may come as a shock to the die-hard Western buff—the Indians not only outshot but outrode their cavalrymen foes.

Major Walsh of the Royal Northwest Mounted Police declared them "superior to the best English regiments." One of General Crook's staff officers described them as "the finest light cavalry in the world." General Charles King rated them "foemen far more to be dreaded than any European cavalry." Major Anson Mills, a captain at the Battle of the Rosebud in 1876, declared, "Their like will never be seen again." General Fred-

erick W. Benteen, also a captain in 1876, gave the red riders of the Plains this high accolade: "Good shots, good riders, and the best fighters the sun ever shone on."

General George Crook, in an official report to the Secretary of War in 1876, stated: "When the Sioux Indian was armed with a bow and arrow he was more formidable, fighting as he does most of the time on horseback, than when he got the old-fashioned muzzle-loading rifle. But when he came into possession of the breechloader and metallic cartridges, which allows him to load and fire from his horse with perfect ease, he became at once 10,000 times more formidable." Crook added: "I have seen our friendly Indians, riding at full speed, shoot and kill a wolf, also on the run; while it is a rare thing that our troops can hit an Indian on horseback, though the soldier may be on his feet at the time."

Corroborating Crook's view of the Indian in warfare, General Nelson A. Miles gave this coolly professional opinion of the Indian's proficiency with improved arms: "The Indian's marksmanship is very accurate within the range to which he is accustomed in killing game, say within 200 yards. But in the use of the long-range rifle, where he must take account of the elevated sights, the distance and the effect of the wind upon the flight of the bullet, he is inexperienced and in no way a match for his more intelligent enemy."

Miles, however, neglected to amplify his statement by admitting that very few rifles with elevating sights came into the hands of the redman, and that he wasted mighty little of his precious ammunition in target

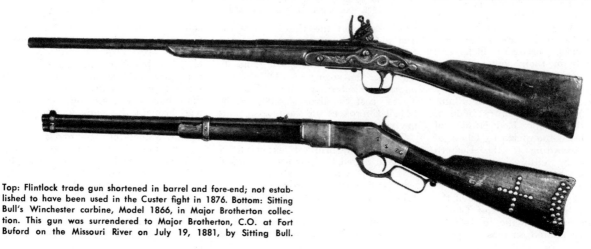

Top: Flintlock trade gun shortened in barrel and fore-end; not established to have been used in the Custer fight in 1876. Bottom: Sitting Bull's Winchester carbine, Model 1866, in Major Brotherton collection. This gun was surrendered to Major Brotherton, C.O. at Fort Buford on the Missouri River on July 19, 1881, by Sitting Bull.

practice; the battle-field was the Indian's rifle range.

In 1866, in the Fetterman fight at Fort Phil Kearney, the Sioux acquired 79 Sharps carbines and Springfield muzzle-loaders from the bodies of the slain soldiers. Two frontiersmen killed in the fight carried 16-shot Henry repeating rifles, caliber 44. These were the first repeating rifles ever taken by the Sioux. A good idea of how the hostile tribesmen were equipped with firearms before this scrap may be obtained from Grinnell, who notes: "Only six of the 81 white men (killed in the Fetterman fight) bore gunshot wounds."

In that year of 1866 a law was passed "allowing any loyal citizen, or proper citizen, to trade with Indian tribes." And so—since guns were what the Indians wanted most—guns were what they got. But there were never enough guns to arm all the fighting men of all the tribes, and even after whipping Crook on the Rosebud on June 17, 1876, and capturing a number of carbines from the troops, only about half the Indians had guns for the climatic struggle with Custer 8 days later. Grinnell wrote that ". . . the guns were of many sorts—muzzle-loaders, Spencer carbines, old-fashioned Henry rifles, and old Sharps military rifles. The Sharps were probably the best guns they had, except those recently captured from the soldiers."

In Thomas B. Marquis' book *Wooden Leg's Story,* the narrator, a Cheyenne, declares: "Guns were not plentiful among us. Most of our hunting had been done with bows and arrows. Of the Cheyennes, Two Moons and White Wolf (chiefs) each had a repeating rifle. Some others had single-shot breechloading rifles. But there was not much ammunition for the good guns. The muzzle-loaders usually were preferred, because for these we could mold the bullets and put in whatever powder was desired, according to the quantity on hand. I believe the Sioux, in proportion to their numbers, had about the same supply of firearms that we had. The Waist and Skirt people (a tribal division of the Cheyennes) had few or no guns; were in every way poor. My muzzle-loading rifle had been lost with my other personal effects when we were driven out and our lodges burned on Powder River." (here Wooden Leg referred to Colonel Reynolds' attack on a Cheyenne village on March 17, 1876).

"6 or 8 guns, I suppose, had been taken from soldiers at the Rosebud fight. I recall seeing only two, a rifle and a revolver, among the Cheyennes. Both of them used cartridges . . ."

"My cap-and-ball six-shooter was my warring weapon. I had plenty of caps, powder and lead for it. I had a bullet mold to make its bullets from the lead. I kept the bullets and the caps in two small tin boxes. The powder I carried in a horn swung by a thong from my shoulders."

In his statement, Wooden Leg pinpoints the reason why the Indians were so poorly armed in comparison to the soldiers; economics. As Vestal has pointed out, ". . . only rich Indians could afford to buy repeaters, and rich Indians were no more numerous per capita than rich white men are."

The going price for even a single-shot breech-loader was 20 buffalo robes or several horses; the price for a repeater three times that. So, unromantically, the lie is given to the persistent myth that the Indians at the Little Bighorn were all armed with Winchesters as opposed to the soldiers' 45-70 single-shot Springfield carbines. The myth began at the Military Court of Inquiry after the disastrous 20-minute battle in which Custer and 206 troopers of the Seventh Cavalry were killed. Major Reno—scornfully called The-One-That-Ran-Away by the Sioux —answered interrogation as to the Indians' armament thus: "The Indians had Winchester rifles and the column made a large target for them and they were pumping their bullets into it."

Question: "The Indians, so far as you observed, were armed with Winchester rifles?"

Answer: "Yes, sir."

Question: "Do you know that they had any other arms?"

Answer: "No, sir."

Lieutenants Varnum and De Rudio backed Major Reno, at least in part. Both officers were cross-examined as to the Winchesters' range, after Varnum had mentioned them in his testimony.

Below the rank of commissioned of-

After the massacre at Wounded Knee, Big Foot lies dead and frozen in the snow.

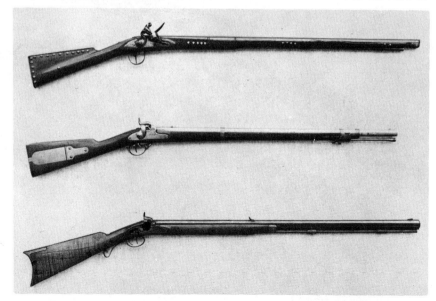

Typical of guns used in the early Canadian West are, from top: flintlock Northwest trade gun; Mississippi rifle, a favorite of land-seeking pioneers and miners in the 1800s; half-stock caplock rifle of Samuel Hawken's pattern.

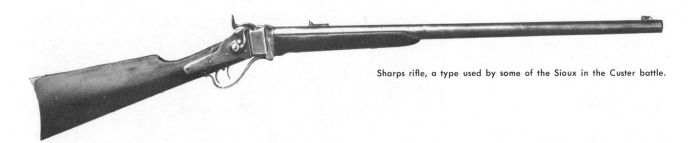

Sharps rifle, a type used by some of the Sioux in the Custer battle.

ficer, the "Winchester story" was considerably different. Sergeant Windolph, in the book *I Fought With Custer,* by Frazer and Robert Hunt, had this to say on the subject:

"It has been generally accepted that all the red warriors were armed with the latest model repeating Winchester rifles and that they had a plentiful supply of ammunition. For my part, I believe that fully half the warriors carried only bows and arrows and lances, and that possibly half of the remainder carried odds and ends of old muzzle-loaders and single-shot rifles of various vintages. Probably not more than 25 or 30 percent of the warriors carried modern repeating rifles."

Sergeant Windolph's estimate is far more logical and reasonable than that of Major Reno. Granting this, it is still improbable that about 500 braves were armed with repeaters. Of 284 long guns turned in by Sioux and Cheyennes in 1877, some 160 were muzzle-loaders according to Army Ordnance records; included in the lot

were 94 percussion rifles by H. E. Leman, six Hawkens, and a weird assortment of Kentuckys, old Springfield and Tower muskets, and one flintlock smoothbore. The balance were cartridge weapons. Thirty-nine repeaters were included in the batch of 124 breech-loaders. In six different calibers, they included four Henrys, 12 Winchesters and 23 Spencers. 123 revolvers were turned in, all but one cap-and-ball. The Ordnance report listed the condition of these weapons in these terms, "would be classed as 'unserviceable' at an arsenal."

Don Rickey, of the Custer Battlefield National Monument Museum, told Stanley Vestal: "On the Custer Battlefield, we have found several types of empty cartridge cases—of other than Army issue. They are mostly 50 caliber (for the Sharps, like the carbine we have that was used by Spotted Wolf, a Cheyenne) and for other 50 caliber arms such as the 1866, 1869 and 1870 models of the Springfield carbine and rifle, which

were retired from Army service by the introduction of the 45-70 Springfield in 1873-74. I have one 50 case that has been purposely altered at the primer pocket end, to enable a hostile to re-prime the cartridge with a common percussion cap—the usual method. It was originally a civilian, Berdan-primed cartridge. We have also found many 44 copper rim-fire cases that would have fit either the Henry rifle or the 1866 Winchester rifle or carbine. Other dug-up items include: a 58 caliber mould for the Minié type bullet used in the Civil War muzzle-loaders (dug up at the site of an Indian village, Little Big Horn valley), two percussion revolvers, and an 1873 Winchester 44-40 carbine."

Rickey did not mention finding any centerfire cartridge cases for the '73 Winchester, which would seem to dispose of the persistent tale that hundreds of braves were armed with this famous rifle in the Custer scrap. Sitting Bull's own Winchester, surrendered to Major Brotherton at Fort

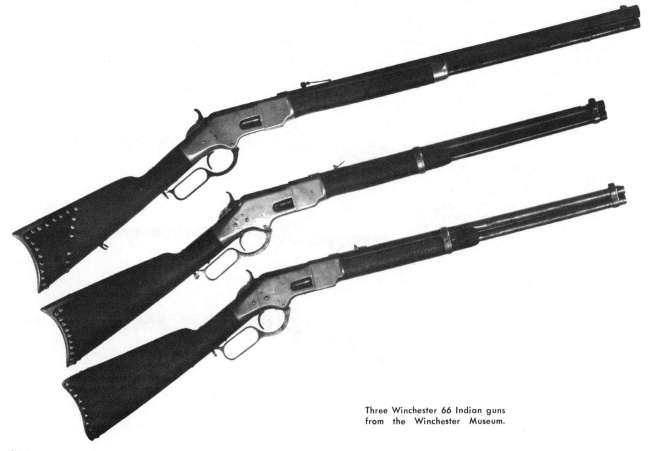

Three Winchester 66 Indian guns from the Winchester Museum.

Reproduction of a color painting by John Barsotti of Columbus, Ohio. The Indians are Apaches.

Buford, July 19, 1881, was a Model 1866 carbine, caliber 44 rimfire, serial number 124,375. This weapon is now in the Major Brotherton Collection at the Smithsonian Institution. The old Bull was reported to have carried a Winchester '73 at the Little Bighorn but, if the story is correct, he parted with it before surrendering to the Army five years later.

The fiery war leader of the Oglala Sioux, Crazy Horse, carried a Model '66 Winchester, as did a few of the other chiefs. Colored pictographs of the battle drawn by Indian participants show lever action rifles with bronze or brass frames in the hands of some of the warriors. Clearly, these weapons were 1860 Henry rifles and Model 1866 Winchesters.

Vestal notes that "when the Army used Gatling guns and Hotchkiss cannon, as at Wounded Knee, the Indian wars came swiftly to an end."

Wounded Knee, to which Vestal refers, is a particularly tragic incident in the annals of the Indian wars; it resulted from an attempt by the Army in 1890 to suppress the so-called "messiah craze," which was causing some unrest among the Sioux in South Dakota. The craze was a sort of religion marked by glorification of the past, ancestor worship, and the belief that an Indian messiah would appear and lead the Indians to victory over the white man. When the Army arrived, many Indians fled their reservations. The Army pursued them,

killed Sitting Bull for resisting arrest on Dec. 15, 1890, and attacked a large party of Indians at Wounded Knee Creek, So. Dak., on December 29. Killed were several hundred men, women, and children. This slaughter was the last "battle" of the Indian wars in the United States. Within a short time the surviving runaways were captured and returned to the reservations.

Even before the brutal massacre of 300 Sioux men, women and children at Wounded Knee in December of 1890, the Apaches had discovered that the White Eyes' "wagon-guns" were sheer murder. When Geronimo ended the 50-year Apache war with the whites by surrendering to General Miles in 1886, the chief laid his hand on a Gatling gun at Fort Bowie and growled: "Heap bad medicine! Goddam—sumbitch!"

The Ghost Dance craze, the murder of Sitting Bull, and the shocking tragedy of Wounded Knee ended the "Indian trouble" between the Mexican and Canadian borders. The last stand of the American Indian in Canada was made in 1897 by a sharpshooting young Cree named Almighty Voice, who was sentenced to 30 days in the guardhouse at the Duck Lake Post of the Northwest Mounted Police for shooting a settler's (some versions say government-owned) steer. Almighty Voice escaped, fleeing into the desolate northern wilderness. During the ensuing chase, and until the ultimate

death of Almighty Voice, 4 Mounties were killed and several wounded. Only after some 61 Mounties had cornered the Cree did their 7- and 9-pound field guns write an end to the saga of Almighty Voice.

So, in a blaze of red raw courage, ended the American Indian's 300 year struggle against the all-conquering white man. Not until World Wars One and Two did the conquerors appreciate the unique fighting qualities of the conquered, when young men of all tribes distinguished themselves in all branches of the Armed Forces. Today, in the steaming jungles of Vietnam, Indian specialists in American uniforms are instructing the Vietnamese in the guerrilla warfare practiced by their ancestors. ●

Bibliography

Guns of the Early Frontiers, by Carl P. Russell, Berkeley, Calif., 1957.

American Heritage Book of Indians, American Heritage Pub. Co., New York, N. Y., 1961.

Firearms in the Custer Battle, by J. E. Parsons and J. S. Dumont, Harrisburg, Pa. 1953.

I Fought with Custer, by F. and R. Hunt, New York, N. Y., 1947. (Story of Sgt. Windolph)

Wooden Leg's Story, by T. B. Marquis, New York, N. Y., 1928.

Report of Major Reno to Chief of Ordnance, *Army & Navy Journal*, Aug. 19, 1876.

On the Border with Crook, by Capt. J. G. Bourke, New York, N. Y., 1896.

Fighting Indian Warriors, by E. A. Brininstool, Harrisburg, Pa., 1953.

Carbine and Lance, by Col. W. S. Nye, Norman, Okla., 1937.

Sitting Bull, by Stanley Vestal, New York, N. Y., 1932.

The Voyageur, by Grace Lee Nute, New York, N. Y., 1934.

Breech Loading

a chronological history of an idea, of a brilliant discovery, that took six centuries to gain acceptance. This detailed and fascinating account is copiously illustrated

Breech-loading shore defense Pierriers or parrot guns, illustrated in Francis Grose's *Antient Armour and Weapons* (London, 1786).

BREECH-LOADING has been invented over and over again. So many of the earliest surviving guns (hand-cannon and larger pieces) were breech-loaders that it is impossible at this late date to do more than guess whether the *first* was a muzzle- or breech-loader. Early breech-loading cannon crop up all over the place. Some Spanish and Majorcan small breech-loading cannon have a removable breech, which is also the cartridge, looking vaguely like a beer mug with a handle. Examples of these guns were discovered accidentally in Madrid when sewer trenches were being dug. These rusty relics can be dated to some time in the mid-13th century, judging from the depth of the layer of debris in which they were found, and by related objects found with them.

In Copenhagen, at the Tojhus Museum, there are several large trestle tables loaded down with cannon found in the North Sea in two different discoveries. These are all beer stein breechloaders. Both the barrels and the detachable breech were embedded in heavy oak planks. The barrels were made of staves of long flat iron held together with rings of iron shrunk on, the rings having been heated white hot. Each barrel was fastened to its stock with four iron rings going around both the barrel and the oak stock. The breech was wedged from the rear to hold it as close as possible to the barrel when the fire was applied to the touchhole. These breechloaders had two advantages over muzzle-loaders. They didn't have to be hauled back from their firing ports to be reloaded, and with several of the beer steins loaded in advance they were rapid fire guns for those days. It has been estimated that a smart gun crew could manage to get off 15 to 20 shots an hour without blowing themselves up by pre-ignition of the charge from an overheated gun barrel. The first discovery, five guns with iron ball and extra chambers, was made in 1846.

Firearms

MASCOLO

PERIERA A BRAGA

by MERRILL K. LINDSAY

Photographs by BRUCE PENDLETON, et al

Breech-loading "beer mug" cannon illustrated in Capo Bianco's text on artillery printed in Venice in 1516.

The guns were still aboard a sunken battleship which had been part of the fleet of Queen Margrethe. She died in 1418, which dates the guns to some time before 1400. These guns, along with other parts of the ship, were discovered on the bottom of the sea, north and east of Anholt in the Kattegut.

Nearly a hundred years later, another warship was located on the other side of the same reef at Anholt. This time six breech-loading cannons with loose chambers were fished up. One still had an iron ball shoved into the breech and the separate chamber still filled with powder was wedged to the back of the barrel with a wooden block. The interesting thing about this later find is that these cannon, of the same vintage as the first ones, were on a ship which had been sunk 160 years later, or in the 1560s. These breech-loading cannon must have worked well to have been kept in use for such a long time. It is interesting to note that these cannon were also used to shoot *langrel* (irregular pieces of scrap iron) at sails and sailors. A barrel of langrel was part of the 1937 find.

Breech-loading hand-cannon and wall pieces picked up on battlefields and at the sites of castle sieges in France are not as easily dateable. Most of them were found hundreds of years ago and are now exhibited in the Musée de l'Armée, at the tomb of Napoleon (des Invalides) in Paris, and in the old fortress (now a museum), la Porte de Hal, in Brussels. About all that is really known about these pieces is where they were found and the date when they were discovered. As they have been in museum collections for at least a couple of hundred years they obviously are not modern fakes. They were often found at the sites of historical battles, such as the battles or sieges of castle or city which took place during the reign of Edward III of England or his Plan-

tagnet successor, Richard. Froissart in his *Chronicles* tells of the use of cannon by the French, the English and the Burgundians, but he does not describe the pieces and we don't know whether they were breech- or muzzle-loaders. The French tradition is that these pieces are all English, but this is not provable. It may just be a French way of saying what nasty people the British are!

Most of the guns in the Paris museums hang from iron straps on the courtyard walls, their breeches open. Few could be considered hand weapons. They are just too big and heavy to have been held at the shoulder. Either they were rested on a wall or parapet, or at some time they had a stand from which they could be fired. Frequently, according to early manuscript illustrations, they were simply laid on the ground, pointed at the enemy, and fired by a soldier who gingerly applied a hot poker to the touchhole and then ran off. As a matter of fact, firing these early pieces was such an unpopular and dangerous business that convicts were often selected for the job. A jailbird would be released, escorted to the cannon by a squad of pikemen and handed a hot poker or a piece of burning match or punk attached to a long stick called a linstock. If he tried to run away he was prodded back into line by the pikemen, who were anxious to see him perform his patriotic duty. If the cannon exploded because of a bad casting, a damaged iron hoop or a particularly potent mixture of gunpowder, well, then the chap had paid his debt to society. If the cannon didn't explode, the jailbird was perhaps let off with a lighter sentence and was the first rung up the ladder on his way to becoming a master gunner.

In England, Italy, Germany and Austria, and especially in Turkey, there are examples of the tremendously big bronze cannon which were cast on the battlefield. Transportation was

too difficult for these great monsters, some of which shot granite cannon balls weighing a thousand pounds, and had bores a man could crawl into. Train loads of horses, sometimes camels, would bring the brass or bronze to a location convenient to where it was to be shot. There, the master gunner, or gunfounder (often a German) would set up his workshop and forge, casting the cannon on the spot. When the war or battle was over, the cannon were sometimes lugged home, but more often they were melted down by the victors to make more cannon when the need arose. Sometimes they were abandoned, to be discovered later by souvenir collectors, who brought them home as trophies. Bronze being scarce and also re-usable, even these did not always survive later wars. Some of these Turkish guns are muzzle-loaders, including examples in Paris and in the Germanisches Museum in Nürnberg, and one of two, cast by Mohammed II for the siege of Constantinople in the 1450's, is now outside the artillery museum in Turin, Italy. The other was melted down by Napoleon.

These siege cannon had all-in-one breeches cast with the barrels. The breeches were of smaller inside and outside diameter than the barrels. The smaller hole was filled with powder and the stone cannon ball was rolled and pushed down the barrel until it rested on the lip of the smaller tube.

Other cannon, such as the one outside of the New Armoury at the Tower of London, and a whole battery of emplacement cannon overlooking the straits of the Bosporus, are breechloaders of massive dimension. The huge breech of such a gun was manhandled up to the barrel after loading. The breech was then screwed into the back of the barrel. In order to rotate it, a gear or key arrangement was cast into the exterior surface of the breech. This gave purchase to the

Henry VIII's shield holds a breech-loading matchlock pistol; *circa* 1500. Joe Kindig collection, York, Pa.

The GUN DIGEST *is pleased and proud to present two comprehensive excerpts on breech-loading arms from Merrill Lindsay's big new book, One Hundred Great Guns.*

This splendid work was several years in the making because the author and his cameraman went up and down the world looking for superbly crafted firearms to photograph in color—a glance at his book, and elsewhere in this volume —will show you that they succeeded in large measure.

Lindsay's chapter, a History of Breechloaders, has been extracted from his new book and specially prepared for the GUN DIGEST *by the author himself for this edition, including extra illustrations in black and white.*

Sixteen pages of brilliant color pictures, also from Merrill Lindsay's new book, will be found elsewhere in this 22nd edition.

crow bars used to rotate the breech as it was wound into the barrel thread.

Latest of the early breech-loading cannon were the "Pierriers." These were shot from ships and also used as shore defense. Francis Grose in 1786 illustrated a shore battery of these guns in his treatise *Antient Armour and Weapons.** These guns are shown mounted on a swiveling device much like a king-sized oar lock. At the breech of the gun, the cascabel is elongated to form a handle for directing or aiming the piece. The breech is cut away for a foot or so with the top half removed to make room for the insertion of the iron ball in the barrel and for the beer mug filled with pow-

* London, 1786.

der that went behind it.

There are many advantages in breech-loading cannon. First, the gun crew did not have to expose themselves in front of the cannon in order to reload. In the second place, with both ends of the piece open, it was possible to inspect the inside of the barrel to make sure that nothing was left over from the previous shot, such as a bit of smouldering charcoal

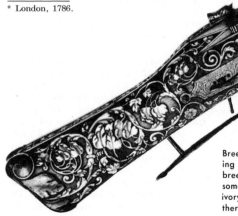

Breech-loading wheel-lock cavalry carbine, using a steel cartridge. One of the earliest breechloaders, the barrel and lock are handsomely carved and the stock is inlaid with ivory. Made around 1550 in Germany or northern Italy, it is now in the Armeria Reale collection in Turin.

which might set off the next charge accidentally. Thirdly, if an over-sized or out-of-round cannon ball got wedged in the barrel the open breech provided easy access for a ramrod to drive out the obstruction, which might otherwise ruin the cannon. Finally, breechloaders were faster to load and more accurate. A ball could be made with a closer tolerance to the bore than a ball which had to be shoved down the muzzle. Crews of muzzle-loading guns had a tendency to use a loose fitting ball, which would roll down the barrel. This, of course, avoided wedging, but it also increased "windage" or the amount of propelling gas which

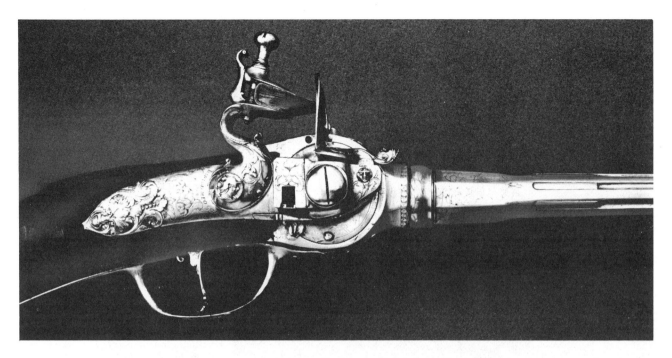

Rotary magazine flintlock breechloader signed *Bartolomeo Cotel*. This Italian gun, dating from the 1690s, is in the Tower of London collection.

could escape around the ball, thus reducing the velocity and accuracy of the projectile. The speed of fire of the breech-loading cannon depended on the number of beer mugs available and on the crews' skill in swabbing, reloading, wedging, and firing. In any event, it was a lot faster than muzzleloading, which required depressing the muzzle, swabbing the barrel to clean and cool it, cleaning the touchhole, loading and ramming down the bagged or loose powder, then the projectile and, finally, resighting the gun before firing.

Despite the many and obvious advantages of breech-loading, there were

a couple of disadvantages, such as backfire when the breech was not fitted closely enough. Another attendant hazard: by cutting away a portion of the breech, or casting the breech with an aperture large enough to admit the powder canister reduced the strength of the whole gun tube. A poor casting or an extra heavy charge could cause the gun to shoot backward, tearing off the back and decimating the gun crew.

Whatever the advantages or disadvantages to breech-loading cannon, there were nevertheless about ten muzzleloaders cast for every breechloader. As time went on, fewer and fewer

breechloaders were cast. Muzzleloaders took over so completely and for so long that it was possible to re-invent breech-loading in complete honesty with no knowledge that it had been around for a long time. Even as late as our own Civil War, the muzzleloaders outnumbered the breechloaders in shoulder weapons and small artillery. Few large breech-loading cannon were used by either of the armies or navies.

The Matchlock

A lot of obscure mechanical genius has been expended on the design of guns over the last 700 years. Practically all of the mechanical devices which were awarded patents as new inventions in the 19th century had been invented and used centuries before, and none of the possible breechloading systems may be exceptioned. The first advance over the handcannon, which required one hand to hold the gun and another to hold the punk or hot poker, was the matchlock. The matchlock let the gunner hold the piece with both hands and allowed him to use his eyes for aiming, rather than having to concentrate his attention on getting the fire into the little touchhole. The matchlock was a simple enough device. At first it consisted of nothing but an "S" shaped piece of wrought iron with a split at one end of the "S" into which the punk, or slow burning match, could be wedged. A nail or screw or rivet through the middle part of the "S" provided a pivot, making a trigger of sorts out of the bottom part of the "S." Pulling on the bottom part of the serpentine made the top curve dip down toward the touchhole, to which a little tray

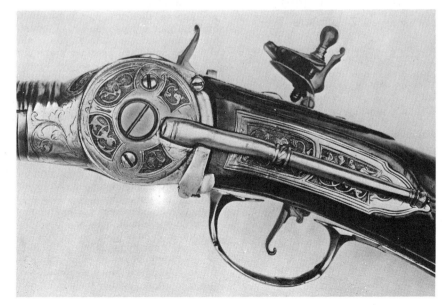

Lorenzoni type of magazine breechloader, made about 1690 by Giacomo Berselli, who probably also built the Cookson guns; 52 caliber smoothbore, with silver inlays and engraving, it is now in the Armeria Reale collection in Turin.

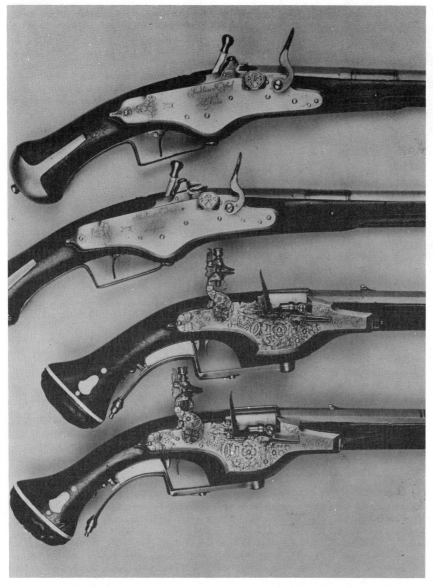

Four Mathias Kalthoff magazine pistols, *circa* 1660, in the Tojhus Museum in Copenhagen. The top two, with the Kalthoff sliding action, are 58 caliber, 21" over-all. The heavily engraved pair are 26" over-all, of 44 caliber.

of priming powder was attached. Nobody knows the date of this simple invention, but long before 1500 the matchlock had been improved by putting the spring inside, and by adding springs and a sear to pull and hold the match end, or cock, out of way of the priming pan when there was no finger pressure. Not too long after this, Peter Peck, a gun and barrel maker in Munich, was building *trap door breechloaders*. A simple back pull of the rear sight caused the spring-loaded top half of the breech to fly open. There, snugly resting in the barrel was an honest-to-God cartridge made of iron, with its own touch-hole connected with the touch-hole in the breech. When the breech was closed for firing, there were two hefty layers of iron or steel between the charge and the shooter. This was a practical and efficient breechloader, and it was built by a gunsmith who

was working 'way back in the early 1500s. The gun was well-made, and even today it shows no signs of the burning effects of hot gases, which would have occurred had the breech and the cartridge been sloppily fitted.

In the Tower of London and in Joe Kindig's collection in York, Pa., there are examples of another kind of matchlock breechloader. These are the shield pistols of King Henry VIII. Probably built by an Italian gunsmith (there is some surviving correspondence, including an offer to build such guns) these shield pistols needed to be breech-loaded. Obviously anyone who needed a shield in front of him to keep off arrows or crossbow bolts was reluctant to get out in front of his shield to reload via the muzzle of his gun. Therefore, these guns have hinged plates on the top of the breech and serpentine match holders which pivot from a fitting on the back of the

shield. Taking up a position of relative security, by a window or behind a castle parapet, the pistoleer could reload at leisure and, having taken aim through a small grilled aperture in the shield face above the projecting gun barrel, shoot.

I don't know how many other examples of matchlock breechloaders exist. One is illustrated in Howard Blackmore's *Guns and Rifles of the World.** It is in the Historical Museum in Bern, Switzerland, and is thought to be of German manufacture from the early 1600's. It looks something like the bolt of a Springfield or a Mauser rifle with a round knob on the end.

The Wheel-lock

While these breech-loading guns and pistols were being made, Leonardo da Vinci and various German clock- and gunmaking families were developing a new type of action. This was the wheel-lock, a mechanical spark-producing mechanism. The wheel-lock eliminated the necessity for a continuously slow burning match. It also speeded up the rate of ignition. It was no longer necessary to adjust the length of burning match between shots. A cumbersome, time-consuming process as the pan had to be cleaned after each shot to get rid of the residue. Then the match was swung into the empty pan with the pan cover open to check for correct length. Finally, the pan could be primed, covered to keep the powder in, and the gun loaded. In other words, breech-loading could add only a little speed to the operation of a matchlock gun. That is at least one of the reasons why, although troops were outfitted with matchlocks until the beginning of the 18th century, they were all issue muzzleloaders.

The breech-loading wheel-lock story is different. The cartridge had its own built-in primed pan and pan cover. You could shoot as fast as you could slip in a new cartridge and crank up the wheel spring. Some of the wheel-locks were not only self-spanning but also reprimed themselves by scraping a little priming powder into the pan from a reservoir.

Wheel-locks were always expensive guns to make and it required not a little skill to build one. It is not surprising that during the wheel-lock period we find many examples of finely made breechloaders. In the Royal Armory in Turin there is a beautiful little cavalry carbine inlaid with ivory which has a hinged breech and a steel cartridge. These cartridges, by the way, were not expendable. They were a lot of work to make, as they had to fit exactly. Many were a complicated piece of hand tooling, with their own pan and pan cover whittled out of the same block of steel. In those days one

* New York, 1965.

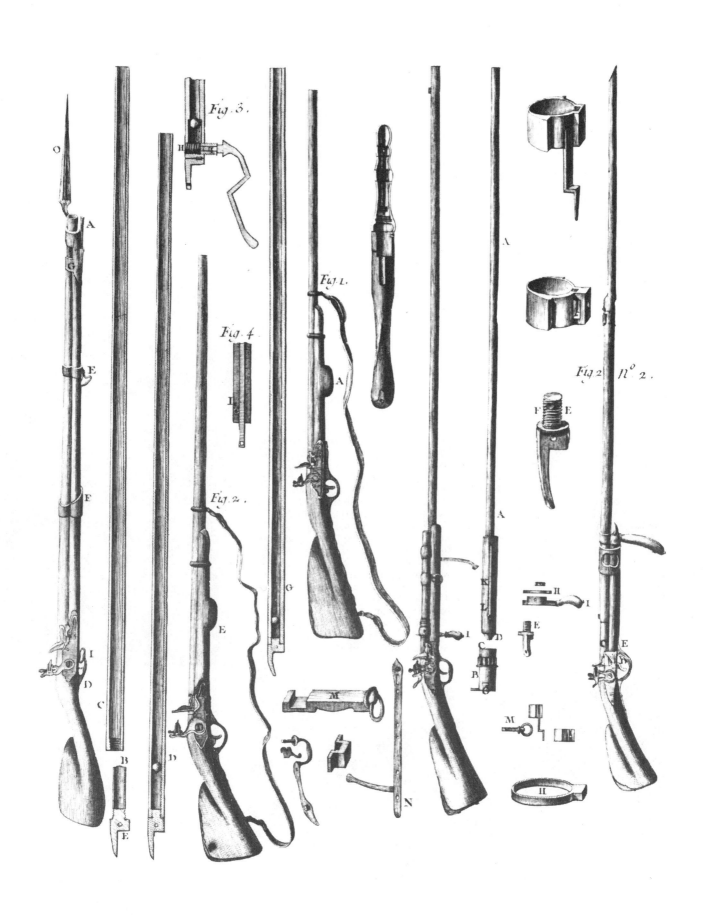

Some military breechloaders, including the Ferguson-Chaumette action, illustrated in Diderot's *Encyclopedia* published in Paris, 1751.

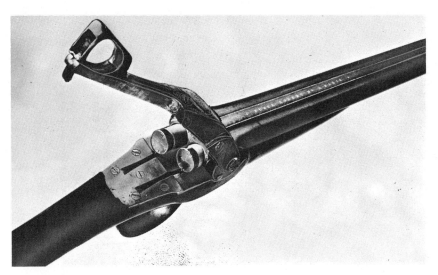

Early French breech-loading shotgun, a 24 gauge pinfire by Robert of Paris. Similar to the Pauly design, this smoothbore was made in the 1830s. Author's collection.

to shoot anywhere but in the general direction. In addition, the gas loss and the weight of the ball slowed the projectile speed to a virtual stand still a few yards after it had left the muzzle.

These turn-off British pistols were made in considerable quantity for a great many years. There are examples of the famous London gunsmith, Trulock, dating from the time of the Restoration, around 1660-1670, and I have two pair of turn-off pistols from a much later period. One pair was made by Griffin a century later and the newest, a tiny pair of muff pistols with tap-action, was made at the very end of the flintlock period, well into the 19th century.

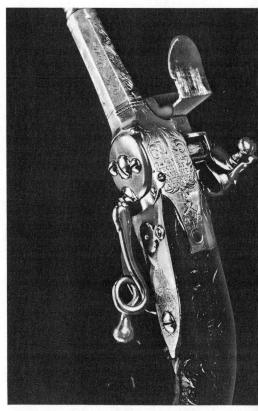

Lorenzoni type of breech-loading pistol. The inscription claims that this repeating breechloader mechanism was invented by August Wetschgli in 1690. Joe Kindig collection, York, Pa.

was lucky to have a couple of cartridges in his pocket, and these he reloaded every time he went out to hunt. The cartridges, being made solidly out of a block of steel, would last as long as the gun, if proper care were taken of them and the black powder residue washed out with water after shooting.

Two different styles of wheel-lock breechloaders are to be seen in the arms collection of the Kunsthistorisches in Vienna. One of these, a pistol with a scroll butt which belonged to the Emperor Rudolph II, has a breech which opens on two hinges on the left side. As the breech stands open, the cartridge can be removed and a new one inserted. The other is the work of Michael Gull, a Viennese gunsmith who introduced many new inventions. As far as I know, he was the first to build a breechloader with a turn-off barrel. These guns required no cartridge. The barrel was simply unscrewed and the powder poured into a cavity in the back. A slightly oversized ball was inserted in the barrel

rear and the two pieces screwed back together. This gave a tight fitting, nearly waterproof load with good breech pressures, thus longer range and better accuracy, especially if the barrel was rifled. Gull built his breechloader in the 1650s. The cannon-barrel Queen Anne English pistols, which employed the same loading system did not come along until the 1680's. They didn't get around much until the first part of the 1700s, which probably accounts for their being called Queen Anne pistols instead of Cromwellian or James II pistols. These guns were the best that the English were to make for another hundred years. They were chambered for a slightly over-sized ball, and their accuracy was notable in comparison with the performance of the contemporary muzzle-loading saddle pistol. The latter was usually loaded with a ball a size or two smaller than the bore which was only held in place in the barrel by a handful of wadding. Such a pistol could not be counted on

While turn-off barrels were certainly the most popular and perhaps the best and safest of the breech-loading systems invented during the flintlock period, there were many other ingenious systems used. For example, there were barrels which slid forward either on a metal frame-work or in a trough in the stock, to open the breech, either for a ball and loose powder charge, or a metal cartridge. The early trap door invention of Peter Peck seems to have been re-invented or rediscovered in England in 1664 by gunmaker Abraham Hill in patent application number 143. Hill says that his gun is loaded "by thrusting for-

Burnside Patent breechloader fires a metallic cartridge with a percussion cap. The U.S. purchased 55,567 during the Civil War. Winchester Museum collection.

ward the sight, and by a square cartridge within the peece near the breech. . . ." Other breechloaders, including a fine sporting flintlock made by Valentin Rewer, opened at the back with a hinge so that the whole stock and receiver dropped down to leave the breech wide open for the removal of the cartridge.

Double Breechloader

One gun, which belonged to Louis XIII of France (it was numbered in his arms cabinet inventory, and is now in the Musée de l'Armée in Paris) is not only a breechloader, but it has an ingenious double breech which pivoted and reversed after the first shot. In American and British legend, a Scotsman named Patrick Ferguson

enough to make way for top loading of both bullet and powder. However, this was by no means an original idea. A Frenchman had patented the same idea in England 50 years before. Isaac de la Chaumette's patent is dated August 12, 1721. In 1751, the idea was well-enough known to have been included in the famous French encyclopedia of Diderot and d'Alembert. Other elevating, screw-mechanism breechloaders were built in Germany, including one in the Kindig collection that works with a small detachable crank handle.

By Ferguson's time, even by Chaumette's, single shot breechloaders were surpassed mechanically by two types of multi-shot breechloaders developed by the Danes and the Italians.

that the repeater will fire 30 shots at one loading.

The Kalthoffs were prolific as well as inventive. Sons, cousins and brothers of old Peter went to London, Paris and Moscow. Departing from the original invention, they devised a number of different repeating systems, all of which seem to have worked well enough for other gunsmiths to imitate the Kalthoff system.

A number of different Italian gunsmiths evolved their own individual systems of breech-loading. The center of this activity, which started in the 1660s, was located around Genoa, Turin and Milan. Examples of three gunsmiths' work survive in the Armeria Reale in Turin. While all are lumped together under the name of

Triplett & Scott magazine breechloader made in Meriden, Conn., *circa* 1860. The barrel, shown in loading position, rotates to extract the case and pick up a cartridge from the stock magazine.

is supposed to have invented another kind of breechloader and used it during the Revolution. There is no question that he did develop a breechloader, for there are a few surviving examples which were made for him by Durs Egg, one of the best of the London gunsmiths. A company of riflemen were outfitted with them and the guns saw limited action against the Americans in the Battle of Brandywine.

The essence of Ferguson's design is a big screw, the diameter of the barrel bore with a very steep pitch to the threads, going through the breech from top to bottom, and attached to a movable trigger guard. One full turn of the trigger guard lowered the screw

The Danish invention came first, a breech-loading magazine gun by one Peter Kalthoff. Built and dated in 1645, it is a wheel-lock with the inscription *Das Erste* (the first), and indeed it was the first of a long series of Kalthoff specials, mostly in flintlock types. The first example had an under-barrel magazine for bullets and a container for loose powder in the stock. It worked via a sliding breech-block, which picked up the ball and then the powder on the side and then fed them into the breech end of the barrel as the block was moved sideways by an under lever which was also the trigger guard. One of the early Kalthoffs, a wheel-lock, claims (per an inscription on the barrel)

one of the designers, Lorenzoni, they are in reality quite different. The only thing some of them have in common is in operating by a side lever instead of by the movement of the trigger guard. Otherwise they are quite dissimilar, with magazines in different places and different loading systems. The Lorenzoni repeater has a unique feature. On the right hand lockplate there is a devil's head carved in the metal. The devil's mouth is open, and when the gun is loaded any excess powder from the priming runs out of this hole.

The two other inventors were Giacomo Berselli, and Pietro Callin of Genoa. The Callin system gets away from the side lever by having a ro-

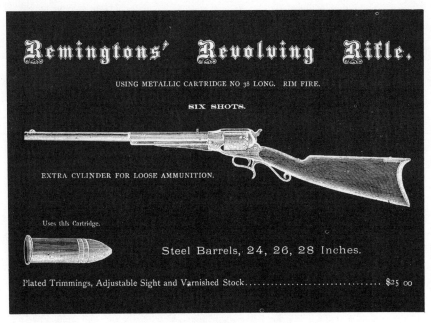

Remingtons' Revolving Rifle.

USING METALLIC CARTRIDGE NO 38 LONG. RIM FIRE.

SIX SHOTS.

EXTRA CYLINDER FOR LOOSE AMMUNITION.

Uses this Cartridge.

Steel Barrels, 24, 26, 28 Inches.

Plated Trimmings, Adjustable Sight and Varnished Stock...................... $25 00

Early Remington revolving rifle, a conversion of a like, earlier percussion cap arm. Note inclusion of spare cylinder for "loose ammunition," or powder and ball.

Sharps percussion breech-loading rifle, the type used in the U.S. Civil War by Col. Berdan's Sharpshooters and other troops.

tating barrel, which picks up the charges as it is turned 90 degrees. Lorenzoni also made a similar mechanism. One thing is certain: these guns worked well when they were in tip-top shape but a little wear or loss of adjustment would allow a train of loose powder to lead fire back to the magazine. Most of the powder magazines were thoughtfully tucked under the shooter's right eye. A fine example of what can happen with this arrangement is to be seen in the Smithsonian Institution. It is a Lorenzoni type side lever pistol, made by the English gunsmith Mortimer. The whole right side of the pistol is shattered, the result of an explosion in the magazine. The Berselli system seems to have been popular in England. At least a few guns which are signed "John Cookson" look like they were made by Berselli. These Cookson-Berselli guns have a side lever for transferring a charge of loose powder and a ball from their separate reservoirs in the buttstock interior.

Even at the end of the 18th century the systems of the Italian gunsmiths were being employed as far away as India. A fine French gunsmith, one Chelembron, was building magazine breechloaders on the turning barrel or Callin system. This invention was still being used in 1860 on a magazine breechloader made in

Meriden, Conn., by Triplett and Scott. In the Meriden gun, the barrel rotates nearly 270 degrees. When the barrel passes a certain point past upside down, it pushes away a swinging gate covering the door to the magazine in the stock. A cartridge is pushed into the breech by a spring carrier in the stock. As the barrel is turned back into shooting position, the magazine gate swings back to keep the rest of the cartridges in the magazine from being expelled. It is an ingenious system and a simple one. It is surprising to me that Triplett and Scott did not have at least as much success with their gun as Spencer did with his.

Pauly's Invention

In 1812 a Swiss inventor/balloonist, Samuel Pauly, built a new kind of gun in his Paris workshop, complete with a kit for loading your own cartridges. A cylinder was provided over which to roll and glue a cardboard sleeve. When properly glued and dried, this was in turn glued to a round brass plate which became the back end of the cartridge. In the center of the plate was a hole for admitting the primer flash and a paper covered fulminate pellet was held in place in the hole with a rosette. Assembled, the cartridge was quite similar to a modern paper shotshell. Pauly had presumably taken Forsyth's invention, which used fulminating pow-

der as a detonator to fire a muzzleloader, and put the primer in the cartridge where it belonged. Pauly's invention was good enough to attract the attention of French army officials. One of Napoleon's generals, the Duke of Rovigo, set up a date for a demonstration. The model gun performed beautifully though it was raining. Pauly got off a string of well-aimed shots in rapid fire sequence. Both the speed of firing and ability to keep on reloading and shooting in the rain woud have been quite impossible with the flintlocks which were issued to Napoleon's troops. Napoleon, however, was not impressed. The military mind of those days did not realize the advantages of increasing the fire power of the individual infantryman. In any event, the waste of ammunition inherent in increasing the rate of firing as well as the cost of modernizing all of the army's muskets was the excuse given. Not only the

French, but all of Europe put off the conversion to breech-loading for nearly another 50 years.

It is true that quite a lot of work was involved in making a Pauly cartridge. Warren Moore, the author of *Guns — The Development of Firearms, Airguns and Cartridges,** owns one of the very rare surviving Pauly loading kits. I have seen it and I've no desire to try it out. It makes loading so complicated that the most dedicated shooter would think twice before discarding his trusty muzzle-

* New York, 1963.

The Austrian Werndl conversion of their muzzle-loading muskets, similar to the Snider and Tabatière (French) conversions in that their breechblocks rotated on the barrel axis.

loader. Nevertheless, the first step toward a self-obturating cartridge had been taken and it was not long before gun designers were coming out with all kinds of ingenious breech-loading systems. Some put the primer cap, which had been invented in 1818, into the end of the cartridge and exploded the primer against an anvil; others put a pin into the side of a metal cartridge, driving the pin into the impact-sensitive material. This was the pinfire system, which has persisted until now!

Even if Napoleon was too busy to understand the significance of Pauly's invention, it did not escape the notice of a German workman in Pauly's shop. Johann Nikolaus von Dreyse worked for Pauly for several years during the experimental phases which led to the Pauly patent. He stayed in Paris working as a gunsmith until 1824 when he went home to Sommerda to work out an improvement of the Pauly invention. The Prussian government got wind of what he was up to and put his operation under wraps. Then one fine day the Prussian army appeared equipped with 300,000 breech-loading cartridge needle guns and trounced the Danes, the Austrians and the French. The needle gun wasn't completely successful, but it did a good job, and the old slow muzzle-loading musket was no match for it. The Dreyse needle gun had two major faults. First, the breech did not always stay tightly sealed under field conditions, and the escaping gases were an annoyance to say the least, sometimes a positive hazard. Second was trouble with the needle itself. It was required to penetrate the entire length of the paper cartridge to detonate the primer pellet lying against the base of the bullet. When the cartridge was fired the needle, of course, was in the midst of the burning gases. The heat of the blast had the undesirable effect of hardening the steel of the needle. The

Three early metallic-cartridge breechloaders. Top: Gibbs-Farquharson-Metford long range target rifle. Lever above guard is a safety. Middle: Frank Wesson No. 1 Long Range rifle; action is very like the Scottish Alex. Henry. Bottom: Sharps side hammer single shot, modified and re-stocked by Frank W. Freund, frontier gunsmith circa 1870-1900.

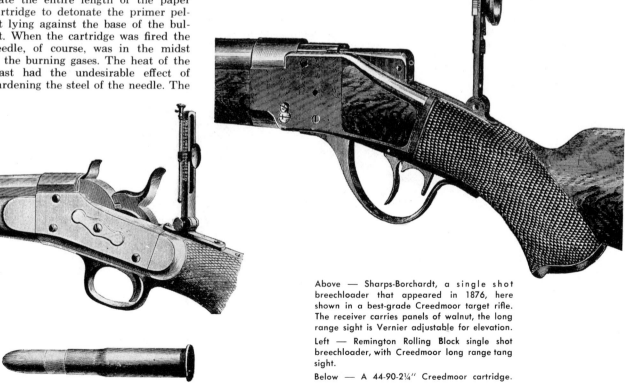

Above — Sharps-Borchardt, a single shot breechloader that appeared in 1876, here shown in a best-grade Creedmoor target rifle. The receiver carries panels of walnut, the long range sight is Vernier adjustable for elevation.

Left — Remington Rolling Block single shot breechloader, with Creedmoor long range tang sight.

Below — A 44-90-2¼" Creedmoor cartridge.

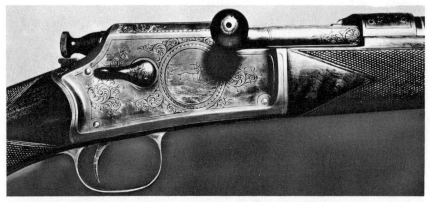

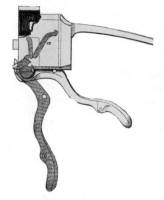

Bolt action breech-loading Winchester built under the Hotchkiss 1883 patent. This gun, engraved by Ulrich, is in the Winchester Museum collection.

Extractor action of the Farquharson single shot, a breechloader that appeared in the 1870s.

needle then became so brittle that a sharp jar might break it.

This may have been the reason why the U.S. Army never got interested in the needle gun although they knew all about it. There are several experimental needle guns in the West Point Museum arsenal, complete with U.S.A. insignia, although they were never issued to troops. It may have been, too, that the army held suspect all breechloaders because of so many complaints from soldiers about singed eyebrows suffered in shooting the Hall breechloader.

Hall Breechloaders

Back in 1811, John Hall had patented a breech-loading flintlock rifle with a removable breechblock. When removed it appeared to be a sort of over-all cartridge with the flint mechanism attached. In 1816 Hall was employed by the Government to supervise the construction of his rifles at the Harper's Ferry arsenal. He built 20,220 rifles. The first were flintlocks, but by far the greater number were built during the percussion period. Despite Sam Chamberlain's enthusiastic account of using the Hall breechblock as a pistol in a tavern brawl

with some Mexicans, the average trooper hated the Halls. More often than not they developed loose-fitting breeches, with sheets of flame coming out of the backsides of the gun while the bullet was meandering down the barrel. Chamberlain had obviously been issued the Hall for use in the War with Mexico in 1846 and '47. The Hall rifle did see action plenty of times from the day it first drew blood in the Seminole Indian wars in Florida in 1818. One who fully appreciated the merits of a breech-loading gun was young Francis Parkman, who lost his Harvard composure and nearly his life for want of one. I'll let him tell you in his own words:

"The chief difficulty in running buffalo, as it seems to me, is that of loading the gun or pistol at full gallop. Many hunters for convenience sake carry three or four bullets in the mouth; the powder is poured down the muzzle of the piece, the bullet dropped in after it, the stock struck hard upon the pommel of the saddle, and the work is done. The danger of this is obvious. Should the blow on the pommel fail to send the bullet home, or should the bullet in the act of aiming, start from its place and

roll towards the muzzle, the gun would probably burst in discharging. Many a shattered hand and worse casualties besides have been the result of such an accident. To obviate it, some hunters make use of a ramrod, usually hung by a string from the neck, but this materially increases the difficulty of loading. The bows and arrows which the Indians use in running buffalo have many advantages over firearms, and even white men occasionally employ them."

Then later: "I . . . shot into her with both pistols in succession. My firearms were all empty and I had in my pouch nothing but rifle bullets too large for the pistols and too small for the gun. I loaded the gun, however, but as often as I leveled it to fire, the bullets would roll out of the muzzle like a squib, as the powder harmlessly exploded. I rode in front of the buffalo and tried to turn her back but her eyes glared, her mane bristled, and, lowering her head she rushed at me with the utmost fierceness . . . . Riding to a little distance, I dismounted thinking to gather a handful of dry grass to serve the purpose of wadding, and load the gun at my leisure. No

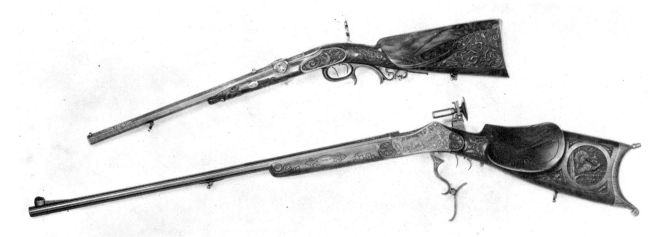

Two early metallic-cartridge breechloaders, both by Stiegele of Munich (Germany). The top gun, a salon or parlor rifle, loads through a hole in the top of the barrel-breech via a right-side handle that rotates 180 degrees to reveal the chamber; the centerfire 6mm rimless cartridge is unknown. The other rifle is a deluxe specimen of the German Schuetzen, *circa* 1885, caliber 8.15x46.5mm.

sooner were my feet on the ground than the buffalo came bounding in such a rage toward me that I jumped back again into the saddle with all possible dispatch . . . . At length bethinking me of the fringes at the seams of my buckskin trousers, I jerked off a few of them, and, reloading the gun, forced them down the barrel to keep the bullet in its place: then approaching, I shot the wounded buffalo through the heart. Sinking to her knees, she rolled over lifeless on the prairie." Only part of his problem was — as he discovered later — he had had a young wounded bull on his hands, not a cow.

This account appeared in Parkman's *The Oregon Trail*, published first in 1847, describing his trip west in 1846.

Having at first hand learned the disadvantages of a muzzleloader on horseback, Parkman was an enthusiastic reporter when his company of hunters on their trip back east ran into an army detachment. Parkman had gone west from Fort Leavenworth, up through what are now the Dakotas and Wyoming, along the trail to Oregon on the Pacific. His band of hunters and Astor trappers had then gone south through the eastern foothills of the Rockies and picked up the Santa Fe Trail heading east. When the party left Leavenworth they had avoided the fort as it was the westernmost outpost of the U.S. Army, and the Army disapproved of civilians wandering unprotected through sometimes hostile Cheyenne and Crow Indian territory. During Parkman's long trip, the U.S. went to war with Mexico. General Kearny set out from Fort Leavenworth with, among others, a company of St. Louis volunteers. These are the civilian soldiers whom Parkman encountered as they were on the way to take Santa Fe, and eventually to relieve the settlers in California.

Parkman describes the St. Louis volunteers' motley mixture of civvies and military uniform, then goes on: "Besides their swords and holster pistols, they carried slung from their saddles the excellent Springfield carbines, loaded at the breech." These cavalry carbines must have been Hall's rifled breechloaders made at Harper's Ferry.

The next step forward was the Sharps rifle, a most notable breechloading invention, patented in 1848. This dropping-block design was the fore-runner of scores of later single shot actions. The original Sharps rifles used paper cartridges, loaded from the breech, the paper envelope containing the bullet and a charge of powder. After inserting the cartridge in the breech, the action was closed by raising an under-lever. This brought up the sharp edged block which sheared off the back of the paper cartridge and exposed the powder in the closed breech to the flame from the percus-

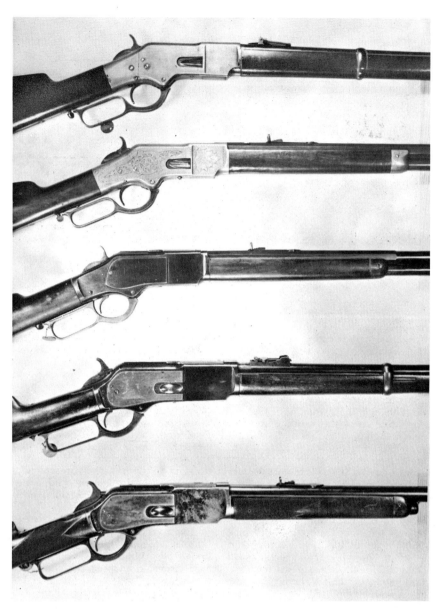

Early metallic-cartridge breechloaders by Winchester. From top: military 1866; engraved 1866; rare 22 rimfire 1873; 1876 carbine and 1876 fancy grade rifle, cal. 50-95 Express.

sion cap. The percussion cap was still outside the gun, placed on a conventional nipple. Later on the Sharps rifles were made to handle metallic cartridges, first the early rimfires and then a variety of centerfire cartridges. The actions of these Sharps was so strong and the guns were so well-engineered that "Old Reliable" was the favorite weapon of a whole generation of hunters. Even the army appreciated the merits of the Sharps action. During the Civil War, the government bought over 80,000 saddle carbines, doubtless because of the advantages a breechloader gave to a man on horseback. Several thousand Sharps rifles were also bought by the U.S., and Berdan's sharpshooters were equipped with them.

Even though the Civil War was fought by both sides with a predominance of muzzle-loading rifled muskets, their long day was ending. Along

with the Sharps came literally dozens of fine to not-so-good breech-loading designs. Most of these were the work of Yankee gunsmiths, lured into the arms competition by the hope of government orders for guns to be used by the armies of the North. Even one army general got into the act. He was General Ambrose E. Burnside, who invented the separately primed Burnside cartridge and also a falling block breechloader to go with it. He supplemented his modest general's pay with government orders for nearly a million and a half dollars worth of Burnside carbines — some 55,000 of them plus millions of rounds of ammunition.

In addition to single shot breechloaders, including Ballards, Peabodys (later known as the Martini-Henry), rolling block Remingtons, Maynards, Stevens, and Frank Wesson's fine guns, there was a host of multi-shot

Pancho Villa's Smith & Wesson 44 rimfire, the engraving and ivory grips carved by L. D. Nimschke, who did a flourishing business with South American generals. Harry Sefried collection.

To me, the funniest patent of all times was issued to one Rollin White in 1865. Despite the fact that breech-loading had been around for at least 600 years, the U.S. patent office actually issued a patent to White for a *cylinder bored end to end.* While it may seem perfectly ridiculous to us, the patent was upheld by the Supreme Court and the assignment of the patent to Smith and Wesson gave them the exclusive right to manufacture cartridge revolvers for the duration of the patent. Colt was thus excluded from the metallic cartridge field, and those manufacturers who tried to get around the patent were fined and required to desist. White collected nearly $70,000 for his well-timed "invention" and breech-loading finally received legal status. ●

repeaters offered to the military. The most successful of these were the Spencers, with tubular magazines in the stock, and (later) the Winchesters with under-barrel tubular magazines, which had evolved out of the Volcanic and Henry rifles.

After centuries, the old muzzle-loaders had finally had it. Even the great armies of the world were compelled to junk their arsenals of front loading guns or convert them to breechloaders. Some of the conversions, such as the Needham side-gate system, are rare collectors' pieces today. Even in England, where the military establishment had clung tenaciously to the huge number of muzzle-loaders left over from the Napoleonic Wars, a fire at the Tower arsenal and a lot of prodding from enlightened civilians, finally broke down the military conservatism. A number of designs were submitted for testing at Woolwich Arsenal and the best was adopted. It turned out to be an American design, the work of Jacob Snider of New York. Snider's rotating breechblock, attached at the side of the barrel, used a thin brass center-fire cartridge. Sniders were issued to British troops in quantity both as conversions of older guns and also of new manufacture from around 1866. They were in constant use by the British in their skirmishes and minor wars around the Empire. Many years later, Kipling tells of the use of the Snider in bush fighting in India.

At the end of the Civil War period in the United States the makers of single shot breechloaders swung into the smaller market for target and sporting guns. While the competition for this business was fierce, the shooting public benefitted. Competition forced manufacturers to high standards of workmanship and finish, and the rifles made for the Creedmoor Matches in the 1870s and 80's were superb examples of the gunmakers' craft.

Single shot rifles were fine for target shooting, and even armies were equipped with them. The original Mauser, granddaddy of all of the world's modern bolt action breech-loaders, was a single shot when it was introduced to replace the Dreyse in the German army in 1872, though it was called the Model 1871. Within eight years, however, a Swiss designer, Frederic Veterli, had designed a magazine rifle, and Benjamin Hotchkiss, an American working in Paris, had developed a bolt action breechloader which Winchester bought and added to their line as the Winchester-Hotchkiss in 1876.

Improvement followed improvement in the next few years. James Lee's built-in box magazine of 1879 was followed by Mannlicher's clip feed in 1885. Mauser adopted the idea of a magazine in 1888. Although the U.S. Army issued side-loading Krag-Jorgensens in 1892, it saw the advantages of clip loading and came out with its own version of the Mauser in 1903. Most of the bolt action sporters of today owe something to the Mauser-Springfield design.

In a nutshell, what put over breech-loading after centuries of experimental designs for every type of ignition, was the Pauly expanding cartridge. This simple idea of a flexible cartridge case that would swell up enough to close off the rearward escape of the expanding gases made breechloaders workable and practical. Quantities of reasonably priced guns could now be made which offered the shooter speed and repeated firing and were no longer a menace to the shooter's eyes and eyebrows. There is no more conservative a group than shooters, so breech-loading, which might have been an overnight success, took some 50 years to find universal acceptance. Pauly, too far ahead of his time, went broke. Eventually he invaded other fields of invention where the atmosphere was not so conservative.

Shooting positions used at Creedmoor (N.Y.) and Dollymount (Ireland) as illustrated in *Rod and Gun*, 1876.

THE DEADLY DEPENDABLE DOUBLE

by ELMER KEITH

M Y WHITE HUNTER John Lawrence, our native trackers Galu-Galu and Goyo, and a local native John had hired because he knew the country were trying to get me a shot at a good rhino. A few days before we arrived at our camp at Manyoni, Tanganyika, a rhino had killed one of the local natives as he was returning home from a beer-bust late at night. The rhino charged from behind in the dark, caught the luckless fellow in the seat of the pants and drove his horn clear up through the heart.

We learned this rhino watered regularly at a certain spring, and the next morning at daylight picked up his tracks there. We trailed him through one thorn thicket after another for the better part of a day. Finally we got close to him. It was late November, with no leaves on the twigs, but the thorn was so thick we couldn't see over 10 feet. Dust dribbled from the boys' fingers showed the air movement was constantly changing. We circled to get the best of it, Lawrence and Galu-Galu ahead of me, Goyo and the local native following. We were soon all down on our

Elmer Keith has for 30 years been one of our leading arms authorities. He has written some seven books, hundreds of articles, and at present he's Shooting Editor of Guns & Ammo.

Who can doubt the double barreled rifle's value? It has proved itself the ultimate weapon on the world's most dangerous game—deadly on elephant, rhino, buffalo . . . dependable under any and all conditions. Here a leading hunter gives the lowdown on this legendary and classic design.

bellies, crawling under the low thorn limbs. We got so close we could hear the bull chewing on the branches, his molars sounding like miniature stamp mills, yet we could see nothing of the huge animal. John and Galu crawled under another low hanging thorn limb, then motioned for me to do likewise. I was carrying my 476 Westley Richards double cradled in my left arm with safety off, ready for action. Though I lay as flat as possible, when I went under the limb one thorn scratched on my shooting jacket. The bull snorted like a steam whistle and crashed off through the thorn instantly, as easily as a hog through a clover patch. Though he was only a few steps away, we couldn't see him. Had he come our way we would have been lucky to get a shot or two in his face and dodge his big feet. At any rate, he was gone and we never did catch up with him.

A Charging Rhino

We trailed up another rhino only to find its horns too short when we did catch up with him at 20 yards, so quietly backed out and let him go. Another day we trailed a big-footed rhino down a deep thorn-choked donga, where we saw several other rhino tracks as well. Finally we caught up with one and John motioned for me to shoot, as it had a very good horn. As I raised the 476, I caught some movement to my left out of the corner of my eye. Taking a closer look I saw little ToTo, a baby rhino not over a week or two old, from his size. Again we carefully backed out, letting that rhino family go its way.

Later, after we had moved over to Mklama Mission east of the Serengetti, we picked up a bull rhino trail and followed it some 5 miles, finally catching up with him in some dense thorn at the foot of some rocky hills. We spread out and I caught a glimpse of his hind legs disappearing into a thorn thicket. I motioned to John. He got my signal and we moved in about 20 yards apart. I came on the rhino facing me at 18 yards, head up and alert. A tree bole covered each shoulder and I was fairly well caught in some wait-a-bit thorn. There was a big bloody patch in the center of the bull's chest, where ticks were eating on him. I decided to give him a heart shot right in the center of that patch of ticks. However as I swung my sights to bear, he decided to get me, dropped his head and charged. My bullet, aimed for his chest, caught him in full stride, right under the base of the front horn on the left side of his snout, and went back and shattered all his upper teeth on that side. The 520-gr. solid put him down in the front quarters. His front legs folded back and he used his chin as a sled runner and continued to kick himself toward me.

I waited for him to get up on all fours, intending to break a shoulder and turn him. When he did get up, at some 8 yards range, I shot for the left shoulder but he dropped again, even as I pulled the trigger, from the effects of my first shot. Instead of breaking the shoulder I hit him in the ribs back of the shoulder and the slug ranged through into his right ham. I was trying to get reloaded while caught in the wait-a-bit thorn, and yelled to John to take him on, as my last shot was too high, over the shoulder in the ribs.

Instantly, John's 416 Rigby cracked. His bullet hit the rhino in the back edge of the right shoulder. We later found it went clear to the left flank, some 60 inches of penetration. The bull jumped to his feet—in fact high in the air—at the impact of John's slug, as though I had never even touched him, swapped ends, luckily for me, and headed out of the thorn into the open. John shot again through a lot of thorn and nicked him at the withers. By this time I was reloaded and tearing my way through the thorn to my right, where it was thinnest. The rhino barged across my front at 30 yards. I swung under his chin and caught him square in the right shoulder, the heavy solid breaking the shoulder and spine and down he went in a cloud of dust, his back toward me. John came up and asked me to pour

the other barrel down between his ears, which I did. This was the only animal that took me on during the trip.

John Lawrence carried and swore by a Rigby 416 bolt action he had used for years. It had a 26″ barrel, a long magnum action and slow-working safety. After his many years in the war he was familiar with the bolt action and very fast in its use, but I thought my short 476 double was much handier. We had some sticky moments on several occasions, when the value of the double rifle was well-impressed on my memory. I carried it myself most of the time, but during a few long treks for elephant Goyo packed it, walking one step in front of me, grasping the barrels near the muzzle with the stock projecting back over his shoulder toward me.

One day we were working through tall reeds in a swamp at the lower end of Lake Manyarra. Water was ankle to hip deep and visibility anything from 6 feet to 10 yards. Suddenly a bull buffalo came to his feet out of the mud, possibly 7 yards in front of us and slightly to our right. Lawrence, Goyo and a local boy with a spear were in front of me. Lawrence swung the long Rigby to bear and the little native pointed his spear. Goyo faded back, but I grabbed the 476 from him as he passed, thumbed off the safety and hung my sights on the bull's nose.

For several seconds the buff grunted hoarsely at us, shaking his heavy, ugly head, while John quietly cussed him out in his best British army vernacular. His horns were only fair and I didn't want to shoot, but it seemed an eternity before he swapped ends and disappeared. Only then did I lower the 476.

Leopard Trouble

Later, at Mklama Mission, we located a pride of lions by their tracks and hung up a kongoni for bait. Next morning we found a huge leopard had fed on the carcass, but the lions had

not found it. We located an even better place for a bait and hung up a big roan bull after removing head and cape, but the local natives swiped our roan before dark. Next morning we moved the kongoni to the new location and saw the big leopard had again been working on it. (I had already killed one leopard, all I was allowed.)

Next morning we were at our hideout in some thorn trees 90 yards from the bait tree at daylight, but nothing showed, so we approached the tree on foot looking for lion tracks. I was in the lead. I had walked under the tree and was just stepping out from under the branches on the far side when a huge leopard sailed over my hat. Instantly my 476 was on his shoulders and had John not yelled, "Don't shoot!" I would have plastered him with both barrels—he'd scared the hell out of me. I know my old Stetson must have been floating on the ends of my hair.

The small rains had come, leafing the tree out, and that big tom had appropriated our bait. The cat had jumped for me, but when John stepped out behind me and the leopard saw there were two of us he arched his back and went over my head. John said if either of us had been alone he would have been leopard bait. I had killed a seven-foot leopard, a beauty, but that old yellow tom looked at least a foot longer and even heavier; a man would have had no chance at all against him.

Down on the Kisigo river, we had trailed elephant all day and I had killed a good bull with heart shots from the 476. We were back-tracking the 6 miles out to the truck trace after hoofing well over 20 miles in the hot sun. John and a local boy were in the lead, next was old Songi packing John's rifle, then Galu-Galu and finally Goyo with my 476 held by the muzzles. My tongue was swollen and I was about done from the heat and no water. Suddenly a bull elephant came charging through the heavy thorn. The whole crew faded

Keith with his bull rhino, the only animal that "took him on" during African safari. The 476 Westley Richards proved adequate for the job.

back past me, but I grabbed my 476 from Goyo's shoulder, snicked off the safety and clipped two more cartridges between my fingers. Not knowing what else to do I swung the big double toward where the trees were bending and waited for him to appear in the clear. I was too damn tired to run or do anything else but stand and shoot. Then John returned and grabbed my shoulder, motioning me back, so I followed him.

We moved back some 10 yards and stopped and the bull stopped also. I had been too done in to realize he was only charging John's scent, as there was a little air movement in his direction. John squeezed my arm and we remained motionless, hardly breathing for some 20 minutes. Then John sent Galu-Galu in to see if the bull was gone. I saw a small rodent go across the trail and into the thorn where the bull had stopped. We could hear him scamper about, but not the slightest sound from the elephant. Finally Galu-Galu came out and told John it had been a big bull that was bleeding from some other hunter's slugs, and he had pulled out. We learned later another hunter had killed a 100-pounder after wounding another bull in that section.

These and other close calls on the trip convinced me that a big double rifle is the best life insurance a hunter can pack when after dangerous game in thick cover. At such short ranges their handiness and power is un-equaled.

Keith vs. the King

We finally got the lion pride on the bait at Mklama Mission. They ate the remains of the kongoni and kept the leopard up the tree that morning, so we tied the hind quarters of my rhino to the tree with a one-inch manila rope. Next morning the rope was broken and we could hear the lions feeding on the rhino but couldn't see them in the thick thorn. I told John we had best get out, as they had not seen nor heard us, and we could hang another bait and return next morning. He agreed, so we killed a zebra, hauled her to the tree with the jeep and hung her up. The next morn we sneaked into our hideout in back of the big thorn tree, leaving the car a mile or so away. Little Galu-Galu was with us.

An open strip some 30 feet wide and 200 yards long ran through some very dense thorn. The bait tree was about 90 yards from the end we had selected to shoot from. In the dim light we could see 8 lions scattered through the open strip. Not 40 yards in front of us, sprawled on his back and snoring, was a fully maned young lion; a few feet farther on a lioness was sleeping and another one had her three spotted cubs at play. Beyond this family a huge old lioness was

Nicely maned male lion taken out of a pride of eight, just after dawn one morning. The 520-gr. soft nose bullet penetrated heart and lodged under skin on far side of animal.

trying to pull down the zebra, and beyond the bait tree a dozen steps an old and big lion lay on his left side, belly toward us.

I had shoved the safety forward on my 476 double long before we reached the tree. I rested the back of my left hand in a crotch of the tree and waited for more light. I wanted to use my scope-sighted 333 OKH but John insisted on the double. Light comes fast there, and soon the birds were flying by overhead. I could make out the front bead but not the bottom of the wide-angle rear sight. I laid the sights on the green grass above the young maned lion and waited.

ACTUAL DIAGRAM
10 CONSECUTIVE SHOTS
100 YARDS
FROM A
DOUBLE 450
EXPRESS
By W.W. GREENER

Finally I could make out my sights. Just then the old boy beyond the bait tree rolled over on his belly and raised his head. One look and I knew he was what I wanted. Placing the sight picture just back of his right shoulder and in line with his heart, I squeezed the trigger.

Pandemonium broke loose. The recoil kicked me back out of the crotch in the tree and I was nearly blinded by the muzzle flash. The big lion swapped ends and made for the thorn at our left, coughing hoarsely as he ran. John tried to get another slug into him, but the lioness got in the way. He did get off a quick shot as the old boy vanished, but missed. The lioness with the cubs disappeared into the thorn to our right, and the other two females followed the big lion into the brush. The young lion did not even wake up from the two rifle shots. Suddenly he sensed something was wrong and rolled over and looked as if he were asking, "Where did everyone go?" Then he jumped to his feet and slid into the thorn to the left. John asked Galu-Galu to go back for the other boys and the jeep.

We started toward the bait tree. John was watching everything on the left, and I on the right. We had not moved 20 yards when we spotted the female with cubs some 7 yards from me in the thorn, her tail swishing back and forth. I hung the 476 on her chest and told John to hold it. He asked what I saw and I told him, and he said if she moved forward to give her both barrels. I waited, my sight picture on her chest. Suddenly she was there no longer, but I hadn't seen where she'd gone in the dim light of the heavy thorn.

We stood back to back for several minutes, until we heard the jeep arrive. Then we walked down to the bait tree and found my old tom dead as a mackerel in the thorn.

My 520-gr. soft nose had taken off the top of his heart and the aorta and lodged under the skin on the off side. It had hit nothing but ribs and meat. John said had he been headed our way he would have lived long enough to reach us easily unless stopped by other bullets. He might have gone 200 yards with the heart shot, if in open country instead of thick thorn.

Double Rifle Advantages

The double rifle is, in effect, two single shot rifles. It has the finest lock work and workmanship possible to put in any rifle. The action is closed against mud, rain, snow or foreign matter, and there is nothing to jam. It has a built-in safety factor in that both locks are hardly going to go haywire at one time. In fact, I have never had any trouble from the locks of my double rifles in many years' usage. A double is short for its barrel length. Most of mine have 26″ barrels, with some 24″ or 25″.

This design balances as well as a fine English shotgun. It has the fastest of all safeties, right on top of the grip under the thumb. You can get off two well-aimed shots with a double in the time it takes to get off one shot, recover from recoil and work the bolt on a bolt action. In real close cover, when you may have to shoot instantly by the feel of the gun, the big double is many times better and faster than the finest bolt or lever action rifle.

I have seen about all bolt actions put out of action from one cause or another. Ejectors, extractors and strikers have broken; soft-headed cases have shed their primers, which lodged in the bolt race and tied up the gun; magazines have jammed.

I've even had the bolt of a 9.5mm

boxlock, a 450-400-3″ at 80 yards, the two barrels grouped only an inch apart. I have owned two Lancaster best-quality, oval-bored rifles that put shots from both barrels right together at 60 yards.

When two barrels are soldered together with ribs, they are very stiff, which seemingly aids accuracy. The better ones are regulated for one load only and you must stick to that factory load or its equivalent handload.

The double rifle should be stocked to fit you perfectly.* You should be able to mount it with your eyes closed, then open them to find the sights aligned. In an emergency you can shoot such a rifle at close range by feel alone. There is no faster sighting equipment than the British wide-angle, shallow-V back sight with platinum center line and a sourdough or bead front, and for close range the

lets pointing back toward the wrist, and even with non-ejector doubles they reloaded very fast. After the second shot was fired and the barrels were still lifted in recoil, they moved the top lever. As the empty cases slid from the chambers they simply brought the left hand over the breech, dunked the next 2 rounds into the chambers, closed the gun and fired again. I can reload very quickly by carrying 2 extra rounds between the second and third fingers of the left hand, rims upward in palm of the hand. When held this way they do not interfere in the least with gripping the barrels of rifles during heavy recoil.

There is a certain weight and barrel length that any hunter can use to best advantage. Tall men can handle 28″ barrels very well but average size men are better off with 26″, the length

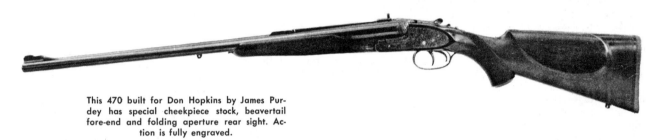

This 470 built for Don Hopkins by James Purdey has special cheekpiece stock, beavertail fore-end and folding aperture rear sight. Action is fully engraved.

Mannlicher-Schoenauer close when the extractor was not over the rim of the case, losing a shot at a fine buck when the rifle only snapped. I couldn't dislodge the stuck cartridge until a bullet from a smaller rifle was dropped repeatedly down the barrel.

Such occurences could be fatal when dealing with dangerous game. Your first mistake on African game can be your last. It's perfectly true that the average sportsman, backed up by a guide or white hunter, is usually safe enough on any game, but I prefer a rifle with which I can handle any situation myself. The big rifle should be carried by the hunter in thick cover. In open country, if you get tired and turn it over to a gun boy, make him walk a step in front of you, grasping the gun near the muzzles, the stock projecting back over his shoulder so you can grab it quickly— as I've had to do on two occasions.

The English make the best double rifles for fit and balance, and in regulating the barrels so they group together. I have several fine Westley Richards rifles that will put bullets from both barrels under a silver dollar at 60 yards, also some Holland & Hollands that will do the same thing. I also have Jim Corbett's venerable tiger rifle, the one with which he killed so many man-eating tigers for the Indian government, some of which had killed several hundred people. When I tried this old No. 2 Jeffery

big white jack or night front sight is fastest to catch.

More drop is needed in a double rifle, as a rule, than on a shotgun, as charging game, except really big stuff, is coming in under the gun, so to speak, especially lion or rhino. With elephants the opposite is true, and the target is getting higher and the angle is changing constantly as the range decreases.

You want nothing on the rifle to catch on limbs, vines, etc., and the sling should be removed. For the same reason you don't want outside hammers.

Repeat Shots

Double rifles can be reloaded very fast, so it is problematical if any bolt gun is faster for four shots. When you fire a heavy caliber bolt gun you must first recover from recoil before you can even reach for the bolt handle to reload, while with the double you can fire that second shot as soon as you recover from recoil. I have seen good fast double men hold 2 cartridges in the left hand under the barrels, bul-

*Note that I say "should be" stocked to fit; not all of my doubles have stocks that were made to my measure, and it is also true that one can, by dint of much practice and handling, obtain good results from a rifle wearing a stock of "standard" dimensions.

That this is true is born out constantly by the millions of hunters who use off-the-shelf guns, and use them fairly successfully or better. Nevertheless, the ideal would be a custom made stock, one that fits the user perfectly.

I personally prefer, while short men are much better off with 24″. There can be no doubt but short barrels are handier in brush and thorn than long barrels.

Use at Extreme Range

Some folks think a double rifle is accurate only at close range. This is a fallacy. I have a best grade Westley Richards 476 that shoots like a match rifle even to long range. I once tried it at 550 yards with the 500-yard leaf turned up. From bench rest, shooting at a snow drift some 3 feet wide and a foot high in the center, a 520-gr. slug from each barrel hit only 3 inches apart in the center of the snow drift.

Sights for Doubles

I do not like a scope sight on a double. They are perfectly satisfactory for shooting non-dangerous game, but I do not want to look through any scope and see only a vast expanse of hide on a charging elephant, with no way of being certain just where the reticle should be placed. A good double is accurate enough for a stalking rifle, but a scope ruins the gun's looks for me and changes its balance also.

Installing a scope on a double not originally intended for one can bring problems, too. Doubles are sensitive to any change in weight or balance and often shoot differently when a scope is added. Or, if regulated originally with a scope, the barrels usually won't group together if the scope is removed.

Capt. E. L. Wadman (an old friend who has spent years in Africa) had his 577-100-750 grouping under a silver dollar at 60 yards, both barrels, then to cut down kick he removed the recoil pad, drilled a couple of big holes and filled them with lead and replaced the pad. Next trial at the range, the barrels grouped a foot apart, the change being in elevation as well as windage. He replaced the lead with heavy dowels and the rifle came back on the money. He's been using that big gun on elephant in Tanganyika for some time now.

I once had a 375 Rimmed Magnum double that shot very well until I had the stock shortened a half-inch and a new pad fitted. Then it no longer grouped both barrels together. I had to experiment at length with handloads to get it working properly again.

Reloading Technique

Reloading for doubles is always a problem. Start by using the exact bullet weight for which the rifle was proved and sighted and then work up with our cooler burning powders until the shots from both barrels move together. Don't tolerate high pressures; this can cause cases to stick and tends to lock primers in the firing pin holes. The gun should open freely and easily, and sticking cases cause undue wear on the hinge pin and extractors.

For straight cases like the 450 Nitro Express, the 500, 577 and 600, the best powders are 3031 and Hi-Vel No. 2; for bottleneck cases like the 450-400, 500-450 and the 475 No. 2, 4064 is good. Straight cases work best with

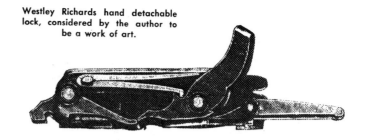

Westley Richards hand detachable lock, considered by the author to be a work of art.

an oversize cork gasket wad run down hard on the powder, and in the big ones — 500, 577 and 600 — two such wads are best pushed down on the powder before seating the jacketed bullets.

The 303 British double rifles are ideal for deer and black bear in timber, and the various 400-360s and 375s are good for any American game. For Africa and the big stuff, I would not recommend anything smaller than the 450 Nitro Express, and for such hunting a man should use just as heavy a caliber as he can handle with accuracy and speed. Small men are probably best off with the 450, 465 and 470, while larger men can handle the 476, 475 No. 2 and the 500 with ease. Really strong men are best fitted with 577s.

The 577 for some reason seems to have more penetration than any other caliber. I know of several elephant being shot through lengthwise with the 750-gr. steel-jacketed solid. George Neary wrote me of following a big bull through dense bush for hours, trying to get a broadside shot. Finally, when it looked as if he was going to lose him, George up and shot him center in the seat of his baggy pants. The bull ran a ways and piled up. Examination showed the 750-gr. solid

had exited from the chest and damaged a tusk.

As another example, Russ Douglas told me of getting a woman within 7 yards of a big bull and asking her to shoot him behind the shoulder. She shut her eyes and gave him both barrels in the belly. He swung on them and Russ had just time enough to throw up his Rigby 577 and 'give the bull both slugs in the chest, then knocked the lady to one side as the bull thundered past them. One of Russ's slugs broke the heavy hip bone and came out of the elephant.

An American going to Africa can rent a good double there, but he should by all means shoot said double at least 20 rounds and get well acquainted with it before ever attempting to use it on great game. Heavy double rifles are not needed in the U.S., though I have seen 465s and 470s used on elk with excellent results. I have personally killed 6 elk with the 450-400-3″ Westley Richards, one with a Watson in the same caliber, and still another with my W-R 400-360.

Tops in Timber

The double is my first choice for all reasonable range timber shooting, and on dangerous game is considered best by the more experienced African hunters. My friend Bob Foster uses a pair of 470s, and John Taylor, who has also killed an awful lot of game, likes the doubles too. John Buhmiller preferred bolt guns until buffalo showed him the need of a big double under certain conditions in dense cover.

A double comes up on game easily and surely and the wide, easily defined rear sight is ideal for such shooting as it never gets fogged up or fills with snow or ice.

For American timber game a lot of fun can be had from the fine old black powder doubles of from 400 to 450 caliber. These can be found on the used market, as a rule, for about the price of a good bolt action, scope-sighted rifle.

Double rifles are made in over-under and side-by-side design. The over-under (usually Continental) is easier to regulate so both barrels shoot together, especially with reduced loads. The Kersten fastening is fre-

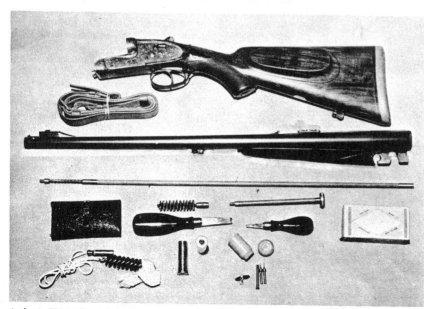

Author's 577 Holland & Holland double rifle, taken down and shown with field trunk contents. This caliber gives extreme penetration on big game—has shot lengthways through an elephant!

quently found in O-U rifles, the Greener cross bolt on lateral doubles. I have seen some very good over-unders from Merkel and Ferlach, in Austria. For dangerous game I much prefer the side-by-side. It is faster and easier to reload, as you don't have to break the gun so far to get the bottom cartridge out of the chamber. Reloading the over-under takes more time — time you may not have. I believe the dangerous game rifle should always be the side-by-side model.

Old black powder expresses often had a bottom lever that swung out to the side to open. Jeffery and others later used and preferred a bottom lever that covered the trigger guard and worked like the famous falling-block Farquharsons, pushing down to open. This style of under lever action is claimed to be one of the strongest and best for 577 and 600 bore rifles, and not

The African buffalo is rated the world's most dangerous game by many experienced hunters. For this one, Keith depended on his best-quality 476 Westley Richards double.

Two of Keith's favorite Westley Richards doubles. Top gun handles the 450-400 3" Jeffery load, a long-time favorite in Africa; bottom gun is the one used by author on safari. Both have hand-detachable locks, auto ejectors.

without justification. It is just as fast as the top-snap type and has a great deal more leverage to open the gun if pins stick in primers or a case sticks in a chamber.

Sidelock or Boxlock?

Many people think a double gun won't shoot well unless it is a sidelock model, and some people — including Jeffery, Holland & Holland, Purdey and Rigby — made their best grade guns only in sidelock form. Purdey even marketed a boxlock, but called it a Wm. Evans, apparently to avoid putting the Purdey name on it.

The weakest part of the double rifle frame is the angle at the junction of the frame's bottom and the standing breech. Holland & Holland and others usually reinforce this point. Some authorities claim the boxlock is not as strong here as the sidelock, because it is cut out for the locks. I have seen shotguns with frames cracked at this point, but have yet to see a boxlock double rifle by a reputable maker that was so cracked.

When it comes to stocking, the sidelock is a poor second. The boxlock has far the stronger design. The sidelock leaves four small fingers and a tiny center section where stock and frame join, and only the usual extended top tang and lower tang, together with the sidelocks themselves, hold the gun together. The sidelock is for this reason much more weakly stocked than any good boxlock, where the wood is left solid and the full width of frame at its

Kersten fastening features double extension rods which bolt securely into place, is used often in over-under double rifles, though here shown in a side-by-side shotgun.

This early damascus-barreled shotgun shows the famous Greener cross bolt fastening used on many lateral doubles; also, the side safety, a design not liked by Keith.

junction.

From the standpoint of design and beauty, I always thought Holland & Holland achieved the best looking and best fitting stock of all, and personally I like the tang extended back over the nose of the comb.

H&H and others described their sidelocks as "hand detachable," and they can be so-detached for examination, etc. If this is done very often, however, the mortise in the wood is bound to wear or chip and the lockwork will no longer be waterproof.

Boxlock rifles usually have about 7 parts to the lock, against some three times as many in a sidelock, so the f o r m e r obviously has less chance to wear or go wrong. The Westley Richards hand detachable locks (which I understand are no longer being made) are works of art, the highest achievement in the gun-making p r o f e s s i o n, for my money. You simply remove the cover-plate from the bottom of the action (some are hinged) when the arm is cocked and the fore-end removed. Then you can lift the locks out with the fingers. They are beautifully damasceened and polished to a high finish. Sometimes an R is inlaid in gold for the right one and an L for the left. At one time this maker even furnished an extra pair in a smal case, if wanted. I never saw any need for the second pair, as the originals never gave the slightest trouble whatsoever.

There is no danger whatever of wear in removing or replacing these locks, and they can be kept in perfect order for that reason. Cleaning or oiling becomes easy. This is a great convenience after being out in a driving rain all day or if the gun is dropped into a stream or lake. I have 8 best-quality Westleys, 7 of which have these detachable locks. I'm sorry they're no longer being made.

Fine double rifles are getting ever harder to come by, as only a few men, most of them living in Britain, are capable of regulating the two barrels. At least two years is now required to building a fine double. However, some fine old ones are kicking around.

Single or Double Trigger?

Many hunters prefer two triggers on their double rifles, claiming they have more instant selection of loads in case they use a solid in one barrel and a soft nose in the other. I like the single trigger. Five of my Westleys, including the 476 I used in Africa and a Lancaster 303, have single triggers and none has ever given me any trouble. With a single trigger you do not have to shift the trigger finger to fire the second barrel in the shortest possible time. On the other hand, heavy rifles like the 577 and 600 often kick the shooting hand loose from its grip and you have to reach for the trigger

It should be noted that nearly all of the several calibers mentioned in this article are no longer available in double rifles. The demand for them is small, the skillful hands needed to make them have nearly disappeared, and the cost of double rifles has soared. Holland & Holland m i g h t be persuaded to make you a double in 465 or 470, maybe (no other calibers can ordinarily be obtained today), and at a cost of some $2500-$3000 and a 2-year — or longer — wait.

Double rifles in good condition, proved for smokeless (Nitro) powder, and in calibers for which there is some hope of finding fresh ammunition, are quite scarce on the used gun market. Any dealer may come up with one, of course, but if you must have a double, your best bet would be an advertisement in the **American Rifleman, Shotgun News,** etc., or a visit to Abercrombie & Fitch in New York City. That firm ordinarily has the widest selection of double rifles — and other imported guns — of any shop we know of.

Before spending hundreds of dollars for a double rifle, make quite certain that factory cartridges are available. ED.

again regardless. I have never seen the need for a *selective* single trigger, as you never change the setting in the presence of game.

For buffalo, some hunters like to use a solid in one barrel and a soft nose in the other. On a broadside shot with a heavy rifle like the 577 or 600, the soft nose is no doubt best when placed in the center of the shoulder in line with the spine, but for most elephant, buffalo, rhino and hippo shooting I much prefer solids. Solids are by all odds the best on such game for any raking or end-on shot.

Automatic safeties should never be installed on double rifles. I have had gunsmith Iver Henriksen remove the automatic feature from the safeties of many double rifles. You have plenty of time to put a safety on, but damn little time to take it off in an emergency, and I want my rifles ready to fire again as soon as reloaded, without having to manipulate a safety. The top tang safety is the best and fastest on a dangerous game rifle. I have seen Continental and Greener guns with side safeties, but they are slow and awkward to move. Only a top safety, right under your thumb as you mount the rifle, should be considered.

Many otherwise fine used double rifles will be found with stocks cracked at the small of the grip. The British are very clever at repairing these and often the crack does not show up until you have fired the rifle a bit. The best answer is to have them restocked to fit you. Gale and Skip Bartlett of Lancaster, Calif., are expert at restocking double rifles and can do a job as good or better than the original makers. George Hoening, Purcell's Gun Shop, Boise, Idaho, is also an expert gunmaker and can resolder ribs and re-regulate barrels. He is one of the very few men I know in this country who can do so. He can also make many parts for them. Knowing this, you might be able to pick up a used gun needing some repairs and thus join the double rifle clan without a large cash outlay. You won't be sorry. ●

My Single-Shot Rifles
An Experience of Sixty Years

by COL. TOWNSEND WHELEN

The dean of firearms writers and editors, Colonel Whelen is the author of many valuable books, notably, The Hunting Rifle *and* Small Arms Ballistics and Design. *His latest volume,* Why Not Load Your Own?, *is the least expensive and most practical book on handloading available. In this article he shares with* GUN DIGEST *readers his long-time affection for single-shot rifles.*

With my Winchester single-shot rifle for the 219 Improved Zipper cartridge, I made my longest kill on a woodchuck.

WHEN I WAS just a little shaver, there was a Winchester single-shot rifle on exhibit in a gun store in my home town. It was for the 40-82 cartridge, had a 30-inch, half-octagon No. 3 barrel, pistol grip stock of fancy walnut, checkered, Swiss butt-plate, target sights, and was nicely engraved. It was my ideal of a fine rifle, and every day after school, while it remained on view, I tramped the two miles downtown to admire it. In some such manner are our tastes formed, and they are likely to remain with us always.

When I was thirteen, my father gave me my first rifle, a Remington rolling block for the 22 rim fire cartridge. Several months later I saw an advertisement of Lyman sights, and I fitted this rifle with a set. I think I have to thank these sights for my becoming a real rifleman, for with them on this little rifle, I soon became quite a good shot, much better than any of my boy friends, and my interest was maintained and matured, as I do not believe it would have been if I had retained the open rear sight on this rifle.

All through my boyhood years I had a lot of fun and sport with this little rifle, and I shot a lot of stuff with it—English sparrows, squirrels, chipmunks, grouse, and one woodchuck. In 1892 I was lucky enough to win a "Fourth of July" rifle match with it in the Adirondack Mountains, and that year I also shot my first buck with it.

When I was eighteen, I enlisted in the Pennsylvania National Guard and had no trouble in qualifying as Sharpshooter with the old 45-70 Springfield single-shot rifle, a very sterling, accurate, and reliable arm. The following year I was shooting on my company rifle team, and I also carried this rifle through the first few months of the Spanish-American War until I won my commission. Following that war I "discovered" the magazine *Shooting and Fishing*, and became much interested in the work of Reuben Harwood with 25 caliber rifles. So I purchased a Stevens No. 44 Ideal single-shot rifle for the 25-20 S. S. cartridge, but it did not seem to shoot nearly as accurately as I was sure I held and aimed it. I know now this was due to the black powder factory ammunition which in small calibers never was worth a hoot for accuracy. Anyhow, still following Harwood's writings, I obtained a Winchester single-shot rifle (low side-wall) for the 25-20 cartridge, with 26-inch, No. 2 half-octagon barrel, pistol grip and shotgun butt, and I placed a gunsling on it. I had John Sidle bush and rechamber this rifle for the 25-21 Stevens cartridge which was Harwood's favorite. Sidle also fitted it with his 5-power Snap-Shot scope which was unique in its day, as it had a much larger field of view than any other scope and was a fine hunting scope for varmints. With this outfit I got much better results but it never entirely satisfied me in accuracy until I had Harry Pope make me a mould for his 80-grain broad base-band bullet, and furnish me with one of his lubricating pumps. Then, with King's Semi-Smokeless powder the rifle shot as well as I could hold it. I had a lot of fine varmint shooting with this rifle in the

hills on either side of the Shenandoah Valley, and when I was ordered to California for station, it proved just the medicine for the Western ground squirrels. For Eastern shooters I will say that these are slightly larger than the gray squirrel, with a shorter and less bushy tail. They live in colonies like prairie dogs and are a great plague to farmers. I disposed of hundreds of them with this little 25-21 rifle. Then one day I expressed it to a gunsmith to have some work done on it, and it was lost in transit. I have ever since mourned it.

In the meantime one season I had a chance to go deer shooting in the North Woods and I got a Winchester single-shot rifle for the 38-55 cartridge and had it fitted with a Sidle scope. Sidle was by far our best scope maker in those days. This gun was poorly balanced and too heavy for a handy hunting rifle, but the scope did save me the embarrassment of shooting a cow in mistake for a deer. About this time I also had a Western hunt in view and I got a similar rifle for the 45-70 cartridge, fitted only with Lyman sights. But despite carefully handloaded ammunition it was not as accurate as the old 45-70 Springfield, and I soon disposed of both these rifles.

Then in 1900 Horace Kephart published in *Shooting and Fishing* his celebrated article on the use of lead bullets in high-power rifles. He had used a Winchester single-shot rifle for the 30-40 Krag cartridge, and the accuracy he obtained with both jacketed and lead alloy bullets was better than anything I had been able to achieve to that date. So an order went in to Winchester for one of these rifles with a 30-inch, Number 3 nickel-steel barrel with .308-inch groove diameter, pistol grip, shotgun butt, and sling. This rifle started a long series of experiments with various loads, methods of resting the rifle, effect of rests on accuracy and location of center of impact, temperature, cleaning, etc., the results of which I gave to riflemen from time to time in the magazine *Arms and the Man*. A little ignition difficulty was experienced, so I had Niedner fit a Mann-Niedner firing pin, .075" in diameter, round headed, with an .055" protrusion, and this trouble ceased. This is an absolutely necessary alteration with all our single-shot actions which were designed in black powder days. By this time I had been shooting for several years on the Army Infantry Rifle Team, and I felt quite sure that my results were fairly free from errors of aim and hold. By this time I had also discovered the bench rest.

In 1906 I got a two months leave and went on a hunt in British Columbia, taking this 30-40 along as my only rifle. It performed there as well as on the range, and I got mule deer, sheep, and goat with it. One very cold day, in a foot of snow, I came on a band of sheep close to timberline. They evidently caught a glimpse of me for they banded together, and started off, but soon slowed down and resumed feeding. I thought I had spotted a ram in the band, and I monkeyed around them for an hour, by which time I was nearly frozen and had to quit. As I left them, it occurred to me to see if I could unload and load my rifle with my hands badly numbed with cold. I was utterly unable to do so in any reasonable time. To my mind this is the only disadvantage of a single-shot rifle as compared with a repeater. Certainly the experience of our older sportsmen the world over with good single-shot rifles has been that they can be fired with all the necessary rapidity under normal conditions. However, I must add one other requirement—the single-shot rifle must extract its fired cases easily. Some don't, due usually to poor chambering or excessive loads.

On a hunt a few days later I came on an enormous rock buttress with two peaks standing up like the ears of a great horned owl. The Chilcotin Indians call this rock "Salina," which is their name for this owl. On a ledge on the face of the cliff was a big goat. I guess the range was about 500 yards, and I could see no way to get closer, so I lay down and took the shot, holding two feet above the goat's back. Of course I missed that, and two other shots I pulled, and the goat leisurely climbed up and disappeared between the two pinnacles. After a lot of climbing and scrambling, I found my way to the back of this rock mass where it was equally precipitous, and while working around at the base of the cliff I heard something above me, and looking upwards I saw the goat or one just like it. At the shot it loosened all holds and, in a shower of small rocks, landed close to me. Then and there I named this rifle "Salina." I continued to use it as a testing piece for many years, and I also hunted a lot with it in Panama from 1915 to 1917. In 1911 I fitted it with a Winchester 5A scope, and thereafter all my dope was recorded in minutes of angle, from which it was easy to determine elevations, trajectory, and bullet drop.

About this time the NRA was developing interest in outdoor shooting with the small bore rifle at 50, 100, and 200 yards. Before this scarcely anyone had shot the 22 at longer distances than 25 yards and little was known of the capabilities of the 22 Long Rifle cartridge at longer distances. So I got another Winchester single-shot for this cartridge, with 26-inch No. 3 barrel, set triggers, and sling. I fitted it with my 5A scope and proceeded to give it a good trial at all distances up to 200 yards. I soon found that various makes of ammunition have quite different results in accuracy. With the makes that proved best it would just about group in 2½ inches at 100 yards. This has proved to be about the best that can be expected of this rifle with this cartridge, and this limitation was what finally caused Winchester to develop their celebrated Model 52 rifle for small bore match shooting. Generally speaking, the old Ballard is the only American single-shot action that has given fine accuracy with the 22 Long Rifle cartridge. However, with this Winchester, I did determine the angles of elevation for all distances, which

had not been known or at least never published before I published my table. Also, before I did this shooting, it was not known that there was so much difference in the accuracy of various makes of cartridges in a certain individual rifle.

Following the loss of my old 25-21 rifle by the express company, I had to have another varmint rifle, so I procured still another Winchester single-shot for the 25-20 S. S. cartridge, and proceeded to develop smokeless powder loads for it. I finally found that the best was the 86-grain, soft point, jacketed bullet with a charge of du Pont Schuetzen powder that filled the case to the base of the bullet. This load shot like nobody's business, and it gave the finest accuracy up to 200 yards that I had obtained up to that time or heard of anyone else obtaining except with Pope muzzle-breech loading rifles. But my elation was short-lived, for the barrel began to pit, and in less than 500 rounds it was ruined.

About this time we had been devoting much study to the cleaning of rifles. It seemed to us that stronger ammonia was the only satisfactory cleaning solution, so I had a new barrel fitted to this rifle and cleaned it immediately after firing with this ammonia. This did not do a particle of good, and again the barrel was ruined in 500 rounds. The same thing occurred with a Winchester Model 92 rifle for the 25-20 W.C.F. smokeless cartridge of Winchester make. When I wrote them a letter of complaint, they stated that I should not blame the rifle for what was evidently the fault of the powder (which they used)!!! However, I excuse them for no one knew much about such things in those days. Of course we now know that the old potassium chlorate primer was the devil in the woodshed. With that primer, in small bores like 25 caliber the relatively small charge of powder did not dilute the primer fouling as it did in larger bores like the 30 caliber, and the primer got in its hellish work at once and fast.

For a while there seemed to be no solution for this problem of smokeless powder in small bores. Then Winchester came out with stainless steel barrels made to order, so I had them build me still another rifle with this barrel, and modelled almost exactly like the fine old 25-21 that I had lost, only it was chambered for the 25-20 W.C.F. repeater cartridge, because I had an idea that the single-shot cartridge would soon be obsolete, which it was. Clyde Baker stocked this rifle, and fitted it with a finger lever that hugged the pistol grip. But before I had time to do much with it, the Kleanbore primer was developed, and this solved all our cleaning and rusting problems. Also at this time the develop-

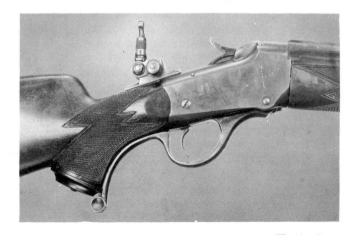

Winchester single-shot rifle for the 25-20 W.C.F. cartridge, with stainless steel barrel. Stock and lock work by Clyde Baker. The first attempt to solve the corrosion problem resulting from chlorate primers.

ment of the 22 Hornet cartridge shifted our work from the older cartridges to the modern high-intensity types. Later, however, I found that I could obtain splendid results with my 25-20 W.C.F. rifle with a load consisting of the 87-grain, soft point, spitzer bullet made for the 250-3000 Savage cartridge, bullet seated far enough out of the case to touch the lands, and a charge of 11 grains of du Pont No. 4227 powder. The trajectory seems to indicate that the velocity is about 2,000 f.s.; evidently a fine wild turkey load. Of course the over-all length of the load is too great for 25-20 repeater rifles.

Up to this time you will note that I had been using Winchester actions exclusively on all my single shots, both because of their strength and durability, and because they were the only new actions that could be procured at that time. After working for some years with the 22 Hornet cartridge in bolt-action rifles, a friend gave me a good Sharps-Borchardt action, so I had Frank Hyde obtain a 22 caliber Remington high-pressure steel barrel with a 15-inch twist, and fit it to this action and chamber it for the 22-3000 Lovell R2 cartridge. Frank also worked over the firing pin, and made the pin retract with the first down movement of the lever, two very necessary alterations with this action. This

Rifle for the 22-3000 Lovell R2 cartridge, with Sharps-Borchardt action. Action and barrel work by Frank Hyde. Stock by William L. Humphrey. Unertl 10X Varmint scope.

rifle, fitted with a 10X Unertl Varmint scope, is a fine, accurate varmint rifle. With good 50-grain bullets and 15.5 grains of 4227 powder it will group reliably, day after day, in about a minute of angle, which is the best that can be expected from this cartridge and a single-shot action. Occasionally a 5-shot group as small as half an inch turns up at 100 yards, but such is a lucky group. This rifle, however, has one peculiarity. Almost invariably the first shot fired from a clean, cold bore strikes from half an inch to an inch above the succeeding group at 100 yards. I think this is because the groove diameter of the barrel is .2235″, while all the bullets I have used so far have measured .224″. This is no drawback because, knowing it I can allow for it, or can fire a fouling shot before starting on the day's hunt.

It has quite generally been proven that with equal barrels and loads, a single-shot action will not give as fine accuracy

as a modern bolt action. There are apparently only two exceptions, the Ballard action for the 22 Long Rifle cartridge, and the Hauck single-shot action, which is a horse of a different color with its better bedding, ignition, and breeching up. I do not mean to imply that there have not been any single-shot rifles that would give gilt-edge accuracy. There have been quite a few, but I would think that any custom riflemaker who guaranteed to produce a single-shot rifle that would average groups under a minute would soon go broke. So far as we have been able to determine, the difficulties with the single-shot action seem to be in the two-piece stock, the breeching up, and the ignition. The single-shot rifle also seems to have a greater jump and barrel vibration than the bolt action. The difference in elevation required between full charges and reduced loads is much greater with it. In this connection it has long been my experience that to get the best accuracy from a single-shot rifle the forearm should not touch the receiver. It should be possible to pass a thin sheet of paper between the two.

The most accurate single-shot rifle that I have owned is one for the 219 Improved Zipper cartridge. I traded Bill Humphrey out of a fine Winchester rifle with 26-inch, No. 3 Diller barrel, .224″ groove diameter and 16″ twist, double set triggers, and a fine stock made by him. I had this chambered for the Improved Zipper cartridge with a very perfect reamer made by Red Elliott. This cartridge is simply the 219 Winchester Zipper case fire-formed to a 30° shoulder angle. You simply fire the factory cartridge in the rifle and it comes out improved. The best load I have found for this rifle has been 32 grains of du Pont No. 3031 powder with the 50-grain Sierra bullet. M.V. is probably around 3,900 f.s. After working up this load and sighting in, it gave three 5-shot groups at 100 yards measuring .65″, .80″, and .80″. For three years I have used this rifle almost exclusively for all my chuck shooting. Its accuracy and very flat trajectory have given a high percentage of hits at long ranges. With it I made the longest first-shot hit I have ever pulled off on a chuck; difficult to pace because it was up and down hill over rough ground, but it was certainly considerably in excess of 300 yards.

The Stevens No. 44½ action is another on which a most excellent and accurate rifle can be built, particularly for cartridges not to exceed the 219 Donaldson in power. My old friend Jim Garland, who has been my companion on many chuck hunts over the past fifteen years, has a glorious piece built on this action. The Diller barrel was chambered and fitted for the R2 Lovell cartridge, and the lock work done by C. C. Johnson. Bill Humphrey made the stock and the scope is a superb 6X Bear Cub Double. With each lot of cartridges that Jim loads for it, usually with 15.5 grains of 4227 powder, he tests it on the bench, and it has never failed to average under an inch, and with some lots of bullets it gives around ¾ inch. He regards it as his best varmint

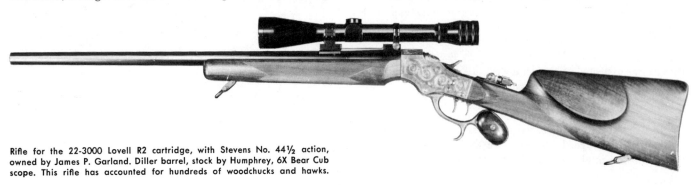

Rifle for the 22-3000 Lovell R2 cartridge, with Stevens No. 44½ action, owned by James P. Garland. Diller barrel, stock by Humphrey, 6X Bear Cub scope. This rifle has accounted for hundreds of woodchucks and hawks.

Squirrel rifle for the 25 Rim Fire cartridge. Ballard action, gunsmithing by Niedner, Shelhammer, and Kornbrath. Lyman Challenger scope. Owned by James P. Garland.

rifle, and its bag numbers in excess of three hundred chucks and hawks. I remember one afternoon two years ago when we were separated by a range of hills. Every two or three minutes I would hear Jim shoot, and towards sundown I wandered over to see what in thunder he had been shooting at. He had a stand on a hill above a creek bottom that was honeycombed with holes, and towards dusk the chucks began to come out. When we went down, we picked up thirty-six of them shot at distances from 150 to 250 yards. Both Jim and I are rather of the opinion that a first-rate riflemaker will turn out a larger proportion of gilt-edge shooting rifles when he uses the Stevens 44½ action than with any other.

Jim also has a superb engraved Ballard for the 25 Rim Fire cartridge, the work of Niedner, Shelhammer, and Kornbrath. With Remington or Peters cartridges it groups the first ten shots at 50 yards in about ¾ inch, and the second ten when it is warmed up a little, in about half an inch, and is his favorite squirrel rifle.

My latest venture in the realm of single shots has been one of the most interesting. Three years ago I took Salina, my old 30-40 Winchester Single Shot, out of the box where it had been in store for several years, well covered in and out with Rig, with the intention of trying some new bullets in it. To my consternation, when I put a patch through the bore it came out with red rust and many bodies of big, black ants. Ants had nested in the bore and their acid had ruined it. One day last year, looking at the old piece that had served me so well for half a century, I decided it was entitled to have something done to rejuvenate it. I had on hand a fine 25 caliber Douglas barrel, .257″ groove diameter and 13-inch twist. So I had H. L. Culver, my metal gunsmith, fit this barrel to the action, and I asked him to chamber it for the Krag case necked down to 25 caliber with a 30° shoulder angle. As it turned out, this case is very similar in shape and capacity to the 25 Donaldson Ace. We called it the 25 Cul-

ver-Krag. Then Bill Humphrey made a beautiful new stock and forearm to my exact dimensions, and Mark Stith fitted one of his 4X Bear Cub Double scopes, and I had just about the finest appearing, best balanced and fitting, and steadiest holding rifle I have ever had in my hands. The intention had been to produce an all-around hunting rifle rather than one for varmint or target shooting, and it has turned out to be just that. I have only worked up one load for it so far—the 100-grain Sierra soft point spitzer bullet and 40 grains of 4350 powder. After sighting in I fired five 5-shot groups with it at 100 yards, measuring 1.75″, 1.12″, .88″, 1.85″ and 1.98″. Before you criticize these groups, consider that they were fired with a rather light-barreled single-shot rifle aimed with a low-power scope having a flat top post reticle, and that the charge was quite a powerful one. It is much more difficult to get a fine grouping with a heavy load than with a light one. Last summer and fall I carried Salina in her new garb for probably a total of 350 miles afoot in my wanderings over the mountains adjacent to my summer home, occasionally gathering in a chuck, crow, hawk, or porcupine, and always hoping for a bear or bobcat which never materialized. I have never carried a rifle that seemed as friendly.

All this pernicious activity with single-shot rifles, covering a period of sixty years, started with that rifle in the gunstore window when I was a little boy, and that is the way with most of our preference for single shots. It is not their superiority that causes us to select and work with them, but rather some romantic or historic association. An urge to acquire and experiment, not always wise, but usually one that gives deep satisfaction. It seems to many of us that the highly efficient bolt action is but a remodeled musket in a way, that the lever action is a product of America's unrivaled quantity-production industry, but that the single shot constructed on fine and beautiful lines by a master riflemaker is a gentleman's piece.

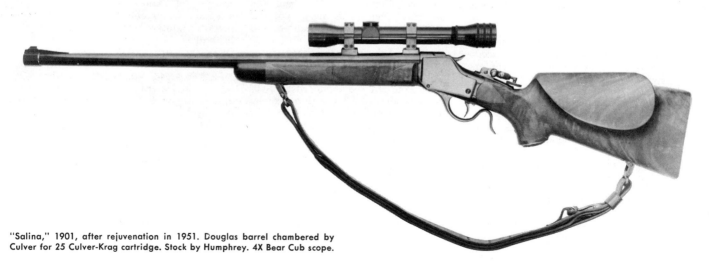

"Salina," 1901, after rejuvenation in 1951. Douglas barrel chambered by Culver for 25 Culver-Krag cartridge. Stock by Humphrey. 4X Bear Cub scope.

RELOADING FOR

An extensive and fully detailed treatise on this specialized phase of cartridge making.

Left—Author recently picked off this coyote with 240 Weatherby Magnum, shown here. The new 6mm round is an instant killer, offering the largest case capacity and velocity practical with the 6mm bore size. Better sectional density and high coefficient of form help buck the wind better. Right—Laramie gunsmith,

RELOADING FOR varmint hunting differs from run-of-the-mill home ammo assembly, mainly in the extra care required to squeeze that cone of fire down as close to one bullet diameter as possible, plus the proper choice of cartridges and bullets.

Varmint rifles are generally small bore from 17- to 25- caliber, launching comparatively lightweight bullets at high velocity. The object is to kill harmful or nuisance vermin humanely. Since no effort is made to save meat, as with deer or other game animals, varmint shooters seek the most explosive effect possible — to achieve instant kills.

Certainly it's possible to kill varmints with deer-class rifles, but calibers above 25 cause quakelike concussions that sorely tax the good hospitality of farmers or ranchers in the area. Also, big bores don't often exhibit that sub-minute-of-angle accuracy so earnestly sought by varminters. Even if inherently super accurate, where is the man who can hold a belching cannon with the precise nicety required to hit a coke bottle-sized ground squirrel at 300 yards or so, for 100 or more rounds? By the time he'd triggered off a day's prairie dog hunting with say a 7mm Remington, the average nimrod would be punchy.

Wildcat 17 calibers go "spat" instead of "boom," spitting 20- to 25-grain pellets, that have a bomb-like effect all out of proportion to their diminutive size. The demand for this mini-caliber appears to be growing

at a great rate. Joyce Hornady made up a biggish batch of 25-gr. 17-cal. bullets and they were sold out overnight! He's now busy making a lot more.

Centerfire 22s are legion, but currently most popular are the 224 Weatherby, 225 Winchester and 22-250 Remington. All share similar velocity figures, and any one is a good choice for every phase of varminting, from squirrels to coyotes and bobcats. Still tops in velocity, killing power and *barrel erosion*, is the 220 Swift, with many advocates in the field, but few in print.

Way out West, where we got a name for wind, and it isn't always "Maria," 22 rifles sometimes adopt two trajectories, one down, the other sideways. That's when the 6mm and 25s take over. The most popular wildcat among predator hunters out here is the formidable 25-06, an '06 case necked down to 25-caliber. Some writers decry it as "overbore capacity," but it puts down critters out as far as you can see them, with all of the conviction of Thor's thunderbolts storming down from Mount Olympus. My 257 Weatherby has more of the same "wrath of the Gods" effect. However, most hunters would as soon pass up the boisterous bang and vigorous push on the shoulder.

Surveys show the 243 Winchester topping popularity polls among California varmint hunters, and the 6mm Remington has a substantial fan club, but I expect the new, super-potent 240 Weatherby to make inroads on

both. A couple of wildcat 6mm cartridges, popular nationwide, are the 240 Page Super Pooper, a 28°-shouldered, blown out version of the 244 Remington, sired by gun writer Warren Page, and the 243 Super Rockchucker, developed by Fred Huntington, manufacturer of "Precisioneered" RCBS reloading tools, years before the 243 Winchester and 244 Remington fostered popular interest in the 6mm. The 243 SRC is a 30-06 case, necked down to 6mm, with the shoulder pushed back to 28°, leaving a slightly longer neck. No fireforming is required. (RCBS, Oroville, California, chambers barrels for both of these cartridges).

The key to varmint loading, regardless of caliber, is proper bullet selection. Squirrel-chuck hunters and predator hunters both want light, fragile bullets, but the latter must avoid those that are too light. One day I watched a friend, shooting 60-grain bullets in a 243 Winchester, lose three coyotes and a bobcat. All went down, apparently with well placed hits, but got up and left the country. We trailed one coyote for over an hour, before it disappeared into thin air. Using 75-grain or heavier 6mm bullets, I have never lost a coyote that was well hit. Recently, I caught a desert wolf through the flanks, as it crossed in front of me, full bore. I watched in wonder as it barreled on, hardly faltering, but recovered in time to correct my lead and drill the fleeing animal through the shoulders

VARMINT HUNTING

by JOHN LACHUK

Anderson, and author look over some chubby Rockchucks shot by the latter during Wyoming trip. Author discovered that his 240 PSP far outranged high velocity 22 centerfire, and held up much better in gale-like winds. He recommends use of heavier bullets for long range shooting with 6mm or 25 caliber.

with a 75-grain Sierra HP from my 240 Page Super Pooper. Traveling at 3400 fps, ahead of 41 grains of 4895, this bullet left a 3-inch exit. It's a tribute to the coyote's stamina that it continued to run with such a wound.

Another coyote, standing head-on, was hit in the chest with my 243 Winchester, pushing an 80-grain Speer spitzer at 3350 fps with 40.3 grains 4895. The animal dropped like a stone. There was no exit wound, but the coyote gurgled like a half-empty fifth of whisky when I picked it up, indicating extensive internal damage.

Sierra's 6mm "Total Destruction" 85-grain boat-tail, with its tender .018″ jacket, tapering to .009″ at the hollow point, makes an excellent long-range chuck or squirrel bullet because it bucks wind and retains velocity better than a flat-based bullet. On a recent rockchuck hunt in Wyoming with Fred Huntington and *Shooting Times* editor, Robert Steindler, I used this bullet in my 240 PSP while Bob used a high velocity 22 bore with 55-grain slugs. An excellent marksman, Bob got more than his share of fat, far-ranging chucks—until the wind started to blow. Then he found himself handicapped by the 22's proclivity to follow the beckoning call of the whistling siren.

Adding five grains to the popular 55-grain weight improves both the 22's long range ballistics and its wind bucking ability. The largely overlooked 60-grain Hornady spire point zips out of a 22-250 at a respectable

3500 fps ahead of 33.7 grains of 4320. The 55-grain spire point, with 34.9 grains of the same powder, takes off 100 fps faster. However, when they both reach 100 yards the 60-grain bullet's 2740 fps almost equals the 55-grain's 2760 fps. At 300 yards, the 60-grain leapfrogs its lighter competition, with 2410 fps against 2390 fps for the 55-grain. The 55-grain has a ballistic coefficient of only .246, while the 60-grain boasts .269, better than a 70-grain Hornady 6mm at .260.

Ballistic coefficient (BC) measures a bullet's wind bucking and velocity retention capabilities. The oft-quoted sectional density (SD) is a fair barometer of bullet performance but it fails to take into account the nose shape of the projectile. To illustrate, compare Speer's 6mm 90-grain spitzer, sectional density of .217, with their 105-grain round nose, SD .254. Looks like the heavy bullet easily bests the light one, but wait! The 90-grain has a ballistic coefficient of .323, the 105-grain's BC is .256. Why? Because the blunt bullet has far greater air resistance.

For the 257 Weatherby and the 25-06, I prefer the heavier bullets, with high ballistic coefficients. They offer super wind bucking plus high velocity retention at long ranges, and that's really what you're buying with a quarter-bore. The 6mm kills varmints as dead as they can get, so you don't need greater killing power. What the 25 has to offer is exemplified in the 100-grain Hornady spire

point, with an impressive BC of .357. Launched at 3500 fps from a 257 Weatherby, it retains 62% of its original velocity at 500 yards. Contrast this with 57% for the 87-grain Hornady 6mm, starting at 3300 fps from a 6mm Remington, and 52% for the 60-grain Hornady 22 with a muzzle velocity of 3500 fps from a 22-250.

I've never experienced ricochets using heavy 25 caliber bullets, and they are grossly destructive. I once loaded my 257 Weatherby down to about 3100 fps, using 117-grain Sierra spitzers, hoping to shoot bobcats without too much pelt damage. I caught one cat full in the chest, and the bullet left a saucer-sized exit, luckily far enough back to allow a fine shoulder mount.

Bores larger than 25 require light weight bullets to avoid ricochets near inhabited areas, and to offer explosive effect on small animals. Sierra's 90-grain hollow point is good in the 270. For the 308 or 30-06, use the 130-grain Speer hollow point or the Sierra 110-grain HP.

Despite the extensive lineup of current factory cartridges, some wildcats have assets worth considering. The 25-06 uses cheap, plentiful brass, requires no fire forming, merely a quick trip through a 270 sizing die and a 25-06 sizer, thence to the powder measure. With today's slow burning powders, it's a more efficient round than when it was created by A. O. Niedner, after World War I.

Not all wildcats have it so easy.

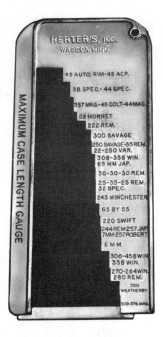

A case-length gauge is an important asset to reloaders. Most varmint cartridges are high intensity rounds that tend to lengthen in firing, especially such as the 243 Winchester, 220 Swift, etc. Frequent trimming is essential to accuracy and safety. Long case-necks may squeeze into the throat, run up high pressures.

The sensitive Lachmiller priming tool helped the author in getting primers seated perfectly square with the case head, and neatly to the cup bottom. Proper primer seating is important to accuracy.

appearing cases, that none-the-less possess excessive headspace, often as much as .040″ to .050″. Reloading and firing such cases is dangerous in the extreme!

Never die-form or resize cases without lubricating with commercial lube supplied by various die makers, or use machinist's soluble oil. Apply just enough lube to give an oily feel to cases. An excess around the shoulder area will result in oil dents.

Reloaders still wage a bitter debate over the relative merits of full-length resizing versus neck-sizing. Being more hunter than target shooter, I usually full-length size, for easy chambering in the field, where a stuck case has more than once cost me a fine trophy. However, when I got my test copy of the new 240 Weatherby Magnum, the cartridge was so new that reloading dies weren't yet available. I sent fired cases to Fred Huntington, and in due course had a full set of RCBS dies, but meanwhile, I had to neck-size using my 240 PSP die. Groups resulting from that exigency were no worse but certainly no better than those fired later after full-length resizing with the proper dies, tending to discount claims that neck-sizing improves accuracy.

Another pro neck-sizing argument states that brass becomes more brittle as it is repeatedly expanded by firing and then resized. Full-length sizing works the body of the case more than neck-sizing, thus logically should shorten case life. However, few failures occur in the body of the case. Normal fatality results from lengthwise cracks in the neck that most

Some go through several reductions in length and/or diameter. It's important that case forming dies support case walls, as they exist, while sizing down the case neck. If die walls are a larger diameter than the case, case walls will buckle before neck sizing occurs. That's why file trim dies can seldom double as forming dies. When die-forming wildcat brass, adjust your final sizing die so cases offer a crush fit in your rifle, to prevent headspace problems. If cases start out too short for your chamber, seat bullets well out, to hold case heads back against the bolt when firing. Another method is to run a slightly oversized expander plug through the case neck and size it back just enough to chamber.

Use near-full loads, never sub-loads to fire-form rimless cases. With light loads, an apparent "bouncing" phenomenon can occur, yielding perfect-

often occur during firing. The greatest enemy of long case life is not the sizing die, but high pressure, usually resulting from too much powder. Cartridge cases, like people, die young when they become gluttons.

To demonstrate how tenacious cases really are, Fred Huntington held a shooting/reloading marathon with four random selected cases, two Remington and two Winchester. They were full-length resized for each loading, in a standard RCBS 30-06 die: Cases were lubed outside only. Leaving the necks dry on the inside, deliberately subjecting them to added strain. Loads were standard velocity and pressure, and the Model 70 Winchester had a normal chamber. Results: One Remington case split at the neck on the 36th firing, the other ditto on the 52nd. The Winchester cases failed in like manner at the 50th and 55th firings. Inasmuch as all failures occurred in the case necks I fail to see how neck-sizing only could have made the cases last longer.

There is at least one disadvantage to neck-sizing. Wall thickness around the circumference of individual case necks can vary .003″ to .004″. Neck-sizing dies, which can't support the case body adequately, tend to offset the necks toward the stronger side. The bullet, held cockeyed to begin with, gets off to a bad start in the rifling and accuracy suffers.

If you don't care to stick with your brass through thick and thin, try inside neck reaming with a line-ream die offered by RCBS, that guides the reamer concentrically, helping to even out wall thickness. Or use the Forster Outside Neck Turner, that trues-up case neck O.D. over a mandrel for about the same effect. Both tools reduce variations between cases for a more consistent bullet pull, further improving accuracy. Full-length

Armory C-H case trimmer is easy to use and fast, keeps cases trimmed, after using case gauge or caliper to set proper length. The chamfering tool (right) is used to remove burrs left inside and outside of the case mouths after trimming.

RCBS case-forming dies provide cases for many wildcat and standard calibers, using cheap, plentiful GI or commercial 30-06 brass. Dies shown form 22-250 brass. Be careful in final sizing of any formed case to make it a crush fit in your rifle, to avoid headspace problems. Use normal, not reduced loads, for fire-forming rimless cases.

This RCBS line-reaming die helps make case necks of uniform wall thickness after they have thickened from brass flowing forward during firing. Be sure to size cases full length, and pull the case necks back over the expander button before reaming.

resize and expand necks before trimming and reaming.

Check case length periodically with a vernier caliper, Pacific's "Big Mike," or a case length gauge from Herter's, McKillen & Heyer, Wilson, etc. Some cases such as the 220 Swift and 243 Winchester, grow .003″ to .006″ each firing with high intensity loads, simultaneously thickening at the neck and require frequent trimming and reaming.

When case necks start splitting, it can be like a plague descended upon your brass. I've lost as many as 8 cases out of 20. To save the rest of the lot of 100, I pulled the bullets and powder, ejected the primers, and annealed the case necks. I'm still using those cases ten reloads later. If you keep track of the number of times your cases are reloaded you can learn to anticipate split necks, and anneal before attrition sets in.

It pays to practice neck annealing with reject brass the first time. I use a common method, as follow: I stand six or eight cases in a ten-inch cake tin, in water within a ¼-inch of their shoulders and play the flame of a Bernz-O-Matic torch inside of each case mouth in turn. When the neck turns red, I tip the case over. The water prevents heat from drawing the hardness of the body and head, where strength is essential to safety. It takes only ten to fifteen seconds per case. Time yourself, so the annealing will be even on all of the cases.

For tapered cases such as the 22-250, "partial sizing" offers most of the advantages of both full-length and neck sizing. Instead of adjusting your full-length sizing die to a firm contact with the shell holder, stop about ⅛-inch short. The diameter of case walls will be reduced but slightly. The neck will be fully sized and held concentric with the body. The shoul-

der area, controlling headspace on rimless cases, will be untouched. Partial sizing reduces cold working of the case body but cases chamber without hesitation and bullets start concentric with the bore. Cases with only a slight taper, such as the 243, won't accept partial sizing because case walls are almost completely sized, squeezing in the shoulder and buckling it outward, in effect lengthening headspace, so the bolt can't close.

All reloaders desire accuracy, but to varmint hunters, it's more than a tender sentiment, it's an absolute necessity! Any load that groups much over an inch at 100 yards makes poor varmint ammo. Frank Snow, president of Sierra Bullets, Inc., and Ferris Pindle, Sierra research engineer, have made some interesting discoveries anent reloading accuracy. They spot check every lot of bullets coming off the line by actually loading and firing them in a heavy bench rifle, mounting a 2-inch, 30x Unertl scope. Shooting is done in Sierra's own 200-yard, underground tunnel. A $3000 counter chronograph automatically reads off instrumental velocities at ten feet and 200 yards simultaneously. Groups average around .200″, for five shots at 100 yards. "If they run over a quarter-inch," says Pindle, "we start to worry!"

Powder charges are metered directly into the cases from a Lyman powder measure, and not weighed, but velocities and pressures are in the low to medium range, where a slight variation in powder weight has less effect. Snow and Pindle use Wilson and RCBS neck-size-only dies most of the time, with a periodic run through an RCBS full-length die. Bullets are seated in a Wilson straight-line die, and concentricity, which they consider very important is checked on a Wilson cartridge spinner.

Bullets are seated .010″ into the lands, a practice that I don't recommend to varmint hunters loading at or near maximum because it runs up pressures erratically at high pressure levels. Accuracy does improve if bullets are not obliged to leap a wide gap from case to rifling, but the bullet ogive should not actually touch the lands. Your rifle magazine likely limits overall length anyway, so the discussion is largely academic, unless you want to single-load—OK for chucks and squirrels, too slow for a coyote darting through distant prickly pear and sage. Seat short bullets at least one caliber deep, to prevent their working loose in the field.

Accuracy depends to a surprising degree upon good primer action. Superior automobile performance requires a hot spark. The same is true of rifle cartridges. Magnum primers, from CCI, Federal and Remington, assure proper ignition of heavily deterent-coated powders such as 4350, 4831 and the Hodgdon ball powders, even in large capacity cases. Intensely cold weather makes powder harder to bring up to kindling temperature. Magnum primers overcome this reluctance to ignite plus helping to keep velocities more uniform and nearer normal in spite of the cold.

Magnum primers also improve accuracy by making up for deficiencies in the rifle's firing mechanism. Frank Snow discovered that short-action bolt rifles shot better when heavy firing pin springs were installed. Coincidentally, ballistician Edward M. Yard found that a heavy blow of the firing pin causes increased flash energy from a primer. Says Mr. Yard, "The difference between a normal and a light blow can be enough to drop a magnum primer to the level of a standard one."

Seat primers uniformly to the bot-

224 Weatherby Magnum has about same ballistics as 225 and 22-250, the latter also offered in Weatherby Varmintmaster rifle, on scaled down Mark V action. Use of 60-gr. bullets in any of these three 22s will make them stand up better in the wind. Ease of deflection by wind is the major failing of 22 caliber varmint rifles.

tom of the primer pockets, both for firm support of the anvils and to prevent a cushioning effect upon the firing pin, making it seat the primer cup fully before it can crush and ignite the primer pellets. No harm will come to primers from seating them well below the case heads. In fact, sensitivity is improved by placing primer pellets under "dry compression."

In the interests of accuracy, I clean primer pockets every fifth or sixth loading, using a Herter's brass bristle brush in a drill press. I also check primer flash holes with a Herter's flash-hole gauge, discarding atypical cases. All of my cases are segregated by make and lot.

A bullet is inherently accurate when its center of gravity coincides with its center of form. In the bore, a bullet is forced to rotate around its center of mass, but once free of confinement, it can, wobble at will around a misplaced center of gravity, and miss the place that you want it to go. Bullets of modern manufacture are, almost without exception, uniform and well balanced, but individual rifles often evidence a strong preference for a particular brand or bullet weight. You must discover the optimum bullet/powder combination for your rifle.

The trick in working up loads for any varmint rifle is to get the job done without wearing out the barrel before you get to take it hunting. Eliminate as many alternatives. as possible with theory, before testing. You may have to consider three or four powders, and perhaps a dozen bullets. Astute study of various reloading tables will reveal which powder offers the best velocity/ pressure ratio. Bear in mind that ball powders, BL-C2, H375, H450, the new W-W powders, etc., cause less bore erosion and also cooperate wondrously well with almost any powder measure. For data see *Hodgdon's Manual* 20. For long barrel life, load under maximum. You won't miss 100 fps or so in the field. Narrow down the bullet list by considering the game you'll hunt. For varmints, you need lighter weight, explosive bullets.

Eliminate unnecessary variables. For instance, I always use CCI 250 Magnum primers—one variable removed. Change only one component at a time, so you know what to blame or credit for a change in performance. Don't mix powder lots or bullets. Stock up on lot numbers that perform well.

Load initial tests of only three rounds each. This is enough to show which loads are grossly inaccurate or show pressure signs. These you abandon without wasting more time and material. Promising combinations are loaded again, in ten-round groups for more decisive testing.

If comparisons are to be valid, accuracy must be tested from a solid benchrest, over a 100-yard range, with no wind. Sandbags fore and aft eliminate muscle tremors. Fire 5-shot groups, allowing 30 seconds cooling between rounds, with the bolt open. Cooling improves accuracy and reduces bore erosion. To assure fair comparisons of various components, scrub the bore with solvent and wipe dry, between strings.

Metal and powder fouling both seriously affect accuracy. Once I took my 300 Weatherby to the range, preparatory to an Idaho elk hunt. Sighting groups at 100 yards printed 3"-4" patterns. The gun had shot much better the year before but, I reasoned, the stock fore-end might have warped slightly during storage. Then, remembering what a cursory cleaning I had performed after the last hunt, I dipped a brass brush in Hoppes, thoroughly scrubbed out the bore, and dried with a patch. The next three shots went into one hole, 12 o'clock-high, right where I zeroed it the year before!

When accuracy testing, take a notebook to the range and record group size and position for each load. If you get a real flyer, and your hold was good, mark the case head with nail polish. If that case delivers a flyer the next time it's loaded, retire it to a second-string batch, reserved for barrel warmups and plinking. Benchrest shooters use this system to weed out bad brass, often winding up with only

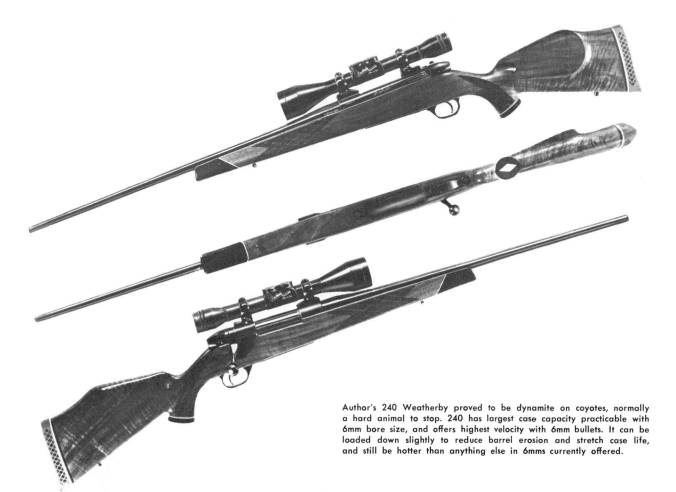

Author's 240 Weatherby proved to be dynamite on coyotes, normally a hard animal to stop. 240 has largest case capacity practicable with 6mm bore size, and offers highest velocity with 6mm bullets. It can be loaded down slightly to reduce barrel erosion and stretch case life, and still be hotter than anything else in 6mms currently offered.

about ⅓rd of their cases eligible for match competition.

Many home experimenters have acquired one of the remarkably accurate, and reasonably priced, Avtron, Herter's B-Square, Oehler, etc., chronographs now available and are blowing primers, separating case heads, and otherwise scaring themselves half to death, vainly trying to match published factory velocity figures. Chances are those numbers were never read off a chronograph! They were interpolated by adding a few fps to convert actual chronograph velocities to "muzzle velocities," plus a little more to equate the elevation to sea level, and an adjustment for temperature, etc. Then, for good measure, the technician subtracts his wife's age and adds his mother-in-law's. Well, it isn't really all that bad, but let's face it, pressure barrels are often 28 to 30 inches long, and usually of tighter bore than production barrels. How can you hope to emulate factory velocities with your super-lightweight 20-incher? (Also remember that two rifles leaving the assembly line the same day, may record velocities as much as 50 fps apart, with the same ammo.) For a candid view of factory velocities, see page 80 of *Speer's Manual For Reloading Ammunition 7.*

Chronograph owners should also buy Homer Powley's P-Max pressure gauge ($49.95), to keep track of pressure as well as velocity in a scientific manner. The 1968 22nd ed. of the GUN DIGEST carried news of a new, easy-to-use pressure measuring system developed by Michael W. York and Don Cantrell. This valuable instrument, which measures absolute pressure—not crusher gauge psi—will be available by the time you read this at less than $300.

A practical way to detect excess pressure is to "mike" the case head just in front of the extractor groove, or on the belt, before and after firing your reloads, to see if expansion has occurred. Some head expansion *may* have taken place on the initial firing, assuming you're getting your brass via factory cartridges. As little as .0005" expansion indicates that your load has exceeded the elastic limits of the brass. This calls for a 5% or more drop in the powder charge. Don't measure the case in front of the solid head portion. Expansion from that point forward is quite normal, even with mild loads. Another excess pressure indicator is expanded primer pockets. Acc-U-Ream provides a set of Go-NoGo gauges for easy detection.

While you can't read primers like tea leaves, they are weather vanes of safety. In his book, *Rifles and Shotguns,* Jack O'Connor offers these guidelines: A primer leak, evidenced as a black smoke ring around the primer, often indicates pressure of some 70,000 psi. Blown primers, that is, primers that *fall out* of the expanded primer pockets when the bolt is opened, warn of about 80,000 psi!

I once had a 243, Savage 110 that handled 41 grains of 4895, behind a 75-gr. Speer bullet, without a whimper. Later, I got a 243 Winchester Model 100, semi-automatic rifle. The identical load displayed severely flattened and cratered primers, most times a red alert for pressure. Examination through a jeweler's loupe disclosed that the case head had pushed back into the hole in the bolt face holding the spring-loaded plunger-type ejector, leaving a round raised spot on the base head. Obviously pressure was far too high. It's not uncommon for one rifle to regurgitate loads that another digests with relish, but I wanted to know why, so I continued firing. On the 6th round, the bolt failed to close fully. With considerable difficulty, I pulled the cartridge, and on the bullet ogive, I saw deep engraving from the rifling lands. Seating the bullets deeper stopped all indications of pressure. However, to be on the safe side, I dropped the charge by one grain, to compensate for the reduced case capacity occasioned by seating the bullets deeper.

Caution and patience should be the handmaidens of handloaders, the patience to start below and work up to maximum loads, and the caution to

High-power 22 centerfire calibers were lacking after WW II. The 220 Swift fell into disfavor, leaving a vacuum that went unfilled for years, until the 224 Weatherby, 225 Winchester and 22-250 Remington appeared. Their only disadvantage is wind-sensitivity that can be improved by using 60-gr. bullets. From left: 222 Rem., 222 Rem. Magnum, 223, 219 Zipper, 22-250, 224 Weatherby, 225 Win., and 220 Swift.

Left—25 caliber is the largest practicable bore size for varmint hunters. Larger bores are troublesome in terms of recoil, noise and possible ricochets. Potent 25s are best with 87/100-gr. bullets. From left: 250-3000 Savage, 257 Roberts, Wildcat 25-06, and 257 Weatherby Magnum. Right—The author considers the 6mm bore size the all-round best compromise for varmint hunting. It combines the low recoil and low noise level of 22 centerfires with potent killing power and boardinghouse reach of quarter-bores. From left: 240 Page Super Pooper, 243 Super Rockchucker, 243 Win., 6mm Rem. and 240 Weatherby Magnum.

drop back again every time a new component is introduced into the formula. Tests by Remington demonstrated that changing the primer mixture alone could vary pressure readings as much as 21,000 psi. How many home loaders reduce charges when they try a new primer?

Reloading errors have a way of compounding themselves. Combine a new, hotter primer with a thick or overlong case neck, plus a bullet seated into the lands, and pressure starts upward. Temperature escalates, causing the powder to burn faster than normal, and pressure leaps, in a vicious cycle that builds on itself, perhaps with disastrous results.

Even simple reloading goofs sometimes have dire consequences. On the range one day, I met a fellow whose face resembled a well-peppered egg, with two white ovals around his eyes. "I was shootin' my '06 Enfield," he said, "when all hell broke loose! If it weren't for my Ray Bans, I'd be in the market for some pencils and a tin cup." (Moral 1: Always wear shooting glasses when testing loads.) His load of 55 grains of 4350 teamed with a 180-gr. bullet, sounded mild enough, but a subsequent lab test revealed, in addition to 4350, generous doses of faster-burning 3031 and 4064. (Moral 2: Dump the powder from your measure back into the correct, *clearly labeled* can as soon as you've finished loading!)

Excess pressure isn't the only rifle wrecker. Normal operating pressures of 50 to 55,000 psi (crusher gauge) can splinter a rifle, if turned loose by a head separation, resulting from excess headspace. If a rimless cartridge is too short for its chamber by as little as .020, the firing pin will drive it forward to solid shoulder contact, then set off the primer. Pressure pushes case walls aganist the chamber where they cling. The case head retreats to the bolt face as pressure mounts, pulling free from the body of the case. 50,000-plus psi will wrench and tear at steel and wood, never intended to withstand such an onslaught.

Excess headspace can result from a sizing die screwed down until it sets the case shoulder back too far. Well made dies, mated with same-make shell holders, should not allow this

The author's reloading bench. Convenient layout offers speed and minimum of confusion. Tools, left to right rear: Akro-Mills steel cabinet for holding dies; Fitz cartridge boxes; Lyman Spar-T turret tool; Lyman-Ohaus D-5 scale, with RCBS Powder Dripper. In front, C-H Armory case trimmer; Wilson case gauge; vernier caliper for checking case length; C-H chamfering tool; plastic loading block; RCBS lube and lube pad; Fitz Flipper with primers; Lyman 55 powder measure.

to happen, but some dies are too short for some rifle chambers. Forcing a Mauser-style extractor over a case rim instead of feeding ammo from the magazine can push a cartridge forward

hard enough to shorten it and cause headspace. Some bolt actions, especially old military rifles, have considerable end play. Hurriedly slamming a round into the chamber can actually "resize" it, to the extent that the bolt can move forward before encountering the barrel, again setting up dangerous headspace.

The most methodical experimentation is for naught if the data are not dutifully recorded. Even a superior memory is a poor reference for technical detail. In the long run, record keeping saves many hours of aggravation. My own method is a simple card file, broken down by calibers and bullet weight. Each 5"x7" *caliber* card lists case length, maximum cartridge length, and shell holder numbers for my various tools. Following *load* cards, subdivided according to bullet weight, list caliber, case brand, bullet weight, brand, style and lot. Below is listed chronographed velocity, date taken, temperature, benchrest accuracy, rifle used and wind conditions. I label all boxes with the labels included in bullet packages, or the excellent and detailed gummed labels available.

For final advice: Gather a library of reloading manuals. Besides the Speer and Hodgdon books, Lyman, Norma and Pacific all publish clear, informative manuals. The new *Hornady Handbook of Cartridge Reloading* boasts a section, devoted to ballistics tables, that is alone worth the $3.50 price of admission! These comprehensive tables enable direct comparisons of velocity, energy, drop and trajectory for all calibers and bullet weights made by Hornady. Tables for over 7,600 loads are among the most complete and easy to follow that I have seen. ●

VARMINT LOAD CHART

Powder/grs.	Bullet/grs.	MV/fps	Powder/grs.	Bullet/grs.	MV/fps
Caliber 222 Remington			50.6/N204	75/Norma HP	3650
25/BL-C(2)	50/Speer SP	3309	47.7/N204	90/Norma HP	3300
24/BL-C(2)	55/Speer SP	3187	41/4895	75/Speer HP	3400
Caliber 222 Remington Magnum			41/4895	80/Speer SP	3368
26.4/4064	50/Horn. Sp.P.	3400	39/4895	90/Speer SP	3234
26.2/4064	55/Horn. Sp.P.	3300	**Caliber 240 Page Super Pooper**		
25.5/3031	55/Sierra SP	3350	48/4350	85/Sierra HPBT	3446
Caliber 223 Armalite (5.56mm)			45/4350	100/Sierra SP	3191
29/H380	50/Speer SP	3113	**Caliber 243 Super Rockchucker**		
28/H335	50/Speer SP	3353	58/4831	85/Sierra SP	3708
27/H335	55/Speer SP	3238	55/4831	100/Sierra SP	3353
Caliber 225 Winchester			**Caliber 240 Weatherby Magnum**		
34/N203	50/Norma SP	3685	58.4/N205	70/Horn. Sp.P.	3850
33/N203	55/Norma SP	3500	55.2/N205	90/Norma SP	3500
33.5/4895	52/Speer HP	3776	54.2/N205	100/Norma SP	3395
33/4895	60/Horn. Sp.P.	3500	**Caliber 250 Savage**		
Caliber 22-250 Remington			33.7/3031	75/Horn. HP	3200
35.5/4895	50/Horn. Sp.P.	3800	38/4064	87/Speer SP	3210
34.4/4895	55/Horn. Sp.P.	3600	**Caliber 257 Roberts**		
34/4895	60/Horn. Sp.P.	3500	48/H380	75/Sierra HP	3563
33/3031	63/Sierra	3500	47/H380	87/Speer SP	3364
Caliber 224 Weatherby Magnum			**Caliber 25-06**		
31.5/3031	50/Speer SP	3827	61/4831	75/Sierra HP	3618
31/3031	52/Speer HP	3679	60/4831	87/Speer SP	3576
30.5/3031	55/Speer SP	3650	55.7/4831	100/Horn. Sp.P.	3300
31.3/4895	60/Horn. Sp. P.	3400	52.4/4831	117/Horn. RN	3000
Caliber 220 Swift			**Caliber 257 Weatherby**		
43.5/H380	50/Speer SP	3947	73/N205	87/Sierra SP	3750
42.5/H380	55/Speer SP	3839	71/N205	100/Horn. Sp.P.	3530
41/H380	63/Sierra SP	3580	69/N205	117/Sierra SP	3350
Caliber 243 Winchester			67/4831	120/Speer SP	3344
48/4831	80/W-W Power Pt.	3288	**Caliber 270 Winchester**		
45/4831	100/W-W Power Pt.	3104	54/4895	90/Sierra HP	3600
40.8/4064	75/Horn. HP	3400	**Caliber 308 Winchester**		
36.2/4064	87/Horn. Sp.P.	3100	62/4831	100/Speer HP	3370
Caliber 6mm Remington			43/4198	110/Sierra HP	3200
49/4831	85/Sierra HPBT	3318	**Caliber 30-06**		
46/4831	100/Sierra SP	3050	53/4320	130/Speer HP	3162
44.2/4320	75/Horn. HP	3500	57/4064	110/Sierra HP	3400
43.7/4320	87/Horn. Sp.P.	3300	54/4895	130/Horn. Sp.P.	3200

THE Winchester Model 70 is certainly one of the finest — if not the finest — production rifles ever made. As received, it adequately meets all requirements for normal use. Still, it is a production made product, hence doesn't have the nicety of hand adjustment a good rifle should have. Given that hand-touch here and there, your M70 will respond with noticeably better accuracy.

It has been my pleasure to "accurize" many M70's in various styles and yards, a two-inch circle at 200 yards, and so on. It means just this to you: since a two-minute rifle is capable of putting its shots into a 6-inch circle at 300 yards, your shot can be as much as three inches from point of aim in any direction. Moreover, there is a "holding" error too, which depends on the power of the scope and the ability of the marksman. If your holding error is two inches at 300 yards, and if the rifle is only capable of two-minute accuracy, it means you can miss your point of aim merely supports the sear. Pulling the trigger moves it out from under the sear, allowing the sear to be pushed down by the firing pin. In the military trigger, on the other hand, the sear and trigger are connected. Pressing the trigger pulls the sear down, allowing the firing pin to move forward. The M70 permits finer, easier adjustment.

Trigger Pull

The first step in adjusting the trig-

Tuning the M70 Winchester

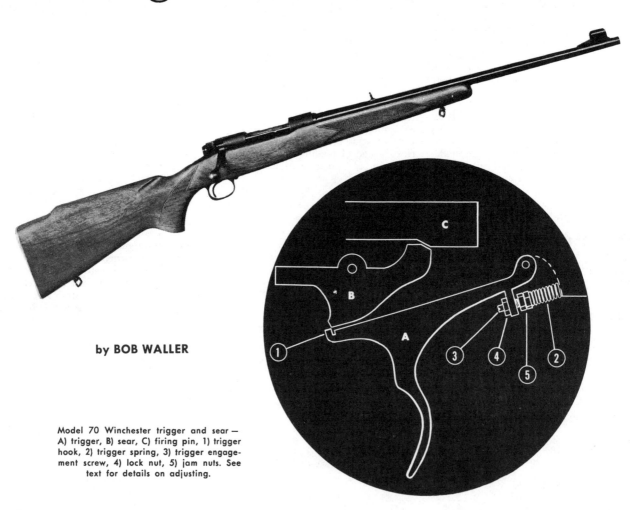

by BOB WALLER

Model 70 Winchester trigger and sear — A) trigger, B) sear, C) firing pin, 1) trigger hook, 2) trigger spring, 3) trigger engagement screw, 4) lock nut, 5) jam nuts. See text for details on adjusting.

calibers. Enough of these were targeted before tune-up to reveal that their accuracy standard was something over two minutes of angle. That's good enough for hunting calibers, perhaps, but not for precise shooting. Each of these rifles responded to the accurizing treatment sufficiently to shrink accuracy down to one minute of angle. "Minute of angle" means one inch for each 100 yards of range, thus a "one-minute rifle" is capable of putting all its shots into a one-inch circle at 100 by up to 5 inches at 300 yards. That's quite a bit even on a deer — and a clean miss on a chuck. The "one-minute rifle" will reduce the error of that rifle by about half.

You can improve your M70 considerably with a little effort. The chief items to correct are bedding and trigger pull. The M70 trigger is of simple and remarkable design, but those who assemble the rifles either don't know what constitutes a good trigger pull, or can't give it the time. The M70 trigger ger is to remove it from the rifle, being careful not to lose the trigger spring. The hook at the front of the trigger engages the sear (1) with a contacting surface of approximately 1/32-inch. This engagement should be reduced to nearly half by careful filing or grinding, being sure not to change the angle. Stone the newly ground surface with a hard Arkansas stone. Again, be very careful not to change angles, round edges or leave a burr at the corner. Before reassembling trigger to rifle, cut

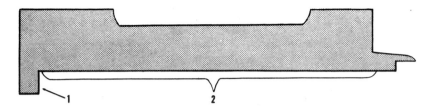

Model 70 receiver must be bedded tightly at rear of recoil lug (1) and all flat surfaces (2) on receiver bottom.

two full coils from the trigger spring (2). Place trigger and trigger spring back on rifle. With bolt closed and firing pin forward, turn trigger-stop screw (3) in until gap between trigger hook and sear is nearly closed. Because there must be room for both parts to move, use a piece of thin paper as a "feeler" gauge, turning the screw up until it just barely grips the paper. This adjustment must be exact, and if it is it removes all backlash. Check your work by cocking and firing. The trigger should not move past the point of release — you should feel no movement of the trigger. This trigger adjustment also must not prevent the sear from moving back into cocking position; it must move freely, without binding. Correct trigger adjustment gives the crisp, clean pull a trigger requires for best accuracy. When this screw is properly adjusted, secure it by turning up the lock-nut (4) tightly.

The two jam nuts (5) are next backed off to give the desired weight of pull. Turning the nuts in to squeeze the trigger spring makes the pull heavier, reduced spring pressure lightens the pull. Check the pull with a scale or weights and, when the desired pull is obtained, jam the nuts tightly together. The M70 trigger can be adjusted from about 2 pounds up safely. A pull of 3 to 4 pounds is about right for normal hunting use. When adjusted, the trigger pull must be checked for safety. Slam the bolt handle closed as smartly as possible; if the sear doesn't hold and the gun fires, you have a very dangerous condition. It can be corrected by putting more tension on the trigger spring. Be very sure that the rifle does not fire when this test is performed. Next, make sure the safety operates normally, and it will if you have followed these instructions. To check: cock the rifle, place safety ON, press the trigger, push safety OFF. If the rifle fires, you have not provided sufficient clearance between sear and trigger. Go back and readjust, being sure the paper moves freely between sear and trigger when firing pin is forward — there *must* be a slight clearance between these parts.

Stock Bedding

The stock bedding on M70 rifles also leaves something to be desired. Most stocks have a gap between the receiver recoil lug and the stock, whereas this lug should bear tightly. Yet the rifles shoot quite well "as is" because the three guard screws hold the generous, flat, bottom-of-receiver surfaces very tightly against the wood. The performance, whatever it is, can be improved by using one of the glass fiber bedding preparations. Use this material only behind the recoil lug. Tighten all three guard screws strongly at first, then experiment with the middle screw as you shoot — sometimes a looser setting of this screw works best.

Winchester usually removes too much wood from the barrel channel for best accuracy. It has been my experience that most M70's shoot best when the last couple of inches of the fore-end bear firmly against the barrel. The remainder of the barrel should be free of contact with the stock or "free-floating."

Free-floating barrels generally don't touch the barrel channel anywhere — with quite heavy barrels the inch or two in front of the receiver is frequently bedded, the idea being to prevent the barrel sagging. Some rifles shoot best free-floating, some don't. I've always felt it best to bed carefully first (which the scanty M70 wood doesn't always allow) and, if this fails to give accuracy, try free-floating. This procedure cannot be reversed, so always try bedding first. Your barrel is not free-floated just because you can

slide a dollar bill between wood and metal. Many shooters are under this false impression. Rifle weight alone is enough to bend the stock, letting the wood and barrel touch, when resting the rifle on its fore-end. All barrels, too, whip and vibrate in firing if the clearance between wood and metal is not ample. Such bedding is far worse than none at all, and good accuracy cannot be obtained. If you free-float, allow at least 1/16-inch clearance all the way around the barrel.

Here's how to tell whether your barrel touches your stock and where it bears: coat the barrel lightly with lampblack (lipstick works well, too!), place barreled action in stock and tighten all guard screws. Now tap receiver ring smartly with a plastic or rawhide mallet. Remove barreled action, then scrape or rasp all contact points to clean wood except the front two inches of the barrel channel. Recoat barrel and test again. In "standard" rifles with fore-end screw, remove and discard the screw and its stud.

You may now have enough fore-end pressure, without shimming, but only shooting will tell you. Super Grade M70's were made with black plastic fore-end tips, hence the two inches of bearing I've suggested should be behind the tip. This plastic tip might loosen under recoil.

Now it's time to shoot, and all shooting is done from a steady bench rest with a scope sight. Three-shot groups are ample. More than three quick shots in a light hunting rifle will cause rapid warming, accompanied by a loss of accuracy not attributable to the rifle. Seldom, if ever, are more than three shots at one time required when hunting.

If accuracy is erratic, you may need additional fore-end pressure. The easiest and fastest way to determine this is to insert small pieces of cardboard (such as business cards), between the barrel and the fore-end tip. Try one thickness of card, then two or more if necessary. You'll discover that the right pressure will vastly improve accuracy.

Once you've got the right pressure, a piece of gasket material of the same thickness as your shim(s) may be glued in place, or bedding compound may be used. The cardboard itself, of course, may be left there.

Model 70 stocks exert heavy pressure on barrel at front 2" of barrel channel on all styles of rifle. Barrel channel should be relieved from here back. In many rifles, shims will have to be inserted.

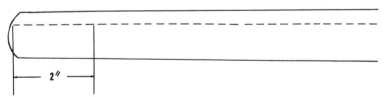

These tuning operations apply to all M70's, bull gun to featherweight. And may I say just a word about the 70 featherweight? It shoots just as accurately as the standard weight for three shots, and it's a much handier rifle to carry or to pack on the trail. I have yet to see a featherweight 70, in any caliber, that won't put a three-shot group in one inch at 100 yards after tuning as outlined here. Moreover, it's as light in weight as a powerful bolt action rifle should be made. ⊕

EXPLODED VIEWS

Completely Detailed Drawings of Famous Firearms

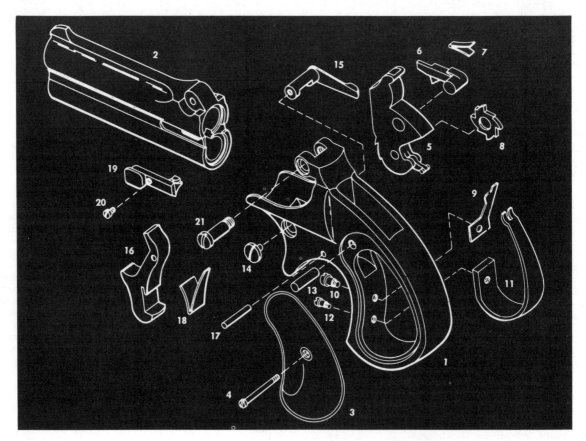

Parts List
1. Frame
2. Barrels
3. Grips (2)
4. Grip Screw
5. Hammer with Stirrup & Stirrup Pin
6. Firing Pin
7. Firing Pin Spring
8. Firing Pin Ratchet
9. Firing Pin Ratchet Spring
10. Firing Pin Ratchet Spring Screw
11. Mainspring
12. Mainspring Screw
13. Hammer Pin
14. Barrel Lock Screw
15. Barrel Lock
16. Trigger
17. Trigger Pin
18. Trigger Spring
19. Ejector
20. Ejector Screw
21. Barrel Hinge Screw

REMINGTON DOUBLE DERRINGER
Caliber 41 Rimfire

Disassembly—Push barrel lock (15) to forward position and swing barrels up. Check chambers to be sure they are not loaded. Remove barrel hinge screw (21) and barrels (2) from frame (1). Remove ejector screw (20) and slide ejector (19) from slot in barrels. Remove grip screw (4) and grips. Cock hammer (5). Place screwdriver between mainspring (11) and inside of frame to maintain tension. Release hammer slowly and disengage mainspring from hammer stirrup. Unscrew mainspring and firing pin ratchet spring screws (10,12) and remove mainspring and firing pin ratchet spring (10) from frame. Drift out hammer pin (13) and remove hammer from frame. Firing pin ratchet (8), firing pin and spring (6,7) can then be removed from hammer. Hammer stirrup is not normally removed from hammer except for replacement. Barrel lock (15) is removed by unscrewing barrel lock screw (14). Trigger (16) and spring (18) are removed by drifting out trigger pin (17).

BELGIAN BROWNING
Hi-Power 9mm

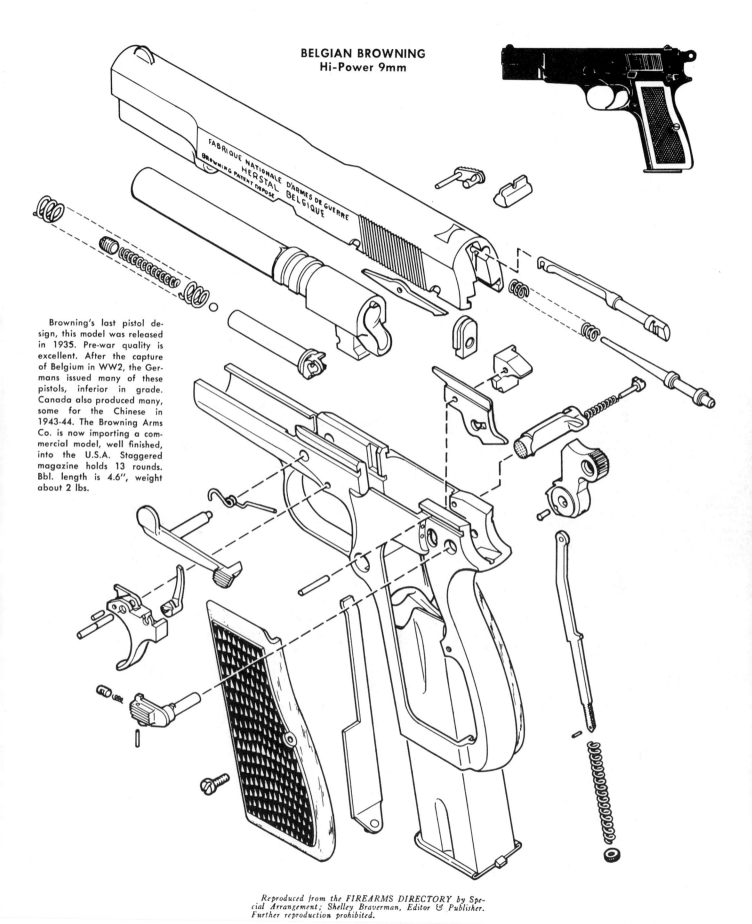

Browning's last pistol design, this model was released in 1935. Pre-war quality is excellent. After the capture of Belgium in WW2, the Germans issued many of these pistols, inferior in grade. Canada also produced many, some for the Chinese in 1943-44. The Browning Arms Co. is now importing a commercial model, well finished, into the U.S.A. Staggered magazine holds 13 rounds. Bbl. length is 4.6", weight about 2 lbs.

FABRIQUE NATIONALE D'ARMES DE GUERRE
HERSTAL BELGIQUE
BROWNING PATENT DEPOSE

REMINGTON AUTOMATIC, Model 51

32 and 380 auto calibers. Overall length, 6½"; barrel length, 3½". Weight, unloaded, 21 oz.

The Remington pocket automatics—the Model 51—and the famous Remington 45 experimental were products of the imagination of J. D. Pedersen, one of the more brilliant arms designers of a century of giants in this field.

The Model 51 entered the line some time shortly after the close of World War I. Precisely when the idea for this pistol was born is hard to determine: Pedersen's basic patent on this arm was filed for on July 30, 1915, and a revised application was filed July 17, 1919; the patent issued August 3, 1920, and was numbered 1,348,733 ("Remington Handguns," Karr and Karr). Several additional patents on the arm were granted in the same year. (An improved ejector was patented in 1924, #1,518,612.)

The Model 51 stayed in the line until 1934. It is generally conceded to have been one of the best pocket automatic, particularly in the design of the grip; the company advertised that "It rests in your palm like the hand of a friend." *Allen P. Wescott and Roger Marsh.*

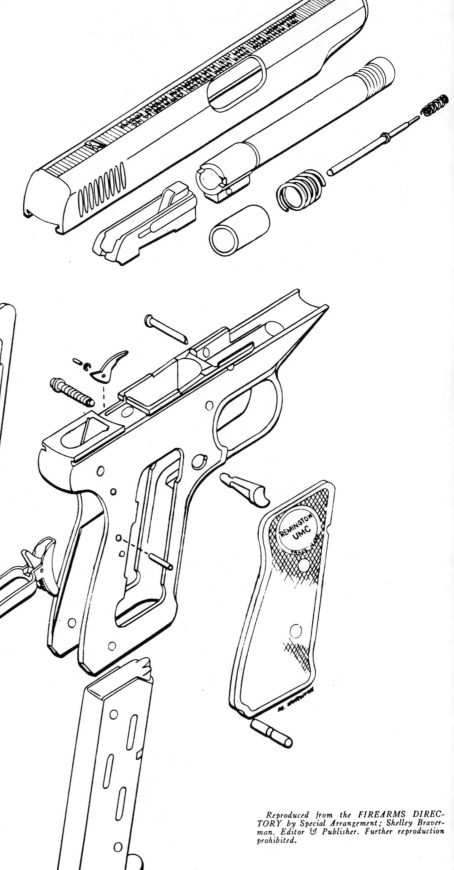

© Firearms Directory

ENFIELD (Model 1917) Cal. 30-06

Developed from British Service Rifles which were being produced in the U.S.A. during World War I, as enough 1903
Springfields could not be made fast enough. The 1917 Enfield
has a 26" bbl. and is 46¼" overall. The D.C.M. disposed of
thousands of these between the wars, and many were converted
to sporters.

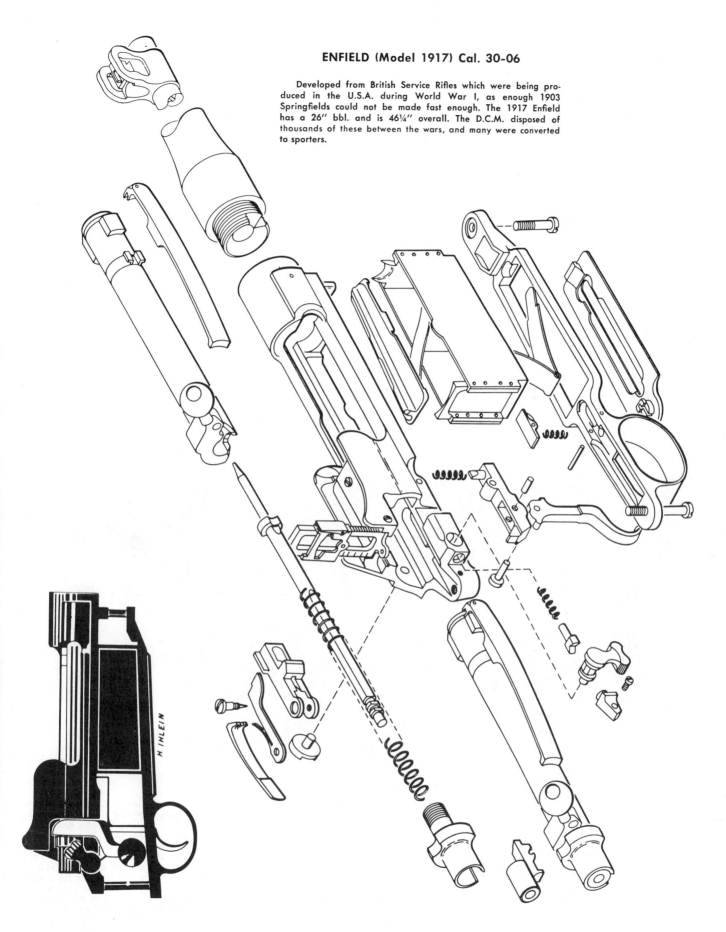

H. IHLEIN

REMINGTON MODEL 1890 FRONTIER REVOLVER

Only slightly over 2000 of the 1890 Remington Frontiers were made, the last of the great line of Remington six shooters. The Model 1890 is identical to the earlier Model 1875 Remington except for the lower contour of the web under the ejector housing, which is cut away in the Model 1890. All parts are interchangeable in both models except where barrels or cylinders are of different caliber. (Model 1875 was made in 44 Remington Center Fire, 44–40, and 45, while Model 1890 was made in 44–40 only.)

Drawing and text by James M. Triggs

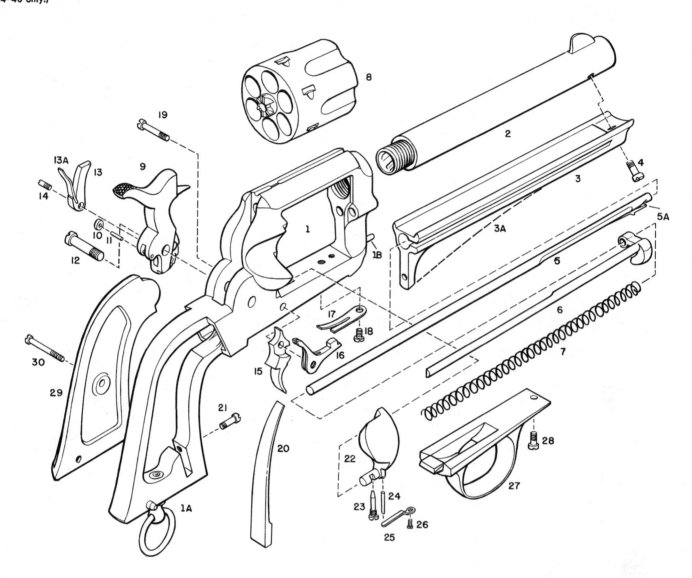

Parts List

1. Mainframe	9. Hammer
1a. Lanyard Swivel Ring Assembly	10. Hammer Roll
1b. Ejector Housing Stud	11. Hammer Roll Pin
2. Barrel	12. Hammer Screw
3. Ejector Housing	13. Hand
3a. Ejector Housing for model 1875	13a. Hand Spring
4. Ejector Housing Screw	14. Hand Stud
5. Base Pin	15. Trigger
5a. Base Pin Catch Spring	16. Bolt
6. Ejector Rod	17. Trigger & Bolt Spring
7. Ejector Spring	18. Trigger & Bolt Spring Screw
8. Cylinder	19. Trigger & Bolt Screw

20. Mainspring	
21. Strain Screw	
22. Gate	
23. Gate Retaining Screw	
24. Gate Plunger	
25. Gate Plunger Spring	
26. Gate Plunger Spring Screw	
27. Trigger Guard	
28. Trigger Guard Screw	
29. Grips (2)-hard rubber	
(model 1875, wood)	
30. Grip Screw	

Disassembly Procedure—Remove the grips. Depress the base pin catch spring (5a) and draw the base pin (5) out as far as it will come. Open the gate (22) and withdraw cylinder from the frame. The ejector housing (3), rod (6) and spring (7) can be removed after unscrewing ejector housing screw (4). Remove trigger guard, unscrew trigger and bolt spring screw (18) and spring (17). The trigger (15) and bolt (16) may be removed after unscrewing their pivot screw (19). Loosen strain screw (21) and drive mainspring (20) out gently from the left side of the frame. Remove hammer screw (12) and ease hammer down in the frame until the hand stud (14) protrudes beneath bottom edge of frame. Unscrew stud and draw hand down out of its slot in the frame, pull hammer up and out of frame. Reassemble in reverse order.

SMITH & WESSON COMBAT MASTERPIECE REVOLVER

Drawing and text by James M. Triggs

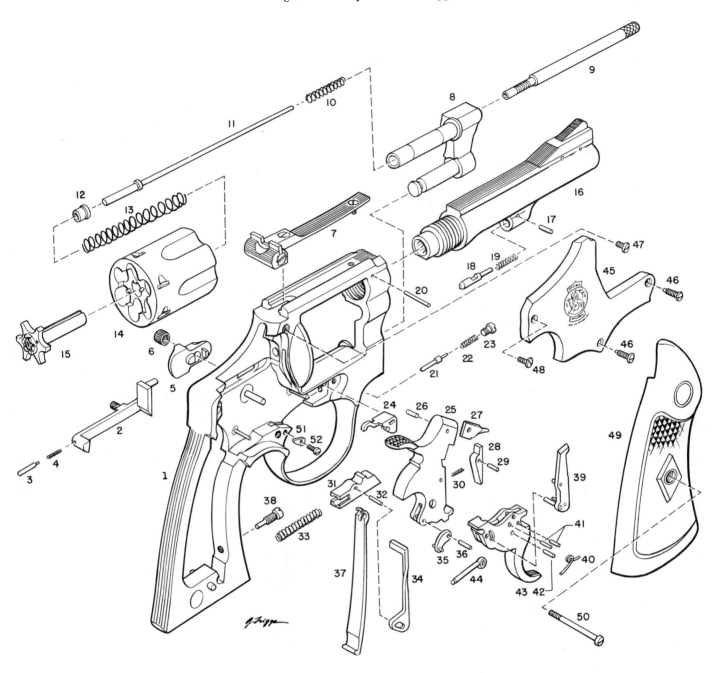

Disassembly Procedure—for the Combat Masterpiece revolver is identical to that followed for the S&W 44 Magnum. This revolver is built on the same frame as the popular K22 and K38 Masterpiece Target revolvers and interior lock parts are the same. In the Combat Masterpiece chambered for the 22 Long Rifle cartridge and in the K22 Masterpiece revolver, the firing pins are inset within the frame and both arms are supplied with a flat hammer. Parts listed here are for the 38 Spec. Combat Masterpiece. The rear sight assembly is shown completely assembled here, see the 44 Magnum view for disassembly.

   *Early production guns had four sideplate screws; currently, only three are used.

Parts List
1. Frame
2. Bolt
3. Bolt Plunger
4. Bolt Plunger Spring
5. Thumbpiece
6. Thumbpiece Nut
7. Rear Sight Assembly, complete (see .44 Mag.)
8. Yoke
9. Extractor Rod
10. Center Pin Spring
11. Center Pin
12. Extractor Rod Collar
13. Extractor Spring
14. Cylinder
15. Extractor
16. Barrel

17. Locking Bolt Pin
18. Locking Bolt
19. Locking Bolt Spring
20. Barrel Pin
21. Cylinder Stop Plunger
22. Cylinder Stop Plunger Spring
23. Cylinder Stop Screw
24. Cylinder Stop
25. Hammer
26. Hammer Nose Rivet
27. Hammer Nose
28. Sear
29. Sear Pin
30. Sear Spring
31. Rebound Slide
32. Rebound Slide Pin
33. Rebound Slide Spring
34. Hammer Block

35. Hammer Stirrup
36. Hammer Stirrup Pin
37. Mainspring
38. Strain Screw
39. Hand
40. Hand Torsion Spring
41. Hand Torsion Spring Pins (2)
42. Trigger Lever Pin
43. Trigger
44. Trigger Lever
45. Sideplate
46. Sideplate Screws (2)
47. Large Head Sideplate Screw*
48. Flat Head Sideplate Screw
49. Grips (2)
50. Grip Screw
51. Trigger Stop
52. Trigger Stop Screw

TYPICAL PENNSYLVANIA ("KENTUCKY") FLINTLOCK RIFLE

Parts List
1. Barrel
2. Front Sight
3. Rear Sight
4. Barrel Lugs
5. Side Plate
6. Side Screws
7. Tang Screw
8. Breech Plug
9. Butt Plate
10. Butt Plate Screws
11. Toe Plate Screws
12. Toe Plate
13. Patch Box Assembly
14. Patch Box Screws
15. Stock (shown partially)
16. Thimbles
17. Escutcheons
18. Barrel Wedges
19. Fore-end Tip
20. Fore-end Tip Pin
21. Ramrod
22. Lock, complete
23. Trigger
24. Trigger Pin
25. Trigger Guard
26. Trigger Guard Pins
27. Lock Plate
28. Sear
29. Sear Spring
30. Sear Spring Screw
31. Sear Screw
32. Bridle
33. Bridle Screw
34. Tumbler
35. Tumbler Screw
36. Hammer
37. Top Jaw
38. Bolt
39. Frizzen Spring
40. Frizzen Screw
41. Frizzen Spring Screw
42. Frizzen
43. Mainspring
44. Mainspring Screw
45. Pan

Because of the varied designs and the many makers of Pennsylvania flintlock rifles, there are hundreds of minor variations in detail. The drawing shows a typical rifle and the procedure outlined will be generally suitable for all early American flintlocks.

Disassembly—In taking these rifles apart, be especially careful of marring the finish or damaging the stock. Take pains with respect to removing screws and driving out wedges or pins, using good quality gunsmith screwdrivers of proper size, and punches or drift pins which fit the pins to be driven out. Judicious use of a good grade of penetrating oil will help to move old parts which may bind from rust or age.

To remove the complete lock, put the hammer at half cock and unscrew the side screws (6) partially. Tapping the heads of these screws gently will loosen the lock plate from its seat in the stock. Unscrew the side screws completely and remove the lock intact. To dismount the lock, compress the mainspring (43) with a spring vise or heavy pliers and remove the mainspring screw (44). Some flintlock mainsprings do not have this screw but are retained in a slot in the lock plate much the same as the mainspring in the 1863 Springfield described elsewhere. Remove the sear spring

screw (30) and spring (29). Remove sear screw (31) and sear (28). Remove bridle screw (33) and bridle (32). Remove tumbler screw (35). Tumbler can usually be driven out of its seat in hammer (36) using a heavy punch or brass drift pin. Frizzen spring (39) is removed by unscrewing frizzen spring screw (41). Frizzen (42) can be removed by unscrewing the frizzen screw (40). Removal of the pan (45) from lock plate (27) is not recommended. Reassemble lock in reverse order.

Barrel (2) is removed from stock (15) by removing tang screw (7) and drifting out wedges (18). Some flintlocks employ pins instead of barrel wedges and the shape and number of escutcheons varies widely. It would be well, unless absolutely necessary for repair or replacement, to leave those parts inletted into the wood alone; the escutcheons, decorative inlays, patchbox, thimbles, fore-end tip, etc.

Butt plate (9), and toe plate (12) are easily removed by withdrawing the screws (10, 11). The trigger guard (25) is usually held into the stock with pins (26) which can be gently drifted out of the stock. Again, caution is in order. Some trigger guards have no pins whatever, being held up solely by tension from the tang screw, which is tapped into the trigger guard in some cases.

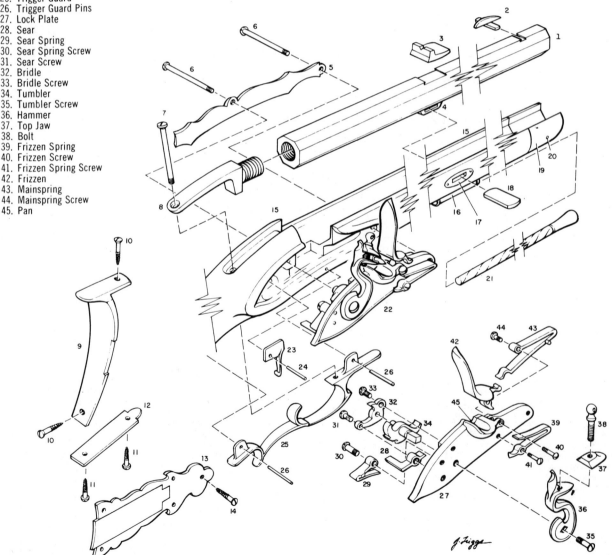

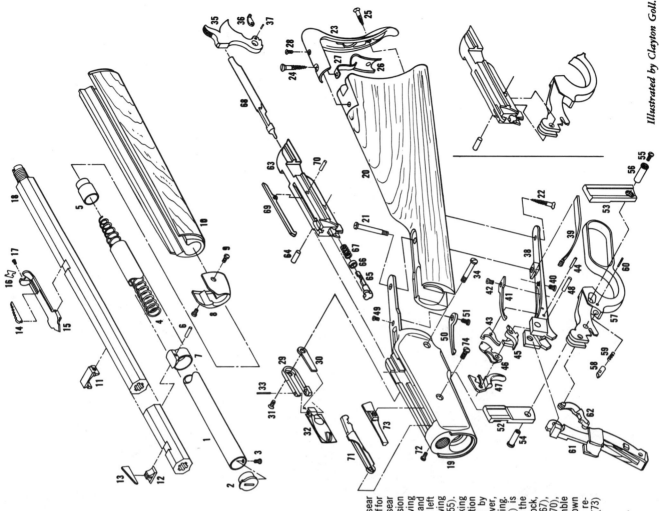

Illustrated by Clayton Goll.

Parts List

1. Mag. Tube
2. Mag. Muzzle Plug
3. Muzzle Plug Screw
4. Mag. Spring
5. Mag. Follower
6. Mag. Ring Pin
7. Mag. Ring
8. Fore-end Tip
9. Fore-end Tip and Tenon Screw (2)
10. Fore-end
11. Fore-end Tip Tenon
12. Front Sight Base
13. Front Sight
14. Rear Sight Elevator
15. Rear Sight
16. Elevation Leaf
17. Elevation Leaf Screw
18. Barrel
19. Receiver
20. Stock
21. Upper Tang Stock Screw
22. Lower Tang Stock Screw
23. Buttplate
24. Upper Buttplate Screw
25. Lower Buttplate Screw
26. Buttplate Slide
27. Buttplate Slide Spring
28. Buttplate Slide Spring Screw
29. Spring Cover Base
30. Spring Cover Screw
31. Spring Cover Spring
32. Spring Cover Leaf
33. Spring Cover Leaf Pin
34. Receiver Screw
35. Hammer
36. Stirrup
37. Stirrup Pin
38. Lower Tang
39. Mainspring
40. Mainspring Tension Screw
41. Sear and Trigger Spring
42. Sear and Trigger Spring Screw
43. Sear Catch
44. Sear Catch Pin
45. Sear
46. Kickoff for Set Trigger
47. Trigger
48. Trigger, Sear, and Kickoff Pin
49. Carrier Stop Tension Screw
50. Carrier Stop
51. Carrier Stop Screw
52. Locking Bolt R.H. side
53. Locking Bolt L.H. side
54. Finger Lever Pin
55. Bushing and Pin Screw
56. Finger Lever Pin Bushing
57. Finger Lever
58. Friction Stud
59. Friction Stud Spring
60. Friction Stud Pin
61. Carrier
62. Carrier Hook
63. Breechblock
64. Lever and Breechblock Pin
65. Ejector
66. Ejector Collar
67. Ejector Spring
68. Firing Pin
69. Extractor
70. Extractor Pin
71. Cartridge Guide
72. Cartridge Guide Screw
73. Cartridge Stop
74. Cartridge Stop Screw

WINCHESTER MODEL 1886

Disassembly—To remove magazine (1), take out mag. muzzle plug (2) by removing mag. plug screw (3), lift out mag. spring (4) and follower (5). Press mag. ring pin (6) from ring (7). Pull toward muzzle to remove mag. tube. Remove ring by turning to right or left. Remove fore-end tip (8) by removing two fore-end screws (9). Remove the fore-end (10). Press out fore-end tip tenon (11). Remove front sight base (12) and front sight (13). Remove rear sight elevator (14), rear sight (15) and elevation leaf (16) by turning elevation leaf screw (17). Unscrew barrel (18) from receiver (19). To disassemble stock (20), remove upper (21) and lower (22) tang screws. Remove buttplate (23) by removing the upper (24) and lower (25) buttplate screw, remove buttplate slide (26) by removing (27) slide spring screw (28).

Disassembly of the receiver consists of removing spring cover base (29) and spring (30) by removing screw (31). To remove spring cover leaf (32), drive out the leaf and base pin (33). Remove receiver screw (34) and lift hammer (35), stirrup (36), and stirrup pin (37) out thru the upper tang hammer slot. The lower tang (38) drops down and out with a set trigger assembly which includes the mainspring (39), mainspring tension screw (40), and sear and trigger spring (41), sear and trigger spring screw (42), sear catch (43), sear catch pin (44), sear (45), kickoff for set trigger (46), trigger (47), and the trigger, sear and kickoff pin (48). Remove carrier stop tension screw (49). Remove carrier stop (50) by removing stop screw (51). Pull down finger lever (57) and using two screwdrivers, remove the right and left hand locking bolts (52) and (53) by unscrewing finger lever pin (54) and bushing pin screw (55). Remove finger lever pin bushing (56), pull locking bolts down and out. The finger lever has a friction stud (58), friction stud spring-(59), removed by driving out friction stud pin (60). The finger lever, carrier (61) and carrier hook (62) are interlocking. Drop finger lever down until breechblock (63) is backed out of receiver far enough to drive out the lever and breechblock pin (64). Pull breechblock, ejector (65), ejector collar (66), ejector spring (67), firing pin (68), extractor (69) and extractor pin (70), out of the receiver as one assembly. Disassemble the breechblock in numbered sequence as shown on drawing. Remove cartridge guide (71) by removing guide screw (72). Remove ctge. stop (73) by removing ctge. stop screw (74).

For assembly, reverse the above procedure.

WINCHESTER

MODEL 94

CARBINE

Designed by John M. Browning, and introduced in 1894, the famous 94 Winchester, originally offered in 32-40 and 38-55, both black powder loads, was the first American sporting repeating rifle adapted (via nickel steel barrels in August, 1895) to handle smokeless powder cartridges. The action incorporated the use of new steel alloys, and the barrels were made on newly designed rifle-barrel drilling tools.

In 1895 the Winchester 30 (30-30) and the 25-35 smokeless powder loads were added to the line, and in 1902 the Model 94 was chambered for the 32 Winchester Special cartridge.

The 30-30 cartridge (30 grains of smokeless powder and a 170-grain bullet) soon became the most popular hunting cartridge in the nation, especially in the West, where the combination of a cartridge power-ful enough for deer at moderate ranges and the light (6½ lbs.) Model 94 carbine began to replace the heavier and shorter-range 73 and 86 Winchesters.

That the 94 Winchester is one of the most popular sporting firearms is evidenced by its fantastic production. The total production of this rifle should soon be approaching the 3,000,000 mark. Number 2,000,000 carbine was presented to President Dwight D. Eisenhower in 1953.

While the 20″ barrel carbine is still in production in 30-30 and 32 Winchester Special carbines, 26″ barrel sporting rifles were produced with round, octagon and semi-octagon barrels in standard and "Fancy" grades, many with engraving and precious metal inlays; some were made in take-down style with the barrel, fore-end and magazine detachable from the action and buttstock.

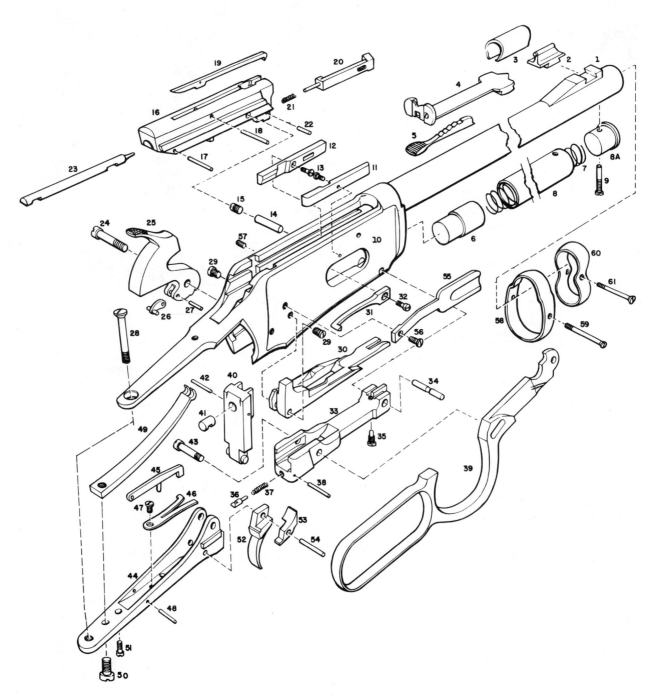

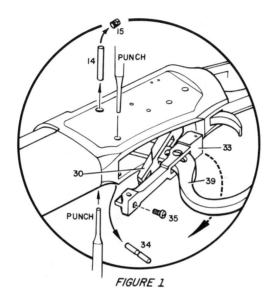

FIGURE 1

Disassembly—To take action down, unscrew upper tang screw (28) and remove buttstock to rear, jarring loose with the hand if necessary. Unscrew finger lever pin stop screw (15) from receiver and drive out finger lever pin (14) with a punch as shown in Figure 1. Remove link pin stop screw (35) and drive out link pin (34). Remove finger lever (39) and link (33) out bottom of receiver as shown also in Figure 1. Unscrew carrier screws (29) from right and left sides of receiver. Drop carrier (30) out bottom of receiver. Remove mainspring screw (50) and mainspring (49) and hammer screw (24). Hold safety catch (45) up and, while pulling back on trigger, remove hammer (25) as shown in Figure 2. Lower tang (44) may be driven out to rear of receiver. Remove locking bolt (40) and breech bolt (16) from receiver as shown in Figure 3. Unscrew spring cover screw (56) and cover (55). Remove carrier spring screw and spring (32, 31).

To remove magazine assembly, unscrew magazine plug screw (9) and plug (8a). Withdraw spring (7) and follower (6) from magazine tube. Remove front and rear band screws (59, 61) and slide fore-end and rear band up on barrel to the front and loosen rear band from fore-end. Magazine tube (8) can now be pulled from its seat in the receiver. Reassemble in reverse order.

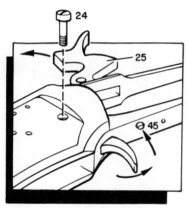

FIGURE 2

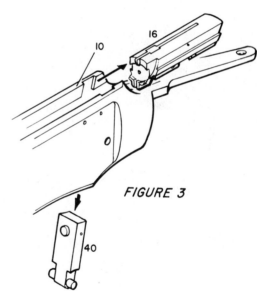

FIGURE 3

Parts List

1. Barrel	16. Breech Bolt	33. Link	50. Mainspring Screw
2. Front Sight	17. Firing Pin Stop Pin	34. Link Pin	51. Mainspring Strain Screw
3. Front Sight Cover	18. Extractor Pin	35. Link Pin Stop Screw	52. Trigger
4. Rear Sight	19. Extractor	36. Friction Stud	53. Sear
5. Rear Sight Elevator	20. Ejector	37. Friction Stud Spring	54. Sear Pin
6. Magazine Follower	21. Ejector Spring	38. Friction Stud Stop Pin	55. Spring Cover
7. Magazine Spring	22. Ejector Stop Pin	39. Finger Lever	56. Spring Cover Screw
8. Magazine Tube	23. Firing Pin	40. Locking Bolt	57. Peep Sight Plug Screw
8a. Magazine Plug	24. Hammer Screw	41. Firing Pin Striker	58. Rear Band
9. Magazine Plug Screw	25. Hammer	42. Firing Pin Striker Stop Pin	59. Rear Band Screw
10. Receiver	26. Hammer Stirrup	43. Finger Lever Link Screw	60. Front Band
11. Cartridge Guide, right	27. Hammer Stirrup Pin	44. Lower Tang	61. Front Band Screw
12. Cartridge Guide, left	28. Upper Tang Screw	45. Safety Catch	
13. Cartridge Guide Screws (2)	29. Carrier Screws (2)	46. Sear and Safety Catch Spring	
14. Finger Lever Pin	30. Carrier	47. Sear & Safety Catch Spring Screw	Note: For clarity, buttstock, buttplate,
15. Finger Lever Pin Stop Screw	31. Carrier Spring	48. Safety Catch Pin	screws and fore-end are omitted in the
	32. Carrier Spring Screw	49. Mainspring	drawing.

ERFURT LUGER, 1918 (M-1914)

Parts List

1. Frame
2. Magazine
3. Magazine Pin
4. Magazine Base
5. Mag. Spring Holder
6. Mag. Spring
7. Mag. Follower
8. Follower Button
9. Grip (2)
10. Grip Screw (2)
11. Locking Bolt
12. Trigger Plate
13. Trigger Lever
14. Trigger Lever Pin
15. Barrel
16. Front Sight
17. Receiver
18. Rear Toggle Pin
19. Rear Toggle Link
20. Front Toggle Link
21. Breechblock
22. Coupling Link
23. Coupling Link Pin
24. Rear Toggle Stop Pin
25. Rear Toggle Pin
26. Breechblock Pin
27. Firing Pin Spring Guide
28. Firing Pin Spring
29. Firing Pin
30. Extractor
31. Extractor Spring
32. Extractor Pin
33. Ejector
34. Trigger Bar
35. Trigger Bar Plunger
36. Plunger Spring
37. Plunger Pin
38. Trigger Bar Spring
39. Trigger
40. Trigger Rebound Spring
41. Mag. Button Spring
42. Mag. Release Button
43. Safety Catch
44. Safety Bar
45. Safety Catch Pin
46. Hold Open Latch
47. Latch Spring
48. Locking Bolt Spring
49. Recoil Lever
50. Recoil Lever Pin
51. Mainspring Guide
52. Mainspring

Disassembly—Remove magazine and check chamber. To disassemble mag., drive pin (3) from base (4), lift out spring holder (5) and follower spring (6). Remove follower (7) by removing button (8).

Remove both grips (9) by removing grip screws (10). Press barrel against firm surface, moving barrel and receiver back on frame until tension is released on the recoil spring; turn locking bolt (11) clockwise to down position and remove trigger plate (12). To remove trigger lever (13), lift lever pin (14) and push out. To disassemble receiver, remove rear toggle receiver pin (18) and remove rear toggle link (19), forward toggle link (20), and breechblock (21) by sliding to the rear of receiver. Disassemble coupling link (22) by removing pin (23). If necessary, remove rear toggle pin stop pin (24). To disengage front and rear toggle links, press out the pin (25) to the right hand side. To disengage breechblock from forward toggle link, press out pin (26). The firing pin spring guide (27), firing pin spring (28), and

firing pin (29) may be removed with a screwdriver. Turn firing pin spring guide counterclockwise and remove from breechblock. Disassemble the breechblock extractor (30) and extractor spring (31) by pressing out extractor spring pin (32). Remove ejector (33) and trigger bar (34) from receiver. Remove trigger bar plunger (35) and spring (36) by pressing out trigger bar plunger pin (37). To disassemble the frame, press out trigger (39) and trigger spring (40) toward left side of the frame. Press inward and to rear on button catch spring (41) to free mag. release catch button (42). Disassemble safety catch (43) and safety bar (44) by removing safety catch pin (45). The safety catch pin may be moved either up and out or down. Lift out hold open latch (46) and remove spring (47). Lift out locking bolt spring (48). Remove recoil lever (49) by pressing out recoil lever pin (50) and lift out mainspring guide (51) and mainspring (52).

Reassemble in reverse order.

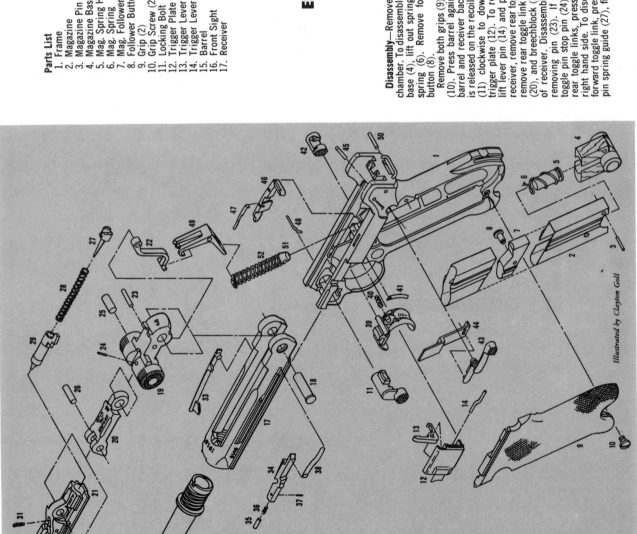

Illustrated by Clayton Goll

Parts List

S1	Barrel Plate Wood—right
S2	Barrel Plate Wood—left
S7	Barrel Plate Screw
S8	Buttplate
S9	Buttplate Screw
S10	Cocking Lever
S11	Cocking Lever Pin
S13	Cocking Lever Lifter
S14	Cocking Lever Lifter Pin
S16	Connector
S26	Connector Stop Pin
S29	Ejector—right
S30	Ejector—left
S31	Ejector Stop Screw
S32	Ejector Extension—right
S33	Ejector Extension—left
S34	Ejector Extension Stop Screw
S35	Ejector Hammer—right
S36	Ejector Hammer—left
S37	Ejector Hammer Pin
S38	Ejector Hammer Spring
S39	Ejector Hammer Spring Guide
S40	Ejector Hammer Sear
S41	Ejector Hammer Sear Spring
S42	Ejector Hammer Sear Pin
S43	Ejector Trip Rod—right
S44	Ejector Trip Rod—left
S50	Firing Pin—over
S51	Firing Pin—under
S53	Firing Pin Spring—under
S54	Firing Pin Retaining Pin
S67	Fore-end Bracket
S68	Hammer—right
S69	Hammer—left
S70	Hammer Pin
S72	Inertia Block
S73	Inertia Block Spring
S74	Inertia Block Spring Guide
S79	Locking Bolt
S81	Mainspring
S82	Mainspring Guide

S90	Selector, Safety
S92	Selector Block
S94	Selector Spring
S99	Sear—right
S100	Sear—left
S102	Sear Spring
S103	Sear Pin
S114	Stock Bolt
S116	Stock Bolt Washer
S117	Stock Bolt Lock Washer
S118	Take Down Lever
S119	Take Down Lever Pin
S120	Take Down Lever Latch
S121	Take Down Lever Latch Pin
S122	Take Down Lever Latch Spring
S125	Tang Piece
S126	Tang Piece Screw—top
S127	Tang Piece Screw—bottom
S128	Top Lever
S129	Top Lever Spring
S130b	Top Lever Spring Retainer
S131	Top Lever Spring Retainer Screw
S132	Top Lever Dog
S134	Top Lever Dog Screw
S138	Trigger
S142	Trigger Pin
S143	Trigger Piston
S144	Trigger Piston Pin
S145	Trigger Piston Spring
S147	Trigger Guard
S148	Trigger Guard Screw
S154	Trigger Spring

Disassembly—Remove fore-end and barrels. Remove one buttplate screw and loosen the other enough to swing buttplate aside. Remove stock bolt (S114) and washers (S116, S117) and remove buttstock by pulling straight back.

Remove mainsprings (S81) and guides (S82) by raising out of sockets in hammers (S68, S69); compress mainspring with screwdriver blade, at the same time exert pressure to slide guides off edge of hammers. Drive out trigger pin (S142); hold inertia block (S72) with one hand and pull trigger (S138) downward with the other; the inertia block can then be raised off the top of the connector (S16), and removed from receiver. Place thin knife blade under selector spring (S94), raising it out of the slot; rotate it one-quarter turn (right or left); this will permit removal of the selector safety (S90) and selector block (S92) as one unit. Remove top and bottom tang screws (S126, S127) and drive tang piece (S125) out from other side.

Remove hammer pin (S70) with drift punch, permitting both hammers to be removed from receiver. Using drift punch, remove ejector trips (S43, S44) pulling straight back. Drive both firing pin retaining pins (S54) out and remove firing pins, noting that the larger pin is in upper position. Remove top lever pin retaining screw (S131) and remove top lever spring retainer (S130b) and top lever spring (S129). With round end drift drive cocking lever pin (S11) from left to right. NOTE: in some cases taper runs opposite and pin must be driven out from right to left. Remove cocking lever (S10). Lift top lever up and draw locking bolt (S79) rearward out of receiver. Place a drift on either side of top lever dog (S132) and rotate on top lever dog screw (S134), clear the hole in the receiver and remove top lever (S128). Remove connector stop pin (S26) and remove connector (S16), piston (S143) and piston spring (S145) from trigger (S138). Reassemble in reverse order.

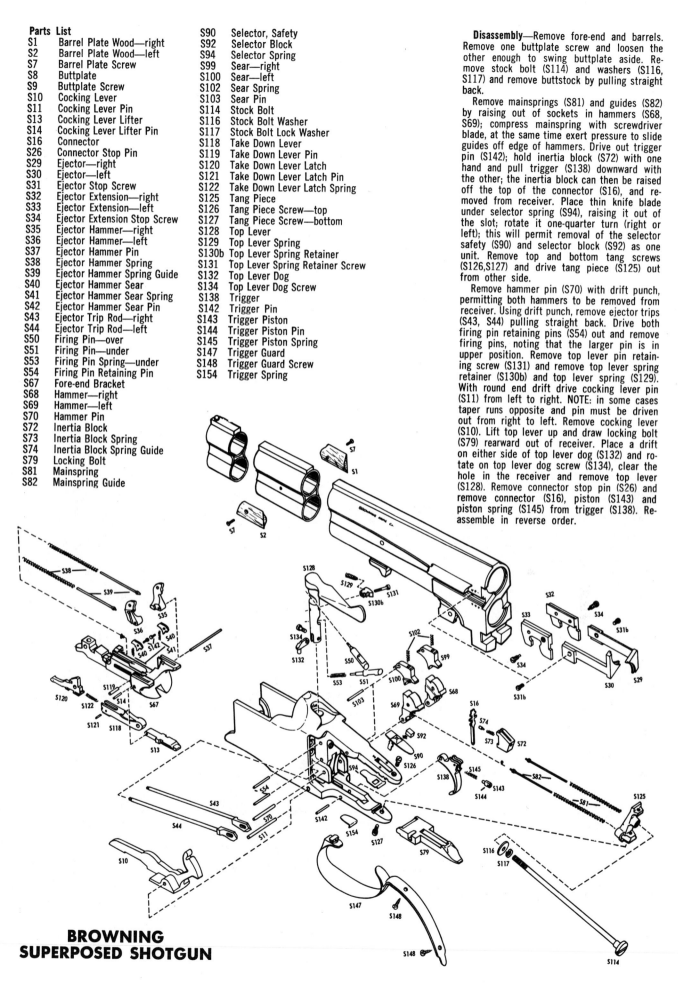

BROWNING
SUPERPOSED SHOTGUN

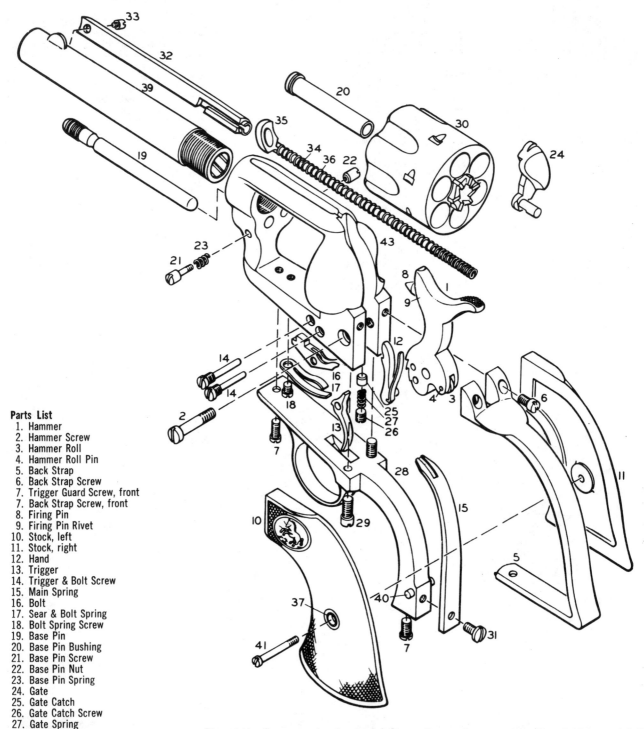

Parts List
1. Hammer
2. Hammer Screw
3. Hammer Roll
4. Hammer Roll Pin
5. Back Strap
6. Back Strap Screw
7. Trigger Guard Screw, front
7. Back Strap Screw, front
8. Firing Pin
9. Firing Pin Rivet
10. Stock, left
11. Stock, right
12. Hand
13. Trigger
14. Trigger & Bolt Screw
15. Main Spring
16. Bolt
17. Sear & Bolt Spring
18. Bolt Spring Screw
19. Base Pin
20. Base Pin Bushing
21. Base Pin Screw
22. Base Pin Nut
23. Base Pin Spring
24. Gate
25. Gate Catch
26. Gate Catch Screw
27. Gate Spring
28. Trigger Guard
29. Trigger Guard Screw, rear
30. Cylinder
31. Main Spring Screw
32. Ejector Tube
33. Ejector Tube Screw
34. Ejector Rod
35. Ejector Rod Head
36. Ejector Spring
37. Escutcheon
39. Barrel
40. Stock Pin
41. Stock Screw
43. Frame

Disassembly—Be sure revolver is unloaded. Open loading gate (24); remove base pin (19) and, with hammer (1) at half-cock position, remove cylinder (30) from right side of frame. On current models base pin is removed by pressing in spring-loaded base pin screw (21); on those revolvers below serial number 165,000, a screw on the front of the frame holds base pin in place.

Remove stock screw and stocks (41,10,11). Remove backstrap screws (6,7) and remove backstrap. Remove mainspring screw (31) and mainspring (15). Remove trigger guard (28) by unscrewing trigger guard screws (7,29). Remove bolt spring screw (18) and sear and bolt spring (17).

Remove hammer screw (2) and trigger and bolt screw (14); trigger (13), bolt (16) and hammer (1) with attached hand and spring (12) may now be taken from frame.

Loading gate (24), gate spring (27) and catch (25) are removed by unscrewing gate screw (26) located in underside of frame. Base pin screw (21), spring (23) and nut (22) may now be removed from frame. Remove ejector tube screw (33) and lift ejector tube (32) from barrel, pushing toward front of barrel to disengage from seat in frame. Ejector rod (34), rod head (35) and spring (36) may now be removed from tube. Reassemble in reverse order.

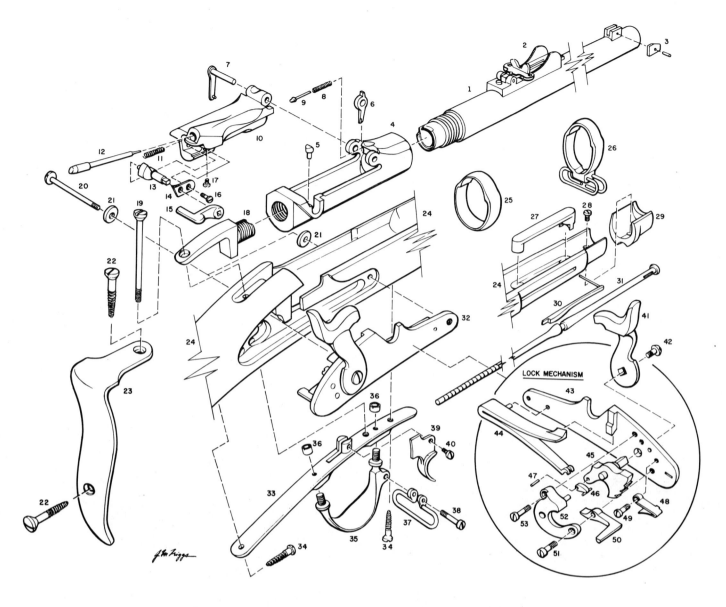

SPRINGFIELD RIFLE — MODEL 1873, 45-70

Disassembly—While there are a number of varieties and variations of the 45-70 Springfields, both in rifles and carbines, procedure for disassembly is generally the same for all. Remove the ramrod (31) and tang screw (19). Put the hammer at halfcock and remove the side screws (20). Remove the lock (32) intact from stock (24). Remove upper and lower bands (25 & 26) by pressing in on band springs (30) and pushing bands forward. Remove barrel and breech assembly intact from stock. To dismount the breech mechanism, remove hinge pin (7) and breech block (10) taking care not to allow extractor (6) and ejector spring (8) and spindle (9) to escape. Unscrew breech block cap screw (16) and remove cam latch (13) with thumb piece (15) and breech block cap (14) intact. Remove cam latch spring (11). Firing pin (12) may be removed by unscrewing firing pin screw (17) from underside of breech block. Trigger mechanism, buttplate and stock tip are all easily removed from stock (24) by removing the screws (22, 34, 28).

To dismount the lock mechanism, compress mainspring (44) with a mainspring vise or heavy pliers and remove from lock plate (43). Remove sear spring screw (49) and spring (48) from lock plate. Remove sear screw (51) and sear (50). Remove bridle screw (53) and bridle (52). Remove tumbler screw (42) from hammer (41). Tumbler (45) may be driven out of hammer with a large punch or brass drift pin. Reassemble in reverse order.

Parts List

1. Barrel
2. Rear Sight Assembly
3. Front Sight & Pin
4. Breech
5. Ejector Stud
6. Extractor
7. Hinge Pin
8. Ejector Spring
9. Spindle
10. Breech Block
11. Cam Latch Spring
12. Firing Pin
13. Cam Latch
14. Breech Block Cap
15. Thumb Piece
16. Breech Block Cap Screw
17. Firing Pin Screw
18. Breech Screw
19. Tang Screw
20. Side Screws (2)
21. Side Screw Washers (2)
22. Buttplate Screws (2)
23. Buttplate
24. Stock (shown partially)
25. Lower Band
26. Upper Band
27. Ramrod Stop
28. Stock Tip Screw
29. Stock Tip
30. Band Springs (2)
31. Ramrod
32. Lock, complete
33. Guard Plate
34. Guard Screws (2)
35. Guard Bow
36. Guard Bow Nuts (2)
37. Guard Bow Swivel
38. Guard Bow Swivel Screw
39. Trigger
40. Trigger Screw
41. Hammer
42. Tumbler Screw
43. Lock Plate
44. Mainspring
45. Tumbler
46. Mainspring Swivel (stirrup)
47. Mainspring Swivel Pin
48. Sear Spring
49. Sear Spring Screw
50. Sear
51. Sear Screw
52. Bridle
53. Bridle Screw

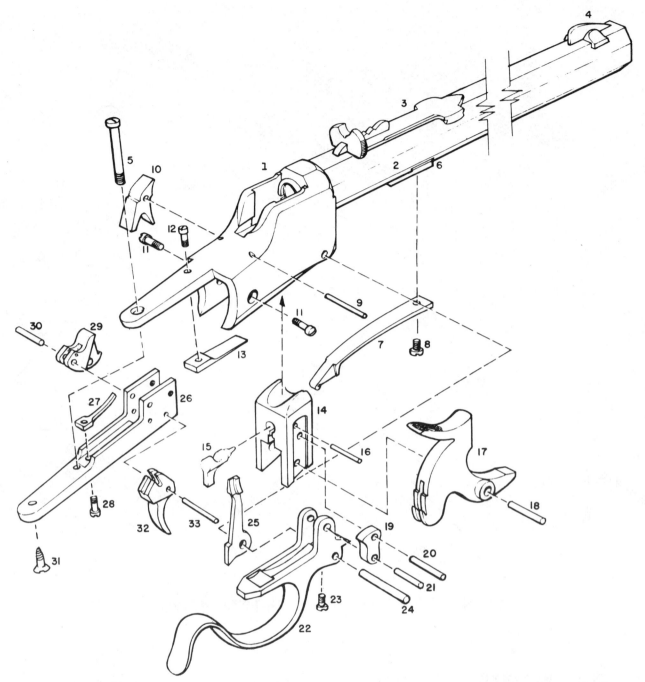

NOTES ON WINCHESTER SINGLE SHOTS

The Winchester Single Shot action was developed and patented (U.S. 220271, Oct. 7, 1879) by John M. Browning in Ogden, Utah. It has been reported that some 600 Browning single shots were made — which the relatively high serial numbers of the known specimens would validate — but against that is the undeniable fact that only a handful of Browning-made single shots exist. The few we do know about are mostly quite plain grade, though there is a fine specimen owned by the Browning Arms Company — figured wood, well-checkered on pistol grip and fore-end, etc.

In 1883 Winchester bought the manufacturing rights to the Browning single shot, the sale also purportedly including the stock of rifles Browning Brothers had on hand.

Winchester made some changes in the basic design to facilitate manufacture, the most obvious being the use of a separate lower tang instead of the integral tang used by Browning.

Over the many years it was made — 1885 to 1920 — the S.S. Winchester appeared in a great range of calibers and models. There were 15 or more rimfire versions alone, from the tiny 22 BB cap to the 44 Henry Flat, while the centerfires ran the gamut from the 22 Extra Long to the 577 Eley, through a total of some 70 different cartridges we know about, perhaps many more. Oddly, perhaps, Winchester's serial number 1 was in 50 Eley caliber!

"High Walls" and "Low Walls" were made, carbines with light 15-inch barrels were offered at the same time as heavy rifles with 36-inch barrels. Sporting and military models were made; plain and extra fancy, engraved grades were available, and total production was about 140,000 units. Parts continued to be available long after 1920, including quite a number of complete actions.

The variant form of the Winchester Single Shot shown on the next page (the property of Harry Siefried, gun designer of Southport, Conn.), is believed to have been an early Winchester toolroom model, perhaps pre-production. No numbers or other stampings appear, and the lever and lower part of the frame are pieced together — but very well-done — by brazing.

For further information on Winchester Single Shots see James J. Grant's "Single Shot Rifles" (New York, 1947) and "More Single Shot Rifles" (New York, 1959), and "The Winchester Book" (Dallas, Tex. 1961) by George Madis. See also Louis Ostendorp's two articles, "Winchester Single Shots" in the 9th ed. of the GUN DIGEST and the same author's "Browning's First Rifle," which appeared in the 10th ed. of the same annual.

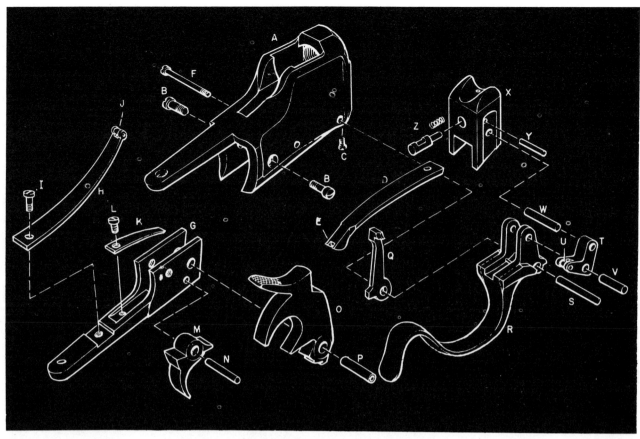

Variant form of the Winchester SS rifle.

WINCHESTER MODEL 1885 SINGLE SHOT RIFLES

Disassembly—Lower finger lever (22) and check action to be sure arm is unloaded. Remove fore-end screw from underside of fore-end and slide fore-end forward and off receiver (1). Remove mainspring screw (8) and mainspring (7) from underside of barrel (2). Loosen finger lever pin stop screw (23) and push finger lever pin (24) out of receiver. Finger lever with attached breechblock (14), hammer (17), link (19) and pins (20,21) may be pulled downward and out bottom of receiver. After removing breechblock, extractor (25) may be dropped out bottom of receiver. Separate these parts by drifting out the respective pins. Remove upper and lower tang screws (5, 31) and pull buttstock off to rear. Remove side tang screws (11) from each side wall of receiver and pull tang (26) out of bottom of receiver. Trigger (32), knockoff (29) and associated parts are easily removed from tang by drifting out their respective pins. Reassemble in reverse order.

Note—While several variations of the Model 1885 action may be encountered, the basic disassembly procedure remains the same.

Winchester Model 1885
Single Shot Rifle

Parts List

 1. Receiver
 2. Barrel
 3. Rear sight
 4. Front sight
 5. Upper tang screw
 6. Mainspring base
 7. Mainspring
 8. Mainspring screw
 9. Sear pin
10. Sear
11. Side tang screws (2)
12. Sear spring screw
13. Sear spring
14. Breechblock
15. Firing pin
16. Firing pin stop pin
17. Hammer
18. Hammer pin
19. Link
20. Link pin, long

21. Link pin, short
22. Finger lever
23. Finger lever pin stop screw
24. Finger lever pin
25. Extractor
26. Tang
27. Knock off spring
28. Knock off spring screw
29. Knock off
30. Knock off pin
31. Lower tang screw
32. Trigger
33. Trigger pin
Note — fore-end, fore-end screw, buttstock, buttplate and buttplate screws are not shown.

Winchester Model 1885
Rifle, a variation

Parts List

A. Receiver
B. Side tang screws (2)
C. Finger lever pin stop screw

D. Finger lever spring
E. Finger lever spring roller
F. Tang/receiver screw
G. Tang
H. Mainspring
I. Mainspring screw
J. Mainspring roller
K. Trigger spring
L. Trigger spring screw
M. Trigger & sear
N. Trigger pin
O. Hammer
P. Hammer pin (hollow to receive
    tang/receiver screw)
Q. Extractor
R. Finger lever
S. Finger lever pin
T. Link
U. Link roller
V. Link pin, short
W. Link pin, long
X. Breechblock
Y. Firing pin stop pin
Z. Firing pin & spring

Peabody-Martini Rifle

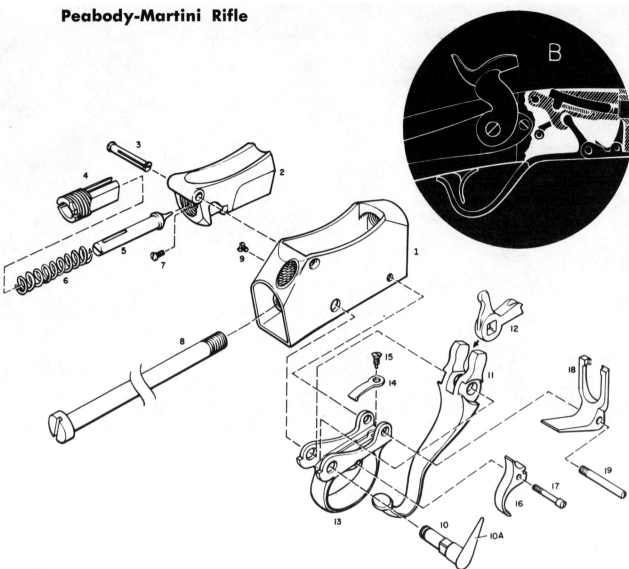

Parts List

1. Receiver
2. Breechblock
3. Breechblock Axis Pin
4. Stop Nut
5. Firing Pin
6. Firing Pin Spring
7. Stop Nut Keeper Screw
8. Stock Bolt (accessible after removing buttplate screws and buttplate).
9. Lever & Tumbler Axis Pin Keeper Screw
10. Lever & Tumbler Axis Pin (with indicator, 10A)
11. Lever
12. Tumbler
13. Guard
14. Trigger Spring
15. Trigger Spring Screw
16. Trigger
17. Trigger Axis Screw
18. Extractor
19. Extractor Axis Screw

Note: Buttstock, buttplate, buttplate screws, fore-end, barrel, and sights are not shown.

A. Section showing relationship of Peabody-Martini internal lock parts.

B. Section of original outside hammer Peabody action.

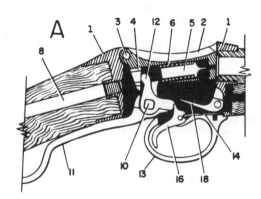

Disassembly—Check action to be sure rifle is unloaded. Split-type breechblock axis pin (3) can be drifted out from right to left. If breechblock axis pin is solid type with keeper screw (similar to No. 9), turn screw to allow pin to be drifted out from right to left. Open breech and press down on front end forcibly while raising lever (11). Remove breechblock (2). Turn keeper screw (9) and drift lever & tumbler axis pin (10) with indicator (10A) out of receiver from left to right. Drop tumbler (12) out top of receiver. Remove extractor axis screw (19) and pull guard (13) out bottom of receiver. Remove lever (11) and extractor (18). To disassemble breechblock (2), turn keeper screw (7) and unscrew stop nut (4) from rear of breechblock. Drop firing pin (5) and spring (6) out rear of breechblock. Reassemble in reverse order.

Gun Digest Index
1944-1973

PART ONE
AUTHOR INDEX

Carhart, Arthur H.
Hunting A Big Mule, 19 ed. 1965, 87.
Carpenter, Russ
Testfire Report, 25 ed. 1971, 321.
Cartwright, B. W.
Flyways of North America, 1 ed. 1944, 77;
2 ed. 1946, 97.
Carver, Wm. A.
Black Powder Pistols, 18 ed. 1964, 77.
Cary, Lucian
Forty-Rod Gun, 18 ed. 1964, 124††; *Madman
of Gaylord's Corner*, 21 ed. 1967, 39††; *Johnny
Gets His Gun*, 26 ed. 1972, 42; *J.M. Shoots
Twice*, 27 ed. 1973, 110.
Chamberlain, Richard H.
Early Loading Tools, 13 ed. 1959, 141; *Milton
Farrow and His Rifles*, 16 ed. 1962, 152**.
Chapel, Chas. E.
Discontinued Metallic Cartridge Arms, 2 ed.
1946, 158; 3 ed. 1947, 155; 4 ed. 1949, 151.
Charles, Jay
U.S. Shoulder Arms, 1966-67, 21 ed. 1967, 97;
U.S. Pistols & Revolvers 1967-68, 22 ed. 1968,
23; *American Handguns 1968-69*, 23 ed. 1969,
94.
Chatfield-Taylor, Robt.
Magnum Megalomania, 17 ed. 1963, 125.
Christensen, Vagn B.
American Signal Pistols & Flares, 22 ed.
1968, 250.
Clark, Sam Jr.
Bullet Making, 5 ed. 1951, 172.
Clede, Bill
Good Gun Manners, 17 ed. 1963, 150.
Cole, D. C.
Flying Shotgun—the Nazi Air Force 3-Barrel,
26 ed. 1972, 110.
Cook, Art
Pellet Guns, 11 ed. 1957, 159.
Cooper, Jeff
The Modern Sporting Pistol, 18 ed. 1964,
192**; *Practical Pistol Shooting*, 25 ed. 1971,
129.
Corson, Bill
23½—The Instead Caliber, 22 ed. 1968, 242.
Cotterman, Dan
New Zing! For Old Barrels, 21 ed. 1967, 205.
Crossman, Col. Jim
Guns of Viet Nam, 21 ed. 1967, 19; *Guns for
Competition*, 22 ed. 1968, 176.
Crum, Gene B.
Bullet Mould Conditioning, 21 ed. 1967, 74.
Curtis, Wm.
High Country Grouse Hunting, 17 ed. 1963,
77.
Daiken, Leslie H.
English Elephant Guns, 12 ed. 1958, 136.
Dalrymple, Byron W.
Big Deal in New Game, 21 ed. 1967, 63;
Home-Grown Exotics, 22 ed. 1968, 169.
Dams, Edward
Shot Loads For Revolvers, 24 ed. 1970, 210.
Datig, Fred A.
The Luger Pistol, 11 ed. 1957, 162.
Davidson, Bill
Handgun Hunting, 27 ed. 1973, 179.
Davidson, Harold O.
Case Capacity Measurement, 25 ed. 1971, 136;
Sighting in the Long Range Magnum, 26 ed.
1972, 257.
Davison, L. P.
Wilhelm Brenneke, 14 ed. 1960, 166**.

Dean, Harry O.
Mossberg Martini, 26 ed. 1972, 20.
Decker, Maurice H.
Guns Will Last a Lifetime, 1 ed. 1944, 104*;
2 ed. 1946, 153; *Take Care of Your Guns*,
4 ed. 1949, 100; *Gun Care, Repair and Blu-
ing*, 5 ed. 1951, 164; *Ammunition Guide*, 3
ed. 1947, 119; 4 ed. 1949, 131; 5 ed. 1951,
190; 6 ed. 1952, 182.
Denny, Robert F.
Firearms Advertising Envelopes, 25 ed. 1971,
23.
Depperman, Bill
Ancestors of the Clay Pigeon, 6 ed. 1952, 60;
When You Hit 'Em, They Break, 7 ed. 1953,
94; *Collecting Old Winchesters*, 8 ed. 1954, 2.
de Haas, Frank
World's Handiest Gun, 14 ed. 1960, 125†; *The
Sharps Side Hammer Rifle*, 22 ed. 1968, 138.
Dickey, Charley
Shooting Preserves, 15 ed. 1961, 79.
Dieckmann, Edw. A.
Those Thundering Clerics, 19 ed. 1965, 111;
Stone Age Guided Missiles, 20 ed. 1966, 129**.
Donnelly, E. F.
The Minie Rifle, 15 ed. 1961, 152†.
Douglas, Ruth C.
Arms—And the Women, 14 ed. 1960, 65.
Downey, Fairfax
The Rockets Red Glare, 26 ed. 1972, 267.
Ducks Unlimited (contributor)
Tips on Decoying, 1 ed. 1944, 72.
Duffey, Dave
Guns and Gun Dogs, 23 ed. 1969, 157.
du Mont, John S.
Paterson and Walker Colts, 7 ed. 1953, 110*;
Caveat Emptor, 11 ed. 1957, 75; *English
Shotguns*, 16 ed. 1962, 91.
Dunlap, Roy F.
Gun Engraving, 9 ed. 1955, 2*; *The Creation
of Precision Rifle Ammunition*, 25 ed. 1971,
264.
Dutcher, John T.
George Schoyen — Riflemaker Extraordinary,
25 ed. 1971, 65††.
Eaton, John
Baggin' a Dragon, 19 ed. 1965, 91.
Edwards, Wm. B.
Story of the AR-10, 12 ed. 1958, 106; *The
Secret Pistol of World War I*, 22 ed. 1968, 220.
Engelhardt, A., Baron
The Story of European Proof Marks, 7 ed.
1953, 2*†; *Development of Proof During the
19th Century: Proof in Great Britain*, 8 ed.
1954, 160*†; *Development of Proof During
the 19th Century: Proof in France: Proof in
Belgium*, 9 ed. 1955, 155*†; *Proof in Modern
Germany*, 10 ed. 1956, 126*†; *Spanish Proof
Marks*, 11 ed. 1957, 29†; *Italian Proof Marks*,
12 ed. 1958, 145†; *Development of Proof in
Austria-Hungary*, 13 ed. 1959, 163†; *Proof in
Modern France*, 14 ed. 1960, 40†; *Proof in
Germany After World War II*, 15 ed. 1961,
144†; *European Proof Marks: Proof in Great
Britain Today*, 16 ed. 1962, 109**.
Etchen, Fred
Trap and Skeet Shooting, 1 ed. 1944, 94*; 2
ed. 1946, 104; 3 ed. 1947, 98.
Fairclough, John
The Camping Rifle, 26 ed. 1972, 208.
Fanta, Ladd
Air Arms Ammo, 23 ed. 1969, 161; *Air Arms
I.Q.*, 24 ed. 1970, 148; *The Air Rifle, Which
One?* 25 ed. 1971, 138.
Fargo, Joe.
Primers for Varmints, 21 ed. 1967, 290.
Farquharson, W. J.
Canadian Vacation Shoot, 19 ed. 1965, 65;
Handsome Rifles, 21 ed. 1967, 110.
Farris, E. M.
Loading the Charcoal Burners, 5 ed. 1951, 186.
Ferris, Ray
The Great Rifle Match, 15 ed. 1961, 83**.
Fitzgerald, Jas. E.
*Some Notes on Mauser and Mannlicher
Rifles*, 6 ed. 1952, 126.
Fix, John
Contact Lenses, 19 ed. 1965, 18**.
Florsheim, Leonard S., Jr.
Retrievers for Your Hunting Pleasure, 8 ed.
1954, 78.
Floss, Frank
Special Delivery Deer, 10 ed. 1956, 58.
Fors, William B.
Antique 22 Cartridge Revolvers, 27 ed. 1973,
93.
Foster, Paul
*Winchester's "Forgotten" Cartridges, 1866-
1900*, 6 ed. 1952, 172*.
Frost, Dan
Tell Me, Elmer, 20 ed. 1966, 64**.
Gaines, Joe
Southern Highland Whitetails, 17 ed. 1963,
161.
Gay, John
You Can't Be Overgunned, 12 ed. 1958, 30.
Glanzer, Ken
Are Round Nose Bullets On The Way Out?
22 ed. 1968, 98.
Glassen, Harold
Hunting the High Alps, 10 ed. 1956, 68.
Gleason, F. W.
Lost Causes, 11 ed. 1957, 36; *Josiah Gorgas
—Armorer of the Confederacy*, 19 ed. 1965,
116**.

Goddard, Col. Calvin
The Criminal Investigative Laboratory, 8 ed.
1954, 147.
Goens, Dale
Stockmaker Supreme, 24 ed. 1970, 146.
Goerg, Alfred J.
Slugging for the High Climbers, 21 ed. 1967,
70.
Goodenough, Tap
Safe Shotgun Shooting, 8 ed. 1954, 96.
Grancsay, Stephen V.
*A Wheellock Sporting Rifle in the George F.
Harding Museum*, 6 ed. 1952, 134*; *Euro-
pean Firearms in the George F. Harding
Museum, Chicago*, 7 ed. 1953, 32*; *Fire-
arms vs. Armor*, 8 ed. 1954, 9; *Cornel Klett,
Hofbuchsenmacher*, 9 ed. 1957, 47††; *The Em-
peror's Pistol*, 11 ed. 1957, 2.
Grant, Bruce
Gun Engraving, 6 ed. 1952, 150.
Grant, Jas. J.
Collecting Single Shot Rifles, 6 ed. 1952, 39;
*Crazy Calibers: F. Wesson, America's First
"Wildcatter,"* 7 ed. 1953, 22*.
Gray, Dr. Otis P.
European Break-Open Guns, 13 ed. 1959,
65†.
Greenwood, Colin
Combat Shooting—a logical start, 26 ed. 1972,
170; *Are Firearms Controls Effective?* 26 ed.
1972, 212.
Grennell, Dean
Powder to Burn, 18 ed. 1964, 101; *The 41
Magnum*, 20 ed. 1966, 257; *New Handguns/
U.S. and Foreign 1969-70*, 24 ed. 1970, 97.
Gross, Stuart D.
Ferlach, U.S.A., 14 ed. 1960, 90.
Hack, Jim
Letters to Jim Hack, 25 ed. 1971, 161.
Hagel, Bob
Too Many Cripples, 14 ed. 1960, 8; *Long
Shots at Big Game*, 17 ed. 1963, 86; *Mystery
Misses*, 18 ed. 1964, 53††; *Remington's Big
Seven*, 18 ed. 1964, 28; *Model 70 Winchesters
—Old and New*, 19 ed. 1965, 32**; *284 Bolt
Action Winchester*, 19 ed. 1965, 193; *Why the
Magnum?* 20 ed. 1966, 139; *Remington's 350
Magnum*, 21 ed. 1967, 178; *1000 Yard Shoot-
ing!* 21 ed. 1967, 276; *The 338—What Does It
Offer*, 23 ed. 1969, 188; *Rough Country An-
telope*, 25 ed. 1971, 17; *Revival of the Sharps*,
25 ed. 1971, 174.
Hall, Edson W.
The 222 Remington, 7 ed. 1953, 164*.
Hall, Thos. E.
Forerunners of the First Winchester, Part I,
11 ed. 1957, 140†; Part II, 12 ed. 1958, 120†;
Part III, 13 ed. 1959, 77†.
Hamilton, Donald
Block That Kick! 22 ed. 1968, 71; *The Quiet
Gun*, 25 ed. 1971, 257.
Hamilton, T. M.
18th Century Gun Cache, 19 ed. 1965, 138.
Hanson, Chas. E., Jr.
The Indian Fusil, 13 ed. 1959, 126.
Harger, Don
How to Hunt Quail, 9 ed. 1955, 152*.
Harper, John A., Jr.
Competitive Rifle and Pistol Shooting, 3 ed.
1947, 47; 4 ed. 1949, 27; *The U.S. and
British Automatic Rifles*, 7 ed. 1953, 29.
Harthan, L. E.
John Farquharson's Rifle, 17 ed. 1963, 48.
Hartley, Hal
Carving a Gunstock, 12 ed. 1958, 199.
Hatcher, Major General J. S.
Modern Gunpowders, 5 ed. 1951, 181; *Rifles
and Shotguns of American Make*, 5 ed. 1951,
2; *Rifles and Shotguns of American Make*,
6 ed. 1952, 6; *Pistols and Revolvers of
American Make*, 7 ed. 1953, 131; *Shotguns
of American Make*, 7 ed. 1953, 96; *Rifles of
American Make*, 7 ed. 1953, 48; *Pistols and
Revolvers of American Make*, 8 ed. 1954, 101;
Shotguns of American Make, 8 ed. 1954, 82;
Rifles of American Make, 8 ed. 1954, 57;
This Year's Shotgun Progress, 9 ed. 1955,
133; *American Handguns Today*, 9 ed. 1955,
114; *What's New in Shotguns Today?* 10 ed.
1956, 207; *Handguns in America, 1955-56*,
10 ed. 1956, 188; *American Rifles 1955-56*,
10 ed. 1956, 158; *Hatcher on Handguns*,
1956-57, 11 ed. 1957, 118; *Rifle Round-Up
1956-57*, 11 ed. 1957, 23.
Hathaway, Laurence J.
Tuning the Single Action Colt, 6 ed. 1952, 91.
Haven, Chas. T.
Our Small Arms and Their Makers, 1 ed. 1944,
55*; 2 ed. 1946, 4; *Military Small Arms of
World War II*, 1 ed. 1944, 55*; 2 ed. 1946, 23;
3 ed. 1947, 15; *From Military To Sporter*, 3
ed. 1947, 33*; 4 ed. 1949, 20; *Foreign Sporting
Arms*, 3 ed. 1947, 40; 5 ed. 1951, 140; *Custom
Rifle Conversion*, 5 ed. 1951, 32.
Hayes, Tom
Rattle Up Your Buck, 18 ed. 1964, 46; *Dream
Rifle*, 21 ed. 1967, 257; *Age of the Autoloaders*,
26 ed. 1972, 94.
Heard, Chas. M.
Hollywood Gunmen, 13 ed. 1959, 186; *Fast
Draw vs. Quick Draw*, 16 ed. 1962, 95.
Hebard, Gil
22 Target Autos, 15 ed. 1961, 34†; *How to Be
a Handgunner*, 16 ed. 1962, 78**; *The Smith &
Wesson 38 Master*, 17 ed. 1963, 184; *U.S.
Handguns, 1963-64*, 18 ed. 1964, 204; *High

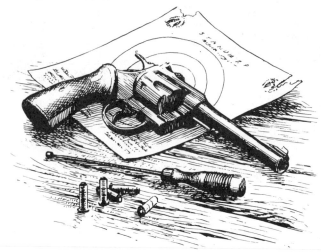

arms Review, 20 ed. 1966, 42; New 2-Bullet NATO Cartridge, 20 ed. 1966, 62; U.S. Rifles & Shotguns, 1967-68, 22 ed. 1968, 54; Reloading Tools & Components, 22 ed. 1968, 119; U.S. Rifles & Shotguns, 1968-69, 23 ed. 1969, 60; South Dakota Safari, 23 ed. 1969, 106; Handloading—1968-69, 23 ed. 1969, 205; Seating Depth vs. Chamber Pressure, 24 ed. 1970, 33; Daisy V/L Rifles, 24 ed. 1970, 128; Handloading—1969-70, 24 ed. 1970, 222; Handiest Tool for Gun Tinkerers, 24 ed. 1970, 255; Handguns 1970, 25 ed. 1971, 149; What Interchangeable 9mm? 25 ed. 1971, 185; Today's Made in Spain Pistols, 26 ed. 1972, 61; Handguns 1971, 26 ed. 1972, 274; High Performance Handgun Loads, 27 ed. 1973, 174; Handguns, U.S. & Foreign 1972-73, 27 ed. 1973, 242.

O'Connor, Jack
Choosing the Big Game Rifle, 1 ed. 1944, 15**; 5 ed. 1951, 7; Outfitting for the Rockies, 5 ed. 1951, 152*; Shotgun Choke and Pattern, 6 ed. 1952, 75†; Tips on Big Game Shooting, 6 ed. 1952, 2†; Gun Games for the Game Shot, 7 ed. 1953, 90*; Crack Rifle Maker, 10 ed. 1956, 25; African Safari, 11 ed. 1957, 52; The Sheep Rifle, 12 ed. 1958, 46**; Shikar in Asia, 13 ed. 1959, 96; The Ones That Shoot Back, 13 ed. 1959, 40††; Rx for the Made-to-Measure Gunstock, 22 ed. 1968, 194††; A Visit to Eibar, 23 ed. 1969, 23; The Killing Power Controversy, 24 ed. 1970, 14††.

Olson, M/Sgt. Ludwig
Original Oberndorf Mauser Sporters, 7 ed. 1953, 142*.

Olt. James R.
The 38 Special, 25 ed. 1971, 168.

Ormond, Clyde
Varmint Rifles, 13 ed. 1959, 122†; First Big Game Rifle, 18 ed. 1964, 89; Muscles for Moose! 19 ed. 1965, 163; Rifles for Desert Ghosts, 21 ed. 1967, 26.

Ormsbee, A. G.
The Story of the Shotgun Choke, 5 ed. 1951, 98.

Ostendorp, Lou
Obsolete Metallic Cartridge Arms, 7 ed. 1953, 211*; 8 ed. 1954, 207*; Winchester Single Shots, 9 ed. 1955, 81; Browning's First Rifle, 10 ed. 1956, 109*.

Page, Warren
It Ain't So, Mac, 6 ed. 1952, 145††; The Swing to the Single Barrel, 6 ed. 1952, 55; White Tails in Three States, 7 ed. 1953, 86*; Slide, 30-06, Slide, 7 ed. 1953, 52; Belted or Blasted, 7 ed. 1953, 44; The Scoop on Scopes, 8 ed. 1954, 193; What's New With Winchester? 8 ed. 1954, 184; Six Gun '53 Style, 8 ed. 1954, 108; Bears I Have Known, 8 ed. 1954, 31; Why Not An Over-Under? 9 ed. 1955, 149; A New Autoloader, 9 ed. 1955, 136; The Search for Accuracy, 9 ed. 1955, 62*; Magnum Shotshells, 10 ed. 1956, 152; A Pair of Sixes, 10 ed. 1956, 18; Goal To Go, 11 ed. 1957, 79; Right on the Button, 11 ed. 1957, 6†; Clay Bird Scattergunning, 12 ed. 1958, 170; Handloading Is Great, 12 ed. 1958, 38†; Old Betsy, 13 ed. 1959, 72; Bullet Bustup, 13 ed. 1959, 9††; Charges are the Bunk, 14 ed. 1960, 10; World Wide Arsenal, 15 ed. 1961, 92**; 243 or 244? 15 ed. 1961, 39; Knock Down Nothing, 16 ed. 1962, 57; The Shotshell Grows Up, 17 ed. 1963, 41; Half Minute Rifle, 18 ed. 1964, 107**; Predictions for PSI, 21 ed. 1967, 16; The Bigger the Cartridge . . . , 22 ed. 1968, 134; It's Not How Long You Make It, 24 ed. 1970, 88; New Mannlicher Rifles, 25 ed. 1971, 50; How Can You Miss An Elephant? 26 ed. 1972, 17.

Palmer, C. M., Jr.
Selecting and Shooting a Target Rifle, 1 ed. 1944, 45; 2 ed. 1946, 45; How To Shoot a Target Rifle, 3 ed. 1947, 49; 4 ed. 1949, 43.

Parmelee, Claude
Scopes and Mounts, 3 ed. 1947, 139; Scope and Mount Review, 4 ed. 1949, 110.

Parsons, Herb
Kids Want to Shoot, 17 ed. 1963, 141.

Parsons, John E.
The Peacemaker and Its Rivals, 5 ed. 1951, 117; The First Winchester, 10 ed. 1956, 29.

Partridge, Derek
Perazzi—The Ferrari of Shotguns, 24 ed. 1970, 136; Guns and Gameshooting, 25 ed. 1971, 164; The Trapshooter—and how he stands, 27 ed. 1973, 19.

Paul, Jan S.
Gunboats for Gun Boxes, 20 ed. 1966, 274.

Phillips, George R.
Armchair Chuck Hunting, 21 ed. 1967, 261.

Phillips, Roger
Ross Rifles, A History, 21 ed. 1967, 264.

Popowski, Bert
Pronghorn Antelope, 19 ed. 1965, 202; Prairie Chicken Comeback, 23 ed. 1969, 83; Buffalo Hunting Today, 24 ed. 1970, 203.

Prudhomme, E. C.
Gun Engraving and the Buyer, 10 ed. 1956, 52*; Gun Engraving, Part II, 11 ed. 1957, 155; Gun Engraving and How To Do It, 12 ed. 1958, 161†.

Pulling, Pierre
New Barrels from Old, 13 ed. 1959, 112; All-Round Gun, 16 ed. 1962, 74**.

Rakusan, J.
The 5.7 Johnson Spitfire, 18 ed. 1964, 166.

Randolph, Lt. Col. Jack
A New Lesson from the Old World, 27 ed. 1973, 228.

Rearden, Jim
Rocky Mountain Goats, 12 ed. 1958, 177.

Reid, Art
Rifled Slugs—how good are they? 24 ed. 1970, 213.

Resman, Bill
Browning versus Winchester, 22 ed. 1968, 40.

Reynolds, Bob
Homemade Pistol Rest, 18 ed. 1964, 184

Riling, Ray
The Arms Collector and His Field, 5 ed. 1951, 149.

Robel, R. J.
They Must Die! 22 ed. 1968, 211††.

Roberts, Major Ned H.
Shooting the Muzzle Loading Cap Lock Rifle, 2 ed. 1946, 70*; 3 ed. 1947, 69.

Robinson, Jimmy
Selecting the Proper Shotguns for Trap and Skeet, 4 ed. 1949, 49; Choosing the Trap and Skeet Gun, 5 ed. 1951, 86*.

Rogoski, Bill
John Marlin, 20 ed. 1966, 4.

Roper, Walter F.
Fun With a Handgun, 3 ed. 1947, 108†; My Favorite Gun—The Super Accurate Single Shot Pistol, 7 ed. 1953, 122*; Blunder Busts! 9 ed. 1955, 52††.

Ruffin, Allen F. Jr.
Trap, Skeet and the Hunter, 26 ed. 1972, 96.

Rusfel, T. R.
Ruger 10/22 Carbine, 19 ed. 1965, 16††.

Russell, A. G.
The Knife Revisited, 27 ed. 1973, 80.

Ryan, Bill
The Upland Game Gun, 5 ed. 1951, 83; Krautbauer Trophy, 22 ed. 1968, 49.

Ryan, Jim
Rocky Mountain Bighorn, 16 ed. 1962, 102; Handloads for Hunting, 18 ed. 1964, 182.

Rychetnik, Joseph
Tips for the Cold Weather Hunter, 19 ed. 1965, 187.

Salisbury, H. M.
The Right Gun for Duck Shooting, 4 ed. 1949, 57**; Duck Gun, Loads and Chokes, 5 ed. 1951, 93**; 3 ed. 1947, 93†.

Samuels, B. F.
Wanted! Gun Designers, 18 ed. 1964, 62; The Right To Bear Arms, 19 ed. 1965, 4; Guide to American Ordnance, 19 ed. 1965, 77; So you want to be a Gunsmith, 20 ed. 1966, 147.

Samuels, Col. H. J.
Binoculars for the Hunter, 23 ed. 1969, 183.

Saxton, Sam B.
The 7mm Magnum in Africa, 18 ed. 1964, 97.

Schumaker, Wm.
Open, Peep, Scope Sights, 18 ed. 1964, 154.

Sear, Arthur W.
Safety Pins, 26 ed. 1972, 223.

Sell, Dewitt
Chicopee Falls, 19 ed. 1965, 92; American Revolver Safeties, 24 ed. 1970, 233; U.S. Handguns Since World War II, 26 ed. 1972, 112.

Sell, Francis E.
I'm Sick of Magnums, 12 ed. 1958, 31; Snapshooting and Snapshooting Rifles, 13 ed. 1959, 88; Shotgun Fallacies, 14 ed. 1960, 69†; 10% Deer Rifle, 15 ed. 1961, 60; Magnum Shotgunning, 17 ed. 1963, 80; Put and Take Choke, 20 ed. 1966, 112; Custom Doubles at Pumpgun Prices, 20 ed. 1966, 166; Hitting's Easier! 22 ed. 1968, 115; Shot Charges and Ranges for the Wildfowler, 23 ed. 1969, 235.

Sellers, Frank M.
Sharps 4-Barrel Pistols, 17 ed. 1963, 153.

Serven, Jas. E.
Catlin and Remington paintings in reproduction, 10 ed. 1956, 149; The Shotgun—A Full History, 17 ed. 1963, 4; Duelling Pistols and Duelling Days, 19 ed. 1965, 8; Smith & Wesson—Pioneers in Cartridge Pistols, 19 ed. 1965, 97**; New Interest in the Old Winchester, 20 ed. 1966, 115; Shot—a History, 20 ed. 1966, 170††; Guns of the Canadian West, 21 ed. 1967, 156; Captain Samuel H. Walker, 23 ed. 1969, 128; Elegant Firearms of the Favored Few, 23 ed. 1969, 195; Guns of the Western History Makers, 25 ed. 1971, 4; Buffalo Bill—Good Man with a Gun, 26 ed. 1972, 144.

Sharpe, Phil
The Art of Handloading Ammunition, 5 ed. 1951, 168*; A Gunbug's Paradise, 5 ed. 1951, 158; Foreign Guns: GI Souvenirs, 5 ed. 1951, 136; Are Ballistics Necessary? 6 ed. 1952, 178;

I Hunted Illegal Deer, 6 ed. 1952, 154; Halger and His Rifles, 7 ed. 1953, 180.

Shaughnessy, Dick
Safe Shotgun Shooting, 8 ed. 1954, 96.

Shaw, Robt. T.
Thar's Guns in Them Sierras, 13 ed. 1959, 110; Turkey Shoot a la Mexicana, 17 ed. 1963, 65.

Sheldon, Frank
Old Gus, 12 ed. 1958, 193.

Sheldon, Col. H. P.
The Fowling Piece, 1 ed. 1944, 68.

Sherwood, Robert
The Mysterious Seven, 21 ed. 1967, 83; A Season with the 6.5 Magnum, 22 ed. 1968, 200.

Shiner, Don
Gunning for Greys, 10 ed. 1956, 84; Talking Turkey, 15 ed. 1961, 147; Crows in the Snow, 17 ed. 1963, 90; Pipe in Your Crows! 20 ed. 1966, 83; Powder Flasks, 26 ed. 1972, 308.

Sipe, Warren
I'm Ready for Them Now, 10 ed. 1956, 66; Deutsche Drillinge, 13 ed. 1959, 136; Confederate Powder Works, 18 ed. 1964, 47; The 9.3x72R, 18 ed. 1964, 26; On Target the Easy Way, 20 ed. 1966, 58**.

Simmons, Dick
Rifle Roundup, 4 ed. 1949, 4; High Velocity Cartridges, 10 ed. 1956, 41; Slappin' Leather, 15 ed. 1961, 86; Rare Stock Woods, 17 ed. 1963, 93**; Locked Breech 380 Autos, 27 ed. 1973, 221.

Smith, E. Stanley
Black Powder Rifles in Pennsylvania, 5 ed. 1951, 70*.

Smith, Pat
Winchester Centennial, 21 ed. 1967, 29.

Smith, Robt. T.
Let's Look at Weatherby's "New Look," 7 ed. 1953, 62.

Snook, Pat
Tune Up for that Hunting Trip, 22 ed. 1968, 164.

Sockut, Dr. Eugene
The Israeli Army, 25 ed. 1971, 40.

Sperbeck, Warren
Table of Comparative Ballistics, Pistol and Revolver Cartridges, 8 ed. 1954, 185; 9 ed. 1955, 194; Table of Comparative Ballistics, Pistol and Revolver Cartridges (Revised 2nd Edition), 23 ed. 1969, 262.

Sprungman, Ormal I.
Waterfowl Shooting with Movie and Still Camera, 10 ed. 1956, 105; Black Brant of Baja, 12 ed. 1958, 65.

Stacy, John R.
Rifle Stocking Made Easy, 17 ed. 1963, 145.

Technical Editors
U.S. Pistols and Revolvers, 1965-66, 20 ed. 1966, 34.

Stanley, Rex
Shooting Steel, 17 ed. 1963, 129.

Stebbins, Henry M.
Cartridge Design, 7 ed. 1953, 183; Used Guns, 8 ed. 1954, 43*; New Wine—Old Bottles, 9 ed. 1955, 102††; The Rifle in Suburbia, 10 ed. 1956, 101; Love That Gun—But Not to Death, 11 ed. 1957, 70†; Junior's 22, 12 ed. 1958, 68; Orphan Cartridges, 13 ed. 1959, 146; Are Shooters Regimented? 14 ed. 1960, 93; Teaching the Young to Shoot, 15 ed. 1961, 9†; Good Old Guns, 16 ed. 1962, 21; Shooting—People-Space, 18 ed. 1964, 179; One and Only Pistol, 20 ed. 1966, 143; Why Ain't Gun Riters Akurate? 23 ed. 1969, 248.

Stegall, Keith
Fast Oil Finish, 9 ed. 1955, 154.

Steindler, Bob
Foreign Firearms — Rifles, Handguns, and Smoothbores, 21 ed. 1967, 119; Arms from Abroad 1967-68, 22 ed. 1968, 152; Foreign Firearms—Handguns, Rifles and Shotguns, 23 ed. 1969, 164; Sporting Arms of the World, 24 ed. 1970, 38; Handguns—U.S. & Foreign 1972-73, 27 ed. 1973, 242; Reloading the 9mm Luger, 27 ed. 1973, 275.

Steinwedel, Louis W.
The Forgotten Gun, 18 ed. 1964, 93; The Flintlock—Father of Firearms, 19 ed. 1965, 122**; The Remington Radicals, 26 ed. 1972, 198; Screw Barrel Pistols, 26 ed. 1972, 288; The Guns of John Brown, 27 ed. 1973, 207.

Stephens, Hal
The Potent 35 Whelen, 10 ed. 1956, 150. The 25 Krag Improved, 17 ed. 1963, 136**.

Stephens, Joseph B.
Guns at the Crossroads, 21 ed. 1967, 173.

PART TWO
SUBJECT INDEX

Rifles—Shotguns

Testfire—Shooters' Needs

ARMS LIBRARY

BALLISTICS

BULLETS & EFFECTS

CLUBS-SAFETY-YOUTH

CIVIL WAR

COLLECTING

FOREIGN WEAPONS

GLOSSARY FOR GUNNERS

GUN CARE

GUN CATALOGS IN FACSIMILE

GUNSMITHS—GUNSMITHING

GUNSTOCKS

HANDGUNS
Combat-Hunting-Plinking

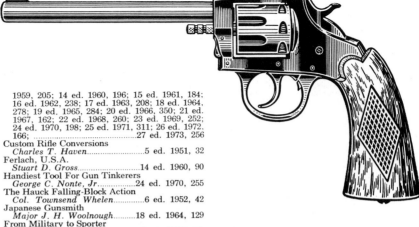

Revolvers

347

Handloader's Digest
Index
1962-1972

PART TWO
SUBJECT INDEX

BEGINNERS

COVERS, INSIDE

Inside Back

Inside Front

GENERAL

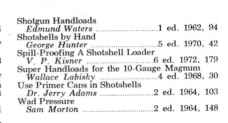